Alexander Ross

Pansebeia

A view of all religions in the world. Sixth Edition

Alexander Ross

Pansebeia

A view of all religions in the world. Sixth Edition

ISBN/EAN: 9783337211011

Printed in Europe, USA, Canada, Australia, Japan

Cover: Foto ©Lupo / pixelio.de

More available books at **www.hansebooks.com**

ΠΑΝΣΕΒΕΙΑ:
OR, A
VIEW
OF ALL
RELIGIONS
IN THE
WORLD:

With the feveral Church-Governments, from the Creation, till thefe times.

Alfo, a Difcovery of all known *Herefies*, in all Ages and Places: And choice Obfervations and Reflections throughout the Whole.

The Sixth Edition, Enlarged and Perfected
By ALEXANDER ROSS.

To which are annexed, the Lives, Actions, and Ends of certain Notorious *Hereticks*. With their Effigies on Copper-Plates.

1 Thef. 5.21. *Omnia autem probate: quod bonum eft, tenete.*

LONDON,
Printed for *M. Gillyflower*, at the *Spread-Eagle* in *Weftminfter-Hall*, and *W. Freeman*, at the Bible, over againft the Middle *Temple-Gate*, in *Fleet-Street*, 1696.

To the Worshipful
ROBERT ABDY,
Esquire.

SIR,

AS Michael and the Devil strove for the dead Body of Moses; and as seven Cities Contested for Homer when he was dead, whom none of them cared for whilst he lived; even so doth it fare with Religion; for the Carkass or Skeleton of which, for the bare sound whereof (being now made a meer Echo, Vox, prætereáque nihil) there is so much contesting, and digladiation in the World; whereas few or none care for the life and substance of Religion, which consisteth in works, not in words; in practising, not in prating; in Scripture Duties not in Scripture phrases: She is as our Saviour was, placed between two Thieves: to wit, Superstition on the right hand, and Atheism on the left. The one makes a puppit of her, sets her out in gaudy accoutrements, bedaubs her native beauty with painting, and presents her in a Meretricious, not in a Matron-like-dress; but the Atheist strips her naked of her Vestments, robs her of her Maintenance, and so exposeth her to the scorn and contempt of the World. But let these men esteem of her as they list, she is notwithstanding the fair daughter of the Almighty, the Queen of Heaven, and beauty of the whole Earth. Religion is the sacred Anchor, by which the Great Ship of the State is held fast, that she may not be split upon the Quick-sands of popular tumults, or on the Rocks of Sedition. Religion is the pillar on which the great Fabrick of the Microcosm standeth. All humane Societies, and civil Associations, are without Religion, but ropes of Sand, and Stones without Mortar, or Ships without Pitch: For this cause, all Societies of men in all Ages, and in all parts of the Universe, have united and strengthned themselves with the Cement of Religion; finding both by experience, and the light of Nature, that no humane Society could be durable, without the knowledge and fear of a Deity which all

The Epistle Dedicatory.

Nations do Reverence and Worship, though they agree not in the manner of their Worship. All their ways and opinions in Religion, I have here presented to the publick view; but to you, Sir, in particular, as to one, whom I know to be truly Religious, not being carried away with the fine flowers and green leaves, but with the solid fruits of Religion, consisting in Righteousness, Peace and Holiness, without which no man shall see the Lord; this is that which will embalm your Name here, and Crown your Soul with true happiness hereafter, when all Humane felicities shall determine in smoak: in this Book are set before you, light and darkness, truth and falshood, Gold and dross, flowers and weeds, corn and chaff, which I know you are able to discriminate, and to gather honey with the Bee out of every weed, with Sampson to take meat out of the eater, with Virgil to pick Gold out of dung, and with the Physician to extract Antidotes out of poyson: Thus beseeching God to increase your knowledge and practice in Religion, and your love to the afflicted professors thereof, I take leave, and will ever be found

Sir, your Humble
Servant to command,
ALEX. ROSS.

THE PREFACE TO THE READER,

Concerning the use of this BOOK.

Christian Reader,

I Understand that some *Momes* have already past their verdict upon this Book, affirming that (seeing the world is pestered with too many Religions) it were better their names and tenets were obliterated than published. To whom I answer, that their assertion is frivolous, and the reasons thereof ridiculous; for the end wherefore these different opinions in Religion are brought into the light, is, not that we should embrace them, but that we may see their deformity and avoid them. Shall Logick be rejected for setting down all the ways of fallacious Arguments? Or Philosophy, for teaching what are the different poysons in Herbs, Roots, Minerals, &c? The Scripture nameth many sins, Idols, and false Gods, must it therefore be reproved of impertinency? The Sea-coast is pestered with many Rocks, Shelves, and Quick-sands, must they therefore be past over in silence in the art of Navigation? Were *Irenæus, Epiphanius, Saint Austin, Theodoret,* and other eminent men in the Church, *fools;* for handling in their Books, all the Heretical, opinions that infested Christianity, both before, and in their times? Do not these Censorious *Momes* know that Truth though comely in it self, is yet more lovely, when compared

pared with falsehood? how should we know the excellency of light, if there were no darkness; the benefit of health, if there were no sickness; and the delights of the spring, if there were no winter; *Opposita juxta se posita clarius elucescunt*: *The Swans feathers are not the less white, because of their black feet; nor* Venus *the less beautiful, because of her Mole.* The Stone is set out by the foil, and the Picture by it's shadow. To infer then, that because the world is pestered with too many Sects and Heresies, therefore we must not mention them, is as much as if they would say, the way to Heaven is beset with too many thieves, therefore we must not take notice of them. But how shall we avoid them, if we know them not; and how shall we know them, if concealed: it's true the world is pestered with too many Religions, and the more is the pity; yet this Book made them not, but they made this Book. He that detects errors makes them not. They that informed the *Israelites* there were Gyants in the Land, did not place those Gyants there. But now I will let these men see the ends for which I have undertaken this task, of presenting all Religions to their view; and they are grounded on the divers uses that may be made thereof. 1. When we look upon the multitude of false Religions in the world, by which most men have been deluded; are not we so much the more bound to the goodness of Almighty God, who hath delivered us out of darkness, and hath caused the day Star of his truth to shine upon, and visit us; who having suffered the World round about us, to sit in the Valley of the shadow of death, and to be overwhelm'd with worse than *Egyptian* darkness, hath notwithstanding in this our *Goshen* abundantly displayed the light of his truth; but how shall we seriously weigh or consider this great mercy, if we do not as well look on the wretched condition of other men, as on our own happiness; which we cannot do, if we know not the errors which make them wretched. What comfort could the *Israelites* have taken in their Land of light, if they had not known that the rest of *Egypt* sate in darkness. 2. When we look upon the different multiplicity of Religions in the world, how that in all times, and in all places, men though otherwise barbarous,

rous, have notwithstanding embraced a Religion, and have acknowledged a Divinity; I say, when we look upon this, do we not admire the impudency of those *Atheists* in this age, who either inwardly in their hearts, or outwardly in their mouths, dare deny the Essence, or else the providence of God; and count all Religions but inventions of humane policy. How can those *Atheists* avoid shame and confusion when they read this Book, in which they shall see, that no Nation hath been so wretched as to deny a Deity, and to reject all Religion, which Religion is a property no less essential to man, and by which he is discriminated from the Beasts, than rationality it self. 3. In the View of all Religions, we may observe how the Children of this world are wiser in their Generation than the Sons of God; for they spare no pains and charges, they reject or slight nothing commanded them by their Priests and Wizards; they leave no means unattempted to attain happiness: See how vigilant, devout, zealous, even to superstition they are; how diligent in watching, fasting, praying, giving of alms, punishing of their bodies, even to death sometimes; whereas on the contrary we are very cold, careless, remiss, supine, and luke-warm in the things that so near concern our eternal happiness. They thought all too little that was spent in the service of their false Gods, we think all is lost and cast away which we bestow on the service of the true God. They reverenced and obeyed their Priests, we dishonour, disobey and slight ours; they observed many Festival days to their Idols, we grudge to give one day to the service of the true God. They made such conscience of their Oaths taken in presence of an Idol, that they would rather lose their lives, than falsifie these Oaths: But we make no more scruple to take the name of God in vain, to swear, and forswear, than if we worshipped *Jupiter Lapis*, meer stocks and stones. Such reverence and devotion they carried to their Idols, that they durst not enter into their Temples, nor draw near their Altars, till first they were purified; they did not only kneel, but fall flat on the ground before their feigned God's; they knock their breasts, beat their heads to the ground, tear their skins, wound and cut their flesh,

A 4   thinking

The Preface to the Reader.

thinking thereby to pacifie their falſe Gods: Whereas we will not debar our ſelves of the leaſt pleaſure or profit to gain Heaven? and ſo irreverent is our behaviour in the Preſence, and Houſe of Almighty God, *before whom the* Cherubims *and* Seraphims *dare not ſtand, but with covered faces,* as if he were our equal, and not our Lord or Father, for (to ſpeak in the Prophets words,) *Mal.* 1. 6. *If he be our Father, where is his honour? and if he be our Lord, where is his fear?* Doubtleſs theſe falſe worſhippers ſhall ſtand up in judgment againſt us, who know our Maſters will, but do it not; is not their zeal in the practice of religious duties, to be preferred to our careleſsneſs; and their ignorance, to our knowledg; which without practice will but aggravate our damnation, *for he that knoweth his Maſters will, and doth it not, ſhall be beaten with many ſtripes*: We are in the right way to Heaven; they are in the wrong way; but if we ſtand ſtill, and walk not, they will be as near their journies end as we. They worſhip Idols, we commit Sacrilege: But is not a Sacrilegious Thief as hateful to God as an Ignorant Idolater? 4. When we look upon the confuſed multitude of Religions in the World, let us learn to tremble at Gods judgments, to make much of the light whilſt we have it, to hold faſt by the truth, to imbrace it with all affection, and the Miniſters thereof; for if once we forſake the right way, which is but one, we ſhall wander all our days after in by-paths, and crooked lanes of errour, which are innumerable: if we reject the thread of God's Word preſented to us by the Church; a thread, I ſay, ſurer than that of *Ariadne*, we ſhall be forced to ramble up and down, through the inextricable *Labyrinth* of erroneous opinions. It ſtood with the juſtice of God to ſuffer men who in the beginning were of one Language and Religion, to fall into a Babel and confuſion, both of tongues and falſe religions, for not retaining the truth; to dig to themſelves broken Ciſterns, which would hold no Water, for rejecting the fountain of living Waters; to ſurfeit upon the poyſonable fleſh of quails, who grew weary of the bread of Angels; and with the Swine to eat husks who would ſlight the wholeſome food of their Fathers houſe. If the *Jews* put God's word from them, and

judge

The Preface to the Reader.

judge themselves unworthy of eternal life, Lo *Paul* and *Barnabas* will turn to the *Gentiles*, *Act.* 13. 46. 5. In reading this Book we shall find, that the whole rabble of vain, phantastical, or prophane opinions, with which at this day, this miserable distracted Nation is pestered, are not new revelations, but old dreams of ancient Hereticks, long ago condemned by the Church, and exploded by the publick Authority of Christian Magistrates: but now for want of Weeders, these Tares spring up again in the Lord's field, and are like to choak the good Corn; unless the Lord of the Harvest send forth labourers into his Harvest. 6. The reading of this Book, may induce us to commiserate the wretched condition of a great part of the World, buried as it were, in the darkness of ignorance, and tyranny of superstition: *To bless God for the light and freedom we enjoy, whereas they are not greater sinners than we; but except we repent, we shall all likewise perish; let us then not be too high minded, but fear, and when we think we stand, let us take heed least we fall:* God hath already permitted divers of those old, obsolete, and antiquated Heretical opinions to break in amongst us; *The times are now come, that Men will not suffer wholesome Doctrine; but having itching ears after their own lusts, get them an heap of teachers, turning their ears from the truth, and giving themselves unto Fables,* 2 Tim. 4. *Thus is the Lord pleased to deal with us, he suffers Heresies to repullulate, that they who are approved among us may be manifested.* He permits Prophets and Dreamers amongst us, but it is as *Moses* saith, to prove us, and to know, whether we love the Lord our God *with all our hearts and with all our Souls,* Deut. 13. To conclude, whereas all Men are desirous of happiness, and immortality, but few walk in the right way that conduceth to it; being there are such multitudes of byeways, as we may see by this Book, let us follow the counsel of the Prophet, *Jer.* 6. 16. *Stand in the ways, behold and ask for the old way, and walk therein, and ye shall find rest for your souls.* And thus good Reader, having shewed thee the true use of this Book, I leave it to thy perusal, beseeching God to keep us from the bye-ways of errour, and to lead us into the way of Truth.

A. R.

The Religions of *Asia*.

The Contents of the First Section.

OF *the Church Discipline, Sacrifices, Ordinations, Publick place,* [*Buildings first erected for Divine Service,*] *and days of Divine Service before* Moses. 2. *Of the Church Government under* Moses; *difference of the High-Priests from other Priests.* 3. *Of the Church-Government from him till* Solomon. 4. *Of the Government after* Solomon, *till the Divisions of the Tribes.* 5. *Of* Solomon'*s Temple, and the outward splendor of the* Jew's *Religion.* 6. *Of the office of the Levites, of the Prophets, Scribes, Pharisees,* Nazarites, Rechabites, Essones, Sadduces, *and* Samaritans. 7. *Of the ancient observation of their Sabbath, of the observation of their passeover, of the feast of Pentecost, tabernacles, new Moons, of trumpets, and of expiation; of their Sabbatical year, and their Jubilee.* 8. *Of their ancient Excommunications, how God instructed them of old, and of the maintenance allowed by the* Jews *to their Priests and Levites.* 9. *Of the Government after the* Jews *were carried captive into* Babylon. 10. *Of the* Jewish *Church-Government at this day, their Prayers, Sabbaths, Feasts, Book of the Law, Passeover, what observable thereupon, and whether to be permitted (among Christians) in the exercise of their own Religion, and wherein not to be communicated with by Christians.* 11. *Of the Jewish preparation for Morning Prayer, Fast in* August, *Beginning of the new year, Feast of Reconciliation, Ceremonies in reading of the Law.* 12. *Their Church-officers, Feast of Dedication, and of* Purim, *Fasts, Marriages, Divorcements, Circumcision, Redemption of the first born, their duty towards the Sick, and Ceremonies about the Dead.*

The Contents of the Second Section.

THe *Religion of the ancient* Babylonians; *of the making, worshipping of Images, and bringing in Idolatry.* 2. *Of* Hierapolis, *and Gods of the* Syrians. 3. *Of the* Phœnicians. 4. *Of the old* Arabians. 5. *Of the ancient* Persians. 6. *Of the* Scythians. 7. *Of the* Tartars, *or* Carthajans, *and* Pagans. 8. *The Religions of the Northern Countries near the Pole. Three ways whereby Satan deludes Men by false Miracles. The fear of his stratagems whence it proceeds? His illusions*

The Contents.

illusions many, our duty thereupon. 9. *Of the* Chinois. 10. *Of the ancient* Indians. 11. *Of* Siam. 12. *Of* Pegu. 13. *Of* Bengala. 14. *Of* Magor. 15. *Of* Cambaia. 16. *Of* Goa. 17. *Of* Malabar. *Pagan Idolaters believe the immortality of the Soul.* 18. *Of* Narsinga, *and* Bisnagar. 19. *Of* Japan. 20. *Of the* Philippiana *Islands.* 21. *Of* Sumatra, *and* Zeilan. 22. *Of the ancient* Egyptians. 23. *Of the modern* Egyptian *Religion.*

The Religions of *Africa* and *America*.

The Contents of the Third Section.

OF *the old* African *Religion.* 2. *The Religion and Church Discipline of* Fez. 3. *Of* Morocco. 4. *Of* Guinea. 5. *Of the ancient* African Æthiopians. 6. *Of the modern* Abyssins. 7. *Of the lower* Æthiopians. 8. *Of* Angola *and* Congo. 9. *Of the Northern Neighbours of* Congo. 10. *Of the* African *Islands.* 11. *The Religions of* America. 12. *Of* Virginia. 13. *Of* Florida. 14. *Of the Religions of West*-Virginia *and* Florida. 15. *Of new* Spain *and* Mexico. 16. *Idolaters their cruelty, and cost in their barbarous sacrifices.* 17. *Of the* Americans, *their superstitious fear, and tyranny thereof.* 18. *Of* Jucatan, *and the parts adjoyning.* 19. *Of the Southern* Americans. 20. *Of* Paria *and* Guiana. 21. *Of* Brasil. 22. *Of* Peru. 23. *Of* Hispaniola.

The Religions of *Europe*.

The Contents of the Fourth Section.

THe *Religion of the ancient* Europæans. 2. *the Roman chief Festivals.* 3. *their Gods.* 4. *their Priests.* 5. *their Sacrifices.* 6. *their Marriage Rites.* 7. *their Funeral Ceremonies.* 8. *the old* Grecian *Religion.* 9. *their chief Gods.* 10. *of* Minerva, Diana, Venus. 11. *How* Juno, Ceres, *and* Vulcan *were worshipped.* 12. *the* Sun *worshipped under the names of* Apollo, Phœbus, Sol, Jupiter, Liber, Hercules, Mars, Mercurius, Pan, &c. 13. *the* Moon *worshipped under divers names and shapes.* 14. *the Earth and Fire, how worshipped, and named.* 15. *the Deity of the Sea, how worshipped* 16. *Death, how named and worshipped.* 17. *the* Grecian *Sacrifices and Ceremonies.* 18. *their Priests and temples of old.*

The

The Contents.

The Contents of the Fifth Section.

THe *Religion of the old* Germans, Gauls, *and* Britains. 2. *of the* Saxons, Danes, Swedes, Moscovites, Russians, Pomeranians, *and their neighbours.* 3. *of the* Scythians, Getes, Thracians, Cymbrians, Goths, Lusitanians, *&c.* 4. *of the* Lithuanians, Polonians, Hungarians, Samogetians, *and their Neighbours.* 5. *of divers Gentile Gods besides the abovenamed.* 6. *the ranks and arms of their Gods.* 7. *with what Creatures their Chariots were drawn.* 8. *of peculiar Gods worshipped in peculiar places.* 9. *the* Greek *chief Festivals.*

The Contents of the Sixth Section.

OF *the two prevalent Religions now in* Europe. 2. *of* Mahomet's *Law to his Disciples.* 3. *Of the* Mahometans *opinions at this day.* 4. Mahomet, *not the Antichrist.* 5. *Of their Sects, and how the* Turks *and* Persians *differ.* 6. *Of the* Mahometán *Religious orders.* 7. *Of their other hypocritical orders.* 8. *Of their seculars Priests.* 9. *Of the* Mahometan *Devotion, and parts thereof.* 10. *Of their Ceremonies in their Pilgrimage to* Mecca. 11. *The rites of their Circumcision.* 12. *their rites about the sick and dead.* 13. *The extent of* Mahometanism, *and the causes thereof.* 14. Mahometanism, *of what continuance.*

The Contents of the Seventh Section.

THe *Christian Religion propagated.* 2. *The decay thereof in the East by* Mahometanism. 3. *Persecution and Heresie the two great Enemies thereof.* 4. Simon Magus, *the first Heretick, with his Disciples.* 5. Menander, Saturninus, *and* Basilides, *Hereticks.* 6. *The* Nicholaitans, *and* Gnosticks. 7. *the* Carpocratians. 8. Cerinthus, Ebion, *and the* Nazarites. 9. *the* Valentinians, Secundians, *and* Ptolemians. 10. *the* Marcites, Colarbasii, *and* Heracleonites. 11. *the* Ophites, Canites, *and* Sethites. 12. *the* Archenticks, *and* Aschothyptæ. 13. Cerdon, *and* Marcion. 14. Apelles, Severus, *and* Tatianus. 15. *the* Cataphrygians. 16. Pepuzians, Quintilians, *and* Artotyrites. 17. *the* Quartidecimani, *and* Alogiani. 18. *the* Adamians, Elcesians, *and* Theodocians. 19. *the* Melchisedicians, Bardesanists, *and* Noetians. 20. *the* Valesians, Cathari, Angelici, *and* Apostolici. 21. *the* Sabellians, Origenians, *and* Origenists. 22. *the* Samosatenians, *and* Photinians.

nians. 23. *the* Manichæan *religion.* 24. *the* Hierarchites, Melitians, *and* Arrians. 25. *the* Audians, Semi-Arrians, *and* Macedonians. 26. *the* Ærians, Ætians, *and* Apollinarists. 27. *the* Antidicomarianites, Messalians, *and* Metangismonites. 28. *the* Hermians, Proclianites, *and* Patricians. 29. *the* Ascites, Pattalorinchites, Aquarii, *and* Coluthiani. 30. *the* Floriani, Æternales, *and* Nudipedales. 31. *the* Donatists, Priscillianists, Rhetorians, *and* Feri. 32. *the* Theopascites, Tritheits, Aquei, Melitonii, Orphei, Tertulli, Liberatores, *and* Nativitarii. 33. *the* Luciferians, Jovinianists, *and* Arabicks. 34. *the* Collyridians, Paterniani, Tertullianists, *and* Abelonites. 35. *the* Pelagians, Prædestinati, *and* Timotheans. 36. *the* Nestorians, Eutychians, *and their Spawn.*

The Contents of the Eighth Section.

OF *the Opinions in Religion held the seventh Century.* 2. *the opinions of the eighth Century.* 3. *the tenets of the ninth and tenth Centuries.* 4. *the Opinions of the eleventh and twelfth Centuries.* 5. *Of the* Albigenses, *and other Sects in the twelfth Century.* 6. *the Sects of the thirteenth Century.* 7. *the Sects of the fourteenth Century.* 8. *Of the* Wicklevites. 9. *the Opinions of the fifteenth Century.* 10. *the Opinions of the sixteenth Century, to wit, of* Luther *and others.* 11. *Of Sects sprung out of Lutheranism.* 12. *Of Protestants.* 13. *Of the other Opinions held in this Century.* 14. *the chief heads of* Calvins *Doctrine.* 15. *Of other Opinions held this age.* 16. *Of divers other Opinions in this Age, and the causes of this variety, and confusion in the Church.*

The Contents of the Ninth Section.

THe *first original of the Monastical life.* 2. *the first Eremites, or Anchorites.* 3. *the manner of their living.* 4. *their Excesses in Religion.* 5. *the preheminence of the Sociable life to the Solitary.* 6. *the first Monks after* Anthony. 7 *the Rules of St.* Basil. 8. *St.* Hierom's *order* 9. *St.* Austin's *order* 10. *If St.* Austin *instituted his Eremites to beg.* 11. *Of St.* Austin's *Leathern Girdle used at this day.* 12. *the institutions and exercises of the first Monks.* 13. *why Religious Persons cut their hair and beards.* 14. *Whence came that custom of shaving.* 15. *of the Primitive Nuns.* 16. *of what account Monks are at this day in the Roman Church.* 17. *How the Monks and Nuns of old were consecrated.* 18. *the Benedictine order.* 19. *of the orders proceeding from them.* 20. *of St.* Bennet's rules

The Contents.

rules to his Monks. 21. *the Benedictines habit and diet.* 22. *Rules prescribed by the Council of* Aix *to the Monks.* 23. *the rites and institutions of the Monks of* Cassinum. 24. *the manner of electing their Abbots.* 25. *the Benedictine Nuns and their rule.* 26. *of the Laws and Priviledges of Monasteries.*

The Contents of the Tenth Section.

OF *new Religious orders sprung out of the* Benedictines; *and first of the* Cluniacenses. 2. *Of the* Camaldulenses, *and Monks of the Shadowy Valley.* 3. *the* Sylvestrini, Grandimontenses, *and* Carthusians. 4. *the Monks of St.* Anthony *of* Vienna: *the* Cistercians, Bernardines, *and* Humiliati. 5. *the* Premonstratenses, *and* Gilbertines. 6. *the* Cruciferi, Hospitalarii, Trinitarians, *and* Bethlemites. 7. *the* Johannites, *or first Religious Knights in Christendom.* 8. *the* Templars. 9. *the* Teutonici, *or* Mariani. 10. *the Knights of St.* Lazarus, Calatrava, *and St.* James. 11. *the orders of Mendicant Friers, and first of the* Augustinians. 12. *of the* Carmelites. 13. *of the* Dominicans. 14. *of the* Franciscans. 15. *of things chiefly remarkable in the* Franciscans *order.* 16. *of the Knights of the Holy Sepulchre, and* Gladiatores. 17. *of the Knights of St.* Mary, *of Redemption, of the* Montesians, *of the order of* Vallis Scholarium, *and* Canons Regular *of St.* Mark. 18. *of St.* Clara, *St.* Pauls Eremites, *and* Boni homines. 19. *the servants of St.* Mary, Cœlestini, *and* Jesuati. 20. *the order of St.* Bridget. 21. *the order of St.* Catherine, *and St.* Justina. 22. *the Eremites of St.* Hierom, *St.* Saviour, Albati, Fratricelli, Turlupini, *and* Montolivetenses. 23. *the Canons of St.* George, *the Mendicants of St.* Hierom, *the Canons of* Lateran, *the order of the* Holy Ghost, *of St.* Ambrose *and* Nemus, *and of the* Minimi *of Jesu* Maria. 24. *the orders of Knight-hood, from the year* 1400. *namely of the* Annunciada, *of St.* Maurice, *of the Golden fleece, of the* Moon, *of St.* Michael, *of St.* Stephen, *of the Holy Spirit,* &c.

The Contents of the Eleventh Section.

OF *Religious orders and Opinions from the year* 1500, *till this day.* 2. *the order of* Jesuits. 3. *of their general rules.* 4. *of their other rules.* 5. *of their rules for Provosts of houses, Rectors of Colleges,* &c. 6. *of their rules for Travellers, Ministers, admonitors,* &c. 7. *of their privileges granted by Popes.* 8. *of other orders in the Church of* Rome. 9. *How Abbots are consecrated at this time.* 10. *Wherein*

The Contents.

10. *Wherein the Christian orders of Knight-hood differ.* 11. *of other orders of Knight-hood besides the French.* 12. *of the orders of Knight-hood in* Germany, Hungaria, Bohemia, Poland, &c. 13. *the orders of the Knight-hood in* Italy. 14. *of the Christian Military orders in the East.*

The Contents of the Twelfth Section.

The Opinions of the Anabaptists, *and wherein they agree with the old Hereticks.* 2. *The Tenets of the* Brownists. 3. *of the* Familists. 4. *the* Adamites, *and* Antinomians. 5. *the Religion of the* Socinians. 6. *of the* Arminians *tenets.* 7. *of the Church of* Arnhem, *and the Millennaries opinions.* 8. *of many other Sects at this day amongst us.* 9. *the Opinions of the* Independents. 10. *the tenets of the* Presbyterians, *where by way of a Catechism, is delivered their whole Doctrine concerning the Ministry, Episcopacy, Presbytery, Lay-Eldership, Deacons, Civil Magistrates, the Election of Ministers, Ordination, power of the Keys, Excommunication.* 11. *Divers erroneous opinions which have been lately revived or hatched since the fall of our Church-Government.*

The Contents of the Thirteenth Section.

The Doctrine of the Church of Rome *concerning the Scriptures.* 2. *their tenets concerning Predestination: the Image of God, original and actual sin, and free will.* 3. *their Opinions concerning the Law of God, concerning Christ, Faith, Justification, and good works.* 4. *their tenets concerning Penance, Fasting, Prayers, and Alms.* 5. *their opinions concerning the Sacraments, and Ceremonies used in those controverted.* 6. *what they believe concerning the Saints in Heaven.* 7. *their Doctrine concerning the Church.* 8. *what they hold concerning Monks, Magistrates, and Purgatory.* 9. *Wherein the outward Worship of the Church of* Rome *consisteth, and first part of their Mass.* 10. *their Dedication of Churches, and what observable thereupon.* 11. *their consecration of Altars,* &c. 12. *The Degrees of Ecclesiastical persons in the Church of* Rome. *Their sacred orders, office of the Bishop, and what colours held sacred.* 13. *Wherein the other parts of the Mass consisteth.* 14. *In what else their outward worship doth consist.* 15. *Wherein consisteth the seventh part of their worship, and of their holy days.* 16. *What be their other holy days which they observe, canonical hours, and processions.* 17. *Wherein the eighth part of their worship consisteth, their Ornaments and Utensils used in Churches dedicated to Christ and the Saints, their office performed to the dead.*

The Contents.

The Contents of the Fourteenth Section.

OF *the Eastern Religions, and first of the* Greeks. 2. *Of the Church dignities, and discipline in the* Greek *Church at this day.* 3. *Of the other Nations professing the* Greek *Religion, chiefly the* Moscovites, *and* Armenians. 4. *Of the Monks, Nuns, and Eremites of* Moscovia. 5. *Of the form of Service in their Churches.* 6. *How they administer the Sacraments.* 7. *The Doctrine and Ceremonies of the* Russian *Church at this day.* 8. *Of their Marriage and Funeral Ceremonies.* 9. *Of the profession of the* Armenians. 10. *Of the other Greek Sects, namely the* Melchites, Georgians, *and* Mengrelians. 11. *Of the* Nestorians, Indians, *and* Jacobites. 12. *Of the* Maronites *Religions.* 13. *Of the* Copthi. 14. *Of the* Abyssin *Christians.* 15. *Wherein the Protestants agree with, and dissent from other Christian Churches.*

The Contents of the Fifteenth Section.

R*Eligion is the ground of all Government, and Greatness.* 2. *By divers reasons it is proved that Religion, of all Common-wealths, and humane societies, is the foundation.* 3. *That Princes and Magistrates ought to have a special care, in setling and preserving of Religion.* 4. *That one Religion only is to be allowed in a Common-wealth publickly.* 5. *In what respect different Religions may be tolerated in private.* 6. *A Christian Prince may not dissemble his Religion.* 7. *Why God blesseth the professors of false Religions, and punisheth the contemners thereof.* 8. *False Religions are grounded upon policy, and what use there is of Ceremonies in Religion.* 9. *The mixture and division of Religions, and of Idolatry.* 10. *How the Gentile Religion in worshiping of the Sun, seems to be most consonant to natural reason; with divers observations concerning Sun-worship, and the knowledge the Gentiles had of a Deity, and the Unity thereof, with some glimmering of the Trinity.* 11. *That the honour, maintenance, and advancement of a Priest-hood, is the main supporter of Religion.* 12. *That the Christian Religion is of all others the most excellent, and to be preferred for divers reasons, being considered in it self, and compared with others; with an exhortation to the practice of Religious duties, which is true Christianity.*

The

The Religions of ASIA.

The Contents of the First Section.

Of *the Church Discipline, Sacrifices, Ordination, Publick place, [Building first erected for Divine Service,] and days of Divine service before* Moses. 2. *Of the Church Government under* Moses; *difference of the High Priest from other Priests.* 3. *Of the Church Government from him till* Solomon. 4. *Of the Government after* Solomon, *till the division of the Tribes.* 5. *Of* Solomon's *Temple, and the outward splendor of the Jews Religion.* 6. *Of the Office of the Levites, of the Prophets, Scribes, Pharisees, Nazarites, Rechabites, Essenes, Sadduces, and Samaritans.* 7. *Of the ancient observation of their Sabbath, of the observation of their passover, of the feasts, of Pentecost, Tabernacles, new Moons; of Trumpets, and of expiation; of their Sabbatical year, and their Jubilee.* 8. *Of their ancient Excommunications, how God instructed them of old, and of the maintenance allowed by the Jews to their Priests and Levites.* 9. *Of the Government after the Jews were carried captive into* Babylon. 10. *Of the Jewish Church Government at this day, their prayers, Sabbaths, Feasts, Book of the Law, passover, what observable thereupon; and whether to be permitted (among Christians) in the exercise of their own Religion, and wherein not to be communicated with by Christians.* 11. *Of the Jewish preparation for morning prayer, Fast in* August, *Beginning of their new year, Feast of Reconciliation, Ceremonies in reading of the Law.* 12. *Their Church Officers, Feast of Dedication, and of* Purim, *Fasts, Marriages, Divorcements, Circumcision, Redemption of the first born, their duty toward the sick, and ceremonies about the dead.*

SECT. I.

Quest. **WAS** there any Religion, Church Government or Discipline in the beginning of the World?

Answ. Yes: For then was the word preached, and Sacraments administred. We read likewise the distinction of clean and unclean Beasts. By Faith *Abel* sacrificed *Heb.* 11. *Noah's* sacrifice was pleasing to God, *Gen.* 8. This could not be will-worship, for such is no ways pleasing to God; it was therefore according to his Word and Commandment. There was also excommunication; for *Adam* and *Eve* for their disobedience was excommunicated out of Paradise, which was then

then the type of the Church ; and every foul not circumcifed the eighth day, was to be cut off from the people of God, *Gen.* 17. The word then being preached (for God preached to *Adam* in Paradife, and doubtlefs he preached to his children out of paradife) the Sacraments adminiftred, and excommunication exercifed, which are the three main points of Church difcipline ; it follows there was then a Church and Church Government.

Q. *Was there then any Ordination ?*

Ordination in the beginning of the World.

A. Yes doubtlefs ; for God is the God if order ; nor was it fit, that he who mediated between God and the People, by preaching, prayer and facrifices, fhould thruft himfelf into that office, without ordination ; therefore God ordained *Adam*, he fome of his Children as *Cain* and *Abel*; whereas *Gen.* 4. we do not read that *Cain* and *Abel* did facrifice, but only brought their Offerings; to wit, that *Adam* might offer them up to God for them : it argueth, that as yet they had not received ordination : and it's likely that ordination then was performed by χειροθεσία or Impofition of hands, which cuftom the Jews retained in ordaining their Levites, *Num.* 8. 10. and after them, the Chriftians in ordination of Minifters, *Act.* 6. 6. 1 *Tim.* 5. 22. which ceremony the Gentiles ufed in Manumiffion of their fervants, and the Jews in ordination of their Synedrion : or the Judges impofed their hands; fo *Mofes* and *Jofhua* laid their hands upon the 70 Elders; and *Mofes* is commanded by God to lay his hands upon *Jofhua* the fon of *Nun*, *Numb.* 27. 18.

Q. *Was there then any publick place of Sacrificing ?*

Churches.

A. Yes upon the fame ground, that God, who is the God of order, will have all things done in his Church with order, and decency ; the meeting alfo together in one place to hear and pray and offer facrifice, did maintain amity amongft God's people. Befides we read, *Gen.* 25. 22. that *Rebecca*, when the children ftrugled in her womb, did not ftay at home, but went, to wit, to the publick place where God's worfhip was, to enquire of the Lord ; and becaufe in this place God ufed to fhew his prefence to his people, by fome outward fign, it was called God's prefence ; therefore *Gen.* 4. 16. *Cain* went out from the prefence of the Lord, that is, he was excommunicate out of the Church : but we muft not conceive, that as yet there were any material buildings for God's fervice ; for in the beginning men conceived it unfit to include God within the narrow bounds of a material Temple, whom the Heaven of Heavens cannot contain; therefore they worfhipped him in the open air, either upon hills, for they thought low places were unbefeeming the moft High God : hence they called every hill God's hill ; or elfe if they were neceffitated to facrifice on the fea fhore or in fome low plane they made their Altars fo much the higher ; which from their altitude, they called *Altaria* ; and thefe places of divine worfhip they named *Temples* from contemplation. The very Gentiles thought it unfit to confine the Sun their chief God to a narrow Temple, feeing the whole World was his

Temple :

Sect. 1. *A View of the Religions of* ASIA. 3

Temple: and after they built Temples for the Deities they would have them for a long time to be ὑπαίθρα, or open roofed.

Q. *Why were the Groves and High places condemned in Scripture?*

A. Because they were abused both by Jews and Gentiles to su- *Groves and* perstition, Idolatry, and all uncleanness; therefore God commands *high places* them to be cut down, Exod. 44. 13. Deut. 7. 5. 12. 3. & 16. 21. *condemned* *Josiah* destroyed them, 2 *Kings* 23. 8. 14. Against their idolatry *in Scrip-* under green trees the prophet *Isaiah* complaineth, Chap. 57. 5. God *ture.* by *Ezekiel* threatneth destruction to the idolaters on the high hills, and under green trees, Chap. 6. 13. such are also reproved by *Hosea*, 4. 13. It's true that in the beginning the People of God had no other Temples but hills and groves; *Abraham* sacrificed upon an hill, Gen. 22. he planted a grove to call upon the name of the Lord, Gen. 12. 1. *Gideon* is commanded to build an Altar upon the top of the rock, *Josh*. 6. 26. Notwithstanding, when the places were abused to Idolatry, God would have them destroyed, Levit. 26. 30. *Hos.* 10. 8. *Amos* 7. 9. *Ezek.* 6. 3, &c. because he would not have his people to give the least countenance to the Gentile idolatry; for suppose they had not upon those places erected any idols, yet they must be destroyed, because such places were abused to idolatry; besides God had given them a Tabernacle and Temple in which he would be worshipped, and to which they should repair from all parts to call upon his name. This Temple also was built upon a hill; they should therefore have contented themselves with the place that God assigned them, and not follow their own inventions, the ways of the Gentiles, who afterward in imitation of the Jews built their Temples on hills, as may be seen by the Samaritans and others. Neither would God be worshipped in groves, because they were places fitter for pleasure and dalliance than devotion; they were dark and obscure places, fitter for the prince and works of darkness, than for the God of light, or children of the day.

Q. *When were buildings first erected for divine Service?*

A. About the building of *Babel*, as *Lactantius* and some others *Buildings* think: for then *Ninus* erected statues to the memory of his father *first erected* *Jupiter Belus*, and to his Mother *Juno*; these statues were placed *for divine* over their Sepulchres and divine honours assigned them; and at *service,* length inclosed within stately buildings, which were their Temples; these they built within consecrated groves; such was the Temple of *Vulcan* in *Sicily*, of *Cybele* in the grove of *Ida*, of *Jupipiter Hammon* in the grove of *Dodone*, of *Apollo* in the grove of *Daphne*, &c. these dark groves were fit to strike a terror in the worshippers, and to perpetrate their works of abomination; and because they had continual lights burning in them, they were called *Luci a Lucendo*, afterwards they became *Asyla*, Sanctuaries or places of refuge; which some think were first erected by *Hercules* his children, to secure themselves from those that he had oppressed. We read that *Theseus* his Temple and *Thebes* built by *Cadmus* were *Asyla* or Sanctuaries; in imitation of whom *Romulus* made one. *Aen.* 8.

Hunc lucum ingentem quem Romulus acer Asylum Retulit.

Christians also in the time of *Basil* and *Silvester* the first, made their Temples places of refuge; which so increased, that Monasteries and Bishops palaces became Sanctuaries; but the exorbitancy of these was limited by *Justinian*, *Charles* the Great and other Christian princes who were content there might be Sanctuaries, because God had appointed Cities of refuge; but the abuses they removed.

Q. *Was there any set day then for Gods Worship?*

Set day of worship.
A. Doubtless there was, though we do not read which day of the week it was; for though God blessed and sanctified the Sabbath day, because of his own rest, and in that it was afterward to be the Jews Sabbath; yet we read not that it was ever kept before *Moses* his time. However it is likely this day was observed before the law among the Hebrews, for *Exod.* 16. as much Manna was gathered on the sixth day as served for two daies.

Q. *What sacrifices were used in the beginning?*

Sacrifice.
A. Burnt offerings, *Gen.* 8. and 22. Peace offerings also *Gen.* 31. 54. for upon the peace made between *Jacob* and *Laban*, *Jacob* offered sacrifice. First fruits also were offered, *Gen.* 4. 4. and Tithes, *Gen.* 14. 20. and 28. 22. The burnt sacrifice called *Gnolah* from *Gnalah* to mount upward (because it ascended all in smoak) was burned to ashes except the skin and entrails. In the peace offering also which was exhibited for the safety of the offerers, the fat was burned, because it was the Lords; the rest was divided between the Priest and the people; the breast and the right shoulder belonged to the Priest to shew that he should be a breast to love, and a shoulder to support the people in their troubles and burthens: For this cause the High Priest carried the names of the twelve Tribes on his breast and shoulders. The first fruits were an handful of the eares of corn as soon as they were ripe; these they offered to God, that by them the whole might be sanctified. Tithes were payed before the law, by the light of nature; because by that light men knew there was a God, to whom they were bound in way of gratitude to offer the tenth of their increase, from whose bounty they had all. They knew also that the worship of God and Religion could not be maintained, nor the Priest sustained, nor the poor relieved without Tithes.

Q. *What form of Church Government was there among the Jews till* Moses?

Jews their Church government from the beginning till Abraham their destruction.
A. The same that was before the flood, to wit, Praying, Sacrificing, preaching in publick places, and solemn days; to which *Abraham* added circumcision. In every family the first-born was Priest; for this cause the destroying Angel spared the first-born of the Hebrews in Egypt.

Under Moses Priests among the Jews.
Q. *What government had they under* Moses?

A. The same that before, but that there was chosen by *Moses* a Chief Priest, who was to enter the Sanctuary once a year with his Ephod, to know the will of God. This was *Aaron*, whose Breeches,

Breeches, Coat, Girdle, and Mitre were of Linen, when he entred into the Sanctuary; the High Priest had his second High Priest to serve in his absence. There were afterward appointed by *David* four and twenty Orders of Priests, every one of which Orders had a chief, or High Priest; the Priest-hood was entailed to the house of *Levi*, because the *Levites* were chosen in stead of the first-born, because they killed the worshippers of the Golden Calf, and because *Phinehas* killed *Zimri* and *Cosbi*. The Priests are sometimes called Levites, and sometimes they are distinct names; for we read that the Levites paid tithe of their tithes to the Priests; their common charge was to pray, preach, sacrifice, and look to the Sanctuary, in which they served with covered heads and bare feet; their Office was also to debar lepers, and all other unclean Persons from the Tabernacle for a certain time. Secondly to excommunicate great offenders, which was called cuting off from the people of God, and ἀποσυναγωγεῖν, to cast out of the Synagogue. Thirdly to anathematize obstinate and perverse sinners, who being excommunicate would not repent. *Alexander* the Coppersmith was anathematized by *Paul*, or delivered to Satan, 1 *Tim.* 1. 20. 2 *Tim.* 4. 14. The Office of the Levites also was to help the Priests in gathering of tithes, and to carry water and wood for the Tabernacle.

Levites among the Jews.

Q. *Wherein did the high Priest differ from other Priests?*

A. The high Priest only had Power to enter into the Sanctuary; he only wore a blew robe with bells, a golden Ephod, a breast-plate, a linen Mitre, a plate of gold on his head; by the Crown or plate was signified Christs Kingly office, by the breast-plate his Priestly, and by the bells his Prophetical office: the high Priest also was only anointed, after the order of Priest-hood was settled; but before this, every Priest was anointed: so he also wore about his paps a broidered girdle to signifie that his heart should be girt and restrained from the love of earthly things. They that took sanctuary, were not to be set at liberty till the death of the high Priest; to signifie that by the death of our high Priest Jesus Christ, we are made free. The high Priesthood was tied to the line of *Aaron*'s first born, the other Priests were of *Aaron*'s other children; the *Levites* were *Levi*'s other Posterity; the high Priest might marry none but a maid; other Priests might marry a Widow, *Levit.* 21. The high Priest might not mourn for the death of his Kindred; other Priests might mourn for their Father, Mother, Son, Daughter, Brother, and husbandless Sister; in other things they agree; for all Priests must be without blemish, all must be represented to the Lord at the door of the Tabernacle, all must be washed, all must be consecrated by offering certain Sacrifices; all must have the blood of the Ram put on the tip of the right ear, the thumb of the right hand, and great toe of the right foot, *Exod.* 25.

Difference of the high Priest from other Priests.

Q. *What Church government was there after* Moses?

A. In the Desart *Eleazer* succeeded his father *Aaron*, and substituted under him *Phinehas* to be chief of the *Levites*. After the *Israelites* entred the Land, the Tabernacle stayed some years at *Silo*; then

Church government after Moses.

then did *Joshua* divide the Land, and designed certain Cities of refuge, which with some other Cities he assigned to the Priests and Levites. The Priesthood did not continue long in the house of *Aaron*, but after the death of *Eleazer*, and three Priests his Successors, this office devolved to *Eli*, of the family of *Ithamar*; who being careless, suffered divers abuses to creep into the Ecclesiastical Government, till God raised *Samuel*, who reformed both the State and Church, by appointing Schools of Prophets, and consistories of Levites. From *Silo* the Tabernacle was translated to *Nob*, from thence to *Gibeon*, when *Nob* was destroyed by *Joab*, and at last it rested in *Jerusalem*. So that all this time there could be no settled Church discipline among the Jews. The Ark also was oftentimes removed, to wit, from *Canaan* to the *Philistines*, from thence to the *Bethshemites*; afterwards it stayed twenty years at *Kirjathjcharim*; after this it remained three months with *Obed Edom*, and at last it was brought by *David* into *Jerusalem*. All

Under David and Solomon. this time neither Tabernacle nor Ark nor Priesthood were settled, till *David* assembled the Levites, and out of them chose *Abiathar* for High-Priest, and *Tsadoc* for chief of the inferiour Priests, who were to deliver the Ark to the Levites to be carried on their shoulders, and withal appointed Singers, and other Musicians: in all 68 of the Levites. He appointed also for the service of the Tabernacle in *Gibeon*, *Tsadoc* and his Brethren. At last, *David* being assured by *Nathan* that his Son *Solomon* should build the Temple, he ordered that 24000 Levites should be set apart for the service of the Temple: to wit, 4000 door-keepers, and as many singers, and 6000 Judges and Governours, and the rest for other Offices. *Abiathar* is made High-Priest, to wait on the Ark at *Jerusalem*. *Tsadoe* is chief of the inferiour Priests to serve in the Tabernacle at *Silo*. *Tsadoc* was *Saul*'s High-Priest, descended from *Eleazer Aaron*'s first born; *Abiathar* of the stock of *Ithamar*, and *Eli*, fled to *David*, who entertained him for his High-Priest; after the death of *Saul*, *David* retained them both, thinking it did not stand with his honour and piety to reject *Saul*'s High-Priest. This *Tsadoc* under *Solomon* was Anointed the second time Priest, as *Solomon* was the second time Anointed King, 1 Chron. 29. 22. and *Abiathar* is deposed for the sins of *Eli* and his Sons; and so in *Tsadoc* the Priest-hood is translated from the house of *Ithamar*, to *Aaron*'s family again. There were also Treasurers ordained, some for the first fruits and tenths, and others for the moneys that were given to the Temple towards the redemption of Vows, first born, and sins: The Priests and Levites were maintained out of the first fruits and Tythes; the other treasure was for maintaining the daily sacrifices and other charges of the Temple; the *Gibeonites*, with others, appointed by *David* and *Solomon*, did help the Levites in their ministration: the Priests, and in their absence, the Levites did administer Justice, both in *Jerusalem*, and in the Cities of Refuge, and ordered Ecclesiastick affairs. There were also sometimes Extraordinary Prophets, besides the ordinary. Its probable that the

ordinary

ordinary prophets were of the Tribe of *Levi*, becaufe the adminiftration and care of holy things belonged to them; but extraordinary Prophets were of other Tribes: thefe medled not with facraments and Sacrifices, which was the Priefts office, nor had they their calling by fucceffion, as the Priefts; nor was the gift of prophecy only tied to the Man, as the Priefthood was; for we read of *Miriam, Hulda*, and divers other women Prophets: and in the Primitive Church, though women muft not fpeak in the Church by Preaching, Praying, or exhorting in an ordinary way as the Minifters ufe, yet they were not debarred to utter their extraordinary Prophecies, if fo be their heads were covered in fign of modefty; but otherwife the Apoftle will not have women to fpeak in the Church, becaufe they muft be in fubjection to their Husbands; and this punifhment is laid on them for being deceived in *Eve*, and hearkening to the counfel of Satan. For, if women did Preach, they might be fufpected to fpeak by that Spirit that deluded *Eve*.

Q. *What was the Ecclefiaftick Government after* Solomon?

A. The renting of the ten Tribes from the other two under *Rehoboam*, did much impair the beauty and magnificence of the Ecclefiaftick ftate. Befides that, it was much defaced by Idolatry; but reformed by *Hezekias*. *Jofias*, and *Jehofaphat*, who took away the high places. Under *Athalia* it was almoft extinguifhed, had not *Jehojada* the High Prieft anointed *Joafh*, who again reformed Religion. He being denied all aid from the Levites out of their Treafure towards the repairing of the Temple, caufed a Cheft to be made into which money given in that kind fhould be put, and imployed by the High Prieft, or by the chief of the inferiour Priefts, and the Kings Scribe or Secretary, towards the reparations of the Temple, whereas before it was collected by the Levites. King *Uzziah* would have burnt Incenfe on the Altar, but was prohibited by *Azariah* the High Prieft, and eighty other Priefts. This *Uzziah* named alfo *Azariah*, though a King, yet was juftly refifted by the Priefts for his pride, facrilege and ambition, in medling with their function; whereby he violated the Laws of politick government, which a King fhould maintain; for confufion muft arife, where offices are not diftinct, but where men are fuffered to incroach upon each others function. 2. He had no calling to the Priefthood; and no man taketh upon him this office but he that is called of God, as was *Aaron*. 3. He violated the law of God, who confined the Priefthood to the houfe of *Aaron*, and Tribe of *Levi*, excluding from that all other Tribes. 4. He was injurious to Chrift, whofe type the Priefthood was, in offering Sacrifices and Incenfe, reprefenting thereby our High Prieft Chrift Jefus, who offered up himfelf a Sacrifice, of a fweet fmelling favour unto God. So *Jehojada* the High Prieft did well to depofe *Athaliah*, who was a ftranger, an Idolater and Ufurper; this was lawful for him fo to do, being High Prieft, whofe authority was great both in Civil and Ecclefiaftick affairs; but this is no warrant for any private man to attempt the like. Befides *Jehojada* was

After Solomon.

was bound to fee the young King righted, both as he was High-Priest, and as he was his Kinfman. *Hezekias* restored all according to King *David's* Institution; he raised great Taxes towards the maintenance of God's Worship, and permitting the Levites to fley the Burnt-offerings, which before belonged only to the Priests Office, and caused the People to keep the Passover in the Second Month, whereas by *Moses* his Institution it should be kept the First Month. He permitted also many, that were not sanctified or cleansed, to eat the Passover against *Moses* his Law, which were Innovations in Religion. *Josias* reforms all abuses, abolisheth Idolatry, repaireth the Temple, Readeth publickly the Law of *Moses*, which was found by *Hilkiah* the High-Priest, and makes a Covenant with God to keep the Law. Under King *Eliakim*, or *Joachim*, Religion was so corrupted, that the Priests, Levites, Prophets or Scribes, with the Elders of the People, condemned the Prophet *Jeremy* to Death. Under *Zedekiah*, both the Church-government and State fell together in *Judea*.

Q. *In the mean while what Church-government was there among the Ten Tribes?*

Church-Government among the Ten Tribes. A. The Kings of *Israel* out of policy, lest the People should return again to *Jerusalem*, and the two Tribes, defaced their Religion with much Idolatrous worship, for executing of which they had their Priests and inferiour Ministers answering to the Levites, but they suffered no Priests or Levites of the Order of *Aaron* to live amongst them. Yet they had their Prophets also and Prophets Children or Scholars: Their two chief Prophets extraordinary, were *Eliab* and *Elisha*. They had also their Elders, who had power of Ecclesiastical Censures; but both Elders and People were ruled by the Prophets, who resided in the great Cities: at last the ten Tribes lost both themselves and Church-discipline, when they were carried away by the *Assyrians*. When *Salmanassar* carried away the *Israelites* into *Assyria*, some remainders of them stayed behind in their own Country; but being oppressed with multitudes of strangers sent thither to New-plant the Countrey, the small number of the *Ephraimites* left behind, were forced to comply with the New Inhabitants, in their Idolatrous religions; now that the *Israelites* were not quite driven out of their Native Country, may be seen in the History of *Josias*, 2 *Chron.*34. 6,7,33. and 2 *Chron.* 35. 18. and 2 *Kings* 23. 19, 20.

Q. *Wherein did the outward splendor of the Jews Religion consist.*

Solomon's Temple, and the outward splendor of the Jews Religion. A. In the Wealth and Magnificence of their Temple, which, for the beauty, riches, and greatness thereof, was one of the Wonders of the World; for besides the abundance of Iron-work, there was in it an incredible quantity of Brass, Silver, and Golden Materials. The great Altar, the Sea or Caldron, the Basis, the two Pillars before the Temple, the twelve Oxen, the ten Lavers, the Pots, the Shovels, the Basins, and other Utensils of the Temple were all of Brass, 1 *Kings* 7. as for Silver, *Josephus* tells us, *lib.* 8. and 9. that there were in the Temple Ten thousand Candlesticks, whereof

most

moſt were Silver, Wine Tankards Eighty thouſand, Silver Phials Ten thouſand, Two hundred thouſand Silver Trumpets, Forty thouſand Snuffers, or Pot-hooks, which he calls Muſical Inſtruments; beſides incredible numbers of Silver Plates and Diſhes, Silver Tables, and the Doors of Silver. This we know, that *David* left Seven thouſand Talents of refined Silver for the Temple, beſides what *Solomon* added, 1 *Chron.* 29. As for Gold, we read that the Oracle and Altar were overlaid with Gold, ſo were the Cherubins, and the whole Houſe overlaid with Gold, and the very Floor alſo, 1 *Kings* 6. Beſides the Golden Altar, *Solomon* made the Table whereon the Shew-bread was, of Gold; the Candleſticks alſo, with the Flowers, and Lamps and Tongs, with the Bowls, Snuffers, Baſons, Spoons, Cenſers, and Hinges, all of pure Gold, 1 *Kings* 7. I need not ſpeak of the Rich Woods, and Precious Stones in the Temple. The Contriver of this Fabrick was God himſelf; the Form of it was Four ſquare; the Courts four; one for the Gentiles, another for the Iſraelites, the third for Women, and the fourth for the Prieſts: the Gentiles might not enter into the Iſraelites Court; for that was counted a Prophanation of the Temple; yet our Saviour, who was frequently converſant in the Court of the Gentiles, accounted that a part of his Fathers Houſe, and the Houſe of Prayer, and it was out of this Court that he Whipped the Buyers and Sellers; this was called *Solomon's* Porch, *John* 10. *Acts* 3. becauſe in that place *Solomon* ſtood when he dedicated the Temple, and uſed there to Pray, or becauſe it ſtood undemoliſhed by the *Chaldeans,* when the reſt of the Temple was deſtroyed. In the Prieſts Court ſtood the Altar of Burnt-offerings, and the Braſen-Sea. In the Sanctuary called the Oracle (becauſe there God delivered his Oracles) ſtood the Ark, the Cenſer, Propitiatory, and Cherubins; it had no Light, nor Window in it; hither the High-Prieſt only had acceſs, and that but once a year, where he burned Incenſe, ſo that he neither could ſee, nor be ſeen. In the Holy Place, which was alſo without Windows, there burned Lights perpetually, to repreſent the Celeſtial Lights; but in the Moſt Holy there was no Light at all, to ſhew, that all outward Light is but Darkneſs, being compared with that Light which God Inhabited, and which no Man can approach unto. Within the Ark were the Two Tables of the Law, the Pot with Manna, and *Aaron's* Rod. The Tables and the Rod repreſented Chriſts Active and Paſſive Obedience; the Golden Pot with Manna, his Two Natures. The Temple was built after the manner of the Tabernacle; but that did far exceed this in ſtability, magnitude, glory, and continuance: In the Tabernacle were but Two Cherubins, in the Temple Four; in the Tabernacle there was but one Golden Candleſtick, and one Brazen Laver, but in the Temple there were ten of each. So this Temple of *Solomon's* far exceeded the other built by *Zerobabel,* wherein was wanting the Cloud, the Celeſtial Fire, the Ark, and the Holy Oyl; beſides, in number of Prophets, Magnifick Structure, and Wealth, it was far inferiour to the Firſt; and yet, in reſpect of Chriſt, the Second did

far

far exceed the First, who supplied the want of the Cloud, Fire, Oyl, Prophecy, *Urim* and *Thummim*. He being all these in a more excellent manner. But we must note, that though the Pot with Manna, and *Aaron*'s Rod were kept in *Moses* his Ark; yet in *Solomon*'s Ark were onely the Two Tables of the Law, 1 *Kings* 8. 9. In the Womens Court stood the *Gazophylacium*, or Treasury, containing the Alms or Gifts that were Offered.

Q. *What else may we observe of* Solomon's *Temple?*

A. That this Temple was to the Jews as their Cathedral or Metropolitan Church; the Synagogues which were not in *Jerusalem* till after the Captivity, did resemble our Parish Churches; in which the Scribes taught, as the Priests in the Temple; and as there was a High Priest for the Temple, so there was for the Synagogue a High Ruler, called *Archisynagogus*. In the Synagogues also they had their distinct Courts, as in the Temple, and an Ark for the Book of the Law; and the same holiness ascribed to the one as to the other, but that they could Sacrifice no where but in the Temple upon the Brazen Altar in the Court of the Priests; which Altar was called *Ariel*, or the *Lion*, because, like a Lion, it devoured the Flesh of the Sacrifices. Upon the Golden Altar Incense was Offered; Christ was represented by both Altars; his Humanity and Passion by the Brazen; his Divinity, Resurrection and Ascension by the Golden Altar, and the Incense thereof mounting toward Heaven. In the Court of the Priest, called, the Holy Place, stood the Table of Shew-bread, on which were Twelve Loaves, which represented the Twelve Tribes; upon each Loaf was a Dish of Frankincense, shewing Christ's Intercession for his People. The Candlestick and Pincers or Snuffers, represented the Doctrine and Discipline of the Church. Some divide the Temple but into three parts, excluding the Court of the Gentiles; to wit, into the Outward Court of the Israelites, the Holy, or Court of the Priests, and the Holiest of all, into which the High-Priest entred once yearly with Blood, Incense and Smoak. It was death for any other to enter there, and even for the High-Priest himself, if he entred above once in a year; *Pompey* and *Heliodorus* took the boldness to enter thither, but the one never prospered after, and the other fell Mad; so dangerous a thing it is to be too bold with Religion. The Brazen-Laver and the Shew-bread in the Priests-Court represented the two Sacraments of the Church, to wit, Baptism and the Eucharist. The Women shewed their Devotion in bestowing their Looking-glasses (which were not of Glass, as ours are, but of Polished Brass) upon the Brazen Laver, *Exod.* 38. 8. a Looking-glass sheweth us the spots of our faces, but Baptism washeth away the spots of our Souls. Two other Temples were built in opposition to that of *Jerusalem*, namely, the Temple of *Samaria*, built by *Sanballat* upon the Mount *Garizin*; the other at *Heliopolis* in *Egypt* by *Onias* the Fourth, whom *Antiochus* had put from the High-Priest-hood. The Second Temple of *Jerusalem*, built by *Zerobabel*, was begun in the second year of King *Cyrus*, *Ezra* 3. 8. and was finished in the ninth year of *Darius Hystaspes*, which was 46 years in all; whereas the first Temple was begun and finished in seven years. *Herod* spent eight years, whether in repairing of the old, or in building of a new is uncertain; yet *Josephus* tells us, that *Herod* pulled down the old Temple, and built a new one; which was six and forty years in adorning and perfecting, of which the Jews are to be understood, *John* 2. 20.

Q. What did the Temple and the Utensils thereof represent to us?

A. As the flitting Tabernacle shadowed out the Church Militant, so the fixed Temple resembled the Church Triumphant; the three Courts represented the three-fold estate of Mankind; to wit, his state in sin before the Law, by the outward Court of the Gentiles; his state under the Law, by the inward Court of the Priest; and his state under Grace by the Holy of Holys. The Temple, as it was built by *Solomon* a peaceable Prince, resembleth the Christian Church erected by Christ the Prince of Peace. The one was built without noise, so was the other. The Temple was built upon a Hill; and the Church, saith Christ, is like a City built upon a Hill. In the Oracle, or most holy place, was neither the light of Sun, Moon nor Candle, resembling the New *Jerusalem* in the Revelation, having the glory of God, and the Lamb for the light thereof, *Rev.* 21. 23. In this place stood the Ark and Golden Censer, with the Tables of the Law, *Aaron*'s Rod, and the Pot with Manna; the Mercy-seat covered the Ark, whereon were the golden Cherubins; Christ's Kingly Office was represented by the Ark crowned with Gold; his Priest-hood by the Censer, and his Prophetical Office by the Mercy-seat, whence God spake to the High-Priest; the Tables of the Law and *Aaron*'s Rod shadowed out his Active and Passive Obedience; the Cherubins looking on the Ark, did signifie Jews and Gentiles looking on Christ their King. The Pot with Manna did adumbrate his Divinity by the one, and his Humanity by the other. The Propitiatory covered the Law, and so hath Christ hid and concealed the Condemning power thereof; in the Sanctuary, or Holy Place, was the Table with the Twelve Loaves, representing the Twelve Tribes, and, in them, all true Israelites, or Church of Christ; on the one side having the Golden Candlestick, on the other the Altar of Incense, besprinkled yearly with the Blood of the Sacrifice: and representing the Preaching of the Word, and Prayer, which by the Death of Christ are made acceptable to God. In the same place also stood the Brazen Altar of Burnt-offerings, and the Brazen-Sea; the one resembled Christ, by whom we are Justified; the other Holiness of Life, by which we are Sanctified: or the Altar of Burnt-offerings did signifie our Eucharist, and the Brazen-Sea our Baptism. The Fire that burned continually on the Altar, did signifie Christ's Divinity; for our God is a consuming fire, saith the Apostle. The Holy Oyl with which the Priest was anointed, shadowed the Graces of the Spirit poured out on Christ's Humanity; with this oyl of gladness Christ was anointed above his Fellows.

What represented by Solomon's Temple and Utensils thereof.

Q. *What*

A View of the Religions of ASIA. Sect. 1.

Office of the Levites.

Q. *What was the Office of the Levites?*

A. Besides that they helped the Priests in gathering of Tithes, some of them did carry Wood and Water for the Tabernacle, which they were bound to carry up and down with its Utensils, to pitch and take it down whilest it was moveable; they were distinguished according to *Levi's* three Sons, into the *Gershonites*, *Cohathites*, and *Merarites*; the first carried the Hangings and Coverings; the second, the chief things of the Sanctuary; the third had the Charge of the Wood-work. In *David's* time some were Judges, some Treasurers, some Singers, and some Porters, 1 *Chron.* 23. 26. The Singers and Porters were divided into 24 Orders, 1 *Chron.* 25. and 26. The Elder Levites were to oversee and teach the Younger, who, from the Thirtieth year of their life, till the Fiftieth, did bear about the Tabernacle. Under them were the *Gibeonites*, or *Nethinims*, whose Office was to draw Water, and hew Wood for the House of God.

Prophets.

Q. *What were the Prophets, Scribes and Pharisees?*

A. Not only were they called Prophets to whom God revealed himself and his purposes in an extraordinary way, but those also that expounded the Scripture, they were also called Fathers, Doctors of the Law, Disputers, Wise Men and Rabbies, from their greatness in knowledge, Which title the Pharisees did appropriate to themselves; their Scholars were called Children, and Sons of the Prophets.

Scribes.

The name of Scribes was given to Scriveners, and publick Notaries; these were called Scribes of the People, *Matt.* 2. 4. and likewise to those that did Write and Expound the Law; such a Scribe was *Esdras*, *Esd.* 7. 6. these were called Doctors of the Law.

Pharisees.

The Pharisees were so called from separation, and by the Greeks ἀφωρισμένοι that is, Separatists; for they separated themselves to a strict kind of Life, and to the Study of the Law, having no commerce with other People, nor communicating with them in Dyet, Apparel, nor Customs. They held a fatal necessity with the Stoicks; and Transanimation with the Pythagoreans: hence they thought, that either the Soul of *John Baptist*, or of *Elias*, or of *Jeremy*, had animated Christ's Body. They preferred Traditions to the Written Word, and placed most of their holiness in Washing, counting it a less sin to commit Fornication, than to eat with unwashen hands; from their daily Washings they were named *Hemero Baptists*; they always washed when they returned from the Market, thinking themselves polluted with the touch of other People. They are noted, *Matth.* 9. 11. for holding it unlawful to eat with Sinners; and *Mark* 7. 4. for their superstitious washing of Cups, Pots, Brazen Vessels and Tables; and *Luke* 18. 12. for Fasting twice in the Week; and *Matth.* 23. 5. for their broad Phylacteries, which were scrolls of Parchment, wherein the Law was Written; so called from φυλάτ(ε)ιν, to keep or reserve; for by these they kept the Law in their Memory: they are noted also for their large Borders and Fringes, *Mark* 23. 5. they wore their Phylacteries on their Fore-heads and Left-arms; and *Hierom* observeth in *Matth.* 23.

Sect. 1. *A View of the Religions of* ASIA.   13

Matth. 23. that they used sharp thorns in their fringes, that by the prickling thereof they might be put in mind of the commandments.

Q. *What were the* Nazarites, Rechabites, *and* Essenes?

A. The *Nazarites* were votaries, *Numb.* 6. so called from *Nazar*, *Nazarites.* to separate; for they separated themselves from wine and strong drink, from coming near the dead, and from the razor: some were *Nazarites* for their life, as *Sampson, John Baptist,* &c. others only for a time, to wit, thirty days; as *Absolom,* who cut his hair the thirtieth day of his vow: such a *Nazarite* was *Paul, Acts* 21. 24. *Nazareth* was a village in *Galilee* where Christ was conceived and bred, and therefore was called a *Nazarite, Matth.* 2. 23. and his Disciples *Nazarites, Acts* 24. 5. but indeed he was the only true *Nazarite*; because he was pure, holy, and separate from sinners; But he was no legal *Nazarite,* for he drunk wine, and went near the dead. These Hereticks were also called *Nazarites,* who taught that with the Gospel should be joyned the Law of *Moses, Acts* 15. 2. Of the *Rechabites,* so called from *Rechab* their Father, *Rechabites.* we read *Jer.* 35. 2, 3, 4, &c. these neither drunk wine nor sowed seed, nor built houses, nor planted vineyards, but like strangers lived all their days in Tents. The *Essenes,* so called from their *Essenes.* skill in curing of Diseases, (for they were much given to the study of Physick) in their opinions were Pythagoreans, ascribing all things to fate, offering no sacrifices but of inanimate things, shunning oaths, pleasures, and wine, and contenting themselves with water only, and mean apparel; their garments were white, and they had all things in common amongst them. They worshipped towards the East, observed the Sabbath more strictly than others; kept seven Pentecosts every year, to wit, every seventh week one, and generally they abstained from marriage; yet some did marry for procreation. They were superstitious in preserving the names of Angels; they were much given to silence, with the Pythagoreans, chiefly at table: none were admitted into their Society without four years probation. There were some of these *Essenes* contemplative only, and lived in gardens, or remote villages, who contented themselves with bread and salt: others were active, and gave themselves to manual labours; these lived in Cities, and fared better, and eat twice a day.

Q. *What were the* Sadduces *and* Samaritans?   *Sadduces.*

A. The *Sadduces* were so called either from *Tsedek* justice, because they would be accounted the only just men in the world; or from *Sadock* the Author of their Sect, who was the Scholar of *Antigonus Socheus*: These rejected all Traditions and Scriptures, except the five books of *Moses*; denied the Resurrection, pains or rewards after this life, Angels and spirits, fate likewise or destiny, ascribing all to mans free-will. They held also that the soul died, and perished with the body. The *Samaritans* held with the *Sadduces,* that there was no Scripture but the Pentateuch; that there was no Re- *Samari-* surrection, nor life eternal, nor any Traditions to be admitted: yet *tans.*

they

they diffented from the *Sadducees* in acknowledging Angels; in worshipping onely upon mount *Gerizim*, whereas the *Sadduces* worshipped also in *Jerusalem*, and kept fair correspondence with the other Jews: whereas the Samaritans and Jews did so hate and abhor each other, that there was no commerce between them, but did curse and excommunicate each other. Of these Jewish Sects, see *Josephus, Philo, Drusius de trib. Sect. Munster, Sigonius, Buxtorfius*, and others.

Q. *How did they anciently observe their Sabbath?*

Jews, their ancient observation of their Sabbath.
A. The day before was the preparation of the Sabbath, called παρασκευή, which began about the sixth hour, that is our twelfth. That day they might not travel above twelve miles, least by coming home too late, they might want time for preparation to the Sabbath, which began in the evening; and which for the excellency thereof, was called the Queen of Feasts, and gave denomination to the whole week: on the Sabbath they must not travel above two thousand paces or cubits; for so far was the distance of the Ark from the Camp. They were so superstitious in keeping of their Sabbath, that they would not fight that day, and so suffered *Jerusalem* to be taken twice: whereas they knew that God commanded them to encompass *Jericho* seven times that day; and that works of charity, necessity, and of Religion, were to be done that day: the preparation for the Sabbath was proclaimed by sound of trumpet; and to shew their zeal to that day, they would keep some more hours than were enjoyned, which additament they called *Sabbatulum*. They would not dress meat that day, because then it did not rain Manna in the desart. Besides the seventh day, which was the Sabbath or rest for men and beasts, they had every seventh year a Sabbath, wherein the ground rested, and their great Sabbath in the end of seven times seven, called the *Jubilee*, in which debtors, prisoners, and mortgagers of lands were made free; when the Passeover fell upon the Sabbath, this was called the great Sabbath, *John* 19. 31. and then there was a preparation for the Passeover, *John* 19. 14. but there was no preparation due to the Passeover but in respect of the Sabbath, which had this privilege above all other Festivals; because God had particularly sanctified this day for his service; being both a memorative day of Gods rest from the works of creation, and figurative of our rest in Heaven; this day is abolished in respect of the ceremonial and judicial part thereof, but in respect of the morality it remaineth still.

Q. *How did the Jews observe their Passeover?*

Their observation of the Passeover.
A. They eat the first Passeover standing, with their loyns girt, shooes on their feet, and staves in their hands, to shew they were in haste to be gone; but afterward; when they were secure out of danger, they eat the Passeover, sitting, or leaning, after the Roman manner: which posture our Saviour observed when he eat the Passeover. The beast that must be eat was a Lamb or Kid, as being cheapest; and because it must be eat up at one time: this Lamb was to be kept four days, to wit, from the tenth day till the fifteenth, that they might have the longer time to think of their deliverance,

liverance, by looking on the Lamb, and withal to search if any defects were in it; for the Lamb must be without blemish; but this custom did not hold long: it must be also a male, and not above a year old. There must not be fewer than ten at the eating of the Lamb; it was killed between the two evenings; that is, between three of the afternoon till sun-setting, which was the first; and from thence till day-light was quite spent; which was the second evening. This killing of the Lamb was rather a Sacrament than a Sacrifice, as not being performed by a Priest, but by private men; and not in the place appointed for sacrifices, but in private-houses. The blood of the Lamb was sprinkled on their thresholds; this ceremony was used but only the first Passeover, as I can find: the Lamb was roasted, not boyled, for the more expedition; and nothing of it must be left, lest it should hinder them in their journey: and it must be eat with sower herbs, to put them in mind of their bitter servitude in *Egypt*: the bread that was eat with it was unleavened, to shew their haft in removing thence; the whole solemnity from this was called the feast of unleavened bread and likewise the Passeover. Albeit properly the Passeover was only the first day, yet the whole eight days were so named. This Sacrament was a true representation of Christ, the immediate Lamb of God, *that takes away the sins of the world*; who is the true Passeover, because the devouring Angel of Gods wrath hast past over our sins; he was killed and roasted by the fire of his Fathers wrath: he is our true food, whom we must eat with sower herbs, and our loyns girt, to shew how ready we must be to undergo the bitterness of afflictions, and to subdue our carnal lusts: we must eat him without leaven; that is, without pride and hypocrisie: now is the time to eat him by faith; for this is the evening of the world in which our Passeover was sacrificed for us. The first and last day of this feast were the two great days; but the days between them were only half holy days. Other Ceremonies of this Feast we will see anon, in the observation of Easter by the Modern Jews.

Q. *What were the feasts of Pentecost and Tabernacles?*

Their feast of Pentecost.

A. Pentecost was kept in memory of the Law given on *Sinai*, fifty days after the Passeover. The first day of the Passeover was called πρώτη called ἀπτέρα; the first Sabbath after this second day, was called δἀτερόπρωτον, that is, the second first Sabbath, *Luke* 16. 1. and because their harvest began at Easter, and ended at Pentecost, therefore they are commanded, *Levit.* 23. 10. to offer a sheaf of the first fruits of their harvest, upon the morrow or second day of their great feast; and on the Pentecost to offer two wave-loaves: the first offering was to sanctifie their harvest, the second was in token of thanks to God for the finishing of their harvest. The feast of Tabernacles was kept in memory of their forty years abode in the Wilderness, when they lived in Tents, and by day were shadowed by a cloud. The first and last days were the chief days, especially the last, called therefore the great day of the feast, *John* 7. 37. and in these long feasts, the first and last days are called Sabbaths. In this

Their feast of Tabernacles.

feast

feast their custom was to hold in their hands branches of trees, which they called *Hosanna*; with this *Hosanna* they honoured Christ; they made booths (therefore the feast was called σκηνοπηγία) in the opening air, in which they lived seven days together, except in time of rain: weak and impotent persons were excused and exempted from these booths, which were made of Citrine trees, Palms, Mirtles, and Willows. The next day after the feast, they compassed the Altar seven times with Palms in their hands, in memory of the encompassing of *Jericho*. During the time of this feast, many bullocks were offered, as may be seen *Numb.* 29. on the last day of the feast they read the last Section of the Law, and began the first, and drew water out of the river *Siloah*, which in the Temple they delivered to the Priests, who poured it with wine on the Altar, the people singing, *with joy shall you draw water out of the wells of Salvation*] *Isa.* 12. 3. This feast was kept the fifteenth day of *Tisri* the seventh moneth; but *Jeroboam* kept it the fifteenth day of the eighth moneth: some think that this feast was kept as a thanksgiving to God for their Vintage; and *Plutarch* calls it θυρσοφοριαν, a bearing about of *Thyrsi*; that is, of Spears wrapped about with Ivy in honour of *Bacchus*. But of these passages see *Hospinian de orig. fest. Munster in Kalender*, and on *Leviticus, Fagius* on *Leviticus*, the *Thalmud tract. de tabern. Scaliger de emend. temp. Josephus in antiq.* Buxtorfius, Tremellius, &c.

Q. *What were their new Moons, and feasts of Trumpets, and Expiation?*

Their new Moons. A. Every new Moon was a festival among the Jews, in which, as on the Sabbath, people repaired to the Prophets for instruction, 2 *Kings* 4. 23. then it was not lawful to buy or sell, *Amos* 8. 4. yet the first new Moon in the beginning of their seventh month called *Tisri*, according to their Ecclesiastical account, but the first month in their civil computation, was called particularly the feast of Trumpets; for though at other feasts they sounded Trumpets, *Their feast of Trumpets.* yet at this feast there was more sounding, to wit, all the day; not so much in memory of *Isaac*'s deliverance from death on mount *Moriah*, nor for the Law given with sound of Trumpets on mount *Sinai*; for the feast of Pentecost was instituted for that, but for the greater solemnity of the new year, from whence they reckoned their Sabbatical years and Jubilees, and dated all their deeds and bargains. This sounding then of Trumpets was a solemn promulgation of the new year, and a preparation for the three ensuing feasts that month, to wit, of Expiation the tenth day, of Tabernacles from the fifteenth to the one and twentieth, and the great feast on the two and twentieth day; but I think this was no particular feast, but the conclusion of the feast of Tabernacles. Of the Sacrifices to be offered in the new Moons, read *Numb.* 28. 11, 15. as for those words of *David*, *Psal.* 81. 3. *blow the Trumpet in the new Moon*, they are most likely to be meant of the first new Moon, or feast of Trumpets. The feast of Expiation was kept the tenth day of *Tisri*; and it was so called, because the High Priest then entred into the Oracle, to expiate his own and the peoples *Their feast* fins: for himself he took a young Bullock and a Ram; for the *of Expia-* people he took a Ram for a burnt-offering, and two he-Goats for *tion.* a sin-offering; the two Goats he presented at the door of the Tabernacle before the Lord; one of these (lots being cast) was sent into the wilderness: this was called the Scape-goat, upon whose head the Priest laid all the sins and evils of the people, to be carried away by the Goat into the wilderness: The other Goat was sacrificed. On this day was their great fast, *Act.* 8. 9. wherein they abstained from all kind of work and delights, so that they might not kindle fire, nor dress meat; notwithstanding their afflicting themselves, the joyful Jubilee was this day proclaimed. Of the Rites used at this day by the modern Jews, we will speak hereafter.

Q. *What was their Sabbatical year, and their Jubile?*

A. Every seventh year was a Sabbath or rest; for then the land *Jews their* did rest from plowing and sowing; then poor debtors that were na- *Sabbatical* tive Jews, and not proselytes or strangers, were released, if they *year.* were not able to pay: by this God would exercise the charity of his people to the poor, and have them rely on his providence, who gave such increase to the sixth year, that it brought forth provision enough for three years; and therefore all things were this time held in common, and they lived as *Adam* did in Paradise, or as people in the golden age, when the earth *sponte suâ* of its own accord brought forth all things; *omnis tulit omnia tellus.* Of this years fertility see *Levit.* 25. 20. The Hebrew servants were this year to be set free, *Exod.* 21. 2. and the Law to be read publickly, *Deut.* 31. 10. The Jubilee, so called from *Jobal*, a Ram, because of the founding of Rams horns at that time was instituted, *Levit.* 25. 8. for the comfort of prisoners, servants and debtors; for then all things were brought back to their former estate; and therefore per- *Their Jubi-* haps it is called Jubilee, from *Jobbel*, to deduce, or bring back, all *lee.* lands that had been sold or morgaged, were restored to the right owners, by which means Families and Tribes were preserved entire without commixtion or confusion, and their ancient inheritances remained whole. This feast was kept every fiftieth year, but was proclaimed the forty ninth, on the day of expiation; and was a type of that great liberty and delivery we have by Christ; which is begun in this world and consummated in that which is to come, where we shall enjoy eternal rest, and shall obtain remission of all our debts, and the possession of that ancient inheritance prepared for us before the foundation of the world. This year of Jubilee also was to put them in mind of their deliverance from the captivity of *Egypt.* As in the Sabbatical year, so likewise in this all things were common; the servant whose ear was boared, is now set free; and the slave that was sold for six years, is now dismissed, although those six years were not ended. The beasts also had liberty to feed where they pleased. But as the Jews did keep no Jubilee in the captivity of *Babylon*, neither have they kept any since Christ. As for their feasts of *Purim*, and dedication, or renovation, called therefore in Greek ἐγκαίνια, we will speak anon. These were all the Festivals kept by the Jews; the three chief besides the Sabbath, were the Passover, Pentecost, and Tabernacles in commemoration of three great benefits, without which no Society or Commonwealth can subsist, to wit, Liberty, Laws, and Defence or Protection. Now for divers reasons God instituted so many festival days. First, because he would have his people keep in mind the benefits he bestowed on them. Secondly, to give him thanks; which they solemnly did, chiefly at Easter, by offering their first fruits; at Pentecost by offering loaves; at the feast of Tabernacles, by sacrificing in that they had now gathered in all their fruits. Thirdly, by these festivals the love and amity of God's people were the more preserved in their often meetings. Fourthly, and so was their devotion the oftner exercised in sacrifices, by which the Levites and poor were relieved. Fifthly, unity of Religion was also by this means preserved. Sixthly, and their obedience also in this was tried. Seventhly, but chiefly Christ, the promised Messiah, was in these feasts represented; for every sacrifice and oblation did shadow forth his death and passion, by whose blood alone, and not by the blood of Goats and Rams, we have obtained eternal Redemption.

Q. *What sorts of Excommunication were used among the Jews?*

Their Excommunications of old.
A. At first they excluded the delinquent out of their Synagogues, *John* 9. 22. but not quite out of the Temple; for he might stand in the gate in time of Divine service; this censure lasted thirty days and more, if the party repented not; and if he died without repentance, he wanted the ceremonies of common burial, and a stone was laid on his coffin, signifying he deserved stoning. They had a higher degree of excommunication, which S. *Paul* calls [*a giving over to Satan*] 1 *Cor.* 5. 5. by the Greeks the party so excommunicated was called ἀνάθεμα, and such were not permitted to come near the Temple. Curses also were denounced against them; *Hymeneus, Alexander,* and the incestuous person are those excommunicated. Their highest degree was *Maran-atha,* that is, the Lord cometh, 1 *Cor.* 16. signifying, that the Lord was coming with vengeance against such; these were totally secluded from the people of God, which is called a cutting off from the people, and a blotting or rasing of their names out of the book of life; answering to those three degrees the Greek Church had; their ὑποπίπτοντες. 2. Ἀφοριζόμενοι. 3. προσκλαίοντες. So the Latine had their *Abstenti, Excommunicati,* and *Anathemata.* The reason why God would have this strict discipline used in his Church, is first, to terrifie the evil doers. Secondly, to preserve the sound sheep from being infected by the scabbed. Thirdly, to keep up the reputation of his Church, which otherwise might be scandalized for conniving at sin. Fourthly, that Gods judgments may be either delivered or prevented; for he is just, and will not wink at sin. Fifthly, that the excommunicate person by his severity may be brought to repentance and amendment of life. They had a peculiar way in-

excommuni-

Sect. 1.   *A View of the Religions of* ASIA.   19

excommunicating the *Samaritans*, to wit, by sound of Trumpet, and singing of the *Levites*, who first by word of mouth pronounced a curse against the *Samaritans*, and those that eat or conversed with them; shewing that they shall never be Proselytes in *Israel*, nor have any part in the resurrection of the just. Then they wrote this curse, and caused it to be read and pronounced in all parts of *Israel*.

Q. How did God instruct the Jews of old?

A. Sometimes by visions and dreams; sometimes by secret inspi- *Jews how* ration; sometimes by a voice from Heaven; sometimes by *Urim instructed* and *Thummim*; that is, light and perfection, which were the pre- *by God of* cious stones on the breast-plate of the high Priest; but ordinarily he *old.* taught them by his word, either written by his holy Pen-men, or unwritten, namely, by Tradition; for God delivered his will this way to *Moses*, and he to *Joshuah*, who imparted this to the Elders, and they to the Prophets. From the Prophets the great Synagogue received these Traditions, till at last they were committed to writing, for the benefit of those Jews which dwelt in *Judea*, about the year of Christ 230. This was called the *Thalmud* of *Jerusalem*; but 500. years after Christ, the Jews at *Babylon* made a more exact collection, and this they called the *Thalmud* of *Babylon*, which contains all their Canon and civil Laws, and this is with them of no less authority than the Scripture. They have besides this their *Kabbala*, which is a mystical kind of learning, consisting most in certain letters and syllables, out of which they raise many mystical whimseys. The *Thalmudists* expect a temporal Kingdom, the *Kabbalists* a spiritual; who also hold that there was an invisible world created 2000. years before this; because the first word in *Genesis* is *Bereshith*, and the first letter thereof is *Beth*, which stands in their Arithmetick for 2000. R. *Jonathan* compiled the *Thalmud* of *Jerusalem*; the other of *Babylon* was made up by R. *Asse*; which is divided into six Parts, sixty Books, and five hundred thirty and two Chapters. It's thought that *Ezra* delivered this *Thalmud* to *Simon* the high Priest, and he to his successors, till at last it came to old *Simeon*, (who took up Christ in his arms) and from him to his Scholar *Gamaliel*. It's most likely that *Pythagoras* had his *Kabbalistical* Philosophy from the Jewish Rabbies: but of these passages see *Galatinus de Arcanis*, *Munster*, *Fagius*, D. *Kimchi*, and the *Thalmud* it self.

Q. What maintenance did the Jews allow their Priests and Levites?

A. Besides certain Cities, and Shares in their Sacrifices and Ob- *Their main-* lations, they allowed them the First-fruits and Tithes, the First- *tenance or* fruits of the Threshing-floor, *Numb.* 15. 20. comprehending the *allowance* First-fruits in the Sheaf, offered at the Passover in the beginning of *to their* Harvest; and the First-fruits of Loaves at Pentecost, in the end of *Priests and* their Harvest, besides the First of their Dough, *Numb.* 15. 20. *Neh.* *Levites.* 10. 37. *Rom.* 11. 10. these First-fruits were called Heave, or Wave-offerings, because they were shaken up and down, to shew that
C 2   God

A View of the Religions of ASIA. Sect 1.

God was Lord of Heaven and Earth; or else from hand to hand to all Corners of the Earth, to signifie, that the whole Earth was the Lord's. The Firstlings of Man and Beast God challeng'd as his own, *Exod.* 13. because he spared the First-born of the *Israelites*, when he smote those of *Egypt*. The Firstlings of Clean Beasts were Sacrificed, the Fat whereof was burned, but the Flesh was given to the Priest. But the Firstlings of Men and Unclean Beasts were redeemed for Five Silver Shekels of the Sanctuary, paid to the Priests for each of them, *Numb.* 18. 15, 16. when they carried up their First-fruits to *Jerusalem*, they had a Pipe playing before them, and a Bull with Gilded-Horns, and a Garland of Olive-branches on his head. As for their Tithes, the Husbandman, according to *Scaliger's* reckoning, out of 6000. Bushels in one year, paid for the First and Second Tithe, and First-fruits 1121 Bushels, which is above a sixth part of the whole, besides the Tithe of their Cattle, and Fruit of their Trees; and so strict were the Pharisees in the payment of their Tithes, that they Tithed *Mint, Anise, and Cummin*, Matth. 23. 23. Out of the first Tithe, paid to the Levites by the Husbandman, was paid a Tithe to the Priest by the Levites. The Second Tithe was paid by the Husbandman, either in Kine or Money, as he pleased. This Tithe was not so great as the first; for if he paid 590. Bushels for his first Tithe, he paid but 531. for his second Tithe: but this second Tithe every third year was spent by the Husbandman at home upon the Poor, and not in *Jerusalem* on the Levites. This year was called the year of Tithes, *Deut.* 26. 12. And though at this day the Jews have no Lands, yet they pay carefully the Tenth of their Increase.

Q. What Church-government had the Jews after they were carried captive into Babylon?

Church-Government in, and after the Captivity of Babylon.

A. They had no setled Government in *Babylon*, being then in Misery and Captivity; yet they had some Elders and Prophets, as may be seen in *Ezek.* 8. 1. After the Captivity, they reformed all things according to King *David's* Institution; but the number of Singers, Door-keepers, and other Officers, came far short of the former. This Government continued in some measure till the time of *Antiochus Epiphanes*, who sold the Pontificate to *Jason*, the Brother of *Onias* the High-Priest: he, by degrees, brought in the Greek Government, and so did the third Brother *Menelaus*; at last it was totally subverted, in the eighth year of *Antiochus*, and again restored by *Mattathias*, and more fully by *Judas, Jonathan*, and his Brother *Simon*: in *Jonathan* the Priesthood was translated from the Family of *Tsadec* to the posterity of *Joiarib*, who came of *Eleazar*. And the Government held out in some sort till *Herod* the First overthrew it, by thrusting out the lawful Priests, and substituting at his pleasure unworthy Men. The like was done by the Roman Governors; then were the Levites deprived of their Tithes by the Chief Priests. The Singers were permitted by *Agrippa* the younger to wear a Linen Garment as well as the Priests; they retained then some Priests and Levites; they had also Scribes and Lawyers, who

exercised

exercised Ecclesiastical Jurisdiction with the Elders of the People. They had also Synagogues of their profession abroad in *Alexandria, Cilicia*, and other places, *Acts* 6. 9. and in *Judea* too, whither the People met to Pray, and hear the Law and Prophets Read. The Synagogues had their Rulers, *Acts* 13. 15. who did Interpret the Law; they were also called Prophets, Scribes and Lawyers. But the Government of the Jewish Church was much pestered by the *Samaritans, Essenes, Sadduces* and *Pharisees*; *Nazarenes*, who rejected the Books of *Moses*; *Hemerobaptists*, who washed themselves daily; and the *Herodians*, who held that *Herod* was Christ. The *Essenes* contemned Marriage, and thought themselves holier than other Men, therefore called ὅσιοι, Saints; they would have had all things equal. The *Samaritans* rejected all Scripture, except the Pentateuch, and were the Sworn Enemies of the Jews. The *Pharisees* were so called from Separation; for they separated themselves from other Men, accounting all prophane but themselves: they placed all Sanctimony in outward shews. The *Sadduces*, so called from Justice, denied Providence, subjected all things to our Will; denied the Souls Immortality, Angels, and the Resurrection. The *Scribes* perverted all by their Sophistical Glosses on the Law. Of these things see *Sigonius, Petram, Josephus,* and others.

Q. *But what Church Government have the Jews at this day?*

A. In *Rome, Venice, Worms, Mentz, Frankford* on the *Moon, Fridburg, Amsterdam,* and in divers places of *Poland, Bohemia,* and elsewhere they have their Synagogues, where they use to Pray together, and to hear the Law Read. Before they come thither they wash themselves, and scrape their Shooes with an Iron fastened in a wall before the Synagogue. They enter with great reverence, bowing themselves towards the Ark, where their Law is kept; and are tied to a Set-form of Prayer, which they must Read in their Books; they that cannot Read must hearken diligently, and say, *Amen,* though they understand not what is Read; for their Liturgy is the old Hebrew, which they generally understand not. They utter divers brief Benedictions, and after them some short Prayers; and because they cannot Sacrifice, being banished from *Jerusalem,* the place appointed for Sacrifice, therefore in stead thereof they Read the Law concerning Sacrifices and Offerings; and some Expositions thereof out of the *Thalmud*, which they understood not. They Pray in particular for the rebuilding of *Jerusalem,* and their return thither, which they daily expect, for which they express great joy and vociferation. Then they Read a long Prayer, collected out of the Psalms, with some part out of the first Book of the *Chronicles,* c. 30. Then they conclude with Singing these words of *Obadiah,* v. 17. *But upon Mount Sion shall be deliverance, and there shall be holiness; and the house of* Jacob *shall possess their possessions,* &c. *And the house of* Esau *shall be stubble,* &c. *And Saviours shall come upon Mount Sion to judge the Mount of* Esau, *and the Kingdom shall be the Lords.* Other Songs also they Sing, much to this purpose; and when they sing or say these words, [*Hearken, O Israel, the Lord*

Jews, their Church Government at this day.

our God is one God] they turn their heads to the four corners of the World, intimating thereby, that God is every where King. There be some of their Prayers which they are bound to say every day twice, Standing Strait, thinking that thereby they shall Merit. But when they utter these words of *Isa.* 6. 3. [*Holy, holy, holy Lord God of Sabbath, the Earth is full of thy glory*] they leap three times. They hold, that whosoever doth speak whilst they are Praying, shall eat burning coals when they are dead. After this, they utter an Execrable Prayer against all Christians and Baptized Jews. Then they Pray for Peace, bowing their heads to the Left, then to the Right hand, and depart out of the Synagogue with their faces still towards the Ark, like Crabs going backward. They use also to go slowly out of the Synagogue, lest by making haste they might seem to be weary of Praying. When they mention the Adoration which is given to Christ by Christians, they spit on the ground in detestation thereof.

Q. *What circumstances do the Jews now observe in Praying?*

Jews, their manner of Prayer. A. They Pray being girt, standing upright, with their faces towards *Jerusalem*, laying their hand on their heart, and bowing their head. They hold it a great sin in Praying, to belch, yawn, spit, or break wind, because they hold the Angels to be there present; but if any be necessitated to break wind, he must beg pardon of God, who hath made him a Body so full of holes; he that Prays must make no interruption, though a Serpent should bite him, or the King of *Israel* speak to him. They are bound to utter an hundred Blessings every day. In Praying they must not touch their naked skin. They hold Sneezing in Prayers to be a good sign, but breaking Wind to be ominous; and they believe that whosoever saith heartily, *Amen*, to their Prayers, hasteneth their Redemption.

Q. *What is the time and order of their Evening Prayer?*

Their times of Prayer. A. About Five in the Afternoon the Door-keeper of the Synagogue with a Hammer knocks at their Doors, warning them to repair to Evening Prayer. When they are come, they sit down, and begin their Service with these words of the 84 Psalm [*Blessed are they that dwell in thy house.*] Then the Precentor, having said or sung some Psalms, and half that holy Prayer called *Kaddesh*, the whole Synagogue saith Eighteen Prayers, according to the number of Bones in a Man's Back. And then the Precentor comes down from his Pulpit, and falls upon his Knees before the Ark, after the example of *Joshua*, Josh. 7. 6. and layeth his Left-hand under his Face, because it is said, Cant. 2. 6. *His left hand is under my head.* This the People do likewise, and with their faces covered, and towards the Ground, they say the Sixth Psalm. Having ended their Evening Prayer, and paused a while, they begin their Night Prayers, which they should say after Supper; but because it would be inconvenient to return late to the Synagogue, and many times they are Drunk after Supper, therefore before they depart, they say some Prayers: but if any have a quarrel with his

Neighbour,

Neighbour, he takes the Liturgy-book and shuts it, clapping his hand upon it, intimating hereby, that he would Pray no more, till his Neighbour were reconciled to him.

Q. *Why do the Jews, beside the Sabbath, keep holy the Monday and Thursday?*

A. *Esdras* appointed that the People should meet three times in a week to be taught the Law, because in the Desart of *Sur* the People wandred three days without Water; that is, say they, without the Law. And because *Moses* went up the second time to renew the Tables of the Law, and to pacifie God's Anger for the Peoples Worshipping the Golden Calf on Thursday, and returned thence on Monday, therefore the devoted Jews use to fast these two days, as the Pharisee did in the Gospel. *Jews hear the Law three times a Week.*

Q. *What Ceremonies observe they about the Book of the Law?*

A. In every Synagogue the Book of the Law is kept within a Chest; this Book is the Pentateuch, Written in Parchment in great Characters, and carried to and fro on two staves, fastened at each end of the Parchment. Before the Door of the Ark, or Chest, hangs a piece of Tapestry, on which divers Birds are figured; because Birds were Pictured upon the Ark of the Covenant. This Book is wrapt in Linen, which is covered with Silk, Velvet, or Tissue. The office of carrying the Law is sold to him that gives most, and the Money is bestowed on the Poor. The two Staves are called the Trees of Life. When the Precentor brings the Book out of the Ark into the Pulpit, then they all Sing these words, Numb. 10. 35. *Let God arise, and let his Enemies be scattered,* &c. After some Anthems are Sung, one comes between the Chasan, or Chief Singer, and him who bought the Office of carrying the Law, and kisses (not the Parchment, for that were too great presumption) but the clothes in which it is wrapped; then with a loud voice he blesseth God, who hath chosen them before all others, and given them a Law. Then the Chief Singer Reads a Chapter, and the Book is kissed again, with blessing of God for giving the true Law. Then it is elevated on high, the whole Congregation shouting, *This is the Law that Moses gave to Israel.* The Women in the mean time being in a distinct Synagogue by themselves, are not permitted to kiss the Book, nor to be there with the Men, to shew what modesty ought to be there: but if he who carried the Book should by chance stumble with it, a long Fast must be injoyned; that fall being held ominous, and a presage of great Calamities. When the Book is wrapped up again within all its Coverings, young and old kiss it, touching it only with their two fingers; and whilest it is carried back to the Ark, they all Sing again, *Return, Lord, to the many thousands of* Israel, Numb. 10. 36. So Prayers being ended, as they are going out of the Synagogue, they say, *The Lord preserve my going out and coming in, from henceforth and for ever,* Psal. 5. 9. *Their ceremonies about the Book of the Law.*

Q. *What is the manner of observing the Sabbath at this day?*

A. Because *Moses* commanded the Israelites to gather as much Manna on the sixth day as might serve them all the seventh; therefore *Their manner of observing the Sabbath.*

fore all that they eat and drink on the Sabbath, is prepared and dreſſed on the Friday: and if the Servants work be more than they can perform before the Sabbath, their Maſters, be they never ſo great and rich, muſt help them, that the Sabbath be not broken: Yet they have three Feaſts that day, one in the evening when they begin their Reſt, the ſecond at noon, and the third in the evening when they conclude their Sabbath. All that day their Tables remain covered: If they do not waſh their heads, hands and feet; if they pare not their nails, beginning at the fourth finger on the left-hand, which parings muſt not be trod upon, but either burned or buried; if they change not their clothes; if the Men cut not their beards, and the Women if they kemb not their heads; if they ſharp not their knives, and make every thing clean in their houſes on the Friday, they eſteem the neglect of any of theſe circumſtances a violation of their Sabbath. Before the Sun go down, the Women kindle their Sabbatarian Lights, which is an ancient Cuſtom, as may be ſeen in *Perſius, Satyr.* 5.

Herodis venere dies, unctáque feneſtra.
Depoſitæ pinguem nebulam vomuere lucernæ.

Except we underſtand here by *Herod*'s days, *Herod*'s Birth-day, which was carefully obſerved by the *Herodian* Sect. Now the reaſon why the Women kindle the Lights, is, becauſe the firſt Woman extinguiſhed the light and glory of Man by her diſobedience. They alſo uſe to haſten their Sabbath, and to enlarge it, by adding a part of the Work-day, that the Souls in Purgatory may have the more liberty and refreſhing, who all that time cool and refreſh themſelves in Water, for which cauſe the Jews are forbid by the Rabbins to draw all the Water out of any place, but to leave ſome for refrigeration of theſe ſcorched Souls. They believe that a good and evil Angel ſtand before their Synagogues, obſerving who Pray and Hear moſt diligently. Theſe Angels wait upon ſuch to their Houſes, where finding all clean and neat, they depart joyfully, though the evil Angel be not concerned, but is forced to ſhew a ſeeming content. They do not put out their Lights all that day, nor muſt they ſnuff them, leſt they ſhould thereby break their Sabbath; nor muſt they that day catch a Flea, or kill a Louſe. If a Jew in his Journey be overtaken by the Sabbath, he muſt ſtay, though in the midſt of a Field or Wood; though in danger of Thieves, Storms, or Hunger, he muſt not budge. They begin their Feaſting on the Sabbath with Conſecrated Wine, and Two Loaves of Bread, in Memory of the double portion of Manna they gathered for the Sabbath: which day they think it not ſufficiently obſerved, except they eat and drink largely in the day time, and kiſs their Wives often in the Night. In their Synagogues they have Read to them Seven of their Chapters by ſeven ſeveral Men, who come in at one door, and go out at another. Theſe Lectures are out of *Moſes* and the Prophets, *Acts* 13. 27. and 15. 21. They Pray for the Souls of thoſe who have violated the Sabbath; who, being in Hell, have ſo much eaſe by their Prayers, as to turn from one ſide to the other.

But

But this Service lasteth not above the Sixth hour, which is our Noon; for, by their Law, they must neither Pray nor Fast beyond this hour. If any Dream of such things as they count ominous, such as the Burning of the Law, the Falling of their Houses, or Teeth, they must Fast till the Evening; and so they must Fast the next day, as a punishment for Fasting on the Sabbath. After Dinner the most of their discourse is about their Use-Money, and other Worldly Business. In the evening they repair to their Synagogues again, and thence to their third Feast. They conclude their Sabbath with Singing, or Caterwawling rather, which they continue as long as they can, for ease of the Defunct Souls: And withal, they Pray that *Elias* would hasten his coming, even the next Sabbath if he please, that he might give them notice of the Messias his coming. Then the richer sort lighting a Torch, taking a Silver Box, full of Spices, with one hand, and a Cup of Wine in the other, they say certain Blessings to God for the Benefits of Light, Wine, Spices, and the Sabbath: and with some ridiculous Ceremonies they end the Sabbath, and begin their Week. Some wash their Eyes and Face with that Consecrated Wine, counting it Medicinable; others sprinkle it about their Houses, against all Charms and Witchcraft. They smell to the Spices, that they may not faint when one of their Souls departeth, which it doth at the end of every Sabbath, and returneth at the beginning of the same; so that every Sabbath-day they have two Souls: Besides, they think Hell-fire stinks in the Week-days, but not in the Sabbath; therefore they smell to the Spices when the Sabbath is ended. They pour out some of their Consecrated Wine on the ground, to refresh *Core* and his Complices, who live yet under the ground in fire. On the Sabbath they will not Light their Candles, make their Fires, Milk their Cows, snuff their Candles, dress their Meat themselves, but have Christians to do such trivial things; and then they brag, that they are the Lords of the World, and the Christians be their servants.

Q. *How do the modern Jews keep their Passover?*

A. The richer sort spend Thirty days in Preparation, and buying of the purest Wheat for their Unleavened Bread, with which also they furnish the poorer sort who cannot buy. The First-born only Fast the Eve before. The Sabbath which immediately preceedeth the Passeover, is very holy among them. In this they have long Sermons concerning the Passeover, and use thereof; this they call the Great Sabbath. They are very cautious in cleansing their Houses, and washing their Utensils three days before *Easter*; being more careful with the Pharisees, to wash the out-side of the Platter, than to purge out the Rapine and Intemperance that is within. The Night before the Passeover, they take great pains to find out all the Leavened-Bread that is in their Houses. They search and sweep every corner and Mouse-hole for crumbs with Wax-Candles; if they find none, they purposely fling down some, that they might not seem to have Prayed and Laboured in vain: All the

Modern Jews, how they keep their Passover.

the crumbs they find, they lay up carefully against the next day, and burn them. They are very curious about the grinding, kneading, and baking of the unleavened bread; the Corn must be ground three days before it be baked; the Mill-stone must be cleansed from all former Meal, and so must the Chest that holds it: The water that is used, must be brought in consecrated Vessels, about the going down of the Sun, covered. The Master of the Family must draw the water himself. The form of their unleavened Cake is round, and full of holes to let in air, lest it should swell. No other ingredient is permitted in the flour but water. About ten or eleven they dine, but soberly, that they may with the better appetite eat their unleavened bread in the evening: But first they repair to their Synagogues, where they sing and pray; only the women stay at home to cover the Tables, to hang the walls with Tapestry, and to expose their Cupboards of Plate, and other riches to be seen, to put them in mind of that wealth which was in the Temple when it was robbed and demolished. Each Master of the Family, if he be rich, hath his Chair of State, wherein he sits like a Prince, to shew that they are now redeemed from the bondage of *Egypt*: The poorer sort sit majestically also in their seats.

Their manner of eating the Paschal Lamb.

Q. *What is the manner of eating the Paschal Lamb at home?*

A. When it begins to grow dark, they run home from the Synagogue; a platter is uncovered, wherein are three Cakes, the uppermost representing the High Priest, the middle the Levite, and the lowermost the people of *Israel*; in another dish is a roasted leg of Lamb or Kid, with an hard Egg; there is also a dish of Pap, or thick stuff, made of divers fruits, with wine spiced, and chiefly Cinnamon, representing the straw and brick of *Egypt*: In another platter there are Lettice, Parsly, Ivy, Raddish, and such like herbs, with another dish of vinegar, to represent the sowre herbs eaten heretofore with the Lamb. Every one hath his draught of wine. The middle Cake is broken into two pieces; the one whereof the Master hides in a Napkin, to shew how the *Israelites* fled with their dough unleavened out of *Egypt*. Then laying hold on the other piece of Cake, they sing, *Such was the bread of affliction our Fathers eat in* Egypt: *Here we are now, the next year we shall be in* Canaan. The platter with the Cakes is carried from the Table to the Children, that they might demand what that is, as we read *Exod.* 12. 26, 27. When the Cakes are set down again, they sing a song of their deliverance; and drink another glass of wine, leaning like Princes in their Chairs. Then some of the Cakes are eaten with thanksgiving, and some of the Herbs dipped in the Pap. And at last the third Cake is broken, and some more of the Herbs are eaten.

Their Modern Ceremonies are Rabbinical.

Q. *By these passages it seems that the Jews do not observe the Passeover, as they are commanded by* Moses.

A. It's true; for the most of their modern Ceremonies are Rabbinical rather than Mosaical. They say, that now they are not tied

tied to the Rites of *Moses*, because they are not in their own Land, but live amongst profane Gentiles, for so they call Christians. But indeed, the true cause why they keep not the old Passeover is, because Christ our true Passeover is sacrificed for us, who hath put an end to all the old Ceremonies: and it is observable, that those Jews who now live in *Canaan*, even in *Jerusalem*, do use altogether the same Rabbinical Rites, and do not sacrifice at all, seeing Christ the Lamb of God, who taketh away the sins of the world, is the only perfect and satisfactory Sacrifice.

Q. *What may we observe concerning the Jews at this day?*

A. That they are a blind, hard hearted, stiff-necked people; who, as the Apostle saith, have always resisted the holy Ghost, and are given up to a reprobate sense: they will not yet part with the veil of *Moses* which is over their eyes; who after so many miracles wrought by Christ and his Apostles, after the accomplishing of all prophecies and types in him, after the finishing of the time prescribed by *Daniel*, of seventy weeks, after sixteen hundred years expectation of a Messiah, since the end of those seventy weeks, after so many calamities which they have suffered for their obstinacy and blasphemies against the Son of God; after so many delusions by *Ben. Cozbah, David, Moses*, and other false Prophets, who gave themselves out to be the Messiah, after so many testimonies and confessions of their own writers, that Christ Jesus was the true Messiah, yet they will not acknowledge it, but continue still in their obstinacy and cruelty against Christ and his members. They brag themselves to be the seed of *Abraham*, and glory in their seal of Circumcision given to him: but if they were of *Abraham*, they would do the works of *Abraham*, they would believe with *Abraham*, who saw the day of Christ, and rejoyced. They can claim no share in the Covenant made with *Abraham*, because they deny and persecute him who is the foundation of the Covenant: they condemn Christians for making and honouring of the Image of Christ and his Saints; which is not so much out of zeal against Images, for they allow the Images of the Cherubins which were in the Tabernacle and Temple, but rather out of spight against Christ and his Saints. They count it Idolatry to honour Christ in his Picture or Image, and yet they consider not that themselves are the greatest Idolaters in the World, in worshipping God according to their own fansie, and not according to his word, which teacheth us, that he is to be worshipped in the unity of Essence, and Trinity of persons, which they deny; thus they worship, though not Images, yet their own imaginations: how often have their Progenitors attempted to reestablish their ancient government, but still in vain, and to their own destruction? witness what they suffered under *Vespasian* and *Titus*, what under *Julian*, when by his permission they began to rebuild their Temple; what under *Hadrian*, when they rebelled, and attempted to set up their earthly Monarchy; what under *Trajan* and *Marcus Antoninus*; what under King *Philip*, called *Longus*, in *France*, when they poy-

Observatious concerning the Jews at this day.

soned

soned the Wells; what shall I speak of their barbarous cruelties, and inhumane savageness under *Andrew* their Captain, in the time of *Trajan*, when they murthered many thousands of people, eating their flesh, wearing their skins, and girding themselves with their guts yet bleeding? of these passages we may read in *Sozomen, Dio, Marcellinus, Paulus Æmilius* the *French* Historian, and others. As they have still been the greatest enemies that ever Christianity had, so do they continue their hatred against us at this day; but being kept under, they dare not do the mischief they would: yet they curse us still, and hold, that the best of Christians is no better than the Serpent, whose head deserved to be trod upon. They think they do God good service if they can cheat a Christian: and they make no conscience to forswear themselves, when they take an oath upon any of our Bibles, thinking they are bound to keep no oath but what they take upon their own *Torah*, or Book of the Law, which is read in their Synagogues. Neither will they swear willingly, but in the Hebrew tongue; counting all other Languages profane, especially the Latin, which they hate, because the Romans and Latin Church have been their greatest subduers and conquerors. They call us Gentiles, Edomites and Devils, and Anathematise us daily. They will not call *Mary* the Mother of Christ, but in derision, *The Mother of him that was hanged.* They are merciless Extortioners, and cunning in the Art of poysoning. Their Religion consisteth most in needless and ridiculous ceremonies, in Rabbinical fables, Cabbalistical whimseys, Thalmudical Traditions, large Fringes and Phylacteries, and in a meer outside; whereas mercy and justice, and weighty things of the Law are neglected and slighted.

Q. *May Christian Princes, with a safe conscience, permit Jews to live in their Territories?*

Jews, whether to be permitted to live among Christians.

A. Yes, conditionally that they communicate not in Religion, nor marry together, nor be too familiar; and that these Jews be obedient to the Civil power, quiet, modest, distinguished by some outward badge, and not to be admitted to any publick office or charge; for they have been tolerated both by the Civil and Canon Law. 2. The Jews in the Old Testament had leave to commerce with the Gentiles. 3. We ought to permit them, upon hope we may convert some of them to the knowledge and love of Christ. 4. We ought by all means to commiserate their condition, because *to them pertaineth the adoption, and the glory, and the covenants, and the giving of the Law, and the service of God, and the promises: whose are the Fathers, and of whom as concerning the flesh Christ came,* &c. Rom. 9. 4, 5. we must consider, *that by their fall salvation is come to the Gentiles; and if the fall of them be the riches of the world, and the diminishing of them the riches of the Gentiles, how much more their fulness?* Rom. 11. 12. let us not then insult over their miseries, *nor boast against the branches; for we are but wild Olives grafted upon them: and if God spared not the natural branches, take heed lest he also spare not thee,* Rom. 11. For *blindness is happened but in part upon*

Israel,

Israel, *until the fulness of the Gentiles do come in*, Rom. 11. And then *all Israel shall be saved*; that is, most of them, according to the Scripture-phrase: For the Angel tells *Daniel, that every one of this people shall be delivered, whose names shall be found in the book,* Dan. 12. 1. So then all the Jews before the last judgment shall be saved, and shall acknowledge Christ the true Messiah; yet not all without exception; but all whose names are written in the book of life; this restriction sheweth, that some will not be saved. 5. By suffering the Jews to live amongst us, we shall be the more induced to acknowledge the goodness of God towards us Gentiles, in receiving us to mercy, when he cast off his own people. By this also we are taught to fear and tremble at Gods judgments; *because for unbelief they were broken off; we stand by faith; let us not be too high minded, but fear; for if we continue not in his goodness, we shall also be cut off*, Rom. 11. Lastly, from the Jews we have our Scriptures; they can be our witnesses to the Gentiles, that our Scriptures are not devised and compiled by us, but by our enemies: out of which Scripture, even to the great grief of the Jews, we can clearly prove, that Christ is the true Messiah; therefore it is convenient that we permit them to live amongst us.

Q. *May Christian Princes permit the Jews to exercise their own Religion?*

A. They may, if so be they dishonour not Christ, nor traduce or molest his Church: For they were better exercise their Religion, than turn Atheists, principally seeing they worship the same God with us, though not in the same manner; and read the same Scriptures, though not in the same sense. For this cause the Primitive Church, and the Imperial Laws suffered them; and Christ himself permitted their Doctors to sit in the chair of *Moses*, and to teach his Doctrine, and counselled the people to obey the same: besides, by permitting the Jews to use their Religion without molestation, by using them courteously, they may be the sooner enduced to embrace Christ; and indeed our cruelties, against them and the wickedness of our lives have been, and are still great obstacles to their conversion. But Christian Princes must be careful that they be not suffered to blaspheme Christ, or abuse his Church: for they are keepers of both Tables, and they do not carry the Sword in vain; they should also use all the gentle means they can to bring them to the knowledge and love of Christ, by instructing them in the grounds of Christian Religion: but violence must be avoided; for faith cometh by perswasion, not by compulsion; neither must their Infants be forcibly baptized against their Parents consent, but when they come to years of discretion they should cause them to be instructed in the Principles of Christianity; nor must their Parents be suffered to hinder them; but whilst they are Infants, they must not be baptized against their Parents will, because that were so take away their right of paternity, which Parents have over their Children, both by the Laws of God, of Nature, and of Nations: besides, the Children of Jews, who are enemies of Christ, cannot

Whether to be permitted amongst Christians to exercise their own Religion.

not be comprehended within the Covenant, and therefore are not capable of the sign of the Covenant till they be of years; and if then they embrace Christ, they are included in the Covenant, and so made capable of the seal thereof. Besides, the forced Baptism of Jewish Children, would be a great scandal to Christian Religion, which would be traduced as a violent way to force Infants to receive that of which they had no knowledge, nor could give their consent to; and so these Children, when they come to years of discretion, might justly repudiate that Religion, which was forc'd on them, when they had neither knowledge of it nor gave consent to it.

Q. In what things must not Christians communicate with Jews?

Wherein Christians are not to communicate with Jews.

A. They must not eat, nor drink, nor bathe, nor cohabit together, nor entertain friendship and familiarity, lest by these means Christians should be infected with their errors and superstition, or lest they should seem to countenance their wicked opinions. 2. Christians must not serve Jews in any kind of service, for then they will brag that they are the Lords of the world, and Christians their slaves: besides, it is unseemly that the children of the free-born (for so we are, being made free by Christ) should serve the sons of the bond-woman; for they are true Israelites, and the sons of *Abraham*, who have the faith, and do the works of *Abraham*: who are Israelites not after the flesh, but after the spirit. 3 Christians must not employ Jews for their Physicians, for this were to ingage them: besides, we know out of Histories how dangerous such Pysicians have proved to Christians, who by reason of their inveterate malice, make no conscience to poyson them, but rather think they are bound to do so. 4. Christians must take heed how they traffick with Jews, lest they be cheated by them, or least they partake of the sins and superstition of the Jews, by selling them such wares as they know they will abuse to their superstitious worship. 5. Let not Christians borrow money of Jews, except they mean to be undone by them; for they have ever been, and are to this day, unconscionable Extortioners. 6. Christians ought not to read their blasphemous books, but to suppress and burn them; for by them our blessed Saviour in his person, offices, preaching and miracles, is highly dishonoured, and his Church traduced: Therefore Pope *Gregory* the ninth, about the year of Christ 1230. caused the *Thalmud*, in which Christian Religion is so much blasted, to be burned; which was performed accordingly by the Chancellour of *Paris*; and about the year 1553. Pope *Julius* the third commanded that all the Jewish blasphemous Books, with both the *Thalmuds*, should be searched out, and flung in the fire: and that their estates should be confiscated, who did harbour or read, print or write such wicked books, or bring them from foreign parts into Christian Territories.

Jews spend eight days in their Easter solemnities.

Q. How many days do the Jews spend in their Easter solemnities?

A. Eight: the two first and the two last are wholly kept with great Ceremony, the other four are but half holy days; This time they
sup

sup plentifully, and drink strenuously, till it be midnight; but they drink up four consecrated cups of Wine, two before supper, and two at or after supper: each of these cups is accompanied with a prayer, and the lasts with execrations against Christians: at supper they eat the other half Cake; and keep open all night their doors and gates, as being perswaded, that then they are safe and secure from all danger; and that they are ready to entertain *Eliah*, whose coming they expect then. During this time, they eat up the whole three Cakes mentioned before, and have divers disputations about what work is fit to be done that time, full of ridiculous subtilties. If during this time they find any leaven in their houses, they touch it not, but cover it till they burn it. Now because they are not certain which is the true fourteenth day of the Moon, when they begin their Easter, they keep the second day as solemnly as the first; and because they know not the true seventh day, therefore lest they should mistake, they observe also the eighth day; after which day they bring leaven into their houses again. The men fast three times after, to expiate for their intemperance during the feast: and for the space of thirty days, they neither marry nor bathe, nor cut their hair, because *Rabbi Akibba* lost by death all his Disciples, being eighty thousand, between Easter and Pentecost.

Q. *How do they now observe their Pentecost?*

A. Pentecost, so called in the New Testament, from the fifty days between Easter and that feast; in the old Law it is called the feast of Harvest, and of first-fruits, *Exod.* 23. 16. Because then their Harvest began, and the time they offered the first-fruits of the Earth. The Jews are very exact in numbring each week and day from Easter to Pentecost, praying continually that God would bring them home again to *Jerusalem*, that in their own Land they might offer to him their first-fruits, as *Moses* commanded them. They keep two holy days at Pentecost, because they know not which is the true day. They produce their Law twice: and by five men they read so much as concerneth that festivity. They strow their Houses, Synagogues, and Streets with Grass, fill their Windows with green Boughs, and wear on their Heads green Garlands; to shew that all places about Mount *Sinai* were green, when they received the Law. They eat that day altogether white meats of milk, to shew the whiteness and sweetness of the Law. They make a Cake or Pye, having seven Cakes in one, to signifie the seven Heavens into which God ascended from Mount *Sinai*.

Their Pentecost.

Q. *How do they keep the feast of Tabernacles?*

A. This third great Feast, which was kept anciently in Booths or Tents, made up of green Boughs, in memory of the forty years peregrination in the Desart, is now observed by the Jews eight days together. The two first and two last are solemnly kept; the other four are but half festivals. They first repair to their Synagogues; then after some praying and singing, they run home to their Tents, but do not stay there all night, as their Ancestors were wont to do. They use to take in one hand Boughs of Palm, Olive and
Their feast of Tabernacles.

and Willow, and in the other a Pom-citron; then they bless God and shake the Boughs towards the four cardinal points of Heaven: then having placed the Law upon the Pulpit, they go round about it seven times in seven days, in memory of the walls of *Jericho*, encompassed seven times. Then having shaken the branches in their hands, they pray against Christians. This feast is kept about the middle of *September*; in which month they believe shall be fought the great battle between *Gog* and *Magog*, in which *Gog* shall be slain, and the Jews restored to their own Land. About night they go abroad in the Moon-light, believing that God doth reveal to them by the shadows of the Moon who shall live or die that year, for then they begin the computation of their year. the shaking of the branches towards the four corners of the world, signifies the destruction of the four great Monarchies, (to wit) the *Assyrian*, *Persian*, *Graecian*, and *Roman*. They make great use of Citrons in this Beast, for they send sixteen men every year into *Spain*, to bring with them as many of these as they can: for by the Citrons, they say, are represented just men, who are as full of their good works, as this fruits is full of seeds.

Q. *How do they keep their new Moons?*

Their new Moons.
A. Their New Moons are but half holy days with them; for in the morning they go to their Synagogues, the rest of the day they spend in eating, drinking and gaming. The day before the new Moon they use to fast; when they first see her, they utter a benediction, and leap three times towards her, wishing that their Enemies may come no nearer to hurt them, then they are able to come near and hurt her. The women have more right to keep this day holy than the men, because they would not part with their Ear-rings and Jewels towards the making of the golden Calf; but willingly parted with them towards the building of the Temple. They give a ridiculous Reason why sacrifices were commanded every new Moon; because, say they, the Moon murmured against God in the beginning; therefore he took her light from her, and appointed sacrifices to expiate her crime.

Q. *Why do the Jews fast in the month of* August?

Fast in August.
A. Because they hold the world was made in *September*, therefore they make that month the beginning of their year; and believe, that about that time God will come to judge the world: for this cause they fast and pray divers days before and baptize themselves in Lakes and Rivers; and where they are wanting, they make pits, which they fill with water; in these they dip themselves over head and ears, thinking this a means to expiate their sins: they frequent their Synagogues and Church-yards, desiring God to pardon them for the good Jews sake who are buried there; and in the same they distribute large Alms to the poor. In some places there, they cause Rams horns to be sounded when they go to their Synagogues, to put the greater terror in them, when they consider their sins, and the horror of Gods judgments. Their fasting ceremonies being ended, they shave and bathe themselves, and begin their year with much mirth and joviality. Q. *What*

Q. *What solemnity use they in beginning their new year?*

A. Because they are commanded by *Moses*, Lev. 23. 24. to keep holy the first day of the seventh month; therefore they begin their Civil year from that day; which after Evening prayer in their Synagogues, they intimate with a cup of Wine, wishing to each other a good year. The younger sort repair to the chief Rabbi for his blessing, which he bestoweth on them by prayer and imposition of hands. Being returned home, they fall to eating, drinking, and making merry. On the Table is set down a Rams head, to put them in mind of that Ram which on this day was sacrificed in *Isaac's* stead; and to signifie, that they shall be the head, and not the tail of Christians. They feed that night plentifully on Fish and Fruit, to shew that they will increase and multiply in good Works, as the Fish do in the Sea; and that their Enemies shall be cut off from all help, as the Fruit is plucked off from the Tree. In the morning they go betimes to their Synagogues to Sing and Pray; the Law is taken twice out of the Ark, and some Lessons read: after which one soundeth a Rams-horn on the Pulpit; if he sounds clear, it's a good sign; if otherwise, they hold it ominous, and a sign of a bad year. This Horn-Trumpet is also in memory of *Isaac's* delivery by the Ram this day, as they hold. The rest of the day they spend in good cheer and mirth. After Dinner they go to the Waters, there to drown their sins. If they see any Fish in the Water, they shake their Clothes, that their sins falling upon those Fishes, may be carried away by them into the Sea, as of old they were by the Scape Goat into the Wilderness. And at night they feast again, and so initiate the year with two days Mirth.

Their Solemnities in beginning the New Year.

Q. *How do they prepare themselves for Morning-Prayer?*

A. They hold it necessary that every Jew, from the Fifteenth of *June* till *Pentecost*, should rise before day, because then the Nights are long; but from *Pentecost* till the Fifteenth of *June*, they may rise after day: their rising will be the more acceptable to God, if they have weeped in the Night, for with such the Stars and Planets do weep; they must let their tears fall down their cheeks, because then God is ready with his Bottle to receive them: these tears may serve them for good use, because when at any time the Enemies of *Israel* send out Edicts to destroy the *Jews*, God is ready with these Bottles to pour them out upon these Writings, and to blot out the Edict, that the Jews may receive no hurt thereby. They hold the morning the best time to enter into the House of God, because *David* saith, *Thou wilt hear my voice betimes in the morning*. In the Evening they say, God commands all the Gates of Heaven to be shut; which are guarded by certain Angels, who are silent till after Midnight; then a great noise is heard in Heaven, commanding the Gates to be opened: this noise is heard by our Cocks here below, who presently upon this clap their wings and Crow, that men thereby may awake: then the evil spirits who had leave to wander up and down in the night, whilst Heaven Gates were shut, lose all power of doing hurt. As soon as they

Their preparation for Morning Prayer.

hear the Cock crow, they muſt ſay this Prayer, as they are taught by their Rabbins ; *Bleſſed be thou, O God, Lord of all the World, who haſt given ſuch underſtanding to the Cock.* When they change their Shirts, the Walls and Bed-poſts muſt not ſee their Nakedneſs, but they muſt change within the Bed-clothes. They muſt not in the Morning put on the left ſhooe before the right ; but at night they ſhould put off the left ſhooe firſt. As they are going out of their Chamber in the Morning, they muſt with a ſubmiſſive mind bow their head to the Ground, in remembrance of the Devaſtation of the Temple at *Jeruſalem* ; but no Man muſt offer to ſay his Prayers till firſt he hath eaſed himſelf at the Stool, and waſhed his hands, becauſe upon them evil Spirits ſit in the Night-time ; and his Face alſo, becauſe it was made after the Image of God ; but they muſt be careful that the right-hand , with which they touch the Law, and Write the Name of God, may no ways be defiled. And when in private they are eaſing of themſelves, they muſt not then think of God, or of his Law, for that will ſhorten their life, as their Rabins ſay. If any Man touch his eye in the Morning with unwaſhed hands, he ſhall be blind ; if his Ears, deaf ; if his noſtrils, they ſhall ſtill be dropping ; if his mouth, it ſhall ſtink ; if any part of his skin, it ſhall be ſcabbed. They muſt not preſume to Pray but in their Four-corner'd-Cloke, from which hangs certain Borders, Laces, or Phylacteries, which they call *Zuzim*; they muſt alſo have their *Tephillin* tied to their heads and hands ; theſe are ſcrowls or bundles of Prayers ; but of theſe and many more of their Superſtitious Ceremonies, ſee *Buxtorfius* in *Synagoga Judaica.*

Q. *How do they prepare themſelves for the Feaſt of Reconciliation ?*

The Feaſt of Reconciliation, and Ceremonies therein.

A. The firſt ten days after the beginning are Penitential, in which they Faſt and Pray. The ninth day every Man, young and old, takes a Cock in his hand ; every Woman and Maid, a Hen. After ſome impertinent Sentences pronounced out of Scripture, each one whirls the Cock about the Prieſts Head, ſaying, This Cock ſhall die for me ; then the Cock's throat is cut, his body flung to the ground, and at laſt Roſted : his guts are caſt upon the top of the houſe, that the Ravens may carry them away and their ſins together. They labour much for white Cocks, which they hold to be pure from ſin ; red Cocks they deteſt, as being full of ſin. The reaſon why they ſacrifice a Cock, is, becauſe the Hebrew word *Gheber* ſignifieth a Man, and in the Thalmud a Cock ; ſo to them the death of a Cock is as much as the death of a Man. After this they go to the Church-yard, confeſs their ſins, and give to the poor the price of their Cocks, becauſe of old they uſed to give their Cocks to the poor. In the afternoon they dip themſelves again in Water, and prepare Light for their next days Service in the Synagogue, where, in the evening, they meet, and reconcile themſelves to each other, where hath been any offence : he that ſeeks to be reconciled, is ſufficiently ſatisfied, though the other be obſtinate ; and thinks himſelf acquitted, in ſeeking for that the other hath refu-

A View of the Religions of ASIA.

sed. If the party wronged die, he that did the wrong goeth to his Grave, and before Ten Witnesses confesseth his fault: they confess also their sins to each other, in some secret place of the Church: they go two and two; the one boweth his body, turning his face to the North; whilst he is confessing, and beating of his Breast, receiveth Thirty nine Stripes on the back of his Fellow with a Leather Thong, whom he repays in the like manner. Having done, they return home, and make Merry with their roasted Cocks and Hens. Over their clothes they put on a white Shirt or Surplice, to shew that now they are White, and pure from sin.

Q. *What other Ceremonies use they in the Feast of Reconciliation?*

A. The ninth day, the Men in the Synagogues, the Women at home, about Evening, light Wax-candles, over which they Pray, stretching out their hands towards the Light; which, if they burn clear, they take it for a good sign that their sins are pardoned, and that they shall be happy: if the Lights be dim, or the Wax melt, it's ominous. Then they Fast, go bare-footed, abstain from Oyl, Bathing, and Carnal Copulation: they spend much of the Night in Singing and Praying, and most of the next day: whilst the Priest extendeth his hands to bless them, they all lay their hands on their Faces, as not daring to look on those sanctified hands of the Priest. At this time they Fast Forty eight hours together; and some have been observed to stand upright and Pray above Twenty four hours without intermission. Some Write, that they use at this time to bribe Satan, that he may not accuse them for their sins.

Q. *What Ceremonies use they when they have Read over the Law?*

A. They divide the Pentateuch into 52 Sections, according to the 52 Sabbaths of the year. The last Lesson, which falls out on that day that immediately follows the Feast of Tabernacles, about the 23d of *September*, is accompanied with Singing, and the Priests Dancing. All the Books are this day brought out of the Ark, with Dancing about it: in the interim, whilst the Books are out of the Ark, a Candle burns within it, to shew that the Law is a Light. In the Synagogue they fling Nuts, Pears, and other fruit to the Youth, who, in scrabling for the same, fall oftentimes together by the ears. That day their Ecclesiastick Offices are proposed to sale, which occasioneth much strife and malice among them. The Money raised on the Offices is for the repair of their Synagogues, and relief of the Poor. At last they conclude all with good Chear and Wine at Supper, and are merry, if while the Law was carried about, he did not stumble that carried it, for that is held very ominous.

Their Rites after the Law is Read &c.

Q. *What are these Church-Offices which they sell yearly?*

A. First, the Office of Lighting the Candles. Secondly, of furnishing the Consecrated Wine, which is spent in their Sabbaths and other Festivals. Thirdly, the Office of folding and unfolding the Book of the Law. Fourthly, of lifting up, and carrying about the said Book. Fifthly, of touching the Sacred Staves on which the Book of Parchment is rolled. Young Men are greedy

Church-Offices sold among the Jews.

of this Office, because they think the touching of these Staves will prolong their life. Sixthly, the Office of Reading the Law. And Seventhly, of supplying his place who is negligent in his office.

Q. *Why do they keep the Feast of Dedication?*

The Feast of Dedication. A. They keep it memory of *Judas Macchabæus*, who Dedicated the Temple the 25 of *November*. After it had been possessed and polluted by the *Græcians*, it was then ordained by *Judas* and his Brethren, and all the People, that this Feast should be kept yearly for eight days together. At that first Dedication was found a small Vessel of Consecrated Oyl; which of it self was not sufficient to hold out above one night, but by Miracle it maintained the Lights for the whole eight days. Now this Feast consisteth in Drinking and Gormandizing, and in Pompous Superstition about their Lights. Yet Christ honoured this Feast with his presence, *John* 10. 22. not to countenance the abuses thereof, but the Institution it self; for all places set apart for the Service of God, ought to be Consecrated and Dedicated to him by Prayer and Decent Ceremonies; therefore *Moses* Dedicated the Tabernacle to God, and *Solomon* the Temple, with great Solemnity and Prayers: when the Temple was Rebuilt, after the Peoples return from *Babylon*, it was Dedicated again; and now the third time it was Dedicated, when it was profaned by *Antiochus*. These second Dedications are called ἐγκαίνεια, that is, Renovations. The Temple was also newly consecrated, or dedicated under *Ezechiah*, after it had been profaned by *Achaz*, 2 *Chron.* 29. The Priests and Levites spent eight days in this dedication.

Q. *What is their Feast of* Purim?

The Feast of Purim. A. That is, of Lots: for *Haman* by lot had appointed the Jews to be Massacred all through the *Persian* Kingdom in one day, to wit, the Thirteenth day of the Twelfth Month, which is *Adar*, or *February*; but the Plotters were Massacred themselves by the Jews the same day. For at *Suse*, *Haman* with his Ten Sons, and Five hundred Men more were slain, and Three hundred the day after: and on the same day through the rest of *Assuerus* his Dominions, were slain by the Jews 75000. So because this day they destroyed their Enemies, and the next day rested themselves, therefore at this Feast they keep two holy days, or rather days for *Bacchus*. In their Synagogues they set up Lights in the night time, and the whole Book of *Esther* is read. As often as they hear the Name of *Haman*, they keep a cruel noise and stamping with their feet. They Read all that passage of the death of *Haman*'s Sons at one breath, to signifie the suddenness of that death. These two days are spent in Singing, Playing, Eating and Drinking. The Men wear Womens Apparel, and the Women Mens, against the Law of God, which they think at this time of Mirth they may lawfully violate. And that the poor may be merry also, the richer sort furnish them with Meat and Drink; and so with this riotous *Bacchanal*, they concluded their Anniversary Feast; for this is the last of the year, having none between this and *Easter*.

Q. *What*

Sect. 1.   *A View of the Religions of* ASIA.

Q. *What Fasting days do the Jews observe now?*

A. They keep the four Fasts mentioned by *Zachary*, Chap. 8. 19. *Their fasts.* to wit, that of the Tenth Month, on the Tenth of *December*, in memory of *Jerusalem* besieged that day by *Nebuchadnezzar*. Secondly, they Fast the Seventeenth day of the Fourth Month, or *June*, in memory of the Two Tables of the Law broken, for the loss of their daily Sacrifice; for burning of the Law; for setting up Idolatry in the Temple; for besieging *Jerusalem* the second time, and for breaking down the Walls thereof. They count, the days from this till the Ninth of the next Month, all unlucky; so that they avoid all great business: and School-masters, during that time, will not beat their Scholars. Thirdly, they Fast the Ninth day of the Fifth Month, or *July*, because then the Temple was burned; therefore they go bare-foot, sit on the ground, read *Jeremiah's* Lamentations, and in the Church-yards among the dead they bewail the loss of *Jerusalem*. From the First till the Tenth of this Month, they abstain from Flesh, Wine, Shaving, Bathing, Marrying, and Pleading, and from all kind of Delights. Fourthly, they Fast the 3d day of *September*, because *Gedaliah*, Governor of those Jews that were not carried away in Captivity, was Treacherously Murdered, as we Read, *Jeremy* 40, and 41. Besides these Fasts, they have others, but not so generally observed: for some of their precifer sort fast every Monday and Thursday. Some Fast the tenth of *March*, because *Miriam* died that day, and the People wanted Water in the Desart. Some Fast the tenth of *April*, for the death of *Eli* and his two Sons, and the loss of the Ark: some Fast the 18th of this Month, for the death of *Samuel*. At *Jerusalem* the Jews used yearly to Fast, in remembrance of the Translation of the Bible out of Hebrew into Greek by the Seventy Interpreters: This Fast was observed the eighth day of *Tebeth*, or *December*, and was a day of much heaviness among them; which must proceed from their pride or envy, or too much superstition; disdaining that their Law should be imparted to the Gentiles, and that this Translation was a profanation thereof. So Superstitious they are in their Fasts, that they will read no passages in the Bible but such as are sad and sorrowful, as the destruction of *Jerusalem*, *Jeremy's* Lamentations, &c. and not any passage that is joyful, such as their delivery from *Egyptian* Slavery, or *Haman's* Tyranny. The only Fast that God commanded, was that upon the day of Expiation: other Fasts were enjoyned by the Prince upon emergent occasions; as the Fast commanded by *Jehosaphat*, by *Joachim* and other Princes. Divers other private Fasts they have upon private occasions. Their Fast is from all meat and drink till the Evening that the Stars appear.

Q. *What is the manner of their Marriages?*   *Their Marriages.*

A. They are Married in the open Air, either in the Streets or Gardens, by their Rabbi's. The Bridegroom wears about his neck a hair-cloth, the end of which the Rabbi puts on the Brides head, after the example of *Ruth*, who desired to be covered with the skirt of *Boaz* his Garment. Then the Rabbi takes in his hand a Glafs full of Wine, over which he pronounceth a Bleffing, praifing God for that Conjunction, and gives it to the Bride-man and his Spoufe that they may drink. Then he takes from the Bridegroom a Gold Ring, and asks of the Standers by if it be good, and worth the Money given for it, and fo puts it upon one of the Brides Fingers: then are the Marriage-writings Read openly. Then the Rabbi takes another Glafs of Wine, over which he Prayeth, and prefents it to the Married Couple to be tafted; but the Bridegroom takes the Glafs and dafhes it againft the Wall, in Memory of the Deftruction of *Jerufalem*: and, for the fame caufe, in fome places, Afhes are put on the Bridegrooms head; fo the Bride, in fign of Sorrow, puts on a Black Cloak, and the Bride-man a Black hood. They are Married in the open Air, that by looking up to Heaven, they may be put in Mind of Multiplying like the Stars. The other Ceremonies ufed before and after Marriage are not to our purpofe, as not being Ecclefiaftical. But we muft know, that befides the Principal Wife, they have others that are fubordinate, which we may call Concubines, who have not the command of the Family, nor gifts or prefents from the Husband, as *Rebecca* had from *Ifaac*, nor Matrimonial Writings, as the chief Wife hath; nor may their Children inherit, but receive Gifts only: thus *Abraham* dealt with the Sons of his Concubines, *Gen.* 25. Their cuftom alfo is firft to be contracted, and after fome fpace of time to be Married; which contract was confirmed either by Writing, or by a piece of Money, or by Copulation; but this laft was punifhable. Their Marriages are accompanied with bleffings and praifes; therefore if they are Married within doors, that Houfe is called *Beth-Hillulim*, the Houfe of Praifes.

Q. *How do they make their Bills of Divorce at this day?*

The Bills of Divorce. A. After the fame manner that they did in the time of Chrift: when any Man is weary of his Wife, he Writes a Bill of Twelve lines only, neither more nor fewer; this he delivers to his Wife before three Witneffes, who fubfcribe and feal the fame, whereby he gives her free power to go whither fhe will, and to difpofe of her felf as fhe pleafeth: but fhe muft not Marry again till after Ninety days, that it may be known whether fhe be with Child or not: the Woman alfo might give a Bill of Divorce to her Husband, of which our Saviour fpeaketh, *Mark* 10. 12. and withal fheweth, that fuch Bills of Divorce were not commanded, but tolerated by *Mofes* for the hardnefs of their hearts; and tells them plainly, that whofoever puts away his Wife, and Marries another, commits Adultery, and fo doth fhe if fhe Marries another, *Matth.* 5. 31. *Peter Martyr* on 1 *Cor.* 7. 10. is miftaken, when he faith, that there is never any mention in Scripture, that the Woman gave a Bill of Divorce to her Husband; but our Saviour tells us, that if the Woman put away her Husband, and Marry another, fhe commits Adultery: but the Man and Woman could not put away one another without a Bill of Divorce, and that before Witneffes.

Q. *After*

Sect. 1.   *A View of the Religions of* ASIA.   39

Q. *After what manner is the Wife separated from her deceased Husband's Brother?*

A. The Widow with five Witnesses repairs to the Chief Rabbi, who asks her certain questions, as, Whether her Husband hath been dead three Months? Whether his Brother be a single Man? Whether the Man present be her Husbands full Brother? What age they are of? And whether they think themselves fit for Procreation? Then he asks of the Woman, if she be fasting? for otherwise she must not spit in his Face. Then he asks of the Man, if the Woman present were his Brothers Wife? If he will Marry her, or suffer his Shooe to be pulled off? If he say he will not Marry, then a Shooe is brought, and put upon his right foot, being bare: then the Woman comes, saying, This my Brother-in-Law refuseth to raise up Seed to his Brother; and so bowing her self, pulls off his Shooe, and spits in his Face, saying, So shall it be done to him that will not build up his Brothers House: and thus they are parted. *The Separation of the Wife from the deceased Husbands Brother.*

Q. *What is the manner of Circumcising their Children?* *Their Circumcision, and Rites thereof.*

A. The Child is first washed, and laid in clean Linen; for if he be foul, or defile himself while he is Circumcised, the Mohel, or Circumciser, is to suspend or interrupt his Prayer, till he be washed again. In the morning of the Eighth day, the God-father seateth himself down in a seat placed near the Ark, and the Mohel near him. Twelve Wax-candles are brought in, to represent the Twelve Tribes. Then two Cups of Red-Wine, the Circumcising-knife, with two Dishes, the one of Oil, the other of Sand. When the Child is brought to the door by the Women, the Congregation riseth up, the God-father takes the Child and sits down in his seat. There is also a seat prepared for *Eliah*, whose coming they expect at the Circumcision. The Child is then Named, and usually by the Name of some of his Ancestors; so that *Luke* 1. 61. it was wondred at, that *Zachary* should Name his Son *John*, seeing none of his Kindred was named with this Name. The Eighth day was so strictly observed, that if it fell on the Sabbath, the Child was then Circumcised: not sooner, lest God should be thought to be tyed to the Sacrament; and because the Child the first seven days after the Birth was held legally unclean, and yet remaining in his Blood, *Levit.* 12. 2, 3. and 22. 27. nor later, lest the Parents should be longer withheld from the comfort of the Sacrament. The penalty of contempt or neglect of Circumcision, was, *a cutting off from the People*, Gen. 17. 14. that is, by Excommunication, or bodily death of the Parents. Therefore God would have killed *Moses*, for not Circumcising his Son: or else by the death of the Son himself, when he comes to years of discretion, if he be not Circumcised either by himself, or by his Parents, or by the Judges.

Q. *How doth the Mohel cut off the fore-skin?*

A. He first rubs it, that it may be the less sensible, then blesseth God for the Covenant of Circumcision; and withal cuts off the fore-

fore-part of the skin, and flings it into the sand, in memory of that promise, *Gen.* 32. 12. *I will make thee as the sand of the sea:* then he spits some red Wine on the wound, and washeth it, and some also on the Childs face, if he faint; and taketh the bleeding member in his mouth, and sucks the blood from it, which he spits into the other Cup of Wine. Then he tears off the remaining skin with his sharp-pointed nails, and layeth the clouts dipt in Oyl in the wound, and bindeth them. Then he blesseth God again, and the God-father takes the other Cup of Wine, and prayeth for the Child. And the Mohel moistneth the Childs lips with wine and his own blood, and prayeth again. If the Child be sick on the eighth day, his Circumcision is deferred till he recover. If he die before the eighth day, he is circumcised at the grave, but without Prayers.

Q. *How do they redeem their first born?*

How they redeem their first born.

A. When the Child is one and thirty days old, he is set upon a Table by the Father, before the Priest, with as much money as two Dollars and a half. After some questions propounded by the Priest to the Father and Mother, amongst others, Whether he esteems more of his Money, or of his Child? he answers, of his Child. Then the Priest takes the money, and layeth it on the Childs head, and propounceth, that he being the first born, and presented before the Lord, is now redeemed. If before this time the Father dies, then the Mother signifieth by a scroll about the Childs neck, that he is the first born, and not redeemed; who when he comes of age, is bound to redeem himself. He is held to be of just age when he is thirteen years old, for then the Parents stand no more charged with his sins, but he must himself bear his own burthen.

Q. *What duty is performed to the sick?*

Their duty to the sick.

A. The Rabbins are bound to visit and comfort them, and prepare them for making their will, if they be rich. They exhort them to be constant in their faith; especially they must believe that their Messias is yet to come: therefore they must make both confession of their faith and of their sins. They pray that their death may be a sufficient expiation for their sins, and that they may have a share in Paradise, and in the life to come.

Q. *How do they use their dead?*

Their ceremonies about the dead.

A. When the party dieth, his kindred tear off a little piece of their garments, because *Jacob* tore his garments when he heard of *Joseph's* death. They mourn also seven days, because *Joseph* did so for his Father. All the water in the house they pour out into the streets. They cover his face, and bow his thumbs, that it resembleth the Hebrew Shaddai, that so they may terrifie Satan from coming near the Corps. His other fingers are stretched out, to shew that now he holds the world no longer, having forsaken it. They wash the body with warm water, and anoint the head with wine, and the yolk of an egg; and cloath him with the white surplice he were on the day of Reconciliation, and then they coffin him.

him. When the Corps is carried out of the houfe, they caſt a ſhell after him, ſignifying that all ſorrow ſhould be now caſt out of that houſe. In the Church-yard a prayer or two is ſaid, then the Corps is buried; the next of kin caſteth in the firſt earth. In their return they caſt graſs over their heads; either to ſignifie their frailty and mortality, *For all fleſh is graſs*; or elſe their hope of the Reſurrection. When they enter the Synagogue, they skip to and fro, and change their ſeat ſeven times. The Mourners go barefoot ſeven days; abſtain from wine and fleſh, except on Sabbaths and Feſtivals. They bathe not in thirty three days, nor pare their nails. They burn candles for ſeven days together, thinking that the departed ſouls return to the place where they left the body, and bewail the loſs thereof. They believe that no Jew can be partaker of the Reſurrection who is buried out of *Canaan*, except God through hollow paſſages of the earth convey his body thither; grounding this conceit upon *Jacob*'s deſire to *Joſeph*, that he ſhould bury him in *Canaan*, and not in *Egypt*. They borrowed divers Gentile cuſtoms in their Funerals, as cutting or tearing their skin, hiring of women to ſing, and minſtrils to play; alſo ſhaving, going bare-footed, and bare-headed, with duſt on their heads, waſhing, anointing, and embalming, beſides beautifying of their Sepulchres, and adding of Epitaphs, &c. They uſed alſo burning of the dead, as may be ſeen in 1 *Sam.* 31. 12. and *Amos* 6. 10. They bury apart by themſelves, and not with thoſe of another Religion. Their common Epitaph is, *Let his ſoul be in the bundle of life, with the reſt of the juſt, Amen, Amen, Selah*. Other vain opinions and ceremonies they have, but not to our purpoſe. Of which ſee *Munſter, Buxtorfius, Margarita, Galatin, Hoſpinian, Fagius,* D. *Kimchi, Aben Ezra,* &c.

The

The Contents of the Second Section.

The Religions of the ancient Babylonians; *of the making, worshipping of Images, and bringing in Idolatry.* 2. *Of* Hierapolis, *and gods of the* Syrians. 3. *Of the* Phœnicians. 4. *Of the old* Arabians. 5. *Of the ancient* Persians. 6. *Of the* Sythians. 7. *Of the* Tartars, *or* Cathaians *and* Pagans. 8. *The Religions of the Northern Countries near the Pole. Three ways whereby Satan deludes men by false miracles. The fear of his Stratagems whence it proceeds; his illusions many, our duty thereupon.* 9. *Of the* Chinois. 10. *Of the ancient* Indian. 11. *Of* Siam. 12. *Of* Pegu. 13 *Of* Bengala. 14 *Of* Magor. 15. *Of* Cambai. 16. *Of* Goa. 17. *Of* Malabar. *Pagan Idolaters believe the immortality of the soul.* 18. *Of* Narsinga, *and* Bisnager. 19. *Of* Japan. 20. *Of the* Philippine *Islands.* 21. *Of* Sumatra *and* Zeilan. 22. *Of the ancient* Egyptians. 23. *Of the modern* Egyptian *Religions.*

SECT. II.

Quest. **W**Hat *kind of Religions, or rather superstitious Government, was there among the ancient* Babylonians.

Answ. They had their Priests called *Chaldeans* and *Magi*, who were much addicted to Astrology and Divination, and had their Schools for education of the Youth in this knowledge. They worshipped divers gods, or Idols rather; the two chief were *Belus*, or *Bel*, or *Baal*, by whom they meant *Jupiter*; the other was *Astaroth*, or *Astarte*, by which *Juno* was understood. They were bound also, by their superstitious discipline, to worship the Sun; and so was the King to offer to him every day a white horse richly furnished. They worshipped also the Fire, under the name of *Nego*; and the Earth, by the name of *Shaca*. To this Goddess they kept a feast for five days in *Babylon*, where, during that time, the Servants were Masters, and the Masters Servants. They worshipped also *Venus*; for maintaining of whose service, the women prostituted themselves to strangers, and received much money thereby: to this purpose they sate and exposed themselves at the Temple of *Venus*, which they call *Militia*. Their Priests used to have their Processions, and to carry their Idols on their shoulders, the people before and behind worshipping. The Priests also were used to shave their heads and beards, and to stand in their Temple with Axes, Scepters, and other weapons in their

Babylonians, their ancient Religion.

hands,

hands, and Candles lighted before them. They held a Divine Providence, but denied the Creation. *Ninus* was the first Idolater, who after the death of his Father *Belus*; set up his Image, and caused it to be adored with divine honours here at *Babylon*, and in the rest of his Dominions. Thus we see that the making of Images, and the worshipping of them, was the invention of the Gentiles; for indeed they were men whom the *Pagans* affirmed to be gods; and every one according to his merits and magnificence, began after his death to be worshipped by his friends; but at length, by the perswasion of evil spirits, they esteemed those whose memories they honoured to be lesser gods: this opinion and idolatry was fomented by the Poets; and not only a preposterous love, and a vain admiration of the worth and merits of dead men brought in idolatry, but likewise *Deisidæmonia*, or a foolish and preposterous fear; *primus in orbe Deos fecit timor*; for the Gentiles did fear their Religion would be in vain, if they did not see that which they worshipped; they would therefore rather worship stocks and stones, than an invisible Deity; but it is ridiculous, saith *Seneca*, *Genu posito simulachra adorare & suspicere ; fabros vero qui illa fecerunt contemnere*: to worship and admire the Image, and to slight the Image-maker; whereas the Artificer deserves more honour than the Art. Against this madness the Prophet *Isaiah* speaketh, Chap. 44. *Men cut down trees, rinde them, burn a part of them, make ready their meat, and warm themselves by the fire thereof; but of the residue he maketh a god, an Idol, and prayeth to it: but God hath shut their eyes from sight and their hearts from understanding*. Divers ways they had in worshipping of their Idols, sometimes by bowing the head, sometimes by bending the knee, sometimes by bowing or prostrating the whole body, and sometimes by kissing the Idol, or by kissing their own hand, if they could not reach to kiss the Idol: of this *Joab* speaketh, *If my mouth hath kissed mine hand when I beheld the Sun shining, or the Moon walking in her brightness,* *Job* 31. 26. But of the Babylonish Idolatry, see *Diodorus, Philostratus, Eusebius, Isidore, Scaliger.*

The making, worshipping of Images, and bringing in Idolatry.

Q. How doth it appear that the Gentile Idols were dead men?

A. By their own testimonies: for *Hermes* in *Asclepio*, as *Apuleius* records, confesseth, *that* Æsculapius, Grand-father to Asclepius, and that Mercury *his own Grand-father, why had Divine worship at* Hermopolis *in* Egypt, *were men whose bodies were buried, the one in* Libya,*the other in* Egypt,*in the town* Hermopolis, *so called from him, but under these names Spirits or Devils are worshipped, which I did draw or intice into their Statues.* Plutarch witnesseth, that the Egyptian good *Osyris* was a man, who because he distinguished every Region in the Camp by their colours, in which Dogs, Oxen, and other beasts were painted; therefore after his death he was honoured under these shapes. In *Cyprian*'s book concerning the vanity of Idols, *Alexander* is informed by *Leo*, the chief Egyptian Priest, that their gods were no other than men. The Greek Poets in rehearsing the genealogy and off-spring of their gods, do intimate, that they were

The Gentile Idols were dead men.

were men. King *Faunus* in *Italy*, made his Grand-father *Saturn* a god; and so he did deifie his father *Picus*, and his wife *Fauna*, who from her gift of prophecying was called *Fatua*, and afterward *Bona dea*. When the Senate made an Act that none should be worshipped at *Rome* for gods, but such as the Senate did allow, did they not by this Act intimate that their gods were but men, and subject to their approbation? *Cicero* in his books of the nature of gods, sheweth that all their Deities, both great and small, were but men; their Temples were their Sepulchres, and their Religion but Superstition. *Virgil* by confessing that the *Trojan* gods were subdued by the *Grecians*, doth acknowledge they were but men. *Sibylla* calls the Gentile gods νεκύων εἴδωλα χαμόντων, that is, the Idols or Images of dead carkasses: the whole story of *Jupiter*, to wit, his birth, education, actions and death, do testifie he is but a man; and if we look on his adulteries, incests with his own sister *Juno*, and his daughter *Minerva*: if on his sodomy with *Ganymedes*, his ravishing of *Europa*, and many others; if on his impiety against his father *Saturn*, whom he drove out of his Kingdom, and forced to hide himself in *Italy*; if, I say, we consider these things, we must needs say that he was so far from being a god, that he scarce deserved the name of a man, but rather of a savage beast, and indeed not unlike in salacity to the Goat his Nurse. Such another god was *Saturn*, a cruel murtherer of his own children, and whose chief delight was to have little children sacrificed to him. What was *Mercury* but a Thief, *Venus* a Whore, *Bacchus* a Drunkard? *Vulcan* was but a Smith, *Apollo* a Shepherd and Mason, *Mars* a Souldier, *Neptune* a Mariner, *Minerva* a Spinister or Weaver, *Saturn* a Husbandman, *Æsculapius* a Physician, &c. in a word, as these were men, so they had no other Deity but what they had from men; therefore I will end with that witty saying, *Si Dii, cur plangitis? si mortui, cur adoratis?* if these are gods, why do you bewail them? if men, why do you adore them? But against these deified men, the Fathers of the Church have written sufficiently; chiefly *Clemens*, *Augustine*, *Eusebius*, *Tertullian*, *Cyprian*, *Lactantius*, *Arnobius*, *Nazianzen*, &c. who tells us, that there was no Religion at all among the Gentiles, seeing every kind of impurity, and impiety was patronized by their gods: and as *Greg. Nazianzen* saith in his third Oration against *Julian*, κακὸν ἦν, ᾗ τίμιον, ᾗ βωμοῖς ᾗ θυσίαις τιμώμενον; that is, to be wicked was not only counted no disgrace, but it was also honoured with Altars and Sacrifices. Therefore justly might the Apostle call the worshippers of such gods, *Atheists*, because they did not worship the true God; but such as were no gods at all, and scarce worthy to be called men. Goodly gods (saith the same Father) who would be drawn to *Æthiopia*, so far off, for the love of good chear; these sure were belly-gods: and withal would undertake a quarrel for the Strumpet *Lucena*.

Q. *What Religious worship, or Idolatrous rather, was used in* Hierapolis *of* Syria?

A. In

Sect. 2. *A View of the Religions of* ASIA. 45

A. In this holy City (for so *Hierapolis* signifieth) was a magnifi- Hierapolis cent Temple, built by *Deucalion*; or as some write, by *Semiramis*; *the Religi-* or, as others, by *Bacchus*. Queen *Stratonice* repaired, or rebuil- *on thereof.* ded rather, this Temple, being decayed. Here men used to geld themselves, and put on womens apparel; such Priests were called *Gall*. Here stood two *Priapi* or *Phalli*, and within the Quire (into which the chief Priest only might enter) stood *Jupiter's* statue, supported with Bulls, *Juno's* with Lyons, having in one hand a Scepter, and a Distaff in the other: In the Temple stood *Apollo*, clothed and bearded, whose Oracles were much consulted; if the petition was liked, the Image would move forward; if otherwise, backward. Here also stood divers other Idols; 300. Priests were maintained here; who did Minister all in white, with their heads covered, and sacrificed twice a day, with singing and musical Instruments, if to *Juno*; but to *Jupiter* no musick. Their high Priest was elected every year, whose clothing was Purple, and a golden Mitre. Not far from the Temple was a deep Lake, in which were kept consecrated fishes: in the midst thereof stood a stone Altar, crowned continually with Garlands; on this odours did still burn. They had divers Feasts the greatest was that of the Fire; where they set divers trees, hung with divers sorts of beasts for sacrifice, on fire, after they had carried about these fires, (in Procession) to their Idols. Here the gelded Priests wound each other, and divers young men at this feast gelded themselves. Here was much confused Musick, Disorder, Fury and Prophecying. Into the Temple none might enter in thirty days, in whose family any died, and then his head must be shaved. He that but lookt upon a dead Corps, was excluded the Temple a whole day. To touch a Dove was abomination, because *Semiramis* was transformed into a Dove; and so it was to touch Fishes, because of *Derceto*, the Mermaid and Mother of *Semiramis*, half a Fish, and half a Woman. To *Hierapolis* were divers Pilgrimages; each Pilgrim was tied to cut his hair on his head and brows; to sacrifice a sheep, to kneel and pray upon the fleece thereof; to lay the head and feet of the sheep upon his own head, to crown himself; to drink cold water only, and to sleep on the ground till his return. The young men were bound to consecrate their hair, then to cut it in the Temple, and to offer it in a Box of Gold or Silver, with their names inscribed thereof. Some other foolish circumstances there were in their superstitious Church-discipline, if I may so call it: of which see *Lucian* in his *Syrian* Goddess; out of whom I have this description. By this, and by what we are to speak of the *Idolatry of* Gentile Idolatry, we may admire the madness of those men, who *the Gentiles* being made, after the Image of God, do subject and enslave them- *and of all* selves to dead Images, to senseless blocks and stones; which have *kinds con-* Eyes, and see not; ears, and hear not: then not without cause *demned.* did *David* say, *That they who made them, are like unto them*; he means those that worshipped them: for not the Artificer, but the Worshipper makes the Idol: So the Poet:

Qui

Qui fingit facros auro vel marmore vultus,
Non facit ille Deos; qui colit ifte facit.

And it is ftrange to fee how cold and fparing we are in the worfhip of the true God, how zealous and expenfive they are in the fervice of their falfe gods; they can cut their flefh, and cry from morning to evening with *Baal*'s Priefts; they can part with their gold and filver, their jewels and ear-rings, to make them a golden Calf; yea, they can offer their Sons and Daughters to be burned in the fire to *Moloch*; and yet there is no fin fo repugnant to God as Idolatry; for it is repugnant to his entity, becaufe *an Idol is nothing in the World*, faith the Apoftle: it is repugnant to his unity, becaufe he is but one; but falfe gods, or Idols, are many: it is repugnant to him as he is verity, becaufe *Idols are lying vanities*: it is repugnant alfo to him as he is life, becaufe Idols are dead and fenfelefs things: it is repugnant to his purity: for Idols are called filthinefs, pollution, and abomination in Scripture: it is alfo repugnant to the love he carrieth to his Church; for it caufeth jealoufie in him, and therefore he calleth Idolatry *Whoredom*, and Idolaters *Adulterers*; and they that worfhip Idols are faid *to go a whoring after other gods*: it is likewife oppofite to Gods goodnefs; therefore Idolatry is particularly called fin, as if it were the only fin in the world: fo *Exod.* 32. 22. *This people is prone to fin*; that is, to Idolatry: fo *Lam.* 1. 8. *My people have committed a fin*; that is, Idolatry: and as it is moft repugnant to Gods nature, fo it is to almoft all his commandments. To the firft; becaufe it makes other gods than he. To the fecond; becaufe it makes graven Images, and worfhips them. To the third; becaufe it takes Gods name in vain, by giving it to the creature, even to ftocks and ftones. To the fifth; becaufe it gives the honour due to Parents unto fenfelefs Idols; for the Idolater *faith to the flock, thou art my father; and to the ftone, thou haft begotten me*, Jer. 2. 27. To the fixth commandment; becaufe the Idolater is an horrible murtherer, in not fparing his own children. To the feventh; for Idolatry is not only fpiritual adultery, but the caufe alfo of carnal pollution, and of unnatural luft; for among the Indians they practifed Sodomy in the fight of their Idols, as a part of that worfhip due to them. Laftly, it is againft the eighth commandment; for the Idolater is a facrilegious Thief, ftealing from God his due and giving it to his Idol, as the Prophet complaineth, *Hof.* 2. 8. There are three infeparable companions of Idolatry; namely, Witchcraft, Covetoufnefs, and carnal Pollution. For the firft, the Apoftle, *Gal.* 5. 20. joyneth Idolatry, and Witchcraft together. The *Ephefians*, as they were given to Idolatry, fo they were to Magical Arts: and as foon as they forfook their Idolatry, they forfook alfo their Witchcraft, and burned their Conjuring Books, *Acts* 19. 19. as *Manaffeh* reared up Altars for *Baal*, fo he ufed inchantments, and dealt with familiar fpirits, and wizzards, 2. *Kings* 21. 6. Hence proceeded diabolical infpirations, and Enthufiafms, Oracles, and many other inchanting tricks. As for Covetoufnefs, it is no wonder

Sect. 2. A View of the Religions of ASIA. 47

der that it accompanies Idolatry; for it is a kind of Idolatry, and so the Apostle calls it: The covetous man worshippeth his god *Plutus*, or *Mammon*, with as great devotion as any Idolater doth his Idol: he saith to the wedge, *thou art my hope, and to the gold, thou art my confidence*; he sacrificeth to his God the poor whom he oppresseth, his own soul also and his body too, which he macerates with care, and deprives of things necessary. King *Ahaz* no sooner gave himself to Idolatry, but he presently shews his sacrilegious covetousness in robbing the house of the Lord of its wealth, 2. *Chron.* 28. As for carnal uncleanness, how much that hath been practised by Idolaters, is known to them that have read Histories; for they did not think their daughters fit for marriage, till first they had been prostituted before their Idols; and though adultery, fornication and sodomy were thought sins, yet these were held vertues, and a part of Religious worship in the presence of their gods; and it is no marvel; for their very gods were Incestuous, Adulterers, and Sodomites; and divers Strumpets after their death were defied, as *Lactantius* instanceth in *Laurentia*, the Wife of *Faustulus*, who for her whoredoms among the Shepherds was called *Lupa*, that is a Whore. Such another was *Leæna* among the *Athenians*; such was *Faula*, *Hercules* his Whore, and *Flora*, who left her estate to the Romans. In a word, Idolatry hath been the cause of all sin and mischief in the world; from whence proceed murthers, rapine, oppression, injustice, intemperance, uncleanness, sorcery, avarice, &c. but from this, that men forsook the living God, who is the punisher of vice, and reward of vertue; and served false gods, who had been wicked men themselves whilest they lived, and patronized wickedness when they were dead.

Q. *What Idolatrous Gods or Devils rather did the ancient* Syrians *worship?*

A. Their chief God was *Baal-Zebub*, or *Beel Zebub*, the Lord of Gods of the Flies, either because his Temple was much infested with Flies, Syrians. or else from the power he had in driving away Flies. He was a great god at *Ekron*, and is called in the Gospel, Prince of the Devils. Some take him for *Jupiter*, others for *Priapus*, others for *Sumanus* chief God of the *Manes*, which some think to be *Pluto*. 2. *Baal-Phegor* or *Peor*, that is, the gaping or naked Lord, so called from the naked posture in which he was worshipped; he was the God of the *Moabites*, His Temple is called *Beth-peor*, *Deut.* 3. 29. some take him for *Priapus*. 3. *Baal* or *Bel*, which signifieth Lord, was a great God or Idol amongst the *Babylonians*, *Sidonians*, *Samaritans*, and *Moabites*, and sometimes among the *Jews*; some take him for *Mars*, others for *Jupiter*, who by the *Phœnicians* is called *Baal Samen*, that is, Lord of Heaven, by which I think they meant the Sun. 4. *Baal-berith*, that is, Lord of the Covenant, *Judg.* 9. 4. by whom they meant *Jupiter*, whose office was to confirm Covenants, and to punish the breakers thereof. *Audiat hæc genitor, qui fœdera fulmine sancit*, Virg. Æn. 12. So *Aristophanes* calls upon *Jupiter* to send his Thunder upon Perjurers, ὁ Ζεὺς ἵησι κεραυτὸν ἐπὶ τῆς ὁπόρκης. Therefore among the Romans, the Herauld of *Fæcialis* in making of Leagues, used as he was killing the Hog, by which they used to confirm their Covenants to call on *Jupiter*. 5 *Dagon* from *Dag* a Fish, because from the navel downwards he was made in the form of a fish, but upward like a man; this was a great Idol among the *Philistines*, and is thought to be the same that *Neptune* or *Triton*. Others who derive the word from *Dagan*, that is, corn, of which he is said to be the inventer, make him all one with *Saturn*. 6. *Astaroth* or *Astarte* was Goddess of the *Sidonians*; the word signifieth a flock of sheep, or sheep-fold; this is thought to be all one with *Juno, Venus*, or *Lucina*, under which names and the form of a sheep, they worshipped the Moon, as they did the Sun under the name of *Jupiter*, and form of a Ram. She is called also by the Greeks ἰεφρία, from ἐρανὸς Heaven, where her aboad is, Ἀςεϳέχα, from her Dominion over the Stars. 7. *Adrammelech*, that is the Kings cloak, or power. *Anamelech*, the Kings Oracle or Answer; these two Idols were worshipped at *Sepharvaim* a town of the *Assyrians*, 2 *Kings* 17. these gods were also honoured in *Samaria*, and so were *Succoth Benoth*, the Tabernacle of Daughters, *Nergal* the light of the *grave*, *Ashima* a fault, *Nibhas* the fruit of vision, *Tartak*, that is, Chained. All which may be seen in the above named chapter of the *Kings*. 8. The *Moabites* worshipped *Chemosh*, the *Ammonites* · *Milchom*, 2 *Kings* 23. *Nisroch* was *Senacherib*'s Idol, 2 *Kings* 19. *Remphan* or *Repham* is the same that *Hercules* the god of *Tyrus*, from *Rephaim*, that is Giants. *Moloch* or *Molech* from *Malach* to reign, was a great Idol among the *Moabites*, and *Ammonites*, and is thought to be the same that *Saturn*, for their Images and sacrifices were much alike; to whom the superstitious Gentiles, and the Jews also offered their sons and daughters to be burned. *Thamuz* mentioned *Ezek*. 8. 14. is by *Hierom* taken for *Adonis*, so call'd from *Adon*, that is, Lord, by which they understood the Sun, as likewise by *Hercules*, many other Idol gods they worshipped: but these mentioned are the chief.

Q. What kind of Discipline was used among the Phœnicians?

Phœnicians, their Religion and Discipline.

A. By their execrable discipline they were bound to offer yearly sacrifices to *Saturn*, or the Devil rather, of young Infants: and in the Temple of *Venus*, to practise not only Whoredom, but Sodomy also; the Phœnicians were bound to prostitute their daughters to *Venus* before they married them. In the Temple of *Venus* were celebrated the annual Rites of *Adonis*, with beatings and howlings, to whom they perform solemn Obsequies. The next day they say he is alive, and then they shave their heads. The women that refused to be shaved, were tied to prostitute themselves to strangers for one day, and by this means money was raised for *Venus*. The Sun also is much worshipped amongst them, whose Priest is crowned with gold, and is clothed with a long-sleeved garment down to the feet. They were also tied by their Discipline to worship *Astarte* in the shape of a sheep, and *Dagon* in the form of a Mermaid. This Idol was called *Atergatis*, and *Dercetis*: in

honour

honour of which the *Phœnicians* abstained from fish, yet her Priests did eat of the fish which they set all day before her. She had also offered to her fishes of gold and silver. Of these passages, see *Eusebius* in his Preparation, *Diodorus Siculus*, *Lucian*, *Pliny*, *Athenæus*, and others.

Q. *What was the Religion and Discipline of the old* Arabians?
A. They worshipped the Sun and Moon, Serpents, Trees, and other such like Deities. The *Nabathæans* burned Frankincense to the Sun on his Altar. They do not bury their dead, but lay them, even their Kings, in Dunghils. Adultery is death among them, but Incest is no sin. They are Circumcised after the example of *Ismael*, at Thirteen years of Age. Their Priests are cloathed with Linen: they wear Mitres and Sandals; they abhor Swines flesh: they pay the Tithes of their Frankincense to their god *Sabis*: the Priests are not to take it by weight, but by measure. They are tied by their Discipline not to gather Cinnamon, till first they Sacrifice; then they divide it with a Consecrated Spear, and assign to the Sun his Portion. In *Panchæa* is a rich and stately Temple, adorned with Statues, and the Priests houses about it. The Priests here rule all, both in Politick and Ecclesiastick Affairs. They are bound to spend their time in singing Hymns, and rehearsing the Acts of their gods. It is not lawful for them to go out of the sacred bounds allotted them: if they do, they may be killed by Law. They hold Mice to be arrant enemies to their gods, therefore they kill them. Of this subject see *Solinus*, *Athenæus*, *Diodorus*, *Boemus*, and others.

Arabians, their Religion and Discipline.

Q. *What was the Religious Discipline of the ancient* Persians?
A. They had neither Temples, Altars, nor Images, holding these improper for their gods: but on the tops of hills offered Sacrifices to Heaven, and to the Sun, Moon, Fire, Earth, Water, and Winds. The Priest useth neither Musick, Vestments, nor Libaments, but only his Tiara or Head Attire, crowned with Myrtle. He Prayeth for all *Persians*, chiefly for the King. He cuts his Sacrifice into small pieces, and puts Herbs under. One of the *Magi* is bound to stand by, and to sing a Hymn of the Genealogy of their gods; for without a *Magus* the Sacrifice is not lawful. Every Man celebrates his own birth-day. To lye, and to be in debt, are heinous crimes with them; so it is to spit, wash, or piss in a River, which with them are hallowed. The *Magi* may with their own hands kill any thing, except a Man, and a Dog. They leave no part of their Sacrifices for their gods, but divide it by the direction of their *Magus* amongst themselves; for they hold that God is satisfied with the Soul of the Sacrificed Beast. To blow the fire with their breath, or to cast any dead thing into it, or dirt, was death. They Sacrificed chiefly to the Fire and Water; the Fire they cherish with dry sticks without their barks, with tallow also and oyl. When they Sacrifice to the Waters, they slay the Beasts in a ditch, and lay the flesh on Myrtle, and Lawrel, the *Magi* burn the same, then they pray and sprinkle on the Earth, Oyl, Milk, and Honey.

Persians, their Ancient Religion.

They used not to slay their Sacrifice with a knife, but with a Mallet or Club. The *Magi* keep the Sacrifice still burning, and pray every day an hour before it. They adored the Sun, whom they called *Mithra*, at his rising, and offered to him white Horses, whose sacred Chariot was drawn with white Steeds before the King when he went to Sacrifice. They had divers Festival days, the chief whereof was that of the Sun. The next was that they called the Destruction of Vices, when they killed poysonable creatures and Sacrificed. Of these *Persian* Rites see *Herodotus, Athenæus, Pausanias*, and others.

Q. *What was the Old* Scythian *Religion?*

Scythians, their old Religion. A. They worshipped first of all *Vesta*, then *Jupiter, Apollo, Venus, Mars*, and *Hercules:* they had neither Images, Altars, nor Temples for any of their gods, except for *Mars*, whose Temples they erected of bundles of Twigs heaped up together. In stead of his Image, they set up an old Iron Sword, to which they offered yearly Sacrifices of Cattel, and Horses; and of Men every hundreth Captive, with whose blood they besprinkle *Mars* his Sword. Then they cut off the right shoulders of the slain Men, and fling them into the Air. They used to wound first, and then to strangle the Beast which they Sacrificed, praying to that God to whom they offered the Beast; they kindled no fire of Wood, for the Country yielded none, but they burned the bones of the Beast to boil the flesh withal; if they want a Vessel, they boil the Flesh in the beasts Paunch; they use no Vows, nor any other Ceremonies. Their chiefest Sacrifices were Horses. But of this, see *Herodotus*, and others.

Q. *What Religious Discipline had the* Tartars, *or* Cathaians *?*

Tartars, their old Religion. A. They worshipped the Sun, Stars, Fire, Earth, and Water, to whom they offered the First-fruits of their Meat and Drink each morning, before they eat and drink themselves. They believe there is one God, maker of all things; yet they worship not, nor pray to him. They place Idols at their Tent-doors, to preserve their Cattel and Milk. To these silk and felt Idols (for of such materials they make them) are offered the first-fruits of milk, meat, and drink, the hearts also of Beasts, which they leave before them all night, and then eat them in the morning; they offer Horses to the Emperour's Idol, which none afterward must ride; they do not break, but burn the bones of their Sacrifices; by their discipline they must not touch the fire with a knife, nor meddle with young Birds, nor pour milk, drink, or meat on the ground, nor break one bone with another, nor make water within their Tents, and divers other such Traditions, which if violated, are punished with death, or else redeemed with much money. They believe another World, but such as this. When one dieth, he hath meat set before him, and Mares milk: his Friends eat a Horse, and burn the bones thereof for his Soul: they bury also with him a Mare, a Colt, and a Horse bridled and sadled; his Gold and Silver also; and they set upon Poles the Horse-hide that was eat, that he may

not

not be without a Tent in the other World; they use to purifie every thing by making it pass between two fires. When they pray, they are enjoyned by their Discipline, to lift up their hands and smite their teeth three times. They use to feed the Ghosts or Spirits with Mares Milk cast in the air, or poured on the ground. They have their Religious Votaries and Monasteries, amongst which there is an Order called *Sensein*, which eat nothing but Bran steeped in hot water. They worship not Idols, nor do they Marry; but they hold Transanimation, and divers other ridiculous opinions, as may be seen in *Johannes de Plano Carpini*, whom Pope *Innocent*, Anno 1246. sent Embassador to the *Tartarian* Court. See also M. *Paulus Venetus*, *Vincentius*, *Bellovack* in *spec. Hist. Mat. Paris*, and others. There is one thing commendable in their Discipline, that they force no Man to embrace their Religion. But *Ortelius* mentioneth a strange custom amongst them, that their Priests on high Trees Preach to them, and after Sermon besprinkle their Auditors with blood, milk, earth, and cow-dung mixed together, and no less strange it is, that they do not bury their dead, but hang them on Trees.

Q. Had the Pagans any knowledge of the Creation?

A. It seems by these *Tartars*, and divers other Gentile Idolaters, of which we are to speak, that many of them had some knowledge of the Beginning of the World, which they learned, not from the Jews, with whom they had no commerce, but from the Heathen Philosophers and Poets; and these were led to believe this truth by the guide of natural reason; for when they considered the continual vicissitudes in the World, the alteration, generation, and corruption of things, the nature of motion and of time, whereof the one presupposeth a Chief Mover; for nothing can move it self; the other consisteth in Priority and Posteriority, which depends upon motion, and suteth not with Eternity; when they observed also the Harmony, Order and Beauty of things, and how every motion and mutation aimed at a certain End, they concluded that this Great Universe could not be ruled, or have existence by chance, but by providence and wisdom; and that therefore this must needs have a Beginning; otherwise we could not know whether the Egg or the Bird, the Seed or the Plant, the Day or the Night, the Light or the Darkness were first. And seeing the World consisteth of corruptible parts, how can the Whole which is made up of such Parts, be Eternal? They found also, that it was repugnant to reason, for so many Eternals and infinite Entities to exist actually together; for every Entity in the World must be Eternal, if it self be Eternal: Besides, that it is against the nature of Eternity to admit *magis* and *minus*, degrees, auction or diminution; which it must needs do, if the World be eternal; for if there have been infinite annual revolutions of the Sun, and infinite monthly revolutions of the Moon, there must needs be something greater than Infinity; for the revolutions of the Moon are far more than of the Sun; by these reasons they were induced to acknowledge a Beginning of the World;

Pagans, their knowledge of the Creation.

World; of which *Merc. Trismegistus* in *Pœmandro* speaketh plainly, in saying, *That God by his word made and perfected the World, dividing the Earth from the Heaven, and the Sea from the Land*, &c. *Orpheus*, in his *Argonautes*, singeth, *How Jupiter hid within his breast the World which he was to bring forth, ᾠδῷ τις πολυαδες, into the pleasant light*, &c. this same Song is Sung by *Hesiod, Homer, Æschilus, Sophocles, Euripides*, and other Poets. *Pythagoras*, as *Plutarch* and *Laertius* testifie, taught, *That the World was made by God.* *Thades, Empedocles, Anaxagoras*, and the other ancient Philosophers, ascribe a Beginning to the World, some from one Element, some from another. The *Platonists* always held the Creation of the World; and the *Aristotelians* affirming, there is a First Mover, must conclude, that the World which is moved, had a Beginning; they say also, that the World doth depend upon God; How then can it be Eternal? seeing dependance and eternity are incompatible. *Aristotle* in his Book *de Mundo*, and in his *Metaphysicks*, saith, *That God is the Cause and Author, not only of living creatures, but also of Nature it self, and of the World.* *Cicero*, in his Books of the nature of the gods, confesseth, *That every thing had a Beginning, and that Man was not created by chance, but by a Supreme Power.* *Seneca, Macrobius, Virgil, Ovid*, and other Latin Poets, except *Lucretius*, affirm the same Doctrine. The *Stoicks* also asserted the Original of the World, and so did the *Epicures*, though these held a beginning fortuital, not providential, ascribing the original of things to chance, not to counsel. This same Doctrine of the Creation is at this day believed by *Turks, Arabians, Persians, Armenians*, the most barbarous People of both *Indies*, as we may see in the progress of this Book: and the greatest Opponents to this Doctrine of the Worlds Creation, as *Pliny, Lucretius, Galen*, and others, are forced sometimes to doubt the truth of their own Tenents.

Q. *Were all Tartars of one Religion or Discipline?*

Tartars, their diversities of Religion.
A. No; for that vast Country containeth several Nations, who were, and some of them yet are, of several Religions. Some Christians, some Mahumetans, and others Pagans, among whom also are divers Sects and Religions. In *Sachion* they have divers Monasteries of Idols; to whom they dedicate their children, and on Festival days Sacrifice Rams to their Idols, for their Childrens preservation, the flesh whereof they eat, but reserve the bones as holy Reliques: the Priests Fee is the Skin, with the Head, Feet, and Inwards, and some part of the flesh also. Before the Corps of any Great Man be buried, they set a Table before it, furnished with all sort of Meats, with the Odour of which they think the departed Soul is refreshed and heartned against the burning of the Body. They cast into the fire with the Body, Pictures of his Men, Women, Horses, and other things, to serve him in the other World. In *Tangoth* they worship Idols with many heads and hands; they have Monasteries where the Monks are Walled up. In *Succuir*, they make Perfumes of Rheubarb for their Idols. In *Caindu* they prostitute their Wives, Sisters

sters and Daughters to Strangers, as an honour due to their Idols. In *Cathai* and *Mangi*, the sick vow to offer their blood to their Idols if they recover; their Sorcerers also cause them to offer to their Idols sacrifices of Rams with black heads, which with spiced drinks they eat up merrily, with singing and dancing, and fling the broth of the sacrifice in the air. In some Provinces of *Cathai* the Monks wear strings about them full of Nut-shells, on which they are still praying: they worship still towards the north, but keep their Church doors open towards the south. Of these see *Paulus Venetus* and *Will. de Rubruquis*, who both travelled in these Countries.

Q. *Of what Religion are the Northern Countries near the Pole?*

A. In *Nova Zembla* (as the Hollanders who travelled thither relate) there is no Religion prescribed by Law; but they worship the Sun so long as he is with them, and in his absence the Moon and North Star. To these they offer yearly sacrifices of Deer, which they burn except the head and feet; they sacrifice also for their dead. The *Samodyes* which are subject to the *Muscovite*, are much addicted to witchcraft and idolatry; among them each kindred have their Temple where they sacrifice; their Priest is he that is eldest, whose ornaments are small ribs and teeth of fishes and wild beasts hanging about them, with a white Garland on his head; in his divine service he doth not sing but howl, and that so long till he become like a mad man, and then falls down as if he were dead, but riseth again, ordereth five Deer to be sacrificed, and then thrusts a sword half way into his belly, still singing or howling rather; the sword he takes out again, heats it in the fire, and then thrusts it in at the Navel, and out at the Fundament; then he lets two men standing by him, pull off his head and left shoulder with a small line, by which they pull the head and shoulder into a kettle of hot water, but he reviveth again, and cometh out whole as he was before; with such jugling illusions do they deceive the people. But of these see *Richard Johnson's* relation in *Hakluit*. Tom. 1.

Religions of the Northern countries near the Pole.

Q. *How many ways can Satan delude men by such false miracles?*

A. Three ways. 1. By local motion, suddenly removing one object from the eye, and substituting in stead thereof another; whereby thus are we deceived in many supposed transformations; as when we think we see Women transformed into Cats, or Hares, or any other creature; the Woman is suddenly conveyed away and the Cat put in her place; such were those transmutations of *Ulysses* fellows into beasts, and of *Diomedes* his company into birds. 2. By darkning the Medium or Air, that we cannot see the object, or by condensing of it so, that the object appeareth bigger than it is, or by altering of it so, that the object appeareth quite other than it is; as we see strange things through some glasses; or lastly, by working on and disturbing of the fancy, which is no hard matter for Satan to do, being a subtle spirit of long experience, and full of knowledge. 3. By working on the outward sensitive

Three ways whereby Satan deludes men by false miracles.

organ,

organ, either by altering the situation thereof; thus by elevating or depressing the eye, we see things double, and otherwise than they are; or by disturbing the vitive spirits, or by casting a mist before the eye. By such tricks the Egyptian Sorcerers made the people believe they had done the same Miracles that *Moses* did. And so the Witch of *Endor* deluded *Saul*, by presenting to him the resemblance of *Samuel*; whereas it was not in the power of Satan to disturb the soul of any just man, and to take it from that place of rest and happiness, where it is under the immediate Protection of the Almighty; yet many learned men are of another opinion, that *Samuel* did truly appear. God so permitting that *Saul* might be convinced of his wickedness, and desertion from God, by the same Prophet, whose counsel he had heretofore despised. Now though Satan deludes oftentimes with false miracles, yet I deny not, but that sometimes by God's permission he doth strange wonders, by the help of natural causes, as he can raise storms, so he did against *Job*'s Children; he can carry his Witches in the Air, so he did carry Christ to the Pinacle of the Temple, and thence to an high Mountain; so the Angel carried *Habakkuk*; he can also make beasts to speak, by guiding their tongues, so the Angel made *Balaam*'s Ass to utter certain words; but he can do no miracle, that is, he can produce such effects as exceed the activity of natural causes; so he cannot raise the dead, or give them life again; he cannot restore sight to the blind, where there is a total privation, nor can he transform men into beasts, being the body of a beast is not capable of an humane soul; nor can the soul of man animate a beasts body, there being no relation between the matter and form, nor is there any disposition, appetite, or aptitude in that matter to receive such a form. This is only the work of God, who changed *Lot*'s Wife into a Pillar of Salt, and *Nebuchadnezzar* into a beast. Satan hath no power over cœlestial bodies, though he be Prince of the Air; he cannot create, nor do those things, which God hath reserved for himself. Therefore when we hear of men transformed into beasts, or raised from the dead, and such like miracles as exceed the course and activity of nature, we may be assured these are no true miracles, but Satanical delusions, especially if they be done to confirm errour, wickedness and superstition; for the end of all true and divine miracles are to establish truth and holiness. Therefore when we read of bringing down the Moon, of driving the Stars backward, and such like impossibilities believed among the Gentiles, we must conclude they were meer delusions of Satan. Such were those wonders ascribed to *Simon Magus*, of making images to walk, of turning stones into bread, of being transformed into a Sheep, Goat, and Serpent, of raising souls from the dead, and such like stuff; all these were meer jugling tricks and Satanical deceptions.

Q. *But why are we so afraid of Satan's Stratagems, seeing the most of them are but illusions?*

A. This

A View of the Religions of ASIA.

A. This fear in us proceeds partly from the guilt of our own conscience; for *Adam*'s sin brought fear both on himself and on his posterity; therefore after he had fallen, he confesseth, that as soon as he heard the voice of God in the Garden, he was afraid: and so we his children do oftentimes fear, where no fear is, and are afraid sometimes at our own shadows, or at the shaking of a leaf. Partly this fear proceeds from want of faith, which Christ reproved in his Apostles; who when they saw Jesus walking in the night time on the Sea, they were afraid, thinking they had seen a Spirit. Besides, the implacable hatred of Satan against mankind, his delight he taketh in affrighting and hurting us, either in our persons, or in our estates, that irreconcileable enmity which is between the Serpent and the Womans seed, is a great cause of this fear in us. Lastly, we are naturally fearful in the dark, because our imagination worketh upon it self, having no outward object to divert it; hence Satan who is the Prince of darkness, useth the opportunity of the night to hurt or to delude us; thus he affrighteth us in the dark in our houses with strange apparitions, motions and sounds; whence some houses have been said to be haunted with Spirits. So in the night he affrighteth travellers with *Ignis fatuus*, or jack in the candle, as we call it, which though it be a natural *Meteor*, yet Satan can move to and fro, purposely to draw travellers into precipices or waters. So in the night time he affrighteth Mariners at Sea, by insinuating himself into those fiery *Meteors*, which like candles, or balls of fire, run up and down the ship; these were deifi'd by the old *Pagans*; if one single flame appeared, they called it *Helena*, and held it an ominous sign of destruction, as she was to *Troy*; if there were two, they named them *Castor* and *Pollux*, and placed their statues in their ships, as we read *Act.* 28. And Seamen use to tell us of many strange sights and apparitions they have seen in the Ocean. Satan also useth to affright men in Churches and Church-yards in the dark, by representing to their Phantasie the shape of dead men in their winding sheets; in the night also strange voices and sounds are heard near deep waters, or rivers, which are taken as presages of some shortly to be drowned there; the like I have heard my self, and have found the event to fall out accordingly; for one day travelling before day, with some company, near the River *Don* by *Aberden*, we heard a great noise, and voices call to us; I was going to answer, but was forbid by my company, who told me they were spirits, which never are heard there, but before the death of some body; which fell out too true; for the next day, a gallant Gentleman was drowned with his horse, offering to swim over. It is strange what *Plutarch* writeth of the voice which from the shoar called upon *Thamus* the Egyptian ship-Master (who then had cast Anchor at *Praxe.e*) telling him that the great god *Pan* was dead. Though the Night mare, which is called *Incubus* and *Succubus*, be a natural disease, as Physicians know; yet Satan had oftentimes made use of this infirmity, to abuse the bodies of men and women

The fear of Satan's Stratagems (though illusions) whence it proceeds.

E 4   in

in their sleep. By all which we see his malice against mankind, and the causes of our fear; which hath wrought so powerfully among the ignorant *Pagans*, that they have planted their whole Religion in the worshipping of these evil spirits; for their gods were none other, as *Porphyry* sheweth, *lib.* 2. *de abstinen. & lib.* 2. *de sacrificio*: For, saith he, *These wicked Spirits delight in shedding of blood, in filthy and obscene speeches, exhorting men to lust, vice, wickedness, and flagitious actions,* &c. *they perswade men that the supreme God delighteth in such impieties,* &c.

Q. *Since the Stratagems and illusions of Satan are so many, what is our duty in this case?*

Our duty respecting the many stratagems and illusions of Satan.

A. Our duty is, 1. To be assuredth at nothing can come to pass, but by the providence of our Heavenly Father, who hath numbred the hairs of our heads, and hath Satan in a chain, so that without permission he could neither afflict *Joab* in his person, children, nor cattel, nor durst he enter into the herd of swine without leave from Christ. 2. Let us remember what Christ hath promised, to wit, that he will be with us, to the end of the world; and if he be with us, who can be against us? Christ came to destroy the works of the Devil; to cast out the strong man, and to tread down Satan under our feet; he hath promised not to leave us Orphans; *he his the good Shepherd that laid down his life for his sheep*, which he holdeth so fast that no man shall take them out of his hand; his name is *Emanuel*, God with us. He was amongst his Apostles, *Luke* 24. when they were assembled together, and in great fear; and so he will be in the midst of two or three gathered together in his name. He is the watchman of *Israel*, that neither slumbers nor sleeps; therefore with *David* let us lie down and take our rest, for he will make us to live in safety. Though we walk through the valley of the shadow of death, let us fear no evil, because the Lord is with us. Let us not be moved; because he is at our right hand; he is our buckler, and our exceeding great reward, therefore let us not fear. 3. Let us put on the whole Armour of God, chiefly the shield of faith, that we may quench all the fiery Darts of the Devil, and let us fight against Satan, as Christ did with the sword of the spirit, which is the word of God. Let us resist the Devil, and he will flee from us. 4. We must remember that God doth sometimes permit Satan to buffet us as he did *Paul*, that he might try our patience, and obedience, that we may be the more watchful of our selves against that roaring Lyon, which compasseth the earth to and fro, seeking whom he may devour; that we may be the more earnest in prayer, that we may adhere the closer to God, and that we may acknowledge his fatherly care and goodness, who will not suffer us to be tempted above measure, comforting our selves in this, that his grace is sufficient for us. 5. We must remember that God hath given his Angels charge over us, to hold us up in their hands, lest we dash our foot against a stone. Christ was no sooner tempted by Satan, but the Angels came and ministred to him. When *Jacob* was persecuted by his brother *Esau*,
God

God sent a multitude of Angels to guard him. The Prophet *Elisha* was encompassed with fiery Chariots, or Angels in that shape, from the *Syrian* Souldiers. Let us not then fear, so long as we know that the Angels of God are round about those that fear him, and delivereth them; and that the same Angels will be ready at our death to convey our souls as they did *Lazarus*, into *Abraham*'s bosom. 6. Let us support our selves against Satan by the assurance of Christ's death, and the remission of our sins; *for blessed is the man whose sins are forgiven him;* therefore let us not be afraid, for *there is no condemnation to them that are in Christ Jesus. It is God that justifieth, who can condemn?* If Satan objects against us, that sin hath abounded, let us answer him in the Apostles words, *grace hath much more abounded.* 7. Let us as our Saviour counselleth us, *watch and pray continually;* our spiritual enemies are many, vigilant, malicious and powerful; nothing will give them advantage over us, but security and neglect of prayer; vigilancy and prayer are Armour of proof against all temptations; with these S. *Paul* armed himself when he was buffeted by the Angel of Satan; therefore saith S. *Hierom. When thou walkest abroad, let prayers arm thee; when thou returnest home, let prayers meet thee: Egredientes domo armet oratio, regredientibus de platea occurrat oratio.* Lastly, let us take heed we do not countenance or approve, or have any commerce with *Necromancers*, or such as take upon them to raise Spirits; for God oftentimes punisheth such vain curiosity; let us beware of too much retiredness; for Satan is most ready to tempt us when we are alone; so he tempted *Eve* when she was alone in the Garden, and assaulted Christ when he was alone in the Desart. Let us take heed also of too much sadness and melancholy; for though this be a natural infirmity, yet Satan by it takes occasion to work mischief; as we see in *Saul*, who is said to have an evil spirit, when he was in his melancholy fit; and we know that in the Gospel mad men, Phreneticks, and Lunaticks are called Demoniacks, because the Devil took occasion by their madness to advance his kingdom of darkness. And let us chiefly endeavour to have a good conscience which is a continual feast, to live an holy life, and to be just in all our ways, and so we shall not need to fear Satan's Stratagems or illusions; *for the righteous man is bold as a Lyon.*

Melancholy its danger.

Q. *Of what Religion were the* Chinois?

A. They were always, and still are Idolaters; except a few gained to Christianity by the Jesuits, and a few Tartars that are Mahumetans. That vast Dominion is full of Temples and Monasteries, replenished with multitudes of Idols, which their cunning Priests feed with the smoak of meats, but they eat the meat themselves. The Priests here have so much power over their gods, that they may beat and whip them when they do not answer their expectation. They have one Idol with three heads, which they much reverence. These represent their three great Philosphers, *Confusius, Xequiam,* and *Tanzu.* Their chief gods are the Sun, Moon, and Stars. They worship also the Devil, not out of love, but fear, that

Chinois their Religion.

that he may do them no hurt; therefore they place his picture in the Fore-castle of their ships. They are Pythagoreans in the opinion of Transanimation; therefore some of them will not kill any living thing. For this cause in *Quinsay* in a walled Park belonging to a Monastery, the Monks feed 4000. living creatures of divers kinds, out of their charity to the souls of Noble men, which were entred into the bodies of these creatures. Their Monks are shaven, are bound to wear beads, to be present at burials, to maintain Celibate whilst they are Monks, to pray two hours together before day. Of these religious Orders there be four sorts, distinguished by their colours, black, white, yellow, and russet. These have their Priors, Provincials, and General; he is carried on mens shoulders in an Ivory Chair, and is cloathed in silk. Their maintenance is not only the Kings allowance, but also the benevolence of devout people, which they procure by begging and praying for them. They have their Nuns also, and Hermits, and consecrated Hills, to which the people make divers Pilgrimages. There are many Colleges for learning, which is of high esteem, among them. Their Secular Priests wear long hair and black cloth, their Regulates are shaven, but neither must marry. They are bound to observe all Festival days, such as the New and full Moons, the Kings birth-day, but chiefly New-years-day, which is the first day of the New Moon in *February*. The people here are very Superstitious in observing their birth-days, and in performing the Funeral Obsequies of their Parents, whom they adore, and bury in the fields, with all solemnity and excessive charges. No man is tied to any particular worship among them, but he may be of what Sect he will. They have abundance of Hospitals for the poor, and no beggars to be seen among them. But for any knowledge of heavenly joys, or hell torments, they have very little or none at all. They are very much afraid when there is any Eclipse of the Sun or Moon, which they hold to be man and wife; for then they think that these two gods are angry with them. Of their many superstitious Ceremonies, and vain opinions in Divinity, see the Discourse of *China*, *Boterus*, *Ortelius*, *Maffeus*, *Linschoten*, and the Jesuits Epistles.

Q. *What was the Religion of the ancient* Indians?

Indians, their ancient Religion.

A. They worshipped their own gods, till *Bacchus* and *Alexander* subdued them, and then the Grecian deities were honoured among them; chiefly *Jupiter*, *Juno*, *Neptune*, and *Berecynthia*: *Hercules* also they honoured in the form and bigness of a Gyant. The River *Ganges* and their tallest trees were honoured as gods among them; therefore it was death to cut down any of them. Dancing to their Idols was held a part of Divine worship; but the *Brackmans* among them worshipped no Images, nor any living creature, were very temperate in their diet, and gave themselves to contemplation of divine things. They abstain from wine and strong drink and women, and lie on skins. Their *Gymnosophists* were Philosophers, who accustomed their bodies to endure all hardness, and their

eyes

Sect. 2. *A View of the Religions of* ASIA. 59

eyes to gaze on the Sun from morning to evening. Of the *Indian* Religion, see *Alexander ab Alexandro, Pliny, Boemus*, &c.

Q. *What is the Religion of* Siam?

A. This Kingdom of the East-Indies (except where the Moors inhabit, and some Christians) is also idolatrous. But especially they worship the four Elements, and accordingly there be four different Sects. Each one desireth to be buried in that Element which he worshippeth: hence some are buried, some burned, some hanged in the air, and some drowned in the water. They hold that God made all things; that the good are rewarded, and the wicked punished; that each man hath two spirits waiting on him, a good and a bad; that the world shall stand 8000. years, and then shall be burned into ashes, whence shall come forth two eggs, and out of them one man and one woman, who shall again replenish the earth. Their religious Orders are so strict, that it's death among them to speak to a woman. They feed on Rice only and herbs, which they beg from door to door. They must not buy nor sell, nor take rents. They are tied to rise at midnight to pray to their Idols. They go still barefooted, and in poor clothes. Every King of this Country at his Coronation is bound to erect a Temple, with high Steeples, and multitudes of Idols. Their Priests go in yellow, being a sacred a colour, resembling the Suns light. They may not nourish any female thing, not so much as a Hen. He that drinks Wine is stoned to death. See the discourse of *China, Boterus, Maginus*, and others.

Q. *What is the Religion of* Pegu?

A. The religious Ceremonies of this Kingdom consisted in mul- *Pegu, its* titudes of Temples, Images, and begging Preachers, who are *Religion.* still preaching and begging. Their Alms are brought to them in the Pulpits whilst they are preaching. The people when they enter into their Churches, at the door wash their feet, and by lifting up their hands to their heads, salute the Preacher first, and then the Sun. When any enters into that Order of *Talipon*, or Preacher, he is first carried in solemnity about the streets on horse-back, with Pipes and Drums, then upon mens shoulders to his house, which is without the Town. They keep holy day every New Moon. They believe multitudes of Gods, and Worlds succeeding each other; that this World hath been governed by four Gods already, who are gone, the fifth is not yet come, after whose death the World shall be burned. After this life they hold some shall live in carnal pleasure, some in torment, and others shall be annihilated. They hold Transanimation, and are bound to fast thirty days every year. They know no women; for whom they allow Nunneries. The people drink the water wherein their Preachers wash themselves, counting it holy. They feed the Devil each morning with baskets of Rice, that he may not hurt them that day. When they are sick, they build him Altars, and pacifie him with flowers, meat and musick. Their Idols are honoured with divers festivals, in which wax lights are burned all night,

and

and the gates stand open, that all those may see and have access to the Idol, who bring presents with them.

Q. *Of what Religion are the people of* Bengala?

Bengala, its Religion.
A. They are not content to worship the River *Ganges*, but to its image also they give divine honours. The River is visited by many Pilgrims, who think themselves happy if they can wash themselves in it. If any can drink of the water thereof at the point of death, he thinks presently by the virtue thereof to obtain Heaven. There is also a Well which they adore; in it they wash away all their sins, and are all clean, both without and within, if they wash in it, and drink thereof. They carry away the Sand of this Well as a sacred Relick, and in recompence leave flowers behind them in the Well. For fear left their Idols should faint with too much heat, there are some who with fans blow the wind for refrigeration. All are bound to enter barefooted into the Idol-Temples. The more horrid and ugly the Idol looks, the more he is worshipped. Sick people are brought and laid before the Idols, which are honoured with lights continually burning before them. Their marriages are made in some water, wherein the Priest and the married couple hold a Cow with her Calf by the tail, and pour water upon it; then the Priest tieth the married persons clothes together; then going round about the Cow and Calf, the Ceremony is ended. The Priest hath for his fee the Cow and Calf, the poor some Alms, and the Idols some Money. About *Jemena* they use to pray naked in the water, and to do penance, by lying flat on the ground, kissing the earth, holding up their hands to the Sun; and turning themselves about forty times. Who desire more of this stuff, let them read *Linschoten, R. Fitzh. Purchas,* &c.

Q. *Of what Religion is the Kingdom of* Magor?

Magor, its Religion.
A. They are for the most part *Pythagoreans,* holding Transanimation: they acknowledge one God, but have many fabulous conceits of him; as that he hath appeared in the world in divers monstrous shapes, to wit, of a Fish, a Snail, a Hog, a Monster resembling Woman in the lower part, and a Lyon in the upper. They worship divers Idols, one chiefly representing a Woman with two heads and many hands; to this Image near this City *Tabor* repair many Pilgrims. The King worshippeth every morning the Image of the Sun, and of Christ also the Son of Righteousness, which he sets on the Crown of his head. See *Oranus* in his Narration of *Magor.*

Q. *What is the Religion of* Cambaia?

Cambaia, its Religions.
A. The People here are so superstitiously Pythagoreans, that there are among them some Religious Orders who are afraid to kill a Gnat or Worm. They are much addicted to fasting and alms giving. Their Religious Persons called *Verteus,* leave no hair on their heads and faces, but a little on their crown. They will not drink their water cold, fearing lest thereby they should slay the soul of the water, which is quickened by boyling. The people here redeem Birds and Beasts appointed to be slain; and if any Bird

Bird be sick or hurt, they carry it to the Hospital. They redeem also Malefactors condemned to die, and sell them for Slaves. For fear left they should tread upon Ants, they will rather go out of the Way than go near their hills. They drink no Wine, nor will eat Eggs, left there should be blood in them. Neither will they eat of Radishes, Onions, or any herb that hath red colour in it. See *Maffeus, Linschoten,* and *Purchas*.

Q. *What is the Religion professed in* Goa?

A. Here are Christians, Jews, Mahumetans, and Pagans who pray to the Sun and Moon, and worship divers Idols of horrible Aspects; but their custom is to pray to the first thing they meet with in the morning, though a Goose or an Ass, and all the day after they pray to it; but a Crow they cannot abide, the sight of that will make them keep in all day. They salute the first appearance of the New Moon with prayers on their knees. Near to every Idol is a Cistern of water, in which they that pass by wash their feet, worship and Offer Rice, Eggs, or such like. When they sow, mow, marry, go to sea, and when the women lie in, they feast their Idols with musick, and other solemnities, fourteen days together, and so do the sea-men after their return home. See *Linschoten*. *Goa, the Religion thereof.*

Q. *Of what Religion are the people of* Malabar?

A. *Pythagoreans* they are, holding not only the Immortality of souls, both of beasts and men, and transanimation, but also a divinity in Elephants, Kine, and other beasts; therefore at *Calecut*, the chief City of this Dominion, and head of a small Kingdom of the same name, there is a stately Temple of 700 pillars dedicated to the Ape. Their *Bramanes*, or Priests (the successours of the old *Brachmanes*) are in such esteem here, that the King will not converse with his new married wife, till one of the chief *Brachmanes* hath had the first nights lodging with her. They hold that God made the world, but because the trouble of governing thereof is so great, therefore hath given the charge thereof to Satan, whom they worship flowers on their Altars, and sacrifices of Cocks. The *Bramanes* wash his Image, sitting on a fiery Throne with three Crowns and four horns in sweet water every morning. The King of *Calecut* eats no meat till it be first offered by his Priest to this Idol. Debtors that will not pay, are arrested by a rod sent from the chief of the *Bramanes*, with which a circle is made about the Debtor, in the Kings name and the said Priest, out of which he dare not go, till the debt be satisfied; otherwise he is put to death. Every twelfth year in the City of *Quilacare* is a Jubilee kept to the honour of their Idol; in which the King of that place, upon a Scaffold covered with silk, before the people, washeth himself, then prayeth to the Idol, and having cut off his nose, ears, lips, and other parts, at last cuts his own throat as a sacrifice to his Idol. His successor, by their discipline, is bound to be present, and to act the same Tragedy on himself at the next Jubilee. See *Castaneda, Barbosa, Boterus, Linschoten,* and *Purchas*. *Malabar, its Religion.*

Q. *How*

Q. *How came the Idolatrous Pagans to believe the immortality of souls?*

Pagans, (though Idolatrous) believe the immortality of the soul.

A. By the meer force of natural reason; for they observed that the soul is incorporeal, not only free from all dependence on the body, in respect of its essence, but also in regard of its inorganical operations, to wit, of Understanding and Will: they found that the more the body decayed and grew weak, the more vigorous, active, and strong was the soul; that it lost nothing of its operations by the loss or decay of the outward senses; that it could comprehend all the world within it self; that it could move it self in an instant, from one end of the world to the other; that it can make things past many years ago, as if they were present; that it can conceive spiritual Essences, and Universalities: all which do prove how far the soul exceedeth the body, and bodily senses, which can reach no farther than to sensible qualities, singularities or individuals, to things, present only, to bodies only. Besides, they observed that the soul could not die, or perish, or corrupt and putrifie as bodies do, because it is immaterial simple, without composition of different substances, and free from contrary and destructive qualities, which are the causes of death, corruption, and putrefaction in bodies. Again, every body is quantitative, sensible, and may be measured, and filled; but the soul hath no quantity, nor is sensible but by its effects, nor can it be measured, nor can the whole world fill it, nor doth it increase or decrease as bodies do; nor can it receive hurt or detriment from any outward thing; and whereas bodily senses are weakned by any vehement object, as the eye by too much light, the ear by a violent sound, &c. the soul is perfected by its object, and the more sublime or eminent the object is, the more is the soul corroborated in its understanding; neither is the soul subject to time and motion as bodies are; for it makes all time present, and is not capable of generation, corruption, alteration, &c. moreover, there is in the soul even of *Epicurus* himself a desire of immortality, which desire cannot be in vain, nor frustrated, because natural, and consequently necessary; and we know that God hath made nothing in vain, but this desire must be in vain if frustrated. And we find that many who have denied the souls immortality in their health and prosperity, have been forced to confess it in their sickness and troubles, and on their death-bed. If we look upon the writings of the learned Gentiles, we shall find them professing this truth; this we may see in the fragments of *Zoroastres*, in *Trismegistus*, in *Phocyllides*, who thus sings.

ψυχὴ δ' ἀθάνατος κỳ ἀγήρως ζῇ διὰ παντός.

That is

The soul is immortal, and void of old age, and liveth always.

And again,

ψυχαὶ ᵹ μίμνουσιν ἀκήραιοι ἐν φθιμένοισιν.

That is,

The souls remain void of fate in death.

Sect. 2. *A View of the Religions of* ASIA.

The *Pythagoreans* believed the same, as we see by their opinion of Transanimation. *Socrates* and *Plato* speak most divinely of the Souls Essence and Immortality; so doth *Aristotle* in his Books *de Anima*; so do the Poets; so doth *Cicero* in *Som. Scip. Erigamus in cælum oculos, tanquam in Patriam, in quam nobis aliquando redeundum est.* Let us (saith he) *lift up our eyes towards Heaven, as our Country to which at last we shall return.* So he saith, *The body is frail, but the spirit is immortal.* So *Seneca, Animus unde demissus est, ibi illum æterna requies manet. Eternal rest remains for the Soul there from whence it came. Animus sacer & æternus, & cui non possit injici manus.* Many such passages may be seen in his Writings: and that generally the Gentiles believed this truth, is plain by their opinion they had of torments in Hell, and of Joys in their *Elysian* Fields.

Q. *Of what Religion are the People of* Narsinga *and* Bisnagar?

A. The rich Indian Kingdom, having these two names from the two chief Cities thereof, is infested with horrible Idolatry. Here is an Idol, to which Pilgrims resort, either with their hands bound, or ropes about their necks, or knives sticking in their arms and legs, which limbs, if they fester, they are accounted holy. Gold, Silver, and Jewels, are given by these Pilgrims to maintain this Idol and his Temple. All these gifts are cast into a Lake, and kept there for the uses aforesaid. This Idol is carried yearly in Procession, with Virgins and Musick going before. Under the Idols Chariot Pilgrims strive to be crushed to death, whose bodies are burned, and the ashes kept as holy Relicks. Some do cut their flesh in pieces, and stab themselves with Knives, to the honour of this Idol, and cast into its face the pieces of their cut flesh. Women also do prostitute themselves to procure Money for the Idols maintenance. He thinks himself blessed that can but touch the Idols Chariot; whereas in other parts of the Indies the Wives burn themselves alive with their Husbands Bodies, or else they are shaven, and live ever after in perpetual disgrace. At the Town *Casta*, the Women are content to be buried alive with their dead Husbands. In some places, when Men make Vows to their Idols, they pay them, by suffering the Priests with sharp hooks fastned to the Cross-yard of a Mast, to lift them up by both shoulders, till the Blood run down on the Mast; then he is let down, and lifted up again by the middle to give thanks to his Idol for accepting his Sacrifice. The Chief Priest of those parts dispenseth with Marriages at his pleasure; and when he gives Licence to the Woman to Marry again, he seals it with a hot Iron on her shoulder. They have divers Festivals, some to their Kine, some to the Sun, and to other of their gods. When the Sun and Moon are Eclipsed, they say it is because they are bit by that Celestial Sign called the Dragon. See *Vertomannus Fernandes*, and the Writers above named.

Q. *What Religion is professed in* Japon?

A. The same Gentilism that is professed in the rest of the Indies, Japon, its with Religion.

with some variation of Ceremonies; but Christianity hath got some footing there, by the industry and painful labours of the Jesuits. The Heathen *Japonians* worship an Image with three Faces, by which they mean the Sun, Moon, and the Elementary World. They have multitudes of Cloysters and Colleges. They have also divers Festivals to their Idols, which they carry in Procession, some on Horse-back, others in Chariots. They believe there are divers Paradises, to which every peculiar god carrieth his own Worshippers; with which imaginary happiness the silly People are so in love, that many use to drown themselves, others to cut their own throats, or to break their necks, by casting themselves down from high Towers; to this they are encouraged by their cunning and covetous Priests, who, out of this, suck no small advantage. Some in narrow holes, receive breath only by a Cane, and so continue fasting and praying till they die. The Priests strangely extort Confession from the People, by putting some of them in scales hanging from high Rocks; from whence they being cast down by their *Gogins*, which they say are Men disguised like Devils, are broken all to pieces. They have a Feast in which they burn multitudes of Lamps at their doors, and walk all night up and down the Streets to meet the Souls of their Friends lately departed, before whom they set meat and drink, and invite them to their houses, that in their three years Journey to Paradise they may not faint for want of provision, seeing that in less time than three years they cannot pass thither. Of these passages see *Maffeus*, *Acosta*, and the Jesuits Epistles.

Philippinæ, *their Religions*.

Q. *What Religion is professed in the* Philippine *Islands?*

A. There are Christians, Mahumetans, and Pagans in those Islands, who worship the Sun, Moon, and Stars, which they hold to be the Children of the Sun and Moon. Their Priests are for the most part Women, who are Sorcerers and Prophetesses. They worship also the Devil in ugly shapes, and so they do that thing which they meet with first in the morning, except it be a Lizard, or other kind of Worm; for the sight of these is held so unlucky, that it makes them leave off all business, and return home. They use to deck their Idols with Ostrich feathers. At the Sacrificing of a Hog they found Cymbals, two old Women with Pipes of Reed reverence the Sun, and in their Sacred Garments, with Hair-laces, and Horns on the head of the elder, dance about the Hog, muttering certain words to the Sun. Then a Cup of Wine is poured on the Hogs head, by the elder of these two Hags, who, at last, kills the Beast, and takes into her mouth a burning Torch, which she bites. The other Witch, with the Swines Blood, marks all that are present in the Fore-head, and then they fall to dressing of the Hog, which the Women only eat up. See *Ant. Pigafetta*, and *Oliver Noorts* Navigation.

Sumatra, and Zeilan *their Religions*.

Q. *What Religion doth* Sumatra *and* Zeilan *profess?*

A. Along the Sea-coasts there are Moors and Christians, but Pagans in the Inland Countries; here the Sea is covered with multitudes

titudes of Islands, in some of which the Priests are tied to nourish their hair, and to have smooth Faces like Women. They gild their Teeth, and are burned in Pitch, if they have Carnal Commerce with a Woman. In *Zeilan*, or *Ceylon*, the blinded People undertake Pilgrimages of a Thousand Leagues, Eighteen miles whereof they wade up to the middle in dirty stinking water, full of Blood-leeches, and Seven Leagues they clamber up a steep Mountain, by the help of Nails and Thorns tied together, there being no other passage. And all this toil is to visit a Stone on the top of this Hill, having in it the Print of a Man's Foot, who, they say, came thither first to Instruct them in Religion. Near the Stone is a springing water, in which they wash, then pray, and with sharp-pointed Instruments cut their flesh, and draw blood, thinking thereby that God is pleased, and that all their sins are pardoned. In this Water the Poor are permitted sometimes by the King to gather Precious Stones, whereof there is store, to Pray for his Soul. There are in this Island many Temples, Priests and Idols, Monasteries also of yellow Monks shaven, and still praying on Beads, who have their Processions in great solemnity, with Dancing and Musick, the Abbot riding upon an Elephant in rich attire, carrying a Golden Rod in his hand, lifted over his head; they pray here to the Devil when they are sick; and to the Image of the Elephants Head for wisdom. They have a huge Statue bearing a Sword in it's hand; they think the World shall not end so long as this Image is in safety. See *Maffeus, Vertimannus, Odoricus, Spilbergius*, &c.

Q. *Of what Religion were the ancient* Egyptians?

A. *Egypt* may be called the Mother of all Superstition and Idolatry; for they entertained an opinion, that all things at first had beginning there of slime or mud, by the heat or influence of the Sun, Moon, and Stars, mixing the Elements in the composition of Bodies, ascribed Divinity to these Celestial Luminaries and Elements, and so erected Temples, Images, Holy-days, and other Divine Rights to them, worshipping the Sun and Moon under the Names of *Osiris* and *Isis*: The *Grecians* under the Names of *Apollo* and *Diana*; the four Elements by the Names of *Vulcan, Juno, Neptune*, and *Ceres*; the five lesser Planets by the Names of *Saturn, Jupiter, Mars, Venus*, and *Mercury*. At length they multiplied their gods so fast, that every Beast, Spring, River, Tree, Trade or Profession in the World, Disease in the Body, Faculty and Passion in the Mind, had its peculiar Deity. And so mad they were upon Idolatry, that of a Man's Yard they made a god, under the Name of *Phallus* and *Priapus*, in memory of *Osiris* his Privities, which, after much toyl were found by *Isis* in *Nilus*, being drowned there by *Typhon* his Brother, who had cut his Body into many pieces, and Buried them in many places. They worshipped Beasts, Birds, Vermin, Leeks and Onions. Their Priests were shaved, and cloathed in pure Linen, abstained from Fish, Wine and Onions. Their Kings, after Election, were chosen into the Society of Priests. They held two beginnings: they Consecrated red Bulls, flung the

Ægyptians, *their Ancient Religion.*

heads

heads of their Sacrifices into *Nilus*, and abstained from Salt. See *Arnobius, Eusebius, Plutarch, Jamblichus*, and many others.

Q. *What devotion did the* Egyptians *use to their deified Beasts?*

Their Idolatrous Worship.
A. They were fed by their Priests in their Temples with choice food: when any dieth, it is wrapped in clean Linen and Embalmed, and buried in a consecrated place, with much Lamentation. All shave themselves in a House where a Dog dieth. Their god *Apis* being dead and lamented, another was found by the Priests, and brought to *Memphis*, where he was placed in *Vulcan*'s Temple, and seven days kept holy for him. By their Law he must live but a prefixed time; then he is drowned in a sacred Spring, and buried with much lamentation. All Beasts are not worshipped in all parts of *Egypt*, but in some places the Crocodile, in other places the Goat, in some Satyrs, in others *Cynocephalus*, or *Anubis*, with his Dogs-head. The Serpent was a great god amongst them, so was the Bull, the Dog, the Cat, the Hawk, and *Ibis*, and two Fishes peculiar to *Nilus*, to wit, *Opyrinchus*, and *Lepidotus*. They worshipped the *Hippopotamus*, Frogs, Beetles, and other Vermine. Their Priests were bound to offer a Cock to the Sun, a Dove to *Venus*, a Peacock to *Juno*, &c. And bloody *Busiris* sacrificed Men to *Nilus*. *Quis illaudati nescit Busiridis aras?* The *Egyptians* hate Swine so much, that if by chance one should touch them, he instantly washeth his Clothes: and Sow-herds are forbid their Temples. They Circumcise Male and Female, and offer Wine to the Full Moon. The Priests wash themselves thrice in the day-time, and twice in the night. They must not eat milk, eggs, or oyl, except with Sallads. Their Priests were Judges, their Gymnosophists were Philosophers, who had their College in a Grove near the Banks of *Nilus*. The *Egyptians* observed divers Feasts to *Isis, Diana, Latona, Mars, Minerva, Mercury, Bacchus, Osiris* and his Nurse. In these Feasts was much disorder and vanity, some beating of themselves, some cutting their Foreheads with Knives, some dancing, some singing, some drinking, some quarrelling. In the Feast of *Bacchus* they were all drunk; in that of *Mars* all mad, knocking down one another with clubs; in the Feast of *Isis* they shewed their folly in tumbling an Ass down from a Precipice. In that of *Minerva*, in burning lights with oyl and salt. But of these and other ridiculous, or rather impious Rites, see *Hospinian, Cælius Rhodiginus, Plutarch, Herodotus, Diodorus Siculus, Eusebius, Strabo, Lucian*, and others.

Q. *How long continu'd this Heathenish Idolatry in* Egypt?

Egyptian Idolatry, continuance thereof.
A. Till the Son of Righteousness shined upon it, and by the bright beams of his Gospel dispelled and scattered all the dark mists of Idolatry, so that *Alexandria*, the chief Nursery thereof, by the Preaching of St. *Mark*, became a Patriarchal Seat, whose Successors have continu'd till this day; but their Residence now is at *Cairi*, where the Metropolitan of *Æthiopia*, or Arch-bishop of the *Abyssins*, receiveth his confirmation from the Patriarch of *Alexandria*. 'Tis true, that *Cambyses*, Son to *Cyrus* King of *Persia*, destroyed

Sect. 2. *A View of the Religions of* ASIA.

ſtroyed many of the *Egyptian* Idols, and *Ochus* his ſucceſſor killed their *Apis:* but theſe were ſhortly after reſtored by *Alexander* the Great, whoſe Succeſſors, the *Ptolemies,* upheld the ſame Idolatry, and ſo did the *Romans,* till by the Preaching of the Goſpel, Darkneſs was forced to give place to Light.

Q. *What Religion is there now profeſſed in* Egypt?

A. Here at this day Chriſtians have their Churches, Jews their Synagogues, and Mahumetans their Moſques: of theſe laſt there be four ſorts, differing in their Laws, Liturgies and Ceremonies. There is a Sect in *Cairo* which liveth altogether on Horſe-fleſh; and another who go naked, giving themſelves to fleſhly luſts openly. The Chriſtians there are *Eutychians,* and are Circumciſed; but it is thought that they have forſaken Circumciſion, by perſwaſion of the Pope's Legates at a Synod held at *Cairo, Anno* 1583. Theſe are called *Cophti,* not from their Profeſſion, but from their Nation: for in the Thalmud *Egypt* is called *Gophti,* and *Ægyptians* in old time *Ægophtia.* They are not rigid *Eutychians,* which were condemned in the Council of *Chalcedon,* for affirming one Nature and one Will in Chriſt; but they are modern *Eutychians,* called *Jacobites,* from *Jacobus* the *Syrian,* who held that Chriſt was true God, and true Man: yet he and his Scholars will not in direct terms affirm there are two natures, leſt they ſhould fall into the error of *Neſtorius,* of the two perſons. Theſe Faſt every Wedneſday and Friday, and have four Lents in the year. They make Infants Deacons, and Baptize them not afore the Fortieth day, and then give them the Euchariſt. They leave out the words in the *Nicene* Creed *from the Son.* They condemn the Council of *Chalcedon,* and admit no General Council ſince that of *Epheſus:* they read publickly the Goſpel of *Nicodemus:* they receive the Euchariſt in both kinds, and in Leavened Bread. To the Sick they neither adminiſter the Euchariſt, nor Extream Unction. They deny Purgatory and Prayer for the Dead. They Marry in the ſecond degree of Conſanguinity: and in their Church-Government are ſubject to the Patriarch of *Alexandria.* There are not above three Chriſtian Churches at *Alexandria,* and ſo many at *Cairo;* about Fifty thouſand Chriſtians in all. Of theſe paſſages ſee *Boterus* in his Relations; *Thevet* in his Coſmography, *Chytræus* of the State of the Church, *Baronius* in his Annals, &c. and *Brerewood's* Collections out of them.

Egypt, its Modern Religions.

F 2   The

THE
Religions of AFRICA and AMERICA.

The Contents of the Third Section.

Of the old African *Religion.* 2. *The Religion and Church-Discipline of* Fez. 3. *Of* Morocco. 4. *Of* Guinea. 5. *Of the Ancient* African Æthiopians. 6. *Of the Modern* Abyssins. 7. *Of the lower* Æthiopians. 8. *Of* Angola *and* Congo. 9. *Of the Northern Neighbours of* Congo. 10. *Of the* African *Islands.* 11. *The Religion of* America. 12. *Of* Virginia. 13. *Of* Florida. 14. *Of the Religions by West*-Virginia *and* Florida. 15. *Of* New Spain *and* Mexico. 16. *Idolaters, their cruelty and cost in their barbarous Exercises.* 17. *Of the* Americans, *their Superstitious fear, and Tyranny thereof.* 18. *Of* Jucatan, *and the parts adjoyning.* 19. *Of the Southern* Americans. 20. *Of* Paria *and* Guiana. 21. *Of* Brasil. 22. *Of* Peru. 23. *Of* Hispaniola.

SECT. III.

Africans, their Religion.

Quest. **W**Hat *was the Religion of the old* Africans ?
A. Their chief gods were the Sun and Fire, to which they erected Temples, and kept the Fire continually burning on Altars to that purpose. The Planets were the *Numidian* and *Libyan* gods. From Gentilism they were converted to Judaism, then to Christianity, and at last to Mahumetanism. We read that *Matthias* the Apostle Preached in *Æthiopia*, and *Simon* another Apostle in *Mauritania*: about the time of *Constantine* Christianity was generally received in the hither and lesser *Africa*; and was by the *Goths* infected with *Arianism*, which made way for *Mahumetanism*. The *Pœni*, or *Phœnicians* and *Carthaginians*, whilst Gentiles, offered Men sacrifices to *Saturn*; and in their supplications they put Infants in the Arms of *Saturn's* Brazen Image made hot with Fire, and so were burned to death. At *Tunis*, near the Lake *Tritonia, Minerva* taught the use of Oyl, and invented the Art of Spinning; therefore she was worshipped as a goddess. *Venus* was a great deity in *Phœnicia*, *Juno* in *Carthage*. At this day the Mahumetans Religion consisteth most in washing and frequenting of the Mosques. See *Alexander ab Alexandro, Jo. Leo, Suidas,* and others.

Fez, the Religion and Church discipline thereof.

Q. *What is the Religion and Church-discipline of* Fez?
A. They are at this day Mahumetans in their profession, and in
their

their Devotion no ways sparing; for there are in the City of Temples and Chappels about 700, whereof some are garnished with many Pillars and Fountains of Marble. Each Temple hath one Priest to say Service, and look to his Churches Revenue, which he bestoweth upon the Church-Officers; namely, the Porters, Cryers, and the Lamp-lighters; these are Night-Officers, but for the Day Cryers, who from their Steeples call the People to Prayers, these have no Pay, but only are freed from Tenths, and all other Payments. In the great Church, which is about a Mile and a half in compass, and hath 31 great Gates, (the Roof whereof is upheld with Twenty Arches in breadth, and 38 in length) are lighted every Night 900 Lamps; some of the greatest are of Brass, with Sockets for 1500 Lamps. About the Walls are divers Pulpits for their Readers, who begin their Lectures shortly after break of day in the Summer: they Read after Sun-set: *Mahumet*'s Law, and Moral Philosophy are Read: then to the Winter-Lectures are allowed large Revenues, Books and Candles. The Priest of this Temple taketh charge of the Orphan's Money, and of the Poor, to whom he dealeth Corn and Money every Holy-day. This Temple hath a Treasurer, and under him Eight Notaries, and Six Clerks, Twenty Bailiffs for the Husbandry, Twenty Lime-kills, and Twenty Brick-kills, for repairing of the Temple, the Revenues of which are 200 Ducats a day. Other Temples of the City are hence furnished when they want. Here are Two stately Colleges for Professors of divers Sciences, and divers Hospitals for Strangers, and the Sick, with all Accommodations. Their Marriages are performed in the Church. They have great Feasting at the Circumcision of the Males. They observe divers Festivals, at some of which the Youth do with Cudgels and other Weapons knock down one another, so that many Murthers are committed. They make Bone-fires on the Feast of St. *John Baptist*, and on *Christmas*-Eve eat Sallads of green Herbs. On *Mahumet*'s birth-day, the Poets make Sonnets in his Praise, which they rehearse publickly, and are rewarded accordingly. In *Fez* are 200 Grammar-Schools; the Youth are bound in Seven years to learn the Alcoran by heart. On *Mahumet*'s birth-day every Boy carrieth a Wax-torch to School, which they light before day, and let them burn till Sun-rising, all this while Singing *Mahumet*'s Praise. Candles are presented to the King that day, of incredible height and bigness, who that night heareth all the Law Read. By *Mahumet*'s Law Sooth-sayers are imprisoned, and yet here are many of that Profession. There are here divers Sects of Mahumetans, some like our Anabaptists, condemning all Learning, and trusting to Enthusiasms; others who think by their Fasting and Good Works, that they are so holy and perfect, that they cannot sin. There be some who hold all Religions to be true, because every one takes that to be God which he worships, and they teach that the Heaven, with the Planets, Stars and Elements, are one God. They have also their Hermits. By their Discipline, Women may not enter their Mosques, because of their

their often Pollutions, and for that *Eve* firſt ſinned. The day after the Child is born, the Prieſt is ſent for to Pray. The Child is waſhed by the Women, who Name it, and then it is Circumciſed; but ſometimes the Circumciſion is put off for divers years. They are very ſtrict in their Faſtings, not taſting any thing, though they ſhould faint, till the Stars appear: the Mufti or High-Prieſt, ſits with the King every day in Judgment, except the Friday, then the King ſits alone. See *Leo, Purchas*, &c.

Q. *What are their times of Prayer?*

Their times of Prayer. A. Two hours afore day, then they Pray for the day. 2. Two hours after day, then they give thanks for the day. 3. At noon, then they give thanks for that half the day is paſt. 4. At Four in the afternoon, then they Pray that the Sun may well ſet on them. 5. At twi-light they give thanks after their daily labours. 6. They Pray two hours after twi-light, and then they deſire a good Night; thus they Pray ſix times in 24 hours; and ſo devout they are, that when they hear the *Sexton* from their Steeples cry to Prayer before day, then may no Man touch his Wife, but prepare to Prayer, by waſhing, or other devotion, either at Church, or in his own houſe: after this his Prayer, the Talby or Prieſt ſits down and reſolves for half an hour all doubts that are moved in matters of their Law. He is counted profane, and diſabled from being Witneſs, who prayeth not ſix times a day. See *Purchas* in his Pilgrimage.

Q. *What is the Religion of* Morocco?

Morocco, its Religion. A. The ſame is there profeſſed that is in *Fez*, but they are not altogether ſo devout in *Morocco*, as in *Fez*; for they have not that number of Magnificent Temples, Colleges, Hoſpitals, and Schools; yet ſome they have, eſpecially one Temple, very large and ſtately, in *Morocco*, with a Magnificent Steeple of incredible height: they have alſo their Hermits, and other Religious Men; in all theſe they come ſhort of *Fez*, by reaſon they are often moleſted by the incurſions of the *Arabians*. They have alſo among them, as in *Fez*, multitudes of Jews, who flocked over thither when they were driven out of *Spain* by *Ferdinand*, and out of *Portugal* by King *Emanuel*. There be alſo among them many Chriſtians, but in miſerable captivity and ſlavery; whereas the *Turks* elſewhere, in Spiritual affairs, ſubject themſelves to the Cailiph of *Cairo*; theſe *African* Kingdoms acknowledge only their ſubjection to the Cailiph of *Bagdat*, or *Babylon*. The *Turks* of *Morocco* and *Fez*, think they merit Heaven if they kill many Chriſtians; therefore they run with as great alacrity to War againſt Chriſtians, as to a Wedding, believing if they die in that War, they ſhall immediately poſſeſs Paradiſe, which is indeed the general belief of all *Turks*. See *Les Eſtats du Monde, Boterus, Leo*, &c.

Q. *What Religion is profeſſed in* Guinea?

Guinea, its Religion. A. Gentiliſm; for they adore Strawen things inſtead of God; of whom they ſpeak blaſphemouſly, calling him evil, black, and the Author of their miſeries: And that they are no ways beholding to him for what they enjoy, but to their own induſtry. They

put

put within their Rings, Wheat, Water and Oyl, for their god to feed upon. Such Rings are worn by many as preservatives against danger. Their Priests use to Preach to them on Festival days, and after Sermon to besprinkle the Infants with Water, in which a Newt doth swim. They consecrate to their Idol the first bit and draught of their meat and drink. But I believe, this black god they rail against, is the Devil, whom their cunning Priests represent to that ignorant People in some black and ugly shape; sometimes of a black Dog. If they paint themselves with Chalk, they think they do good service to their god. When he is angry with them, they use to bribe the Priest with gold; so Fishermen use to do, when they have no success at Sea. The Priest with his Wives walk in Procession, knocking his breast and clapping his hands, then hanging some bows from the trees on their necks, and playing on a Timbrel, the Priest flings Wheat into the Sea, to appease the angry god. They have certain trees in great veneration, consulting with them as with Oracles, using divers foolish ceremonies. They worship a certain Bird, which hath Feathers like Stars, and a voice like a Bull. The Tunie is a sacred Fish with them, and not to be touched. So are the Mountains, whose tops they daily feed, or the Priests rather, with meat and drink. When one dieth, the Priest makes gods of Straw to accompany the dead in the other World, Wine and good chear are sent with him, and Servants, with his Wives; If he be the King, these are slain to wait upon the King, and their heads advanced upon Poles round about the Grave. They hold it a sin to spit on the ground. The Tuesday is their Sabbath. They use Circumcision and some other Turkish ceremonies. See *G. Arthur Dantiscanu, Mercator, Bertius*, &c.

Q. *Of What Religion were the* African Æthiopians *anciently?*

A. Gentiles; for they worshipped some immortal gods, as the Sun, Moon, and the World; some mortal, as *Jupiter, Pan, Hercules*; But some of them who dwelt near and under the Line, did not worship, but curse the Sun still when he rose, because his excessive heat offended them. When their Queen went to *Solomon*, she being instructed by him in the knowledge of the true God, upon her return planted the Jewish Religion in her Country; but the Eunuch of Queen *Candace* being baptized by *Philip*, brought home with him the Christian Faith, which hitherto they have retained. See *Diodorus, Boemus, Strabo, Sardus, Damianus à Goez*, &c. *Æthiopians of Africa, their ancient Religion.*

Q. *What Religion do these* Æthiopians, *or* Abissyns *profess?*

A. Christianity; yet Gentilism is retained in some part of *Prestor-John*'s ample Dominions. The Christians Circumcise both Male and Female on the eighth day, in memory of Christ's Circumcision. The Males are Baptized Forty days after, and the Females Eighty. They abstain from certain Meats, and use some Mosaical Ceremonies. They are very rigid in their Fastings; they begin their Lent ten days before ours; some Friars eat no bread all the Lent, some not in a whole year; but are contented with Herbs, without Salt or Oyl: They keep a Fast of three days after *Their Religion at this day.*

ter *Candlemaſs*, in memory of *Nineveh*'s Repentance. Some Friars all that time eat nothing, and some Nurses give their children suck but once a day. He that Marrieth three Wives is Excommunicated. Queen *Candace* after her Conversion consecrated the two Magnificent Temples of the Sun, and Moon, to the Holy Ghoſt and the Cross. Afterward these two Temples were given to the Monkiſh Knights of St. *Anthonies* Order, with two large Monasteries. The *Abyſſins* in their Liturgy mention the three firſt General Councils, but not that of *Chalcedon*, because they are *Eutychians*, or *Jacobites*. Their Patriarch is only a Monk of St. *Anthonies* Order, and so is the Patriarch of *Alexandria*, by whom the *Æthiopian* is conſecrated, and is in ſubjection to the See of *Alexandria*. They obſerve here both Saturday and Sunday with equal devotion. In the Euchariſt the Prieſt adminiſters Leavened Bread, except on the Thurſday before Eaſter; for then it is unleavened, becauſe that day Chriſt inſtituted the Supper. And the Deacon gives the Wine in a Spoon. They receive all ſtanding, and in the Church only; all that day after they muſt not ſpit till Sun-ſet. They give the Euchariſt to Infants immediately after Baptiſm. They believe Traduction of Souls. They are careful to confeſs their ſins to the Prieſt, and ſtill after a Confeſſion receive the Euchariſt. The Patriarch only excommunicates, and none but Murtherers uſually. Inferiour Prieſts and Monks labour for their Maintenance, but the Biſhops, Deans, and Prebends, have large Revenues and Benefices. They permit their Clergy to Marry once, and have Pictures in their Churches, but not Images. Betwixt Eaſter and Whitſuntide, they eat fleſh on Fridays. Every *Epiphany* day they Baptize themſelves in Lakes or Rivers. So do the *Muſcovites* in memory of Chriſt's Baptiſm the ſame day. They uſe no Confirmation, nor Extreme Unction. See *Damianus à Goez, Alvarez* in his *Æthiopian* Hiſtory, and others.

The lower Æthiopians, their Religion.

Q. What is the Religion of the lower Æthiopians?

A. Theſe were not known to the Ancients, but they are found by Navigators to be, for the moſt part, Gentiles, though divers *Moors* live among them; Yet ſome of them worſhip but one God. They ſuperſtitiouſly obſerve divers days of the Moon. They feaſt the dead with bread and boyled fleſh. They puniſh Witchcraft, Theft, and Adultery with death. They may Marry as many Wives as they pleaſe, but the firſt is the Chief, and the reſt are her ſervants. They pray to the Dead in White Garments. In *Monomotapa* and ſome other places thereabouts, the Jeſuits have Converted divers to Chriſtianity; many whereof are fallen back again to Gentiliſm. See *Emanuel Acoſta* of the Eaſtern affairs, and *Boterus*, &c.

Angola, its Religion.

Q. What is the Religion of Angola and Congo?

A. In *Angola* they are all Heathens. In the midſt of their Towns they worſhip Wooden Idols reſembling Negroes, at whoſe feet are heaps of Elephants Teeth, on which are ſet up the Skulls of their Enemies killed in the Wars. They believe they are never ſick but when

Sect. 3. AFRICA and AMERICA.

when their Idol is angry with them; therefore they please him by pouring at his feet the Wine of Palms. They use to wash and paint and new cloath their dead, and bury with him meat, drink, and some of his goods, at whose grave they shed the blood of Goats. They are much addicted to divination by birds; and their Priests are in such esteem, that they think life and death, plenty and famine are in their power. In the Kingdom of *Congo* they worship some monstrous creatures instead of God. But they were converted to Christianity by the *Portugueze, Anno* 1490. At the City of *Banza*, afterward called S. *Saviour's*, was erected a Cathedral Church for the Bishop, who was there received by the King in great magnificence. This Church had 28 Canon Residents. All their Idols of Beasts, Birds, Trees, and Herbs, with their Conjuring Characters were burned. Divers Religious persons and Jesuits were sent from *Portugal* thither to erect Schools and Colleges for Divinity and the Arts. See *Purchas, Lopez, Maffeus, Osorius* of the Acts of *Emanuel*. *Congo, its Religion.*

Q. *What Religion do the Northern Neighbours of* Congo *profess?*

A. In *Loango* under the Line, they worship Idols and are Circumcised. Every Tradesman appeaseth his God with such things as belong to his Trade: the Husbandman with Corn, the Weaver with Cloth, &c. At the death of their Friends they kill Goats, to the honour of their Idols, and make divers Feasts in memorial of the dead. They will rather die than touch any meat which is prohibited by their Priests. At *Kenga* the Sea-port of *Loango*, there is an Idol kept by an old Woman, which is once a year honoured with great solemnity and feasting. There is another Idol at *Morumba* Thirty Leagues Northward, where Boys are Sworn to Serve this God, and are initiated with hard diet, ten days silence, abstinence from certain Meats, and a cut in their Shoulder, the blood of which is sprinkled at the Idols feet. Their Trials of life and death, are in the presence of this Idol. At *Anzichi* they are Circumcised, worship the Sun and Moon, and each Man his particular Idol. In some of these neighbouring Coutreys the People are Man-eaters, and worship the Devil, to whom, when they offer sacrifice, they continue from morning till night, using Charming Vociferations, dancing and piping. See *Lopez, Barros*, and others. *The Religions of its Northern Neighbours*

Q. *Of What Religion are the Islands about* Africa?

A. In some of them are Mahumetans, in some Christians, but in most Heathens. In *Socotera*, an Island near the mouth of the Red-Sea, whence we have our best *Aloes*, they are *Jacobites*, and are governed by their *Abuna* or Priest. They much reverence the Cross. They have Altars in their Churches, which they enter not, but stand in the Porch. In *Madagascar*, or the great Island of St. *Lawrence*, there are many Mahumetans upon the Coast, but more Idolaters within the Land, who acknowledge one Creator, and are Circumcised; but use neither to pray nor keep holy-day. They *African Islands their Religions.*

punish

punish Adultery and Theft with death. In the Isle of St. *Thomas*, under the Line, are Christians and Moors. In divers Islands are no People at all, in the *Canaries* are Christians; before they were Idolaters, and had many Wives, whom they first prostituted to their Magistrates, and this uncivil civility they used to strangers instead of Hospitality. They bury the dead by setting them upright against a Wall, with a staff in their hand; and if he was a great Man, a Vessel of Milk by him. *Madera* is also possessed by Christians, and so be the other Islands on this hither part of the *African* Coast. See *Ortelius*, *Mercator*, and other Geographers.

Q. *What Religion was professed among the* Americans ?

America, *the Religi- on thereof.*
A. Before the *Spaniards* came thither, they were all Pagans; who as they were distinguished into divers Nations, so they worshipped divers gods, after divers manners; but they did generally acknowledge the Sun and Moon for the chief gods. In *Canada* they worshipped the Devil, before the *French* came thither, and in most places there as yet they worship him; who, when he is offended with them, flings dust in their eyes. The Men Marry two or three Wives, who, after the death of their Husbands never Marry again, but go still after in Black, and besmear their Faces with Coal-dust and Grease; they do first expose their Daughters to any that will lie with them, and then give them in Marriage. They believe that after death their Souls ascend into the Stars, and go down with them under the Horizon into a Paradise of Pleasure. They believe also that God stuck a multitude of Arrows in the Beginning into the Ground, and of these sprung up Men and Women. They have divers ridiculous opinions of God, as that he once drank much Tobacco, and then gave the Pipe to their Governour, with a command that he should keep it carefully, and so doing he should want nothing; but he lost the Pipe, and so fell into want and misery. Such senseless conceits have these people, who as they are savage in their carriage, so in their understanding they are little better than beasts. They use to sing the Devils praises, to dance about fires, which they make to his honour, and leap over them. They bemoan the dead a great while, and bring Presents to the Grave. Many of these ignorant Souls were Converted to Christ by the Industry of the Jesuites, *Anno* 1637, and 1638. See Father *Paul*'s Relation of New *France*. See also *Chaplain* and *Jaques Cartier*, &c.

Q. *What is the Religion of* Virginia ?

Virginia, *its Religion.*
A. Before the *English* planted Christianity there, they worshipped the Devil, and many Idols, as yet they do in many places there. They believe many gods, but one principally who made the rest; and that all creatures were made of Water, and the Woman before the Man, who by the help of one of the gods, conceived and bore Children. They are all Anthropomorphites, giving to their gods the forms of Men, whom they worship with Praying, singing, and offerings. They hold the Souls Immortality, rewards and punishments after this life, the one in Heaven, the other in a burning pit

towards

towards the West. The Priests are distinguished from other People by Garments of Skins, and their hair cut like a Comb on their Crowns. They carry their gods about with them, and ask Counsel of them. Much of their devotion consisteth in howling and dancing about fires, with Rattles, or Gourd, or Pumpion rindes in their hands, beating the ground with stones, and offering of Tobacco, Deer-suet, and Blood on the Stone Altars. They undertake no matters of consequence without advice of their Priests, the chief whereof is adorned with Feathers and Weasels Tails, and his Face painted as ugly as the Devils. They bury their Kings (after their bodies are burned and dryed) in white skins, within arches and mats, with their wealth at their feet, and by the Body is placed the Devil's Image. The Women express their sorrow with black paint, and yellings for Twenty four hours. None but the King and Priest may enter these houses, where the Images of Devils and their Kings are kept. Instead of saying Grace at Meat, they fling the first bit into the Fire; and when they will appease a Storm, they cast Tobacco into the Water. Sometimes they sacrifice children to the Devil. But of these passages, see *Hackluit*, and *Purchas* out of him.

Q. *What is the Religion of* Florida?

A. Their chief Deities are the Sun, and Moon, which they honour with dances and songs. Once a year they offer to the Sun a Harts Hide stuffed with Herbs, hanging Garlands of fruits about his Horns, so presenting this gift towards the East, they pray the Sun to make their Land produce the same fruits again. But to their Kings, they use to sacrifice their first-born Males. Much of their Devotion, like the rest of barbarous Savages, consisting in singing, dancing, howling, feasting, and cutting off their own skins. Adultery in the Woman is punished with whipping. In some parts of this Country the next of Kin is permitted to cut the Adulteresses Throat, and the Woman to cut the Adulterers. In some parts also of the Country they worship the Devil; who, when he appears and complains of Thirst, humane blood is shed to quench his thirst. When a King is buried, the Cup wherein he used to drink, is still set upon his Grave, and round about the same are stuck many Arrows; the People weep and fast three days together; the Neighbour Kings his Friends cut off half their hair. Women are hired, who for six months howl for him three times a day. This honour the King and Priest have, that they are buried in their houses, and burned with their houses and goods. See *Benzo, Morgares, Hackluit*, &c.

Florida, its Religion.

Q. *Of what Religion are the Nations by West-*Virginia *and* Florida?

A. Few of them are yet known, but such as by Navigation are found upon the Sea-coasts, and some Islands conquered by the *Spaniards*, are worshippers of the Sun, and Water: because the Sun by his heat, and the Water by its moisture produce all things; therefore when they eat, drink, or sacrifice, they use to throw up

*Religions of the Nations by West-*Virginia *and* Florida.

in the air, towards the Sun, some part of their Food. The *Spaniards* took advantage of this Superstition, and made these People believe they were Messengers sent thither to them from the Sun; whereupon they submitted, holding it impious to reject the Messengers, which their chief god had sent them. They worship also here Idols, and in some places the Devil, and observe the same Superstitious Ceremonies in the burial of their Dead, that their Neighbours do. See *Hackluit*.

Q. *What was the Religion of* New-Spain ?

New-Spain, *its Religion.*

A. They were gross and bloody Idolaters before the *Spaniards* brought them to the knowledge of Christ, who requires of his Disciples no other Sacrifice but that of a contrite heart; he having shed his own blood, that we might spare the shedding of ours. These wretched *Americans* acknowledge one chief God, yet they worshipped many: Principally the Sun, to whom they offered the heart of the Sacrifice; even of Men: neither did they eat or drink, or smell to a Flower, till they had cast up in the Air to the Sun some portion of their Meat and Drink, and some leaves of their Flowers. At *Mexico* they worshipped many Idols, but three principally; the first was called *Vitziliputzli*, placed in an Azure coloured Chair, with Snakes heads at each corner. On his head were rich Plumes of Feathers with Gold: in his left hand was a white Target, in his right a Staff; at his sides he had four darts. Perhaps by this Image they represented the Nature of God; by his blew Chair they might signifie Heaven his Seat; by the Snakes Leads, his Wisdom; by the Feathers and Gold, his Glory; by his Target, Protection; by the Staff, Direction; and by the four Arrows, his Power, extending over the four parts of the World; East, West, South, and North; or else, which is more likely, they represented the Sun by this Idol, whose aboad is in the Azure Skie, and his Arrows or Beams are extended to the four quarters of the World: the feathers may signifie his lightness; and the Gold, his Glory; his Target and Staff may shew that the Suns heat is both defensive and offensive. Near to this Idol stood a Pillar of less work and beauty, on which was another Idol, called *Thaloe*; perhaps by this they meant the Moon. They had a third Idol of black Stone, with four darts in his right hand, looking angrily; this they worshipped as the god of Repentance; this Idol, with the others, was richly adorned with Gold and Jewels. In *Cholula* they worshipped the god of Wealth or Merchandising; they had also an Idol of Paste, or Dough, which was consecrated and made every Year, to which rich Presents were brought, and stuck in the Paste. They made gods also of their chief Captives, to which they gave divine honours, for Six, sometimes for Twelve Months, praying and sacrificing to him, and carrying him in Procession; but at last the Priests kill him; the Chief Priest pulls out his heart, offers it smoaking to the Sun; then he is opened, cut in pieces, and eaten. They adored many other gods and goddesses with many heathenish Superstitions. Of which see *Joseph Acosta* in his History of the *Indies, Gomara, Peter Martyr of Millan*, &c.

Our

Sect. 3.   AFRICA and AMERICA.

Out of this discourse we may see what cruelty is used among Idolaters in their barbarous sacrifices; how lavish also they are of their gold, silver, and jewels, with which they adorn their Idols; this hath been always the Devils policy, by outward splendor and wealth to draw ignorant and covetous-minded people to follow Idolatry; for such a bewitching quality there is in the splendor of gold, silver, and stones, that both the eyes and hearts of Men are drawn after them: to this purpose, *Lanctantius*, lib. 2. *instit. auri, gemmarum & eboris pulchritudo ac nitor perstringit oculos: nec ullam religionem putant ubi illa non fulserit; itaque sub obtentu deorum; avaritia & cupiditas colitur*; the beauty of Gold, Jewels, and Ivory, do so dazel many eyes, and captivate their hearts, that they think there is no Religion where these shine not; therefore under pretence of worshipping God, covetousness and desire is worshipped. Hence Idolatry may be truly called covetousness; and this by the Apostle is called Idolatry. Not without cause then did God forbid the Israelites to make to themselves gods of gold and silver, as knowing what force these Metals have to draw Mens Minds after them. And indeed some of the wise Gentiles themselves laughed at the Vanities of those who bestowed so much gold on their Idols; *Aurum Vasa Numæ, Saturniaque impulit æra*, saith Persius; the gods were better worshipped in *Numa's* earthen Vessels, than they were afterward in Gold; and then he offereth to God a sincere heart, is more accepted than he that bestows on *Jupiter* a golden beard; *Dicite pontifices, in sacro quid facit aurum*; and yet the access of gold and silver in their Statues and Temples is stupendious, as *Lipsius* sheweth *de mag. urb. Romæ*. And the *Romans* were come to that height of Superstition, that they thought a Bull was not a fit sacrifice to their gods, if his horns had not been gilded, or his forehead adorned with plates of gold: see *Virgil. Et statuam ante aras auratâ fronte juvencum:* and *Livy l.* 5. sheweth, that to *Apollo* was sacrificed, not only an Ox with gilded horns, but also *capræ albæ auratæ*, white Goats with horns gilded; and *Val. Flac. l.* 3. *Arg.* speaketh of *lectas auratâ fronte bidentes*, of Sheep with gilded horns. And long afore the *Romans*, this golden superstition was used, as may be seen in *Homer's Iliad.* 3. where *Nestor* promised to sacrifice to *Minerva* an Ox χρυσὸν κέρασιν περιχεύσας, pouring gold about his horns. *Joseph Acosta* relates in his History of *America*, what magnificent Temples and rich Images of gold and precious stones the *Indians* dedicated to their Idols. Against all such vanities *Arnobius* in his Book against the Gentiles disputeth elegantly, shewing that God is not taken with such toys as Temples, Altars, and Sacrifices; but, *cultus verus in pectore est*, his true worship consisteth in the breast; and as our Saviour saith, neither in the Temple of *Samaria*, nor of *Jerusalem*, but in spirit and truth,

Idolaters, their cruelty and cost in their Barbarous Sacrifices.

Persius, his notable saying.

> *Quin damus id superis de magna quod dare lance*
> *Non possit magni Messalæ. lippa propago ;*
> *Compositum jus, fasque animo, sanctosque recessus*
> *Mentis, & incoctum generoso pectus honesto !*
> *Hæc cedo ut admoveam templis, & farre litabo.*

An honest upright sincere and sanctified heart, saith *Persius*, is above all the Temples and Sacrifices in the World.

Mexico, its Priests and Sacrifices.

Q. *What Priests had they at* Mexico, *and what Sacrifices.*

A. Besides their inferiour Priests, they had one chief, whose habit was a Crown of rich Feathers on his head, Pendants of Gold, with green stones at his ears, and under his Lip an azure stone ; his office was to receive the Body of the dead King at the Temple door, with a Mournful Song, to open the Breast of the sacrificed man, to pull out his Heart, to offer it to the Sun, and then to fling it to the Idol, to which the Man was sacrificed. The inferiour Priests in the interim holding the legs, arms, and head of the Sacrificed wretch, whilst his heart was taken out. They used also to flay off the skins of Men, and cloath some therewith, who went about dancing, and forcing People to offer them Presents, or else they would strike them over the face, with the bloody corner of the skin. The Priests office also was to burn Incense before their Idols every morning, noon-tide, evening, and at midnight for them, with Trumpets and Coronets, they sounded a long time, which done, they burned the Incense in Censers with much reverence, and then they beat themselves, and draw blood with sharp Bodkins. They did Preach also on some Festival days to the People. The Revenues of the Priests were great ; the Temples in state, magnificence, and wealth, exceed ours. The Priests were all anointed, and wore their hair long, for they never cut it. They did sometimes anoint themselves with an Unguent made of venomous beasts, which made them without fear, and armed them with cruelty. They painted their skins black. They washed the new-born Children, and let them blood in their ears ; they performed Marriages by asking the Parties mutual consent, and tying together a corner of the Womans Veil, with a corner of the Man's Gown, and so brought them to the Bridegrooms house, causing the Bride to go seven times about the Hearth. They buried the dead either in their Gardens, or on Mountains; sometimes they burned the Body ; and if he was a Great Man, they killed his Chaplain and his Officers to attend him, burying also Wealth with him, that he might not want in the other World. The Priest used to attire himself; in these great Funerals, like a Devil with many Mouths, and Glass-eyes, and with his Staff stirred and mingled the ashes. When the King died, the Priests were to sing his Elogies, and to sacrifice Two hundred Persons to serve him. Adultery was punished with death, and so was dishonesty in their Nuns and Monks, of which there were two great

Cloysters at *Mexico*. But who will see these particulars handled at large, let them read *Joseph Acosta*, and *Lopez de Gomara*.

Q. *Had the* Americans *any knowledge of Christian Religion?*

A. Concerning Christ they knew nothing; some small knowledge they had of a Supream God, whom they called *Wirochoca*, and of the Creation; of the Immortality of Souls, of a Life after this, wherein are punishments and rewards; and some of them, as *Lerius* witnesseth, believe the Resurrection of the Flesh; and if we will believe *Acosta*, they have some knowledge of the Trinity, which they worship under the Picture of the Sun with three heads; they have some Tradition likewise of *Noah*'s Flood, and that all Mankind was drowned, except six Persons who saved themselves in a Cave; some in *Brasil* believe, all were drowned except their Progenitors, who were preserved to propagate Mankind. The *Indians* also report, that the Sun hid himself in a certain Lake within an Island, during the time of the Deluge, and so was preserved; this is not unlike the Poetical fiction of *Diana* and *Apollo*, how they were begot in the Isle *Ortygia*, called afterward from their first appearance *Delos*, by this intimating, that after the Flood, by reason of thick Fogs and Mists arising out of the moist earth, the Sun and Moon were not seen in many days; but these vapours being spent, and the Earth dry, the Moon was first seen, and then in some few hours afterward the Sun. The Tradition which they have of the Flood, cannot be that of *Ogyges* King of *Attica*, which happened about Six hundred years after *Noah*'s Flood, and which drowned only the Country about *Athens* and *Achaia* in *Peloponnesus*; nor was it that of *Deucalion*, which happened in the 82d. year of his Age, about Two hundred and fifty years after the former, and Seven hundred eighty two years after *Noah*'s Flood; for this drowned only *Thessaly*, and some part of *Italy*, of which the *Americans* could have no knowledge; seeing many places nearer never heard of these Floods, it is most likely then that their Tradition was grounded on *Noah*'s Flood; for as *Noah*'s Posterity Peopled all the World, so they dispersed the Memory of this Flood wherever they planted; for we find this deluge not only mentioned by *Moses*, but also by *Berosus*, *Alexander*, *Polyhistor*, *Abydenus* the Historian, as he is cited by *Eusebius*, *Plato* in *Timæo*. *Plutarch* Writing of *Deucalion*'s Flood, speaketh of the Dove sent out of the Ark, which relates to *Noah*'s Flood; and *Ovid* describing the same Flood, Writes according to the Mosaical description of the first and universal deluge; whereas that of *Deucalion* was but of a particular Country: So *Lucian de Dea Syria*, Writes of *Deucalion*'s Flood, as if he had read the sixth and seventh Chapter of *Genesis*, of *Noah*'s Flood; for he sheweth how all flesh had corrupted their ways upon the Earth, how all their Works were ἔργα ἀδίμικα, works of Injustice and Violence; how the rain fell, the Fountains of the great Deep were opened, the Waters so prevailed, that all flesh died, πάντες ὄλοντο. He sheweth also how he was preserved with his Wife and Children in a Great Ark; and how all the Beasts that live

Marginal notes: Americans acknowledge a Supream God, a Trinity, the Immortality of Souls, a Life after this, and have some Tradition of Noah's Flood.

live on the Earth, two and two entred into the Ark, &c. And, lastly, how he built an Altar after his deliverance. This description is directly of *Noah*'s Flood, not of *Deucalion*'s; besides, *Mela*, *Solinus*, and *Pliny*, Write, that *Joppe*, the Maritime Town of *Syria*, was of great Antiquity, as being built before the Flood; which cannot be meant of *Ogyges*, or *Deucalion*'s Flood, which were only in some places of *Greece*, and went not so far as *Syria*; neither was it any great Antiquity for *Joppe* to be built before these Floods; for many Cities besides this were built before; therefore doubtless is meant *Noah*'s Flood. Lastly, *Josephus* saith, that *Omnes barbaricæ historiæ Scriptores*, all the Barbarian Historians have mentioned this Flood.

Q. *What Festival days were observed in* New Spain?

New Spain its Festival days.
A. Every Twentieth day, which was the last of their Month, was holy, and then were Men Sacrificed. At the first appearance of Green Corn, Children were Sacrificed, so when the Corn was a Foot above the Ground, and again when it was two Foot high, holy-days were kept, and Children Butchered. In some of their Feasts they sacrificed a Woman, and with her skin coveted a Man, who danced about the Streets two days together. In one of their Feasts, which the *Mexicans* kept in their *Canoes* upon the Lake, a Boy and Girl were drowned to keep company with the gods of the Lake. In *May* they kept the Feast of *Vitziliputzli*, in which his Image made of Paste, richly adorned, was carried by Maidens attired in White, on their shoulders to the Court, and thence by the Young Men in the Stairs of the Temple, and thence to the top with Musick; much adoration, vain ceremonies, and wicked sacrificing of Men were used that day. In *May* also was kept the Feast of Pennance and Pardon; in which a Captive was sacrificed. After much profane adoration, the People took up earth and eat it, desiring pardon for their sins, and bringing rich presents to their Idol, and whipping themselves on the shoulders. Much Meat is presented that day to the Idols, and then to the Priests, who five days before had eat but one meal a day. The Merchants had their peculiar god, and festival day, in which they sacrificed a Man, after they had given him for nine days divine honours. His heart they offered about Midnight to the Moon, perhaps because she is the Mistress of the Waters, on which Merchants use to Traffick; or because they are more beholding to her Light in the Night than others are. Concerning these Festivals, their Schools and Seminaries, their belief of the Souls Immortality, of their Rewards and Punishments, of their Nine severa. places appointed for them, see *Acosta*, *Gomara*, and P. *Martyr* in his Decads.

Q. *What was the Religion of* Jucatan, *and the parts adjoyning?*

Jucatan, its Religion, and Parts adjoining.
A. In *Jucatan* they were Circumcised, and yet gross Idolaters, but curious Workmen in Carving and adorning their Images. They had in their houses Images made like Bears, which they worshipped as their Houshold gods, with Singing and Incense. In hollow Images, they caused Boys to Answer the Peoples Peti-

tions, as if God had spoke to them. When they wanted rain, or were in any danger, they had their Proceſſions, and Pilgrimages to theſe Idols. In *Nicaragua*, they worſhipped the Sun, and divers Idols. All their Prieſts, except Confeſſors, married. The ordering of the Sacrifices, and their numbers, depended meerly on the Prieſts, who uſed to go about the Captives three times ſinging mournfully, and then with their flint knives ſuddenly open their Breaſts. They divide the body thus; the Prelate hath his heart, the King his hands and feet, the Taker his Buttocks, and the People the reſt. The heads are ſet on trees, under which they ſacrifice men and children. They have their Idolatrous Proceſſions, in which for the honour of their Idol, they wound themſelves, and for the deſire of future happineſs, they offer themſelves chearfully for Sacrifices. Whilſt the Prieſt anoints the cheeks and the mouth of the Idol with blood, the others ſing, and the People pray. The Prieſt makes marriages, by joyning the little fingers of the Bridegroom and Bride near a fire; but the Lords are permitted for honours ſake, firſt to corrupt the Bride. The Adulterer is beaten, and the Adultereſs is divorced. He that forceth a Virgin is a ſlave, except he pay her Dowrie. But if a ſlave force his Maſters daughter, they are both buried alive. See *Penzo*, *P. Martyr*, and *Gomara*.

Q. *What was the Religion of the Southern Americans?*

A. They generally worſhip the Sun and Moon, with divers Idols, and the Devil in divers ſhapes; they believe the Souls immortality. Their Prieſts are their Phyſicians, and therefore in great eſteem, and exceeding rich, for they have all the goods of him whom they cure. When they go to wars, they carry their gods with them, of whom they ask Counſel of all affairs; and then they keep Lent for two months. They puniſh in ſome places theft and murther with the loſs of Ears and Noſe; in other parts with death. Theſe faults in the Nobility are puniſhed with the loſs of their hair only. In ſome places they hold it a part of their devotion, to offer their daughters to be defloweréd by their Prieſts. When it thunders and lightens, they ſay the Sun is angry with them. When there is an Eclipſe, they faſt; the married Women ſcratch their Faces, and pluck their hairs; the maidens draw blood with ſharp fiſh-bones. When the Moon is Eclipſed, they ſay the Sun is angry with her. When a Comet is ſeen, they beat drums, and hollow, thinking by this to drive it away. They uſe to conſult with, and invocate the Devil. The Prieſts learn Phyſick and Magick when they are young, being two years ſhut up in Woods; all that time they keep their Cells, ſee no Women, nor eat fleſh. They are taught by their Maſters in the night. The dead are buried either at home, or being dried at the fire, are hanged up. The bones at laſt are burned, and the skull preſented to the Wife, to be kept by her as a Relick. In their *Lent* faſts they abſtain from Women and Salt. See *P. Martyr*, *Gomara*, *Linſchoten*, *Cieza*, &c.

Southern America, the religion thereof.

Q. *Of what Religion are the people of* Paria, Guiana, *and along the river* Debaiba, *or St.* John?

A. Here

Paria Gui-ana, and Debaiba, their Religions.

A. Hereabout they be very zealous in worshipping of the Devil, and Idols, to whom they sacrifice men, and then eat them. When their gods are angry, they macerate themselves with fasting. Their Priests are stoned or burned, if they marry against their Vow of Chastity. They believe rewards and punishments after this life. The spot in the Moon they hold to be a man imprisoned there for Incest with his Sister. They feed yearly the departed souls with *Maiz* and Wine. They held the souls of great Men only, and such as were buried with them, immortal. Their great mens Funeral Pomps are celebrated yearly with much lamentation, drinking, and bestial ceremonies, both men and women casting aside all modesty. He that will know more of this stuff, let him read the forenamed Authors.

Q. What is the Religion of Brasil?

Brasil, its Religion.

A. They acknowledge the immortality of the soul, and believe that there are rewards and punishments after this life: For they hope, that if they kill and sacrifice many of their enemies, they shall be carried beyond the Mountains into pleasant Gardens, there to dance and rejoyce with their fore-fathers. They stand in much fear of the Devil, who is still vexing of them; therefore they chiefly worship him; and when they go abroad, they commonly carry fire with them, as their defence against the Devil, who they think is afraid of fire. They have their solemn festivals, which they celebrate with dancing, howling, and tatling. The Husband hath power to kill the adulterous Wife. Their marriages are without any Ceremonies. They bury their dead upright in a pit, with their goods. The Husband plays the Midwife to the Woman, washeth, painteth, and nameth the Child by the name of some wild beast: they have some knowledge of *Noah*'s flood. Of these passages see *Maffeus, Lerius Stadius,* &c.

Q. What Religion did the people of Peru *profess?*

Peru, its Religion.

A. Their chief god was *Wiracocha*, by whom they understood the maker of all things; next to him they worshipped the Sun, and the Thunder after him: the Images of these three they never touched with their bare hands: they worshipped also the Stars, Earth, Sea, Rainbow, Rivers, Fountains and Trees. They adored also wild beasts, that they might not hurt them; and in sign of their devotion, when they travelled, they left in the cross ways, and dangerous places, old shooes, feathers, and if they had nothing else, stones. They worshipped the Sun, by pulling off the hairs from their Eye-brows: when they fear, they touch the Earth, and look up to the Sun. They worshipped also the dead bodies of their Emperours, and indeed every thing they either affected or feared. They have some glimring knowledge of the beginning of the world, of *Noah*'s flood, and they believe the end of the world, which still they fear when the Sun is eclipsed, which they think to be the Moons husband: they held their Priests in such esteem, that no great matter was undertaken by Prince or People without their advice. None had access to the Idols but they; and then only when they

are

are clothed in white, and proftrate on the ground. In facrificing they abftain from Women; and fome out of zeal would put out their own eyes. They ufed to confult with the Devil, to whom they facrificed men, and dedicated boys in their Temples for *Sodomy*. They had alfo their Temples richly adorned with Gold and Silver, and their Monafteries for Priefts and Sorcerers. Their Nuns were fo ftrictly kept, that it was death to be defloured: after fourteen years of age they were taken out of the Monaftery, either to ferve their Idols (and fuch muft be Virgins ftill) or elfe to ferve as Wives and Concubines to the *Ingua*, or Emperor. They are very frequent and ftrict in their confeffions, and chearfully undertake what penance is enjoyned them. But the *Ingua* confeffeth only to the Sun: after confeffion they all wafh in baths, leaving their fins in the water. They ufed to facrifice Vegetables, Animals, and Men, chiefly Children, for the health or profperity of their *Ingua*, and for victory in War: In fome places they eat their men-facrifices, in others they only dried and preferved them in filver Coffins; they anoint with blood the faces of their Idols, and doors of their Temples, or rather flaughter-houfes. See *Acofta, Cieza, Gomara*, &c.

Q. *What feftival days did the* Peruvians *obferve?*

A. They had feafts and Sacrifices every month of the year, in which were offered multitudes of fheep of different colours, which they burned. The *Ingua*'s Children were dedicated in thefe Feafts, their ears were pierced, then they were wiped, and their faces anointed with blood, in fign that they fhould be true Knights to their *Ingua*. In *Cufco* during this month and feaft, no ftranger might remain; but at the end thereof they were admitted, and had a morfel of bread prefented to each man, that they fhould by eating thereof teftifie their fidelity to the *Ingua*. In the fecond month, which is our *January* (for in *December*, in which the Sun returns from *Capricorn*, was their firft month) they flung the afhes of their facrifices into the River, following the fame fix leagues, and praying the River to carry that prefent to *Wiracocha*; in three following months they offered one hundred fheep. In the fixth they offered one hundred fheep more, and made a Feaft for their *Maiz*. In the feventh they facrificed to the Sun. In the eighth and ninth months, two hundred fheep were offered. In the tenth one hundred more, and to the honour of the Moon; burned torches, wafhed themfelves, and then were drunk four days together. In the eleventh month they offered one hundred fheep, and upon a black fheep poured much Chica or Wine of *Maiz*, to procure rain. In the twelfth month they facrificed one hundred fheep and kept a feaft. They have alfo their fafts which continue in mourning and fad proceffions two days, and the two days after are fpent in feafting, dancing, and drinking. See *Jof. Acofta.*

Peruvians, their feftival days.

Q. *What was their belief of the departed Souls?*

A. That they wander up and down, and fuffer hunger, thirft, and cold; therefore they carry them meat, drink and clothes. They ufed alfo to put gold, and filver in their mouths, hands and bofoms;

Peruvians. their Belief of the departed fouls.

soms; much treasure hath been digged out of graves. But they believed that the souls of good men were at rest in glory. The bodies were honoured after death, sacrifices were offered to them, & cloaths. The best beloved Wife was slain and attendants of all sorts. To the *Ingua*'s Ghost young children were sacrificed, and if the Father was sick, many times the Son was slain, thinking this murther should satisfie death for the Father. Of these, and other their impious Ceremonies, see *Acosta*. By these horrible murthers committed among the poor Americans, we may see what a cruel and barbarous tyrant superstitious fear is, and what wretched slaves they are who are captivated by this tyrant, far more savage than *Mezentius*, *Phalaris*, *Busyris*, or any other tyrannical butcher that ever was; for there is no Tyrant so powerful, or barbarous, but may be avoided by flying from him to remote places; but who can fly from that superstitious fear, which a man doth carry continually about him? *Quid terras alio calentes Sole mutamus? patria quis exul se quoq; fugit?* a man may fly from his country, saith *Horace*, but not from himself; this tyrant haunts the superstitious wretch continually, as the evil Spirit did *Saul*. Again, no Tyrant can tyrannize over a man longer than he lives; death sets every slave at liberty; but this Tyrant leaves not his slave in death, but with the Terrors of future torments in hell, doth vex his soul when it is departing hence; *Curæ non ipsa in morte relinquunt*; there is no slave so wretched and miserable, no pain so great, no captivity so unpleasing, no chains so heavy, no prison so loathsome, which in sleep are not forgotten; for then the slave is at liberty, the pain is eased, the chains are light, and the darkest dungeon, is then a beautiful Pallace; but this *Deisidemonia*, as the Greeks call it, this superstitious fear will not permit its captivated slave to rest or take any quiet, but affrights him in his sleep with horrid dreams, and hideous phancies, so that sleep which should be his comfort and ease, becomes his tormenter. Besides, Temples and Altars, which use to be Sanctuaries for Delinquents, are no ease or Sanctuary at all to the superstitious sinner; any servant might be defended from his Master by laying hold of the Altar; but no Altar, no Temple, no Sacrifice can Privilege the superstitious soul, who is still jealous and fearful of his cruel gods; and what wonder is it, if we consider the nature of those insatiable Devils, whom they worship, who are never satisfied with the blood of beasts, men, women, and children, but are still thirsting after more, with the horse-leech; if these be the gods which the Gentiles serve, surely, as *Plutarch* saith, they had been in no worse condition if the *Typhones*, and *Giants* had overthrown these gods: for they could not have been more cruel, nor have expected more bloody victims. And doubtless as the same *Plutarch* saith, these poor wretches do not love their gods, but rather hate them, because they still fear some hurt and mischief from them; therefore as some men flatter, and give rich presents to Tyrants, not because they love them, (for indeed they hate them) but that they may not receive hurt by them; so deal superstitious men with their gods.

And

And in truth *Plutarch* is not altogether mistaken, when he makes Superstition worse than Atheism; for the Atheist holds there is no God, but the superstitious honour, such sordid, base, and cruel gods, that it were far better there were no gods than such; for it is less impiety to say there is no God, than to give his sacred Honour to such wicked, greedy, barbarous, and bloody-sucking Devils. I had rather (saith he) men should say there is no *Plutarch*, than that they should say, *Plutarch* is an inconstant, fickle, cholerick, a revengeful and cruel man. And so he concludes, that Superstition is the cause of Atheism and Impiety; because men looking upon the ridiculous gestures, impurity, cruelty, injustice, madness, undecency, and all kind of villainy perpetrated in their Temples, concluded, it were better to have no Gods, than such abominable Deities. But see *Plutarch* himself in his Book of Superstition.

Q. *What was the Religion of* Hispaniola?

A. They worshipped the Sun and Moon, which they say at first shined out of a Cave; and their tradition is, that out of two Caves came mankind; the biggest men out of the greatest Cave, and the least men out of the lesser Cave. They worship also divers Idols with ugly shapes, by which the Devil useth to speak to them; these they call *Zemes*, to which they kept divers festivals. In these they had their publick dances, with the musick of shells tied about their arms, thighs, and legs. The King sits drumming when the people present themselves, having their skins painted with divers colours of herbs. When they sacrifice, they use with a sacred hook, thrust down their throat, to turn up their stomach. Then they sit down in a ring, cross-legged, and wry-necked, about the Idol, praying their sacrifice might be accepted. In some places the women dance about their Idols, and sing the praises of their ancient Kings; then both Sexes on their knees offer Cakes, which the Priests cut, and give to every one a piece; this each man keeps as a holy Relick all the year against dangers. If any fall sick, the Priests impute this to their neglect in the Idols service; therefore exhort them to build a Chappel, or dedicate a Grove to their god. They think the Ghosts of the dead walk, who assault such as are fearfull, and vanish from them who are not afraid. Their several Rites are like those of the other Pagan Countries. See *P. Martyr*.

Hispaniola, its Religion.

Out of what I have written concerning the Idolatry of *Asia, Africa*, and *America*, we may conclude with *Tertullian, lib. de Idolat.* that every sin, by what name soever it be called, or of whatsoever quality it is, may be comprehended in the sin of Idolatry, *Idololatriæ crimine expungitur*, to use his own phrase; that is, every sin is made up, and attains to its perfection and consummation in Idolatry: so that as he sheweth in that book, there is no such murtherer as the Idolater, who not only destroyeth the bodies of men and beasts to please his Idol, but likewise murthereth his own soul: there is no such Adulterer as he, who not only goeth a whoring after false gods, but adulterates the truth; for every false god is adultery; there is no such thief as he, for not only much robbery and oppres-

Idolatry further condemned.

sion is committed to maintain false worship and Idolatry, as *Arnobius* instanceth in the Romans, who to maintain the worship of their gods, did rob all other gods and nations, and with their triumphant gold (*Persius* calls it *aurum ovatum*) adorn their Images: But besides this theft, the Idolater robs God of his right and honour, giving it to such as are not gods. I will not speak of the uncleanness, drunkenness, wantonness, and other sins which accompany this master-sin, which *Tertullian* calls *Principale crimen generis humani, summus sæculi reatus,&c. devoratorium salutis*: the main wickedness of mankind, the chief guilt of the world, the devourer or destroyer of mans happiness and salvation; therefore he will not have any Christian to paint, or make graven Images to be worshipped, affirming that it is flatly against the law of God, and likewise against their vow in baptism, to forsake the Devil and his Angels: how do they forsake him, if they make him? if they make it their trade to live by him, how have they renounced him? can they deny with their tongue, what they confess with their hand? destroy that with their words, which they build up with their deeds? confess one God, and make many? preach the true God, and yet make false gods? If any say that he worships none, though he makes them, *Tertullian* will answer him: That he who makes false gods, doth really worship them; not with incense and sacrifice, but with his wit, sweat, industry and skill, which he impends on the making of them; he is more than their Priest; for without him they could have no Priest. How can a Christian put forth that hand to touch the Body of our Lord, by which he hath made a Body for the Devil? And as it is Idolatry, saith he, to carve or paint Idols, so it is any ways to adorn them, to build houses or temples for them, so that all such Artificers are guilty of Idolatry; so are judicial Astrologers, who call the Stars by the names of Idols, and take upon them to foretell future contingencies by them; so are School-masters, who teach the Genealogies and Fables of these false gods; this severity indeed was needful in the beginning of the Gospel, when Gentilism was to be suppressed, that way might be made for Christianity; but now Pagan Idolatry being quite extinguished among us, there is no danger in reading or teaching of Heathen Authors. He condemneth also Merchants that bring home or sell incense, or any thing else whereby Idols are worshipped. So he will not have Christians to be present at the solemnities, shows, or festivals of Idols, nor to give any countenance to them, or to wink and connive at them, or to call them gods, or to swear by them, for that is to take the name of the true God in vain; nay, he will not permit Christians to light candles, or set up bayes in their doors, which upon solemn days was an honour due to the Emperor, because that ceremony had some resemblance with Gentile Idolatry.

The

Sect. 4.   87

THE
Religions of EUROPE.

The Contents of the Fourth Section.

The Religion of the Ancient Europeans. 2. *The* Roman *chief Festivals.* 3. *Their Gods.* 4. *Their Priests.* 5. *Their Sacrifices.* 6. *Their Marriage-Rites.* 7. *Their Funeral Ceremonies.* 8. *The old* Græcian *Religion.* 9. *Their chief Gods.* 10. *Of* Minerva, Diana, Venus. 11. *How* Juno, Ceres, *and* Vulcan *were worshipped.* 12. *The* Sun *worshipped under the names of* Apollo, Phœbus, Sol, Jupiter, Liber, Hercules, Mars, Mercurius, Pan, *&c.* 13. *The* Moon *worshipped under divers names and shapes.* 14. *The Earth and Fire, how worshipped and named.* 15. *The Deity of the Sea, how worshipped.* 16. *Death, how named and worshipped.* 17. *The* Græcian *Sacrifices and Ceremonies.* 18. *Their Priests and Temples of old.*

SECT. IV.

Quest. **W**Hat was the Religion of the ancient Europeans?

Answ. The same Paganism was professed among them, that was in the other parts of the World, and which is yet professed in *Lapland, Finland,* and some parts of *Norway, Lithuania,* and Samagotia, whose Religion is Idolatrous, whose Knowledge is Magick, and whose Actions are Barbarous. The chief gods that were worshipped in *Europe,* were the Sun, Moon, Stars, Elements, Rivers, Fountains, Trees; and indeed so many great and small, that according to *Varro's* computation, they exceeded Thirty thousand in number. If we speak of the Religions professed among the *Greeks* and *Romans,* we shall speak in a manner of all; because they had almost all *Europe* under their Dominion, and before their Conquest the same Idols were worshipped by all, but under different Names. *Numa* taught the *Romans* to worship their gods, by offering Corn and Cakes besprinkled with Salt, and to erect Temples, but no Images, thinking it both absurd and impossible to represent that Incomprehensible power by outward shapes and forms. But many years after *Tarquinius Priscus* taught them according to the *Græcian* manner, to set up Images to their gods. Then were the Vestal Nuns chosen, who were to continue so Thirty years; the first ten they were learners, the second ten years practitioners in their office,

G 4   but

but the third ten years teachers of the Novices. If they committed Whoredom, they were burned or buried alive; if the sacred fire went out by their neglect (which was held ominous) they were Scourged. Then were the Priests of *Mars* called *Salii*, instituted at first but Twelve, afterwards Twenty four. These were chosen out of the *Patricii*, and they were in *March* to dance solemnly with their Targets called *Ancilia*, one of which fell down from Heaven. These Festival Dances were dedicated to *Mars*. They had their *Augures*, or Diviners. They had their *Triumviri*, called *Epulones*, who had the charge of the holy Feasts; and other *Triumviri*, who had the charge of the *Sybils* Books. *Arvales* had the care of the Fields: *Feciales* of the Wars. All these were Orders of Priesthood, to which may be added *Flamines*, of which there were as many as there were of their greater gods. *Jupiter*'s Priests were called *Diales*, the Priests of *Mars*, *Martiales*, of *Romulus*, *Quirinales*, &c. He that had the charge of these Priests, of the Sacrifices, and of Festivals, was called *Rex Sacrificulus*, or the King of Priests, because anciently Kings did exercise the Priests Office. But above them all was the Pontifical College, which at first consisted only of Eight, but *Sylla* enlarg'd them to Fifteen; these were to assist the Chief Pontifex or Pope, in whom alone was the Supream Power of all Religion, of Sacrifices, Holy-days, Priests, Vestals, Vows, Funerals, Idols, Oaths, Ceremonies, and whatsoever concerning Religion; besides the care of the Wooden-bridge called *Pons sublicius*. He had more Privileges and Honours than the Kings themselves; for he might ascend the Capitol in his Litter, which was not lawful for others. And whatsoever Criminal fled to him, he was that day free from Punishment; neither was he bound to give an account of any thing he did.

See Alex. ab Alexandro, Plutarch, Pliny, Cicero, Gellius, Fenestella, Letus.

Q. *What were the Roman Chief Festivals?*

A. *Saturnalia*, to the honour of *Saturn*, about the Suns going into *Capricorn*; then the Servants were better than their Masters; this Feast they had from the *Greeks*. *Feriæ Latinæ*, to *Jupiter*; this Feast was kept upon the Hill *Albanus*, mid-way between *Alba* and *Rome*, by the *Romans* and *Latins*. *Quinquatria* was a Feast of five days, to the honour of *Minerva*; it was kept after the *Ides* of *March*; the first day was for Sacrifice, the other three for Sword-players, and the last for Lustration. *Natalitia*, to the *Genius*; in which Feast it was held abominable to shed the blood of some Beasts, and ominous, seeing those Birth-Feasts were wholly dedicated to Mirth and Joy. *Vertumnalia*, were Feasts to *Vertumnus* the god of Merchandising; it was kept in the Month of *October*. *Lupercalia* in *February*, to the honour of *Pan Lycæus*, the god of Shepherds, who keeps the Sheep from the Wolves: This Feast *Evander* brought with him out of *Arcadia* into *Italy*; in it the Young Men used to run up and down the Streets naked, with Leather thongs in their hands, striking gently all such as they met: young Ladies used purposely to offer their naked hands to be struck by them, hoping hereby to become Fruitful. *Agonalia*, were Feasts kept in *January*,

Their chief Festivals.

ry, either to the honour of *Janus*, or elſe of *Agonî*, the god of Actions and Enterprizes. *Carmentalia* in *January* alſo, to the honour of *Carmenta*, *Evander*'s Mother, who was a Propheteſs. *Feralia*, ſo called *à ferendis epulis*, from carrying Meat to the Graves of their Friends; this Feaſt was kept in *February*, to the *Manes* or Infernal Ghoſts. *Terminalia* in *February* alſo, to *Terminus* the god of Marches and Bounds; this Feaſt was obſerved to keep amity between Neighbours, that they might not differ about the bounds of their Lands, *Saliaria* in *March*, to the honour of *Mars*, whoſe Prieſts called *Salii*, went about Dancing with the *Ancilia*, or Targets in their hands. *Liberalia*, which the *Greeks* call *Dionyſia*, were kept in *March*, to the honour of *Bacchus*, or *Liber*, whoſe Prieſts that day did ſacrifice with Ivy Garlands on their heads. *Cerealia*, in *April*, in memory of *Proſerpina*, found again by *Ceres*. The Ceremonies of this day were performed by the *Roman* Matrons, but originally this was a *Greek* Feaſt. *Palilia* in *April*, to *Pales* the Goddeſs of Shepherds. *Vinalia* in *April* too : this Feaſt was alſo called *Veneralia*, becauſe kept to *Venus*, in whoſe Temple much Wine was poured out, the Gardens dedicated, the Sacrifices offered to her. *Robigalia* to *Robigo*, the god of Smut; this Feaſt was kept in *April*, that the Corn might not be ſmutty. *Compitalia* in *May* : theſe Feaſts were kept in *compitis*, Streets and High-ways, to the *Lares*, and their Mother *Mania*, to whom Children were wont to be Sacrificed, till *Junius Brutus*, in ſtead of theſe, commanded the heads of Poppies and Onyons to be offered. *Lemuria* in *May*, ſo called from the *Lemures*, or Night-Ghoſts; which they pacified with this Feaſt, in which they uſed to fling Beans, thinking thereby they drove theſe Ghoſts out of their houſes. *Matralia* in *May*, were Feaſts to *Matuta*, which the *Greeks* call *Leucothea*; no ſerving-Maids were admitted into this Feaſt, except one, whom each Matron was to ſmite on the cheek, becauſe *Matuta* was jealous, that her Husband loved her Maid better than her ſelf, whereupon ſhe grew Mad, and drowned her ſelf, with her Son *Melicerte*, and ſo was made a goddeſs; ſhe was alſo called *Ino*. *Neptunalia* in *June*, were celebrated to the honour of *Neptune*; *Portunnalia*, to *Portumnus* the god of Harbours, in *Auguſt* this Feaſt was kept in the harbour of the River *Tibris*. *Conſualia*, in *Auguſt*, to the honour of *Conſus* the god of Counſel; in this Feaſt the Aſſes and Horſes were crowned and kept from work. In the ſame Month were kept *Vulcanalia* to *Vulcan*. *Meditrinalia* in *October*, to *Meditrina* the goddeſs of Phyſick; for in this Month they uſed to taſt of old and new Wine for a Medicine. *Auguſtalia* the ſame Month, in memory of *Auguſtus* his return to *Rome* from his Victories and Conqueſts. *Fontinilia*, in *October*, in which Feaſt all Fountains and Wells were crowned with Garlands. *Mercurialia* to *Mercury*, in *November*, and *Brumalia* the ſame Month to *Bromus*, or *Brumus*, that is, *Bacchus*. In *December* were kept not only *Saturnalia*, Feaſts to *Saturn*, but alſo *Opalia*, to his Wife *Ops*. And *Angeoralia* to *Angerona* the goddeſs of Anguiſh and Grief. And then alſo was the Feaſt called *Laurentialia*,

See Plu-
tarch, Alex.
ab Alexan-
dro, Joseph
Scaliger,
Rosinus,
and o-
thers.
Their chief
gods.

lia, to *Acca Laurentia*. Besides these and many other set-Feasts, they had others, called *Conceptiva*, and *Nundinæ*; of all which,
Q. *What God did the Romans worship?*
A. Their chief Deities were Twenty, namely, *Jupiter* the God of Thunder, *Juno* of Riches, *Venus* of Beauty, *Minerva* of Wisdom, *Vesta* of the Earth, *Ceres* of Corn, *Diana* of Hunting, *Mars* of Wars, *Mercury* of Eloquence, *Vulcan* of Fire, *Apollo* of Physick, *Neptune* of the Sea, *Janus* of Husbandry, *Saturn* of Time, *Genius* of Nativities, *Orcus* of Hell, *Bacchus* of Wine, *Tellus* of Seeds, *Sol* the Sun, and *Luna* the Moon. But indeed under all these names they understood the Sun, to whom for his divers effects, and operations, they gave divers Names, as *Macrobius* sheweth. Besides these, they worshipped many other Deities of less note; As, *Bellona* the goddess of War, *Victoria* of Victory, *Nemesis* of Revenge, *Cupido* of Love, *Gratiæ*, or *Charites* of Thanks, *Penates* Man's tutelar Gods, *Lares* the Houshold gods, *Parcæ* the goddesses of Destiny, *Furiæ*, or *Eumenides*, the goddesses of Punishments; *Fortuna* the goddess of Providence. All these were called *Dii majorum Gentium*: there were others whom they named *Indigites*, these were Men who for their Merits were Canonized and made Gods. Such were *Hercules, Faunus, Evander, Carmenta, Castor* and *Pollux, Æsculapius, Acca Laurentia, Quirinus*, &c. And not only Virtuous Men, but the Vertues themselves were deified; these had their Temples, Sacrifices, and Festivals. Such were the *Mind, Vertue, Honour, Piety, Hope, Chastity, Peace, Concord, Quietness, Liberty, Safety*, and *Felicity*; Besides these, they had inferiour Gods, whose Merits deserve not Heaven, nor scarce Veneration; these they called *Semones*, as it were *semi-homines*, half-men; such were *Priapus, Vertumnus, Hippona, Nænia*; and all these petty gods which waited upon every servile office and action of Man; such were *Nascio* the goddess of Birth, *Cunina* of Cradles, *Rumina* of sucking, *Potina* of Drinking, *Educa*, or *Edusa* of Eating, *Carnea* of Flesh, *Juventus* of Youth, *Volupia* of Pleasure, *Lubentia* of Lust, or Desire, and many more of this sort. They had also their gods of Marriages, as *Jugatinus* the god of joyning; *Domiducus* who had the Bride home; and many more of this kind. Child-bearing Women had their several goddesses, as *Partunda, Egeria*, and many more. Mens actions also had their Deities; such were *Horta* the goddess of exhorting, *Volumna* of Willing, *Laverna* of Stealing, *Nenia* of Funerals, *Libitina* of Graves, or Coffins. The Rusticks had their peculiar gods, as *Robigus* the god of Smut, *Stercutius* of Dung, *Rubona* of Oxen, *Hippona* of Horses, *Mellona* of Honey, *Pomona* of Fruit, *Pales* of Fodder, *Flora* of Flowers, *Terminus* of Bounds, *Pan* of Shepherds, *Silvanus* of Fields and Woods, *Priapus* of Seeds and Gardens, besides many more. And so ridiculous they were in multiplying Deities, that Cinques and Privies had their *Cloacina*; Fevers their *Febris*; Fear and Paleness had their gods, to wit, *Pavor* and *Pallor*: they worshipped also foreign gods, as *Isis, Serapis, Osiris*, the Deities of *Egypt*; *Sanctus*, or *Dius Fidius*, the *Sabines* god:

and

and many more which they borrowed of those Nations they subdued. But we must observe, that although the ignorant multitude among the Gentiles did worship many gods, yet the wiser sort acknowledged but one true God; thus *Mercurius Trismegistus*, the ancientest of the Philosophers, confesseth, there is but one Unity the root of all things; one goodness of infinite power, the Author of life and motion in the World. So *Pythagoras*, who first assumed the name of Philosopher, saith, that God is one, and all in all; the light of all Powers, the Beginning of all things, the Torch of Heaven, Father, Mind, Life, and motion of the Universe. *Empedocles*, who succeeded *Pythagoras*, sheweth, that from this one Entity, proceed πάντα ὅσα ἦν, ἐστὶ, ἢ ἔσται, all things that have been, are, and shall be. This same is acknowledged by *Parmenides*, *Thales*, *Anaxagoras*, *Simæus*, and other Philosophers of that age. *Socrates* confirmed this truth by his death: *Plato*, his Scholar, calleth God τὸ ὄν, that Entity which hath being of himself, αὐτοφυῆ, begot of himself, the beginning, middle, and end of all things, &c. *Jamblichus* calls God αὐταρκῆ, sufficient in himself; αὐτοπάτερα, Father to himself; τὸ ἀγαθὸν, goodness it self; the fountain and root of all things, intelligent and intelligible, &c. *Prochus* Writeth, that he is King of all things, the only God, who produceth all things of himself; the end of ends, and first cause of all operations, the Author of all goodness and beauty, by whose light all things shine, &c. *Simplicius* saith, that from this divine beauty proceed all beauties, and all truths from this Divine Truth, the Beginning of all Beginnings, the source and original of all goodness, the Cause of causes, God of gods, &c. *Plotinus* to the same purpose makes God the original of all things, and who only is sufficient in himself, giving being to all, &c. The same doctrine is taught by his Scholar *Porphyry*, and likewise by all the other *Platonists*. This was also the general Tenet of the Stoicks, as may be seen in *Epictetus*, who sheweth, that above all things we must learn to know there is but one God, the Governour of all things, &c. who is not ignorant of our works, words, and thoughts, &c. *Cicero* tells us, that nothing is more excellent than God, by whom the World is Governed, who is subject and obedient to none. So *Seneca*, we must find out something more ancient than the World, whence the Stars had their original, &c. he calls God the Soul and Spirit; the preserver and keeper of this Universe, the Lord and Architect of this great work, &c. The same is acknowledged by *Chrysippus*, as he is cited by *Plutarch*; there cannot (saith he) be found out any other beginning or original Justice, but from *Jupiter*, who is the common nature, fate, and providence of all things. The *Peripateticks* maintained the same Doctrine, as may be seen in *Aristotle*'s Physicks, Metaphysicks, and *de Mundo*; he acknowledgeth a first, infinite, and eternal Mover, who is only wise, and the cause of causes. He is the Father of gods and Men, the preserver of the World, the mover of Heavens, Sun, and Moon, &c. His Scholar *Theophrastus* to the same purpose confesseth, that from this

But one God acknowledged by the wiser sort of Gentiles.

this one principle, all things have their exiſtence and conſiſtenc
that God made all things of nothing ; *Alexander Aphrodiſæus*, a
the reſt affirm the ſame truth; and not only the Philoſophers, b
likewiſe the Poets aſſented to this doctrine. *Orpheus* ſings thu
εἶδ᾽ τίς ὅτι ἔτερος, χωρὶς μεγάλη βασιλῆ^Θ : there is none other b
this great King, whoſe ſeat is in Heaven, and is compaſſed w
clouds, who ſeeth all things, and is ſeen of none, *&c.* To t

Of theſe, ſee *Auguſtine* in the *City of God. Lactantius, Cicero, Plutarch, Roſinus*, and others.

ſame purpoſe *Phocyllides*, εἷς Θεὸς ὅτι σοφὸς, δυνατὸς γ᾽ ἅμα καὶ
ἀνολβ^Θ : there is one wiſe God, powerful and bleſſed. But
this ſubject I will ſpeak more hereafter, concerning the Sun
could alledge *Homer, Heſiod, Sophocles, Virgil, Ovid,* and other Po
to this purpoſe; but this work is already performed by *Juſtin M.
tyr, Euſebius, Clemens, Lactantius, Pleſsis*, and others; who likew
have inſerted many verſes out of the *Sibyls*.

Q. *What Prieſts had the* Romans ?

Their Prieſts.

A. Of theſe we have ſaid ſomewhat already, but we will ſ
ſomething more. Their ancienteſt Prieſts were *Luperci,* the Prie
of *Pan, Lycæus, Potitii,* and *Pinarii* of *Hercules.* Of Divinati
by Chirping of Birds, *Augures* ; of Divining by Poultry, *Pullai*
They that had the care of Altars, and looked into the intrals of t
Sacrifice, were called *Aruſpices*, and *Extiſpices.* Curiones w
the Prieſts that had care of each *Curia* or Ward in the City :
Romulus divided *Rome* into 33 Wards, and aſſigned to each of th
a Prieſt, or *Curio.* Over theſe were *Curio maximus,* that is,
Archbiſhop. The Prieſts which *Romulus* ordain'd to the meme
of *Titus Tatius,* King of the *Sabines,* were called *Sodales Tatii.* T
Prieſts that went always covered with Threaden Caps, or Hoo
were called *Flamines quaſi Filamines,* whereof there were div
ſorts, as we have already ſhewed. Of the *Veſtal* Prieſteſſes, a
the *Salii,* as alſo of the *Feciales, Rex Sacrificulus,* and *Pontifex ma
mus,* we have ſaid. The Prieſts that had the charge of the *Sil*
Books, were at firſt but two, called *Duumviri* ; then they were
creaſed to ten, *Decemviri* ; at laſt to fifteen, called *Quindecemv
Fauna,* or *Fatua,* who for her loyalty to her Husband, was cal
Bona Dei, had her peculiar Prieſteſſes. The Prieſts of *Cybele,* M
ther of the gods, were called *Galli,* whoſe Chief, or Archbiſhop v
called *Archi-gallus;* there were alſo other Prieſts called *Triumviri,* a
Septemviri Epulonum, who had charge of the publick Feaſts a
Games. Beſides theſe, every Idol had his Prieſt ; and theſe h
their under-officers, or ſervants, called *Camilli.* The ſervants
Flamen Dialis were called *Flaminei.* They had their Church-w
dens, called *Editui* ; their Trumpeters and Sackbutters, called

Of theſe, ſee the fore-named Authors.

bicines, and *Tibicines* ; *Popa* were thoſe that bound the Sacrifice
Victimarii that killed them. Their Criers that went before
Prieſts to injoyn the People to forbear working during the time
Sacrificing, were called *Preciæ.* The Women that were hired
Sing the Praiſes of the Dead, were named *Præficæ.* Their Gra
Digeſters, *Veſpillones.*

Q. *What sort of Sacrifices did the ancient* Romans *use?*
A. They used to offer a day before the Solemn Sacrifice, a Pre- *Romans,* parative Sacrifice, called *Hostia Præcedanea*. Their *Succedanea their Sa-* were Sacrifices which succeeded when the former were not satis- *crifices.* factory. Weathers that were led to be Sacrificed with a Lamb on each side of them, were called *Ambigui*: *Bidentes* were sheep sacrificed, having two horns, and two eminent teeth. *Ambervales* were sacrifices carried in their Processions about the Fields. *Amburbales* were Processions and Sacrifices about the City. Heifers sacrificed which had never been tamed, or put under the yoke, were called *Injuges*. The Priest having brought the sacrifices to the Altar, used to Pray, laying his hand on the Altar, Musick in the mean time sounding. Then he layeth on the head of the beast Corn, or a Cake, with Salt and Frankincense; this was called *Immolatio*, from *mola* the Cake. Then followed *Libatio*, which was the tasting of the Wine, and besprinkling thereof upon the beasts head; this done, the hairs between the horns of the beast being pluckt out, were flung into the fire, this they called *Libamina prima*. Then the beast was killed, the blood received in Vessels, and in the Intrails searched, at last the beast is cut in pieces, one piece was wrapped in Meal, and then burned on the Altar; this was called *Litare*. After this they went to Feasting, Singing, and Dancing: Now every particular god had his sacrifice; white beasts were sacrificed to their supernal gods, black to the infernal. The Bull was the proper sacrifice of *Jupiter, Neptune, Mars, Apollo, Luna,* and the *Heroes*. The Ram was sacrificed to *Mars* and the *Heroes*. Wine was offered to *Ceres* and *Liber*. The Goat to *Æsculapius* and *Liber*. Milk and Honey to *Ceres*. A Horse to *Sol* and *Mars*. A Lamb to *Juno* and *Faunus*. A Dove to *Venus*. A Doe to *Pan* and *Minerva*. A Hind to *Diana*. A Hog to *Sylva-* Of these *nus.* A Cock to the *Lares*. A Sow to *Cybele*, and a Sow to *Ceres*. particulars A Hen to *Æsculapius*, and a Child to *Saturn*, &c. But this last was see *Servi-* abolished by the *Romans*. To each god also they assigned his par- *us on Vir-* ticular Bird. The Eagle to *Jupiter*. The Cock to the Sun. The *gil, Rosinus,* Magpie to *Mars*. The Raven to *Apollo*, &c. They had also their *Alex. ab* peculiar Trees. *Jupiter* the Oak. *Pallas* the Olive. *Venus* the *Alex. and* Mirtle. *Pluto* the Cypress. *Bacchus* the Vine. *Hercules* the Pop- the Latin lar. *Apollo* the Lawrel, &c. Poets.

Q. *What Religious Rites did the* Romans *use in their Marriages?*
A. In their Marriages they used Prayers, in which they called *Their Mar-* upon the chief Wedding gods, to wit, *Jupiter, Juno, Venus, Dia- riage-Rites na,* and *Pytho,* or *Suadela*. Before they married, they consulted with their *Auspices*; who encouraged, or discouraged them, according to the Birds they saw; the best *Auspicium* was either two Crows, or two Turtles; these signified long and true love; but to see one of these alone was ominous. After this sight they went to their prayers, and in the Temple before the Altar, were married, first sacrificing a Hog to *Juno, Cui Vincla jugalia curæ,* for she had the chief care of marriages: The gall of the sacrifices the Priests flung

flung away, to shew there should be no gall in a married life. They must not marry upon unlucky days; such were the days after the *Calends*, *Nones*, and *Ides*; these were called *dies atri*, or black days; such a day was that which was kept in memory of *Remus*, killed by his brother, called *Lemuria* or *Remulia*. Neither must they marry on Funeral-days, nor on Festivals, nor when there was any Earth-quake, or Thunder, or stormy weather, no such commotions must be in marriages. The Bride was besprinkled with water, to signifie her purity, and in the Entry or Porch, she must touch the fire and water, placed to shew she must pass through all difficulties with her Husband. In the Wedding-chamber were placed certain Deities, or rather Idols, to shew what was to be done in that place; these were *Virginensis*, *Subjugus*, *Prema*, *Partunda*, *Manturna*, *Venus* and *Priapus*. Their other Rites, which were rather politick than religious, I touch not, as not being to my purpose.

See Scaliger de re Poetica, Alex. ab Alex. Rosinus, Servius, Del Rio in Senecam, &c.

Q. *What were their religious Rites in Funerals?*
A. The Corps was wont to be washed, anointed, crowned by the Priest, and placed in the porch of his house, with a Cypress tree before it. Every thing that was to be employed in the Funeral was to be bought in the Temple of *Venus Libitina*, to shew that the same Deity which brought us into the world, carrieth us out of it. The eyes of the dead bodies were closed upon the going out of the breath, but opened again in the Funeral Pile, that by looking towards Heaven, they might signifie the soul was gone thither; which also they express by the flying of the Eagle out of the same pile where the Emperors body was burned. The place for the burial was appointed by the *Pontifices* and *Augures*. Before the pile were wont to be sacrificed Captives, to pacifie the infernal ghosts: But this being held too cruel, Gladiators were appointed to fight; and for want of these, Women were appointed to tear their cheeks; but this custom was forbid by the Law of the twelve Tables. The Priests after the fire was burned, gathered the bones and ashes, washed them with wine, put them in an Urn, and besprinkled the people three times with Holy-water. For the number of three was sacred; so was seven and nine: therefore upon those days they used to keep festivals in memory of the dead. Altars adorned with Cypress boughs, and blue Laces, were wont to be erected to the Ghosts, and on them Frankincense, Wine, Oyl, and Blood.

Their Funeral Rites.

Of these and other customs see Virgil, and Servius on him: Kirchmanus, also Rosinus, Rhodiginus Alex. ab Alex. Gyraldus, and others.

Q. *Why was the burying of the dead held an act of Religion?*
A. Because it was held an act of justice and mercy both to bury the dead: of justice, that earth should be restored to earth, and dust to dust; for what could be more just, then to restore to mother earth her children, that as she furnished them at first with a material being, with food, raiment, sustentation, and all things needful, so she might at last receive them again into her lap, and, afford them lodging till the Resurrection, whereof some of the wiser Gentiles were not ignorant. It was also an act of mercy to hide the dead

Burial of the dead, an act of justice and mercy.

dead bodies in the earth, that those organs of such a divine soul might not be torn by wild beasts and birds and buried in their maws. That disconsolate mother of *Euryalus* in the Poet, is not so much grieved for the murthering of her Son, as for that he should be made a prey to the birds and beasts.

Heu terrâ ignota, canibus data præda Latinis   Æn. l. 9.
Alitibusque jaces.

It was held among the Egyptians one of the greatest punishments that could be inflicted, to want the honour of burial: and with this punishment *Jehoiakim* the son of *Josiah* is threatned, *Jer.* 22. 19. that he should be buried with the burial of an Ass, and cast forth beyond the gates of *Jerusalem*. And the Milesian Virgins were terrified from hanging themselves by the Law of their Senate, that such self-murderers should have their bodies dragged naked through the streets in the same rope wherewith they hanged themselves. *Mezentius*, in the Poet, doth not desire *Æneas* to spare his life, but earnestly intreats to afford him burial.

Nullum in cæde nefas, nec sic in prælia veni ;   Æn. l. 10.
Unum hoc per (siqua est victis venia hostibus) oro
Corpus humo patiare tegi, &c.

So *Turnus* intreats for the same favour from *Æneas, Si corpus spoliavi lumine mavis, Redde meis,* Æn. 12. The right of Sepulture hath been held so sacred among all civil Nations of the Gentiles, that the violation thereof hath by their Laws been counted Sacrilege. Therefore they have ascribed to their gods the patronage of Funerals and Sepultures: for this cause they called the law of interring, the law of their gods, νόμον δαιμόνων. *Isocrates* in *Panathenaico* sheweth that the right of Sepulture is not so much humane as divine: ἐκ ὡς ὑπ' ἀνθρωπίνης κείμενον φύσεως, 'ἀλλ' ὡς ὑπὸ δαιμονίας προςτεταγμένον δυνάμεως. The burying of the dead is commended by the Pagan Writers as a work of humanity, mercy, clemency, piety, justice and religion; therefore the Latin phrase yet doth intimate how just a thing it is to bury the dead, when they call Funerel Deities, *justa exequiarum,* or *justa funebria*. We read in *Homer, Iliad.* 24. how angry *Jupiter* and *Apollo* were with *Achilles* for abusing and neglecting to bury the body of *Hector*: shewing, that *Achilles* had lost all mercy and modesty: ἔλεον μὲν ἀπώλεσεν ἰδὲ οἱ αἰδὼς γίνεται, &c. And to shew how religious an act it is to bury the dead, the Gentiles assign the care of Funerals and Sepultures to certain gods, which they called *Manes*, whose chief was *Pluto*, called therefore *Summanus:* hence all Tombs and Monuments were dedicated *Diis Manibus;* and therefore they who offered any violence to Tombs, were said to violate the *Manes ; Deorum Manium jura sancta sunto.* Of this you may see more in our *Mystagogus Poeticus.* It was counted an execrable thing, if any should light upon a dead body unburied, and not cast earth upon it; therefore the high Priest among the Jews, albeit he was not to be present at any funeral, yet if by chance he found a dead corps, he was to bury it himself. And so careful were the Jews

in

in this duty, that the bodies of Malefactors were to be buried after Sun-set. Horace brings in the dead corps, promising a reward from *Jupiter* to him that should cast some earth upon it. *Multaque merces unde potest tibi defluat aquo ab Jove*, *Neptunoque*: but if he refuse to do this work of humanity, *piacula nulla resolvent*, no sacrifice should be able to expiate his crime. And to make men more careful of this last duty to the defunct, the Poets feigned that the souls of those dead bodies which lay unburied, did wander up and down an hundred years without any rest, neither were they admitted into πύλας 'Αΐδαο, as *Homer* speaks, that is, the gates of *Pluto*; nor where they received by *Charon* over the River *Styx* (as *Virgil* sings) till the bodies be interr'd.

Nec ripas datur horrendas, nec rauca fluenta
Transportare prius quàm sedibus ossa quierunt.

Hence is that *Patroclus*, in *Homer*, doth so earnestly sollicite *Achilles* to bury him: the like earnest suit doth *Palinurus* in *Virgil* put up to *Æneas* for the same favour. And because want of burial was counted one of the greatest disgraces and punishments that could be inflicted on the dead, therefore self-murderers were debarred from the honour of interment, which as the Poet saith, *Est solus honos Acheronte sub imo.*

Q. Of what Religion were the Græcians?

Greeks and Gentiles, their Religions and gods.

A. They and the Romans differed little in their superstitions. The Romans worshipped twenty principal gods, the *Græcians* but twelve of them; to wit, *Jupiter*, *Saturn*, *Bacchus*, *Apollo*, *Mars*, *Minerva*, *Diana*, *Venus*, and *Juno*, *Ceres*, *Mercurius*, *Vulcan*; their Altar was called Βωμὸς τ̃ δώδεκα Θεῶν, The Altar of the twelve gods; but indeed *Neptune*, *Hercules*, *Proserpina*, and others, were in no less esteem among them. By these gods they were wont to swear; and as the *Romans*, so did they make Deities of the Creatures, of passions, of accidents, and of their own ignorance, in erecting an Altar to the unknown God, Θεῷ 'Αγνώςῳ, *Acts* 17. Their chief god was *Jupiter*, whom they call the Father and King of gods; so *Homer* often. Him they acknowledged their Deliverer, their Counsellor, their Law-giver, and Defender of their Towns: hence these Epithets of 'Ελάθειος, Βυλαῖος, Νόμιος, πολιῆχος, μητίετα. that is, a Councellor, often in *Homer*; ὕπατος κρειόντων, the chief Commander, or Ruler of the World; so *Virgil*:

Qui res hominumque Deûmque
Æternis regit imperiis.

But yet *Homer* is permitted to abuse the supream God with the Title of an adulterer, and of an impotent god, who was subject to the Fates, and bound by the other gods till *Thetis* loosed him. He makes him also false in his promises to *Agamemnon*, a laughing stock to *Juno* and *Minerva*, a slave to Love, subject to sleep, a makebate among the other gods. So that albeit both the Greeks and Romans worshipped the same *Jupiter*, yet the Romans being a wiser people, spake always reverently of him, as may be seen in the Prince of Poets, *Virgil* triumphant, who in this respect, as in many

many other cases is to be preferred before *Homer*, as I have shewed elsewhere. Their next god was *Apollo*, or the Sun, whom they made the chief god of Shepherds: as they armed *Jupiter* with thunder, so they did *Apollo* with his silver bow: therefore called ἀργυρότοξ۰, by *Homer*. They made him the Author of Divination: Hence his Oracles were famous every where. They that died suddenly, were said to be killed by him: they made him also the god of Musick and Physick. He was called *Alexicacus* and *Apotropaius*, that is, a Deliverer from, or a turner away of evil. The mysteries of these things we have unfolded elsewhere, in *Mystagogo Poetico*. He had a rich Temple at *Delphos*, beautified with much gold, therefore called *Pindarus* πολύχρυσον, and he from his golden bow, χρυσότοξ۰. He invented the Cythron, and *Mercury* the Harp: they were therefore worshipped both upon one Altar. *Apollo* from his sight and knowledge of all things, was called σκοπός. *Mercury* was worshipped as the god of Musick also, and of Merchandizing. He had the charge of Wrestlers: therefore was called ἐναγώνι۰: and because with his rod he used to conduct the souls to and from Hell, he was named πομπαῖ۰. He was also the Messenger and Herauld of the gods: and because he had the charge of doors, to keep them from thieves, he was called προπύλαιος: and from the invention of four useful Arts, to wit, Letters, Musick, Wrestling, and Geometry, he was called τετράγωνος, four square, and so was his statue. *Homer* calls him ἄγγελον ἀθανάτων, the Angel of the gods. And the Greek Epigrammatist names him ὑπηρέτην, the servant of the gods: and ἐπίσκοπον, the Bishop of Wrestlers. But this god was a notable thief, for he stole from *Jupiter* his Scepter: from *Neptune* his Trident: from *Mars* his Sword: from *Venus* her Girdle: from *Vulcan* his Tongs.

See the Greek Poets and their Interpreters.

Q. *What were their other chief gods whom they worshipped?*

A. *Saturn*, a cruel god, who both devoured his own children, and could not be pacified but by the sacrificing of Infants. In honour of him, they kept the feast called κρόνια, *Saturnals*; and afterwards the Romans worshipped him bare-headed; but the other gods with their heads covered. He was bound by *Jupiter* for his injustice, and thrust down to Hell; and yet they hold his government most happy, and under him the golden Age. He found out the use of the Sithe or Pruning hook, with which he is painted; and taught the Italians husbandry, for which he was highly honoured by them. From him, not only the *Capitol* was called *Saturnius*, but also the whole Country of *Italy*, *Saturnia Tellus*. *Bacchus* or *Liber*, by the Greeks called *Lyæus*, *Dionysius*, *Bromius*, was a great god amongst them, and worshipped with *Ceres* upon the same Altar; therefore *Pindarus* calls him πάρεδρον Δαμάτερος, the assessor of *Ceres*. He was called Νυκτίλι۰, from his Night-sacrifices; ἀγλαιόμορφος, from his beauty; and μυριόμορφος, from his different shapes; for sometimes he was a goat, sometimes a man, and sometimes a bull, to shew the different disposition of drunkards. They called him δίγονον, because twice born; first of *Semele*, then of *Jupiter*. Κισσοστέφανον, crowned with Ivy, and a multitude more of such Epithets they give him, as may be seen in the Greek Epigrammatist. His feasts or *Bacchanals*, were so full of disorder, riot, immodesty, and madness, that the Senate ordered this Greek feast should not be used in *Rome* or *Italy*. *Mars* for his hard armour and hard heart, and brazen face, was called by the Greeks, χάλκιΘ-; and by *Pindarus*, χαλκάρματος, carried in a brazen Chariot. *Homer* calls him ὠκύτατον, the swiftest of all the gods. Yet was over-reached by *Vulcan* the slowest, to let us see that strength is overcome many times by Policy; he was married to *Venus*; for souldiery, and venery are seldom separate. He is by *Homer* joyned with *Minerva*; Arts and Arms do meet together; he was a great god among the Grecians, but greater among the Romans, to whom they dedicated Priests, Feasts, and divers Temples, not only for being their tutelar god, but also because he was *Romulus* his Father; this mad god, for so he is called by *Homer*, μαινόμνΘ-, was wounded by *Diomedes*; and he is termed their ἀλλοπρόσαλλΘ- inconstant, mutable, false, and treacherous. A brave god! miserable is that Country where this god domineers, whose greatest enemies are *Jupiter* and *Minerva*; that is, peaceable Princes, and wise Councellours.

Of these see the Greek and Latine Poets.

Q. *What were* Minerva, Diana, *and* Venus?

A. These were also *Grecian* deities. *Minerva* was the *Athenian* chief goddess, from whom they were named *Athenians*. Her Festivals were called *Panathenæi*, and her chief Temple *Parthenium*; for she from her perpetual cœlibate was stiled παρθένΘ-. She hath the next place in Heaven, among the gods, to *Jupiter*, and wears his arms and target called *Ægis*, to shew that King's should never be without wise and learned men, next to them. When she came out of *Jupiter*'s brain, she made a noise brandishing with her Spear, at which mortals were affrighted; therefore she is called ἐγχέσιμος, and *Pallas*; the wisdom of a Governour being expressed either by his words or actions, keeps the people in awe, she had her *Palladium* at *Athens*, as well as at *Troy*, and at *Rome* had divers Temples called *Minervia*. *Diana* the sister of *Apollo* was worshipped by the *Greeks* in the habit of a woman armed with a Bow and Arrows. So she was afterward by the *Romans*, to whom they erected divers Temples, the chiefest whereof was upon the hill *Aventine*. She is called by *Pindarus* ἱππόσοιν a horse-driver; for by her they understood the Moon, to which they assigned horses, to signifie her motion, and anciently a golden Chariot drawn by white hindes; from her delight she took in arrows, she is called by the same Poet ἰοχέαιρα, by which are meant her beams; she was painted also with a Torch in her hand, as *Hecate* is always, to shew that she and *Hecate* was all one; and by this Torch was meant her light; she was also the same with *Proserpine*, and is called *Triformis* from the Moon's three different shapes: but she was a cruel goddess, who would not be satisfied without humane sacrifices; in *Arcadia* she was worshipped in the form of a Virgin, covered with a hindes skin, having a Torch in one hand, two Serpents in the other, and on

Greeks, their gods, how worshipped and painted.

her shoulders her bow and quiver. Of these mysteries I have written sufficiently in *Myst. Poet.* *Venus* was worshipped in armour by the *Lacedæmonians,* because she overcame *Mars,* her worship consisted in Flowers and Frankincense. She was sometimes placed upon the same Altar with *Mercury,* to shew how well Beauty and Eloquence agree. She was had in honour more in *Rome* than in *Greece,* because from her, as being the mother of *Æneas,* the *Romans* deduced their Original; therefore she was honoured with many Temples at *Rome*; she was the chief deity that was worshipped by the women: Harlots honoured her for gain; honest Virgins for Beauty; Matrons for concord with their husbands; Widows for new Husbands; and all for Fecundity: she being held the author of all these. She was painted in a Chariot drawn sometimes with Doves, sometimes with white Swans; she was crowned with Mirtle and Roses; she was begot of the Sea froth. All which express to us the qualities of love.

See *Pausanias, Capel-la, Bocca-tius, &c.*

Q. *How were* Juno, Ceres, *and* Vulcan *worshipped by the* Greeks?
A. At *Corinth,* *Juno* was worshipped in the habit of a Queen, with a Crown on her head, on which were carved the Graces and the hours, sitting in a throne of gold, and white Ivory; having in one hand a Pomegranate, and in the other a Scepter with an Owl on the top thereof. By *Juno* they mean the Moon; therefore her Statue and Throne were of white materials. Hence *Homer* calls her λдυκώλενον having white arms. The Moon is Queen of the night, therefore she hath her Crown, Throne, and Scepter; the Owl being a night bird, was fitly dedicated to her that was Lady of the night. She was the goddess of riches and fecundity, and the same with *Lucina*: therefore she hath the Promegranate, a Symbol of plenty; as she is the Moon, the hours attend her; as the giver of riches, the Graces; for bounty and good turns require thanks. In some *Græcian* Temples her Image is drawn by Peacocks, to shew that pride and wealth go together, and that rich people delight in gaudy and glorious apparel. At *Argos* she was worshipped with Vine branches about her, treading on a Lions skin, in contempt of *Bacchus,* and *Hercules,* *Jupiter's* two bastards; the one glorying for finding the use of Wine, the other for killing the Lion. *Juno* was called τελεία perfection, because she had the charge of marriage, in which mans perfection consisteth, and ὁμόφρων as being *Jupiter's* wife and sister; her sacrifices in *Greece* were *Hecatombæa,* a 100. beasts: at *Rome,* she was honoured with divers Names, Temples and Sacrifices; the *Calends* of every month were dedicated to her, and her solemnities were kept in *February.* *Ceres* was worshipped in a Chariot drawn by two Dragons, with Poppy heads in one hand, and a burning Torch in the other, with a sheaf of Corn on her head. What all these meant, we have shewed elsewhere. The secret or mystical sacrifices of *Ceres Eleusina,* were not to be divulged; for no profane person was to be admitted to them; for the Priest going before uttereth these words, ἕκας ἕκας ὅστις ἀλιτρός. The *Roman* Priests proclaiming the same in

'their tongue, *Procul procul este profani*. The *Arcadians* did so honour *Ceres* and *Proserpina*, that in their Temples they kept fires perpetually burning. In her sacrifices Hogs were offered, but no Wine. The Priests of *Ceres* were called μέλισσαι, that is, Bees, to shew both their diligence, purity and chastity. She was worshipped also at *Rome*, where she had her Priests and Temples, and great solemnities in *April*, called *Ludi Cereales*. In *Vulcan*'s Sacrifices a Torch was lighted, and delivered from one to another, to signifie, that the Torch of our life is imparted from the father to the son by generation. He was worshipped in the form of a lame man, with a blue cap, to shew us the nature of the fire whereof he was god. At *Rome* he was also worshipped, but his Temple was built by *Romulus* without the City, because *Mars* his corrival had his Temple within the City, of which he was the tutelar god.

See Cartarius, Martianus Capella, Scaliger, Spandanus, &c.

Q. *Did the* Greeks *and* Romans *worship these gods only?*

A. Yes, innumerable more; or rather the same deities above named under other names: for *Apollo, Phœbus, Sol, Æsculapius, Jupiter, Liber, Hercules, Mars, Mercurius, Pan,* &c. are different names of one and the same Sun, which was the chief god worshipped among the Gentiles. *Luna, Hecate, Diana, Juno, Lucina, Venus, Ceres,* &c. do signifie the Moon. *Vesta, Ops, Cybele, Rhea, Ceres, Berecynthia, Magna Mater, Tellus, Pales, Flora, Fauna, Bona Dea, Proserpina,* &c. do signifie the Earth, and the benefits we receive thence. *Neptune, Nereus, Glaucus, Proteus, Triton, Consus, Oceanus,* &c. signifie the Sea. *Pluto, Plutus, Proserpina, Charon, Cerberus,* &c. are but different names of one and the same infernal deity. And as the same god had different names, so he had different sorts of worship; for the Sun, under the name of *Apollo*, was worshipped in the form of a beardless youth, with yellow hair, carrying in one hand a Cythron, in the other Arrows and his Bow. As *Sol*, he was honoured in a flaming ship full of rich waters, carried about the world, by which light is imparted to all. As *Phœbus*, he was adored in a golden Chariot drawn by four horses swift and fiery, in one hand he holdeth a glittering Target, in the other a burning Torch, on his head a golden Crown beset with twelve precious Stones. As *Æsculapius*, he is set forth sitting in a Chair, in the habit of a grave man with a long beard, crowned with Bayes, holding in one hand a knobbed staff, and with the other leaning on a Serpents head. Sometimes he is described with two Cocks in his hand, and certain fruits and herbs in his lap, by which the properties of Physicians are represented; for the Sun is the great Physician. As *Jupiter*, he was worshipped sitting in a Throne, with a Scepter in one hand, and an Eagle in the other, by which was expressed his power and dominion. As *Bacchus* or *Liber*, he was set out like a naked youth, with horns on his head, a Crown of Ivy, and sometimes of fig-leaves, with the *Thyrsus* or Vine-spear in his hand, sitting in a Chariot drawn by Tygers, and Panthers. Which may signifie both the power, influence and raging heat of the Sun. As *Hercules*, they honoured him clothed with a Lions Skin, Crown'd with

Sect. 4.   *of* EUROPE.   101

with Poplar leaves, and the Club in his hand knocking down the Hydra. We have shewed the meaning of these in *Myſtagog. Poetic.* and that the Sun's courses through the Twelve Signs were adumbrated by *Hercules* his twelve labours. As *Mars*, he was adored with a Helmet on his head, a Spear in one hand, and a Bow in the other. As *Mercury*, he was worshipped like a young man on a square stone, having wings on his head, and on his feet, with a Sword in his hand killing many-eyed-*Argus*: by which was meant the Sun's perpetual vigour, in that he was resembled by a Youth; the Wings shewed his swiftness, the Square-stone the four seasons of the Year, or four Climates of the World. His killing of *Argus* shewed the confounding of the Star light by the Sun's presence. As *Pan* he was expressed and adored under the form of a Satyr, with a red face, long beard, horns on his head, a spotted skin about him, having in one hand a Pipe, in the other a Shepherds staff; his beard and horns signified his beams; his speckled skin, the Heaven speckled with Stars; the Pipe, the harmony of his motion; and the staff, his power. Much more might be said of this subject.

But see the Mythologo-gifts, and what we have written in Myſtag. Poetic.

Q. *Under what names and shapes did they worship the Moon?*

A. As *Hecate* she was worshipped under the shape of a monster with three heads, by which they signified the Moon's threefold form she assumes, according to her access and recess to and from the Sun. As *Luna* at her first appearance, she was honoured with white and golden garments, and a burning Torch, to shew the increasing of her light; when she was half full, with a Basket of Fruit, to shew how the fruits fill and grow with her: but when she was at full, with a dark coloured garment, to signifie the decreasing of her light. As *Diana*, she was worshipped in the habit of a woman, with a torch flaming in one hand, two snakes in the other, a bow and arrows on her shoulders, sitting in a Chariot drawn with white Deer, all which signified partly her light, and partly her motion. Her light is a help to hunters: therefore she was worshipped in the habit of a hunter. As *Juno* she was honoured in the ornaments of a Queen, sitting in a chariot of brass, silver and gold, which signified both her light, beauty and dominion over the night. As *Lucina*, she was crowned with the herb *Dictamnus*, or Dittany, which is good for Women in labour: and a burning torch in her hand, to shew the hot fits, and sharp pains of Child-bearing Women, upon which the Moon hath great power. As *Venus*, she was resembled by a beautiful Woman naked, crowned with Roses, and rising out of the Sea, by which they signified the light and beauty of the Moon, when she ariseth. As *Ceres*, she was represented by a Matron with a sheaf of Corn on her head, and a Lamp in her hand, to shew, that from her proceeds both light and plenty.

Moon, how worshipped.

Q. *What names and worship did they give to the Earth and Fire?*

A. They were called *Veſta*; and under that name worshipped in the habit of a Virgin, sitting on the ground, and crowned with white Garlands, whose Temple was built round, and in it a perpetual red.

Earth and Fire how worshipped.

H 3

petual fire kept by the Nuns of *Vesta*. These two Elements were joyned together, because fire is begot, both in, and of the Earth. The Virgins habit signified the purity of the Fire; her sitting, the immobility of the Earth; the white Garlands, the purity of the Air or Firmament, compassing the Earth and Fire; the roundness of the Temple shewed the rotundity of the Earth. The Earth also was called *Rhea, Ceres, Berecynthia, Magna Mater, Cybele, Ops*, &c. She is called *Vesta à Vestiendo*, because she is clothed with herbs, grass and trees: *Rhea*, from ῥέειν, to flow; because waters are still flowing in and upon her. *Ceres*, or *Geres*, from Corn-bearing, and supporting all things. *Berecynthia*, from the Hill *Berecynthus* in *Phrygia*, where she was worshipped. The Great Mother, because she generally nourishes and maintains all earthly creatures. *Cybele*, from κύβος, a Cube, to shew the stability of the Earth. *Ops*, from the help we have by her. *Proserpina à serpendo*, from the creeping things within her, and from the herbs which creep out of her. *Tellus*, from *Terra*, the Earth, which was worshipped in the habit of an old Woman, with Towers on her head, having in one hand a Scepter, in the other a Key; clothed in a garment embroidered with herbs, flowers and trees, and sitting in a Chariot drawn with Lions, to shew, that the Earth supporteth all Towers and Castles, produceth all herbs and trees; is the predominant Element in compounded bodies, signified by the Crown, Key, and Scepter: the motion of her Chariot on four wheels, signifieth the motion, not of the Earth, but of her Inhabitants in the four seasons of the year; the Lions, and all earthly creatures, though never so strong and fierce, are subject to the Laws of terrestrial nature. Of the manner how *Ceres* was painted and worshipped we have said already. By *Proserpina*, they meant the Earth, as she is fruitful, and cherisheth the seeds cast into her. For this cause she is called *Bona Dea*, from the many good things she affords us; and *Faunia à Favendo*, from favouring and cherishing us. *Pomona*, from the fruits; and *Flora*, from the Flowers she produceth: and *Pales*, as she furnisheth fodder to the cattel: therefore she was held the goddess of *See the* Shepherds, and her Feasts *Palilia*, were kept without shedding of *Mythologist.* blood; then were the Cattel purified with Sulphur, Rosemary, Savin, and Bayes, and made to pass through flames of Stubble and Hay.

Q. *What worship had the Deity of the Sea?*

Sea how A. He was called *Neptune*, and worshipped in the form of an an-
worshipped. cient Man, with a Crown on his head, holding his Trident in one hand, and embracing his Wife *Amphitrite* with the other. Between his legs was a Dolphin. His Chariot drawn with Horses. The Sea's swift motion was represented by the Dolphin and Horses; and its Dominion over all other waters, by the Crown and Scepter. He was called *Consus*, from Council; to shew, that Princes Counsels should be hid, as the cause of the ebbing and flowing of the Sea is. He was called *Neptunus à Nubendo*, from covering the Earth. *Nereus*, and his Wife *Thetis*, were Sea Deities, and indeed the

Sect. 4. *of* EUROPE.

the same with *Neptune*; so was *Oceanus*, whose Chariot was drawn by four Whales: *Proteus* is also the same, though those are held by most to be different gods, yet in effect all is but one and the same deity; so were the *Tritons* and *Nereids*, though these, with the *Sirenes*, are thought by some to be Monstrous Fishes. The *Tritons* of all were counted *Neptune*'s Trumpeters, to shew the noise and roaring these we of the Sea. Old *Glaucus* is also the same Sea god with the rest; have spoken who is described and worshipped in the form of an old Man, with ken fullong hair and Beard dropping with water, his breast beset with ly in Sea-oars, and below the Navel like a Fish. *Mystagogo Poetico.*

Q. *What worship and names did they give to Death?*

A. Death was held a Deity, and worshipped under the name of Death how *Pluto*, or *Plutus*, sitting in a dark Throne, with a black Ebony *worshipped.* Crown on his head, a Rod in one hand, to drive together the dead Bodies, and a Key in the other, to lock them in. At his feet was placed the Three-headed-Dog *Cerberus*, all which was, to shew the condition of the Dead. The Cypress-tree stood always by him; he was called ἀγυιλαῶ, from gathering, or driving people together. Death is the great King of darkness, who drives all Men, rich and poor, wise and fools, Kings and beggars into one place; *omnes eodem cogimur.* Death is called *Cerberus*, that is, a devourer of flesh: For it consumes all flesh. This is the black dog, as *Seneca* calls him, which is still barking at, and biting of Mortals; he is called *Bellua centiceps* by *Horace*, the Hundred-headed-Beast; for death hath a hundred ways to seize upon us: The same death is expressed by *Charon* to some, by *Acheron* to others; for to good Men who Of these depart hence with a clear Conscience, death is comfortable; but *things see* to the Wicked, whom the furies of an evil Conscience do torment, *more in* Death is terrible and comfortless, expressed by the word *Ache-* Mystag. *ron.* *Poet.*

Q. *What was the manner of Sacrificing in* Greece?

A. None came near the Altar till they were first purified, neither Greeks, must the Sacrifice be laid on the Altar, till it was also lustrated or *their sacri-* purified with Meal and holy water, called χέρνιψ. The standers- *ficing.* by were besprinkled with this water, after a Fire-brand taken from the Altar had been quenched in it, and then some holy flower or meal was cast on them. This done, the Priest prayed, then the Victim was brought to the Altar, with the head upward, if it was dedicated to the superiour gods; but if to the inferiour, with his head downward. The Fat, Heart, Spleen, and Liver, were offered to the gods; the rest of the Beast was eat up by the Priests and People, spending the rest of the day in gormandizing and drunkenness. When the *Greeks* sacrificed to *Vesta*, and the *Romans* to the *Lares*, they left nothing of the Sacrifice; hence *Lari sacrificare & Θυῆν Ἑστίᾳ*, was to eat up all. The poorer sort offered δυλήματα, that is, Meat or Cakes, the same with the *Roman Mola*, which, by the richer sort was mingled with Wine and Oyl. These frugal sacrifices are called by *Pindarus* λιταὶ θυσίαι, supplicating sacrifices, intimating, that there is more devotion in these mean sacrifices, than

H 4 many

many times in those that are most costly; for it is not the sacrifice, but the heart of the sacrificer God requires. They used to try if their Victim would prove acceptable to their Gods, by putting the Cake on the head between the Horns, which were in solemn feasts gilded; if the beast stood quiet, it was fit to be sacrificed; if otherwise, it was rejected. In all sacrifices *Vesta* was first invocated ἀπ' Ἑστίας ἄρχου, to shew both the antiquity and necessity of fire in sacrificing. Their custom also was to sacrifice in the morning to the Gods, in the evening to the *Heroes*, or Demi-gods. The *Greeks* did not as the *Romans*, grind the Corn which they laid on the head of the Victim, but laid it on whole, ὅτι σύμβολον τῆς παλαιᾶς τροφῆς, saith *Suidas*, to shew the manner of the ancient Feeding, before the grinding of Corn was invented. This whole Corn was called ὖλαι. They were wont also after their sacrifice and feast, to burn the Tongue of the Beast, and besprinkle it with Wine, as *Homer* sheweth, γλώσσας δ' ἐν πυρὶ βάλλον ἀνιστάμενοι δ' ἐπέλειβον: This was to shew, that after Drinking and Feasting, the Tongue should be silent: and nothing divulged what was then spoken. This was also done in honour of *Mercury* the God of Eloquence and of Sleep; for about sleeping-time the Tongue was sacrificed. The *Grœcian* Priests used to dance or run about the Altars, beginning first at the Left hand, to shew the motion of the Zodiack, which is from the West, called by Astronomers the left-part of the World: then they danced, beginning at the right-hand, to shew the motion of the first Sphear, which is from East to West. Their bloody sacrifices were called impure; but Frankincense, Myrrh, and such like, were named by them, ἁγνὰ θύματα, pure offerings. The flesh of the Victims were called *Theothyta*, but by the Christian Doctors *Idolothyta*. They that gathered the consecrated Corn were named *Parasiti*. They that met to sacrifice were called *Orgeones*, from ὀργιάζειν, to sacrifice. *Phylothytæ* were those who superstitiously, upon all occasions, were given to sacrifice. Sacred Feasts were called θοίνα, from Θεὸς, and οἶνΘ-, because much Wine was drunk to the honour of the Gods; and therefore μεθύειν is to be drunk, because they used to be drunk μετὰ τὸ θύειν, after they had sacrificed. The burning of Incense, or such like, before the Sacrifice, were called *Prothymata*.

See *Suidas*, *Eustathius*, *Rhodiginus*, *Albinæus*, &c.

Q. *What Priests and Temples had the Ancient* Greeks?

Their Priests and Temples.

A. As they had multiplicity of Gods, so they had of Priests anciently. The Priests of *Jupiter* and *Apollo* were young Boys, beautiful and well-born. The Priests of *Cybele* were gelded; *Ceres*, *Bona Dea*, and *Bacchus* had their Women-Priests. *Bellona*'s Priests used to sacrifice with their own blood. The *Athenian* Priests, called *Hierophantæ*, used to eat Hemlock, or Cicuta, to make them impotent towards Women. No man was made a Priest who had any blemish in his body. Their Garments and Shooes were white, if they were the Priests of *Ceres*. Purity was the chief thing they observed outwardly. They that sacrificed to the Infernal Gods, wore Black Garments, but Purple if they were the Priests of the

Celestial

Celestial Deities. They used also to wear Crowns or Myters, with Ribbands, or Laces. Their office was not only to Pray and Sacrifice, but also to purifie with Brimstone and Salt-water. Their Chief-Priests, called *Hierophantæ*, were the same in Authority with the *Pontifices* at *Rome*. The *Athenian* noble Virgins, called κανηφόροι, from bearing on their shoulders the κάνης, which was a basket or chest of Gold, in which the first-fruits and other consecrated things were carried in their *Panathenaian* pomps to the honour of *Minerva*; I say these Virgins did much resemble the Vestal Nuns at *Rome*. The πρέσπολος, or νεωκόρης, was a Bishop, or overseer of the Sacred Mysteries: πυρφόρος was he that attended the Sacred Fire on the Altar; they had their κήρυκες, Criers, or Preachers, and ναοφύλακες, Church-wardens, and other Officers. Now for their Temples. At *Athens*, the Temple of *Minerva* was built in the highest part of the City; so was *Jupiter*'s Temple at *Rome* built in the Capitol. The Temple of Mercy, called *Asylum*, which was a Sanctuary for Delinquents, was erected at *Athens* by the Sons of *Hercules*. *Theseus* had erected one before, called *Theseum*, in imitation of which *Romulus* at *Rome* built such another. At first the Gentile Gods had no Temples at all, but were worshipped either on Hills or in Groves. *Cecrops* was the first (as some think) who built a Temple in *Athens*, and *Janus* in *Italy*. Before that time they had no other Temples, but the Sepulchres and Monuments of the Dead. The Temples of the Celestial Gods were built upon the ground, of the Infernal under. In the Country of *Sparta*, *Jupiter* had a Temple called σκοτιτάς, from the darkness thereof, being obscured with Groves. There was also γῆς ἱερόν, the Chappel of the Earth, and μοιρῶν, the Chappel of the Destinies, the place where they had their Assemblies and Sermons, called σκιάδη. Their Temples were called μέλαθρα, from the black Smoak of their Sacrifices and Incense; ναός, or according to the Attick νεώς, was the general name for Temples, because the Gods dwelt in them; and because they were consecrated and holy, they were named ἱερά. Σηκός was that part of the Temple where the Idol stood, the same with the Latin *Delubrum*; τέμενος, from τέμνειν, to cut or separate, did signifie the Temple, as it was set apart and separated from other buildings. Such honour they gave to their Temples, that they durst not tread on the threshold thereof, but leapt over it; nor must they pass by any Temple without reverence to it: there they kept their Treasures for the more security; Sacrilege being held then an execrable crime, and so it was held an impiety to walk in the Temple of *Apollo Pythius*, and punishable with death by the Law of *Pisistratus*. Hence the Proverb, when any danger was expressed, or impiety, ἐν πυθίῳ κρεῖττον ἦν ἀποπατῆσαι, it had been better you had walked in the *Pythium*; the word also ἀποπατέω signifies easing of the body, which that none might do, the Images of Serpents were set over the gates of Consecrated places; *Pinge duos angues, sacer est locus. extra me ite.* Their matrimonial and funeral Rites were the same with the *Romans*.

But of these passages, see the Scholiast on Aristophanes, Suidas, Pol. Virgil, Cerda on Tertullian, Rhodiginus, Turnebus, and others.

The

The Contents of the Fifth Section.

The Religions of the old Germans, Gauls, *and* Britains. 2. *Of the* Saxons, Danes, Swedes, Moscovites, Russians, Pomeranians, *and their Neighbours.* 3. *Of the* Scythians, Getes, Thracians, Cymbrians, Goths, Lusitanians, *&c.* 4. *Of the* Lithuanians, Polonians, Hungarians, Samogetians, *and their Neighbours.* 5. *Of divers Gentile-gods besides the above-named.* 6. *The Ranks and Arms of their gods.* 7. *With what creatures their Chariots were drawn.* 8. *Of peculiar gods worshipped in peculiar places.* 9. *The Greek chief Festivals.*

SECT. V.

Germans, Gauls, and Britains, their Religions.

Quest. OF what Religion were the Germans, Gauls, and Britains?

Answ. The *Germans* at first had neither Images nor Temples, but abroad worshipped the Sun, Moon, and Stars. Mother *Earth* was in chief esteem among them; to her they dedicated a Chariot in a Grove, which was lawful only for the Priest to touch. He was never to leave the Chariot, which was always covered with Cloth, and was drawn by two Oxen in Procession; then Holy-days were appointed; at the end of her journey, she, with the Chariot and Cloaths were washed in a certain Lake, but the Ministers who performed this work, were never seen any more, but were swallowed by the Lake, and the goddess restored again by her Priest to her Grove. The Ancient *Gauls* worshipped *Mercury* in the first place, as being the god of High-ways, Journies, Gain, and Merchandizing: After him they worshipped *Apollo, Jupiter, Mars,* and *Minerva.* They, and the *Germans,* were wont to sacrifice Men sometimes; so did the ancient *Britains,* which, with the *Gaules,* had the same Religion and Priests, called *Druids,* from the Oaks, under which they used to Teach, and Sacrifice; for they Expounded all Religious Mysteries, taught the youth, decided Controversies and Suits in Law, ordained Rewards and Punishments; and such as obeyed not their Decrees, they Excommunicated, debarring them from all Divine Exercises, and all commerce with Men. These *Druids* had one Chief over them, whose Successor was always elected. They were free from paying Taxes, from serving in the War, and had many other Priviledges. They committed not the Mysteries of their Religion to Writing, but to the memory of their Disciples, who spent many years in learning by heart their Precepts in Verse. They believed the Immortality of Souls, they read

Philosophy to their Scholars: It is thought by some, that *Diana's* Temple stood where St. *Paul's* Church in *London* stands now. And *Minerva* had her Temple at *Bath*, and *Apollo* in *Scotland*, near *Dalkeith*. The *Saxons* worshipped the Seven Planets, among which *Thor*, the same with *Jupiter*, was chief; from him *Thursday* was denominated. The next was *Wodan*, or *Mars*, *Wednesday* is so called from him. *Frea*, or *Frico*, was *Venus*, to whom *Friday* was dedicated, as *Tuesday* to *Tuisco*, the Founder of the *German* Nation.

See *Tacitus*, *Cæsar's* Commentaries, *Camden*, and others.

Q. *Under what shapes and forms did the old Saxons worship their gods?*

A. They worshipped the Sun under the shape of half a naked Man set upon a Pillar, whose head and face was all beset with fiery rayes, holding on his breast a flaming wheel, by which they signified the Suns heat, light, and motion. They worshipped the Moon under the form of a Woman, with a short Coat, and a Hood with long Ears, with the picture of the Moon before her breast; they gave her also piked shooes. *Verstegan* cannot find the reason of this habit; but perhaps the reason may be this, if I may have leave to conjecture; they gave her a short Coat, to shew the swiftness of her motion; for a long coat signifieth a slow motion; therefore they painted *Saturn*, whose motion is the slowest of all the Planets, with a long Coat. The Hood, or Chapron, with long ears, was to represent her horns, or else to shew that sounds are heard afar off in the Night, which is the time of her Dominion. Her piked shooes also may resemble her horns. *Tuisco*, their third Idol, is set out in the skin of some wild Beast, with a Scepter in his hand, this is thought to be the first and most ancient of that Nation, from whom the *Germans* call themselves *Tuytshen*, or (as the *Flemings* pronounce it) *Duytshen*, as *Verstegan* observeth; but I think that under this name they worshipped *Mars*; for, as *Tacitus* Writes, *Mars* was one of the *German* gods. His hairy garments doth shew the fierce and truculent disposition of that Warlike god; besides that, hairy *Sylvanus* is thought to be the same that *Mars*; his Scepter may signifie the power and command which Soldiers have in the World. But it is more likely by this Idol they meant *Mercury*; for, next to the Sun and Moon, he was, as *Tacitus* saith, the *German's* chief god. His Scepter and hairy garment may signifie the power and command that Eloquence and Musick have over the most brutish natures; and of these two faculties *Mercury* was the Inventer. And we must know, that as the *Romans*, next to the Sun and Moon, honoured *Mars* the Patron of their City, for which cause they dedicated to him the third day of the week; so the *Germans*, for the same cause, dedicated to *Mercury*, their chief Founder and Patron, the same day, which, from his Name, *Tuisco*, is called *Tuesday*, yet retained among us. Their fourth Idol was *Woden*, from whom *Wednesday* is so called. He was the *German's Mars*, and is called *Woden*, from being Wood, or Mad, intimating hereby the fierceness of Souldiers, and fury of War. He is

Old Saxons worshipped their gods under divers shapes and forms.

painted

painted with a Crown on his head, a Sword in his hand, and in compleat Armour. Their fifth Idol is *Thor*, which was their *Jupiter*, for they made him the god of the Air, and Commander of Winds, Rain, and Thunder: they painted him sitting in a Chair of State, with a Scepter in his right hand, a golden Crown on his head, encompassed with Twelve Stars, by which they meant that he was King of the upper Regions, and Commander of the Stars: from him *Thursday* is named, as among the *Romans*, *Dies Jovis* from *Jupiter*. Their sixth Idol was *Friga*, from her our Friday is denominated, and was the same that *Venus* among the *Romans*; she is painted in the habit of a Man in Arms, with a Sword in one hand, and a Bow in the other; so among the *Romans*, she was *Venus armata*, and *barbata*, Armed, and Bearded; she is called by the Greeks Θεις, in the *Masculine*, and by *Aristophanes*, ἈφεἰδυῖΘ-, so by *Virgil*, *Deus; descendo .c ducente Deo flammam inter & hostes.* Their seventh Idol was *Seater*, whence comes the name *Saturday*, dedicated to him; *Verstegan* will not have this *Seater* to be the same that *Saturn*, because he was otherwise called *Crodo*, but this is no reason, for most of the gods had different names; the Sun is called *Apollo*, and *Phœbus*; the Moon, *Diana*, *Lucina*, *Proserpina*. The goddess of Wisdom is called *Pallas*, and *Minerva*, &c. Doubtless then this Idol was *Saturn*, as his Picture shews; for he is set out like an old Man, and so he is Painted among the *Romans*; the Wheel in his Left-hand signifieth the Revolution of Time, the Pail of Water in his Right-hand, wherein were Flowers and Fruits, and the Pearch under his Feet, do shew the Dominion Time hath over Sea and Land, and all things therein contained, for all sublunary things are subject to Time and Change. His long Coat, as I shewed before, did signifie the slowness of *Saturn*'s Motion, which is not finished but in 30 years. Other Idols they worshipped, but of less note, of which see *Verstegan*.

Q. *What was the Religion of the* Danes, Swedes, Moscovites, Russians, Pomeranians, *and their Neighbours?*

Danes, Swedes, Muscovites, and their Neighbours their Religions.

A. The *Danes* and *Swedes* worshipped the same gods that the *Saxons* did. They call upon *Thor*, or *Jupiter*, when the Pestilence is among them, because he ruleth in the Air: In the time of War they call upon *Woden*, or *Mars*: In their Marriages they Invocate *Frico*, or *Venus*. They had also their *Heroes*, or Demi-gods; they used to kill nine Males of each kind of sensitive creatures, and to pacifie their Gods with the blood thereof, then to hang up their bodies in the Grove next the Temple, called *Ubsola*. In some parts of *Saxony* they worshipped *Saturn*, under the name of *Crodo*, like an Old Man standing on a Fish, holding in his hand a Wheel and a Pitcher. *Venus* they worshipped in the form of a naked Woman, standing in a Chariot drawn with two Swans, and two Doves. On her head she wore a Garland of Myrtle; in her Right-hand she had the Globe of the World, in the other Three Oranges. Out of her Breast proceeded a burning Taper. The Three *Graces* naked with Fruit in their hands waited on her. In *Westphalia* they worshipped

ped an Idol all in Armour, holding a Banner in his right hand with a Rose, and in the left a pair of Scales. On his breast was carved a Bear, on his Helmet a Lion : It seems by the Idol they understood *Mars*. The *Rugians* near the *Baltick*-Sea worshipped *Mars* in the form of a Monster with seven Faces, and seven Swords hanging by his side in their Scabbards ; he held the eighth sword naked in his hand. The same *Rugians*, as also the *Bohemians*, worshipped an Idol with four heads, two of them looking forward, and two backward ; in its Right-hand it held a Horn, which the Priest every year sprinkled with Wine ; in the Left-hand a Bow : This also seems to be *Mars*. The *Sclavi* adored an Idol standing on a Pillar, with a Plow-share in one hand, a Lance and Banner in the other ; his head was beset with Garlands, his Legs were booted, and at one of his heels a Bell did hang. Some of them did worship an Idol on whose Breast was a Target, in which was ingraven an Oxe head. It had a Pole-axe in its hand, and a little Bird sitting on its head : All these may seem to represent *Mars*. The *Muscovites* and *Russians* adored an Idol called *Perun*, in the shape of a Man holding a burning-stone in his hand, resembling Thunder ; a fire of Oaken-wood was continually maintained burning, to the honour of this Idol : It was death for the Ministers, if they suffered this Fire to go out: It seems this was *Jupiter*'s Image. The *Stetinians* in *Pomerania* worshipped a Three-headed-Idol, and used to ask Oracles, or advice of a Black Horse : the charge of which was committed to one of the Priests. In the Countries about *Muscovia*, they worship an Idol called *Zolata Baba*, the Golden Hag. It is a Statue like an Old Woman holding an Infant in her Bosom, and near to her stands another Infant: To this Idol they offer the Richest Sable Skins they have. They Sacrifice Stags to her, with the blood whereof they anoint her face, eyes, and her other parts : The beasts entrails are devoured raw by the Priests. With this Idol they use to consult in their doubts and dangers.

See *Saxo Grammaticus, Cranzius* on *Vandalia, Olaus, Guaguin*, and other Historians.

Q. *What Religion did the* Scythians, Getes, Thracians, Cymbrians, Goths, Lusitanians, *and other* Europeans *profess* ?

A. The same Gentilism with the rest, adoring Idols of stocks and stones, in stead of the true God, or rather they worshipped the Devil, as appears by their inhumane humane sacrifices. The *Scythians* used to sacrifice every hundred captive to *Mars* : So did the *Thracians*, thinking there was no other means to pacifie that angry and butcherly god, but by murthering of men. Of the same opinion were the old *Germans*, who sacrificed men to *Mercury*. The *Cymbrians* or *Cymerians* by their women-Priests used to murther and sacrifice men. These the devils girt with brass girdles, and in a white surplice, used to cut the throats of the captives, to rip up their bowels, and by inspection to foretell the event of the war, and withal to make drums of their skins. The *Goths* did not think they pleased the Devil sufficiently, except first they had tormented the poor captive by hanging him upon a tree, and then by tearing him

Scythians, Getes, Thracians, Cymbrians, Goths, *&c.* their Religions.

him in pieces among brambles and thorns. These *Goths* or *Getes* believed that the dead went into a pleasant place where their God *Tamolxius* ruled; to him they used still to send a Messenger chosen out among themselves by lot, who in a Boat of five Oars went to supplicate for such things as they wanted. Their manner of sending him was thus; They took him hand and foot, and flung him upon the points of sharp Pikes, if he fell down dead, they concluded that the God was well pleased with that messenger; if otherwise, they rejected him as an unworthy messenger; therefore they chose another to whom they gave instructions before he died, what he should say to their God; and so having slain him upon their Pikes, committed the dead body in the boat to the mercy of the Sea. The *Lithuanians* used to burn their chief captives to their Gods. The *Lusitanians* ripped open the bowels of their captives in their divinations, and presented their right hands, being cut off, to their Gods. The *Sclavi* worshipped an Idol called *Suantovitus*, whose Priest, the day before he sacrificeth, makes clean the Chappel, which none must enter but he alone, and whilst he is in it, he must not draw his breath, but hold his head out of the window, lest with his mortal breath he should pollute the Idol. The next day the people watching without the Chappel door, view the Idols cup; if they find any of the liquor which was put there wasted, they conclude the next years scarcity, but otherwise they hope for plenty; and so they fill the cup again, and pray to the Idol for victory and plenty; then pouring out old Wine at the Idols feet, and offering to him a great Cake, they spend the rest of the day in gormandising. It is held a sin and a dishonour to the Idol not to be drunk then. Every one payeth a piece of money to the Idols maintenance; to which also is paid the third part of all booties taken in the war. To this purpose, the Idol maintained

See *Olaus Magnus, Saxo, Guaguinus, Johannes Magnus, Aventinus*, &c.

three hundred horse, whom the Priest payed, being the Idols treasurer. In *Lithuania, Russia*, and the adjacent places, the Rusticks offer a yearly sacrifice of Calves, Hogs, Sows, Cocks, and Hens, about the end of *October*, when their fruits are all gathered in, to their Idol *Ziemiennick*; they beat all these creatures to death, then offer them with prayers and thanksgiving; which done, they fall to eating and drinking, flinging first pieces of flesh into every corner of the house.

Q. *What did the* Lithuanians, Polonians, Hungarians, Samogetians, *and their Neighbours profess?*

Lithuanians, Polonians, Hungarians, &c. their Religions.

A. Their chief God was the Sun. They worshipped also the Fire, which they continually maintained by Priests chosen for that purpose. They ascribed also Divinity and worship to Trees, and the taller the Tree was, the more adoration it had. When Christianity began to be preached among the *Lithuanians*, and were exhorted to cut their Trees, none would venture to touch these Gods, till the Preachers encouraged them by their example; but when they saw the trees cut down, they began to lament the loss of their gods, and complained to their Prince of the wrong done to

them

them by the Christians, whereupon the Preachers were commanded presently to abandon the country, and so these dogs returned to their vomit. They adored also Serpents, which they entertained in their houses, and used by their Priests to ask Oracles or advice of the Fire, concerning their friends when they fell sick, whether they should recover health again. The same Idolatry was used by the *Polonians* or *Sarmatians*. The *Hungarians* or *Pannonians* did not only worship the Sun, Moon, and Stars; but also every thing they first met with in the morning. Most part of *Livonia* is yet Idolatrous, worshipping the Planets, and observe the heathenish customs in their burials and marriages. In *Samogethia* a country bordering on *Prussia*, *Livonia*, and *Lithuania*, they worshipped for their chief god, the *Fire*, which their Priests continually maintained within a Tower on the top of an high hill, till *Uladislaus* King of *Poland* beat down the Tower, and put out the fire, and withal caused their Groves to be cut down, which they held sacred, with the Birds, Beasts, and every thing in them. They burn the bodies of their chief friends, with their horses, furniture, and best cloaths, and withal set down victuals by their Graves, believing that the departed souls would in the night-time eat and drink there. The like superstition is used by the *Livonians*. So the *Lapponians* are at this day, for the most part, Idolatrous; they hold that no Marriage which is not consecrated by fire and a flint, is lawful, therefore by striking of the flint with iron, they shew that as the like sparks of fire flie out by that union, so children are propagated by the conjunction of male and female. Many parts also of *Muscovia* at this day continue in their Gentilism. *See Olaus, Munster, in his Geography, and others.*

Q. *What other gods did the Gentiles worship, besides those above named?*

A. It were tedious to mention all; I will only name some of them. *Æolus* was god of the Wind, *Portunus* god of Harbours, *Agonius* god of Action, *Angerona* goddess of Squinzes, *Laverna* or *Furina* goddess of Thieves, *Aucula* goddess of maid-servants, *Carna* goddess of hinges, *Aristæus* god of honey, *Diverra* goddess of sweeping, *Feronia* goddess of Woods, *Dice* goddess of Law-suits, *Fidius* of Faith, *Aruneus* of diverting hurt from Corn, *Hebe* of youth, *Meditrina* of Medicines, *Mena* of womens monthly flowers, *Myodes* or *Miagrus*, the same with *Belzebub* the god of Flies, *Limentinus* of thresholds, *Peitho* goddess of Eloquence, *Aius* of speech, *Pecunia* of money, *Thalassius* of marriage, *Vacuna* goddess of leisure or idleness, *Vitula* goddess of youthful wantonness, *Sentinus* of sense, *Tutanus* of defence, *Vallonia* of Vallies, *Vitunus* of life, *Collina* of hills, *Jugatinus* of the tops of mountains. We cannot meet with any creature, action, passion, or accident of mans life, which had not its peculiar deity. *Gods of the Gentiles. Of these see Austin, Tertullian, Lactantius, Plutarch, Arnobius, Eusebius, &c.*

Q. *How did they rank and arm their gods?*

A. Some of them they called Supernal, as *Saturn*, *Jupiter*, *Apollo*, *Mercurius*, *Mars*, *Vulcan*, *Bacchus*, *Hercules*, *Cybele*, *Venus*, *Minerva*, *Juno*, *Ceres*, *Diana*, *Themis*. Some they named infernal, *How Rank-ed and Armed.*

as

as *Pluto, Charon, Cerberus, Rhadamanthus, Minos, Æacus, Proserpina, Alecto, Tisiphone, Megæra, Chimera, Clotho, Lachesis, Atropos.* Some were deities of the Sea, as *Oceanus, Neptune, Triton, Glaucus, Palemon, Proteus, Nereus, Castor, Pollux, Phorbus, Melicerta, Amphitrite, Thetis, Doris, Galatæa,* and the other Sea-Nymphs, called *Nereides.* The Countrey gods, and of the Woods, were *Pan, Sylvanus, Faunus, Pales* the *Satyres,* &c. There were three deities called *Graces,* or *Charities,* to wit, *Æglia, Thalia, Euphrosyne.* Three Fatal Sisters, called *Parcæ*; to wit, *Clotho, Lachesis, Atropos*; Three furies, called *Eumenides,* to wit, *Alecto, Megara, Tisiphone.* The chiefest of their gods they did thus arm; namely, *Saturn,* with the Sithe. *Jupiter* with Thunder. *Mars* with the Sword. *Apollo* and *Diana* with Bows and Arrows. *Mercury* with his *Caduceus,* or Rod. *Neptune* with the Trident, or three-forked Scepter. *Bacchus* with the *Thyrsus,* or spear woven about with Vine-leaves. *Hercules* with his *Clave,* or Club. *Minerva* with her Lance and *Ægis,* or Target, having on it *Medusa*'s head. *Vulcan* with his Tongs, &c.

Of these see the Poets, and their Commentators.

Q. *With what Creatures were their Chariots drawn?*

Their Chariots how drawn.

A. *Jupiter, Sol, Mars,* and *Neptune,* had their Chariots drawn by Horses. *Saturn* by Dragons. *Thetis, Triton, Leucothoe,* by Dolphins. *Bacchus* by Lynces and Tygers. *Diana* by Stags. *Luna,* or the Moon, by Oxen. *Oceanus* by Whales. *Venus* by Swans, Doves, and Sparrows. *Cybele* by Lions. *Juno* by Peacocks. *Ceres* by Serpents. *Pluto* by four black Horses. *Mercury,* in stead of a Chariot, had wings on his head and heels. The mystical meaning of these things we have opened.

In Myst. Poet.

Q. *In what peculiar places were some gods peculiarly worshipped?*

In what peculiar places worshipped.

A. Though *Apollo* was worshipped in many places: as in the wood *Grynaum* in *Ionia*; on *Phaselis,* a hill in *Lycia*; in *Tenedos,* an Isle of the Ægean Sea; in *Delos* and *Clatos,* two of the *Cyclad* Islands; on hill *Cynthus* in *Cyrrha,* a Town of *Phocis*: at *Rhodes,* on hill *Soracte*; on *Pernassus,* and other places; yet he was chiefly worshipped at *Delphi,* a Town of *Phocis.* So *Venus* was honoured in *Cyprus,* and in *Paphos,* a Town of the same Isle; and in the Isle *Amathus* in the *Ægean* Sea, on Hill *Eryx*; and in *Sicily,* and elsewhere; yet her chief worship was at *Paphos.* So *Juno* was worshipped at *Samos,* an Isle of the *Icarian* Sea; at *Argos* and *Mycenæ,* Towns of *Achaia,* and in other places; yet she was principally honoured at *Carthage* in *Africa. Minerva* was worshipped in *Aracynthus,* a Hill of *Ætolia*; in *Pyreus,* a Hill of *Attica,* and elsewhere; yet she was chiefly honoured at *Athens. Bacchus* was worshipped at *Nysa,* a Town of *Arabia*; at *Naxos,* one of the *Cyclades*; but chiefly at *Thebis* in *Bætia. Diana* was worshipped at *Delos,* on Hill *Cynthus*; at *Ephesus,* and elsewhere. *Hercules* was honoured at *Gades*; at *Tylur,* a Town near *Rome*; at *Tyrintha,* near *Argi*; at *Thebis* in *Bætia,* &c. *Jupiter*'s worship was maintained at *Rome,* in *Libya,* on hill *Ida* in *Crete,* and elsewhere. *Mars* was adored at *Thermodon* in *Scythia,* on *Rhodope,* a hill in *Thracia*; among the *Getes,* and other Nations. *Vulcan* was chiefly honoured at *Lemnos,*

Quirinus at *Rome*, *Faunus* in *Latium*, *Isis* in *Egypt*, *Æsculapius* in *Epidaurus*, a Town in *Peloponnesus*, *Cybele* in *Phrygia*, chiefly on the hills *Ida*, *Berecinthus* and *Dindymus*. *Fortune* was honoured in *Antium* and *Præneste*, a Town of *Italy*, &c. Who would know more of these let them consult with the Poets.

Q. *What were the* Greek *chief festivals?*

A. The *Greek* were these: *Anacalypteria*, kept by the Rusticks Greeks, to *Ceres* and *Bacchus*, upon the taking in of their fruits; but I find *their chief* that the feast of *Proserpina*'s wedding with *Pluto*, called *Theo-* *Festivals*. *gamia*, was called *Anacalypteria*, and so was the third day of each marriage from ἀνακαλύπτομαι, to disclose or discover, because then the Bride, who before had been shut up in her fathers house, came abroad to her husbands house; and so the Presents that were given her by her Husband that day, were called *Anacalypteria*. 2. *Anthesteria* were Feasts kept to *Bacchus*, so called from *Anthesterion*, the month of *February*, in which they were kept. But some will have this to be the month of *November*; others of *August*, which is most likely, because then grapes are ripe, and the Athenian children were crowned with Garlands of flowers. This feast also was called *Dionysia*, 3. *Alctis* was a feast at *Athens*, kept to *Icarus*, and *Erigone*. 4. *Anthesphoria*, kept to the honour of *Proserpina*, who was carried away by *Pluto* as she was gathering of flowers; ἄνθος is a flower: It was called also *Theogamia*, a divine marriage. 5. ἀπατεία, was an Athenian feast kept four days; *Erasmus* mentions only three. 6. *Ascolia*, were Attick feasts kept to *Bacchus*, from ἀσκὸς a bladder; because in the middle of the Theatre, they used then to dance upon bladders that were blown and oyled, only with one foot, that by falling they might excite laughter; this dancing was called *Ascoliasmus*, of which *Virgil* speaks: *Mollibus in pratis unctos saliere per utres.* 7. Βοηδρόμια, were Athenian feasts in the month of *September*, called by them *Boedromion*: this feast was kept with vociferation and running. 8. χαρίσια, were love feasts, in which kinsfolks entertained each other with good chear and gifts. 9. χύτεια, were feasts at *Athens*, wherein all kinds of seeds were boiled to *Bacchus* and *Mercury*, in a pot called χῆδον; this feast was kept about the midst of *November*. 10. διαμαστίγωσις, was the scourging-feast among the *Lacedæmonians*, in which the prime youth were whipt in the presence of their friends at the altar of *Diana*. 11. Διάσια, the feasts of *Jupiter*; they were called also *Στυγία*: Here they were not very jovial, but sad, and σκυθρωποὶ, of sowre countenance. 12. ἐλαφηβόλια, from ἔλαφος and βάλλω, were Feasts kept to *Diana* in *February*, called *Elaphebolion*, wherein Stags were sacrificed to *Diana*. 13. *Ephestia* at *Thebes*, were feasts kept to the honour of *Tyresias* the Prophet, who had been both man and woman; therefore that day they cloathed him first in mans apparel, and then in a womans habit. 14. γαμήλια from γάμῳ Marriage: this was *Juno*'s feast kept in *January*, called *Gamelion*; and she having the charge of marriages, was called *Gamelia*. 15. *Hecatombæ* to *Juno*, in which a hundred sacrifices were offered, and divers

I shews

shews or sports exhibited to the people: He that overcame was rewarded with χαλκῆ ἀσπις, a brazen Target, and a Myrtle garland. This feast was called also ἡραῖα from *Juno*'s name; and the month of *July*, in which this feast was kept, is named ἑκατομβαιῶν. 16. ἐλευηφόρεια Athenian feasts, in which certain holy Reliques were carried about in a chest called ἑλένη, by the Priests called *Helenophori*. 17. ὑακίνθια were *Lacedæmonian* feasts, kept to the honour of *Apollo*, and his Boy *Hyacinthus*, whom he lost; therefore *Lycander* calls him πολύθρηνον, much lamented. 18. *Hypocaustria* were feasts to *Minerva*, for avoiding the dangers that come by firing, from ὑποκαίειν, to kindle or burn. 19. ὑσεια, was a feast at *Argos*, so called from ὕς a Sow, because by them then this beast was sacrificed to *Venus*. 20. λαμπάδεια, so called from λαμπτήρ, a Torch, or Lamp: This feast was kept to *Bacchus*, into whose Temple, in the night they used to carry burning Torches, and to place goblets full of Wine in all parts of the City. 21. μεγαλήσια were the feasts of *Cybele*, called *Magna Mater*, in which were exhibited divers spectacles to the people in the month of *April*. 22. μεταγείτνια, was *Apollo*'s festival, who was called *Metageitnius*; and the month in which it was kept was named μεταγειτνιών, which some say is *May*, others *July*. 23. μονοφάγια, was a feast among the *Ægeans*, in which it seems they eat all of one dish, or else but once a day, or else each man apart. These are called μονοφάγοι. 24. μουνυχία, the feast of *Minerva*, kept in the harbour of *Athens*, called *Munichium*. The month of *March* was also called μουνυχιών. 25. νηφάλια were sober sacrifices without Wine; therefore called ἄοινα; at *Athens* these sacrifices were performed to *Venus Urania*; likewise to *Mnemosyne*, *Aurora*, *Sol*, *Luna*, the Muses and the Nymphs, and even to *Bacchus* himself. Sometimes they offered instead of Wine ὕδωρ μελίκρατον, water mingled with honey. 26. νυκτηλία were the night sacrifices of *Bacchus*, whence he was called νυκτήλιος. 27. οἰνιστήρια, were Athenian feasts, so called from the great cup of the same name, which being filled with Wine, beardless youths οἱ μέλλοντες ἀποκείρειν ἢ χόλλω faith *Athenæus, being to cut* their long hair offered to *Hercules*. 28. *Ornea*, the festivals of *Priapus*, who was called ὀρνεάτης, from *Ornis*, a Town of *Peloponnesus*. 29. ὠσχοφόρεια an Athenian feast, in which the Noble youth carried ὄσχας, Vine branches into *Minerva*'s Temple. The feast was instituted when *Theseus* returned mourning from *Crete*, upon the report of his Fathers death *Ægeus* 30. παναθήναια, the chief Athenian feast to the honour of *Minerva*; it was celebrated every fifth year. In this were divers shews; the youth then used to dance in armour, called πυρρική, from *Pyrrhus* the inventer. The Image of *Pallas* was then carried in a Ship called *Panathenaica*, in which the sail called *Peplus*, was spread; and on this was woven the Giant *Enceladus*, slain by *Pallas*. In this Feast they used to run with lamps or torches; and so they did in the Feasts called *Ephestia* and *Promothea*; He that overcame, had for his reward καρπὸν ἐλαίας, the Olive fruit, that is, a pot of Oyl, whereof *Pallas* was the Inventer, and none but he, could by the Law carry any Oyl out of the Attick Countrey. 31. πυανέψια, were Feasts dedicated to *Apollo* in the month πυανεψιῶν, which some take for *October*, others for *July*. This Feast was so called from πύανω, from beans, or other kind of *legumina* consecrated to *Apollo* 32. σκίρα, an Athenian Feast to *Minerva*; the month in which it was kept was called σκιρροφοειῶν, from bearing about in procession σκίερν or σκιάδιον, a Fan to make a shadow from the Suns heat. The Fan was carried by *Minerva*'s Priest, accompanied with the Gentry of *Athens* out of the Tower; from this they called *Minerva, Scirada.* The month of this feast was thought to be *March*. 33. θαργήλια, this feast was dedicated to *Apollo* and *Diana* at *Athens*, in the month of *April*, which was called θαργηλιῶν. In it the first fruits of the earth were offered to these gods, and boyled in the pot called θάργηλΟ. 34. θέοινα were feasts to *Bacchus* the god of Wine, who was therefore θέοινΟ, and his Temple θεοίνιον, commonly called; this was an Athenian feast. 35. θεόξενα, were feasts dedicated to all the gods together. This feast by the Latines is called *dies pandicularis*, and *communicarius*. *Theoxenia* also were games exhibited to *Apollo*, who was called *Theoxenius*, and this κοινὴ ἑορτὴ common feast was at *Delphi*, consecrated peculiarly to *Apollo*. This feast was so called παρὰ τὸ ξενίζειν τοῖς θεοῖς, because all the gods were entertained at a feast. *Castor* and *Pollux* were the authors of this feast; for when *Hercules* was deified, he committed to these *Dioscuri* the care of the *Olympick* games, but they devised this new feast of *Theoxenia*. It was chiefly observed by the Athenians in honour of foreign gods; for among them θεοὶ ξενικοὶ τιμῶν, saith *Hesychius*, the foreign gods were worshipped. This feast is called by *Pindarus* ξενίαι τραπέζαι, hospitable tables, and the sacrifice ξενισμὸς. 26. ϑύα was the Feast of *Bacchus*, in whose Temple three empty Vessels in the night-time were filled with wine, but none knew how, for the doors were fast locked and guarded. *Thuia* also was the first Priestess of *Bacchus*, from which the rest are called *Thyadæ*. 37. τριετηρικὰ were the feasts of *Bacchus* every third year, in Latine *Triennalia* and *Triennia*; of which *Ovid, Celebrant repetita Triennia Bacchæ.* Some other festivals the Greeks observed, but of less note.

Of these see Suidas, Athenæus, Rhodiginus, Gyraldus, Hesychius, Tertullian, Austin, Plutarch, Iul. Pollux, the Scholiast of Aristophanes Menvesius, and others.

The Contents of the Sixth Section.

Of the two prevalent Religions now in Europe. 2. *Of* Mahomet'*s Law to his Disciples.* 3. *Of the* Mahometans *opinions at this day.* 4. Mahomet, *not the Antichrist.* 5. *Of their Sects, and how the* Turks *and* Persians *differ.* 6. *Of the* Mahometan *Religious Orders.* 7. *Of their other Hypocritical Orders.* 8. *Of their secular Priests.* 9. *Of the* Mahumetan *devotion, and parts thereof.* 10. *Of their Ceremonies in their Pilgrimage to* Mecca. 11. *The Rites of their Circumcision.* 12. *Their Rites about the sick and dead.* 13. *The extent of* Mahometanism, *and the causes thereof.* 14. Mahometanism, *of what continuance.*

SECT. VI.

Mahumetans, their Religion.

WHat *are the two prevalent Religions this day in* Europe? *A.* Mahometanism, and Christianity. The former was broached by *Mahomet* the *Arabian*, being assisted by *Sergius* a *Nestorian* Monk, with some other Hereticks and Jews, about Six hundred years after Christ; for *Mahomet* was born under *Mauritius* the Emperour, *anno Christi* 591, and under *Heraclius, anno* 623. He was chosen General of the *Saracen* and *Arabian* Forces, and then became their Prophet, to whom he exhibited his impious doctrine and law, which he pretended was delivered to him by the Angel *Gabriel.* But his Book, called the *Alcoran*, was much altered after his death, and divers different copies thereof spread abroad, many of which were burned, and one retained, which is now extant. This is divided into 124 Chapters, which are fraughted with Fables, Lyes, Blasphemies, and a meer hodge-podge of fooleries and impieties, without either Language or Order, as I have shewed in the Caveat I gave to the Readers of the *Alcoran* ; yet to him that readeth this Book a thousand times, is promised a Woman in his paradise, whose eye-brows shall be as wide as the Rainbow. Such honour do they give to their ridiculous Book called *Musaph*, that none must touch it till he be washed from top to toe; neither must he handle it with his bare hands, *See Lanicerus, and others.* but must wrap them in clean linen. When in their Temples it is publickly read, the Reader may not hold it lower than his girdle ; and when he hath ended his reading, he kisseth the Book, and layeth it to his eyes.

Their Law.

Q. *What Law did* Mahomet *give to his Disciples ?*
A. His Law he divides into Eight Commandments. The first is to acknowledge only one God, and only one Prophet, to wit, *Mahomet.*

Sect.6. *A View of the Religions, &c.* 117

Mahomet. 2. The second is concerning the duty of Children to their Parents. 3. Of the Love of Neighbours to each other. 4. Of their Times of Prayer in their Temples. 5. Of their yearly Lent, which is carefully to be observed of all for one Month, or Thirty days. 6. Of their Charity and Alms-deeds to the Poor and Indigent. 7. Of their Matrimony, which every Man is bound to embrace at 25 years of age. 8. Against Murder. To the observer of these Commands he promiseth Paradise; in which shall be Silken Carpets, pleasant Rivers, fruitful Trees, beautiful Women, Musick, good Chear, and choice Wines, store of Gold and Silver Plate, with precious Stones, and such other conceits. But to those that shall not obey this Law, Hell is prepared, with Seven Gates, in which they shall eat and drink Fire, shall be bound in Chains, and tormented with Scalding Waters. He proveth the Resurrection by the Story of the Seven Sleepers, which slept 360 years in a Cave. He prescribes also divers Moral and Judicial Precepts, as abstinence from Swines flesh, blood, and such as die alone: also from Adultery and False Witness. He speaks of their *Fridays* devotion; of good Works; of their Pilgrimage to *Mecca*; of Courtesie to each other; of avoiding Covetousness, Usury, Oppression, Lying, casual Murther, Disputing about his *Alcoran*, or doubting thereof. Also of Prayer, Alms, Washing, Fasting, and Pilgrimage. He urgeth also Repentance, forbiddeth Swearing, commends Friendship, will not have Men forced to Religion; will not have Mercy or Pardon to be shewed to Enemies. He urgeth Valour in Battel, promising Rewards to the courageous, and shewing, that none can die till his time come, and then is no avoiding thereof.

Q. *What other opinions do the* Mahumetans *hold at this day?*
A. They hold a fatal necessity, and judge of things according to the success. They hold it unlawful to drink Wine, to play at Chess, Tables, Cards, or such like Recreations. Their Opinion is, that to have Images in Churches is Idolatry. They believe that all who die in their Wars, go immediately to Paradise, which makes them fight with such chearfulness. They think that every Man who lives a good life, shall be saved, what Religion soever he professeth; therefore they say, that *Moses*, *Christ*, and *Mahomet*, shall in the Resurrection appear with three Banners, to which, all of these three professions shall make their repair. They hold that every one hath two Angels attending on him; the one at his right hand, the other at his left. They esteem good works meritorious of Heaven. They say, that the Angel *Israphil*, shall in the last day sound his Trumpet, at the sound of which, all living creatures (Angels not excepted) shall suddenly die, and the Earth shall fall into dust and sand; but when the said Angel soundeth his Trumpet the Second time, the Souls of all that were dead shall rise again: then shall the Angel *Michael* weigh all Mens Souls in a pair of Scales. They say there is a terrible Dragon in the Mouth of Hell; and that there is an Iron-bridge, over which the wicked are conveyed, some

I 3   into

into everlasting Fire, and some into the fire of Purgatory. They hold that the Sun at his rising, and the Moon at her first appearing should be reverenced. They esteem Polygamy no sin. They hold it unlawful for any Man to go into their Temples not washed from head to foot; and if after washing, he piss, go to stool, or break Wind upward or downward, he must wash again or else he offends God. They say, that the Heaven is made of Smoak; that there are many Seas above it; that the Moons light was impaired by a touch of the Angel *Gabriel*'s Wing, as he was flying along, that the Devils should be saved by the *Alcoran*. Many other favourless and senseless opinions they have, as may be seen in the Book called *Scala*, being an Exposition of the *Alcoran*, Dialogue-wise.

Q. Was Mahomet *that great Antichrist spoken of by St.* Paul, 2 Thes. 2. *and by St.* John *in the Apocalypse* ?

Mahomet, not that Great Antichrist spoken of by Saint Paul, and Saint John.

A. No; For *Mahomet* was an *Arabian*, descended from *Ismael* and *Hagar*: but *Antichrist* (if we will believe the ancient Doctors of the Church) shall be a *Jew*, of the Tribe of *Dan*. 2. *Antichrist* shall come in the end of the World, and as the Church anciently believed, immediately before Christ's second coming; but *Mahomet* is come and gone, above a thousand years ago. 3. The Ancient Fathers believed, that the Two Witnesses which shall oppose *Antichrist*, and shall be slain by him, are *Henoch*, and *Elias*; but these are not yet come. 4. The Tradition of the Primitive Church was, that *Antichrist* should reign but Three years and a half, supposing that this period of time is meant by time and times, and half a time: but *Mahomet* we know reigned many more years. 5. *Antichrist* will wholly oppose himself against Christ, vilifie him, set himself up in his stead; and to extol himself above all that is called God: but *Mahomet* doth speak honourably of Christ, in calling him the Word of God, the Spirit of God, the Servant of God, the Saviour of those that trust in him, the Son of a Virgin, begot without the help of Man, as may be seen in his *Alcoran*. 6. Our Writers, as *Forbes*, *Cartwright*, &c. hold, that *Antichrist* is described, *Revel*. 9. under the name of that Star which fell from Heaven, having the Key of the bottomless pit, and under the Name of *Abaddon*, and *Apollyon*; but that *Mahomet* with his followers are set out in that same Chapter under the four Angels bound in the great River *Euphrates*. 7. The Apostle, 2 *Thes*. 2. saith, *That Antichrist shall sit in the Temple of God as God, and shall exalt himself above all that is called God*. But this cannot be meant of *Mahomet*, for he never sat in the Temple of God, whether by this word we understand the Temple of *Jerusalem*, or the Church of Christ; for he, and his Disciples separated themselves from the Church of Christ; and will have no Communion with Christians. 8. Antichrist is to come with signs and lying wonders, and by these to raise his Kingdom. But *Mahomet* came with the Sword, and by it subdued the Neighbouring Nations, so that neither he, nor his followers, did, or do pretend to any wonders. 9. Our Writers say, that Antichrist is not to be taken for a particular Person, but for a whole

Com-

Company or Society of People under one head; but *Mahomet* was a particular Person. 10. Antichrist is to be destroyed by the breath of the Lord's Mouth; but *Mahomet* died a natural death. By all these Reasons then it appears, that *Mahomet* cannot be that great *Antichrist* who is to come in the end of the World. Yet I deny not but he was an Antichrist in broaching a Doctrine repugnant to Christ's Divinity. Such an *Antichrist* was *Arius*; likewise in persecuting Christ in his Members, he may be called *Antichrist*; and so might *Nero, Domitian, Dioclesian*, and other Persecutors. Besides, the number of the Beast 666 is found in *Mahomet*'s Name, and so it is found in divers other Names. If we consider the miseries, desolation and blood that have followed upon the spreading of Mahometanism in the World, we may, with *Pererius* on *Revel.* 6. conclude, that *Mahomet* is signified by death, which rideth on the Pale Horse, followed by Hell or the Grave; to whom was given power over the fourth part of the Earth, to kill with the Sword, with Famine, &c. for he was the death both of Soul and Body to many Millions of People; upon whose wars followed Destruction, Famine, Pestilence, and many other Miseries, in that part of the World, where he and his Successors have spread their Doctrine and Conquests.

Q. *Are all the* Mahometans *of one Profession?*

A. No: for there be divers Sects amongst them; but the two main Sects are, that of the *Arabians*, followed by the *Turks*; and of *Hali* by the *Persians*. To this *Hali Mahomet* bequeathed both his Daughter and his *Alcoran*, which the *Persians* believe is the true Copy, and that of the *Turks* to be false. This *Hali* succeeded *Mahomet*, both in his Doctrine and Empire; whose Interpretation of the Law they embrace for the truest. As the Saracen *Caliphs* of old, exercised both the Kingly and Priestly Office; so both are claim'd by the Modern *Persian*; for both were performed by *Mahomet* and *Hali*. But to avoid trouble, the *Persian* Sophi contents himself with the Secular Government, leaving the Spiritual to the *Muftued Dini*, who is as the *Mufty* in *Turky*. These two Sects differ in many points: for the *Arabians* make God the Author both of good and evil; but the *Persians* of good only; the *Persians* acknowledge nothing Eternal but God; the *Turks* say that the Law is also eternal; the *Persians* say, that the blessed Souls cannot see God in his Essence, but in his Effects or Attributes; the *Turks* teach, that he shall be visible in his Essence. The *Persians* will have *Mahomet*'s Soul to be carried by the Angel *Gabriel* into God's presence when he received his *Alcoran*. The *Turks* will have his Body carried thither also. The *Persians* Pray but three times a day, the *Arabians* five times; other differences they have; but these are the chief Doctrinal differences: the main is about the true *Alcoran*, the true interpretation thereof, and the true Successor of *Mahomet*; for they hold *Eubocar, Osmen*, and *Homar*, whom the *Turks* Worship, to have been Usurpers, and *Hali* the only true Successor of *Mahomet*, whose Sepulcher they visit with as great devotion, as the *Turks* do the other three.

See *Byrrius, Loriceri- us, Knoles, Camerarius Jnxim, &c.*

Q. *What*

Mahometans, their Religious Orders.

Q. *What Religious Orders have the* Mahometans?

A. Moſt of their Religious Orders are wicked and irreligious. For thoſe whom they call *Imalier*, and *Religious Brothers of Love*, are worſe than Beaſts in their Luſts, ſparing neither Women nor Boys; their Habit is a Long Coat of a Violet Colour, without Seam, girt about with a Golden Girdle, at which hang Silver Cymbals, which make a jangling ſound; they walk with a Book in their hand, containing Love-Songs and Sonnets, in the *Perſian*-Tongue; theſe go about Singing, and receive Money for their Songs, and are always bare-headed, wearing long Hair, which they Curle. The Order of *Calender* profeſſeth perpetual Virginity, and have their own peculiar Temples, or Chappels. They wear a ſhort Coat made of Wool and Horſe-hair, without ſleeves, they cut their Hair ſhort, and wear on their heads Felt-hats, from which hangs tufts of Horſe-hair, about a hand-breadth. They wear Iron-Rings in their Ears, and about their Necks and Arms; they wear alſo in their Yard an Iron or Silver Ring of 3. *lib.* weight, whereby they are forced to live chaſtly; they go about Reading certain Rimes, or Ballads. The Order of *Derviſes* go about begging Alms in the Name of *Hali*, Son-in-law to their god *Mahomet*. They wear two Sheep-skins dried in the Sun, the one whereof they hang on their Back, the other on their Breaſt; the reſt of their body is naked. They ſhave their whole body, go bare-headed, and burn their Temples with an hot Iron. In their Ears they wear Rings, in which are precious Stones, they bear in their hand a knotty Club. They are deſperate Aſſaſſinates, will Rob and Murther when they find occaſion; they eat of a certain Herb called *Aſſerad*, or *Matſlach*, which makes them Mad; then they cut and ſlaſh their Fleſh; the Madder they are, the more they are Reverenced. In *Natolia*, near the Sepulchre of a certain Saint of theirs, is a Convent of theſe Monks, being above Five hundred, where once a year there is kept a general Meeting of this Order, about Eight thouſand, over whom their Superior, called *Aſſambaba*, is Preſident. On the Friday after their Devotions they make themſelves drunk with *Aſſerad* in ſtead of Wine; then they fall to dancing in a round, about a Fire, Singing Ballads, which done, with a ſharp knife they cut Flowers and Figures on their skins, for the Love of thoſe Women they moſt affect. This Feaſt holdeth Seven days, which ended, with Banners diſplayed, and Drums beating, they depart all to their ſeveral Convents, begging Alms all the way that they March. Their Fourth Order called *Torlachs*, are cloathed like the *Derviſes*, but that they wear alſo a Bears Skin inſtead of a Cloak, but they go bare-headed and ſhaven; they anoint their heads with Oyl againſt Cold; and burn their Temples againſt Defluctions. Their Life is beaſtly and beggerly, living in ignorance and idleneſs; they are begging in every corner, and are dangerous to meet with in Deſart places, for they will rob and plunder; they profeſs *Palmeſtry* like our *Gypſies*, who uſe to pick ſilly Womens Pockets as they are looking in their hands. They carry

Sect. 6.   *of* EUROPE.   121

carry about with them an old Man, whom they worship as a Prophet; when they mean to have Money from any Rich Man, they repair to his house, and the old Man there Prophesieth sudden destruction against that House; which, to prevent, the Master of the House desires the old Man's Prayers, and so dismisseth him and his train with Money, which they spend wickedly; for they are given to Sodomy and all Uncleanness. *See Menavino, Nicholaus Nicholai, Septemcastrensis, &c.*

Q. *Are there no other hypocritical Orders amongst them?*

A. Yes, many more. Some whereof go naked, except their Privities, seeming no ways moved either with Summers heat, or Winters cold; they can indure cutting and slashing of their flesh, as it were insensibly, to have their patience the more admired. Some will be honoured for their Abstinence in eating and drinking sparingly and seldom. Some profess Poverty, and will enjoy no earthly things. Others again profess perpetual Silence, and will not speak, though urged with Injuries and Tortures. Some avoid all Conversation with Men. Others brag of Revelations, Visions and Enthusiasms. Some wear Feathers on their heads, to shew they are given to Contemplation. Some have Rings in their Ears, to note their subjection and obedience in harkning to Spiritual Revelations. Some bear Chains about their Necks and Arms, to shew they are bound up from the World; some by their mean Cloaths brag of their Poverty. Some, to shew their love to hospitality, carry Pitchers of clean Water, which they proffer to all that will drink, without taking any Reward. Some dwell at the Graves of the Dead, and live on what the People offers them. Some of them have secret Commerce with Women, and then give out that they Conceive and bear Children without the help of Men, purposely to extenuate the miraculous Birth of *Christ*. Some are *Antinomians*, affirming, that there is no use of the Law, but that Men are saved by Grace. Some are for Traditions and Merits, by which Salvation is attained, and not by Grace. These addict themselves wholly to Meditation, Prayer, Fasting, and other Spiritual exercises; there be some, who be accounted Hereticks, for they hold that every Man may be saved in his own Religion, and that *Christ*'s Law is as good as *Mahomet*'s; therefore they make no scruple to enter into Christian Churches, to Sign themselves with the Cross, and besprinkle themselves with Holy-water. These Votaries have their Saints, to whom they have recourse in their wants, and to whom they assign particular Offices: some have the charges of Travellers, some of Children, some of Child-bearing-Women, some of Secrets, and such like. They have also their Martyrs, Reliques, and Lying Miracles. *See Georgievitz, Septemcastrensis, Busbequius and others.*

Q. *What Secular Priests have they?*

A. They have eight Orders, or Degrees; 1. The *Mophti*, or their Pope, on whose judgment all depend, even the Great *Turk* himself, both in Spiritual and Secular Affairs. 2. The *Cadelescher*, who, under the *Mophti*, is Judge of all Causes, both Civil and Ecclesiastical. 3. The *Cadi*, whose Office is to Teach the People, *Their Secular Priests.*

4. *Modecit*,

4. *Modecis*, who have the Charge of Hospitals. 5. *Antiphi*, who publickly Read the Heads of *Mahometan* Superstition, holding in one hand a naked Sword, in the other a Scimiter. 6. *Imani*, who in their Temples have charge of the Ceremonies. 7. *Meizin*, who on their Towers Sing and call the People to Prayer. 8. *Sophi*, who are their Singing-Men in their Temples. The higher Orders are chosen by the Grand-Signior. The inferior by the People, who have a small Pension from the *Turk*, which being insufficient to maintain them, they are force to work and use Trades. There is required no more Learning in them, but to Read the *Alcoran* in *Arabian*, for they will not have it Translated. To strike any of these, is the loss of a hand in a *Turk*, but of life in a Christian. In such esteem they have their beggarly Priests.

Their Devotion.

Q. *Wherein doth the* Mahometans *Devotion consist chiefly?*

A. In their multitudes of Mosches, or Temples, the chief of which is Saint *Sophi* in *Constantinople*, built, or rather repaired by *Justinian*. 2. In their Hospitals, both for Poor and Strangers. 3. In their Monasteries and Schools. 4. In their Washings, whereof they have three sorts. One of all the Body. Another of the private parts only. The third of the hands, feet, face, and Organs of the Five Senses. 5. In giving of Alms either in Money or in Meat; for their manner is to sacrifice beasts, but not as the *Jews* upon Altars; these beasts they cut in pieces and distribute among the Poor. Their other sacrifices, which either they offer, or promise to offer when they are in danger, are so divided, that the Priests have one share, the Poor another; the third they eat themselves. 6. In making of Vows, which are altogether conditional; for they pay them if they obtain what they desire, otherwise not. 7. In adorning their Temples with multitudes of Lamps burning with Oil, and with Tapestry spread on Mats, upon which they prostrate themselves in Prayer. On the Walls are written in Golden Letters, *There is but one God, and one Prophet Mahomet*. 8. In Praying five times a day, and on *Friday*, which is their Sabbath (because *Mahomet's* Birth-day,) six times, bowing themselves to the ground, twice as often as they Pray. Whosoever absents himself, chiefly on *Friday*, and in their *Lent*, is punished with Disgrace, and a Pecuniary Mulct. 9. In divers ridiculous Ceremonies acted by their Priests, as pulling off the Shooes, which all People are tied to do when they enter into the Temple; in stretching out the hands and joyning them together, in kissing the ground, in lifting up the head, in stopping of the Ears with the fingers, in Praying with their Faces to the South, because *Mecca* is there, in wiping their eyes with their hands, in observing a Lenten Fast for one Month in a year, changing the Month every year, so that they Fast one whole year in Twelve; and then they abstain from all Meat and Drink, till the Stars appear. In plucking off their hairs at the end of their Fast, and in Painting of their Nails with a Red colour. 10. In Pilgrimages to *Mecca*, in Circumcision of their Children, in Feasting at the Graves of the Dead, and in other such vain Ceremonies.

See Georgieovitz, Knolles, Purchas, &c.

Q. *What*

of EUROPE. 123

es obferve they in their Pilgrimage to Mecca ? *Their Pil-*
s undertaken and performed every year, and *grimage to*
that he who doth not once in his life go this *Mecca.*
ffuredly damned ; whereas Paradife and re-
ured to them that go it. The way is long and
reece, being fix Months journey, and dange-
rabian Thieves, Mountains of Sand, with
overwhelmed ; and want of Water in thofe
efarts. Their chief care is to be reconciled
there is any difference, before they go ; for
iind them all Grudges and Quarrels, their
iem no good ; they begin their Journey from
eeks after their *Eafter*, called *Bairam*, being
abi on Dromedaries, and 200 *Janizaries* on
pieces of Ordnance, a Rich Vefture for the
n Velvet Covering, wrought with Gold, to
ich the *Baffa* delivers to the Captain of the
els that carry thefe Veftures are covered with
many fmall Bells ; the night before their de-
great Feafting and Triumphs. No Man may
this Pilgrimage, and every Servant is made
The Camel that carrieth the Box with the *Al-*
Cloth of Gold and Silk, the Box with Silk
ey, but with Gold and Jewels at their entring
ns alfo and Singers encompafs the Camel, and
ufed in this Pilgrimage. They ufe divers
y when they meet with Water. When they
Ioufe of *Abraham*, which they Fable was mi-
iveth a new Covering and a new Gate ; the
Pilgrims, which hath a vertue in it to Pardon
e Ceremonies performed, they go round about
n times ; then they kifs a Black Stone, which
n thither from Heaven ; at firft it was White,
ig of Sinners, it is become black ; then they
ie Pond *Zunzun*, without the Gate five paces
fhewed to *Hagar*, when fhe wanted Water fo
they drink, and Pray for Pardon of their fins
at *Mecca*, they go to the *Hill of Pardons*, 15
ere they leave all their fins behind them, after
rmon, and Prayed, and offered Sacrifices. Up-
nuft not look back to the Hill, leaft their fins
hence they repair to *Medina*, where *Maho-*
iought to be ; but by the way they run up a
hey call the Mount of Health ; they run, that
all their fins. Thence they come pure to the
ich notwithftanding they may not fee, being
Silk Curtain, which by the *Eunuchs*, being 50
on the Tomb, and to light the Lamps, is taken
ims Captain prefenteth the new one ; without,
each

each man gives to the *Eunuchs* handkerchiefs, or such like, to touch the Tomb therewith; this they keep as a special Relique. When they return to *Egypt*, the Captain presenteth the *Alcoran* to the *Bassa* to kiss, and then it is laid up again; the Captain is Feasted, and presented with a Garment of cloth of Gold. They used to cut in pieces the Camel with his Furniture which carried the *Alcoran*, and reserve these pieces for holy Reliques. The *Alcoran* also is elevated, that all might see and adore it, which done, every one with joy returns to his own home.

See Verto-man, Lanicerus, and others.

Q. *What Ceremonies use they about their Circumcision?*

Their Circumcision.

A. They are circumcised about eight years of age; the Child is carried on horse back, with a Tullipant on his head to the Temple, with a torch before him, on a spear deckt with flowers, which is left with the Priest as his Fee, who first nippeth the end of the skin of the Childs yard with pincers, to mortifie it, then with his Scissors he nimbly cuts it off, presently a powder is laid on to ease the pain, and afterwards salt. The childs hands being loosed, looketh as he is taught by the Priest, towards Heaven, and lifting up the first finger of his right hand, saith these words: *God is one God, and Mahomet is his Prophet.* Then he is carried home in state after some prayers and offerings at the Church. Sometimes the child is circumcised at home; and receiveth his name, not then, but when he is born. They feast then commonly three days, which ended, the child is carried with Pomp to the Bath, and from thence home, where he is presented with divers gifts from his Parents Friends. Women are not circumcised, but are tied to make profession of their *Mahometan* faith.

SeeGeorgiovitz, and others.

Q. *What Rites do they observe about the sick and dead?*

Their Rites about the sick and dead.

A. Their Priests and chief friends visit them, exhort them to Repentance, and read Psalms to them. When any dieth, the Priest compasseth the Corps with a string of beads, made of *Lignum Aloes*, praying God to have mercy on him; then the Priests carry it into the Garden, wash it, and cover it with its own garments, with flowers also and perfumes, and his Turband is set on his head. Women perform this office to the body of a Woman. This done, the body is carried to the Temple with the head forwards, and set down at the Church-door, whilst the Priests are performing their service; then it is carried to the burial-place without the City: the Priests that Pray for his soul, are paid for their pains, and feasted at home. Some part of their good chear is set on the grave, for the soul to feed on, or for alms to the poor. They believe there are two angels, who with angry looks, and flaming fire-brands, examine the dead party of his former life, whom they whip with fiery torches if he be wicked; if good, they comfort him, and defend his body in the grave till the day of judgment; but the bodies of the wicked are knocked down nine fathoms under ground, and tormented by their angry angels, the one knocking him with an hammer, the other tearing him with an hook, till the last day; against this torment the *Turks* use to pray at the

graves

graves of the dead. The Women there do not accompany the dead to the grave, but stay at home weeping, and preparing good chear for the Priests and others of the departed mans friends. They believe that when the Corps hath been in the grave one quarter of an hour; that a new spirit is put into it, is set upon its knees, and is examined by the foresaid angels of his faith and works. They believe also that it is a work of charity, and conducible to the soul of the defunct, if the Birds, Beasts, or Ants be fed with the meat which they set on the graves of the dead. *See Menavino, Bellonius, &c.*

Q. *How far hath this* Mahometan *Superstition got footing in the world?*
A. Though it be not so far extended as Gentilism, yet it hath over-reached Christianity; not in *Europe*, where Christianity prevaileth, but in *Africa* where it hath thrust out the ancient Christian Churches, and erected the half-Moon instead of the Cross, except it be among the *Abyssins*, and some small places held by the *Spaniard* or *Portugal*: But in *Asia* it hath got deeper footing, having overrun *Arabia*, *Turky*, *Persia*, some part of the *Mogul*'s country, and *Tartaria*, only here and there some small Congregations of Christians are to be found; in *America* indeed it is not as yet known. Now the reasons why this superstition is not so far spread, are these. 1. The continual jars, frivolous debates, and needless digladiations about questions in Religion among Christians, which hath made the world doubt of the truth thereof, and takes away the end and scope of Religion, which is to unite mens affections; but the remedy is become the disease, and that which should cure us, woundeth us. 2. The wicked and scandalous lives, both of Christian Laity and Clergy: for the Mahometans generally are more devout in their religious duties, and more just in their dealings. 3. The Mahometans conquests have in those parts propagated their Superstition. 4. Their Religion is more pleasing to the sense than Christianity; for men are more affected with sensitive pleasures, which *Mahomet* proffers in his Paradise, than with spiritual, which are less known, and therefore less desired. 5. The greatness of the *Turkish* tyranny over Christians; the rewards and honours they give to those that will turn *Musulmen*, or *Mahometans*, are great inducements for weak spirits to embrace that Religion; for a Christian Runnegado that will receive Circumcision among them, is carried about the streets with great joy and solemnity, is presented with many gifts, and made free from all taxes; for which very cause, many, both *Greeks* and *Albanians*, have received circumcision. 6. The liberty which is permitted to multiply Wives, must needs be pleasing to carnal-minded men. 7. They permit no man to dispute of their *Alcoran*; to call any point of their Religion in question; to sell the *Alcoran* to Strangers, or to translate it into other languages: It is death to offend in many of these; which is the cause of much quietness and concord among them. 8. They inhibit the profession of Philosophy among them, and so they keep the people in darkness and ignorance, not suffering the light to appear and to detect their errours. 9. They teach, that all who live a good life shall be saved,

Their Superstition how far spread,

Men are much taken with moral outsides, w[hich ex]
ceed Christians; for they are more modest
generally than we; Men and Women conv[erse not]
miscuously, as among us; they are less sum[ptuous in]
dings; less excessive and phantastical in thei[r appa]
ring in their diet, and altogether abstemiou[s from wine]
reverent in their Churches, so that they wil[l not suffer]
paper to be trod upon, or lie on the ground
kiss it, and lay it in some place out of danger
the name of God and *Mahomet*'s Law is
they are also more sober in their speeches a[nd more]
obedient to their Superiors than we are. 12.
pleasing to our nature than private revenge,
is prohibited, but by the Mahometan Law
are to hate, and to kill their enemy, if the[y]
had infected most of the Eastern Churches
wonder if they received *Mahomet*'s Doctrine
upon *Arius* his Heresie. 14. They suffer n[o]
Christ, but honour him, and speak reverent[ly]
of *Moses* and *Abraham*; which makes that n[o Chri]
stians are in those parts much averse from, o[ur]
Religion. 15. They have been always very
in gaining Proselytes, and yet force no man[.]
like Reasons, let us not wonder at the great e[xtent of Maho]
nism in the World.

Q. *Of what continuance is Mahometanism?*

Mahometa- A. *Mahomet* was born in the year of Ch[rist]
nism, of of St. *Gregory* the Pope, and *Mauritius* the E[mperor]
what conti- *Genebrard* he lived 63 years, of which he sp[ent in sprea]
nuance. ding of his Doctrine, then died in the year o[f]
stance being Emperor, and *Eugenius* the first
metanism hath lasted already above 100 year[s, to the confu]
sion and vexation of the Church of Christ, an[d dishou]
nour of Christian Princes, who if they had [spent some]
of that blood against the Turks, which the[y have]
sinfully shed in their own private quarrels, th[ere had not been at]
this day any remainder of that damnable Se[ct, which hath]
continued a scourge to the Church of Christ[, longer than any]
did against God's people of old. For the E[gyptians vext the]
Israelites scarce 200 years; the *Canaanite* 2[0 years; Midian]
18 years the *Philistines* 40 years; the *Assyria[ns and Babylonians*, from]
the first to the last, did not vex and oppress [God's people]

years; afterward they were oppressed by *Antiochus Epiphanes* 40 years, the Christian Church from *Nero* till *Constantine* was afflicted about 260 years; and afterward by the *Goths* and *Lombards* near 300 years. But this oppression of the Church by *Mahomet* hath, as I said, lasted above a thousand years. The Reasons are divers, as I have shewed in the former question; to which may be added these, 1. By this long Persecution and Tyranny of the Turks, God will try and exercise the Faith, Patience, Constancy, and other Virtues of his people, which would corrupt and putrefie like standing water, or *Moab* settled upon the Lees, not being poured from vessel to vessel. How can the courage of a Souldier be known but in a skirmish? or the skill of a Mariner, but in a storm; *Marcet sine adversario virtus*; that tree, saith *Seneca*, is most strongly rooted in the ground, which is most shaken with the wind. *Nulla est arbor fortis & solida, nisi in quam venti sæpius incursantes, ipsa enim vexatione constringitur, & radices certius figit.* 2. God is pleased to continue this tyranny and power of the Mahometans, to the end that Christian Princes may love each other, and stick close together against the common Enemy; that their Military Discipline might be exercised abroad, and not at home: For this cause the wisest of the Romans were against the utter destruction of *Carthage*: fearing left the Romans wanting an Enemy abroad, should Exercise their Swords against themselves, which fell out accordingly. For the same cause, God would not utterly destroy the *Philistines, Ammonites, Moabites,* and other neighbouring Enemies of the *Jews*. But such is the madness of Christians, that though we have so potent an Enemy close at our doors ready to devour us, yet we are content to sheath that Sword into our own bowels, which we should employ against the common Foe. 3. God will have this Sword of Mahometanism to hang over our heads, and this Scourge to be still in our eyes, that thereby we may be kept the more in awe and obedience; that if at any time we start aside like a broken Bow, we may return again in time, considering God hath this Whip ready and at hand to correct us. Thus God left the *Canaanites* among the *Jews*, to be pricks in their eyes, and goads in their sides: *I will not* (saith the Lord) *drive out any from before them of the Nations which* Joshua *left when he dyed; that through them I might prove Israel, whether they will keep the way of the Lord to walk therein*, &c. *therefore the Lord left these Nations without driving them out hastily.* See *Judg.* 2. 21, 22. & 3. 1, 2, 3, &c. 4. God is content to continue this Mahometan Sect so long, because Justice is exercised among them; without which, a State or Kingdom can no more stand, than a tree without a root, or an house without a foundation: they are also zealous and devout in their way; and great enemies to Idolatry, so that they will permit no Images to be painted or carved among them; knowing that God is not offended so much against any sin as against Idolatry, which is spiritual adultery, most destructive of that matrimonial conjunction between God and us. 5. The Lord by the long continuance

nuance of Mahometanifm, will punifh the perfidioufnefs and wickednefs of the Greek Emperours, as likewife the multitude of Herefies and Schifms hatched in that Church. 6. This Sect of Mahometanifm is fo made up of Chriftianifm, Judaifm, and Gentilifm, that it abates the edge of any of thefe Nations, from any eager defire of its extirpation.

The Contents of the Seventh Section.

The Chriftian Religion propagated. 2. *The decay thereof in the Eaft by* Mahometanifm. 3. *Perfecution and Herefie the two great Enemies thereof.* 4. Simon Magus *the firft Heretick with his difciples.* 5. Menander, Saturninus, *and* Bafilides, *Hereticks.* 6. *The* Nicholaitans *and* Gnofticks. 7. *The* Carpocratians. 8. Cerinthus, Ebion, *and the* Nazarites. 9. *The* Valentinians, Secundians, *and* Ptolemaians. 10. *The* Marcites, Colarbafii, *and* Heracleonites. 11. *The* Ophites, Cainites, *and* Sethites. 12. *The* Archonticks *and* Afcothyptæ. 13. Cerdon *and* Marcion. 14. Apelles, Severus, *and* Tacianus. 15. *The* Cataphrygians. 16. Pepuzians, Quintilians, *and* Artotyrites. 17. *The* Quartidecimani, *and* Alogiani. 18. *The* Adamians, Ecclefians, *and* Theodofians. 19. *The* Melchifedecians, Bardefanifts, *and* Noetians. 20. *The* Valefians, Catheri, Angelici, *and* Apoftolici. 21. *The* Sabbellians, Originians, *and* Origenifts. 22. *The* Samofatenians *and* Photinians. 23. *The* Manichæan *Religion.* 24. *The* Hierachites, Melitians, *and* Arians. 25. *The* Audians, Semiarrians, *and* Macedonians. 26. *The* Ærians, Ætians, *and* Apollinarifts. 27. *The* Antidicomarianites, Meffalians *and* Metangifmonites. 28. *The* Hermians, Proclianites, *and* Patricions. 29. *The* Afcites, Partalorinchites, Aquarii, *and* Coluthiani. 30. *The* Floriani, Æternales, *and* Nudipedales. 31. *The* Donatifts, Prifcillianifts, Rhetorians, *and* Feri. 32. *The* Theopafchites: Tritheits, A***, Melitonii, Ophei, Tertullii, Liberatores, *and* Nativitarii. 33. *The* Luciferians, Jovinianifts, *and* Arabicks. 34. *The* Collyridians, Paterniani, Tertullianifts, *and* Abelonites. 35. *The* Pelagians, Prædeftinati, *and* Timotheans. 36. *The* Neftorians, Eutychians, *and their Spawn.*

SECT. VII.

Chriftianity its beginning.

Queft. **W**Hat *is the other great Religion profeffed in* Europe? *A. Chriftianity,* which is the Doctrine of Salvation, delivered to man by Chrift Jefus the Son of God, who affuming our nature of a pure Virgin taught the Jews the true way to happinefs, confirming his doctrine by figns and miracles; at length fealed sealed it with his blood; and so having suffered death for our sins, and rose again for our Justification, he Ascended to his Father, leaving Twelve Apostles behind him to propagate this Doctrine through the World, which they did accordingly, confirming their words with Miracles, and their own blood; and so this light of the Gospel scattered all the Fogs and Mists of Gentile Superstition; at the sight of this Ark of the New Covenant, the Dagon of Idolatry fell to the ground: when this Lion of the Tribe of *Judah* did roar, all the Beasts of the Forest, that is, the Pagan Idols, or Devils rather, hid themselves in their Dens. *Apollo* complained that his Oracles failed him, and that the Hebrew Child had stopped his Mouth. When it was proclaimed at *Palotei* by *Thanas* the *Ægyptian* Shipmaster, that the great God *Pan* was dead, all the evil Spirits were heard to howl and bewail the overthrow of their Kingdom; *Porphyry* complained that the Preaching of Christ had weakened the Power of their gods, and hindred the gain of their Priests. The Bones of *Babylas* so hindred *Apollo*, that he could deliver no Oracle while they were there. The *Delphick* Temple fell down with Earthquake and Thunder, when *Julian* sent to consult with the Oracle. Such was the irresistible power of the Two-edged Sword which came out of Christ's mouth, that nothing was able to withstand it. The little Stone cut of the Mountain without hands, smote the great Image of *Nebuchadnezzar*, and brake it in pieces; to the Doctrine of Twelve poor weak Fishermen, did the great Potentates of the World submit their Scepters. Thus the Stone which the Builders refused, became the head of the corner; it was the Lord's doing, and it's marvellous in our eyes. The terrible Beast, which with his Iron Teeth destroyed all the other Beasts, is destroyed by the weakness of Preaching, against which, the more the *Roman* Empire struggled, the more it was foiled, and found by experience, that the Blood of Martyrs was the Seed of the Church, which conquered the great Conquerors, not with acting, but with suffering; not by the Sword, but by the Word, and more by their death, than by their life: like so many *Samsons*, triumphing over these *Philistines* in their Death and Torments.

Q. 2. *Seeing the power of Religion was so irresistible in the beginning, that it carried all like a torrent before it, How came it to grow so weak within 600 years, that it yielded to* Mahometanism?

A. When God saw that the ungrateful professors of Christianity began to loath that Heavenly Manna, and to covet for Quails of new Doctrine, he gave them leave to eat and poyson themselves therewith. He was not bound to cast Pearls before Swine, and to give that which was holy to Dogs. In his just Judgments he removed the Candlestick from those who rejected the Light, and delighted themselves in darkness; it was fit the Kingdom of God should be taken from them, and given to a People that should bring forth the fruits thereof. They deserved to be plagued with a Famine, who grew wanton and spurned against their Spiritual Food. Besides, when the Devil perceived he could do no good by open hostility and persecution, but the more burthen he laid upon the Palm, the more it flourished, and the oftner he flung the Gyant of Religion to the Ground, the stronger it grew with *Antæus*: he resolved at last to joyn the Foxes Tail to the Lions skin, and to try whether the heart of the Sun would not make the Traveller sooner forsake his Cloak, than the impetuosity of the Wind. He choaks all Zeal and Sincerity with the baits of Wealth and Honour; he poysons them with Ambition, Pride, Covetousness, and Envy; the evil Man sowed the Tares of Dissention and Heretical Doctrines in the Lord's Fields; the Spiritual Husbandman grew careless and idle, the Shepherds neglect their Flocks, the Dogs grow dumb, and so the Lord's Sheep are suffered to stray, and become a prey to the Wolves. The Watchmen being inebriated with honour, wealth, ease and security, fall asleep on the Walls, and let the Enemy seize on the Lord's City. It was not then the weakness of Christian Religion that was the cause of *Mahomet's* prevailing; for the heat of the Sun is not weak, though it cannot soften the Clay; nor is the good Seed that is cast into barren ground to be blamed, if it do not fructifie; neither is the Preaching of the Gospel impotent and weak, because it doth not always edifie. All the Water in the Sea cannot mollifie a Rock, nor all the Rain in the Clouds fecundate a Stony barren ground. The Subject must be capable, or else the Agent cannot operate. *Mahometanism* then prevailing upon Christianity, proceeded from the voluntary perverseness of Mens hearts, from the Malice and Craft of the Devil, and from the Just Judgments of the Almighty.

Q. 3. *What were the Engines that Satan used to overthrow Religion in the beginning?*

Religion, by what Engines battered.

A. Open Persecution and Heresie; with the one he destroyed the Bodies, with the other he poysoned the Souls of Christians. Persecution, with *Saul*, killed its Thousands; but Heresie, with *David*, Ten thousand. Persecution was the Arrow that did fly by day, but Heresie the Pestilence that raged in the darkness. Persecution was the Pruning-knife that lopped the branches of Religion, but Heresie the Ax laid to the Root of the Tree. Persecution was the Dragon that drove the Woman into the Wilderness, but Heresie the Beast that spake Blasphemies. Open Persecution began in *Nero* a Tyrant, but Heresie in *Simon* a Witch. Open Persecution began about 66 years after Christ's Ascention, but Heresie immediately after Christ's departure, about the sixth year, in the beginning of *Caligula's* Reign. Persecution is the wild Boar of the Forest, but Heresie the little Fox that eateth up the Grapes of the Lord's Vineyard.

Q. 4. *Who was the first Heretick that opposed the Orthodox Religion, and what were his Opinions?*

Hereticks and Heresies, namely, Simon Magus.

A. Simon, called *Magus*, because he was a Witch; a *Samaritan* by Birth, and a Christian by Profession; he would have bought the Gifts of the Holy Ghost for Money, *Acts* 8. 13. He denied the Trinity, and affirmed himself to be the true God. He taught, that

Sect. 7.   *of* EUROPE.   131

that the World was made by the Angels, not by God. And that Christ came not into the World, nor did he truly suffer. He denied also the Resurrection of the Flesh, and permitted promiscuous Marriages. He likewise affirmed, that the true God was never known to the Patriarchs and Prophets. This Point was afterward maintained by *Menander, Cerinthus, Nicholas, Saturninus,* and *Basilides,* succeeding Hereticks. Upon this Doctrine also the *Tertullianists* and *Anthropomorphites* grounded their Heresie, in ascribing a Humane Body to God. His denying of the Trinity, begot afterwards the *Sabellians, Samosatenians, Montanists, Praxians, Photinians,* and *Priscillianists.* His Heresie of the Creation of the World by Angels, begot the *Marcionites, Manichees,* and the *Angelick* Hereticks, who worshipped *Angels.* In saying that Christ came not, nor suffered, he gave occasion to the Heresies of *Valentinians, Cerdonians, Marcionites, Aphthardocites, Docites, Samosatenians,* and *Mahometans.* Upon his denial of the Resurrection, *Basilides, Valentinus, Carpocrates, Apelles,* and the *Hierarchites,* grounded their Heresies. Besides, *Epicurism, Libertinism,* and *Atheism* got vigour hereby. By permitting Licentiousness and promiscuous Copulation, he gave occasion to the *Basilidians, Gnosticks, Machinees, Acatians, Eunomians,* and *Mahometans* to live like Beasts, and to slight Marriage. Besides these impious Opinions, he held Magick and Idolatry lawful. He gave to the Angels barbarous Names. He slighted the Law of *Moses,* as being not from God; and blasphemously denied the Holy Ghost to be a Substance, but a bare Virtue or Operation, and caused his Disciple to worship his Whore *Helena,* or *Selene,* for a Goddess.

See *Austin, Irenæus,* and *Epiphanius* upon this subject, in their Books they wrote against Heresies.

Q. 5. *Why did* Simon Magus *and his Scholars, with many other Hereticks since him, besides* Jews *and* Mahometans, *deny the Trinity?*

A. Partly the Malice of Satan, who hates and persecutes the Truth; partly the Pride of Hereticks, who would seem wiser than the Church; partly their Ignorance, because by natural reason they cannot comprehend this ineffable Mystery, and partly Malice against Christ, whose Divinity is denied by *Jews* and *Mahometans,* bred this Heresie, notwithstanding the Truth is plainly set down both in the Old and New Testament, asserted by all the Greek and Latin Fathers, confirmed by all General Councils, and proved by all Orthodox Divines, that it is no more repugnant to natural reason, for the Father, Son and Holy Ghost to be one God, than for the Soul, Mind and Body to be one Man : but because this Doctrine is sufficiently proved by all Divines, both ancient and modern, and all objections to the contrary answered and refused, I will forbear to set down what is so plain and obvious, already handled by so many Pens, and will only shew that the Doctrine of the Trinity was not unknown even by the Light of Nature to the Gentile Philosophers, Poets and Sybils : *Zoroastes* speaketh of the Father, *who having perfected all things, hath delivered them to the Second Mind, which Mind,* (saith he) *hath received from the Father*

Trinity denied by Simon Magus *and his Scholars, with others besides.* Jews *and* Mahometans *; and why.*

K 2   *knowledge*

knowledge and power. Here is a plain testimony of the First and Second Person. Concerning the Third, he saith, *That the Divine Love proceedeth from the Mind or Intellect*; What else is this Divine Love but the Holy Ghost? The *Chaldæan Magi*, which were their Philosophers, acknowledged Three Beginnings, to wit, *Ormasses, Mitris,* and *Ariminis,* that is God, the Mind and Soul. *Mercurius Trismegistus* taught his *Ægyptians, that God, who is life and light, begot the* World, *who is the other* Intellect, *and Maker of all things; and together with him another, who is the* Fiery *God, or* Spirit; here the Three Persons are distinctly named. He sheweth also, *that the subtil intellectual Spirit, by the power of God, did move in the Chaos*; this is consonant to the words of *Moses, the Spirit of God moved on the waters. Orpheus* Singeth the Praises *of the great God, and of his word which he first uttered. Pythagoras* and his Scholars were not ignorant of this Mystery, when they placed all perfection in the number of Three, and made Love the Original of all things. *Zeno* the *Stoick* confesseth, *that* λόγος, *the Word, is God, and the Spirit of Jove. Socrates* acknowledgeth *God to be the* Mind, *or* Intellect, *that the Essence of God is his* Idea, *which he begets by the knowledge of himself, and by which he made the World. Numenius* the *Pythagorean, Plotinus, Jamblicus,* and others, do Write very plainly of the three *Hypostases,* or Persons in the Trinity, so that no Christian can Write more fully, as may be seen in their own words, as they are alledged by *Du-Plessis* in his Book of the Truth of Christian Religion, who citeth also certain Oracles of *Serapis,* the *Ægyptian* chief Idol, or Devil, and of *Apollo,* out of *Suidas*; by which we may see how the evil Spirits are forced to confess the Trinity. I could also alledge the Testimonies of the *Sybils* to the same purpose; but because I study brevity, and these Heathen Testimonies, and *Sybilline* Verses, are cited by *Clemens Alexandrinus, Origen* against *Celsus, Cyril* against *Julian, Eusebius* in his Preparation. S. *Augustine* in his Books of the City, *&c.* I forbear to insist any more on this Subject. And as the Gentiles gave Testimony to this plurality of Persons, so did the *Jews* also, though now they reject this Doctrine, thinking that we, by worshipping the Trinity, do worship three Gods; but their Ancient Rabbins do prove the Trinity out of the Old Testament, as *Rabbi Simeon,* the Son of *Johai* brings a place out of *Rabbi Ibba,* upon *Deut.* 6. *Hearken, O Israel, the Lord our God is one God.* In the Hebrew thus, יהוה אלהינו יהוה אחד *Jehovah Elohenu Jehovah Echad.* He shews, that the first *Jehovah* is God the Father; the second word *Elohenu,* our God, is God the Son; for so he is called by the Prophet, and Evangelist, *Emanuel, God with us.* The third word *Jehovah,* is God the Holy Ghost. And the fourth word *Echad,* that is, *One,* is to shew the Unity of Essence in this plurality of Persons. Many other passages I could alledge out of the Writings of the Ancient Rabbies to confirm this Truth; but this is already performed by *Galatinus* in his Books *de Arcanis Catholicæ veritatis.*

Q. 6. *Who*

Sect. 7.   *of* EUROPE.

Q. 6. *Who were* Simon's *principal Scholars, and what were their opinions?*

A. Menander, a Samaritan alſo, and a Magician. He flouriſhed *Menander.* at Rome, in the Time of *Titus,* about 49 years after Chriſt. He held the ſame impious Opinions that *Simon* did ; but differed from him in ſaying, that himſelf, and not *Simon,* was the Saviour of the World ; and that therefore all ſhould be Baptized in his Name, and not in the Name of *Simon,* or Chriſt, and that all ſuch ſhould in power excel the Angels, and ſhould live Immortally here ; ſo he denied the Reſurrection of the Fleſh. To him ſucceeded *Saturni-* *Saturninus.* *nus,* and his Fellow-Scholar *Baſilides,* about the Fifteenth year of *Adrian* the Emperour, and after Chriſt the Hundreth. *Saturninus* was of *Antioch,* and infected *Syria* with his Poyſon, as *Baſilides* did *Ægypt.* *Saturninus* held the ſame impieties with *Simon* and *Menander,* but differed from them in ſaying, that the World was made only by Seven Angels, and not by all, againſt the Will and Knowledge of God. He taught alſo that ſome Men were naturally good, and ſome naturally evil; and that nothing muſt be eat that hath life in it, which was the Doctrine afterward of the *Manichees.* And impiouſly affirmed that ſome of the ancient Holy Prophets ſpake, and were ſent by Satan. *Baſilides* alſo was a *Simonian* Heretick, *Baſilides.* but differed from him, in holding, there were ſo many Heavens as days in the year, to wit, 365. The Chief God he called 'Αβραξας, in the Letters of which Name are contained 365. He held alſo, that this inferiour World and Man was Created by the 365th, or laſt Heaven. He taught alſo, that the Superiour God *Abraxas* begot the *Mind,* this the *Word :* Of the *Word* came *Providence,* and of *Providence Wiſdom :* Of *Wiſdom* the *Angels* were begot, the laſt of which was the God of the *Jews,* whom he calls an ambitious and turbulent God, who had attempted to bring all Nations in ſubjection to his People. He ſaid that Chriſt was ſent by *Abraxas* to oppoſe the Turbulent God of the *Jews,* and doth not call him *Jeſus* and Saviour, but *Goal,* a Redeemer. He held it un- See *Iren.* lawful to ſuffer Martyrdom for Chriſt ; He permitted Idolatry, and *us, Auſtin,* taught, that no voluntary ſin was pardonable, and that Faith was *Theodoret,* not the Gift of God, but of Nature, as alſo Election. The other *Tertullian,* Errors which this *Egyptian* held (for he was of *Alexandria*) were *Epiph. ni-* the ſame that *Simon* maintained.   *H, &c.*

Q. 7. *What was the Religion of the* Nicolaitans *and* Gnoſticks ?

A. The *Nicolaitans,* ſo called from *Nicholas,* one of the Seven *Nicolai-* Deacons, *Act.* 6. and whoſe Works Chriſt hated, *Rev.* 2. gave *tans.* themſelves to all uncleanneſs and fleſhly luſts, teaching, that Men ought to have their Wives in common. They made no ſcruple of eating things offered to Idols. At their Meetings or Love-Feaſts, they uſed to put out the Lights, and commit promiſcuous Adulteries with each others Wife. They taught, that the World was made by the copulation of light and darkneſs, out of which Angels, Dæmons, and Men were procreated. Man's Seed and Menſtruous

Gnosticks. struous Blood were with them Sacred, and used by the *Gnosticks* in their Divine Service, whereby they brought an odium upon Christianity. They would not have God, but Angels Creators of this inferiour World, which Angels they called by divers barbarous Names. *Nicholas*, the Father of this Sect, was by Birth an *Antiochian*, whose Doctrine began to spread about the beginning of *Domitian*'s Reign, after Christ 52 years, before St. *John*'s Banishment into *Pathmos*. The Professors of this Sect did long retain the Name of *Nicolaitans*, but were called *Gnosticks* from γνῶσις, Knowledge, which proud title they gave themselves, as if their knowledge had been transcendent above other Men. But their Knowledge was so whimsical, that neither they, or any else understood it; they babled much concerning their *Æones*, and of *Jaldabaoth*, who made the Heavens, and all things we see, of Water. They ascribed divers Sons to their Chief *Æon*, to wit, *Ennoia*, *Barheloth*, and *Prunicon*, which they named Christ. They held, that most things were procreated of the *Chaos*, and the *Abysse* of water and darkness. They taught also, that in faithful Men were two Souls, one holy, of the Divine Substance, the other adventitious by Divine Insufflation, common to Man and Beasts. These are the Souls that sin, and which pass from Man to Beast, after the opinion of *Pythagoras*, they held also there were two Gods, a good and an evil; as the *Manichees* afterward did. They made *Jesus* and *Christ* two distinct Persons, and that *Christ* descended in *Jesus* when he was Thirty years old, and then he wrought Miracles. On this Doctrine the *Eutychians* and *Nestorians* grounded their Heresies. They would have none to suffer Martyrdom for Christ, who they said conversed on the Earth after his Resurrection 18 Months. This Heresie was much spread in *Asia* and *Ægypt* about 129 years after Christ, and in *Spain* it flourished after Christ 386 years. Out of this Sink, the *Valentinians*, *Manichees*, and *Priscillianists* sucked their Poyson.

See *Irenæus, Tertullian, Austin, Theodoret,* &c.

Q. 8. *Of what Religion were the* Carpocratians?

Carpocrates.
A. *Carpocrates*, by birth an *Alexandrian* in *Ægypt*, who flourished about the year of Christ 109. in the time of *Antoninus Pius*, and was contemporary with *Saturninus*; this *Carpocrates*, I say, taught, there were two opposite Gods; that the Law and good Works were needless to those that had Faith; that we could not avoid the rage of evil Spirits, but by doing evil, for that was the way to please them. Therefore they gave themselves over to Magick and a Libidinous life. They taught also, that Christ was a meer Man, and that their Master *Carpocrates* was the better Man; hence sprung up the *Samosatenians* and *Arrians*. They said also, that Christ was begot as other Men, of *Joseph* and *Mary*; and that only his Soul ascended into Heaven. They held *Pythagorean* Transanimation, but denied the Resurrection, and that this World was not made by God, but by Satan. Because their Disciples should not publish their abominable Mysteries, they put a mark by a Bodkin on their right Ear. *Carpocrates* carried about with him his Punk *Marcellina*.

See the Authors above-named, *Eusebius* also, and *Clemens Alexandrinus*.

Q. 9. *What*

Sect. 7. *of* EUROPE. 135

Q. 9. *What was the Religion of* Cerinthus, Ebion, *and the Nazarites?*

A. *Cerinthus* being a *Jew* by Birth, and Circumcised, taught, that all Christians ought to be Circumcised: He lived in the time of St. *John* the Apostle, who would not enter into the same Bath with that pernicious Heretick, he spread his Heresie in *Domitian*'s time, about 62 years after Christ. He held the same impious Tenets that *Carpocrates*, and taught, that it was *Jesus* who died and rose again, but not Christ. He denied the Article of Life Eternal, and taught, that the Saints should enjoy in *Jerusalem* carnal delights for 1000 years; the maintainers of this whimsie afterward were the *Origenists, Chiliasts*, or *Millenaries*, and on this *Mahamet* founded his paradise. *Ebion* was a *Samaritan* by birth, but he would be esteemed a *Jew*. He lived also in *Domitian*'s time. He denied Christ's Divinity, and held the necessity of the Ceremonial Law, with *Cerinthus*: and that the use of flesh was unlawful, because all flesh was begot of impure generation. The *Ebionites*, of all the New Testament, admitted only St. *Matthew*'s Gospel, because it was Written in *Hebrew*. The *Ebionite* Heresie did not continue long under the Name of *Ebion*, but under other Names, to wit, *Sampsei*, and *Elcesitæ*. Against these Hereticks, St. *John*, who lived in their time, wrote his Gospel, to prove Christ's Divinity; and rejected St. *Paul*'s Epistles, because they refel the Ceremonial Law. As for the *Nazarites*, or *Nazarens*, they were before *Cerinthus* and *Ebion*, about the end of *Nero*, 37 years after Christ. They were the first that retained Circumcision with Baptism, and the Ceremonial Law with the Gospel. They were led much with private Revelations and Enthusiasms. They had more Gospels than one; to wit, the Gospel of *Eve*, and that which they called the Gospel of *Perfection*. They were much addicted to Fables. *Noah*'s Wife they called *Ouria*, which signifieth Fire in *Chaldee*; she oftentimes set the Ark on fire, which therefore was so many times Rebuilt. They make her also the first that imparted to Mankind the knowledge of Angels.

Cerinthus.

Ebionites.

Nazarites.

See *Epiphanius, Eusebius, Austin,* &c.

Q. 10. *What was the Heretical Religion of the* Valentinians, Secundians, *and* Ptolemaians?

A. The *Valentinians*, who, from their whimsical knowledge were called *Gnosticks*, had, for their Master, *Valentinus*, an *Ægyptian*, who lived in the time of *Antonius Pius* Emperour, about 110 years after Christ. He taught, that there were 30 *Æones*, Ages, or Worlds, who had their beginning from *Profundity* and *Silence*; that being the Male, this the Female. Of the Marriage or Copulation of these two, were begot *Understanding* and *Truth*, who brought forth eight *Æones*. Of the *Understanding* and *Truth*, were begot the *Word* and *Life*, which produced ten *Æones*. The *Word* and *Life* brought forth *Man* and the Church, and of these were procreated twelve *Æones*; these 8. 10. and 12. joyned together, made up the 30. the last of these 30 being abortive, produced the Heaven, Earth and Sea. Out of his imperfections were procreated divers

Valentinians.

K 4 evil,

evils, as darkness, out of his fear; evil spirits, out of his ignorances; out of his tears, springs and rivers'; and out of his Laughter light. They also taught, that Christ's Body was meerly Spiritual, and passed through the Virgin, as through a Conduit or Pipe. Evil was natural (they said) to the Creature, and therefore they made God the Author of evil; which afterward was the Doctrine of the *Manichees*. They held, that only the Soul was redeemed, and that there should be no Resurrection of the Body. Faith (they taught) was natural, and consequently Salvation, which all did not obtain, for want of good Works; this was the *Pelagian* Doctrine afterward. They made three sorts of Men; to wit, Spiritual, who are saved by Faith only: these they called the Sons of *Seth*; hence the *Sethian* Hereticks. The second sort are animal, or natural, who are saved by Works, and are of *Abel*; hence the *Abelites*. The third sort are carnal, who cannot be saved, these are of *Cain*; hence the *Cainite* Hereticks. They eat of things offered to Idols, slighted good Works as needless, and rejected the old Prophets. *Valentinus* his chief Scholar and Successor, was *Secundus*, whose Disciples, called *Secundians*, changed the Name, but retained the Doctrine of *Valentinus*, permitting all kind of vicious life, in that they held, Knowledge without good Works, would bring Men to Heaven, *Valentinus* held, that the Æones were only the defects of the Divine Mind; but *Secundus* said, they were true Essences, subsisting by themselves. He added also Light and Darkness to the eight principal Æones, and so made up ten. To *Secundus* succeeded *Ptolemæus* in *Valentinus* his School. He gave to *Bathos*, or *Profundity*, two Wives; to wit, 'Εννοια, that is, *Cogitation*; and Θέλησις, that is, *Will*. By the former Wife *Bythus*, he procreated Νῦν, the *Mind*; and by the other he begot 'Αλήθειαν, the *Truth*. *Ptolemæus* also slighted the Old Law.

Secundians.

Ptolemæans, See *Irenæus* Epiphanius, Austin, with his Commentator *Danæus,* &c.

Q. 11. *Of what Opinion were the* Marcites, Colarbasii, *and* Heracleonites?

A. Marcus was a notable Magician, who lived under *Antoninus Pius,* about 115 years after Christ. His Scholars called themselves *Perfect,* and bragged, that they were more excellent than *Peter* or *Paul.* They denied Christ's Humanity, and the Resurrection of the Flesh. They held two contrary beginnings, or God's; to wit, Σιγὴ, that is, *Silence*; and λόγος, that is, *Speech*. From these the *Marcionites* and *Manichees* borrowed their two Principles. They retained their Æones of *Valentinus,* but reduc'd them to four; to wit, *Silence, Speech,* and two unnamed; so, in stead of the Christian *Trinity,* they held a *Quaternity*. They taught, that all Men, and every member in Man's Body, were subject to, and governed by certain Letters and Characters. They Baptized not in the Name of the Father, Son, and Holy Ghost; but in the Name of the Father unknown, of Truth the Mother of all, and of him who descended upon Jesus. By Magical words they bragged, that they could turn the Sacramental Wine into Blood, and bring down the Grace of God from Heaven into the Chalice. The *Colarbasians,*

Colarbasians.

Sect. 7.   *of* EUROPE.   137

Larbasians, so called from *Colarbus*, or *Colarbasus* the Author of that Sect, ascribed the life, actions and events of Man, and all Humane Affairs to the seven Planets, as Authors thereof. They held also but one Person in the Deity, called by different Names. They divide Jesus from Christ, as the *Nestorians* afterward; and taught, that Christ was a Flower compacted and made up of 30 *Æones*. *Heracleon*, Father of the *Heracleonites*, lived above 100 years after Christ. These divided the *Æones* into good and bad, and held two beginnings, to wit, *Profundity* and *Silence*. *Profundity* they held to be the most ancient of all; and that of this with *Silence*, all the other *Æones* were procreated. They said, that Man consisted of a Soul, Body, and some Third Substance; they held it no sin to deny Christ, in danger of life, with the Mouth, if so be the Heart believed in him. They used in their Prayers Superstitious and Magical words, to drive away Devils. And they thought, by anointing their Dead with Water, Oyl and Balsam, to free them from Eternal Death. *Heracloo-nites.* See *Tertul. lan, Irenæus, Epiphanius, Austin*, &c.

Q. 12. *Of what Religion were the* Ophites, Cainites, *and* Sethites?

A. These were called also *Ophei*, and *Ophiomorphi*, from ὄφις, the Serpent which they worshipped. This Sect began about the year of Christ 132. They taught, that Christ was the Serpent which deceived *Eve*; and that he, in the form of a Serpent entred the Virgins Womb. In the Eucharist they used to produce a Serpent, by Inchanting words, out of his Hole, or rather Box, in which they carried him about; neither did they think that the Sacramental Bread was Consecrated, till that Serpent had first touched it, or tasted thereof; they denied also the Resurrection of the Flesh, and Christ's Incarnation. The *Caini* were so called, because they worshipped *Cain* as the Author of much goodness to Mankind, so they worshipped *Esau, Core, Dathan, Abiram,* and *Judas*, who betrayed Christ, saying, that he fore-knew what happiness should come to Mankind by Christ's death, therefore he betrayed him. Some of this Sect were called ἀντίτακ), that is, resisters of God, for they opposed him what they could in his Laws, therefore rejected the Law of *Moses* as evil, and worshipped the wicked Angels, whom they pleased by their evil actions; they taught also, that we were evil by nature, and that the Creator of the World was an Unknown God, and envious to *Cain, Esau,* and *Judas*. The *Sethites*, so called from *Seth, Adam*'s Son, whom they worshipped, lived most in *Egypt*. About the same time that the *Cainites* flourished. They thought that *Seth* was born of a Superior *Virtue*, which they called *Mother*. She of the chief God brought forth *Seth* the Father of all the Elect: So they make *Seth* a part of the Divine Substance, who came in place of *Abel*, who, by the envy of some Angels, stirring up *Cain* against him, was slain. They prate also, that by the cunning of some Angels, some of *Cain*'s Posterity were preserved in the Ark, from the Flood which was sent by this great Mother to punish the *Cainites* for the Murthering of *Abel*. Of this *Ophites. Cainites. Sethites.*

posterity

posterity of *Cain* proceed all wicked Men. They denied the Resurrection, and held, that the Angels had carnal commerce with Women, and of this copulation two Men were produced, the one Earthly, the other Heavenly, being an Hermaphrodite, who was created to God's Image, who, as they blasphemously taught, is an Hermaphrodite, and so *Adam* also. They made Christ, who was born of the Virgin, to be no other than *Seth*.

See the above named Authors.

Q. 13. *What Religion did the* Archonticks *profess, and the* Ascothyptæ ?

Archonticks.

A. These were the last of the *Valentinian* Hereticks, called *Archontici*, from ἀρχὸν, or ἀρχόντων, that is, *Principalities*; these they worshipped as inferiour Gods, Father of the Angels, and creators of the world; of *Photenia* the Mother, were the angels begot by these *Archontes*. One *Peter* an *Anchorite*, and a Monk of *Palestina* was author of this Sect, in the time of *Constantius* the Son of *Constantine*, about the year of Christ 308. These spawned another Sect, which they called *Ascothyptas*, because they brake in pieces all the Plate and vessels used in the Sacrament; for they rejected the Sacraments of the Church. They despised good works, and gave themselves to all uncleanness, and slighted the Old Testament, and denied the Resurrection, and Sacraments, as is said, thinking it unlawful to represent Spiritual and Heavenly things by corporeal and earthly. They thought that the Devil begot *Cain* and *Abel* of *Eve*; both these Sons were Reprobates. And that a man who hath knowledge and faith, may be saved, let his life be never so vitious, and that the Devil was the Son of the Jewish, but not of the Christian God. They also affixed to each Heaven or Sphear an angel, as the *Peripateticks* did an *Intelligence*.

Ascothyptæ.

See Austin, Theodoret, Isidorus,

Q. 14. *What was the Religion of* Cerdon *and* Marcion ?

Cerdon.

A. *Cerdon* lived about the time of *Valentinus* the Heretick, under *Antoninus Pius* Emperour, 110 years after Christ; he taught that there were two contrary Gods; the one a God of mercy and pity, the other of justice and severity, whom he called evil, cruel, and the maker of the world. The former God he called good, and the Father of Christ, and Author of the Gospel; but *Moses* Law they rejected and the Old Testament, as proceeding from the other God, to wit, of justice. The *Cerdonians* also denied the Resurrection of the flesh and Humanity of Christ; affirming that he was born of a Virgin, nor suffered but in shew. *Marcion,* by birth a *Paphlagonian* near the *Euxin* Sea, was *Cerdon*'s Scholar, whose opinions he preferred to the Orthodox Religion out of spleen, because his Father Bishop *Marcion* excommunicated him for Whoredom, and because he could not without true repentance be received again in the Church; therefore he professed and maintained *Cerdon*'s Heresies at *Rome*, in the time of *M. Antoninus Philosophus*, 133 years after Christ, but he refined some points, and added to them some of his own phansies. With *Cerdon* he held two contrary gods, and denied Christs incarnation of the Virgin, and therefore blotted his Genealogy out of the Gospel, affirming his body

Marcion.

ly to be from Heaven, not from the Virgin. He denied that this world by reason of the Ataxie and Disorder in it, could be the work of the good God. He rejected the Old Testament and the Law, as repugnant to the Gospel; *which is false; for there is no repugnancy.* He denied the Resurrection, and taught that Christ by descending into Hell, delivered from thence the souls of *Cain, Esau,* the *Sodomites,* and other reprobates, translating them into Heaven. He condemned the eating of flesh, and the married life; and renewed baptism upon every grievous fall into sin. If any of the *Catechumeni* died, some in their name were baptized by the *Marcionites.* They also baptized, and administred the *Eucharist* in presence of the *Catechumeni,* against the custom of the Church. They permitted Women also to baptize. They condemned all Wars as unlawful, and held transanimation with the *Pythagoreans.*

See *Epiphanius, Eusebius, Austin, Theodoret, &c.*

Q. 15. *What was the Religion of* Apelles, Severus, *and* Tatianus?

A. *Apelles* whose Scholars were called *Apellitæ,* was *Marcion's* Disciple, and a *Syrian* by birth. He flourished under *Commodus* the Emperour, about 150 years after Christ. He taught that there was but one chief God, to whom was subordinate a fiery God who appeared to *Moses* in the bush, who made the world, and gave the Law to the *Israelites,* and was their God. He gave to Christ a body compacted of the Starry, and Elementary substance, and appeared in the shape only of man. This body when he ascended, he left behind him, every part thereof returning to their former principles; and that Christs spirit is only in Heaven. He rejected the Law and Prophets, and denied the Resurrection. *Severus,* author of the *Severians,* was contemporary with *Apelles* under *Commodus,* 156 years after Christ. He used the company of one *Philumeni* a Strumpet and Witch. He taught his disciples to abstain from Wine, as being poyson, begot of Satan, in the form of a Serpent, with the Earth. The world he said was made by certain powers of Angels, which he called by divers barbarous names. He hated Women and Marriage, denied the Resurrection, the Old Testament, and Prophets, using instead of them, certain Apocryphal Books. *Tatianus,* a bad Scholar of a good Master, *Justin Martyr,* was a *Mesopotamian* by birth, and lived under *M. Antoninus Philosophus,* 142 years after Christ; his Disciples were called *Tatiani* from him, and *Encratiæ* from ἐγκράτεια, temperance, or continence, for they abstain from Wine, Flesh, and Marriage. They were called also *Hydro Paristatæ,* users of Water, for in stead of wine they made use of water in the Sacrament. They held that *Adam* was never restored to mercy after his fall; and that all men the sons of *Adam* are damned, without hope of salvation, except the *Tatiani.* They condemned the Law of *Moses,* the eating of flesh, and the use of wine, and held Procreation of children to be the work of Satan; yet they permitted, though unwillingly, Monogamy or the marrying once, but never again; they denied that God made male and female, and that Christ was the seed of *David.*

Apelles.

Severus.

Tatianus.

S *Irenæus, Tertullian, Eusebius, Austin, Theodoret, Epiphanius, &c.*

Qu. 16.

Cataphrygi- **Qu. 16.** *Of what Religion was the* Cataphrygians?
ans.

A. Montanus Difciple to *Tatianus*, who was his contemporary, was author of this Sect, who for a while were from him called *Montanifts*; but being afhamed of his wicked life, and unhappy end, they were afterward from the Country where he was born, and which was firft infected with his herefie, called *Cataphrygians*, καταφρύγας: they were named alfo *Tafcotragita*, becaufe they ufed in praying to thruft their fore-fingers into their Noftrils, to fhew their devotion, and anger for fin. *Tafcus* in their Language, fignifieth a long ftick or ftaff, and *Druggus* their Nofe, as if you would fay *Perticunafati*, as the Interpreter of *Epiphanius* tranflates it. They loved to be called *Spirituales*, becaufe they bragged much of the gifts of the Spirit; others that were not of their opinion, they called natural men. This Herefie began about 145 years after Chrift, and lafted above 500 years. He had two Strumpets which followed him, to wit, *Prifca* and *Maximilla*, thefe forfook their Husbands, pretending zeal to follow *Montanus*; whereas indeed they were notorious Whores: they took upon them to prophefie, and their dictates were held by *Montanus* as Divine oracles, but at laft, he and they, for company hanged themfelves. He blafphemoufly held himfelf not only to be in a higher meafure infpired by the Holy Ghoft, than the Apoftles were, but alfo faid, that he was the very Spirit of God, which in fome fmall meafure defcended on the Apoftles; he condemned fecond marriages, and yet allowed Inceft. He trufted altogether to Revelations and Enthufiafms, and not to the Scripture. In the *Euchariſt*, thefe Wretches mingled the Bread with Infants Blood; they confounded the Perfons of the Trinity, affirming the Father fuffered.

See *Epi-*
phanius,
Eufebius,
Auſtin,
Theodoret,
Ifidore, &c.

Q. 17. *What was the Religion of the* Pepuzians, Quintilians, *and* Artotyrites?

Pepuzians. *A.* Thefe were Difciples of the *Cataphrygians*: *Pepuzians* were fo called from *Pepuza*, a Town between *Galatia* and *Cappadocia*, where *Montanus* dwelt; and *Quintilians*, from *Quintilla*, another whorifh Prophetefs, and companion to *Prifca* and *Maximilla*. They held *Pepuza*, to be that new *Jerufalem* foretold by the Prophets, and mentioned in the Epiftle to the *Hebrews*, and in the *Revelations*. In this they faid we fhould enjoy life eternal. They preferred Women before Men, affirming that Chrift affumed the form of a Woman, not of a Man. And that he was the authour of their wicked Tenets. They commended *Eve* for eating the forbidden fruit, faying, that by fo doing, fhe was the author of much happinefs to man. They admitted Women to Ecclefiaftical Functions, making Bifhops and Priefts of them, to Preach, and adminifter the Sacraments. They mingled alfo the Sacramental Bread with humane *Artotyrites.* Blood. The *Artotyritæ* were fo called from offering Bread and Cheefe in the Sacrament inftead of Wine, becaufe our firft Parents offered the fruits of the Earth, and of Sheep, and becaufe God accepted *Abel*'s facrifice, which was the fruits of his Sheep, of which Cheefe cometh; therefore they held cheefe more acceptable than Wine.

Quintilians.

of E U R O P E.

ts they were *Pepuzians*, and differed from them See *Epi-*
ng; therefore they were called *Artotyritæ*, from *phanius,*
ɪɛ́s cheese. *Aust in,*
vas the Religion of the Tessarescæ Decacitæ, or *Theodoret,*
ɪd of the Allogiani?
ɪf these were so called from observing *Easter* on
ɪf the Moon in *March*, after the manner of the
de St. *John* the author of that custom, which *Quartade-*
ɛ Orential Churches, till Pope *Victor* excommu- *cimani.*
ɪismatick, in dissenting from the custom of the
This controversie fell out about the 165 year
ɪen being Emperour, and from the first Origi-
d 200 years. This Heresie was condemned by
and ordered that *Easter* should be kept after
Western Church, which derived their custom
These Hereticks also denied repentance to those
m; which was the *Novatian* Heresie. *Alogia-* *Alogiani.*
ɪ the privative, and λόγ۞ the word, because
to be the word, and consequently they denied
on and *Cerinthus* had done before, *Samosatenus,*
ohmetans afterward. These *Alogiani* rejected
and his Apocalypse, as not written by him, but
ɪs ridiculous; for *Cerinthus* denied *Christ's* Divi-
ɪhn *asserteth, in writing, that the Word was God.*
ɛre named also *Berilliani* from *Berillus* a Bishop
ught that Christ was a man, and then became, See *Epipha-*
The first broacher of this Heresie is thought to *nius, Austin.*
ɪne man, who lived about the time of *Severus* *Theodoret,*
ɪrs after Christ, from him they were called *Ar-* *Isidore, &c.*

ɪs *the Religion of the* Adamians, *and* Elcesians, *and*

t. or *Adamites*, so called either from one *Adam* their *Adamians.*
am the first man, whose nakedness they imitate,
ter the *Gnosticks*, and were called *Prodiciani* from
they followed. Of this Sect there be many extant
held it unlawful for men or women to wear
igregation and assemblies, seeing their meetings
dise on earth, where they were to have life Eter-
ɪven; as *Adam* then in his Paradise, so Christians
naked, and not cloathed with the badges of their
hey rejected marriages as diabolical; therefore
ɪous copulation in the dark; they rejected also
l, as needless, seeing he knew without us what
Elcesei, so called from *Elcesa*, an impostor; *Elcesians.*
a spotted kind of Serpent, which they represen-
able dispositions, were much addicted to judici-
ooth-saying. They held two Priests, one below
n, a meer man, and one above; they confound
Christ

Chrift with the Holy Ghoft, and fomtimes they call him Chrift's Sifter, but in a mafculine name, to both which Perfons they give longitude, latitude, and locality. To water they afcribe a Divinity, and fo they did to two Whores, *Marthus* and *Marthana*, the duft of whofe feet and fpittle they worfhipped as holy reliques. They had a certain Apocrypha Book, the reading whereof procured remiffion of fins; and they held it no fin to deny Chrift in time of Perfecution. This Herefie began to fpread, about 210 years after Chrift, under *Gordian* the Emperor. See *Origen*, who writ a-

Thedocians. gainft it. The *Theodocians* fo called from one *Theodocus*, or *Theodoti-*
Of thefe *on*, who lived under *Severus* Emperor, 170 years after Chrift. He
Hereticks was a *Bizantian* by birth, and a Tanner by profeffion, who
fee *Tertul-* taught that in times of perfecution we may deny Chrift, and in fo
lian, Eufe- doing, we deny not God, becaufe Chrift was meerly man, and
bius, Epi- that he was begotten of the feed of man. He alfo added to, and
phanius, took from the writings of the Evangelifts what he pleafed.
Auftin,The-
odoret, &c.   Q. 20. *What was the Religion of the* Melchifedecians, Bardefa-nifts, *and* Noetians?

Melchife-   A. The former were called *Melchifedecians* for believing that
decians. Melchifedeck was not a man, but a Divine power fuperior to Chrift, whom they held to be a meer man. One *Theodocus* Scholar to the former *Theodocus* the Tanner, was another of this Sect, who lived
Bardefa- under *Severus* about 174 years after Chrift. The *Bardefanifts* were
nifts. fo called from one *Bardefanes*, a Syrian, who lived under *Verus* the Emperour, 144 years after Chrift. He taught that all things, even God himfelf were fubject to Fate, or a Stoical neceffity, fo that he took away all liberty, both from God and man; and that vertue and vice depended on the Stars. He renewed alfo the whimfies of the *Æones*, by which he overthrew Chrifts Divinity, and
Noetians. denied the Refurrection of the flefh. The *Noetians*, fo called from *Noetus*, born in *Smyrna*, taught that there was but one Perfon in the Trinity which was both mortal and immortal, in Heaven God, and impatible; on earth Man, and patible. So they made a Trinity, not of Perfons, but of Names and Functions. *Noetus* alfo
See the taught, that he was *Mofes*, and that his brother was *Aaron*. This
Authors Heretick was buried with the burial of an Afs, and his City *Smyr-*
already *na* was overthrown eight years after he had broached his Herefie.
named. He lived about 140 years after Chrift, under *M. Antonius*, and *L. Verus* Emperours.

   Q. 21. *Of what Religion were the* Valefians, *the* Cathari, Angelici *and* Apoftolici?

Valefians.   A. The *Valefians*, fo called from one *Valens*, an Arabian, who out of the doctrine of the *Gnofticks* or *Tatians* condemned Marriage and Procreation. Therefore his Scholars after the example of *Origen*, gelded themfelves, thinking none can enter into Heaven but Eunuchs. *Whereas the Eunuch, Chrift fpeaks of, be fuch, as by continence fubdue the lufts of the flefh*; This Herefie fpringing under *Julianus Philippus* Emperour, about the year of Chrift 216. The
Cathari. *Cathari* καθαροί, fo called by themfelves, as if they were purer than

of EUROPE.   143

ived moſt of their Tenets from *Novatus*, hence
vatians. This *Novatus* lived under *Decius* the
ſt 220 years. He was an African born. This
e Time of *Arcadius*, to wit, 148 years; they
ɔ thoſe who fell after Baptiſm, they bragged
ty and good works. They condemned ſecond
ous. They uſed rebaptization, as the *Dona-*
They rejected alſo Oyl or *Chriſm* in Baptiſm.
lſo called from worſhipping of Angels; it ſeems *Angelici.*
ɡun in the Apoſtles time, who condemneth it;
ſortly after the *Melchiſedecians*, about the year
: *Apoſtolici* were ſo called from imitating the *Apoſtolici.*
les, theſe were the ſpawn of the *Encratites*, a-
iſt 145. They rejected all married people as
, and held that the Apoſtles perpetually ab-
ʒe. They had all things in common, holding
n, who had any thing peculiar to themſelves.
ance and reconciliation to thoſe that fell after
f the Evangeliſts, they uſed Apocrypha books, See the
ling to the Egyptians; the acts of *Andrew* and Authors
:eticks were called alſo *Apotactitæ* by the La- above na-
reeks *Ἀποτακτικοί*, from renouncing of the med.

the Religion of the Sabellians, Origenians, *and*

were indeed all one in opinion with the *Noeti-*
rew more famous than the other; for *Sabellius*
was a better Scholar than *Noetus*. Sabellianiſm *Sabellians.*
bout the year of Chriſt 224, under the Perſe-
They held there was but one Perſon in the
followeth that the Father ſuffered; therefore
tripaſſiani. This one Perſon or *ὑποςάσις*, ſay
:rs names, as occaſion ſerves. The *Origenians*
ɔne *Origenes* a Monk, who lived in *Egypt*, and *Origenians.*
y. Theſe condemned marriage, extolled concu-
enemies to propagation, committing the ſin of
ject ſuch books of the old and new Teſtament,
irriage. The *Origeniſts* or *Adamantians* were *Origeniſts.*
nous *Origen*, who for his conſtancy in times
or his inexhauſted labours, was named *Ada-*
ɔegan to ſpread about the year of Chriſt 247,
Emperour, and continued above 334 years.
ed firſt in the council of *Alexandria* 200 years
again in the fifth general council of *Conſtanti-*
the firſt; they held παλιγγενεσίαν, or a revolu-
:heir eſtate and condition after death, into the
verſe in the world; and ſo denying the perpe-
tate either in Heaven or Hell, by conſequence
rrection of the fleſh. They held alſo that the
                                        puniſhment

punishment of the Devils and Reprobates should last only 1000 years, and then should be saved. They taught that Christ and the holy Ghost do no more see the Father, than we see the Angels; that the Son is coessential to the Father, but not coeternal; because, say they, the Father created him, as he did also the holy Spirit. That the souls were created long before this world, and for sinning in Heaven were sent down into their bodies, as into Prisons. They did also overthrow the whole historical truth of Scriptures, by their allegories.

See Eusebius, Epiphanius, Austin, Theodoret, &c.

Qu. 23. *What was the Religion of the* Samosatenians, *and* Photinians?

Samosatenians.

A. *Paulus Samosatenus* was so called from *Samosata*, where he was born, near *Euphrates*. His Scholars were called *Paulinians* and *Samosatenians*, and afterward *Photinians*, *Lucians* and *Marcellians*, from these new teachers. Their belief was, that Christ was meerly man, and had no being till his Incarnation. This Heresie was taught 60 years before *Samosatenus*, by *Artemon*, and was propagated afterward by *Photinus*, *Lucian*, and *Marcellus*, *Arrius* and *Mahomet*. They held that the God-head dwelt not in Christ bodily, but as in the Prophets of old, by grace and efficacy, and that he was only the external, not the internal word of God. Therefore they did not baptize in his name; for which cause the Council of *Nice* rejected their baptism as none, and ordered they should be rebaptized, who were baptized by them. This Heresie under the name of *Samosatenus* brake out about 232 years after Christ, and hath continued in the Eastern parts ever since. The *Photinians*, so called from *Photinus*, born in the lesser *Galatia*, held the same Heresie with *Samosatenus*, and began to propagate it about the year of Christ 323 at *Syrmium*, where he was Bishop, under *Constantius* the Emperor; and before him, *Marcellus* his Master, under *Constantine* the Great, publickly taught it, affirming also, that the Trinity was the extention of the Divinity, which is dilated in to three, and contracted again into one, like wax being contracted, may be dilated by heat. This Heresie was much spread under *Valens* the *Arrian* Emperor, 343 years after Christ.

Photinians.

See the forenamed Authors.

Q. 24. *What was the* Manichean *Religion?*

Manichees.

A. *Manes*, a *Persian* by birth, and a Servant by condition, was Father of the *Manichean* Sect; which was the sink of almost all the former Heresies, for from the *Marcionites* they derived their opinion of two Principles, or Gods; one good, the other bad. With the *Encratites* they condemned the eating of Flesh, Eggs, and Milk; they held also with the *Anthropomorphites*, that God had Members, and that he was substantially in every thing, though never so base, as dung and dirt, but was separated from them by Christ's coming, and by the Elect, *Manicheans* eating of the fruits of the Earth, whose intestines had in them a cleansing and separating vertue. They condemned also the use of Wine, as being the gall of the Princes of darkness. With *Marcion* also they rejected the Old Testament, and curtilated the New, by excluding Christ's

Genealogies

Genealogies; and said, that he who gave the Law, was not the true God. They babled also, that there was a great combat between the Prince of darkness, and of light; in which, they who held for God, were taken captives, for whose redemption God laboureth still. With the *Ophites*, they held, that Christ was the Serpent which deceived our First Parents; and, with divers of the precedent Hereticks, not only did they deny Christ's Divinity, but his Humanity also; affirming, that he feigned himself to suffer, die, and rise again; and that it was the Devil who truly was crucified. With *Valentinus*, they taught, that Christ's Body was fixed to the Stars, and that he redeemed only our Souls, not our Bodies; With the former Hereticks, they denied the Resurrection, and with *Pythagoras*, held Transanimation. With *Montanus*, *Manes* held, that he was the true *Paraclet*, or comforter, which Christ promised to send. With the Gentiles they worshipped the Sun, Moon, and some Idols; with *Anaxagoras*, they held, the Sun and Moon to be Ships; and told, that one *Shacla* made *Adam* and *Eve*. They made no scruple to swear by the creatures; they gave to every Man two contrary Souls, which still struggle in him. With the Poets they held, that the Heaven was supported by the shoulders of one whom they called *Laturanius*. They make the Soul of Man, and of a Tree, the same in essence, as being both of them a part of God; with the former Hereticks also they condemned Marriage, and permitted promiscuous copulation; and that not for procreation, but for pleasure. They rejected Baptism as needless, and condemned Alms-giving, or Works of Charity; they make our will to sin natural, and not acquired by our fall; as for sin they make it a substance, communicated from Parents to Children; and not a quality, or affection. These wicked opinions raged in the world 340 years after *Manes* was excoriated alive for Poysoning the *Persian* King's Son; these Hereticks were three Sects; to wit, *Manichees*, *Catharists*, or Puritans; and *Macarii*, or blessed.

Of those see Clem. Alex. andrinus, Epiphanius Theodoret, and Austin, who had been himself a Manichee.

Q. 25. *What was the Religion of the* Hierachites, Melitians, *and* Arrians?

A. The *Hierachites*; so called from *Hieracha*, an *Ægyptian*, and a Monk, who lived shortly after *Origen*, under *Galljenus*, 234 years after Christ, taught, that Married People could not enjoy Heaven; nor Infants, because they cannot Merit; they admitted none in their Church, but those that lived single. They denied that Paradise in which Man was Created, had any earthly or visible being. They held *Melchisedeck* to be the Holy Ghost, and denied the Resurrection. The *Meletians* (so called from *Meletius*, a *Theban* Bishop in *Ægypt*; who, because he was deposed for offering to Idols, in Spleen he taught the *Novatian* Heresie, in denying pardon of sins to those that fell, though they Repented) rejected all from their Communion, who, in time of Persecution, fell from Christ, though they afterward Repented. They used Pharisaical washings, and divers Judaical Ceremonies, and in their Humiliations, to appease God's Anger with dancing, singing, and gingling of

Hierachi, &c.

Meletians,

Arrians.

See *Epiphanius,*
Austin, Eusebius,
Ruffinus,
Socrates,
and *Theodoret,* in their Histories.

small bells. This Heresie began under *Constantine* the Emperour 286 years after Christ. The *Arrians* so called from *Arrius* a *Lybian* by birth, and a Presbyter of *Alexandria* by Profession, were called also *Exoucontii*, for saying that Christ was ἐξ ἐκ ὄντων, created of nothing. This Heresie brake out under *Constantine* 290 years after Christ, and over-run a great part of the Christian world. They held Christ to be a creature; and that he had humans body, but no humane soul, the divinity supplying the room thereof. They held also the Holy Ghost a creature, proceeding from a creature, to wit, Christ. The *Arrians* in their *Doxologies* gave glory not *to the Father, and to the Son, and to the Holy Ghost*, but *to the Father, by the Son, in the Holy Ghost*. They rebaptized the *Orthodox* Christian and baptized only the upper parts to the *Navel*, thinking the inferiour parts unworthy of baptism.

Q. 26. *What was the Religion of the* Audians, Semiarrians, *and* Macedonians?

Audians.

A. The *Audiani* so called from *Audæus* a *Syrian*, who appeared under *Valentinian* the Emperour 338 years after Christ, were named afterwards *Anthropomorphytæ*, for ascribing to God a humane body: these, as afterward the *Donatists*, forsook the Orthodox Church, because some wicked men were in it. They held darkness, fire and water eternal, and the Original of all things. They admitted to the Sacrament all Sorts of Christians, even such as were profane and impenitent. The *Semiarrians* were those who neither would have Christ to be ὁμοούσιον, of the same individual, essence with the Father, as the Orthodox Church held; nor yet ὁμοιούσιον, of a like Essence, but ἑτερούσιον, of a different Essence, but of a like Will: and so they taught, that Christ was not God in Essence, but in Will only and Operation. This Heresie also held that the Holy Ghost was Christ's creature. It began under *Constantius* the Emperour 330 years after Christ. The chief author thereof was one-eyed *Acatius*, Bishop of *Cæsarea Palestina*, successor to *Eusebius*; hence they were called *Acatiani*. The *Macedonians* so called from *Macedonius*, Bishop of *Constantinople*; held that the Holy Ghost was a creature, and the servant of God, but not God himself; and withal that by the Holy Spirit was meant only a power created by God, and communicated to the creatures. This Heresie sprung up, or rather being sprung up long before, was stiffly maintained under *Constantius* the Son of *Constantine* 312 years after Christ; and was condemned in the second Oecumenical Council at *Constantinople* under *Theodosius* the great. These Hereticks were called πνευμαλομάχοι, fighters against the spirit.

Semiarrians.

Macedonians.

See *Socrates, Sozomen, Theodoret, Isidore, Austin, Epiphanius,* &c.

Q. 27. *Of what Religions were the* Ærians, Ætians, *or* Eunomians, *and* Apollinarists?

Ærians.

A. The *Ærians* so called from *Ærius* the Presbyter, who lived under *Valentinian* the first, 340 years after Christ, held that there was no difference between a Bishop and a Presbyter, that Bishops could not ordain, that the dead were not to be prayed for; that there should not be set or anniversary fasts, and with the *Encratites*, or

Apotactitæ

Apotactitæ admitted none to their communion, but such as were continent, and had renounced the world. They were called *Syllabici* also, as standing captiously upon Words and Syllables. They are said also to condemn the use of flesh: the *Ætians* were called so from *Ætius* a Deacon, whose successor was *Eunomius*, about the year of Christ 331 under the Emperor *Constantius*; he was Bishop of *Cyzicum*, whose Disciples were called *Eunomians*, and *Anomei*, for holding that Christ was no way like the Father. They were called also *Eudoxiani*, *Theophraniani*. When they were banished, they lived in holes, and caves, and so were called *Troglodite* and *Gothici*, because his Heresie prevailed much among the *Goths*, by means of *Ulphillas* their Bishop. These Hereticks held that God could be perfectly here comprehended by us, that the Son was neither in power, Essence, or Will, like the Father, and that the Holy Ghost was created by the Son; that Christ also only assumed mans body, but not his soul. They permitted all kind of licentiousness, saying, that faith without good works could save. The *Eunomians* did rebaptize the *Orthodox* professors, and baptized in the name of the Father uncreated, the Son created, and the Holy Ghost created by the Son. The *Apollinarists* so called from *Apollinaris* Presbyter in *Laodicea*, divided Christ's humanity in affirming that he assumed mans body and a sensitive soul, but not the reasonable or intellective soul of man, because that was supplied by the divinity; from this division they were named *Duplares* and *Dimoiritæ*. In stead of the Trinity, they acknowledge only three distinct degrees of power in God, the greatest is the Father, the lesser is the Son, and the least of all the Holy Ghost. They held that Christ's flesh was consubstantial with his Divinity, and that he took not his flesh from the Virgin, but brought it from Heaven. They held that Christ had but one will, that mens souls did propagate other souls, that after the Resurrection the Ceremonial Law should be kept as before. This Heresie brake out 350 years after Christ, under *Valens* the Emperor.

Ætians.

Eunomiani.

Apollinærists.

See the Authors above named.

Q. 28. *What did the* Antidicomarianites, Messalians, *and* Metangismonites *profess?*

A. The former of these were so called, because they were ἀντίδικοι Μαείας, adversaries to *Maries* Virginity. Whence they were named *Antimaritæ*, and *Helvidians*, from *Helvidius* the author, who lived under *Theodosius* the great, 355 years after Christ: These held, that *Mary* did not continue Virgin after Christ was born, but that she was known by *Joseph*, whereas she was indeed ἀειπάρθενος a perpetual Virgin. The *Messalians* were so named from the *Chaldaick* word, *Tsalah*, which signifies to pray, therefore in *Greek* they were called εὐκταί from εὐχή, prayer, because they did pray continually; and *Martyriani* for worshipping as a Martyr one of their Sect, who was killed by a Souldier. They were called also *Enthusiastæ* from their pretended inspirations, and *Euphemitæ* from εὐφημίαι, praises or eulogies which they sung to God, and *Satanici* from worshipping of Satan, whom they held to be the go-

Antidicomarianites.

Messalians ans.

vernour

vernour of mankind. They held that nothing was required to salvation, but prayer; therefore they rejected Faith, Preaching and Sacraments; and taught that God was visible to our bodily eyes, and that Satan was to be worshipped that he might do no hurt; they bragged, that they could visibly expel Satan, whom they could see come out of the mouth like smoak, and in form of a Sow with her Pigs, into whose place the Holy Ghost did visibly succeed. They live idly, and hate working, so that they excommunicate any of their Sect that labour; they condemn all Alms-giving, except to those of their own Sect: they allow lying, perjury, and dissembling in Religion. They slighted the Sacraments, and held that Baptism was of no use, but only for sins past. This Heresie prevailed under *Valentinian* and *Valens*, Emperours, 341 years after Christ. The *Metangismonites* were so call'd from μεταγγισμὲνΘ-, that is transvasation, or putting one vessel, or ἀγγῖον, in Greek, into another; for they held that the Son was in the Father, as a lesser vessel in a bigger; and so they make the Divine Essence bigger and lesser than it self, they held also that God was corporeal.

Me'angismonites.
See Philaster, Austin, Damascen, Theodoret, &c.

Q. 29. *What was the Religion of the* Hermians, Proclianites, *and* Patricians?

Hermians.

A. The *Hermians* or *Hermogonians*, so called from *Hermius* or *Hermogenes* an African under *Severus* the Emperor, 177 years after Christ, are by Saint *Austin* reckoned the same with the *Seleucians*. These held that the elements or matter of the world was coeternal with God. That the angels were made of spirit and fire, and that they were the creators of mens souls. That evil was partly from God, partly from the matter; that Christ in his ascension left his body in the Sun; they denied that there was ever any visible Paradise; that there shall be any Resurrection, and that Baptism by water was to be used. The *Proclianites* were so called from one *Proclus* or *Proculus*, an obscure man, who held the Hermogenian opinions, and withal taught that Christ was not yet come in the flesh. The *Patricians* were so called from one *Patricius* whom *Danæus* thinks lived under *Arcadius* the Emperour, 387 years after Christ. These held that no God, but Satan made mans flesh, and that therefore men may lawfully kill themselves to be rid of the flesh; they admit and reject what Books of the Old Testament they please.

Proclianites.
Patricians.
See Austin, Isidore, Gratian, and others.

Qu. 30. *What did the* Ascitæ, Pattalorinchitæ, Aquarii, *and* Coluthiani, *profess?*

Ascitæ.

A. The *Ascitæ* so named from ἀσκΘ-, a Bottle, used to carry about Bottles filled with Wine, and stopped, bragging that they were the new Evangelical Bottles filled with new Wine; and such they held necessary for all good Christians to carry about; in this they placed the main of their Religion. These, and divers other heresies, like *Jonas* his gourd were quickly up and quickly down. The *Pattalorinchitæ* were so named from πάτ]αλΘ- a staff or stick, and ῥίγχΘ- the Nose, for they used to thrust their fingers into their Nose, and Mouth, to hinder them from speaking; for they placed

Pattalorinchitæ.

all

all their Religion in silence. Hence they were called *Silentiarii*. The *Aquarii* were so called from *Aqua*, water, because in stead of *Aquarii.* pure Wine, they offered Water in the Sacrament. These were the spawn of the *Severians, Encratites,* and *Helcesaites*. The *Coluthi-* Coluthiani. *ani* were so called from *Coluthus* Presbyter of *Alexandria*, and cotaneous with *Arrius*, under *Constantine*, 290 years after Christ. Their opinion was, that God could not be the author of punish- See *Phila-* ment, because it is evil; whereas *Amos* the Prophet shews the con- *ster, Austin,* trary, *that there is no evil in the City, which the Lord hath not done, Theodoret, Amos* 3. 6. and in *Esay*, the *Lord formeth the Light and Darkness, Isidore,&c. making peace, and creating evil*, Isa. 45. 7.

Q. 31. *What were the Religious Tenets of the* Floriani, Æternales, *and* Nudipedales ?

A. The *Floriani* were so called from *Florinus*, or *Florianus*, a Ro- Floriani. man Presbyter, who lived under *Commodus* the Emperour, 153 years after Christ. These Hereticks were spawned by the *Valentinians*, whose Doctrines, concerning the *Æones*, and other of their Tenets they maintained, and withal, that God made evil and sin ; *whereas* Moses *tells us, that all things which he made were very good.* They retained also the *Jewish* manner of keeping *Easter*, and their other Ceremonies. *Æternales*, from the opinion of the World's Eter- Æternales. nity ; for they held there should be no change after the Resurrection, but that the World should continue as it is now. This Heresie in *Philaster* and *Austin*, hath neither Name, nor Author. The *Nudipeda-* Nudipedales *les* were those, who placed all Religion in going Bare-foot ; because Moses and *Joshua* are commanded to pull off their shooes, and *Isaiah* See *Phila-* to walk bare-foot; *whereas these were extraordinary, and peculiar Pre-* ster, Austin, *cepts and Signs of particular things, not enjoyned to be imitated.* &c.

Q. 32. *What was the Religion of the* Donatists, Priscillianists, *the* Rhetorians, *and the* Feri ?

A. The *Donatists*, so called from *Donatus* a *Numidian*, who, be- Donatists. cause *Cecilian* was preferred before him to the Bishoprick of *Carthage*, accused him, and all the Bishops that Ordained him, to be *Traditores*, that is, such as had delivered the Bibles to be burned by Idolaters, under the Persecution of *Maximinus* : though this Accusation was found false, yet *Donatus* persisted obstinate, and separated himself, and his Congregation, from all others, accounting that no Church, where any spot or infirmity was to be found; and that such a pure Church was onely to be found among the *Donatists*, and yet they would have no Man to be forced, or urged to a godly life, but must be left to himself, *which was to open a Gap to all impurity*, they did also slight the magistracy, and would not suffer them to punish Hereticks. They held the efficacy of the Sacraments to depend upon the dignity of the Minister, and not on the Spirit of God; they rebaptized also the *Orthodox* Christians, as if their baptism had not been baptism. They held it no sin to kill themselves, rather than to fall into the hands of the Magistrate; and so they made no scruple to kill others that were not of their faith, when they found any advantage. They used certain Magical purifications,

rifications, and bragged much of Enthusiasms and Revelations. They also, with the *Arrians*, made the Son less than the Father, and the Holy Ghost than the Son. This Heresie was divided into divers schisms, the chief whereof were the *Circumcellians*, so called from their Cells and Cottages in which they lived, to shew their austerity; these made no bones to murther all they met, that were not of their Religion, so that they were more dangerous than Highway Robbers. The *Donatists* were named also *Parmenianists*, from *Parmenianus*, one of *Donatus* his Disciples. At *Rome*, they were named *Campates* from the Camp, or Field; and *Montenses* from the Hill where they used to hide themselves. The *Priscillia-*
Priscillia- *nists*, were so named from *Priscillianus* a *Spaniard*, who under
nists. *Gratian* the Emperour, spread his Heresie first in *Spain*, 348 years after Christ. From thence, like a canker, it run through all the West: his Heresie was made up of former Heresies; for with the *Manichees* he held that the world was made by an evil God. With the *Sabellians* he confounded the persons of the Trinity; with the *Origenists*, he taught that mens souls were made before their bodies in some receptacle of Heaven; and with the *Manichees*, that they were parcels of the Divine Essence. With Astrologers they held that all humane events depend on the Stars; and with the *Stoicks*, that we sin necessarily, and coactively. With the *Gnosticks* they condemned marriage; with the *Encratites*, the eating of flesh; with the *Audians* they allowed lying, and perjury in matters of Religion; and with the *Gnosticks* they rejected the
Rhetorians. ancient Prophets, as fanatical and ignorant of the will of God. The *Rhetorians* so called from one *Rhetorius*, held the same Tenet, which the *Mahometans* do at this day, namely that every man shall be saved by the Religion he professeth, and that therefore no Reli-
Feri. gion should be forced, but men should be left to their own choice,
See Phila- and will. The *Feri*, or wild Hereticks, were such as held it un-
ster, Austin, lawful to eat or converse with men; therefore they held none
Isidore,&c. should be saved, but such as lived alone: They taught also that the holy Ghost was a creature.

Q. 33. *What were the* Theopaschitæ, Tritheitæ, Aquei, Melito-
Theopas- nii, Ophei, Tertullii, Liberatores, *and* Nativitarii?
chitæ. A. The *Theopaschites*, held that the Divinity of Christ suffered as
Tritheitæ. there had been in him but one nature, because one person. The *Tritheits* divided the Essence of God into three parts; the one they called the Father, the other the Son, and the third the Holy Ghost;
Aquei. as though each of the persons had not been perfectly God. The *Aquei* held that the water was not created but coeternal with God;
Melitonii. this Heresie was culled out of the *Hermogenian* and *Audian* Tenets. The *Melitonii* so named from one *Melito*, taught that not the soul, but the body of man was made after God's Image, and so with the
Ophei. *Anthropomorphites* they made God Corporeal. The *Ophei*, so cal-
Tertullii. led from one *Opheus*, held there were innumerable worlds. The
Liberatores *Tertullii*, from one *Tertullus*, taught that the souls of wicked men should be converted into Devils, and Savage Beasts, *Liberatores*, are

are those who taught that Christ by his descending into Hell, did **Nativita-**
set at liberty all wicked that then believed in him. *Nativitarii*, were **rii.**
such as taught that Christ's Divine Nativity had a beginning, because
it is written, *Psal.* 2. [*Thou art my Son, this day have I begotten thee,*] Of which
so they acknowledged the Eternity of his Essence, but not of his Fi- **see Phila-**
liation. These were but branches of former Heresies, broached by **ster, Austin,**
obscure or unknown authors, and of short continuance. **Isidore,&c.**

Q. 34. *What were the* Luciferians, Jovinianists, *and* Arabicks?

A. The *Luciferians*, so called from *Lucifer* Bishop of *Caralitanum* **Luciferi-**
in *Sardinia*, who lived under *Julian* the Apostate, 333 years after **ans.**
Christ, taught with the *Cerinthians*, and *Marcionites* that this
world was made by the Devil. That mens souls were corporeal,
and had their being by propagation or traduction. They denied
to the Clergy that fell, any place for repentance, or reconciliation;
neither did they restore Bishops or inferior Clerks to their dignities,
if they fell into Heresie, though they afterward repented. This
was the Doctrine of the old *Novatians*, and *Meletians*; these *Luci-*
ferians were named also *Homonymians*, for using the word flesh am-
biguously in their disputations. The *Jovinianists* were so called **Jovinia-**
from *Jovinian* a Roman, who lived under *Jovinian*, the Emperour, **nists.**
335 years after Christ. These held with the Stoicks that all sins
were equal; that after baptism we could not sin: that fasting was
needless, that Virginity was not better than the married life, and
that the blessed Virgin in bearing Christ, lost her Virginity. The
Arabicks, were so named from *Arabia*, the Country where this **Arabicks.**
Heresie was broached and maintained, under *Philip*, the Emperour,
217 years after Christ, they held that mens souls died with their **See the a-**
bodies, and that both in the last day should rise again. From this **bove named**
Heresie they were called Θνητοψυχῖται, that is, mortal souls; not **authors and**
much different from them are the *Psychopanuychitæ* of this age, **Hierom.**
who make the soul sleep in the Grave with the body, till the Re- **against Jo-**
surrection. **vinian.**

Q. 35. *What were the* Collyridians, Paterniani, Tertullianists,
and Abelonitæ?

A. The *Collyridians* were hatched also in *Arabia*, and so named **Collyridi-**
from a kind of Cakes or Buns, which the Greeks call κολλυρίδας; **ans.**
these Cakes they presented every year with great ceremony to a
certain Maid sitting in a Chair of State, and covered with a veil,
in honour of the Virgin *Mary*: these flourished under *Theodosius* the
great, 357 years after Christ. *Paterniani* so called from one *Pater-* **Paterniani.**
nus an obscure fellow, were named also *Venustiani*, from *Venus*,
which by their venereal actions, they honoured more than God;
These held that all the lower parts of mans body, from the Navel
downward, were made by the Devil; and therefore they gave
themselves to all lasciviousness and uncleanness, therefore they
were called ηθιοσκοπται, deriders of good manners and honesty.
The *Tertullianists* were so called from that famous Lawyer and Di- **Tertullia-**
vine *Tertullian*, who lived under *Severus* the Emperour, about 170 **nists.**
years after Christ. He being excommunicated by the Roman
Clergy

Clergy for a *Montanist*, fell into these heretical opinions; to wit, that God was corporeal, but without delineation of members; that mens souls were not only corporeal, but also distinguished into members, and had corporeal dimensions, and did increase and decrease with the body; and that the soul had its Original by propagation or traduction. He held also that the souls of wicked men after death, were converted into Devils; that the Virgin *Mary* after Christs birth, did marry once, and with the *Cataphrygians*, he bragged much of the Paraclet or Spirit, which they said was poured on them in a greater measure, than on the Apostles. He condemned all use of arms, and wars among Christians; and with the *Montanists* rejected second Marriages, as no better than adultery. The *Abelonitæ* were so called from *Abel, Adam*'s Son; these taught that *Abel* was married, but had no carnal commerce with his Wife, because there is no mention made of his children, as there is of *Cain*'s and *Seth*'s. For this cause these *Abelites* did marry Wives, but not use them as Wives for propagation, for fear of Original sin, whereof they would not be authors; therefore they condemned copulation, as a work of the flesh, and altogether Satanical. But for the conservation of their Sect, they used to adopt other mens Children. This Heresie sprung up under *Arcadius* the Emperor, 370 years after Christ, in the Territories of *Hippo*, where Saint *Austin* was Bishop. This Heresie lasted not long.

Abelonitæ.

Of which see. *Austin.*

Q. 36. *What Tenets in Religion held the* Pelagians, Prædestinati, *and* Timotheans?

Pelagians.

A. The *Pelagians* were so called from *Pelagius* a Britain by birth, and a Monk at *Rome*, afterward a Presbyter, under *Theodosius* the younger, 382 years after Christ. They were named also *Cælestiani* from *Cælestius* one of *Pelagius* his Scholars. These taught that death was not the wages of sin, but that *Adam* should have died, though he had not sinned. That *Adam*'s sin was hurtful onely to himself, and not to his posterity; that concupiscence was no sin, that Infants did not draw original sins from their Parents, that Infants might be saved without baptism, that they should have life eternal, but out of the Kingdom of God; that man after the fall had freewill to do good, and ascribed no more to grace, but that by it we had our nature, and that by our good works we obtain grace; they rejected the Doctrine of predestination, *perhaps because the Hereticks called* Prædestinati, *made Predestination a cloak for all wickedness, security and desperation*; for they taught that the Predestinate, might sin securely, for he could not be damned; and that such, as were not Predestinate, should never be saved, though their life were never so holy. This Heresie was not long before *Pelagianism*, and is the same with that of the *Libertines*. The *Timotheans*, so called from *Timotheus Ælurus*; (that is, the Cat, from his bad conditions) sprung up under *Zeno* the Greek Emperour, 447 years after Christ. These taught that the two natures of Christ were so mixed in the Virgins Womb, that they ceased to be what they were before, and became a third substance made up of both, as a mixed

Prædestinati.

Timotheans.

mixed body is made up of the Elements, which lose their names Of the *Ti-*
and forms in the mixtion. These Hereticks afterward lost the *motheans*
name of *Timotheans* from *Timotheus* their Author, Bishop of *Alex-* see Pet.
andria, and were called *Monothelites*, and *Monophysites*, from ascri- *Lombard,*
bing onely one will, and one nature to Christ. Of the *Pelagians* *Evagrius,*
see *Austin*, and the other Fathers who have written against them. *and Nice-*
  Q. 37. *What was the Religions of the* Nestorians, Eutychians, *phorus.*
and of those Sects which sprung out of them?

  A. The *Nestorians* were so called from *Nestorius* Patriarch of *Nestorians.*
Constantinople, who broached his Heresie under *Theodosius* the
younger, 400 years after Christ. He taught that in Christ were
two distinct persons, to wit, the Son of God, and the Son of
Mary; that the Son of God in Christ's Baptism descended into the
Son of *Mary*, and dwelt there, as a lodger doth in a house; therefore he will not call the Virgin *Mary* Θεοτόκον the Mother of God,
but χριστοτόκον, the Mother of Christ. Besides he made the humanity of Christ equal with his Divinity, and so confounded their
properties and operations. This Heresie was but the spawn of
some former Heresies, chiefly of *Manicheism*, and *Arrianism*. It
was condemned in the Council of *Ephesus* under *Theodosius* the younger, in which *Cyril* Bishop of *Alexandria* was President, and the
author *Nestorius* was deposed and banished, where his blasphemous tongue was eat out with Worms, and his body with *Core*
and his seditious complices swallowed up by the Earth. The *Eu-* *Eutychians*
tychians so named from *Eutyches, Archimandrite*, or Abbot of *Con-* *and their*
stantinople, who lived in the latter end of *Theodosius* the younger, *spawn.*
held opinions quite contrary to *Nestorius*, to wit, that Christ before the Union, had two distinct natures, but after the Union
onely one, to wit, the Divinity which swallowed up the Humanity, and so they confounded the property of the two natures,
affirming that the Divine nature suffered and died; and that God
the Word, did not take from the Virgin humane nature. This
Heresie was first condemned in a Provincial Synod at *Constantinople*; then it was set up again by *Dioscurus* Bishop of *Alexandria*,
in the theevish Council of *Ephesus*, called λῃστρικὴ, and at last condemned by the General Council of *Chalcedon*, under *Marcian* the
Emperour. From the *Eutychians* sprung up the *Acephali*, or headless Hereticks, so called, because they had neither Bishop, Priest,
nor Sacrament amongst them; these held that in Christ were two
natures, which notwithstanding they confounded, as they did also
the Properties, saying that the humanity lost it self and properties,
being swallowed up by the divinity, as a drop of Vinegar is lost
in the Sea. *Severus* Bishop of *Alexandria* was author of this Sect,
under *Anastasius* Emperour, 462 years after Christ. They were
called also *Theodosians*, from *Theodosius* their chief Patron, and
Bishop of *Alexandria*. 2. The *Monophysites* were all one with
the *Eutychians*, differing onely in name. 3. The *Agnoeta*, so called from ἀγνοία, ignorance, because they held that Christ's Divinity, which with them onely remained after the Union, was ignorant

tant of the day of Judgment, and where *Lazarus* after his death was laid. This Heresie was revived by *Theodosius* Bishop of *Alexandria*, under *Mauritius* the Emperour, 572 years after Christ. 4. The *Jacobites* so called from *Jacobus* the Syrian, held the same opinions that the *Eutychians*; and scoffed the Christians with the name of *Melchites*, because they followed the Emperour in the Faith. These under *Phocas* the Emperour drew all *Syria* into their Heresie, 575 years after Christ. 5. The *Armenians* so named from *Armenia*, infected with that Heresie, held that Christ took not a humane body from the Virgin, but that it was immortal from the first minute of its conception; hence they were called φθαρτολάτραι and σκηνολάτραι; they again in scorn called the Orthodox Christians *Manicheans* and *Phantasiasts*; these held a Quaternity of Persons, and that the Divinity suffered; and kept their *Easter* after the Jewish manner. They sprung up under *Phocas* the Emperour, 577 years after Christ. 6. The *Monothelites* in words held there were two natures in Christ, but in effect denyed them, by giving him one Will onely. All these branches of *Eutychianism* were condemned by the fifth General Council held at *Constantinople* under *Justinian*, the first who confirmed the Council of *Chalcedon*, to which these διακεινόμενοι, or doubting Hereticks (for so they call themselves) would not subscribe. At last sprung up *Mahometanism*, 589 years after Christ. Of which we have spoken already. Of all these see *Isidore*, *Theodoret*, *Evagrius*, *Nicephorus*, *Socrates*, *Sozomen*, and others.

The

The Contents of the Eighth Section.

1f the opinions in Religion held the seventh Century. 2. The opinions of the eighth Century. 3. The Tenets of the ninth and tenth Centuries. 4. The opinions of the eleventh and twelfth Centuries. 5. Of the Albigenies *and other Sects in the twelfth Century.* 6. *The Sects of the thirteenth Century.* 7. *The Sects of the fourteenth Century.* 8. *Of the* Wicklevites. 9. *The opinions of the fifteenth Century.* 10. *The opinions of the sixteenth Century, to wit, of* Luther *and others.* 11. *Of Sects sprung out of Lutheranism.* 12. *Of Protestants.* 13. *Of the other opinions held this Century.* 14. *The chief heads of* Calvin's *Doctrine.* 15. *Of other opinions held this age.* 16. *Of divers other opinions in this age, and the causes of this variety and confusion in the Church.*

SECT. VIII.

Quest. **W**Hereas we have had a view of the different Heresies in Christian Religion, the first 600 years after Christ; now let us know what were the chief opinions and authors thereof in the seventh Century.

Answ. The Heicitæ professed a Monastical life, but withal taught that the service of God consisted in holy dances and singing with the Nuns, after the example of *Moses* and *Miriam,* Exod. 15. *upon the overthrow of* Pharoah *in the Red Sea.* Gnosimachi were haters and despisers of all learning, or Book-knowledge; teaching that God required nothing from us, but a good life. *Of this we have too many in this age.* But *Christ tells us that life Eternal consists in knowledge: And God complaineth by the Prophet, that his people perish for want of knowledge;* So *Christ sheweth that destruction fell on* Jerusalem, *because she knew not her day; and the Lord complained that his people had less knowledge than the* Ox *or the* Ass. *Therefore God hath given lips to the Priest, to preserve knowledge, and Christ by his own knowledge hath justified many, saith the Prophet.* The Armenii taught that the holy Ghost proceeded onely from the Father, and not from the Son. That Christ rose from the dead on the Sabbath day; *whereas the Scripture tells us plainly, that he arose the third dead.* They observed also the Jewish sacrifices. They used first to baptize the Cross, then to worship it. They taught it was not man that sinned, but Satan by tempting him: and that man had not propagated by carnal Copulation, if he had not sinned. They denied Original sin, and held that all who died before Christ, were damned for *Adam*'s sin.

Hereticks of the seventh Century.

They

They afcribed no efficacy to the Sacraments, an abfolutely neceffary. They placed the Childrer fants, if they were of faithful Parents, in cart unfaithful, in Hell. They never baptized wi the *Eucharift*. They held baptifm without chrif ufed rebaptization. They permitted the husbar trimony when he pleafed, and denyed prayers the eternity of hell fire. And that the fouls we the Refurrection. And taught that then there fh at all, but that they fhould be converted into were fo called from *Chazus*, which in their lang Crofs: for they taught that the Crofs was onely therefore they were named *Staurolatra*, or Crofs-profeffed alfo *Neftorianifm*. The *Thnetopfyhita* died with the bodies. *Theocatagnoft.e* were fu fome of God's actions and words. *Ethnophron* Chriftians, who with Chriftianity taught *Gentile* Lampetians fo called from *Lampetius*, their there fhould be no diftinction of garments amc They condemned alfo all vows. The *Maron* one *Maron*, held with *Eutyches*, *Diofcorus*, and Chrift had but one nature and will; thefe wer ciled to the Church of *Rome*.

See *Dama-fcen, Nicephorus, Sanderus, Baronius,* &c.

Qu. 2. *What opinions were held in Religion wi tury?*

Hereticks of the eighth Century.

A. The *Agonyclita* held that it was fuperft bow the knees, or proftrate the body: therefore ftanding. The *Iconoclafte*, or *Iconomachi* taugh try to have Images in Temples. The *Aldeber Aldebertus* a French-man their author, believe Reliques brought to him by an Angel, from the world. They equalled him with the Apo Pilgrimages to *Rome*; they held that his hair: well to be worfhipped, as the reliques of St. Pe that he knew their fins, and could forgive the on. The *Albanenfes* held that all Oaths we there was no original fin, nor any efficacy in tl ufe of extream unction, nor of confeffion; nor on; that the Sacraments loft their efficacy, i Priefts; that there was no free-will; fome v tranfanimation, and the eternity of the world ar fore-fee evil. That there fhould be no Refurr Judgment, nor Hell.

See *Sanderus, Baronius, Gualtorus,* &c.

Q. 3. *What were the opinions held in the nir ries?*

Hereticks of the ninth and tenth Centuries.

A. Claudius Bifhop of *Taurinum*, condemned ges, Invocation of Saints, and taught that bap til of the crofs, was no baptifm. One *Godefcalku* was a French-man held the Herefie of the *Pr*

God would not have all men to be saved; and consequently that Christ died not for all. *Photius* a *Grecian* denyed the Procession of the holy Ghost from the Son, and held that there was no reward for the good or bad, till the general Judgment; that there was no Purgatory; he condemned second marriages, and prayers for the dead; he held it no sin to hurt an enemy, even with lying and perjury. Fornication with him was no sin, he dissolved marriages at pleasure. He maintained usury, sacrilege, and rebaptization; and taught that Children were not to be baptized till the eighth day. He gave the Eucharist to Infants; the cup to the Laity; denied extream Unction; and administred the Sacrament in Leavened Bread. *Johannes Scotus* a benedictine Monk, and Scholar of *Bede* (not *Duns Scotus subtilis*) held that in the Eucharist was only the figure of Christs body. *Bertramus* a Presbyter taught, that the body of Christ which is in the Eucharist, was not the same who was born of the Virgin. The same opinions were maintained by some in the tenth Century. *See the above named Authors.*

Qu. 4. *What were the opinions of the eleventh and twelfth Centuries?*

A. *Berengarius* Archdeacon of *Anjou*, taught that Christs body was not corporally, but figuratively in the Sacrament: *Horibert* and *Lisoius* in *France*, taught Manicheism. The *Simoniacks* held it lawful to buy and sell Church preferments. The *Reordinantes*, would admit no Simoniack Priests till they were reordained. At *Millan* a new Sect of *Nicolaitans* brake out, teaching the necessity of promiscuous Copulation. *Sabellianism* brake out also this age. In the twelfth Century, *Marsilius* of *Padua* taught that the Pope was not Christ's successor: that he was subject to the Emperor: that there was no difference between Bishops and Priests, and that Church-men should not enjoy temporal estates. The *Bongomillii*, whose author was one *Basil*, a Physician, renewed the Heresies of *Arrius*, the *Anthromorphites*, and the *Manichees*. They rejected the Book of *Moses*, made God with a humane shape, taught that the world was made by evil angels, and that *Michael* the Arch-Angel was incarnate. They condemned Image-worship, and despised the cross, because Christ died on it. They held the Churches baptism to be the baptism of *John*, but their own to be the true baptism of Christ: they slighted the Church-Liturgy, and taught there was no other Resurrection, but from sin by repentance: they held also that men might dissemble in Religion. At *Antwerp* one *Taudenius*, or *Tanchelinus*, being a Lay-man, undertook a Reformation, teaching that men were justified, and saved by faith onely; that there was no difference between Priests and Lay-men; that the Eucharist was of no use, and that promiscuous copulation was lawful. The *Petrobrusians* so called from *Peter de Bruis* of *Antwerp*, held that baptism was needless to Infants; and likewise Churches were useless, that crosses should be broken, that Christ was not really in the Eucharist, and that prayers for the dead were fruitless. One *Peter Abailard* taught that God was of a compounded *Hereticks the eleven and twelfth Centuries.*

pounded Essence, that he was not the Author of all goodness; that he was not only eternal; that the angels helped him to create the world; that power was the property of the Father, wisdom of the Son, goodness of the Holy Spirit. He denyed that Christ took our flesh to save sinners, or that the fear of God was in him; he said that the Holy Ghost was the soul of the world, that man had no free-will; that all things, even God himself, were subject to necessity, that the Saints do not see God, that in the life to come there should be no fear of God, and that we are in matters of faith to be directed by our reason. His chief Disciple was *Arnoldus Brixiensis*, who denied also temporalities to the Clergy. *Gilbert Porretanus* Bishop of *Poytires*, taught that the Divine Essence was not God, that the Proprieties and Persons in the Trinity were not the same; that the Divinity was not incarnate in the Son. He rejected also merits, and lesned the efficacy of baptism. The *Henricians* so called from one *Henry* of *Tholouse* a Monk, and fomented by *Henry*, the Emperour, taught the same Doctrines that *Peter de Bruis* did, and withal that the Church-musick was a mocking of God. The *Patareni* taught also the same things. The *Apostolici* so named from saying they were Apostles immediately sent from God, despised marriage, all meats made of Milk; the baptizing of Infants, Purgatory, prayers for the dead, invocation of Saints, and all Oaths. They held themselves to be the onely true Church. One *Eudon* gave himself out to be the Judge of the quick and dead. The *Adamites* started up again in *Bohemia*. The *Waldenses* so called from *Waldo* of *Lions*, who having distributed his wealth, professed poverty; he rejected Images, prayers to Saints, Holy-days, Churches, Oyl in Baptism, Confirmation, the *Ave Mary*, auricular confession, indulgences, purgatory, prayers for the dead, obedience to the Prelates, distinction of Bishop and Priest, Church-canons, merit, Religious orders, extream unction, miracles, exorcisms, Church-musick, Canonical-hours, and divers other Tenets of the Church of *Rome*. They held that Lay-men might Preach, and consecrated the Bread, and that all ground was alike holy. They rejected all prayers, except the Lords-prayer, and held that the Eucharist consecrated on the Friday, had more efficacy than on any other day. That Priests and Deacons falling into sin, lost their Power in consecrating, and Magistrates in governing, if they fell. That the Clergy should possess no temporalties, that the Church failed in Pope *Sylvester*'s time. They rejected the Apostles Creed, and all Oaths; but permitted promiscuous copulation; and taught that no man ought to suffer death by the sentence of any Judge.

See *Baronius, Genebrard, Sanderus, Gualterus,* &c.

Q. 5. *What were the* Albigenses, *and what other Sects were there in this twelfth Century.*

Albigenses, and their opinions.

A. These not long after the *Waldenses*, swarmed in the Province of *Tholouse*, and were overthrown by *Simon* Earl of *Montferrat*; these taught that they were not bound to make profession of their faith; they denyed Purgatory, Prayers for the Dead, the

real

real Presence, private confession, images, bells in Churches, and condemned the eating of flesh, eggs and milk. The Romish Writers affirm that they held two Gods; that our bodies were made by Satan, that the Scriptures were erroneous, all Oaths unlawful, and Baptism needless. They rejected the old Testament and Marriage, and Prayers in the Church; they held there were two Christ's, a good born in an unknown Land, and a bad born in *Bethlehem* of *Judea*; that had God had two Wives, of which he begot Sons and Daughters; and more such stuff, as may be seen in the above-named Authors. The *Correrii* held the *Petrobrusian* Tenets, and withal that the Virgin *Mary* was an Angel; that Christs body was not glorified in Heaven, but did putrefie as other dead bodies, and so should remain after the day of judgment. They taught also that the souls should not be glorified till the Resurrection. *Joachimus Abbas* taught that in the Trinity, the Essence generated the Essence, which opinion was condemned in the general council of *Lateran*, under *Innocent* the third: not long after started up *Petrus Jehannes*, who maintained the errour of *Joachimus*, and withal taught that the reasonable soul was not the form of man; that the Apostles preached the Gospel after the literal, not after the spiritual sense; that grace was not conferred in baptism; that Christ's side was pierced with a Lance whilst he was yet alive, *which is directly against the words of Saint John*; therefore this opinion was condemned in the Council of *Vienna*; he held also *Rome* to be *Babylon*, and the Pope to be Antichrist.

See *Baronius, Sanderus, Bellarmin, Vicgas*, and the Authors above named.

Q. 6. *What opinions in Religion were professed in the thirteenth Century?*

A. *Almaricus* a Doctor in *Paris*, taught that if *Adam* had not sinned, there had been no procreation, nor distinction of Sex. This was condemned in the Council of *Lateran*, under *Innocent* the third. He held that the Saints do no ways see God in himself, but in his creatures. He denyed the Resurrection, Paradise, and Hell, also the real presence, invocation of Saints, Images and Altars. He said that in the Divine mind might be created *Ideas*. He transformed the mind of a contemplative man, into the Essence of God; and taught that charity made sin to be no sin. *David Dinantius* taught that the first matter was God, *which was to make God a part, and the meanest part of all his creatures*. *Gulielmus de sancto amore*, taught that no *Monks* ought to live by alms, but by their own labours, and that voluntary poverty was unlawfull, the same doctrine was taught by *Desiderius Longobardus*, affirming it a pernicious opinion that men should leave all for Christ. *Raymundus Lullius* taught that in God were different Essences, that God the Father was before the Son; that the holy Ghost was conceived of the Father and the Son, *whereas the Doctrine of the Church is that he proceeds from the Father and the Son; not by way of Generation or Conception, but of Eternal and Spiritual, dilection*; he also taught that it was injustice *to punish* any man for opinions in Religion or Heresie. Tho *Whippers* taught that whipping of themselves

Hereticks of the thirteenth Century.

selves with rods full of knots and sharp pricks did more expiate and abolish sin, than confession; that this their voluntary whipping was before Martyrdom, which was inflicted by outward force: that now there was no use of the Gospel, nor of the Baptism of Water, sith the Baptism of Blood was better; that holy water was needless; that no man could be saved who did not scourge himself. They also held perjury lawful. The *Fraticelli* whose author was one *Hermannus Italus*, held community of Wives lawful, which Doctrine they put in practise, at their meetings to pray; then putting out their lights, they used promiscuous copulation: and the children born of such commixtion, they put to death. They taught that all things amongst Christians should be in common; that Magistracy did not consist with Christianity, and that the Saints did not see God till the day of Judgment. *Gerardus Sagarellus* of *Parma*, whose disciples were named *Pseudo-apostoli*, that is, false Apostles, because they bragged that they did imitate the Apostles poverty, therefore they would not take or keep money, or reserve any thing for the next day; he taught that to make vows, or to swear at all, was unlawful; that marriages might be dissolved by such as would embrace their Religion; and that they were the only Christians; they were enemies to Tythes, and to Churches, which for prayer they accounted no better than Hogs-Styes.

See the above named Authors.

Q. 7. *What were the opinions in Religion of the fourteenth Century?*

A. The *Beguardi* who professed a Monastical life, taught that we might attain to as much perfection and beatitude in this life, as in Heaven; that all intellectual natures were blessed in themselves, not in God; that it was a sin to kiss a Woman, but not to lie with her; because nature inclined to this, but not to that. That perfect and spiritual men were freed from obedience to superiors, from fasting, praying, and good works, and that such men could not sin, nor increase in grace, being perfect already. They would have no reverence to be used in the Eucharist, nor at all to receive it, for that did argue imperfection. The *Beguinæ* professed the same Tenets, and withal, were against vows and voluntary poverty. The *Beguini* taught that wealth consisted not with Evangelical perfection, and therefore blamed Pope *John* 22, for permitting the *Franciscans* to have corn in their barns, and wine in their cellars. They held that the state of *Minorites* was more perfect than that of Bishops; that they were not bound to give an account of their faith when they were demanded by the Inquisitors; and that the Pope had no power to dispense with Vows. The *Lollhards*, so called from *Walter Lolhard* their author, held that *Lucifer* was injuriously thrust out of Heaven; that *Michael* and the blessed Angels should be punished eternally; that *Lucifer* should be saved; that the blessed Virgin lost her Virginity after Christ's birth; and that God did neither see, nor would punish sins committed under ground; therefore they gave themselves to all uncleanness in their

Hereticks of the fourteenth Century.

their vaults and caves. *Richardus Armacanus* taught that voluntary poverty was unlawful; and that Priests could bless, and confer orders as well as Bishops. One *Janovesius* taught that in the year 1360 on *Whitsunday*, Antichrist would come, who should pervert all *Christians*, and should mark them in their hands and Fore-heads, and then should be damned eternally: and that all *Jews*, *Saracens*, and *Infidels*, who were seduced by Antichrist, should after his destruction be converted to Christ, but not the Christians that fell off from Christ. The *Turelupini* taught that we should not be ashamed of those Members we have from nature; and so, like the *Cynicks*, they gave themselves openly to all uncleanness; they held also that we were not to pray with our voice, but with the heart only.

See the above named Authors.

Q. 8. *What were the Tenets of the* Wicklevites, *who lived in this Century?*

A. They were so called from *John Wickliff* an *Englishman*, and taught that the substance of bread and wine remained in the Sacrament; that neither Priest nor Bishop, remaining in any mortal sin, could consecrate, or ordain; that the Mass had no ground in Scripture; that outward confession was needless where there was true contrition: that a wicked Pope had no power over the faithful; that Clergy-men should have no possession; that none should be excommunicate by the Church, but he who is first excommunicate by God; that the Prelate who excommunicates a Clerk appealing to the King, is a Traitor; and so he is that being excommunicate, refuseth to hear, or to preach; that Deacons and Priests may Preach without authority of the Bishop; that the King might invade the Churches Revenues; that the people may punish their Kings; that the Laity may detain or take away their Tythes; that special prayers for any man were of more force than general; that religious orders were unlawful, and that such should labour with their hands; that it was a sin in *Constantine*, and others, to enrich the Church; that the Church of *Rome* was Satans Synagogue; they rejected the Popes election by Cardinals Indulgences, decretal Epistles, the Popes excommunications, and his supremacy; they held also that *Austin*, *Bennet*, and *Bernard* were damned for instituting religious orders; that God ought to obey the Devil; that he who gives alms to Monasteries should be excommunicate: that they are *Simoniacks* who pray for their Parents or Benefactors: that Bishops reserved to themselves the power of ordination, confirmation, and consecration for lucres sake: that Universities, Degrees and Scholars of Learning, were hurtful to the Church. These, and such like Tenets of *Wickliff*, are set down in the Council of *Constance*, where they were condemned. Other opinions are fathered upon him: to wit, that man had no free-will: that the sins of the Predestinate were venial; but of the Reprobate, all mortal; that the Saints were not to be invocated; nor their reliques kept, nor the cross to be worshipped, nor Images to be placed in Churches: they rejected also Vows, Canonical-hours, Church-Musick, Fasting, Baptizing of Infants, Benedictions, Chrism

Wickliff's opinions.

See Flori-mundus Raymundus of the original of Heresies, Genebrard, Bellarmine, Patreolus, Gregory de Valentia, and and others

and Episcopacy. He held also that the brother and sister might marry, that every creature may be called God, because its perfection is in God.

Opinions and Heresies of the fifteenth Century. John Hus

Q. 9. *What opinions were taught in the fifteenth Century?*

A. *John Hus* of *Bohemia* publickly maintained the Doctrine of *Waldus* and *Wickliff*, and withal taught that St. *Peter* was never head of the Church, that the Church is only of the Predestinate: that Saint *Paul*, when he was a Persecutor, was not a member of Satan: that the Divinity and the Humanity, made up one Christ, whereas the personal union consisted indeed, not between the two Natures, but between the Person of the *Word* and the Humane Nature: That the Pope was subject to *Cæsar*: that the Pope was not Head of the Church, nor Vicar of Christ, nor Successor of *Peter*: that Bishops were murtherers, in delivering over to the secular power such as did not obey them; that Canonical obedience was a humane invention; that Priests, though excommunicate, ought to Preach: that Excommunication, Suspensions, and Interdicts, were invented to maintain the Clergies pride. These, and such like points did he defend, for which he was condemned in the Council of *Constance*. These same opinions were maintained by *Hierom* of *Prague*, for which he was also by the same Council condemned the next year. One *Pickard* of *Flanders* renewed in *Bohemia* the Heresie of the *Adamites*. The *Hussites* divided themselves into three Sects, to wit, the *Pragenses*, the *Thaborites*, so called from mount *Thabor*, where Christ was transfigured, which name, *Zisca*, their Captain gave them, calling the Castle where they used to meet, *Thabor*, as if they had seen there Christ's Transfiguration: The third Sect were called *Orphans* after *Zisca*'s death, as having lost their Father and Patron: all these used barbarous cruelty against Priests, Monks, Churches, Images, Reliques, and such as professed the Roman Catholick Religion the *Moscovites* or *Russians* fell off to the Greek Religion, and held that the Pope was not the chief Pastor of the Church; that the Roman Church was not head of the rest. They rejected also the Latine Fathers, the definitions, canons, and decrees of the general councils, and used leavened bread in their Eucharist. One *Rissuich* a *Hollander*, taught that the Angels were not created; that the Soul perished with the body; that there was no Hell, that the matter of the Elements were coeternal with God. He blasphemed Christ as a Seducer, and not the Son of God. He held that *Moses* never saw God, nor received his Law from him; that the Scriptures were but Fables; that the Gospel was false; *and such like blasphemous stuff did he spue out, for which he was burned.*

Hierom of Prague. Hussites.

See the above named Authors. Opinions of the sixteenth Century. Luther his opinions.

Q. 10. *What opinions did the Sixteenth Century hold?*

A. *Martin Luther*, an *Augustin* Friar, taught that Indulgences were unlawful; that the Epistles to the *Hebrews*, the Epistle of *James*, the second of *Peter*, the two last of *John*, the Epistle of *Jude*, and the *Apocalypse*, were not canonical. He opposed the invocation of Saints, Image-worship, Free-will, the Popes Supremacy,

macy, Excommunication, temporal poſſeſſions of the Clergy, merits of Works, poſſibility of fulfilling the Law, the Monaſtical life, cœlibate, canonical obedience, diſtinction of Meats, Tranſubſtantiation, Communion under one kind, the Maſs, auricular Confeſſion, Abſolution, Purgatory, extream Unction, and five of the Sacraments. He held alſo that general Councils might erre; that *Antichriſt* was not a particular perſon; that Faith only juſtified; that a faithful man may be aſſured of his ſalvation; that to the faithful, ſin is not imputed; that the firſt motions are ſin; that Sacraments did not confer grace. Divers other opinions are fathered upon him by his adverſaries, as may be ſeen in the above-named Authors. The *Anabaptiſts*, ſo called from Re-baptizing, had for their Author one *Nicholas Stork*, who pretended familiarity with God by an Angel, promiſing him a Kingdom, if he would reform the Church, and deſtroy the Princes that ſhould hinder him. His Scholar *Muncer* raiſed an army of 4000 Bores and Tradeſmen in *Suevia* and *Franconia* to maintain his Maſters dreams; but they were overthrown by Count *Mansfield*. *John* of *Leyden*, a Taylor, renewed the ſame dreams, and made himſelf King of *Munſter* of the *Anabaptiſts*, whoſe Viceroy was *Knipherdoling*; but this phantaſtical Monarchy was ſoon deſtroyed, the Town taken after 11 months Siege, where the King and his Viceroy, with their chief Officers, were put to death. Their Tenets were that Chriſt was not the Son of *Mary*, nor true God; that we were righteous not by faith in Chriſt, but by our own merits, and ſufferings. They rejected original ſin, Baptiſm of Infants, communion with other Churches Magiſtracy among Chriſtians, Oaths, and puniſhments of Malefactors. They refuſed to ſwear allegeance to Princes; and held that a *Chriſtian* may have many Wives, and that he may put away his Wife if ſhe be of another Religion, and marry another. That no man muſt poſſeſs any thing in proper, that re-baptization may be uſed; that before the day of Judgment, the godly ſhould enjoy a Monarchy here on Earth; that man had free-will in ſpiritual things; and that any man may Preach, and give the Sacraments.

Anabaptiſts.

Of theſe ſee the above-named Authors, and beſides, Pontanus, Bullinger, Sleidan, Oſiander, and others.

Q. 11. *What are the Anabaptiſts of* Moravia?

A. Theſe at firſt called themſelves Apoſtolical, becauſe they did imitate the Apoſtles in going bare-foot, and in waſhing one anothers feet, in having alſo all things in common amongſt them. But though this cuſtom be now left, yet at this day in *Moravia* they have a common Steward, who doth diſtribute equally things neceſſary to all. They will admit none into their Society, but ſuch as have ſome trade, and by their handy-work can get their livings. As they have a common Steward for their temporals, ſo they have a common Father for their ſpirituals, who inſtructs them in their Religion, and prayeth with them every morning before they go abroad to work. Theſe publick prayers, are to them inſtead of Sermons. They have a general Governour or Head of their Church, whom none knoweth but themſelves; for they

Anabaptiſts of Moravia.

they are bound not to reveal him. They communicate twice in the year; the men and women sit promiscuously together. On the Lords day they walk two and two through the Towns and Villages, being clothed in black, and having staves in their hands. They are much given to silence; at table for a quarter of an hour before they eat, they sit and meditate, covering their faces with their hands: the like devotion they shew after meat. All the while their Governour stands by, to observe their gesture, that if any thing be unbeseeming, he may tell them of it. When they come to any place, they discourse of the last Judgment, of the eternal pains of Hell, of the cruelty of Devils, tormenting mens bodies and souls; that so they may affright simple people into their Religion; then they comfort them by shewing them a way to escape all those torments, if they will be but re-baptized, and embrace their Religion. They observe no festival days, nor will they admit of any disputations.

Of these see Florimundus Raymundus de origine Hæres. Sects sprung out Lutheranism.

Q. 12. *What Sects are sprung out of* Lutheranism?

A. Besides the Anabaptists already mentioned, there be *Adiaphorists*, of which *Melanchton* is thought to be Author; these hold the customs and constitutions of the Church of *Rome* to be things indifferent, and that they may be professed, or not professed, without scruple. 2. *Ubiquitaries.* These hold that Christ's Humanity as well as his Divinity, is every where; even in Hell. *Brentius* is thought to be Father of this opinion. *But if Christ's humanity be every where, then we must deny the Articles of his Resurrection, Ascension, and coming again to Judge the quick and the dead, for what needs there such motions, if he be every where.* 3. *Majorists*, so called from one *George Major*, one of *Luther's* disciples, who taught that no man, (nay not Infants) can be saved without good works. *But its ridiculous to expect good works from Infants who have not as yet the use of reason, nor organs fit for operation.* 4. *Osiandrists*, so called from *Andrew Osiander* a *Lutheran*, who taught that Christ's body in the Sacrament suffered, was corruptible and died again, *directly against Scripture, saying that Christ being risen from the dead, dieth no more, death hath no more dominion over him.* He taught also that we are not justified by faith or works, but by the Essential righteousness of Christ dwelling in us. *But the Essential righteousness of Christ is the Righteousness of his Divinity, which is not communicable, nor separable from him.* 5. *Augustinians* in *Bohemia*, these taught that none went to Heaven or to Hell, till the last Judgment: *whereas Christ tells the contrary to the good thief,* This day thou shalt be with me in Paradise, *and affirmeth that the Soul of* Lazarus *was carried by Angels into* Abraham's *bosom, and* Dives *into Hell. Wherefore did Christ ascend to Heaven, but that we might be where he is. They make also dormice or swallows of mens souls, saying, that they sleep till the resurrection; if St. Stephen when he was dying had known this Doctrine, he would not have called upon the Lord Jesus to receive his spirit.* The story also of *Lazarus* and *Dives* doth overthrow this conceit. They say also that Christ's humane nature is not as yet ascended into Heaven, *which*

which *directly overthroweth our* Creed *in that article; as likewise the Scriptures, and withal the hope and Comfort of a Christian.* 6. *Stancarians* so called from one *Francis Stancarus* a *Mantuan*, who taught that Christ justifieth us, and is our Mediator only according to his humane nature; whereas our redemption is the work of the whole person, and not of one Nature alone. 7. *Adamites* so called from one *Adam* author of the Sect; they use to be naked in their Stoves and conventicles, after the example of *Adam* and *Eve* in Paradise. And therefore when they marry, they stand under a Tree naked, having only leaves of Trees upon their privities; they are admitted as brethren and sisters, who can without lust look upon each others nakedness; but if they cannot, they are rejected. 8. *Sabbatharians*, so called because they reject the observation of the Lords day, as not being commanded in Scripture, and keep holy the Sabbath day only, because God himself rested on that day, and commanded it to be kept. *But they forget that Christ came to destroy the Ceremonial Law, whereof the Sabbath, in respect of the seventh day, was a branch; and therefore Christ himself brake it, when he commanded the sick man whom he cured, to carry home his bed on that very day.* 9. *Clancularii* were those who professed no Religion with their mouth, thinking it sufficient to have it in their heart. They avoid all Churches and publick meeting to serve God; thinking their private houses to be better than Temples, *whereas they should remember, that private prayers cannot be so effectual as publick, neither is it enough to believe with the heart, except we also confess with the mouth; for he that is ashamed to confess Christ before men, shall not be confessed by Christ before his Father, and his only Angels.* 10. *Davidistæ*, so called from one *David George* a *Hollander*; he gave himself out to be the *Messiah*, sent by the holy Spirit, to restore the house of *Israel*, that the Scriptures were imperfect, and that he was sent to bring the true Law and Doctrine, that the soul was pure from sin, and that the body only sinned; *whereas indeed they both concur in the act of sinning, and therefore are both punishable, especially the Soul which is the chief Agent, the Body is but the Instrument.* He taught also that a man may have many Wives to replenish spiritual Paradise, that it was no sin to deny Christ with the mouth, so long as they believed on him in their heart. He rejected also the books of *Moses*. 11. *Mennonists*, so called from one *Mennon* a *Frieslander*. They deny Christ to be born of *Mary*, affirming that he brought his flesh from Heaven; he called himself the Judge of man and Angels. 12. *Deistæ* and *Tritheistæ*, who taught there were three distinct Gods differing in degrees. One *George Paul* of *Cracovia* is held to be the Author of this Sect. 13. *Antitrinitarians.* These begins the spawn of the old *Arrians* and *Samosatenians*, deny the Trinity of Persons, and the two natures of Christ, their author was *Michael Servetus* a *Spaniard*, who was burned at *Geneva*. 14. *Antimarians*, who denyed *Mary's* Virginity, affirming she had other children besides Christ, because there is mention made of Christ's brethren in the Gospel; *this is the old He-*

resie of Cerinthus, and Helvidius; *whereas they consider not that in Scripture those of the same kindred are called brothers. So is Lot called* Abraham's *brother*; and Laban, Jacob's *Uncle, is called his brother.* 15. *Antinomians*, who reject the Law, affirming, there is nothing required of us but faith, *this is to open a wide gap for all impiety. Christ came not (as he saith himself) to abolish the Law, but to fulfil it. If there be no use of the Law, then they must deny Gods justice; and that it is now an useless attribute of the Divinity.* 16. *Infernales*, these held that Christ descended into no other Hell but into the grave only, and that there is no other Hell but an evil Conscience; *whereas the Scripture speaketh of Hell-fire, prepared for the Devil and his Angels, and calls it the bottomless pit*, &c. 17. *Boquinians*, so called from one *Boquinus* their Master, who taught that Christ did not die for the wicked, but only for the faithful, *and so they make him not to be the Saviour of mankind, and of the world, but a particular Saviour only of some*; *whereas Saint* John *saith, that Christ is the reconciliation for our sins, and not for ours only, but also for the sins of the whole world,* 1 John. 2. 2. 18. *Hutists*, so called from one *John Hut*, who take upon them to prefix the very day of Christ's coming to judgment, *whereas of that day and hour knoweth no man, nay not the Angels in Heaven.* 19. *Invisibles*; so called because they hold that the Church of Christ is Invisible; *which if it be, in vain did he compare it to a City built upon a Hill; in vain also doth he counsel us to tell the Church, if our brother will not be reformed, in vain also doth the Apostle warn Bishops and Presbyteries to look to their flock, to rule the Church which Christ hath purchased with his blood,* Act. 20. *How can he be called the Shepherd of that flock which he never saw?* 20. *Quinuinistæ*, so called from one *Quintinus* of Picardy a Taylor: he was author of the *Libertines*, who admit of all Religions. Some of them mockt at all Religions, as that *Lucianist* who wrote a book of the three Impostors. Some of them deny the souls immortality, and doubt whether there be any other Deity except Heaven and Earth. 21. The Family of Love, whose author was one *Henry Nicholas* a Hollander. They reject all Sacraments, and the three last petitions of the Lord's Prayer. They say that Christ is only the Image of God the Fathers right hand, and that mans soul is a part of Divine Essence. 22. *Effrontes*, so called from shaving their fore-heads till they bleed, and then anoint them with oyl, using no other baptism but this; they say the Holy Ghost is but a bare motion inspired by God into the mind; and that he is not to be adored: *all which is directly repugnant to Gods word, which proves that the Holy Ghost is true God.* Thou hast not lied, *saith* St. Peter, unto man, but unto God, *meaning the Holy Ghost. This Sect took up their station in Transylvania.* 23. *Hofmanists*, these teach that God took flesh of himself, *whereas the Scripture saith, that Christ was made of a Woman.* They deny pardon to those that relapse into sin; *and so they abridge the grace of God, who wills us to repent, and thereupon receives us into favour.* 24. *Schewenkfeldians*, so called from one *Gaspar Schewenkfeld* a *Silesian*, he taught that the Scripture was

needless

needless to Salvation, and with the old *Manichees*, and *Valentinians*, that Christ was not conceived by the holy Ghost in the Virgins Womb, but that God created a man to redeem us, and joyned him to himself, and that this man became God, after he ascended into Heaven; they confound the Persons of Father and Son, and say that God did not speak these words, *This is my beloved Son.* That Faith is the very Essence and Nature of God. That all Christians are the Sons of God by Nature, procreated of the Divine Essence. That the Sacraments are useless; that Christ's body is every where. Of these Sects, and many more of less note, see *Florimundus Raymundus*; hence we may see what a dangerous Gap hath been made, since *Luther* began to oppose the Church of *Rome*, for the *little Foxes to destroy Christ's Vineyard*; *what multitudes of Tares have grown up amongst the good Corn in the Lords field*; *what troublesome Frogs, worse than those of Egypt, have crawled into most mens houses*; *what swarms of Locusts have darkened the Sun of Righteousness, whilst he was shining in the Firmament of his Church.*

Q. 13. *What other opinions in Religion were maintained this age?*

A. *Carolostadius*, Arch-Deacon of *Witeberg*, and *Oecolampadius*, Monk of the Order of S. *Bridget*, opposed *Luther*'s Doctrine in the point of the real presence, shewing that Christ was in the bread only Sacramentally, or significatively. The *Libertines*, whose author was one *Quintinus* a Taylor of *Picardy*, taught that whatsoever good or evil we did, was not done by us, but by Gods Spirit in us; that sin was nothing but an opinion; that in reproving of sinners, we reproved God himself; that he only was regenerate who had no remorse of conscience, that he only repented, who confessed he had committed no evil: that man in this life may be perfect and innocent; that the knowledge we have of Christ and of our Resurrection, is but opinion; that we may dissemble in Religion, *which is now the opinion of Master Hobbs*; and lastly, they slight the Scriptures, relying on their own inspirations; and they slight the Pen-men of the Holy Ghost calling St. *John* a foolish young man, St. *Matthew* a Publican, St. *Paul* a broken vessel, and St. *Peter* a denyer of his Master, *Zuinglius*, Canon of *Constance*, held the doctrine of *Carolostadius* against *Luther*, concerning the real presence. *David George*, a Glasier in *Gaunt*, taught that he was God Almighties Nephew, born of the Spirit, not of the flesh, the true *Messiah*, and third *David* that was to reign on Earth; that Heaven was void of Inhabitants: and that therefore he was sent to adopt Sons for that Heavenly Kingdom. He denied Spirits, the Resurrection, and the Judgment, and Life eternal. He held promiscuous copulation with the *Adamites*; and with the *Manichees*, that the soul was not polluted with sin; that the souls of Infidels shall be saved, and the bodies of the Apostles, as well as those of Infidels, shall be burned into Hell fire, and that it was no sin to deny Christ before men; therefore they condemned the Martyrs of folly, for shedding their Blood for Christ, *Melanct-*

See *Prate-*
olus, San-
derus, Ge-
ebrard,
Cochlaus,
Gualterus,
&c.

hon was a *Lutheran,* but not altogether so rigid; so was *Bucer,* except in the point of Christ's real presence; *Westphalus* also, but he denyed original sin, and the Holy Ghosts procession from the Son; and that Christ did not institute the Lent fast, nor was any man tied to keep it.

Q. 14. *What were the chief Heads of* Calvin's *Doctrine?*

Calvin's
Doctrine.

A. That in this life our faith is not without some doubtings and incrudelity; that the Scriptures are sufficient without traditions, that an implicite faith is no faith; That the Books of *Tobias, Judith,* part of *Hester, The Wisdom of Solomon, Ecclesiasticus, Baruch, The History of Bell and the Dragon,* and the Books of *Maccabees* are no parts of the Canonical Scripture; that the *Hebrew* Text of the old Testament is only Authentical, and so the *Greek* of the new Testament; that the Scripture in Fundamentals is clear of it self, and is a sufficient Judge of controversies; that the Elect have saving faith only, which can never totally and finally be lost; that predestination to life or death, depends not on mans foreseen merits or demerits, but on Gods free-will and pleasure; that no sin comes to pass without the will of God; that the Son of God received not his Essence of the Father, nor is he God of God, but God of himself; that Christ, in respect of his humanity, was ignorant of some things; that the Virgin *Mary* was obnoxious to divers sins and infirmities; that Christ is our Mediator in respect of both natures; that Christ was in the state of damnation when he suffered for us, but did not continue in it; that Christ by his suffering merited nothing for himself: that he descended not truly into Hell, but by suffering the pains of Hell on the cross; that there is no *Limbus Patrum,* nor Purgatory; that our Prayers avail not to the dead; that the torments of the evil angels were deferred till the day of Judgment; that Christ came not out of the grave whilst it was shut; that the true Church of God consisteth only of the Elect, and that it is not visible to men; that the Church may erre; that St. *Peter* was not Bishop of *Rome,* nor the Pope his Successor, but that he is Antichrist; that the Church and Magistrate, cannot make Laws to bind the conscience; that cœlibate and the monastical life is unlawful, and consequently the vows of chastity, poverty, and obedience; that man hath not free-will to goodness; that concupiscence or the first motions, before the will consents, are sins; that all sins are mortal, and none in themselves venial; that in this life our sins are still inherent in us, though they be not imputed to us; that we are justified by faith without works, and that faith is never without charity: that the best of our works deserve damnation; that here we may be assured of our justification and salvation; that the Church-Liturgy ought not to be read in Latine, but in the vulgar tongue: that faith is a more excellent vertue than charity; that there is no merit in us: that in this life we cannot possibly fulfill the Law: that to invocate the Saints, to worship Images and Reliques, or the cross, is Idolatry: that usury is not altogether unlawful: that Lent and other set Fasts are not to be kept:

kept: that there be only two Sacraments, Baptism, and the Lords Supper: and that the Sacraments cannot justifie or confer grace: that the Baptism of water is not of absolute necessity, nor depends the efficacy of it from the intention of the Minister, nor ought it to be administred by private Men or Women, in private houses. That Christ is not corporally in the Eucharist: that in the want of Bread and Wine, other materials may be used, and that wine alone, without water, is to be used; that there is no Transubstantiation, nor ought to be any adoration of the Bread, that the Cup should be administred to all, that extream unction was only temporary in the Church: that the Clergy ought to marry. He rejected also the Church Hierarchy, and ceremonies, and exorcisms, penance, and confirmation, Orders, Matrimony, and extream Unction from being Sacraments.

Doctrine. See Calvin's own works, Beza, and others that have followed Calvin's Tenets.

Q. 15. *What other opinions in Religion were held this age?*

A. *Servetus* a *Spaniard*, who was burned at *Geneva* taught with the *Sabellians*, that there was but one Person in God, and that there was in Christ but one nature, with *Eutyches*; he denyed the Holy Ghost, and Baptism to Infants, which he would have to be deferred till the thirteenth year of their age. He held also that God was Essential in every creature. *Brentius* a *Lutheran* taught that Christ's body, after its Ascension, is every where, whence sprung up the *Ubiquitaries. Castellio* a School-Master in *Geneva*, held that the Canticles was not Scripture, but a Love-ballad between *Solomon* and one of his Concubines. One *Postellus* taught that men of all Sects, and Professions should be saved by Christ. *Osiander* held that we were justified not by faith, but by the Essential righteousness of God, which he said was the formal cause of our justification. One *Stancarus* a *Mantuan*, taught that Christ justified us, not as he was God, but as he was man. *Amsdorphius* wrote a Book to prove that good works were pernicious to salvation. One *George Major* taught that Infants could not be justified for want of good works. *John Agricola* affirmed that the Law was altogether needless, and that Christians were not tied to the observations thereof. Hence sprung up the Antinomians. One *Steumbergerus* in *Moravia*, denyed the Trinity, the Divinity of Christ, the Holy Ghost, and Virginity of *Mary*; he rejected also Baptism and the Lords day, affirming we had no command in Scripture to keep that, but the Sabbath only. One *Okinus* taught that Polygamy, or multiplicity of Wives was lawful: One *Valentinus Gentilis* of *Naples*, denyed the Trinity, and rejected the Creed of *Athanasius*. One *Paulus* of *Cracovia* in *Poland*, denyed also the Trinity and Unity of Essence, and taught that neither the Second nor Third Person were God; that Satan was created evil; that mans intellect is eternal; that one free-will was a passive power moved necessarily by the appetite; that God was the Author of sin, and that the will of man in sinning was conformable to the will of God; that it was not adultery to lie with another mans Wife; that we must believe nothing, but what is evident to sense or reason;
that

that the same body which dieth, riseth not again; that the soul perished with the body; that there should be no care had of burial; that separated souls could not suffer corporeal fire. And that God being a Spirit, should not be invocated by our mouth, but by our heart. One *Swinkfeldius* taught that the Scripture was not the Word of God, nor that our faith depended on it, but it rather on our faith. That Christ brought his body with him from Heaven. That Christ's humanity became God after his ascension; that every man was endowed with the same essential vertues of justice, wisdom, &c. which were in God. That the power and efficacy of Gods word preached, was the very Son of God. In *Moravia* there started up some professors called *Nudipedales*, because they were bare-footed; these, in imitation of the Apostles, forsook houses, lands, business, and children, and lived together in common avoiding the society of other people. Another Sect sprung up, which called themselves *Free-Men*; teaching that they were freed from obedience to Magistrates, from Taxes, Tythes, and other duties; that after Baptism they could not sin. That they were not only like God, but already deified. And that it was lawful among themselves (but no where else) to have Women in common.

Of these see Patreolius, Genebrard, Raymundus, Sanderus, Gualterus, and others.

Qu. 16. *Were there no other opinions held in this Century?*

Christian Religion pestered with diversity of opinions.

A. Yes, many more: so vain and luxurious are the wits of men, in finding out many inventions, and shaping to themselves, forms, and *Ideas* of Religions, every one esteeming his own the best, and as much in love with his own imaginations, as *Narcissus* was with his shadow in the water, or *Deucalion* with his own picture. Some reject Scriptures, others admit no other writings but Scriptures. Some say the Devils shall be saved, others that they shall be damned, others that there are no Devils at all. Some hold that it is lawful to dissemble in Religion, others the contrary. Some say that Antichrist is come, some say not; others that he is a particular man, others that he is not a man, but the Devil; and others, that by Antichrist is meant a succession of men; some will have him to be *Nero*, some *Caligula*, some *Mahomet*, some the *Pope*, some *Luther*, some the *Turk*, some of the Tribe of *Dan*; *and so each man according to his fancy will make an Antichrist.* Some only will observe the Lords day, some only the Sabbath, some both, and some neither. Some will have all things in common, some not. Some will have Christ's body only in Heaven, some every where, some in the Bread, others with the Bread, others about the Bread, others under the Bread, and others that Christ's Body is the Bread, or the Bread his Body. And others again, that his Body is transformed into his Divinity: Some will have the Eucharist administred in both kinds, some in one, some not at all. Some will have Christ descend to Hell in respect of his Soul, some only in his Power, some in his Divinity, some in his Body, some not at all: some by Hell, understand the place of the damned, some *Limbus Patrum*, others the wrath of God, others the grave.

Some

Some will make Christ two Persons, some give him but one Nature and one Will; some affirming him to be only God, some only man, some made up of both, some altogether deny him: some will have his Body come from Heaven, some from the Virgin, some from the Elements; some will have our souls Mortal, some Immortal, some bring it into the body by infusion, some by traduction; some will have the soul created before the world, some after: some will have them created altogether, others severally: some will have them corporeal, some incorporeal: some of the substance of God, some of the substance of the body: *So infinitely are mens conceits distracted with variety of opinions, whereas there is but one Truth, which every man aimsat, but few attain it; every man thinks he hath it, and yet few enjoy it.* The main causes of these distractions are pride, self-love, ambition, contempt of Church and Scripture, the Humor of Contradiction, the Spirit of Faction, the desires of Innovation, the want of preferment in high Spirits, Anger, Envy, the benefit that ariseth to some by fishing in troubled waters: the malignant eye that some have on the Churches prosperity, the greedy appetite others have to Quails, and the Flesh-pots of *Egypt*, rather than to *Manna*, though sent from Heaven: the want of contempt of Authority, Discipline, and order in the Church, which like Bulwarks, Walls, or Hedges, keep out the wild Boars of the Forest from rooting up the Lords Vineyard, and the little Foxes from eating up the Grapes thereof. Therefore wise Governours, were forced to authorise Bishops, Moderators, or Superintendents (call them what you will) for regulating, curbing, and punishing such luxurious wits, as disturbed the peace of the Church, and consequently of the State, by their fantastical inventions, knowing that too much liberty was no less dangerous than Tyranny, to much mercy as pernicious as cruelty: and a general permission in a Kingdom or State, no less hazardous to the publick tranquility, than a general restriction.

The Contents of the Ninth Section.

The first Original of the Monastical *Life.* 2. *The first* Eremites *or* Anchorites. 3. *The manner of their living.* 4. *Their Excesses in Religion.* 5. *The preheminence of the Sociable life to the Solitary.* 6. *The first Monks after* Anthony. 7. *The Rules of St.* Basil. 8. *St.* Hierom's *order.* 9. *St.* Austin's *order.* 10. *If St.* Austin *instituted his* Eremites *to beg.* 11. *Of St.* Austin's *Leathern Girdle used at this day.* 12. *The Institutions and exercises of the first Monks.* 13. *Why Religious persons cut their Hair and Beards.* 14. *Whence came that custom of Shaving.* 15. *Of the Primitive Nuns.* 16. *Of what account Monks are at this day in the* Roman *Church.* 17. *How the Monks and Nuns of old were consecrated.* 18. *The Benedictine order.* 19. *Of the orders proceeding from them.* 20. *Of St.* Bennet's *rules to the Monks.* 21. *The Benedictines Habit and Diet.* 22. *Rules prescribed by the Council of* Aix *to the Monks.* 23. *The Rites and Institutions of the Monks of* Cassinum. 24. *The manner of electing their Abbots.* 25. *The Benedictine Nuns and their Rules.* 26. *Of the Laws and Privileges of Monasteries.*

SECT. IX.

Quest. **H**Aving taken a view of the Opinions in Christian Religion for 1600 years; it remains that we now take notice of the strictest observers thereof: therefore tell us who they were that separated themselves from other Christians, not so much in opinion, as in place and strictness of living; and what was the first original of this separation?

Eremites, or Anchorites.

A. When the Christian Religion in the beginning was opposed by persecutors, many holy men and women to avoid the fury of their persecutors, retired into desart places, where they gave themselves to fasting, prayer, and meditation in the Scriptures. These were called *Eremites* from the Desart where they lived and *Monachi* from their single or solitary life; And *Anchorites* from living a part by themselves. Such were *Paul* the *Eremite, Anthony, Hilarion, Basil, Hierom,* and others. Afterward the *Eremites* growing weary of the Desarts, and Persecution at an end, betook themselves into Towns and Cities, where they lived together, and had all things in common within one building which they called *Monastery, Covent,* or *Cloyster.* These Monks were called ϑεραπδ ται Worshippers, ἀσκηται Exercisers or Wrestlers in Christianity; *Clerici* also, as being the Lords inheritance; and *Philosophers* from their study and contemplation of Divine and Humane things.

These

Sect. 9. *A View of the Religions*, &c.

These houses were called *Coenobia*, because they held all things among them in common, and *Claustra* or *Cloysters*, there they were inclosed because from the rest of the world. φροντιστηρια, Schools of cares and discipline, and ασκητηρια, places of exercise. As the men had their peculiar Houses or Cloysters, so had the women, who were willing to separate themselves from the world; these were called *Nonnæ*, or *Nuns*, from the *Egyptian* word *Nonnus*, for there were the first Monasteries; from their solitary life they are named *Moniales*, and from their holiness *Sanctimoniales*; and from the *Roman*, phrase *Virgines Vestales*; now, because these holy men and women lived at first in caves and subterraneal holes, they were named *Mandritæ*; for *Mandræ* signifies caves or holes; and *Troglodita*, from these *Ethiopians* in *Arabia* near the Red Sea, who lived on Serpents flesh and Roots, whose skins were hardned with the nights cold, and tanned with the Suns heat. They were so called απο τῶν Τρωγλων, from their caves where they dwelt.

Q. 2. *Who were the first* Eremites, *or Anchorites?*

A. If we take *Eremites* for such as have lived in Desarts for a while, to avoid persecution; then we may say that *Eliah*, *John Baptist*, and *Christ* himself were *Eremites*. For they were forced sometimes to live an *Eremitical* or solitary life in desarts. But if by *Eremites* we understand such as wholly addicted themselves to an Eremitical or solitary life, from the world and worldly affairs, that they might the more freely give themselves to fasting, prayer, and contemplation, then the first *Eremite* we read of, since Christ, was *Paul*, the *Theban*: who having lost in the Persecution under *Decius*, both his Parents, and fearing to be betrayed by his Sisters Husband, betook himself to a cave at the foot of a Rocky Hill, about the year of Christ 260, and there continued all his life, to wit, from fifteen years of age till he died, which was the one hundredth and thirteenth year of his life. All which time he saw no body but *Antoninus*, who being ninety years old, by divine instinct came to *Paul* on the day he died. This *Antoninus* instituted this *Eremitical* life in *Egypt*. Being twenty years old, he sold his Estate, and bestowed it on the poor; then in remote places he lived alone, but that sometimes he would visit his Disciples. At 35 years he betook himself to the Desart, till he was 55. Then he returned to the Cities, and Preached Christ there. Afterward he returned again to the Desart, where he spent the remainder of his life, and died the 105 year of his age, and after Christ, 361. To him succeeded *Hilarion*, the first *Eremite* in *Palestina* and *Syria*. Then *Paul* surnamed the Simple, *Amon* an *Egyptian*, with divers others.

See *Hierom.* in the life of *Paul* and *Anthony*, and in his *Chronicle*. See also *Marcellus*, *Sozomen*, *Sabellicus*, in their Histories, and others, Eremites, *their first manner of living*.

Q. 3. *How did these first* Eremites *live?*

A. They spent their time in working, sometimes in preaching, praying, fasting, and meditating, and sometimes in composing differences between *Christians*, in visiting the sick, and in such holy exercises did they place their Religion. *Paul* the *Theban* was content with a Cave instead of a Palace; with a piece of dry bread
brought

174   *A View of the Religions*   Sect. 9.

brought to him by a Raven every day, instead of delicate chear, with water in stead of Wine; and with the leaves of Palms in stead of rich apparel: And to avoid idleness, he would work sometimes with his hands. *Anthony* contented himself with bread, salt, and water; his dinner-time was at Sun-setting; he used to fast sometimes two days together, and to watch and pray whole nights; he lay on the bare ground: disputed often times with the *Arrians* and *Meletians*, in defence of *Athanasius*, did intercede many times with the *Emperour Constantine*, for distressed Christians, and was always ready to compose their quarrels. *Hilarion* was content to live in a little hovel which he made himself of shells, twigs and bulrushes, four foot broad, and five foot high, spending his time in praying, fasting, curing of diseases; casting out Devils. His garment was sack-cloath, which he never put off; his food, roots, and herbs, which he never tasted before Sun set; Six ounces of Barley bread contented him from 30 years till 35, from that time till 63, he used Oyl to repair his decayed strength: From 64 till 80, he abstained from bread. That he might not be idle, he made him baskets of bulrushes, and used to lie on the ground. Thus did these Primitive *Eremites* spend their time; *Not in chambering and wantonness, surfeiting, and drunkenness; but in temperance, sobriety, continence, hunger, thirst, heat and cold, reading, praying, preaching, and fasting, not placing Religion in saying, but in suffering; not in good words, but in good works; not in talking of Scripture, but in walking by Scripture.*

See Hierom, Sozomen, Nicephorus, and others describing their lives: And Athanasius in the life of Anthony, if that Book be genuine.

Q. 4. *Wherein did some* Eremites *exceed in their Religious, or rather, superstitious kind of Living?*

A. As Jealousie is too much Love; so is Superstition too much Religion; *but* too much of one thing (as we say) *is good for nothing: Ne quid nimis* should be in all our actions. *God will have mercy, and not sacrifice:* He will say, *Who required these things at your hands?* Such kind of *bodily exercise,* as the Apostle saith, *availeth little*; It is not a torn skin, nor a macerated body, nor a pinched belly that God requires, but *a broken and contrite spirit*; *a renting of the heart, and not of the garment*; and therefore the excess of *Eremitical* penance is ἐθελοθρησκία, Will-worship, and not that which God requireth, to wit, *mercy and justice; to relieve the oppressed; to comfort the comfortless; to visit the fatherless, and widows, and to keep our selves unspotted of the world:* To place Religion in abstinence from certain meats, is against the Apostles rule, 1 Tim. 4. saying, *That every creature of God is good, and nothing to be rejected, which is received with thanksgiving.* Altogether to abandon the society of Christians, is contrary to St *Paul's* counsel, Heb. 10. *Let us consider one another, to provoke unto love and to good works, not forsaking the fellowship that we have among our selves, as the manner of some is*; under pretence of forsaking the world, to go abandon all care of Friends and Family, is condemned by the Apostle, 1 Tim. 5. *If any man hath not a care of his Family, he hath denied the Faith; and is worse than an Infidel.* They that willingly

Their too great rigour.

deprive

deprive themselves of the means of doing good to their neighbours, transgress the Law of God which commands us *to love our neighbours as our selves*. These subsequent examples will shew how far some men have exceeded the bounds of Christianity, and out-run Religion, by too much superstitious devotions and excessive pennance. One *Asepesima* lived 60 years together in a Closet, all which time he never was seen of any, nor did he speak to any. The like is recorded of one *Didymus*, who had lived ninety years by himself. One *Batthæus* an *Eremite* of *Cœlosyria*, fasted so long, till worms crawled out of his teeth. One *Martinus* tied his leg with an Iron Chain to a great Stone, that he might not remove thence. One *Alas* never tasted bread in eighty years together. *John Sormany* the *Egyptian* stood praying within the Cliff of a certain Rock three years together, so long, till his legs and feet, with continual standing swelled with putrified matter, which at last broke the skin and run out. One *Dominicus* an *Eremit* wore continually next his skin, an Iron coat of Male; and almost every day used to scourge himself with whips in both hands. Some have killed themselves with hunger, some with thirst, some with exposing themselves to excessive heat, have been stifled; others by extremity of cold, have bin frozen to death; as if God took delight in self-murther, which in him to affect were cruelty, and in any to act, were the greatest impiety. Some again not content with ordinary ways of *Eremitism*, have spent their days within hollow-pillars, whence they were named *Stylitæ*, neither admitting the speech nor sight of any man or woman. *O curas hominum! O quantum est in rebus inane!* what need all this toil? Christ saith, *that his Yoak is easie, and his Burthen light*; but these men laid heavy burthens on themselves, which God never required; he made man *Animal politicum*, a sociable creature, therefore said, *It was not good for man to be alone. Wo to him that is alone*, saith *Solomon*. Besides no place, though never so remote and solitary, can privilege a man from sin. *Lot* was righteous among the wicked *Sodomites*, and yet in the solitary cave committed Incest with his two Daughters; what place could be more retired than Paradise, and more secure than Heaven; yet *Adam* fell in Paradise, and the Angels fell in Heaven.

They that will read the superstitious sufferings of these men above-named, and of others, let them look in Sozomen, Theodoret, Socrates, Nicephorus Evagrius, &c. Sociable preferred to the solitary.

Q. 5. *Whether is the solitary life in a Desart, or the sociable life in a Covent to be preferred?*

A. 1. The sociable life, because the end of our creation was not to live apart, like wild beasts, but together, like men. 2. Because we are bound to help each other, by Counsel, Instruction, Admonition, Exhortation, to bear one anothers burthens, to comfort the comfortless, to support the weak, to cloath the naked, to feed the hungry: for as the Orator said, we are not born for our selves, but our Parents, Country and Friends, challenge a share in us. 3. Because he that liveth alone, as he sins against his creation, and humane society, so he sins against himself, in that he debars himself of those comforts and aid, both spiritual and corporal

which,

which he hath in a sociable life. 4. Because God is more present with many, than with one. *Therefore his Church, which he promiseth to be with till the end of the world, and on which he hath bestowed the Spirit of Truth, to conduct her into all Truth, and which he hath built upon the Rock, so that Hell gates shall not prevail against her;* his Church I say, is a congregation, and consisteth not of one, but of many; and Christ hath promised that *where two or three are gathered together in his name, he will be in the midst of them.* 5. Because God is better praised and more honoured of many together, than by one alone; therefore *David will praise God, and declare his name in the great Congregation.* Christ will have *our light to shine before men, that they seeing our good works, may glorifie our Father which is in Heaven.* This cannot be done by him that lives amongst wild beasts in a Desart. How can he honour God by the exercise of Justice, Mercy, Charity, Humility, and other vertues, chiefly of his patience, in suffering injuries, and of his obedience to superiors? How shall he find out his own infirmities and failings, seeing self love is in every man, and no man can so well pry into himself as another; and *the heart of man is deceitful above all things?* 6. And lastly, no man can be so secure from danger of enemies, as when he is in company; and therefore Satan is more ready to assault man by temptations, when he is alone, than when he is in the company and society of others. So he set not upon Christ when he was in *Jerusalem*, but *when he was led by the Spirit into the Desart,* therefore, *wo to him that is alone, for when he falls, there is not a second to help him up.* As then in the body natural, God did not separate one member from another, but united them all in one bulk, under one head, to be animated by one heart or soul, that they might help each other, so hath he done in the body Politick of Mankind.

Monks who were the first.

Q. 6. *Who were the first Monks after* Anthony?

A. The *Thabennesii*, so called from *Thabenna*, an Island in the Province of *Thebais*. In this, one *Pachomius* an *Eremite*, about the time of *Constantius*, *Constantines* Son, assembled divers Monks together, and by the advice of an Angel (so goeth the story) prescribed them these rules; to wit, that they should live together in one House, distinguished into divers Cells, and in each Cell should remain three Monks, but should all eat in one Hall. No man must be forbid to eat or fast; they must sleep not lying on beds, but sitting in their chairs: they must wear Goat skins, which they must never put off but when they communicate; then they must come only with their hood, with which their heads must be covered when they eat, that they may not be seen to eat; for in eating they must neither cast their eyes off from the Table, nor must they speak. No stranger must be admitted without three years trial. They must pray twelve times in the day time, likewise in the evening, and in the night, a Psalm preceeding each prayer. The Monks were divided into 24 Orders, according to the number of the Greek letters,

See *Sozomen, Nicephorus* and *Vincentius* in his, *Spec. Hist.*

Sect. 9. *of* EUROPE. 177

Qu. 7. *What were the Religious rules that Saint* Basil *prescribed to his Monks?*

Monks of Saint Basil and their rules.

A. Saint *Basil,* Presbyter of *Cæsarea* in *Cappadocia,* being molested by *Eusebius,* Bishop there, to avoid trouble and disturbing of the Church, retired to a Monastery in *Pontus,* where he preached to the Monks of that place; and departing thence, travelled about the country of *Pontus,* and perswaded the *Eremites,* who lived apart in caves and cells of the Desarts, to unite themselves in Monasteries, and withal prescribed to them these 95 subsequent rules, which were embraced by most of the Eastern Monks. The Rules were these. 1. To love God with all their heart, soul and strength, and their neighbours as themselves. 2. To ground this Love of God upon his power, glory, and excellency, as he is in himself; and on his goodness, mercy, and bounty towards us. 3. That the love of our neighbour be grounded on the command and will of God, and on his love toward us his enemies; for if God hath so highly loved us that were his enemies, shall not we, when he commands us, love our neighbours? 4. That they should not live any longer asunder, but together, because of the mutual helps, comforts, instructions, exercise of vertue, efficacy of prayers, security from dangers which are in the sociable, not in the solitary life. 5. That they should forsake the delights and vanities of the world, and with the Apostle, *to crucifie it, and to be crucified to it.* 6. That they should dispense their wealth to the poor and indigent. 7. That none be admitted into their Fraternity without probation. 8. That Infants be also admitted, but not without the consent of their Parents. 9. That they study to be continent, and sober in their diet and behaviour. 10. Is set down the measure of their eating and drinking, and simplicity of food. 11. That there be no affectation or contention for superiority of place at the Table, but that all things be done there with order and decency. 12. That their apparel be plain, simple, and homely; and that they were a girdle, after the example of *John Baptist,* and the Apostles. 13. That they walk not after their own sense and pleasure, but as they are directed by God's word. 14. That they be obedient to their Superiours, but chiefly to God. 15. That they should serve God with the same affection as *David* did, when he said, *As the Hart brayeth for the Rivers of water, so doth my soul after thee, O God.* 16. That he who is their Governour, should consider whose Minister he is; and that he should be as tender of his charge, as a Nurse over her child. 17. That he reprove at first gently, and in the spirit of meekness; but that he esteem of the obstinate as Heathens and Publicans. 18. That he suffer not the least offence to go unreproved, seeing the least is a breach of God's Law. 19. That repentance be in sincerity. 20. That it be accompanied with good works. 21. And with confession. 22. That if a man relapse into sin, he may use more sincerity in his repentance than before; for it seems the disease was not perfectly cured. 23. Let him that reproveth be as a Father, or a Physician; and he who is reproved, as a Son, and a

N Patient.

Patient. 24. That no man defend or excuse himself in his evil courses. 25. That among them all things be in common. 26. That men of Estates bestow on their kindred what is their due, and the remainder on the poor. 27. That none return to their Parents houses, except it be to instruct them, and by their Superiors leave. 28. That none give way, through idleness, for their minds to waver, or wander up and down. 29. That to avoid idle and sinful dreams in the night, let every one be diligent in meditating on the Law and the Word of God by day. 30. That with the same affection which Christ shewed in washing of his Disciples feet, should the strong and whole serve the sick and infirm. 31. That they should love one another, as Christ hath loved us. 32. That their speech be not idle, but *seasoned with salt, and edifying.* 33. That they should abstain from upbraiding or defaming words. 34. That they who either defame, or patiently hear their brother defamed, be excommunicated. 35. That they give not place or scope to anger. 36. That *they set their affections on Heavenly, not on Earthly things.* 37. That they neither sorrow nor rejoyce, but when they see God honoured or dishonoured. 38. That they take heed of worldly cares, and too much security. 39. *That whatever they do, may be done to the glory of God.* 40. That they beware of pride. 41. That by a mean esteem of themselves, they may learn humility. 42. That every one be obedient to another, *as servants are to their Masters, or as Christ was obedient to his Father.* 43. That no man give occasion of scandal or offence to his brother; that every one do his duty with chearfulness, without grudging; that reconciliation may be made where there is any difference. 44. *That they judge not, lest they be judged.* 45. That they be truly zealous against sin. 46. That no man do his own will, nor undertake any thing without leave, seeing Christ *came not to do his own will, but the will of him that sent him.* 47. They that be thankful to God, *who hath made them partakers with the Saints in light.* 48. That they instruct no vices in their duties. 49. That they debar not any man from entring into their Convent upon trial; and withal, that they give them no offence. 50. That in their Fasting they use moderation and devotion. 51. That no man scorn to wear an old garment when it is given him. 52. That every man observe the hour appointed for eating. 53. That they give their alms with due consideration, and according to the discretion of the Superiour. 54. That a younger Brother, instructing his elder, do it with reverence; and that no man disturb the Orders settled in the Monastery. 55. That great care be had of the Utensils belonging to the Monastery. 56. If any be necessarily detained from publick prayer and singing, that then he pray and praise God in his heart. 57. That they be reverent in their prayers, and not suffer their minds to wander, seeing the eyes of God are upon them. 58. That the Steward, and other Officers of the Convent, be prudent and faithful in their dispensation. 59. That there be diversity of rewards, according to the diversity of works. 60. That he who returns to God by repentance, must weep, and be sorry for his former

former life, and hate his former actions. 61. That they should not be dismayed who have not wealth to give to the poor, seeing they have forsaken all for Christ. 62. That they take heed of affected ignorance, and consenting to other mens sins. 63. That they must not be silent, or connive at their Brothers offences, but must reprove him. 64. That they should never be without compunction and care, by reason of the remainders of sin in them. 65. That they indeavour to be *poor in spirit*, which is to forsake all for the love of God. 66. That they persevere in doing good till the end of their life. 67. That though in respect of themselves, they must not care what they eat, or what they drink; yet, that they may be helpful to others, they must labour with their hands. 68. That to think of meat and drink out of season is a sin. 69. That sack-cloath be worn for humiliation, other garments for necessity; that in speaking, they be neither too loud nor too low. 70. That the Eucharist be received with fear, reverence, and faith. 71. They observe when it is fit to speak, when to be silent. 72. *That they have always the fear of God before them; That they avoid the broad way, and strive to enter in at the narrow gate.* 73. That they beware of covetousness, vain-glory, and vanity in apparel, to please men. 74. That they abstain from all defilement of the flesh, and endeavour *to be pure in heart.* 75. That they hate sin, *and take delight in Gods Law.* 76. That they try their Love to God, *by their thankfulness to him, by obedience to his commands, and by denying themselves,* Their Love to their neighbour; by *fellow feeling and sympathy in his prosperity and adversity.* 77. That they should imitate God and Christ, in *loving their enemies.* 78. *That they should be angry; but sin not; that they give place to anger, and not resist evil, but being persecuted, either to suffer, or fly.* 79. That they strive for the peace of conscience; and *like new born babes, receive the sincere milk of God's Word, without resisting.* 80. That no man be puffed up with a conceit of his own worth, nor brag thereof, or glory therein. 81. *That they beg true wisdom from God, and acknowledge him the Author of all good.* 82. That they may know what it is, *to be holy, to be just, not to cast pearls before Swine, and to be content with their daily bread.* 83. That no Brother alone visit a Sister but in company, and that by permission; and for edification, to avoid offence. 84. That reproof be joyned with gentleness; and that none rely on his own judgment.

85. *That they bear one anothers infirmities.* 86. *That they pray against temptations.* 87. That they do not speak, or act any thing rashly, but advisedly. 88. That in giving, *they should chiefly have regard to those of the houshold of faith;* and that every one must not be a dispenser, but he only to whom that charge is committed. 89. *That they labour not for faith,* as some do, *without charity; and that they hide not their Talent in a Napkin.* 90. They must distinguish between fury, which is always evil; and just indignation against sin in their brother. 91. That Satan is not the cause of sin in any man, but as he consents to it; therefore *the more watchful should every man be over his own heart.* 92. If any man, being in debt, en-

ter into the Monastery, he ought to pay his debt, if he be able. 93. That when a Sister confesseth, the Priest-Confessor do nothing but by order and decency, and in the presence of the Mother or Abbatess. 94. If Satan strive to hinder any good action, they must not leave off their holy purpose and resolution. 95. *That no man be wise in his own eyes, nor trust in his own strength, but in the Lord.*

These Canons we may read more fully in Saint *Basil*'s Works. *Ruffinus* translated them into Latine; And here we may see that such a Monastical life is not to be condemned: for these Monks were not to be idle, but to work with their hands; therefore their Monasteries were called 'Ασκητήρια, places of Exercise, and the Monks 'Ασκηταὶ, Exercises, which signifieth not only the exercise of their hands, but also of their minds; as *Hospinian* observes out of *Budæus*. These Monks were tied to wear a white garment.

Q. 8. *What Religious Order did Saint* Hierom *erect?*

S. Hierom.

A. S. *Hierom*, who was coetaneal with S. *Basil*, being offended at the Heathenish lives of Christians in *Rome*, betook himself, with some others, into *Syria*, where he lived in the Desart for a time, giving himself to study, prayers, and meditation; afterward returning to *Rome*, was so hated there by the Clergy whose vices he sharply reproved; that he betook himself again to his Monastical life in *Syria*, where *Paula* a noble *Roman* Matron, erected four Monasteries, three for Women, and one for Men, in *Bethlehem*, near the stable where Christ was born. In this Convent Saint *Hierom* lived many years with divers of his friends, spending his time in devotion, writing, and meditating on the Bible, and educating also of divers noble youths, to whom he read Rhetorick, and the Poets: And thus he ended his days the 91 year of his life, and of Christ 421. The *Monks* of his Order are called *Hieronymiani*, whose garments are of a swart or brown colour: Over their coat they wear a pleated cloak divided; they gird their coat with a leather girdle, and wear wooden shooes. There is also an Order of *Eremites* of Saint *Hierom*, set up by *Charles Granellus* a *Florentine*, about the year of Christ 1365. These *Hieromites* flourished most in *Italy*, and *Spain*, and have large revenues.

Monks of S. Hierom.

See Sabellicus, Polydore, Virgil, Baronius, Erasmus on the life of S. Hierom, and his Antidote to Rusticus the Monk.

Q. 9. *Of what Religious Order is Saint* Augustine *held to be Author?*

Monks of S. Austin.

A. Of these who are called *Canon Regulars*, bearing Saint *Augustine*'s name, and of the *Eremites* of Saint *Augustine*. Which of these two Orders was first instituted by that great light and Doctor of the Church, is not yet certain; we find that this holy man was at first a *Manichee* till he was 31 years of age, and professed *Rhetorick* at *Rome* and *Millan*; but by the perswasion of *Simplicianus*, and reading the life of *Anthony* the Monk, he became a convert, and in a Garden with his Friend *Alipius*, as he was bewailing his former life, he heard a voice accompanied with the Musick of Children, saying to him, *Tolle, lege, Tolle, lege,* that is, *Take up and Read;* looking about, and seeing no body, he took this for a

Divine

Sect. 9. *of* EUROPE. 181

Divine admonition, and so taking up the Bible, the first passage he lighted on was this: [*Not in surfeiting and Drunkenness, not in Chambering and Wantonness, but put you on the Lord Jesus,* &c.] Upon this in resolving, to become a Christian, he went with *Alipius* to *Millan,* where they were both baptized with his Son, by Saint *Ambrose* Bishop there. After this having spent a few years in fasting, prayer, and study in the Holy Scripture, he was called to *Hippo* in *Africa,* where he he was at first Presbyter, and then Bishop. He built a Monastery within the Church of *Hippo;* where he lived with other learned men as in a Colledge, and from thence sent abroad divers Divines to be Clergy-men in *Hippo,* and Bishops to other places. Now whereas Saint *Austin* was first an *Eremite,* and lived in the Desart, before he erected a Collegiate life in *Hippo,* it is likely that the *Eremites* of his Order are more ancient than his Monks or Canons. But some doubt, whether either of these Orders were instituted by him, as divers other Orders who profess to live after his Rule; as the *Scopetini* instituted by *Steven,* and *James* of *Sena,* and confirmed by *Gregory* 11. about the year 1408. The *Frisenarii* called also *Lateranenses;* these sprung up in the Territory of *Luca* in *Hetruria,* which *Eugenius* 4. ratified. The Order of Saint *George* in *Alga* instituted at *Venice* by *Laurentius Justinianus, Anno* 1407. and confirmed by Pope *John* 22. These wear a Blue habit. The *Dominicans,* also, *Brigidians, Jesuati,* Servants of the blessed Virgin *Mary, Hieromites, Antonians, Trinitaries,* Brothers of Saint *John* of *Jerusalem, Cruciferi,* brothers of Saint *Peter* the Confessor, Brothers of the Lord's Sepulchre, *Eremites* of Saint *Paul,* with divers others. The habit of the Canons regular is a White Cloath Coat, open before, and down to their feet. This is girded to their body, and over it they wear a Linen Surplis to their knees, and over that a short black cloak to their elbows, with a hood fastned to it; their crowns are shaven like other *Friars;* and when they go abroad, they wear a broad hat, or a black corner'd cap. But Saint *Austin's Eremites* wear a black coat, with a hood of the same colour; underneath there is a White little coat. Their Girdle is of Leather with a Buckle of Horn. After the example of these *Monastical Canons,* there were *Ecclesiastical Canons* erected, who instead of an Abbot, had the Bishop for their Governour; these were seated near the Cathedral Church, which sometimes was called *Monastery,* and corruptedly *Minster,* these Canons, whilst they lived strictly according to their rule, were named *Regular;* but when they fell off from their strict way of living, and medled with worldly business, they received a new name of *Canons Secular. Volatteran* reckoned 4555 Monasteries of Canons in *Europe.* 700 in *Italy,* whereas now are scarce 60. Popes 36, Cardinals 300, of Canonized Saints 7500.

Q. 10. *Did Saint* Austin *institute his* Eremites *to beg?*

A. It is not likely, for S. *Austin* never begged himself, but did live by his learned and pious labours; Christ and his Apostles did live idlely, and by begging; S. *Paul* laboured, *working with his own hands, beg.*

With him see Sabe- licus, Vol. Virgil, Crantzius, Baleus, Alphonsus, Alvarez de Guicciard. &c. Monks of S. Austin are not l-

hands, and said, 1 Cor. 4. *That he who will not work, shall not eat.* And 2 Thes. 3. *That it is a more blessed thing to give, than to receive.* A begger was not suffered in Israel, and amongst God's people it was held a curse to beg; therefore *David* wished that his Enemies might beg their Bread; and sheweth that the children of the righteous shall never be driven to beg. Besides, they that are able to work and will not, but live upon the alms of such as are sick and impotent, are robbers of the poor and weak. I deny not, but Christ undertook voluntary poverty, because he confesseth, *Luke*. 6. *That the Son of man had not whereon to lay his head*, and *Luk*. 8. 3. *That the Women did minister to him of their goods*; and elsewhere, *That he had neither House of his own to be born in, nor a Chamber of his own to eat his last Supper in, nor an Ass of his own to ride on, nor a Grave of his own to lie in.* Yet we do not read that he begged, or lived idlely; for he went about preaching, working miracles, and doing good; therefore he needed not to beg; for he that will thus imploy his life, shall not want, nor need to beg. And so if the Monks would take pains in praying and preaching, they needed not to be Mendicants; *For the labourer is worthy of his wages, no man goeth a Warfare on his own charges; he that serveth to the Altar, must live by the Altar; and he that soweth Spiritual things, should reap Temporal.* I deny not also, but there were Lazarus, the two blind men in the Gospel, the Cripple in the Acts, who did beg; but then the Jewish government was much altered from its first purity, and their Laws much neglected or corrupted, by their subjection to the *Romans*. Again that Christ and his Disciples needed not to beg, is plain, *by the common purse among them, whereof* Judas *was the carrier*. Now Christ assumed voluntary poverty, though he did not begg; to shew that he came to suffer want, and that his Kingdom was not of this world; and to sanctifie our poverty to us, and to teach the rich of this world, that they trust not in uncertain riches; and that the poor should not be dejected, seeing Christ himself was poor. God also, to humble us, doth suffer us sometimes to be in want. So he dealt with *Elias*, when he asked bread of the Widow; and *David*, when he desired bread of *Abimelech*; and *Lazarus*, when he begged at the rich mans door: but this is seldom, and to let us see, that on earth we have not true happiness. Again, I deny not but a single man, who hath no charge of Wife, Children, and Family, may renounce his wealth, that he may be the less burthened with the cares of this life, and the more apt for prayer and contemplation; but this is not lawful in him who hath the charge of Wife and Family, for whom he ought to provide, *If he be not worse than an Infidel.* To be brief, these Monks, who can work, or preach, and will not, ought not to beg; for wages are due to those that work, not so much out of charity, as out of justice.

Q. 11. *Was that leathern Girdle ever worn by S.* Augustine, *with which the Monks of this Order used to cure Diseases, and ease Pains in the body?*

A. 1. That

A. 1. That Saint *Austin* ever wore this Girdle, is not known to me, nor can it be proved but by their own traditions. 2. That this Girdle hath miraculously cured Diseases, and assuaged Pains, is believed by divers Lay people, even by some Princes, who have for this end, wore the same. 3. That wonderful cures have been wrought by this Girdle, is assevered by divers, but how truely, I know not. 4. God sometimes, by weak means, produceth strange cures; as by *Christ's Spittle, Saint* Peter's *Shadow, Saint* Paul's *Handkerchief,* the *Hem of Christ's Garment.* 5. God permits Satan sometimes to do strange things, that they who will not believe the truth, may be deluded. 6. Many strange cures are to be ascribed to the force of immagination, rather than to such weak outward means. 7. To deny all miracles which have been written, is too much temerity; and to believe all, is too much credulity. 8. We read of miracles not only done by *Moses, Christ,* and his *Apostles,* but also by the Sorcerers of *Egypt, Simon Magus, Antichrist, Apollonius,* and others. 9. As Scriptures at first were proved by miracles, so miracles are now to be proved by Scriptures; for such miracles as are not consonant to God's word, are not true. 10. Divers of the *Roman* Church doubt the truth of many of their miracles; *Canus Loc. l.*11. *c.* 6. calls *the Author of the Golden Legend, a man of a Brazen Face, and a Leaden Heart. Espencœus* upon 2 *Tim* 4. saith, *That the Legends are full of Fables.* Cajetan Digr. 12. Opusc. de concep. Virg. cap. 1. tells us, *That it cannot be known infallibly, that the miracles on which the Church groundeth the Canonisation of Saints be true, because the Credit thereof depends on mens reports, who may deceive others, and be deceived themselves.*

Q. 12. *What were the Institutions and exercises of the first Monks?*

A. At first they used to work, when occasion served; to eat and drink soberly, to go decent in their apparel, to fast and pray often, to possess all things in common; to Read, Meditate, Preach, and hear the Word of God, to study Temperance, Continency, Modesty, Obedience, Silence, and other Vertues. They were divided into tens, and hundreds; every nine had their *Decurio,* or tenth man to overlook them, and every hundred had their *Centurio,* to whom the ten *Decurions* were subject, they had their distinct beds; at the ninth hour they met to sing and hear Sermons, at Table they sit silent, and content themselves with Bread, Herbs, and Salt; the old men onely drink Wine; in the night they had their hours of Prayer; in the Summer they dine, but sup not: The chief Governour they called Father in *Syriack,* Abbot, who for his learning was eminent, and for his life exemplary. These ancient Monks used to wear Hoods and Girdles, they went also with staves, and scrips of Goat-skins. But in *Egypt* they wore on shooes, because of the heat of that Country. The affairs of the Convent was committed to some Brother, till he grew weary of it: but in *Mesopotamia, Palestine,* and *Cappadocia,* the Brothers did serve by turns weekly; at the end of the week, the servant did wash the feet of his Brothers, and so resigned up his office to the next. In moſt places they obſerved the third, ſixth, and ninth hours for prayer; none were admitted into the Monaſtery, till they were firſt tried by waiting ten days together without the the Gate, and patiently enduring all the opprobrious ſpeeches that ſhould be uttered againſt them; then did the Abbot receive them with a long exhortation, admoniſhing them of their duties and chiefly exhorting them to Mortification, Humility, Silence, Obedience, Meekneſs, Patience, Sobriety, Submiſſion, Confeſſion of their infirmities, and ſuch like duties. Then are theſe Probationers ſtript of their own Garments, and cloathed in Monks habit, and are tied one whole year under ſtrict diſcipline; if there be diſ-like on either ſide, they receive their own cloaths again from the Steward, and are diſmiſſed the Monaſtery. Small offences among theſe Monks were puniſhed with publick humiliation and acknowledgement, the offender lying flat on the ground, till the Abbot bid him riſe; but great faults were puniſhed with ſtripes, or expulſion: during their ſitting at Table, they were to hearken to what was read out of the Scripture, to the end, they might be taken off from idle talk, and that their minds might be fed as well as their bodies, ſeeing *not by bread alone man doth live, but by every word that cometh out of the mouth of God.* Theſe primitive Monaſteries alſo were ſubject to the Biſhops of the Dioceſſe, without whoſe leave they were not to go abroad from their Convents. *I do not find that in theſe Primitive Monaſteries they were tied to ſet Faſts, to the three Vows of Chaſtity, Poverty, and Obedience, or to different cloths and colours; or to ſtay longer in the Monaſtery, than their own liking.*

See *Caſſianus, Hierom, Eraſmus, Vadianus,* &c.

Q. 13. *Why did Religious Perſons cut their Hair and Beards?*

A. Becauſe long Hair was abuſed among the Gentiles to Pride, Luxury, and Superſtition. It did argue alſo Effeminateneſs, Childiſhneſs, or Slaviſhneſs; for in ſome places ſlaves uſed to wear long hair, which when they were made free, they laid aſide; ſo children, when they came to years of puberty, cut their Hairs, and offered them to *Apollo,* who by the Poets is called *Crinitus,* and κυρίτροφ⸱, the nouriſher of Hair; the Gentiles gave long Hairs to their gods; So *Jupiter, Apollo, Bacchus, Neptune, Æſculapius,* are deſcribed with long Hair. Nature gave the Woman long Hair, to diſtinguiſh her from the Man; therefore men with long Hair were noted for effeminate, and in deriſion called τειχοπλόκαι, Hair-trimmers. The Apoſtle reproves it in men; therefore the Clergy by the Canons of Councils and Decretals, are forbid to nouriſh their Hairs, but to cut them; yet I do not find that they uſed in thoſe times to ſhave, or were enjoyned to do ſo, but rather the contrary: therefore *Optatus Milevitanus, L. Cont. Parmen.* reproves the *Donatiſts* for ſhaving the *Catholick Prieſts:* and *Clemens Alexandrinus, L.* 3. *Pædag. cap.* 11. ſaith, that the Hairs are to be clipt with Sciſſors, not ſhaved with a Rafor. And the reaſon why ſhaving was then prohibited among the Chriſtians, was becauſe it was uſed by the Gentile Prieſts in honour of their Idols; for in the time of the Primitive Chriſtians, were the Prieſts of *Iſis* yet extant,

Why they cut their hair and beard.

extant, who used to shave their Heads: for this cause God would not have the Jewish Priests to shave, seeing he would not have them to be like the Idolatrous Priests, nor would he have them to shave in Funerals, *Levit.* 21. Now the reasons why Monks and Clerks, were shaved among Christians, and that onely on the top of their Head, so that their hairs hanging about their Ears, represented a Crown, were these. 1. To resemble the Crown of Thorns which Christ wore: 2. To shew that Christ's Priests are also spiritual Kings. 3. They shave off their Hairs, to shew that they should lay aside all superfluities of the flesh, and sinful lusts; but the Crown of the Head must be bare, to shew that the mind must be free for contemplation. 4. Their naked and bare Crowns were to shew their nakedness, purity, and simplicity of their lives. 5. To shew their repentance and conversion; for such were commanded to cut their Hairs, before they were admitted again into the Church. 6. To discriminate the Christian Monks from the Jewish *Nazarites*, who wore long Hair, as *Moses* did a Veil, to shew that the mystery of redemption was not as yet revealed. 7. They cut or shave to avoid the uncleanness and inconveniencies that accompany long Hair. 8. To shew their contempt of the world, and of those vain Effeminate men, who pride themselves in their long Hair. 9. They shave their beards, that they may look smooth like Children and Angels, who are always painted young, by this shewing, they should be Children in malice, and Angels in innocency.

Con. Agath.
Can. 11.
Tolet. 3.
Cap. 12.

See *Platina Baleus*
Pol. Virgil,
Bellarmin,
and others.

Q. 14. *Whence came the custom of shaving, or cutting the Hair of Head and Beard among Religious persons?*

A. Some will have Saint *Peter* to be the first Christian that was shaven on the crown, at *Antioch*, by the Gentiles in derision. Others ascribe this custom to *Anicetus*, who lived about 165 years after Christ; but this is rejected by *Bellarmine*. Others again will have the Fourth Council of *Toledo*, about the year of Christ 631, to enjoyn this shaving of the crown; and in the Council of *Aquisgran, anno Christi* 816, the Monks are enjoyned to shave in *Easter* week. But shaving of the Beard is not so ancient; for it came in with the Doctrine of Transubstantiation, taught by *Peter Lombard, Anno* 1160, and established by *Innocent* 3. in the Council of *Lateran*, in the year 1200. The reason of this shaving was, lest any hairs of the beard might touch the body or blood of Christ; or lest any crum of the bread, or drop of the wine might fall upon, or stick to the beard. In the time of *Epiphanius*, about 400 years after Christ, it was not the custom among *Monks* to cut their beards; for he inveighs against the *Monks* of *Mesopotamia*, for wearing long hair like Women, and cutting their beards, which also was the custom of the *Messalian* Hereticks. But that this custom of cutting the beard was not generally received by the Clergy, appears in the *French Story*; for *Francis* the first caused the Church-men with a great summ of money to redeem their beards which he threatned to cut: but indeed the custom of shaving was used among the

Their shaving, whence it came.

Gentile

Gentile Priests; for which reason God would not have his Priests to shave, that they might not seem to follow the wayes of Idolaters. The Egyptian Priests, by shaving off all their hairs, did signifie that the Priests should be pure and clean, and free from all pollution. They used also in Mourning and Funerals to cut their hairs; so *Statius* saith, *lib. 6. Theb. Tergoque & pectore fusam Cæsariem minuit*, and to cut the hairs of the dead, which they laid on the Tomb, or cast into the fire, as a sacrifice to *Pluto* and *Proserpina*, as may be seen in *Euripides* and *Homer*: Of this custom speaketh *Virgil*, in the death of Queen *Dido*;

> *Nondum illi flavum Proserpina vertice crinem*
> *Abstulerat, Stygioque caput damnaverat Orco, &c.*
> *Sic ait & dextra crinem secat, &c.*

They used also to spread their cut hair upon the Coffin, as *Heliodor*. l. 6. sheweth ἔτιλλε τὰς τρίχας, κ᾽ ἐπὶ κλίνη ἐπέβαλλε. And as they offered the hairs of the dead to *Orcus*; so they did of children to the Rivers, from whence they held all things had their Original, or else to *Apollo* and *Hercules*, that is, the Sun; for by the heat of the Sun, and the moisture of Water, hairs are procreated. But in their marriage Solemnities, they used to offer their hairs to *Diana*, or *Juno*, *cui vincla jugalia curæ*; for she was held the Goddess of Marriage. Childrens hair were cut with Ceremony in the Temples, and preserved in boxes or cases of Gold and Silver. Sea-men in danger of shipwrack used to cut their hairs, thinking thereby to appease the Angry Sea-gods. Among some *Gentiles* the hairs were cut in sign of liberty; among others in token of servitude: It was a punishment to cut the hair among the Germans, *Tacitus de mor. Ger.* sheweth of the Women there, who for adultery, had their hair cut: *Accisis crinibus nudatam domo expellat maritus*; Such also as stood guilty of capital crimes were shaved; as *Nicolaus Damascenus* sheweth, and *Philostratus* in the life of *Apollonius*. But sometimes again guilty persons wore long hair, and were forbid to shave; to be half shaved was the badge of a slave; *Frontes literati, & capillum semirasi, & pedes annulati*, saith *Apuleius, l. 9*. Slaves were stigmatized on the fore-head, half shaved, and had rings about their feet. *David*'s *servants were sent back by the Ammonites half shaved*. Sometimes shaving was a note of Effeminateness; sometimes of Craft; sometimes of Foolishness; sometimes of Liberty; and sometimes (as is said) of Slavery. But however it was used among the Gentiles, it is expresly forbid to

Lev. 19.
Isa. 7. 20.
and 15. 2.
Jer. 48. 37.

the Jews, and threatned as a punishment. Yet among Christians it is indifferently used; but among the Monks and Priests it is used as a mark of distinction; and to shew, that as dead men were shaved among the Gentiles, so that our Monks are dead to the world and as the Gentiles thought by cutting their hair, to pacifie their angry Gods, so the Monks, by laying aside all fleshly superfluities, strive to avoid God's wrath. This I should like well, if they were as careful about the thing signified, as they are about the sign: See *Hadri-* . And as shaving was sometimes a sign of Liberty, so I wish it were *an Junius,* among them, who was as they pretend, they are free from the *Pol. Virgil,* world, so they were free also from the Devil, and the flesh, and *Hospinian,* from those sins that enslave them; for *he that committeth sin, is Schedius,* *the servant of sin;* yea a servant of servants, whatsoever badges of *Bellar-* liberty he pretend. *mine, &c.*

Q. 15. *Were there any Religious Women, which we call* Nuns, *in the Primitive times of the Church?*

A. Yea: For we read of *Marcella, Sophronia, Principia, Paula,* Nuns in the *Eustochium,* and others, who did profess chastity, and contempt Primitive of the world, and an earnest desire of Heavenly things. This re- times. tired life they undertook of their own accord, and not by force; for every one is not capable of perpetual Virginity, nor were they tied to it by vow: For the Apostle saith, *That if a Virgin, marry, she sinneth not.* Indeed such Virgins as had dedicated themselves to God and a single life, if afterward finding their own inability to persevere, did marry, these marriages were thought scandalous, yet lawful; *For it is better to marry than to burn;* therefore they were not rescinded; and the parties so marrying, were evil reported of for their inconstancy; for this cause penance was injoyned them. And afterward *Jovinian* made it capital for any man to marry, or to solicite a Nun, because the *Donatists* of his time defloured divers Nuns. Such married couples were Excommunicated by the Church, perpetually imprisoned, or put to death, by the Civil Magistrate, and the Marriage absolutely disannulled as incestuous. Before *Constantine*'s time, I do not read of any Monasteries or Nunneries erected for Women, by reason of frequent persecutions, and the uncertain condition of Christians then: but after that peace was established in the Church, Houses were built for Virgins, but yet with liberty to be elsewhere, for *Eustochium* the Virgin lived with her own Parents, and so did the Virgin *Demetrias*; and we find in *Cyprian, Hierom,* and *Austin,* that such Virgins had liberty to go abroad, to hear Sermons in the Church, and to receive the Eucharist with the rest of God's people; they were enjoyned to be modest and frugal in their cloaths and diet; not to converse with men; not to walk alone; not to bathe, except their hands and feet; to fast and pray often; to be vailed; to abstain from wine; to wash the Saints feet; not to be idle, but either to sing, pray, hear, or be working with the needle. And seeing hair was given to the Woman as an ornament and badge of distinction, and for modesty; therefore Nuns of old were not shaven, as now, but were prohibited by the Council of *Gangren, Can.* 17. to shave at all. Yet in the Syrian and Egyptian Monasteries, Nuns at their admission used to offer their hairs to the Abbatesse, because it was not Lawful for them to wash or anoint
their

their heads therefore to keep their heads the cleaner from filth and vermin, they cut their hair. It's likely they learned this custom from the Vestal Virgins at *Rome*, who used to cut their hair, and offer it on the Tree *Lotos*, called *Capillata*, as *Pliny* sheweth.

They that will read more fully what is written of the Primitive Nuns, let them read Basil, Athanasius, Cyprian, Hierom, Austin, &c. *who have written largely of this subject.*

Q. 16. *In what account are Monks at this day in the* Roman *Church?*

Monks, in what account at Rome *at this day.*

A. They are of that high esteem, that their very garments are counted sacred, and that there is power in them to cure diseases, to work miracles, to drive away evil spirits, to further them towards Heaven, so that some Kings and Princes have desired to die in a *Franciscan* Hood. 2. They count this the state of perfection, the Angelical life, the life that *Eliah* and Saint *John Baptist*, *Christ* and his *Apostles* did embrace, and a life meritorious of Heaven. 3. Whereas in the beginning Monks were altogether Laymen, and not to meddle with any other employment but what was proper to their profession, to wit, prayer, fasting, virginity, poverty, and obedience: now they are admitted into, and privileged with all Ecclesiastick Dignities, from the Door-keeper, even to the Papacy. 4. The married life, amongst many of them, is accounted pollution, compared with the Monastical; *Notwithstanding the Apostle tells us that Marriage is honourable, and Christ honoured it himself with his presence and first miracle*; and would be born of a Virgin, but after she was espoused to a husband. 5. Such is the respect they give to this life, that they prefer it to all natural affection and duty between Parents and Children, to which not onely we are tyed by nature, but also by a special command from God. *Hierom* commends *Paula* in her Epitaph for abandoning Brother, Kindred, and her own Children, whose tears she slighted, preferring this kind of life to them all; but this preposterous zeal is condemned by the Council of *Gangra, Can.* 15. 6. So likewise they preferr it to the mutual duty and stipulation that is between Man and Wife, permitting, yea teaching, that they may forsake each other, and enter into a Monastery; which is *to put asunder those whom God hath joyned together*; to defraud one another of due benevolence, and by this means occasion adultery. The Apostles counsel is, *that the married couple should not defraud one another, except it be for a time, by consent, to give themselves to prayer, seeing the man hath not power over his own body, but the woman; and so the man hath power over the woman.* 7. They will not permit Monks and Nuns ever to Marry, though they have not the gift of continency, accounting all such Marriages Sacrilege; whereas the first Monks were left to their own freedom, and not constrained to stay longer than their conveniencies would permit: and in the Primitive times of the Church, marriages contracted after the vow of continency made, were not dissolved, but
held

held lawful; onely the parties for their inconstancy were enjoyned penance, and the man made incapable of Ecclesiastical employment: Neither were their Monks forced to vow chastity, seeing every one is not capable thereof, and much mischief hath proceeded from this constrained vow: but men were left to their own freedom. Neither was it at that time counted a more hainous sin for a Monk to marry a Nun, than to keep a Concubine. The modern Monks are permitted to wear Rings; to converse in Kings and Princes Courts; and such is the opinion they have of Monasteries, that they think a man cannot sufficiently repent him of his sins, or be truly mortified, except he be shut up in a Convent.

See Erasmus, Polyd. Virgil, Hostinian, Baronius, Bellarmin, &c.

Q. 17. *How were the Monks and Nuns of old consecrated?*

A. The Monks after prayers and exhortation made by the Priest, is by the same signed with the sign of the Cross, and shaved or polled rather; then is his old garment taken off, and he is cloathed in a Monastical habit, and with other holy men present, is made partaker of the Divine mysteries. The Nuns were consecrated either by the Bishop or the Priest, and by them covered with a Veil; if the Abbatess presumed to do this, she was excommunicated: Twenty five years of age was then held a fit time for Virgins to be Veiled, but now they may at twelve, or before; the days of the year for receiving their Veil, and Consecration, were the Epiphany, Easter-eve, and the festival days of the Apostles, except in case of death. The Virgin to be consecrated, was presented to the Bishop in her Nuns habit; then before the Altar with Musick and burning Tapers, the Priest before he puts on her Veil, thus saith, *Behold Daughter, and Forget thy people, and thy Fathers House, that the King may take pleasure in thy beauty:* To this the people cryed *Amen,* and so the Veil is cast over her, and all the Religious Matrons present do kiss her, after the Priest hath blessed and prayed for her: in this Veil is placed as much Sanctity, as in Baptism; and that such Virgins as depart out of this world without it, are in danger of damnation.

How consecrated anciently. See Ambrose, Tertullian, Hierom, Austin, and Dionysius the Areopagite, in his Hierarchy, if that Book be his.

Q. 18. *What was the Religious Order of the Benedictines?*

A. *Benedict* or *Benet* in *Umbria,* a country of *Italy,* being weary of the Wars and Tumults there, retired himself into a Desart place, after the manner of *Anthony* the *Theban,* to whom did flock multitudes of people; from thence he goeth to *Cassinum,* an ancient Town where he settled, and prescribed Laws to his Monks, after the manner of Saint *Basil.* He is said to found twelve Monasteries, over which he placed twelve Abbots, that were his Disciples. His chief Monastery, *Cassinum,* was richly endowed by *Tertullus,* a Roman Patrician, who bestowed on it, Castles, Villages, Lands, and large possessions. *Equitius,* a Senator, followed his example, and conferred large revenues on it, and so did divers others after him. This Order did quickly spread through *France, Germany, Sicily, Spain, England,* and other places. By the means of *Maurus,* his Disciple, who was Son to *Equitius* the Roman Senator,

Benedictine Monks.

nator, near *Orleans*, the firſt Monaſtery of *Benedictines* is founded, conſiſting of one hundred and fourty Brothers, which number was not to be altered. By *Placidus*, Son to *Tertullus*, the Roman Patrician, *Benet* ſet up a Monaſtery in *Sicily*. By *Leobardus*, he erected a Monaſtery in *Alſatia*, four miles from *Straſburg*; he planted alſo a Monaſtery at *Rome*, near the Lateran Church, in the time of *Pelagius*. By *Donatus*, a *Benedictine* Convent is erected in *Spain* about the year of Chriſt 590. By *Auſtin*, Arch-Biſhop of *Canterbury*, the *Benedictines* got footing in *England*, *Anno* 596. And ſo by degrees they ſpread through other places; chiefly in *Germany*, by *Boniface* the German Apoſtle, and Biſhop of *Mentz*, *Anno* 545. Theſe *Benedictines* were afterward divided into divers Sects, Namely the *Cluniacenſes*, inſtituted in *Burgundy*, by one *Otho*, an Abbot, to whom *William*, Sirnamed the Godly, *Dean* of *Aquitain*, gave a Village called *Maſtick*, Anno 916. The *Camalduenſes* were erected by one *Romoaldus* a *Benedictine*, on the top of the *Appenin* Hills. The *Valliſumbrenſes*, ſo called from *Vallis Umbroſa*, on the ſide of the *Appenins* were erected by one *Gualbertus* a Florentine, *Anno* 1060. The *Monteliuetenſes* were ſet up by one *Bernard Ptolomeus* at *Sienna* in *Tuſcany*, *Anno* 1047. The *Grandimontenſes* about the ſame time were inſtituted by one *Steven*, a Noble-man in *France*. The *Ciſtertians*, ſo called from *Ciſtertium* in *Burgundy*, about the ſame time were erected by one *Robert*, Abbot of *Moliſmenia*. Saint *Bernard* was of this Order, who about the year of Chriſt 1098, was made Abbot of *Claravallis*, whoſe Monks were called from his Name *Bernardines*, who are all one with the *Ciſtertians*, ſaving, that the *Ciſtertians* wear all white; but the *Benardines*, a black Gown over a white Coat. The *Celeſtini*, ſo called from Pope *Celeſtinus* the Fifth, their Founder, whoſe former name was *Peter Moroneus*. This Order was confirmed by *Gregory* the Tenth, in the Council of *Lyons*. All theſe were branches of *Benedictines*. The *Camalduenſes*, *Monteliuetenſes*, and *Ciſtertians* wear white; the Monks of the Shadowy Valley, Purple; the *Celeſtines*, Skie colour, or blew. The *Grandimontenſes* wear a Coat of Mails, and a black Cloak thereon.

See *Antoninus*, *Sabellicus*, *Bruſchius* of the German Monaſteries, *Baleus* in his Centuries, &c.

Q. 19. *What other Orders proceeded from the* Benedictines?

Benedictines, Authors of other Orders.

A. *Benet* may be called the founder and author of all the Religious Orders that were in the Weſt, for 666 years together, that is, till the times of the *Dominicans*, and *Mendicants*; ſo that there were of *Benedictine* Monks reckoned by *Trithemius*, lib. 4. cap. 4. above fifteen thouſand Abbies; out of which proceeded multitudes of *Cardinals*, *Arch-Biſhops*, *Biſhops*, *Abbots*, and other eminent men, beſides *Popes*. The *Gregorian* Order was a branch of the *Benedictine*. *Gregory* the great, afterward Pope, was at firſt a Monk, who, after his Fathers death, erected on his own charges ſix Monaſteries, in *Sicily*, and at *Rome* converted his Fathers houſe into a Monaſtery, and dedicated it to Saint *Andrew*; to theſe Monks he preſcribed the rule of Saint *Benet*, and aſſigned to them a large dark or brown coloured cloak to be worn, on which was woven a red croſs in the breaſt;

breast; these did not shave their beards. The Monks called *Gerun-* *dinenses* were after the Order of *Bennet*, instituted by *John* Bishop of the *Gerundinenses* in *Portugal*, about the year of Christ 610. He was warned in a dream to build a Monastery, which he did, and had it ratified by the Pope. He gave them a white Garment to wear, with his own arms on the breast thereof; they were ordered to wear four Ribbands, to wit, two red, and two green. This order was erected under Pope *Boniface* the Fourth. The rule which *Bennet* prescribed to his Monks, was written out by Pope *Gregory* the great, and confirmed by *Eugenius* the Second.

Of these passages, see Platina, Francus in his Chronicles, Sabellicus, Volaterran, Trithemius, &c.

Q. 20. *What were the Rules which St.* Bennet *prescribed to his Monks?*

A. He first sheweth what the duty of the Abbot is, namely; to be careful of his charge, to be holy, just, wise, and charitable in his deeds; and to be powerful in his words, to exhort, correct, reprove, to beware of partiality, and dissimulation, and chiefly of covetousness, and pride, not to do any thing of himself without advice of the Convent; he enjoyneth all to be obedient, silent, humble to be watchful to prayer in the night; he prescribes what Psalms they are to sing every day and night; and what Psalms in their canonical hours. That *Hallelujah* should be said continually between Easter and Pentecost; that they should praise God with *David* seven times a day; to wit, in the morning, at the first, third, sixth, and ninth hours; in the evening, and completory, and at midnight. Particular Psalms are appointed for each of these canonical hours; that they must pray with all reverence. That there be Deans chosen in each Monastery to ease the Abbot; That every Monk have his own bed to sleep in, that a candle burn by them till the morning; That they sleep in their cloaths girt, that at the Ringing of the bell they may be the more ready for prayer; divers degrees of Penance are injoyned according to the degrees of offences; That the Abbot use all the means he can to reclaim the excommunicate persons, that the lost Sheep may be brought home with joy; That if no correction will prevail, the obstinate person be expelled the Convent; who upon repentance may be received three times; but never after the third time; That the Steward of the Monastery be a man of discretion, government, and trust; That the Abbot keep an Inventory of all utensils belonging to the Convent; That all things be common among the Brothers; That there be no grudging or murmuring; That every one serve in the kitching, and in other places when his turn is; That a special care be had of the sick and infirm, so likewise of the aged and children; That there be chosen a weekly Reader, to read in time of refection; That each man be content with a pound of bread for a day; and that only the sick be permitted to eat flesh; That wine be drunk sparingly; That from Easter to Pentecost, the Brothers may have their refection at the sixth hour, and their supper in the evening; in the Summer let them fast every fourth and sixth day in the week, till the ninth hour. The other days let them dine at the

Benedictines, their rules prescribed by Saint Bennet.

sixth

sixth hour; from the midst of *September* till Lent, let them have their refection at the ninth hour; but in the Lent time at the evening, so it be by day light; That after the Completory there be no speaking at all; if any come late to prayers, or to the Table, he is to stand a part by himself, and to be last served, and shortned in his victuals; if any for some great offence be excommunicated out of the Oratory, he shall make satisfaction by prostrating himself before the Oratory; that they shall not only give themselves to prayer and meditation, at the appointed hours, but shall also labour some part of the day with their hands, to keep them from idleness; That they observe Lent withal strictness; that they use strangers with all reverence and chearfulness, and that the Abbot salute them with a holy kiss, and wash their feet; That none receive letters, or tokens from their Parents, without the Abbots leave; That the Abbot cloath his Monks as he findeth the seasons of the year requireth; That no Novice be admitted into the Monastery, without sufficient trial of his constancy, and patience; That if a Priest desireth to enter into a Monastery, he submit himself to the Laws thereof; and that he have the next place to the Abbot; That Noble-men, who offer their Children to God in the Monastery, swear, they will never give them any part of their Estate, but that it be conferred on the Convent; That if a stranger Monk desire to continue in the Monastery, he be not denied, so his life be not scandalous; If the Abbot desire to have a Priest or Deacon ordained, let him choose one of his own Convent; that he shall be Abbot whom the whole Convent, or the greater and better part shall choose; That the Provost or *Præpositus* be chosen by the Abbot, to whom he must be subject; That the porter be an ancient and discreet man, who may receive and give answers, and that the Monastery be provided with Water, and a Mill, and other necessaries within it self, lest the Brothers should wander abroad; if the Abbot enjoyn to any Monk impossibilities, he must with reverence and submission excuse his inability; if the Abbot urge it he must obey, and trust to God's assistance; That in the Monastery none presume to depend, or strike, or excommunicate another: But that they be obedient and loving to each other; That they be zealous for God's Glory, and when they are working, be still singing of Psalms.

These Rules are set down at large in Hospinian, out of Gregory, and contracted by Isidore, Hispalensis. Their Habit and Diet.

• Q. 21. *What Habit and Diet do the* Benedictines *use?*

A. Their habit is a round coat, a hood called *Cucalla, Cappa,* and *Melos* from *Melis*, a brock, gray, or badger, because it was wont to be made anciently of the skin of that beast. *Scapulare* is so called from *Scapulis* the shoulders, which this covereth. In Winter their hoods are lined. They were not want to wear breeches but when they travelled into the countrey. The colour of their upper garment is black; under which they wear a white wollen coat with sack cloath, and they go booted. The ancient *Benedictines* were wont, after they were Bishops, to wear the habit of their former profession; and to this they were enjoyned by the eighth General Council held at *Constantinople*; they were also tied by their rule to lie in their coats and hoods, and to wear courſe cloath; *but now* *Of the Be-* the caſe *is altered, and, So it was in Saint* Bernard's *time, who* ne diſtinct complains againſt the Monks luxury in apparel, wearing, Non quod Habit and utilius, ſed quod ſubtilius: Silk garments to ſhew their pride, but not Diet, ſee of cloath to keep them warm.* Their ſimple and courſe Diet, as it more in Po- was preſcribed by *Bennet,* is changed into dainty fare; they now lid. Virgil, eat fleſh and drink Wine plentifully; of this *Hugo de Sancto Victo-* Sabellicus, re complaineth. Antoninus,

Q. 22. *What Religious Rules did the Second Council of* Aquiſgran Turrecre- *or* Aix *preſcribed to be obſerved by the Monks?* mata, &c.

A. This Council being held the eight hundred and ſixteenth *Rules pre-* year after Chriſt, ordered that no Lay-man or Secular Prieſt be *ſcribed to* received into a Monaſtery, except he become a Monk; that the *the Monks* Monks do ſwear, that in the *Paraſceve* they uſed nothing but bread *by the* and water. That before they go to ſleep the Prior beſprinkle them *Council of* with holy water; That the tenth part of their alms be given to Aix. the poor; That they bathe not without the Priors leave; That particular Pſalms be ſung for the dead; that they bow not their knees in Whitſun-week, nor faſt: but they muſt faſt the Ember weeks, and on the Eves of the Apoſtles; that in caſe of neceſſity the Brothers walk with ſtaves: that in uncertain theft, there be a ſuſpending from Supper, till the guilty party confeſs; that at Chriſtmas and Eaſter for eight days together, they that will, may eat the fleſh of Birds; that all Monks, if they can, learn their rules by heart; that in the Kitchin, Mill, and other ſuch places, they work with their own hands; that the Delinquent caſt himſelf on the ground before his Abbot, or Prior; that they kiſs no Women; that in Lent they waſh each others Feet. At the Lords Supper let the Abbot waſh and kiſs the Feet of his Brethren. In Eaſter, and Whitſun-week, and on Chriſtmaſs, and other Feſtival Days, let there be no ſpeaking in the Cloyſter, but hearing Gods word read. That the Abbot exceed not the proportion of his Monks in eating, drinking, cloathing, ſleeping, and working; and that he be not given to gadding abroad; that the Servants, after the refection of the Brothers, eat by themſelves; and that the ſame Leſſons be read unto them, which were read to the Brothers; that *Hallelujah* be omitted in the Septuageſima. The Novice muſt neither be ſhaved nor cloathed with a Monk's Garment, till his time of probation be expired, and promiſe made by him of Obedience, according to Saint *Bennet*'s rule. That none be ſet over Monks, but he that is a Monk. That in Lent the Brothers do work till the ninth hour, then repair to Maſs; and in the Evening let them take their refection. *Theſe are the chief Duties, to which Saint* Bennet*'s Monks are enjoyned by the aforeſaid Synod. And whereas at firſt the Monks were Lay-men, and had no Prieſt, but ſuch as came from abroad; at laſt they were permitted to have Prieſts of their own, and that they ſhould receive Tythes, Firſt-fruits, Oblations and Donations, as well as other Prieſts, by* Gregory *the Great,* Boniface, *and other Popes, as may be ſeen in* Gratian.

Q. 23. *What were the Rites and Institutions of the Monks of Cassinum?*

Monks of Cassinum.

A. This was the first Monastery of *Benedictines*, where divers Rites were observed, which are not in *Bennet's* Rule. The chief are these. Fourteen days before *Easter* all the Altars are stript from their ornaments, and covered with black; the Images are veiled; *Gloria Patri* is not sung. Three nights immediately before *Easter*, the Night-Service continueth till the Morning, and is joyned to the *Mattins*; no Bells are rung; the lights are put out; the Abbot washeth the Monks feet. In the Parasceue late, a little bread and water is taken. On *Easter* Eve in the Night time the Tapers are kindled. On *Easter* Day, before *Mass*, there is a Procession with Burning Tapers, and Holy Water, the Priests singing and praying. The two next days after, Crosses, Holy waters, and Relicks, are carried about with the Gospel, and burning Tapers, with singing and saluting each other with Holy kisses, the Priests being in their rich Copes. Six several times in the Year, they enter into the *Refectory* singing; namely, on *Christmas* day; on the *Epiphany*; on *Palm Sunday*; on the *Holy Sabbath*; on *Easter*-day; and the third day in *Easter* week. Every Lord's day they have Twelve Lectures, and so many on their chief Festivals; namely, *Christ's Nativity*, the *Epiphany*, the *Purification* of *Mary*, the two Martyrs, *Faustinus* and *Juletta*, S. *Scholastica*, S. *Bennet*, *Ascension* day, the Festivals of the Apostles, S. *Lawrence*, S. *Mary*, S. *German*, S. *Andrew*; On these Eves they fast, they do not kneel, nor work; but on the lesser Festivals they read but eight Lessons, and afterwards they work. Their Meat and Drink is measured to them, according to the Discretion of the Abbot. When they receive new Garments, which is about S. *Martin's* day, they march singing with Tapers burning in their hands, into the Vestry, or Wardrobe, where this Gospel is read. [*Be not careful what you shall eat, nor what you shall drink, nor for your bodies, with what they shall be cloathed.*] They having prayed, they lay down their old Garments, and receive new. They begin their Lent on *Quinquagesima* Sunday; and a few days before they receive wax for lights, with which they are to read in the night time. They confess to one another twice a day; in the morning of their failings by night; in the evening of their failings by day. They must not walk either within or without the Convent with a staff, except they be weak. What work soever they are about in the Kitchin, or elsewhere, they sing Psalms. They are shaven all together on certain days, namely, at *Easter*, *Ascension* day, the first of *August*, the first of *September*, and the first of *October*, and at S. *Martin's* day, and *Christmas*. If *Easter* fall out late, they are shaved a little before *Septuagesima*, and in the *Quinquagesima*.

These Rites besides their Ceremonies about the dead, are Recorded by Theodomarus, the twelfth Abbot of that Monastery, and out of him set down by Hospinian de Orig. Monachatus Abbates, how Elected.

Q. 24 *What is the manner of Electing their Abbots?*

A. Each Monastery is to choose an Abbot from among themselves, either by general consent, or of the better part: If there be none among them fit for that place, then they may chuse out

of

of some other Monastery; when he is chosen, it is not in their power to depose him. If a Clergy-man be chosen Abbot, he must leave off his former Function. Two Abbots must not be chosen for one Monastery; nor must one Abbot be over two Monasteries; they must not meddle with Secular Affairs. If an Abbot do not punish grievous Enormities, he is to be sent to another Convent, where he is to do Pennance; but not in his own because of the strict Subjection and Obedience, by which the Monks are tyed to their Abbots. If the Convent chuse an unfit Man for their Abbot, the Bishop of the Diocess, with the Neighbouring Abbots, or the Prince of the place, may depose him, and choose another. Now Princes ordinarily choose such as they please, and impose them upon the Monks: But the Abbot, when he is chosen, must be consecrated by the Bishop of the Diocess, who hath power to visit the Monasteries within his Jurisdiction, and to correct what is amiss. If the Abbot shall refuse to submit to the Bishop, he is suspended from the Communion till he Repent. Neither must he alienate any thing that belongs to the Convent without the Bishop's consent; if he do otherwise, he must be degraded, and the things alienated restored again by the Bishops command. What is conferred by Devout persons on the Monastery, must not be converted by the Abbot to his own particular use. No man must erect a Monastery without the Bishops consent; nor must the Abbot travel into a Foreign Country without leave from his Diocesan, who must not do any thing that may tend to the prejudice of the Monastery; which if he do, he is to be Excommunicated; neither must he, without the consent of the other Abbots, depose an Abbot, or alienate the things belonging to the Monastery, for the Abbot's offence. In case of injury, the Abbot may appeal from the Bishop to the Prince, or to a Council; and some Abbots there are, who, with their Monasteries, are only subject to the *Pope*, as *Cassinum*. The Monastery of Saint *Maximinus*, near *Trevers*, is subject only to the Emperour in Temporals, and to the Pope in Spirituals. Anciently the Election of the Abbot was ratified by the Emperour, or Prince, in whose Dominion the Monastery was; but afterwards the Pope extorted this Power from the Emperour, and drew all investitures to himself; to whom the Abbots swear allegiance and Fealty. The Ceremony used by the Emperour in the Abbot's confirmation, was the delivering of a Staff and Ferula into his hand, to put him in mind of his pastoral Office.

Of these passages see Bresschius in his German Monasteries, Balaeus In his Centuries, Hospinian, and others.

Q. 25. *What were the Nuns of this Order, and what were their Rules?*

A. *Scholastica*, Sister to *Bennet*, erected the Order of *Nuns*, after *Bennet's* Rule. They are not permitted to be God-mothers in Baptism, nor to go abroad, except in case of great necessity, and that with some ancient Women. They must give themselves to Singing, Prayer, and Meditation, and must observe the Canonical hours. They must not speak with any man, except in publick before witnesses. None must be admitted into the Nunery with-

Nuns of St. Bennet's Order, and their Rules.

out one Years Probation at least. If any be found Unchaste, after three Whippings she is fed with bread and water for one whole year in prison. None must wear silks; they are consecrated and veiled by the Bishop alone. When the Nun is cloathed with her sacred Vestments, she approacheth to the Altar, holding in each hand burning Tapers; there she kneeleth, and having heard the Gospel read, the Bishop prayeth for her perseverance in patience, chastity, sobriety, obedience, and other virtues. The Abbatess ought to be a woman of Discretion, Gravity, and Religion; who should be careful and vigilant over her Charge; who must not suffer any man to speak either with her self, or with her Nuns, after Sun-set, till the morning, and that before witnesses. She must not go abroad without the Bishops leave, and upon urgent Necessity, and must leave in the interim a Deputy to look to her charge; neither must she go abroad without some Nuns to accompany her. No young woman must be chosen Abbatess, nor any under sixty years of age. No woman must be suffered to come into the Monks Convent, nor must men be permitted to enter the Nunnery, except the Priest to officiate, who must stay no longer than whilest he is officiating. The Monasteries of men and women must be built apart, to prevent scandal and the Temptations of the Devil. The Abbatess must not presume to impose hands, to ordain Priests, or to veil the Virgins.

Of these things see Gregory, and the Councils, chiefly of Tours, Foro-julium, the sixth of Constanti-nople, of Paris, under Ludo-vicus and Lotharius, &c. Monaste-ries, and their Laws.

Q. 26. *What Laws were prescribed for Monasteries?*

A. 1. That they should be built in such places, where all Conveniencies may be had, that the Brothers may not have occasion to gad abroad. 2. That they may not, being once dedicated, be converted to Secular uses; but if the Monks live disorderly, they may be thrust out, and Secular Canons be put in their place. So likewise the Houses of Secular Canons may be converted into Monasteries. 3. That in Synods or other publick Meetings, the Abbot of *Cassinum* take the place before all other Abbots, because of the Antiquity, and Dignity of that Monastery, being the Mother of all other Monasteries in the West. 4. They were exempted from all Civil Exactions, and Secular affairs, that they might the more freely serve God. 5. Every Monastery was permitted to have an Advocate, who was a Lawyer, to maintain the Priviledges, Lands, and Revenues of the Convent; for the ease of the Monks, who were not to meddle with Secular Affairs; but the Advocate was to do nothing without the consent of the Abbot, and his Monks, nor they without him in secular business. 6. Most Monasteries were Erected not only to be houses of Devotion, but also Schools of good Learning; in which the learned Languages and liberal Sciences were professed. For this cause *Oswald*, King of the Angles, as *Bedal. 3. cap. 3.* witnesseth in his History, gave large possessions and Territories for building of Monasteries, in which the youth might be educated; and so *Gregory* the Great, employed divers Monasteries in *England*, for extirpating of the Pelagian Heresie. *Baleus cen. 13. Maidulfus Scotus* the Philosopher, Erected ed the Monaſtery of *Malmesbury*, in which he ſet up a School for the Greek and Latine tongue, where he read the Arts himſelf, as *Baleus Cent.* 14. *cap.* 16. ſheweth. For the ſame end were the Monaſteries of Saint *Denys* in *Paris*, of *Millan*, of *Rhemes*, of Saint *Gall*, of *Tours*, of *Trevers*, and many more erected; ſo were the Canons houſes, near Cathedrals, built for this end, that Youth might there, as in Colleges and Schools, be taught and educated; that from thence able Divines might be ſent abroad to preach the Goſpel. Therefore the Canons were enjoyned to maintain Profeſſors of Divinity, and to aſſign Prebendaries for their ſuſtinance.

7. Though in the beginning Monks were Lay-men, and lived not upon Tythes, but on their Lands and Rents, or on their own Labours, yet afterward when they were admitted into the Prieſthood, and permitted to preach, and Adminiſter the Sacraments, they were inveſted with Tythes, Oblations, firſt Fruits, and other Eccleſiaſtical Duties. *Paſchalis* the Second, about the year of Chriſt 1100. ordained that no Monk ſhould pay Tythes of their own Labours. And afterward Pope *Adrian*, exempted from paying of Tythes, the *Ciſtertians*, Saint *Johns* Knights of *Jeruſalem*, and the Templers. 8. Monaſteries had the ſame Privileges that Lords have over their Vaſſals; namely, to demand Mortuaries, which was the chief horſe, or other beaſt belonging to the party deceaſed. 9. Great Men and Princes thought no priſon ſo ſure as a Monaſtery; therefore the Greek Emperours uſed to ſhut up in Monaſteries their rebellious Children, and potent Subjects whom they ſuſpected, either of greatneſs or Ambition. So *Ludovicus Pius* was ſhut up in a Monaſtery by his Son *Ludovicus* the ſecond: Divers other examples are extant upon Record. 10. Princes had ſuch a Conceit of the Sanctity of Monaſteries, that they thought they could not make ſufficient ſatisfaction to God for their ſins, except they had for ſome time ſhut themſelves up in Monaſteries. 11. The *Benedictine* Monks by the Rule of their Founder, were not to eat fleſh, except Birds at *Chriſtmas* and *Eaſter*; yet they may drink Wine, except in Lent: But Children, Aged, and Sick people were diſpenſed to Eat Fleſh. 12. When Children by their parents are ſhut up in monaſteries, though afterwards, when they come to Years of Diſcretion, they ſhould deſire to remove, yet they may not by the Laws of the Convent; becauſe (ſay they) thoſe who are once Dedicated to God, may not return to the world again: For this they alledge the Example of *Samuel*, who in the Temple, being Dedicated by *Hannah* his Mother to the Service of God, perſiſted therein. But this was not the Cuſtom of the firſt Monaſteries, which left men to their own Liberty; and the Pope hath power to diſpenſe with Monaſtical Vows; ſo he did, when he diſmiſſed out of the Monaſtery *Caſimir* of *Polonia*, whom the People choſe for their King; in Memory whereof, the *Polonians* were enjoyned by *Clement* 2. to ſhave their Crowns like Monks, and the Knights at certain Feſtivals to wear white Surplices, like Prieſts, in time of Divine Service. 13. Of Monks and Lay-men

were

Fraternities. were instituted *Fraternities*. For many devout Seculars, not being able to use the Habit, or be subject to the rigid Rule of the Monks, were notwithstanding willing to partake of their Prayers and merit of their Order; so that at certain times they had their Meetings for relieving of the Poor, for Prayers and publick supplications, in which they had their processions in Sackcloath, and their faces covered with Linen, whipping their naked backs in sign of Repentance. Of these *Fraternities* were divers Families, to wit, of St. *Sebastian*, St. *Rotch*. St. *Ann*. St *Anthony*, St. *Dominic*, St. *Martin* of the *Rosary*, and divers others. Of these passages see *Bruschius, Baleus, Pol. Virgil, Surius* in the Lives of the Saints, the Centuries of *Magdeburg, Isidor*, and divers others.

The Contents of the Tenth Section.

Of New Religious Orders sprung out of the Benedictines *and first of the* Cluniacenses. 2. *Of the* Camaldulenses *and Monks of the Shady Valley.* 3. *The* Sylvestrini, Grandimontenses *and* Carthusians. 4. *The Monks of Saint* Anthony *of* Vienna, *the* Cistertians, Bernardines, *and* Humiliati. 5. *The* Præmonstratenses, *and* Gilbertines. 6. *The* Cruciferi, Hospitalarii, Trinitarians, *and* Bethlemites. 7. *The* Johannites, *or first Religious Knights in Christendom.* 8. *The* Templars. 9. *The* Teutonici, *or* Mariani. 10. *The Knights of S.* Lazarus, Calatrava, *and S.* James. 11. *The Orders of the Mendicant Fryers, and first of the* Augustinians. 12. *Of the* Carmelites. 13. *Of the* Dominicans. 14. *Of the* Franciscans. 15. *Of things chiefly remarkable in the* Franciscan *Order.* 16. *Of the Knights of the Holy Sepulchre, and* Gladiatores. 17. *Of the Knights of Saint* Mary *of Redemption, of the* Montesians, *of the Order of* Vallis Scholarium, *and* Canons Regular, *of Saint* Mark. 18. *Of St.* Clara, *St.* Paul's *Eremites, and* Bonihomines. 19. *The Servants of St.* Mary, Celestini, *and* Jesuati. 20. *The Order of St.* Bridget. 21. *The Orders of St.* Katherine, *and S.* Justina. 22. *The Eremites of S.* Hierom, *S.* Saviour, Albati, Fratricelli, Turlupini, *and* Montolivetenses. 23. *The Canons of S.* George, *the Mendicants of S.* Hierom, *the Canons of* Lateran, *the Orders of the Holy Ghost, and of S.* Ambrose *and* Nemus, *and of the* Minimi, *of* Jesu Maria. 24. *The Order of Knight-hood, from the Year* 1400. *namely, of the* Annunciada, *of Saint* Maurice, *of the Golden Fleece, of the Moon, of S.* Michael, *of S.* Stephen, *of the Holy Spirit,* &c.

SECT. X.

Quest. I. **W**Hat *New Religious Orders did there spring up in the West, upon the Decay of the* Benedictines, *and what were the* Cluniacenses.

A. After the *Benedictines* had flourished in the West about 400. Years, namely, from the time of *Justinian,* till *Conradus* the first, about the 900. Year of Christ; out of this Root sprung up new branches, who being offended at the loose lives of the *Benedictines,* and that they had fallen off from their Founder's Rule, resolved to retain the old Rule of *Bennet,* but to add some new Statutes thereto, and to underprop the old decaying house, with new posts. The first that began this Reformation was *Berno,* who built a Monastery near *Cluniacum,* over which, when he was dying, he placed one *Odo* to be

Abbot

Abbot thereof; which *Odo*, was the first indeed, that revived *Bennet*'s rule, and inforced it with new additions, and so from the place his Monks were called *Cluniacenses* and not *Benedictines*; by their rule the Abbot must eat with his Brothers, and not always with Strangers; a revolting Monk may be received again above three times; fearing least the wandring Sheep should become a prey to the Wolf. They renewed the custom of dipping the consecrated bread into the Cup; which was used in case of necessity to Children and the sick; and afterward was promiscuously used by all at the Communion, till it was condemned by Pope *Julius*, 340 years after Christ: But this custom revived again *Anno* 580. and was condemned again by the third Synod of *Bracara*: At last *Anno* 920. it was revived by these Monks of *Cluniacum*. When any is to be admitted into their Order, they are brought to the Monastery, there they are clipped, shaved, washed, and stript of their old cloathes: and then being new cloathed, are admitted. These Monks at first were very strict, but afterwards became more loose.

Monks or Cluniacenses.

Of them see Bernard, and Peter Cluniacensis, Sabellicus, Antonius, Cassander, &c.

Q. 2. *What were the* Camaldulenses *and Monks of the Shady Valley?*

A. About the year of Christ 1030. according to *Sabellicus*, one *Romualdus* of *Ravenna*, perceiving how the Rule of *Bennet* was neglected, began to lay the foundation of a new Order in the Field *Camaldulum*; whence he gave the Name of *Camaldulenses* to his Monks. He erected, as we said before, a Monastery upon the top of the *Appenines*; having obtained a place from one *Modulus*, who dreamed he had seen in his sleep, Ladders, reaching from that place to Heaven, on which he saw Mortals cloathed in white, mounting upwards; whereupon *Romualdus* procureth the place buildeth a Convent, and gave his Monks white Hoods to wear. He enjoyned them also silence, except in time of Divine Service, and yet some to keep their rule of silence the more strictly, will not joyn with the rest, but pray by themselves: Two days every week they feed on Bread and Water, which is their fast; and sit bare-footed on the ground. About half a mile from thence are wooden Crosses, which women must not go beyond, under pain of the Pope's curse. The Order of *Vallis Umbrosa*, or the Shadowy Valley, was instituted, *An*. 1060. by one *John Gualbert*, a *Florentine*, as is said: This *John* having forgiven his enemy, who had killed his Brother, (for which mercy shewed to his Enemy, in a certain Abby Church, whither he went for Devotion, he was thanked (so the story goeth) by a Crucifix there, which bowed its head to him) resolved to renounce the world, came to the Shadowy Valley, where there were two Monks living. In that place he makes up a like house of boards; but his Fame grew so great, that many, both Clergy and Laymen flock to him; And the Lady of the Soyl being Abbatess, bestowed the ground upon him, with other large possessions. So he being made Abbot, by the consent of the Monks, who were gathered together there, proposed Saint

Monks, or Camaldulenses.

Monks of the Shadowy Valley.

Bennet's

Sect. 10.   *of* EUROPE.   201

Bennet's Rule to be obſerved; which he enlarged by cauſing Lights to burn ſtill in the Night, both in their Chappel and Dormitory; and ordering that they ſhould wear no other cloath, but what they made of the wool of their own ſheep. He reformed divers Monaſteries, and placed over them Provoſts of his own chooſing: He built alſo divers in *Lombardy*, and elſewhere; for which he was Canonized, *and by Alexander* 2. *and Gregory* 7. others his Order was ratified. Their habit was of a purple, or as Popes; write, of an Aſh-colour. *See Surius de Vitis Sanctorum, Volatteran, Pol. Virgil, Antoninus, Sabellicus,* &c.

Q. 3. *What were the* Sylveſtrini, Grandimontenſes, *and* Carthuſians?

A. The *Sylveſtrini* were ſo named from one *Sylveſter*, who inſtituted this order after the Rule and Habit of the Monks of *Vallis Umbroſa*. This Order was begun in the Marquiſate of *Anchona* in *Italy*. The *Grandimontenſes* were ſo called from the Voice that three times uttered theſe Words in *Grandi Monte*; that is, in the Great Hill, where one *Peter* was adviſed by the ſame Voice to build his Monaſtery. This *Peter* was Diſciple and Succeſſor to one *Steven*, who in the Year 1076. erected this Order in *Gaſcony*, where on the Hill *Muretum* he built him a Cottage, after he had wandered through many Deſarts. He preſcribes a Rule to his Diſciples, patched up of *Bennet's* Rule, and of the Rites of the *Canons Regular*, of Saint *Auſtin's* Monks, and of his Eremites. He, as we ſaid before, wore on his naked body a Coat of Mail, his bed was a hard board, without either ſtraw or coverlet; with often kneeling, kiſſing of the ground, and beating it with his Fore-head and Noſe, he made his hands and knees hard like a *Callus*, or Corn, and his Noſe crooked. This Order at firſt was ruled by a Prior; afterwards Pope *John* 22. gave them an Abbot. *Monks or Sylveſtrini. Monks, or Grandi-montenſes.*

The *Carthuſians* or *Charter* Fryers were inſtituted by *Bruno*, born in *Collen*, and profeſſor of Philoſophy in *Paris*, about the Year of Chriſt 1080. upon this occaſion; being preſent at the ſinging of the Office for his fellow Profeſſors now dead (a Man highly reputed for his Holy life) the dead Corps ſuddenly ſitteth up in the Bier, and cryeth out, [*I am in Gods juſt Judgments condemned*] theſe words were uttered three ſeveral days: At which *Bruno* was ſo affrighted, that a man held ſo pious, was damned, what would become of himſelf and many more? Therefore concluded there was no ſafety for him, but by forſaking the world: Hereupon he with ſix of his Scholars betook themſelves to a hideous place for dark Woods, high Hills, Rocks, and wild Beaſts, in the Province of *Dolphini* near *Grenoble*; the place was called *Carthuſia*; whence his Monks took their name, and there built a Monaſtery, having obtained the Ground of *Hugo*, Biſhop of *Grenoble*, who alſo became a Monk of that Order. By their Rule, theſe Monks ſhould wear ſackcloath or a hair Shirt next their skin, a long white cloath coat looſe, with a hood, and a black cloak over, when they walk abroad. The Lay-Brothers wear a ſhort Coat to their Knees. They Eat no fleſh at all, they buy no fiſh, but eat them *Carthuſi-ans.*

when

when offered; they eat Branny bread, and drink Wine mingled with Water. On the Lords Day, and fifth Day of the Week, they feed only upon cheese and Eggs. On the third Day or Saturday, on pulse, or pot-herbs; on the second, fourth and sixth, upon Bread, and Water only. Every one dresseth his own Meat; they eat apart, and but once a day. Yet on the chief Festivals of *Christmas, Easter, Whitsuntide, Epiphany, Purification,* the twelve *Apostles, John Baptist, Michael, Martin,* and *All Saints,* they eat twice a day, and together at one Table, and then may talk together; at other times, they must keep silence. Every one hath his own cell, wherein they pray, read, meditate, and write books: but in these Cells they observe the Canonical hours; but in their Mattins and Vespers they keep in their Churches, and have Mass on these days, wherein they eat twice. They are not suffered to go abroad, except the Prior and Procurator, and that upon the affairs of the Convent. They are limited to enjoy a certain quantity of Land, a certain number of sheep, Goats, and Asses, which they must not exceed. They must admit no Women into their Churches, nor were they to have in one Convent above twelve Religious Men, besides the Prior, and Eighteen Converts or Lay-Brothers, with a few servants, who are not to come into the Quire where the Prior and his Brothers sit, but these are in a lower Quire by themselves. They never admit any again into their society, who once leaves them. *These were the ancient Rules, to which, they were tyed, but in some things are fallen off now.* The Monks of this Order have a meeting or chapter yearly at *Carthusia,* about their own affairs; hither two Monks out of every Cloister do repair, where they stay Fourteen Days: This Order was confirmed by Pope *Alexander* the third, Anno. 1178. they came in to *England, Anno.* 1180, and seated themselves at *Witham,* near *Bath.*

See *Baleus, Surtius, Panvinius* in his Chronicles, *Genebrard, Pol. Virgil, Vincentius,* &c.

Q. 4. *What were the Monks of St.* Anthony *of* Vienna, *the* Cistertians, Bernardines, *and* Humiliati?

St. *Anthony's Monks of Vienna. Monks,* or *Cistertians.*

A. About the year of Christ 1105 Saint *Anthony's* Monks of *Vienna,* were set up by *Gastho* and *Gerondus,* two Noblemen of that place, and were to live according to Saint *Austin's* Rule; of which we have already said. The *Cistertians* began about the year 1098 by one *Robert* Abbot of *Molismenia,* who, as we have said, taking Offence at the loose lives of the *Benedictines,* by the perswasion of *Steven Harding* an Englishman, forsook that society; and being accompanied with one and twenty other Monks, came to *Cistertium* in *Burgundy,* where they Erected their Convent. Here they resolved to stick close to the Rule of Saint *Bennet,* and to cut off all the superfluities of Apparel and Dyet, introduced by the loose Monks of that Order. And because they did not find that Saint *Bennet* ever possessed Churches, Altars, Oblations, Tythes, and Sepulchers, or that he had Mills, Farms, or that he ever suffered Women to enter into his Convent, or that he buried there any, except his own Sister; therefore they meant to abandon

all

all these things and to profess Poverty with Christ: They would not suffer their Monks to Meddle with Husbandry, or any Secular affairs; and with Saint *Bennet* they ordered, that their Monastery should consist but of twelve Monks and an Abbot. They must keep silence, except it be to the Abbot or Prior. If any Monk run away from his Monastery, he must be forced back again by the Bishop. The *Cistertians* must be contented with two coats, and two hoods; they must work with their hands, and observe strictly their Fasts; they must salute strangers by bowing their head and body; and in imitation of Christ, must wash their feet. No Fugitive is to be received into the Convent, after the third time. The Abbots Table must be furnished for strangers. This Order was confirmed by Pope *Urban* the second, *Anno*. 1100. and came into *England Anno* 1132. Their Colour was gray, whence in the beginning they were named *Grisei*. The *Bernardines*, so called from Saint *Bernard*, Abbot of *Clarivallis*, were the same with the *Cistertians*, but that, as we said before, they wear a black coat over a white cloak: yet on Festivals they wear the *Cistertians* habit, to shew whence they came. The *Benardines* and *Cistertians* are not subject to Advocates or Bishops. And Pope *Alexander* the third, ordered, that if the Bishop refused to bless the abbot, he might receive Benediction from his own Monks. The *Humiliati* arose in *Germany* about the year of Christ 1164. in the time of *Frederick Barbarossa*, who in his Wars against *Lombardy*, brought captive thence into *Germany* multitudes of men, with their wives and children; these growing weary of their long exile; cloth themselves in white, and approaching to the Emperor, fall down at his feet, begging pardon for their Delinquency; from this posture they were called *Humiliati*, the Emperour being moved with their tears and habit, gave them leave to return home into their countrey: who being returned, resolved to live a Monastical life; therefore they built Monasteries, in which they gave themselves to Prayer, Fasting, Meditation, and making of Cloath. *Innocent* the third, did first ratifie this Order, and then their succeeding Popes. They wear a plain coat, a *Scapular*, and a white cloak over it; they follow *Bennet*'s rule in some part.

Monks, or Bernardines.

Monks, or Humiliati.

Of these Orders see Polydor, Sabellicus, Antoninus, Volatteran, Balaus, Trithemius, Crantzius, and others.

Q. 5. *What were the* Præmonstratenses *and* Gilbertines?

Answ. One *Robert* of *Lorrain* or *Nobert*, as others write, Arch-Bishop of *Magdeburg*, to which Church he procured the Title of Primate of *Germany* from the Pope; This *Nobert* I say, being offended at the dissolute Lives of the Monks, betook himself into a Desert, in the Diocess of *Liege*, with thirteen others. He went about Bare-footed in the midst of Winter, preaching Repentance, about the Year of Christ 1119. These Monks lived after the Rule of Saint *Austin*, which they say, was delivered to them in Golden Letters, from himself in a Vision. They were named *Præmonstratenses*, from the place where they first settled in the Diocess of *Landunum*, called *Præmonstratum*, or *Præmonstratenses*. because this place in a Vision, was *Præmonstratus*, or foreshewed

Monks, or Præmonstratenses.

to

to them. There habit is a white coat, with a Linen Surplice, under a white Cloak. *Calixtus* the second confirmed this Order, and gave them the Title of *Canons Regular exempt* ; their Abbot by their Rule muſt not wear a Mitre and Gloves, whereas other Abbots wear both, with Rings alſo on their fingers, and ſtaves in their hands. All the Abbots of this Order, or their Deputies, are to meet once a Year at *Præmonſtratum,* to conſult about the Affairs of their Order. If any out of Stubbornneſs refuſe to come, a penalty may be inflicted on him, by the other Abbots, which neither Biſhop, nor Arch-Biſhop can take off, but the Pope alone. The Abbots alſo have power of Excommunication and Abſolution, in reference to the Monks under their power : If Differences ariſe, they muſt compoſe them among themſelves, and not appeal to Secular Courts. They muſt not keep or feed Deer, Dogs, Hawks, Swine, or any ſuch thing as may bring ſcandal upon their Order. If their Dioceſan refuſe to give them Ordination, they may receive it of any other Biſhop ; they were exempted from the Biſhops Juriſdiction. Theſe and many other Privileges Pope *Innocent* the third beſtowed on them ; they had no Schools among them for Education of the Youth : They came into *England* about the Year 1145. and ſeated themſelves in *Lincolnſhire.* They had liberty from the Pope to have Nunneries cloſe to their Monaſteries. The *Gilbertines* were ſo called from one *Gilbert* of *Lincolnſhire,* who in the Year 1148. inſtituted this Order, and Erected in a ſhort time thirteen Monaſteries ; to which he preſcribed ſtatutes collected out of the Rules of *Auſtin* and *Bennet.* This Order was confirmed by Pope *Eugenius* the third. *Gilbert*'s chief Cloyſter was at *Sempringham* in *Lincolnſhire,* where he was born ; in which were 700. Friars and 1100. Nuns.

See Balæ-us, Cap-grave, and Scrop in Chron. Mathæus Pa is, Crantzius, Trithemius, Sigibert's Continuator, &c.

Q. 6. *What were the* Cruciferi, Hoſpitalarij, Trinitarians, *and* Bethlemites ?

Monks, or Cruciferi.

A. Theſe *Cruciferi, Crucigeri,* or as we call them, Cruched Friers, came into *England, Anno* 1244. and had their firſt Monaſtery at *Colcheſter* ; but were inſtituted as the ſtory goeth, by *Cyriacus* Biſhop of *Jeruſalem,* in memory of the croſs which *Helena* found by his direction. Theſe were to carry a Croſs in their hand ſtill when they went abroad ; afterward in the year 1215. they were reſtored or confirmed by Pope *Innocent* the third, or rather newly inſtituted, becauſe the great commotion raiſed in *Rome* by the *Albigenſes,* was ſuppreſſed by the *Croyſado*'s, or Army of Chriſtians, whoſe Badge on their Garments was a Croſs ; theſe were then going for *Syria* againſt the Infidels. This Order was ratified by Pope *Innocent* the fourth, and *Alexander* the third.

Monks, or Crucigeri.

They wear a sky coloured habit by the appointment of Pope *Pius* the ſecond. *Polydor* takes the *Cruciferi* for another Order, becauſe they wear a black cloak, and carry not in their hands, but on their breaſts a white and red Croſs, and obſerve S. *Auſtin*'s rule. The

Monks, or Hoſpitalarii.

Hoſpitalers of the Holy Ghoſt had their beginning at *Rome,* about the year

year 1201. and were confirmed by Pope *Innocent* the third; they had the same rule and privileges that other Monks had before them. Their chief office was to take care of, and lodge the sick and poor, and to bury them when they were dead. The *Trinitarians*, *Monks, or* or order of the Trinity, began, *Anno* 1211. by *John Matta*, and *Trinitari-* *Felix Anachoreta*. These two were warned in a dream to repair *ans.* to Pope *Innocent* the third, to obtain of him a place for their order; he likewise being warned in a dream to entertain them; confirms their order, cloaths them both in white cloaks, with a red and sky-coloured Cross wrought on the breast of the same, and calls them *Brothers of the Holy Trinity, and Monks of the Redemptions of Captives:* for their charge was to gather money for redeeming captive Christians from the Infidels. This Order came into *England Anno* 1357. Two parts of all their Revenues they were to reserve for their own Maintenance, the third was for the Captives: By their Rule three Clergy, and three Lay-Brothers may cohabit with one *Procurater*, who was not to be called by this name, but by the name *Minister*: Their Garments must be of white cloth; they must lie in woollen, and must not put off their breeches when they go to bed. They may ride on Asses, but not on Horse-back: They are to fast, as other Orders do, and to eat flesh upon Sundays only, from *Easter* till *Advent* Sunday, and from Christmas till *Septuagesima* Sunday: Likewise on the *Nativity, Epiphany, Ascension*, and on the *Assumption*, and *Purification* of *Mary*, and on *All-Saints* days. They are to labour with their Hands; to hold a Chapter or meeting every Sunday for regulating of their Convent: and a general Chapter is to be kept every year, on the *Octaves of Pentecost*. Their Minister must be chosen by common consent of the Brothers, he must be a Priest, every Convent must have his Minister; and over these must be a great Minister. None must be admitted into this Order till he be past twenty years of age. They must shave, but the Lay-Brothers may *Monks or* permit their Beards to grow. At certain times of the Year, the *Bethle-* Faithful that are Dead must be absolved in the Church-yard. *mites,* Their Rules concerning Love, Sobriety, Continency, and other *See Bala-* Christian Virtues, are the same that we have mentioned before in *us, Poly-* the Rules of *Basil, Austin, Bennet*, &c. The *Bethlemites* about the *dor, Sabel-* year 1257. had their first residence in *Cambridge*. They were ap- *licus, Vo-* parelled like the *Dominicans* or *Prædicants*, but on their breasts *latteranus,* they wore a red Star like a Comet, in memory of that Star, which *Panvinius,* appeared, at Christ's Nativity. *Genebrard,*
Mat. West-
Q: 7. Who were the first Religious Knights in Christendom? *minster,&c.*
A. The *Johannites*, or Knight-Hospitallers of Saint *John* Bap- *Knights,* tist, who got leave of the *Calypha* of *Egypt* to build a Monastery in *Hospitallers* *Jerusalem*, which they dedicated to the Virgin *Mary*: The first *of St. John.* Abbot and Monks of this Convent were sent thither from *Amalphia* in *Italy*. The same *Amalphitans* built also at *Jerusalem* a Nunnery for such Women as came on Pilgrimage thither. The first Abbatess hereof was Saint *Agnes*, a noble Matron; these Monks of
Jerusalem

Jerufalem for the greater Eafe of poor Pilgrims built an Hofpital, to receive them in, and withall a Chappel, or Oratory to the Honour of Saint *John* Baptift; or as fome think, to *John Eleemofynarius*, fo called from his bounteous Alms to the poor; he in the time of *Phocas*, was Patriarch of *Alexandria*; this Hofpital, was maintained by the *Amalphitans*. The *Hofpitallers*, Anno 1099. when *Jerufalem* was taken by the Chriftians, began to grow Rich, Potent, and in great Efteem, both with King *Godefrid*, and his Succeffor *Baldwin*; their Order was confirmed by Pope *Honorius* the fecond; fo having obtained much Wealth, they bind themfelves by Vows to be Hofpitable to all the *Latin* Pilgrims, and to Defend with their Arms Chriftianity againft all Infidels. They follow the Rule of Saint *Auftin*, and inftead of canonical Hours fay fo many *Pater-Nofters*: They go armed, having a Belt with a white Crofs: over which they wear a black Cloak with a white Crofs: Many of them in time of Peace wear a black Crofs; but in time of War a Red one: They have a Mafter over them, whom they chufe themfelves. Their firft Mafter was *Gerard*; the next *Raymundus de Podio*, a *Florentine*, chofen in the year 1103. In every Province they have alfo a Prior. Every one that Enters into this Order voweth to God, the Virgin *Mary*, and Saint *John* Baptift, Obedience, Poverty, and Chaftity; they are tyed three times yearly, to wit, at *Chriftmas*, *Eafter*, and *Whitfuntide*, to receive the Eucharift; they muft not ufe Merchandizing, nor be Ufurers, nor make Wills, nor make any their Heirs, or alienate any thing without confent of their Mafters; none born of *Infidels*, *Jews*, *Saracens*, *Arabians*, and *Turks*, muft be admitted into this Order; nor Murderers, nor Married men, nor Baftards, except they be of Earls or Princes: They muft have fpecial care of ftrangers, and of the fick, to lodge them; they muft admit only fuch as are found and ftrong of Body, Nobly defcended, and at leaft Eighteen Years old. They are diftinguifhed into three Ranks; to wit, Priefts or Chaplains. 2. Serving-men. 3. Knights: Thefe laft muft be of Noble Extraction. When Chriftian Princes fall at variance, thefe Knights muft fide with neither, but ftand Neutrals, and endeavour to reconcile them. Pope *Hadrian* the fourth exempted them from paying of Tythes to the Patriarch of *Jerufalem*, who claimed them as his due. Pope *Alexander* the third, for their brave Exploits againft the Infidels, exempted them alfo from Tythes, and the Jurifdiction of Bifhops. At length about the Year 1299. when the Weftern Princes by reafon of their Domeftick Wars, could Afford thefe Knights no Help, they were forced by the Governour of *Damafcus* called *Capcapus*, to quit all their Caftles, Land, and Garrifons they had in *Syria*, and totally to abandon that Country, in the year 1300 after almoft 300. years poffeffion; and fo having got a Fleet of Ships, they invade, and take the Ifle of *Rhodes* from the *Turks*, Anno 1308. and poffeffed it againft all Oppofition 214 years: From this they were called the Knights of *Rhodes*: And had eight feveral Families, and eight
Provinces

Knights Hofpitallers of Rhodes.

Provinces of *Europe*, to wit, in *Gallia*, *Avernia*, *Francia*, *Italy*, *Arragon*, *England*, *Germany*, and *Castile*. Each of these provinces hath a *Prior*, these *Priors* choose the great Master; they have also their *Marshal*, *Hospitaller*, *Baily*, *Treasurer*, and *Chancellor*; these send out of their Provinces to the great Master young men Nobly born, who gives them their Oath to be chast, poor, and obedient, and to promote the Well-fare of Christendom against the Infidels; and so he is admitted Knight of the Order. Here they stay five years, and have fifty ducats yearly Pension for their service; then they are sent home into their Country, and by the great Master are set over some House. If in the election of the great Master there be equal suffrages, one chief Knight is chosen for Umpire, who by his suffrage ends the controversie. The great Master in spiritualities is only subject to the Pope; in his temporalties, to secular Princes. After these Knights had possessed *Rhodes* 212 years, and had endured a siege of six months, for want of help from the western Princes, were forced to deliver up the Island to the *Turk*, Anno 1523. From thence they sailed to *Candy*, where they were entertained a while by the *Venetians*; at last they resolved to seat their great Master in *Nicea*, a Town under *Charles* Duke of *Savoy*, upon the *Ligustick* Sea, in the Province between *Marseilles*, and *Genua*, being a fit place to discry and suppress Pirates. But when *Buda* in *Hungary* was taken by the *Turk*, fearing least *Solomon* would assault *Italy*, they fortifie *Nicea*, and from thence remove to *Syracuse* in *Sicily*, which then with the Kingdom of *Naples* belonged to *Charles* the Emperour; there they stoutly defended the Christian Coasts from *Turks* and *Priates*; but *Charles* the Emperour perceiving they might do more good if they were seated in *Malta*, gives them that Island, which they accept Anno 1529. promising to defend *Tripolis*, to suppress the Pirates, and to acknowledge the Kings of *Spain* and both *Sicilies* for their Protectors, to whom every year they should present a Falcon. This Island they stoutly defended against *Solomon* for five months, Anno 1565. who was forced to leave it. The great Masters revenue is ten thousand Ducats yearly, besides some thousands of Crowns out of the common Treasury, and the tenth of all goods taken at Sea. They have for the most part six Gallies, every one being able contain five hundred men, and sixteen great Canons.

Knights of Malta. See Crantzius, Polydor, Jacobus de vitriaco, in hist History of Jerusalem, Volatteran, Æmilian Hospinian, &c.

Q. 8. *What were the* Templars?

A. About the year of Christ 1123. not long after the institution of the *Johannites* or *Hospitallers*, *Hugo de Paganis*, and *Gaufrid de S. Aldemaro*, with seven other prime Men vowed to secure the High-ways, and to defend from Robbers all Pilgrims that came to visit the Holy Sepulchre. And because these had no Habitation, *Baldwin* King of *Jerusalem*, assigned them a place in his own Palace near the Temple to dwell in; whence they were called *Templarii*: They lived after the manner of the *Canon Regulars*, possessing nothing in Propriety, but were sustained by the bounty of the Patriarch, and Christian Pilgrims. Thus they continued Nine

Templars.

Years,

Years, till the Year 1122. Then did *Honorius* the second, Bishop of *Rome*, with the Patriarch, Erect them into an Order, assigning a white Cloak to be worn by them; afterwards Pope *Eugenius* added a red Cross: These in a few Years by their valour, and care of Pilgrims, grew mighty numerous, and rich; so that sometimes in publick Meetings, three Hundred Knights have been together, besides infinite numbers or Brothers; they had above Nine thousand Manners in Christendom, whereas the *Hospitallers* had but Nineteen. They had the same Rule prescribed them, that other Monks had, to wit, Obedience, Poverty, Chastity, Gravity, Piety, Charity, Patience, Vigilance, Fortitude, Devotion, and such like Virtues. When any of them were taken Prisoners by the Infidels, they were to be redeemed only with a Girdle and a Knife. They were exempted from the Bishops jurisdiction by Pope *Calixtus* the second, in the Council of *Rhemes*, Anno 1110. And from Tythes to Pope *Alexander* the third. It was excommunication to lay violent Hands on any Templar. At last this Order with their Pride and Luxury became so odious, that having continued two hundred years, they were utterly routed out of *France* by King *Philip* the fair, and likewise out of their Kingdoms by the Instigation of Pope *Clement* 5. In *France* they were put to death, and their Estates confiscated to the Pope and King. But in *Germany* their lives were spared, and their Estates bestowed on the *Hospitallers*, and the *Teutonick* Knights of St. *Mary*. Some think they were put to death for worshipping Images covered with Mens skins, for sacrificing men, for burning a child begot of a *Templar*, and a Nun; with the fat of which Child they anointed their Image; and for divers other crimes, *Yet doubtful whether true or false*.

See *Matthew Paris*, *Antoninus*, *Volatteran*, *Sabellicus*, *Pol. Virgil*, *Paucerus*, *Crantzius*, *Balæus*, *Hospinian*, *P. Æmilius*, &c.

Teutonicks, or Marians, and their instalment.

Q. 9. *What were the* Teutonici, *or* Mariani?

Answ. These were a mixt Order of *Johannites* and *Templars*, for they both used Hospitality to Pilgrims, and defended them in the High ways from Robbers. They were called *Teutonici* from their Country, for they were *Germans* that undertook this Order, who living in *Jerusalem*, bestowed all their Wealth on the Maintenance of Pilgrims, and by the Patriarchs leave, assigned to them our Ladies Chappel, from this Chappel of Saint *Mary*, they were named *Mariani*. The chief promoters of this Order, were the *Lubikers* and *Bremers*, with *Adolphus* Earl of *Holstein*, who with a Fleet of Ships, assisted the *Christians*, besieging *Ptolemais*, and provided Tents, with all Necessaries for the sick and Maimed Souldiers. This Order was erected before *Accona* or *Ptolemais* by the King of *Jerusalem*, the Patriarch, divers Arch-Bishops, Bishops and Princes of *Germany* then present, and was confirmed by the Emperour *Henry* the sixth, and Pope *Cælestine* the third, who assigned them a white Cloak, with a black Cross; and added a white Target with a black Cross also, and gave them leave to wear their beards, and granted Indulgences, with other Acts of Graces, to those that should undertake or promote the Order; they had Power to bestow Knight-hood on such as deserved, and are

enjoyned

enjoyned to follow the Rule of Saint *Auſtin* : But none muſt be admitted into this Order, except he be a *Teutonick* born, and nobly deſcended. Their charge was to be ready on all occaſions, to oppoſe the Enemies of the Croſs; and are tied to ſay two hundred *Pater-Noſters*, *Creeds*, and *Ave Maries* in twenty four hours. When the Holy Land was loſt, theſe Knights came into *Germany*, on whom the Pope and Emperour *Frederick* the ſecond, *Anno* 1226. beſtowed the Country of *Pruſſia*, conditionally that they ſubdue the Infidels there; which they did in the ſpace of fifty three years, and ſo got the full poſſeſſion thereof. Upon the River *Viſtula*, where they had raiſed a Fort againſt the enemy, they built their chief City, and called it *Marienburg* : they ſet up three great Maſters, the one in *Germany*, the ſecond in *Livonia*, and the third in *Pruſſia*; this was over the other two: They aided the *Polonians* againſt the *Lithuanians*, much of whoſe Country they ſubdued; which cauſed great Wars between theſe *Teutonicks* and the *Polonians*, after that *Poland* and *Lithuania* were united under one Prince. After many bickrings, at laſt the *Polonian* forced the great Maſter to ſwear fealty to him, to admit into this Order as well *Polonians* as *Germans*, and make them capable of Offices, that what Land ſoever the *Teutonicks* obtain, they ſhould hold the ſame in Fee of the King. This occaſioned a War between *Albert*, Marqueſs of *Brandenburg*, and the *Polander* King *Sigiſmund*, to whom for want of help from the Emperour, being then imployed in Wars againſt *France*, and the *Turk* of *Hungary*, he was faign to ſubmit, and to acknowledge the King for his Lord. Then he obtains *Pruſſia*, but changed his title from Maſter to Duke of *Pruſſia*, *Anno* 1393. *Venceſlaus* King of the *Romans* and *Bohemians*, drove all the *Teutonick* Knights out of *Bohemia*, and ſeized on their eſtates. The Knights are thus inſtalled. The *Commendator* placeth him that is to be Knighted in the midſt of the Knights; then asketh every one of them, if they find any exception againſt him, either for his body, mind, or parentage, the ſame is demanded of the Party to be Knighted, and withal, if he be skilful in any uſeful Art, if in debt, if married, or if he have any bodily infirmity; if he hath, he muſt not enter into that Order: then he is commanded to kneel, and by laying his Hand on the Goſpel, and Rule of the Order, to vow and promiſe obedience, chaſtity, poverty, care of the ſick, and perpetual War with the Infidels; which done, the *Commendator* promiſeth to him ſufficient bread and water, and courſe cloath for his life time; then he riſeth, and having kiſſed the Maſter, and each one of his Brothers, he ſitteth down in the place appointed for him. Then the Maſter, or *Commendator* exhorts the Brothers to obſerve their Rule carefully: After this, he is Inaugurated, his kindred attend on him to the Church with a Torch burning before him, in which are faſtned thirty pieces of Silver and a Gold Ring. Then he kneels before the Altar, and riſeth again behind the Offertory, and ſo are delivered to him a Sword, Target, Spurs, and a Cloak, which were all conſecrated before; then the *Commendator* draweth his Sword, with which he

See Poli- is girt, and with it ſtrikes his Target twice, ſaying, *Knight-hood*
dor, Crant- is better than ſervice, and with the ſame Sword ſtriking him on
ſius, Fuch- the back, ſaith, *Take this blow patiently, but no more hereafter;*
cius, Tri- then the *Reſponſory* being ſung, the reſt of the day is ſpent in Fea-
themius. P. ſting and Drinking.
Æmilius,
Peucerus, Q. 10. *What were the Knights of Saint* Lazarus, *of* Calatrava,
Slexdanus, *of Saint* James *and divers others?*
Urſpergen. A. The order of St. *Lazarus* was inſtituted about the year of
Seulvin, Chriſt 1119. and being almoſt extinct, was renewed by Pope
Frank. Ho- Pius 4. they wear a dark-coloured garment with a red Croſs be-
ſpinian, &c. fore their breaſt. This Order is highly eſteemed by the Dukes of
Knights of Savoy, who alſo were inſtituted the Knights of the *Annunciada* in
S. Laza- memory of the *Annunciation* of *Mary;* he ordained fourteen of the
rus. prime Nobility to be of this College, on each of whom he beſtowed a golden Collar, with the Virgins Picture hanging at it, within the Links of the Collar are engraven theſe four Letters, F. E. R. T.
which was the Motto of *Amadeus* the great, who took *Rhodes.* The
meaning is *Fortitudo Ejus Rhodum Tenuit;* the annual ſolemnity is
held on our Lady Day in the Caſtle of St. *Peter* in *Turin.* But
this is ſcarce to be reckoned among the Religious Orders. The
Of Calatra- Knights of *Calatrava,* are ſo called from that Province in *Spain;*
va. they were inſtituted *Anno* 1121. or as ſome ſay 1160. by *Sanctius*
(others write) by *Alphonſus* King of *Spain,* in the County of *Toledo,*
where the *Templars* had a Monaſtery, who not being able to reſiſt
the *Saracens,* were forced to give place to theſe new Knights, who
were of the *Ciſtertian* Order. They wear a black Garment with a
red Croſs; the revenues of their Maſter is forty thouſand Crowns
yearly; they are enjoyned by their Rule to ſleep in their cloaths
girded; to be ſilent in the Chappel, Hall, Kitchen, and Dormitory; to eat fleſh but on Sundays, Tueſdays, and Thurſdays, and
but of one kind, and but once a day, and muſt faſt Mundays,
Wedneſdays, and Frydays, for the exaltation of the Croſs till
Eaſter, if they be at home; If any lay violent Hands on them,
they ſhall be Excommunicated. In the Lands that they ſhall ac-
quire from the *Saracens,* it ſhall not be lawful for any to build
Churches, or Chappels without leave from the Knights; who
alſo chuſe their own Clergy; other Immunities and privileges
they have, as may be ſeen in the Confirmation, or Bull of Pope
Innocent the third, which is extant in the Second Book of his De-
Of Saint cretal Epiſtles. The Knights of Saint *James* in *Spain,* were inſti-
James. tuted under Pope *Alexander* the Third, who confirmed this Order,
and were to follow Saint *Auſtin's* Rule. The firſt Maſter was Pe-
Divers Or- ter *Ferdinand,* whoſe yearly Revenue is one hundred and fifty
ders of Thouſand Crowns. They were inſtituted *Anno* 1170. The great
Knight- Maſter is next to the King in power and ſtate; they wear both in
hood. Who Peace and Wars a Purple Croſs before their Breaſt, reſembling the
may d ſee Hilt of a Two-handed Sword called *Spatha;* therefore theſe
more of the Knights are called *Milites* Sancti *Jacobi de Spatha;* and the Order
F. from *Compoſtella* is named *Compoſtellanus.* Many other Orders of
Orders of Knight-
Knight-

Knight-hood there are in *Christendom*, as of Saint *George* in *England*, of Saint *Andrew* in *Scotland*, of Saint *Michael* in *France*, of the *Lily* in *Navarre*, of Saint *Mark* in *Venice*, of the *Dove* in *Castile*, of the *Golden Fleece* in *Burgundy*, of Saint *Maurice* in *Savoy*, of Saint *Stephen* in *Tuscany*, and many more which are rather Secular, than religious Knights. The *List* of which may be seen in our continuation of Sir Walter Raleigh's *History*.

hood, may read Sebastian Frank in his Chronicle, Panvinius in his Appendix to Platina, and in his Chronicle, Polyd. Hospinian, and others. Friers Mendicants. Monks, or Augustinians. Eremites of St. Austin.

Q. 11. *What were the Order of* Mendicant Friers?

A. Of these were four sorts; namely, *Augustinians, Carmelites, Prædicants*, and *Minorites*. The *Augustinians* were erected by *William* Duke of *Aquitania*, about the year 1150. from whom they were named *Guilehelmites*, but afterwards Pope *Innocent* the fourth, understanding that there were many sorts of *Eremites* in divers parts of the world, living under different Titles and Rules, he invited them to live under one Head, and to profess one Rule, to wit, that of Saint *Austin*. But this Pope dying in the interim, *Alexander* the fourth succeeded, to whom Saint *Austin* appeareth in a vision, having a great hand, but small limbs; by this he is warned to perfect the Union which *Innocent* began, which he did accordingly, and so he unites them all in one Order, and calls them by one Name, to wit, the *Eremites* of Saint *Austin*, whose rule he commanded they should follow, and be subject to one General Prior, and so dispensed with their former Rules and Observations. Withal he enjoyns them to forsake the Desarts, and to live in Cities, that they might teach the people. To this end he gave them divers privileges; and so did *Honorius* the fourth, about the year of Christ 1290. They wear a black coat with a Hood of the same colour, and under a white short coat, a leathern girdle with horn buckles. They came into *England*, Anno 1252. before *Alexander's* vision, and by their Sermons indeavoured to advance King *Richard* the Third, his Title against the Heirs of King *Edward*. These *Eremites* did spread so fast through the World, that there were reckoned of this Order about 2000 Convents. These Monks have three Rules to which they are bound, given them by Saint *Austin*, as they say. The first is, that they possess nothing in property, but have all things in common; that they be not sollicitous what they shall eat or drink, or wherewith they shall be cloathed; That none be admitted without trial; That none depart, or carry any thing out of the Monastery, without the Superiours leave; That no man maintain any point of Doctrine, without acquainting the Superiour with it; That secret Faults be first reproved, and if not repented of, punished: In Persecution let them repair to their *Præpositus*. Their second Rule contains the Times and Manner of their Praying and Singing; their times of Working, reading and refreshing; of their Obedience, Silence, and Behaviour, both at home and abroad, and how Contumacy must be punished. The third Rule contains their duties more largely; as that they must love God above all things, that they maintain Unity; that meat, drink, and cloath, be distributed as need is; that all things be common,

common, that there be not pride, contempt, or vain glory amongst them; here they are enjoyned to prayer, reverence, devotion, abstinence; silence, contentments: to hear the word read at table; to be careful of the sick and infirm; to be modest in Apparel, Words and Gesture, in their Looks, when they chance to see a woman; to reprove immodesty in their Brothers, to receive no Letters nor Gifts without the Superiours knowledge, to have their cloaths well kept from Moths, to beware of murmuring and repining; that to conceal any thing, shall be counted theft, that they be not too nice in washing their cloaths; That in sickness the Physician be advised with; That they may bathe sometimes; That the sick want not any thing needful for him; That there be not strife, envy, nor evil words among them; That the Superiour use not harsh words in reproving; That he shew good example to his Brothers in holy Conversation; That he be wise, humble, and careful of his charge; and that the duties here enjoyned may be the better performed, these Rules must be read once every week; which rules are followed, and observed, not only by all the Canon Regulars, and the Eremites of Saint *Austin's* order, but also by the *Mendicants*, except the *Minors*; and likewise by the *Dominicans*, the Servants of our Lady, the *Brigidians*, *Jesuati*, Canons Regular of St. *George*, *Montolibetenses*, Eremites of St. *Hierom*, *Hyeronymites* simply, *Cruciferi*, *Scopetini*, *Hospitalarii*, St. *Antonii*, Trinitatis, *Servitæ*, *Feruerii*, *Ferieri*, or of St. *John* of *Jerusalem*, *Crucifori with the Star*, the *Friers* of St. *Peter* the confessor de *Magella*; *Sepulchritæ*, or Brothers of the Lords Sepulchre; The *Friers* of the *Valischolarii*, *Victoriani*, *Gilbertini*; The Eremites of St. *Paul*, whom some think to be all one with the *Augustinians*; *Fratres de Pœnitentia*, *Coronati*; The Knights of St. *James de Spatha*, and divers more, who notwithstanding differ in their habit, exercises, and manner of living.

Monks of S. Austin. See Alphonsus Alvares Guerrera, and Hospinian out of him. See also Polydor, Antoninus, Sebastian Frank, Satellicius, Volateranus, Balæus, &c.

Monks or Carmelites.

Q. 12. *What were the* Carmelites?

A. These were *Eremites*, whose Habitation was in Caves and Rocks within the Hill *Carmel*, famous for the *Prophets*, *Elias* and *Elisha*. About the Year of Christ 1160. or as others 1121. *Almericus* Patriarch of *Antioch*, and the Popes Legate came thither, and gathered these dispersed *Anchorites* into one body, and built them a Monastery on the top of the Hill near the Well of *Elias*, by which stood an ancient Chappel of our Lady; Perhaps from this Chappel, the *Carmelites* were called the Virgins Brothers. The same *Almericus* translated into Latine the Book concerning the institution of the first Monks, written in Greek by *John*, Bishop of *Jerusalem*, for benefit of these *Carmelites*; and placed over them a Latine Governour in the time of Pope *Alexander* the Third, who began his Popedom *Anno* 1170. The Governours name was *Bertholdus Aquitanus*; some think this Order was instituted 40. years after, to wit, in the Papacy of *Innocent* the third: Their second Governour was *Brochard* of *Jerusalem*, who made them a rule, much after the Rule of Saint *Basil*; which in the year 1198. was abridg-
ed

Sect. 10.   *of* EUROPE.   213

ed and confirmed by *Albert*, Patriarch of *Jerusalem*, who tyed them to fasting, silence, and canonical Hours; and the Lay-Brothers to *Peter* the *Eremites* Beades or Prayer, and to our Ladies Psalter. They were as yet tyed to no Vow, but that of obedience to their Superiours. They came into *England* about the year 1240. *Ralph Fresburn* was the first Governour here, and *Hunfrid Neckton* the first *Carmelite* that read School Divinity in *Cambridge*, and was of that Order the first Doctor of Divinity. This Order came into *Lithuania*, Anno 1427. Whilst they were in *Syria*, their Garment was a striped cloak of party colours, which they say was used by the Prophet *Eliah*; but Pope *Honorius* the third, or as some say the fourth, took from them this Habit, as not beseeming or agreeable to Religion; and instead thereof gave them a white cloak, and a white hood, and under, a coat with a scapulary of hair colour. The use of the white cloak was confirmed by Pope *Nicholaus* the fourth. Whilst they used the former habit, they were highly esteemed by the *Egyptians*, and maintained by the *Sultan*; but when they began to wear the Popes new Livery, he expelled them out of *Egypt*, and burned down their Monastery and Chappel. *Honorius* the fourth, exempted them from the Jurisdiction of Princes and Bishops. *Gregory* the ninth, forbad to injoy possessions, or revenues, but to beg from door to door. *Honorius* the fourth will have them called instead of *Carmelites*, *Brothers of the Virgin Mary*: *Alexander* the fourth, allowed them Prisons to punish their Apostates, and *John* 23. took them into his immediate protection, and by a vision was warned to keep them out of Purgatory. Many of the *Carmelites* fell off from their first strictness of Life, and gave themselves to all riot and voluptuousness; whereupon they were divided into two Sects: the one were called *Observantes*, the other *Non Observantes*; to undertake this Order is held meritorious, and three years Indulgence is promised to him that shall at any time call them brothers of Saint *Mary*. In many of their Cloysters they have the Picture of *John* Baptist in their Habit, because he is named *Eliah*; and they say that *Eliah* did wear this Habit, they have charged now (I mean the *Non Observantes*;) their Hair-coloured coat into black.

Of these passages See *Bals. us, Sabellic. Mant. an. Eclog. 10. Scrope, Vincentius in Specul. Hist. Polyd.* &c.

Q. 13. *What were the* Dominicans?

A. These were so called from *Dominicus* a *Spaniard* their first Author; they sprung out of the *Humiliati*, and were instituted by *Innocent* the third; *Anno* 1205. the chief end of their institution was to write, expound and preach the word of God; whence they are named *Prædicantes* or *Prædicatores*. *Dominicus* was by Pope *Innocent* the third, *Anno* 1207. imployed with twelve Abbots of the Order of *Cistertians*, to preach down the Doctrines of the *Albigenses*. He by his preaching, so incensed the Princes against them, that they took arms, and killed above One hundred thousand of them. *Dominicus* with twelve more, accompanied by *Fulco*, Bishop of *Toledo*, went to *Rome*, where he petitioneth *Innocent* the third, to confirm his order; who was somewhat averse,

Monks or Dominicans.

Friers Prædicants.

till

till he dreamed that he saw *Dominicus* supporting with his shoulders the Church of *Lateran* that was ready to fall down; hereupon he adviseth *Dominick* to pitch upon some Rule, and he would ratifie it; *Dominick* returns presently to his Disciples being sixteen together, acquaints them with the Popes Intention; they all resolve to profess the rule of Saint *Austin* the preacher: In the interim *Innocent* dieth, *Honorius* the third succeeded; who confirmed their rule and institution. *Dominick* added some things to St. *Austin's* rule. He divided his Monastery into three parts, one for himself and contemplative Brothers, the other for contemplative Sisters, the third was for both Sexes, that were given to the active Life: These were called Brothers and Sisters of Saint *Dominick*; or the Souldiers of *Jesus Christ*, for as *Dominick* with the Spiritual, so these with the corporal sword were to subdue Hereticks. The *Dominicans* are tyed to reject all kind of Wealth, Money and Possessions, that their work of preaching may not be hindred. To hold every Year a general Chapter. To fast seven months together; namely, from Holy Rood day in *September*, till *Easter*; and at all other times on Friday to abstain from flesh, except in times of Sickness. To lie in Blankets, not in Sheets; nor on Feather-beds. To be silent, to wear a white coat, under a black cloak, which they say was prescribed by the Virgin *Mary*, to one *Reginaldus* in his sickness. To have low built Monasteries answering to their poverty and humility: To be content with the Title of *Friers Prædicants*, whereas before they were stiled *Friers* of the blessed Virgin *Mary*. To celebrate on every Saturday *the Office of the Virgin Mary*, except in Lent, and on Festival days. To disperse themselves through all parts of the world, for preaching the Gospel. To choose them a General Master, whose subordinate Prelates should be called **Priors** but not *Abbots*. The first that was elected Master General was *Dominicus* himself, *Anno* 1220. who died the next year after. The *Prædicants* do not promise to live according to their Rule, or to keep it (because not to perform such a promise is a mortal sin) but only to obey according to the Rule; *Because in this case Omission or Transgression obligeth not to sin, but to the Punishment, as they think*. For Dominick's *good Service against the* Albigenses, *he is made by* Honorius *the third, Master of the sacred Palace. And so the* Dominicans *are ordinarily Master of this place. And because a* Dominican *poysoned* Henry *the seventh, Emperour, in the Eucharist, therefore the Pope inflicted this punishment on the Order, that their Priests should ever after in the Eucharist use their left Hand.* *Antoninus* writes that *Dominick*, received a staff from *Peter*, and a Book from *Paul*, with a Command to preach the Gospel every where; hereupon his Disciples dispersed themselves into all parts. *Dominick* himself went to *Rome*, where by the concession of the Pope and Cardinals, he gathered together in one Convent all Nuns dispersed through divers places of the City, where they had the Church of St. *Sabina* assigned them; forty four of them met together, and took upon them the profession and habit of St. *Dominick*,

nick. The order of the *Prædicants* increased so fast, that in the same time of *Sabellicus*, about the year of Christ 1494. were reckoned 4143. Monasteries of *Dominicans*, in which were 1500. Masters of Divinity; besides divers Cloysters of them in *Armenia* and *Æthiopia*, and 150. Convents of *Dominican* Nuns, in Divers parts of *Europe*. The cause of this great increase of *Prædicants*, was partly the mortified life, humility, and abstinence of *Dominick*; for they write of him that he preferred bread and water to be the best cheer; a hair-shirt to the finest Linen, a hard board to the softest Bed, and a hard stone to the easiest Pillow. He did use to wear an Iron chain, with which he beats himself every night, both for his own sins, and the sins of the world, for which also he did frequently weep, and pray whole nights together in Churches. He offered himself twice as a ransom, to redeem others: And partly the cause was, his frequent vision and miracles, (which whether true or false, I leave for others to judge;) partly also by receiving Children and Infants, into their society before the years of probation; besides the great respect which the Popes carried towards this order; for *Gregory* the ninth, canonised *Dominick*, *An.* 1233. They were subject to no Ordinary, but to the Pope: They had many privileges granted them, as to preach in any mans Pulpit without asking leave of the Bishop; to make Noble-men and their Ladies confess to them, and not to their Curates; to administer the Sacraments when they pleased, to be exempt from all Ecclesiastical censures; and this priviledge they had from Pope *Innocent* the fourth, that no *Dominican* could change his Order, or enter into any other.

Of these passages see Mat. Paris, Antoninus, Vincentius in Speculo, Hist. Sabellicus, Florentius, Crantzius, Theodoricus de Apolea in vita Dominici, Surius, de vit. Sanct. Frank in Chron, &c.

Q. 14. *What were the* Franciscans?

A. They are so named from *Francis* an *Italian* Merchant, who before his conversion was called *John*. He living a wicked and debauched life in his younger years, was at last reclaimed by a vision, as the Story goeth, of a Castle full of Arms and Crosses, with a voice telling him, that he was to be a spiritual Souldier. Afterward as he was praying, he was warned by a Voice to repair the decayed Houses of Christ; which he did by stealing money from his Father, and bestowing it on the Reparation of Churches; whereupon his Father beats him, puts him in prison, and desinherits him he rejoyceth at this, stript himself naked of all his Garments, which he delivers to his Father, shewing how willing he was to relinquish all for Christ. Within a short while he gathered many Disciples, to whom he prescribeth this Rule, *Anno* 1198. That they shall be chast, poor, and obedient to Christ, to the Pope, and to their Superiors; That none be admitted into their Order, till they be duly examined and proved; That the Clergy in their Divine Service follow the Order of the *Roman* Church, and the Lay-Brothers say 24. *Pater Nosters* for their *Mattens*, &c. That they fast from *All Saints*, till *Christmas*, &c. That they enter not into any house, till they say, Peace be to this house, and then they may eat of what is set before them; That they meddle not with money, nor appropriate any thing to themselves:

Franciscans.

that

that they help one another; that Pennance be impofed on thofe who fin; that they have their publick Meetings or Chapters, and that they chufe their provincial Minifters, and thefe muft chufe a General Minifter over the whole Fraternity; that their preachers be men of approved Gifts, and that they preach not abroad without leave from the Bifhop; That they ufe Brotherly admonition and correction, that they give themfelves to Prayer, modefty, temperance, and other vertues, and that they enter not into *Nunneries*, except fuch as are authorized; that none go to convert *Saracens* or other Infidels, but fuch as are fent by the Provincial Minifters; that they all remain conftant in the Catholick Faith, and that none break this Rule, except he will incurr the curfe of God, and of the two bleffed Apoftles, *Peter* and *Paul*. This Rule *Francis* ftrengthened by his will and Teftament which he enjoyneth to be read, as often as they fhall read the rule. This rule and order was confirmed by Pope *Innocent* the third, but not till he was warned by vifions of a Palm-tree growing and fpreading under him, and of a poor man fupporting the decaying *Lateran*, and until he had tried *Francis* his obedience, which he fhewed by wallowing in the mire with Swine, as the Pope advifed him. This order was alfo confirmed again by Pope *Honorius* the third, and by Pope *Nicholaus* the third in his Decretal Epiftles, which he enjoyned fhould be read in Schools. *Francis* would not have his Difciples to be called *Francifcans* from his name, but *Minores*, and fo he would have the Superiours or Governours of his order to be called not Mafters, but Minifters, to put them in mind of their humble condition, and to follow Chrifts advice to his Difciples, *Whofoever will be great among you, let him be your Servant.*

Who would know more fully thefe paffages, let him read Bonaventure in the life of Saint Francis, Antoninus Sebaft. Frank, Trithemius in Chron. Balzus. Mat. Paris, Vincentius, &c. Monks, or Francifcans Schifms, Families, Rules and Privileges. Friers Minorites. ¶

Q. 15. *What things elfe are obfervable in the* Francifcan *Order?*

A. 1. *Francis* divided his Difciples into three Claffes or Ranks; the firft was of the *Friers Minorites*, whereof himfelf was one, and whofe life was moft rigid; For they were neither to have Granaries, nor two *Coats*. The fecond was of Ladies and poor Virgins, who from Saint *Clara* were named *Clariffæ*; this Order was not fo ftrict as the former. The third was of *Penitents* inftituted for Married people, who defired to do Pennance;. thefe might enjoy propriety in their goods. The firft fort was for contemplation and action too; namely, in preaching; the fecond for contemplation only, the third for action only. This third Order is not properly called Religious, becaufe they may continue in their married eftate, and enjoy propriety. Thefe are called *Friers Penites* of *Jefus Chrift*; and *Sacci* from their fack-cloth which they wore; and *Continenses*, not that they vowed continency, but becaufe certain days every week, they abftain from carnal Copulation. The Women are called *Sifters Penitents*. The firft Order were not to permit any of the third Order to enter their Churches in time of interdict. This Order was condemned in *England, Anno* 1307. but is again advanced by *Peter Tuxbury* a *Francifcan* Minifter, and allowed in the Chapter at *London*, 2. Many Families
sprung

sprung out of this Minorit Order; namely, *Observantes, Conventuales, Minimi, Caputiani, Collectanei,* who gathered or collected the moneys; *Amadeani, Reformati de Evangelio, Chiacinicum barba, de Portiuncula, Paulini, Bostaini, Gaudentes, de Augustinis* with their open shooes, and *Servientes.* 3. *Francis* himself wore a short Coat without any Artificial tincture: instead of a girdle, he used a cord, and went bare-footed; hence after long alteration among his Disciples about their habit and shooes, it was ordered, that they should wear Soles only, having no more upper Leather than to tye the shooes. That they should travel either on foot, or upon Asses. And whereas they could not agree about the form, measure, and colour of their habit, (for Saint *Francis* in this determined nothing,) the matter is referred to Pope *John* 22. who leaves it to the Arbitrement of their General and Provincial Ministers. At this day they wear a long coat with a large hood of gray, or hair colour, bare-footed, and girded with a cord. 4. Such Vertue hath been held in a *Franciscan* Garment, that divers Princes have desired to be buried in it, thinking thereby to be safe from the Devil. So we read of *Francis* the second Marquess of *Mantua*, of *Robert* King of *Sicily*, and divers others, who have by their last Will ordered that they might be Interred in a *Seraphick* Habit. And yet we read that *Francis* himself died naked, because he would be like Christ, who hung Naked on the Cross. 5. I read of divers Schisms among the *Franciscans* about the form of their habit; one I find in the time of *Crescentius de Eseyo* their sixth General Minister, *Anno* 1245. Some among them bragging much of the Spirit, would not live after St. *Francis* rule, but after their own, accounting themselves the Saints. These despised a long habit, and would go in short cloaks. Another Schism they made in the Province of *Narbon, Anno* 1315. after the death of Pope *Clement.* 5. During the vacancy of the Popedom almost two years. These Monks choose their own Ministers and Governours, and flung away the habit of their Order as prophane, wearing short Garments, imprisoning and excommunicating the *Obedientes*. Pope *John* 22. condemned these *Minorites* as Hereticks; and the *Fratricelli* starting up at that time condemned the same Pope of Heresie, for saying Christ and his Disciples had a common stock among them, whereof *Judas* bore the bag. Another Schism they had about the year 1352. Some petitioned the Pope for leave to Live after the Letters of Saint *Francis* his Rule; and not after the gloss, as they all did. They obtain four places to reside in, and in each of them twelve Brothers. But these aiming at liberty rejecting the rule of their Order, and wearing short undecent Garments, were suppressed by Pope *Innocent* the sixth. Another Rupture was among them, during the Schism of the Church, begun by *Urban* the sixth, who sat at *Rome*, and *Clemens* at *Avinion*; for the *Minorites* of *England, France,* and *Spain*, chose them one General; and those of *Italy, Germany*, and *Hungary* another, *Anno* 1431. They divided themselves into *Conventuales*, and *Observantes*; these despising the

Conventual

Conventual Prelates, chose their own Governours, calling the others profane and impious. These touch no Money, eat no flesh, and wear no shooes: They multiplyed exceedingly in all parts, chiefly in *Italy*. They were confirmed by the Council of *Constance*, and divers Popes. 6. *Francis* prohibited his Monks to meddle with Ecclesiastical Preferments, to be called Lords or Masters, to hear confessions, to eat flesh, to wear rich apparel, and to dwell in sumptuous houses, *Bonaventure* their eighth General, ordered that they should continue singing till the Epiphany, *Glory to thee O Lord, who was born of a Virgin*, &c. He taught them also to exhort the people to salute the Virgin *Mary* at the ringing of the Bell, after the *Completory*; in memory of the Angel saluting her that hour. Pope *Gregory* the eleventh limited the power of the *Minorites* Protectors, that they should not meddle with any, except he disobey the Pope and Church, Apostatize from the Faith, and forsake his rule. *Honorius* the third decreed, that no *Minorite* should ever forsake his order. The *Minorites* obtained this favour, that they might make Masters of Divinity among themselves; whereof *Alexander de Ales* was the first. 7. The *Franciscans* did increase so fast in all parts, that from the year 1211. till the year 1380. being the space of 169. years, there were erected in *Christendom* above 1500. Monasteries of this order. *Sabellicus* recordeth that in his time were Ninety thousand *Minorites*. The cause of this increase was partly their diligence and sedulity in making Proselites, partly their privileges, and partly their pretended sanctity and mortification, but chiefly their incredible miracles and visions of *St. Francis*, which are obtruded on the peoples belief; as his five wounds, his bearing of *Christ* in his arms, his mansion in Heaven next *Christ*, and much other stuff to this purpose, with which their Legends are fraught.

Poverty, three-fold.

Of these things see the Authors above named.

8. There be three sorts of poverty among the *Mendicant Friers*; one is to have nothing, either in common or in propriety; and this is the *Franciscan* poverty, which is the greatest of all: another is which the *Dominicans* profess; that is, to have nothing in propriety, yet something in common, as books, cloaths, and food. The third is, and the least, to have somethings both in common and in propriety, but only such as necessity requires, for food and raiment; and this is the poverty of the *Carmelites* and *Augustinians*.

Q. 16. *What were the Knights of the Holy Sepulchre, and the Gladiatores?*

Knights of the Holy Sepulchre.

A. These ascribe the original of their Order to *St. James* our Lord's Brother, and Son of *Alphæus*; but it's more likely that this Order began when *Jerusalem* was taken by *Godfry of Bulloign*; at this day, it is quite extinct. When *Jerusalem* was taken by the *Soldan*, these, *Anno Christi* 1300. with all the other religious Knights of Christendom were driven out of *Syria*; yet the care of the holy Sepulchre, which these Knights had charge of, was committed to the *Franciscans* by the *Soldan*, who of all the Christian profession suffered none to stay in *Syria* and *Jerusalem*, but the *Armenians, Syrians, Georgians, Greeks,* and *Franciscans*, the Pope allows

lows eight of this Order with a Christian Knight, who is their *Guardian*, to keep the Sepulchre. The manner of installing the Knights of the Sepulchre was this: The Knights after preparation, being brought within the Sepulchre, where Hymnes are sung, and Prayers said, declares kneeling, that he is come to be made Knight of the most Holy Sepulchre of our Lord, that he was nobly descended, and had means sufficient to maintain him; withal promiseth to hear Mass daily, to expose his life and estate against the Infidels, to defend the Church of God and Ministers thereof, from their persecutors, to avoid unjust Wars, Duels, filthy Lucre, and such like, to maintain peace among Christians, to shun oppression, perjury, rapine, blasphemy, and all other grievous sins. Then the *Guardian* laying his hand on the Knights head, bids him be a stout, faithful, and a good Soldier of our Lord *Jesus Christ*, and of his holy Sepulchre. Upon this, he gives him a pair of Guilded Spurs, with a naked Sword, signing him three times with a Cross, and bidding him in the Name of the Trinity, use the Sword to his own and the Churches defence, and to the confusion of the enemies thereof; then the Sword being sheathed, is girded to the Knight by the *Guardian*; the Knight riseth, and bending his knees and bowing his head over the Sepulchre, is by the *Guardian* struck on the Shoulder three times with the Sword, saying, *I ordain thee Knight of the Holy Sepulchre of our Lord Jesus Christ, in the Name of the Father, Son, and Holy Ghost.* This he repeats three times, and crosseth him three times, then kisseth him, and puts a Golden Chain about his Neck, with a double Red Cross hanging at it; at last, the Knight having kissed the Sepulchre, the Monks present sing *Te Deum*, and after a short Prayer, he is dismissed. This order was by Pope *Innocent* the Eighth, *Anno* 1483. made one with the Knights of *Rhodes*. The order of *Gladiators* began in *Livonia* much about the time that the *Teutonicks* began in *Jerusalem*, *Anno* 1204. They were called *Gladiatores*, from carrying on their Cloak two Red Swords across. *Albert* Bishop of *Riga* began this Order, and allowed a third part of his Churches Revenues towards the Maintenance thereof. Their Habit was White, on which were woven two bloody Swords in manner of a Cross as is said; to signifie their innocency, and war-fare against the *Pagans*; whom they converted to Christianity, not only in *Riga* the Metropolis, but in most places of *Livonia*. Pope *Innocent* gave them all the Lands they could subdue there. The rule they professed was the same with that of the *Templars*; but by the Popes perswasion, both the *Cruciferi* and *Gladiators* incorporated themselves into the *Teutonick* Order.

Gladiators.

See *Crantzius L. 7. Functisius. L. 10. Munster in his Geography, Balæus cent. 4. &c.*

Q. 17. *What were the Knights of St. Mary of Redemption, of Montesia, and the order of* Illis Scholarium, *and Canons Regular of St. Mark?*

A. The Knights of St. *Mary de Mercede*, or of *Redemption*, because their charge was to redeem captives, was instituted by *James* King of *Arragon*, who in the year 1212. subdued the Isles *Baleares*.

Of S. Mary of Redemption.

ares. This order began about the year 1232. and is confirmed by *Gregory* the Ninth. They wear a White Garment, with a Black Cross. They are of the *Cistertian* order. The Knights of *Montesia,* are so called from that place in the Kingdom of *Valentia.* They were instituted much about the time of the former Knights of *St. Mary* by the same King *James,* and confirmed by the same Pope *Gregory* the Ninth; the badge of this order is a Red Cross, and are also *Cistertians.* The order of *Vallis Scholarium,* began *Anno* 1217. by one *Guilelmus Richardus,* a Scholar of *Paris,* who with *Edward* and *Manasses* professors of Divinity, betook themselves to the Desart in *Chambany,* where they set up a new order, but after the rule of St. *Austin.* They borrowed also some things of the *Cistertians,* that the Prior should visit all the Churches of his order without exacting any temporalities, that they held a general Chapter every year; that they wear no linen Shirts, nor sleep on Feathers-beds; that none eat flesh, but such as are sick and weak. The place where they first resided in was call'd *Vallis Scholarium.* This order was confirmed by Pope *Honorius* the third. The order or Congregation of St. *Mark*'s *Canons Regular* began in *Mantua,* about the year 1231.

Of Monte-sia.

Monks of Vallis Scholarium.
Monks, or St. Mark's Canons Regular.
See Panvinius in his Chronicle, and Genebrard. See also Volaterran L. 21. Balæus. Polydor, Hospinian, and others.
Nuns of St. Clara.

Q. 18. *What was the order of* St. Clara, St. Paul's Eremites, *and* Boni homines?

A. *Clara,* was of the same Town *Assisium* with *Francis,* and his intimate acquaintance; she was Daughter to *Ortulana,* who undertook Pilgrimages both to *Rome* and to the holy Sepulchre; in her child-hood she wore sack-cloth next her skin, and would never hear of Marriage. She stole away from her Parents, cut off her Hair, and could not be drawn away by any persuasions from her intended course of life. About the year 1215. at the Church of St. *Damianus* she instituted the Order of *Poor Ladies,* called from her name *Clarissa,* and from the place the Nuns of St. *Damian.* Near this Church in a Cottage she lived two and forty years, afflicting her Body with Fasting, Watchings, and all kind of hardness. Next her flesh she wore the bristly side of a Hogs skin, lay on hard boards, went bare-footed. In Lent and other Fasting times, she used only bread and water, she tasted Wine only upon Sundays; her Rule was that of the *Franciscans.* Pope *Innocent* the third, or, as others say, *Honorius* the third, confirmed this order. She could not be perswaded by Pope *Gregory* the Ninth, to reserve any of her possessions, but forsook all for Christ, as she thought. St. *Paul*'s *Eremites* in *Hungary* were instituted in the year 1215. after the rule of St. *Austin* by *Eusebius* of *Strigonia,* and was confirmed by *Gentilis* the Pope's Legate, *Anno* 1308. They came into *England,* and seated themselves in *Colchester,* *Anno* 1310. The order called *Boni Homines,* or *Boni Viri;* that is, good men was instituted by *Edmund,* Son to *Richard* Earl of *Cornwall,* who had been elected Emperour. These did follow St. *Austin's* rule, and wear a sky coloured Garment.

Eremites of St. Paul in Hungary.
Monks, or Boni Homines. See Polydor, both in his History, and in his Inventions, Frank in his Chronicles. Balæus in his Appendix. Antoninus in his Titles, &c.

Q. 19. *What*

Sect. 10. *of* EUROPE. 221

Q. 19. *What were the* Servants *of St.* Mary *the* Cœlestini, *and* Jesuati?

A. One *Philip Tudert* a *Florentine* by birth, and a Physician by profession, instituted the order of Saint *Maries Servants,* they follow the rule of St. *Austin*; they wear a short black Coat, and over that, a long black Cloak pleated about the shoulders. They were confirmed by Pope *Bennet* the eleventh, and seven other Popes after him. They are permitted to carry a Satchel or Bag to put the Alms in, which they beg. In *Italy* there be eight and forty Monasteries of these *Servants.* This order was initituted *Anno* 1282. or as others say, 1285. The *Cælestini* were so called from Pope *Cælestine* the fifth, who having before his Popedom lived an *Eremitical* life in divers Desarts, at last erected this order after the rule of St. *Bennet,* and procured it to be confirmed by Pope *Gregory* the tenth, in the General Council of *Lyons.* Their habit is of sky colour with a Hood. *Cælestine* their Author being elected Pope, and cheated out of it by *Boniface* the eighth, who by a cane and a hole in the Wall, spake to him to relinquish his Popedom; which he did, thinking an Angel had spoken to him: I say, *Cælestine* returned again to his Eremitical life, which he could not long enjoy; for Pope *Boniface* put him in prison upon Jealousie, where he died. These Monks came into *England, Anno* 1414. The *Iesuati* began at *Sena* by *John Columbanus,* and *Francis Vincent, Anno* 1365. they were called *Jesuati* from using the name of *Jesus* often in their Mouths. Pope *Urban* the fifth, approved them, and enjoyned them to wear a White Garment, a White cover for their head, a leather girdle, and to go bare-footed, using only wooden soles. These Monks were afterwards called *Apostolici.*

Monks or St. Maries *servants.*

Monks, or Cælestini.

Monks, or Jesuati. See Frank in Chron. Sabellicus Enne. 9. Crantzius, L. 9. Volaterranus L. 21 Polidor, L 7. Surius Tom. 3. De Vit. Sanct. &c.

Q. 20. *What was the Order of Saint* Bridget?

A. Bridget not that of *Scotland,* who lived about the year, 530. but a Princess of *Sweden, Anno* 1360. obtained a confirmation of her Order (which she received immediately from Christ, as she said) by Pope *Urban* the fifth. Her Rule was according to that of St. *Basil's.* The Monks and Nuns may have their Convents continguous, and the same Church, but the Brothers must officiate below, the Sisters above. Both Sexes must use gray cloaks and coats, with a red cross thereon. They must have nothing in propriety, touch no money, must lie only upon straw. The fashion, colour, and measure of their cloaths are set down; on their Veil they must wear a white linen Crown, on which are sowed pieces of red cloath, representing drops of blood, and so placed that they may resemble the cross. The Sisters are enjoyned how to officiate, and what prayers they shall use every day, to be silent, to avoid conference with men, except it be at a window, upon urgent occasion, on Sundays and great Festivals, and that only from nine till the vening. She that openeth not her Window at all, shall have the greater reward in Heaven. Days of Fasting are prescribed them; none must be admitted into the Order, without a years probation:

Monks and Nuns of S. Bridget's Order.

Then

Then she muſt be examined and conſecrated by the Biſhop, who is to bring her into the Church with a Red Croſs carried before her, having the Crucifix on the one ſide, and the Virgins Image on the other, to put her in mind of Patience, and Chaſtity: two Tapers burning muſt be carried before the Croſs; then the Biſhop conſecrates a Ring, and prayeth. She having teſtified her conſtant Reſolution to that kind of life, the Biſhop by putting the Ring on her finger, Marrieth her to Chriſt, and prayeth; ſhe comes to the Altar and offers, then returns to her place again. Her new Cloaths are alſo conſecrated, and ſhe is called by the Prieſt to come bare-footed to the Altar, the Biſhop prayeth again, and withal puts on her the coat of her profeſſion, her ſhooes, hood, and cloak, which he tieth with a wooden button, in memory of Chriſts wooden Croſs, to which her mind ſhould be faſtned. Then her Veil was put on, the Biſhop at every action, and parcel of her cloathes prayeth, and at laſt her Crown, the Biſhop praying that ſhe may be crowned with joy. She returns to her place, and is called again to the Altar, where ſhe falls on her face, the Biſhop with his Prieſts read the *Litany*, abſolves her, and gives her the Euchariſt; her Coffin which during the time of the Maſs ſtood there, is carried by four Siſters, ſprinkling duſt on it, into the Convent; at the gate whereof ſtands the Abbateſs with her *Nuns*, the Biſhop with two Tapers carried before him, and the Prieſts ſinging, brings the new *Nun*, and recommends her to the care of the *Abbateſs*, which ſhe receives, ſhuts the Gate, and brings her into the Chapter. The firſt eight days ſhe is tyed to no Diſcipline. At Table and in the Quire ſhe ſitteth laſt. The number of the Siſters is ſixty, and no more. Thirteen Prieſts according to the number of the Apoſtles, whereof Saint *Paul* was one; four *Evangeliſts*, or Preachers; repreſenting the four Doctors of the Church, *Ambroſe*, *Auſtin*, *Gregory*, and *Hierom*; and eight Lay-men. All theſe together make up the number of the thirteen Apoſtles, and 72. Diſciples. The Prieſts Garments ſhall be of courſe gray, on which ſhall be worn a red Croſs, and in the mid'ſt a round piece of white cloath, to reſemble the Hoſt which they daily offer. The four *Evangeliſts* ſhall carry on their Cloaks a white circle, to ſhew the incomprehenſible Wiſdom of the four Doctors which they repreſent. Within theſe circles Red pieces of cloath ſhall be inſerted like Tongues cloven, to ſhew, their Learning and Eloquence. The Lay-brothers ſhall wear on their cloaks a white Croſs, to ſhew Chriſts innocency, with five pieces of red cloath, in memory of Chriſts five wounds. The number of Brothers in the Convent, muſt not exceed five and twenty, who are to be bleſſed by the Biſhop, after the ſame manner that the Siſters were; but inſtead of a Ring, the Biſhop ſhall hold the Prieſt by the hand, and for a Vail, ſhall lay his hands on his head; and inſtead of a Crown, ſhall uſe the ſign of the Croſs. The Abbateſs ſhall be among the thirteen Prieſts, as *Mary* was among the Apoſtles; ſhe ſhall have for Confeſſor, him whom the Biſhop alloweth. Confeſſion muſt be made at leaſt three times yearly, and

every

every day if need be, to such Priests as the Confessor shall chuse; the Priest shall be diligent in Preaching, Praying, and Fasting. Every Thursday shall be a Chapter held, wherein the Delinquent Sisters may be punished with Fasting, standing without doors in the Church yard, whilst the other Sisters are within at Divine Service, and with prostrating her self on the ground, till the Abbatess take her up, and intercede for her Absolution. If a Sister possess any thing in propriety, and dieth before she confesseth it, her Body is layed on a Bier at the Church door, where they also say an *Ave-Mary* for her, and then is absolved, and after Mass is carried from the Quire to the Church door by the Sisters, where the Brothers receive her, and bury her. Neither the Abbatess, nor any Sister must receive gifts or have any thing in proper. Every one after the first foundation, must bring their yearly revenues to be imployed by the Abbatess, but after the number of Sisters is filled, and a Revenue settled, they that came after need bring nothing. If any die, her cloaths and allowance in dyet shall be given to the poor, till another be choosen. Every year before the Feast of *All Saints* let there be an Audit of Expences kept; if any thing remain over and above the expences, let it be reserved for the next years expences, or bestowed on the poor, on whom also the Nuns old cloaths must be conferred. Every Novice must bring a Present or Alms gift to the Convent, but nothing that hath been got by oppression, cheating, stealing, or any other sinistrous means; such gifts must be restored again, and so must gifts doubtfully got be rejected; and if the Convent stand not in need of any present, let it be given to the poor. In every Church must be thirteen Altars, on each of which one Chalice, but on the high Altar two Chalices, two pair of Flaggons, so many candlesticks, one cross, three censers, one for daily use, the other two for solemn Feasts, a *Cibary* for the Host; let there be no Gold nor Silver in the Convent, except where the Holy Reliques are kept; let every one have her office or service-Book, and as many other Books as they will, for good Arts; Let each Altar have two Altar-cloaths; Let no Sisters be admitted under eighteen, nor Priest or Brother under five and twenty years of age; Let the Sisters imploy their time in devotion, labouring with their hands and about their own affairs, after the manner of Christ and his Mother; Let Rich and Poor have the same measure of Meat and Drink; and let not any afflict their body too much; for not their own correction, but gods mercy must save them. Let the Sisters confess at the Lattess of the windows, where they may be heard, but not seen; but in receiving the Eucharist, they may be heard and seen. But they must do nothing without the leave of the Abbatess, and some witnesses, except in time of confession. Priests must not enter the Nunnery, except to give the Sacrament in the Agony of death, and that with some witnesses; all the Priests and Brothers may enter to perform Funeral obsequies. The Bishop of the Diocess must be the Father and Visitor of the Monasteries and Nunneries, the Prince of the Territory

tory shall be the Protector, and the Pope the faithful Guardian; without whose will no Convent shall be made. Let there be a hole like a grave still open in the Convent, that the Sisters may pray every day there with the Abbatess (taking up a little dust between her fingers) that God who preserved Christs body from the Corruption of the grave, who would also preserve both their bodies and souls from the corruption of sin. Let there be a Bier or Coffin at the Church door with some earth, that all commers-in, may remember they are dust, and to dust shall return: to the observers of this rule Christ promiseth his aid, who revealed himself to St. *Briget*, and councels her to convey it to the Pope to be confirmed. So goeth *the story, as it is set down by* Hospinian, *who translated it out of the* German *into the* Latine *tongue: this Order came into* England, Anno 1414. *and was placed at* Richmond. *There be few of these elsewhere, except in* Sweden.

See *Antoninus*, B.1. *Isus, Nauclerus*, *Trithemius Cranzius*, &c.

Q. 21. *What was the Order of* S. Katherine, *and of* S. Justina ?

St. Katherine of Senae.

A. *Katherine* born in *Senae* in *Tuscany*, in her Childhood vowed Virginity; and in a dream saw *Dominick* with a Lily in his hand, and other Religious Founders, wishing her to profess some of their Orders. She embraced that of *Dominick*, in which she was so strict, that she abhorred the Smell of Flesh, drunk only Water, and used no other cheer but Bread and raw Herbs. She lay upon boards in her cloaths. She girt her self so close with an Iron Chain, that it cut her skin; she used to watch whole nights together, and scarce slept half an hour in two days, in imitation of *S. Dominick*. She used to chastise her self three times every day with that Iron Chain, for an hour and half at a time, so that the blood run from her shoulders to her feet. One chastisement was for her self, the other for the dead, and the third for those that were alive in the World. Many *strange stories are recorded of her, as that Christ appeared and Married himself to her with a Ring; that he opened her side, took out her old Heart, and put a new one in stead of the former; that he cloathed her with a bloody coloured garment, drawn out of the wound in his side; so that she never felt any cold afterwards: and divers other tales to this purpose.* Some say this order began *Anno* 1372. others *Anno* 1455. The Nuns of this order wear a white garment, and over it a black Veil, with a head-covering of the same colour. The order of St. *Justina*, was instituted by *Ludovicus Barbus*, a *Venetian*, *Anno* 1409. after the ancient discipline of *Benedict*. This rule was enlarged by *Eugenius* the fourth, and confirmed by *John* 24. The Monks of this order are careful not to eat out of the Convent with seculars, and to wash the Feet of strangers.

Nuns of St. Katherine.

Monks of St. Justina.

See Frank in Chron. Polyd.Virg. Hospinian, Antoninus. Franc. Mydius, &c.

Eremites of St. Hierom.

Q. 22. *What were the Eremites of Saint* Hierom, *of Saint Saviour, the* Albati, Fratricelli, Turlupini, *and* Montolivetenses ?

A. St. *Hierom*'s Eremites in *Spain*, under St. *Austin*'s rule was instituted about the year 1366. in *Urbinum* a City of *Umbria* in *Italy* in the time of Pope *Gregory* the ninth, and was confirmed by *Gregory* the twelfth. Of this order there is in *Italy* five and twenty Convents. They differ in their habit, and other things, little or nothing

thing from the other Monks of St. *Hierom*. The Canons of St. *Saviour* were inſtituted alſo in *Italy*, near *Senæ*, in a place called *Scopetum*, whence they are named *Scopetini*. They follow St. *Auſtin*'s rule. Their Author was one *Francis* of *Bononia*, Anno 1366. in the time of Pope *Urban* the fifth, and were confirmed by his ſucceſſor, *Gregory* the eleventh, Anno 1370. They wear a white Cloak, with a white Hood above a white linen Gown. *Albati* were ſo called from the white linen they wore; theſe in the time of Pope *Boniface* the Ninth, Anno 1399, came down from the *Alpes* into *Luca*, *Flaminia*, *Hetruria*, *Piſa*, and other places of *Italy*, having for their guide a Prieſt cloathed in white, and carrying in his hand the Crucifix: He pretended ſo much Zeal in Religion, that he was held a Saint. *Theſe People increaſed to ſuch a vaſt body, that* Boniface *the Ninth grew Jealous, their Prieſt aimed at the Popedom; therefore ſent out ſome armed men againſt them, apprehended their Prieſt, and put him to death; upon which the whole multitude fled, every Man returning to his houſe.* Theſe made profeſſion of Sorrow, weeping for the ſins and calamities of thoſe times; they eat together in the High-ways, and ſlept all promiſcuouſly together like beaſts: they are by moſt reckoned among the *Hereticks*, and not religious Orders, and ſo are the *Fratricelli*, or *Beghardi*; who would be counted the third Order of *Franciſcans*; they were called *Fratricellæ*, Brothers of the Cells and Caves where they dwelt. Their Women were named *Beghinæ*, and *Beguttæ*. Theſe ſprung up Anno 1208. they went with their faces covered, and their heads hanging down; their lives were flagitious, and their opinions heretical, as we have already ſhewed among the Hereſies; therefore they are condemned by *Boniface* the eighth, *Clement* the fifth, and *John* the twenty ſecond: yet *Gregory* the eleventh, and *Eugenius* the fourth, defended ſuch of them, againſt whoſe life and faith, no juſt exceptions could be taken: *Gregory* about the year 1378, *Eugenius*, Anno 1431. The *Turlupini* alſo, though they would have been thought a religious order, were heretical in their Tenets, and therefore condemned and burned, Anno 1372. *Montolivetenſes*, or Monks of Mount *Olivet* began 1407, when the Church was divided between three Popes. In this diſtracted time many of *Senæ* betook themſelves to the next Hill, which they called Mount *Olivet*, and cloathed themſelves in white, profeſſing St. *Bennet*'s rule. They were confirmed by Pope *Gregory* the twelfth. There were others of the ſame name long before theſe, but *Boniface* the eighth, Anno 1300. put them down, and executed their Author at *Viterbium*; he only wore a linen cloath about his waſt, the reſt of his body naked.

Q. 23. *What were the Canons of St. George, the Mendicants of St. Hierom, the Canons of Laterane, Order of the Holy Ghoſt, of St. Ambroſe ad Nemus, and of the Minimi of Jeſu Maria?*

A. The *Canons Regular of St. George*, called alſo *Apoſtolici*, were inſtituted by *Laurence Juſtinian*, Patriarch of *Venice*, Anno 1407.

they were confirmed by *Gregory* the twelfth. They wear a linen Surplice over their Garments, and a black hood, but out of the Cloyster they wear a black Cloak, with a black Hat. There be two orders more of this name; the one wear white, the other blue; they abstain from Flesh, except in their sickness, and are not tyed by Vows to their profession. The Mendicants of St. *Hierom* were instituted by *Carolus Florentinus*, *Anno* 1407. and are confirmed by *Gregory* the twelfth: they profess St. *Austin*'s Rule; they wear dark-coloured cloaths, and over their Coat a pleated Cloak divided, they use a leathern girdle, and wooden Shooes. The Canons of *Lateran* make St. *Austin* their Author; these were expulsed, St. *John Lateran*, by Pope *Calixtus*, after they had been seated there by *Eugenius* the fourth, who expelled the *Seculars* thence; but *Paul* the second, called back the *Regulars*, and by degrees expelled the *Seculars*. Their Cloak, Scapulars, and Hood are black. The order of the *Holy Ghost* was instituted near *Venice*, by *Gabriel* of *Spoletum*, *Anno* 1407. They use the same Habit that the *Canons Regular* do wear. The Brothers of St. *Ambrose ad Nemus*, were instituted at *Milan*; and confirmed, *Anno* 1433. They wear dark coloured Cloaths, and profess St. *Austin*'s rule. The *Minimi* of *Jesu Maria*, were instituted by one *Francis Paula*, a *Cicilian*, *Anno* 1471. he made three rules; one for the Brothers, another for the Sisters, and the third for both Sexes called *Tartiarii*. He would have the Brothers to be called *Minimi*, and the Sisters *Minimæ*, to teach them humility. They were enjoyned to keep the Ten Commandments, to observe the Church Laws, to obey the Pope, and to preserve in their Vows of Chastity, Poverty, Obedience, and Fasting. This was allowed by *Julius* the second, *Innocent* the eighth, *Sixtus* the fourth, *Alexander* the sixth, and *Leo* the tenth. They abstain altogether from flesh, they wear only course linen, and wander up and down bare-headed, and bare-foot.

Mendicants of S. Hierom.

Canons of Lateran.

Monks of the Order of the Holy Ghost.

Of S. Ambrose ad Nemus.

Monks or Minimi of Jesu Maria.

See *Surius Tom.* 2. *de vit. Sanct.* with other Authors already named.

Q. 24. *What Orders of Knight-hood were there erected in Christendom after the year* 1400 ?

A. The Knights of the Annunciation of *Mary*, by *Amadeus* the fifth, Earl of *Savoy*, and first Duke thereof, *Anno* 1420. of this Order we have already spoken. The Order of *Maurician* Knights was instituted by *Amadeus* the seventh, *Anno* 1490. to the honour of St. *Maurice*, whose Ring was delivered to *Peter* Earl of *Savoy*, that by him he might be conveyed to his successors, as a Badge of their Right to, and Soveraignty over that Countrey. The Knights of the Golden Fleece were instituted by *Philip* the good Duke of *Burgundy*, and Father to *Charles*, whom the *Switzers* defeated and flew. This *Philip* on his Wedding-day, with *Isabel* the King of *Portugal*'s daughter, erected this Order, *Anno* 1429. which he called by the name of the Golden Fleece, in memory of *Jason*, and those other Worthies, who ventured their lives for that Golden Fleece, to encourage Christians to venture their lives like courageous *Argonautes*, for the Defence and Honour of the Catholick

Knights of the Annunciation.

Of Saint Maurice.

Of the Golden Fleece.

lick Church. There were appointed thirty one Knights of this Order, the chief whereof was the Duke of that Dukedom. "Of these Knights we have spoken already in the History of the World; in the Impression by me owned, as before is mentioned. The Knights of the *Moon* were instituted by *Reiner*, Duke *Of the Moor* of *Anjou*, when he obtained the Kingdom of *Sicily*, *Anno* 1464. These Knights wore a silver half Moon on their Arm, and were bound to defend one another in all dangers, and never to fall at Variance among themselves. The Knights of Saint *Michael* the Arch-Angel were instituted by *Lewis* the French King, *Anno* 1469. These wear a Golden Chain, at which hanged the Image of Saint *Michael* treading on the Infernal Dragon. This picture his *Of Saint* Father, *Charles* the seventh, wore in his Banners; and it is worn *Michael.* by his Posterity, in memory of Saint *Michael*, who was seen in the Battel at the bridge of *Orleans*, fighting against the *English*, whom he forced to raise their Siege. The King appointed there should be of this Order 36 Knights, whereof himself should be the first. They are tied to hear Mass every day. The Knights of Saint *Stephen* were instituted by *Cosmo* Duke of *Florence*, and *Of Saint* confirmed by Pope *Pius* the fourth, *Anno* 1561; in imitation of *Stephen.* the Knights of *Malta*. They differ from the *Johannites*, that instead of a white, they wear a red Cross set in Gold. They may also marry once, which the *Johannites* could not do. Their seat is in *Ilua* an Island in the *Ligustick* Sea. They are called Saint *Stephen's* Knights, not from *Stephen* the first Martyr, but from *Stephen* Bishop of *Florence*, who was canonized, or from Pope *Stephen*. The Knights of the *Holy Spirit* were instituted by *Henry Of the Holy* the *French* King, *Anno* 1579. Of the Knights of St. *George* in *Spirit.* *England*, or of the *Garter* instituted by King *Edward* the third, *Anno* 1351. And of the Knights of the *Star*, set up by King *John* the first of *France*, in memory of that *Star* which appeared at Christ's Nativity, the Knights also of *Jesus Christ* in *Portugal*, and of the Knights of *Alcanthara* in *Castile*, we have already spoken. He that will see more, let him Read *Panvinius in Chron. Sabellicus, Enne. 9. Crantzius. L. 9. Frank in Chron. Polyd. L. 7. Volaterran L. 21. Girard. Hist. Lib. 15. Baleus Cent. 5. Heutereus L. 4. rer. Burgund. Tilius, Hist. Franc. Genebrard. in Chron. Hospinian de orig. Monach.* and the Continuation of Sir *Walter Raleigh's* History of the World, *in the Edition by me owned.*

The Contents of the Eleventh Section.

Of Religious Orders and Opinions from the Year 1500. *till this day.* 2. *The Order of* Jesuites. 3. *Of their general Rules.* 4. *Of their other Rules.* 5. *Of their Rules for Provosts of Houses, Rectors of Colleges*, &c. 6. *Of their Rules for Travellers, Ministers, Admonitors*, &c. 7. *Of their privileges granted by Popes.* 8. *Of other Orders in the Church of* Rome. 9. *How Abbots are consecrated at this time.* 10. *Wherein the Christian Orders of Knight-hood differ.* 11. *Of other Orders of Knight-hood besides the French.* 12. *Of the Orders of Knight hood in* Germany, Hungary, Bohemia, Poland, &c. 13. *The Orders of Knight-hood in* Italy. 14. *Of the Christian Military Orders in the East.*

SECT. XI.

Quest. I. **W**Hat *Religious Orders and Opinions in Religion are there sprung up in these latter times, that is, from the Year* 1500. *till this day, in the Christian World?*

Orders of Poor Pilgrims.

A. In the Year 1500. started up a new Order, called *Poor Pilgrims*; these came out of *Italy* into *Germany* bare-foot, and bare-headed; some covered their Bodies with Linen, others with Gray cloth, carrying every one in his hand a wooden Cross, but without scrip or bag, staff or money; drinking neither wine nor beer; feeding all the week, except on Sunday, upon Herbs and Roots sprinkled with Salt: They abstained altogether from Eggs, Butter, Milk, Cheese, Fish, and Flesh. In the Church they stretch out their Arms in manner of a Cross, and Praying fell flat on the ground. They stayed not above four and twenty hours in any place, they went by couples begging from Door to Door. Among them were Divers Priests, Deacons, and Sub-Deacons: this Pennance they undertook voluntarily, some for three years, others for five or seven; as they pleased, and at the end of their years returned home, and betook themselves again to their callings: They excluded from their Pilgrimage only Monks and Women. About six years after, was instituted the Order of *Indians*, under Pope *Julius* the second, and *Maximilian* the first Emperour. "These were of the *Carmelite* Race; and were "called *Indians*, as I suppose from their Intention, to convert the "*Indians* then Discovered: They wore black cloaths, and over them white Gowns, as appears by that Verse of *France, Medius: Qui tegimus pura pallia pulla toga.* Under Pope *Clement* the seventh was instituted the Order of *The Society of Divine Love*; these were

Of Indians.

Devout

Devout people, who met in retired places, remote from the com- *Of Divine* pany of the vulgar: here they Prayed, Sung, Adminiſtred the Sa- *Love, or* craments, and did other Acts of Devotion; they were called alſo *Theatini.* Theatini from *Theatinum*; the Biſhoprick of which place was rejected by *John Peter Carraſa*, that he might the more freely enjoy that Devout life, and give himſelf the more ſeriouſly to contemplate Divine Myſteries, and to regain the Honour of the Clergy, ſo much degenerated from their former Integrity. He refuſed alſo the Biſhoprick of *Brunduſium*, which Charles the Fifth would have conferred upon him, yet afterwards he was content to change his Name from *John Peter* to *Paul* the fourth, and to accept the Popedom. Of this Society alſo were *Cajetan* the *Apoſtolical Protonotarie*, *Boniface* a Noble man of *Piemont*, and one *Paul* a *Roman*. In the Year 1537. was inſtituted the Order of *Paulini*, by a cer- *Of Paulini.* tain Counteſs called *Gaſtalia* at *Mantua*, hence her Diſciples were named *Gaſtalini*. The Brothers and Siſters of this Sect were by their own ſtrength thus to tame their fleſh; they were to lie two and two together in one bed, but with a cross laid between the *See Hoſpi-* man and the woman, that they might not touch one the other. *nian Franc.* This courſe they were to uſe ſo long, till they had quite ſubdued *Modius,* the tickling of the fleſh. But this order laſted not long; for the *Nauclerus,* inconveniences found in it occaſioned the extirpation thereof. *and others.*

Q. *What is the Order of the* Jeſuites?
A. This Order which is called the *Society* of *Jeſus*, (becauſe *Of Jeſuites.* they take upon them to advance the Name, Doctrine, and Honour of *Jeſus* more than other Orders heretofore,) was inſtituted about the year 1540. by *Ignatius Loyola of Cantabria*, who being *Ignatius* at firſt a Souldier, and receiving ſome wound in the *French* War, *Loyola.* of which he lay ſick above a year, reſolved upon recovery of his health, to renounce the world; and wholly to addict himſelf to the advancing of the name of *Jeſus*, for this cauſe being ſix and twenty years of age, he forſakes all, and travels to *Jeruſalem*; thence (having done his devotion to the holy Sepulchre) returns into *Spain*, where at *Complutum* and *Salamantica*, he gives himſelf to ſtudy; in the interim he took upon him to preach Mortification, both by his Doctrine and mean Habit, Though as yet he was furniſhed neither with ſufficient Learning, nor was he called; wherefore he was impriſoned, and examined by the Inquiſitors, and being found Zealous for the Roman Faith, was diſmiſſed, and thence goeth to Paris, where he ſtudied ten years in great poverty and weakneſs of body, and was at laſt made Maſter of Arts. In the year 1536. he returns to *Spain* with ten more of his profeſſion, and from thence to *Rome*, to have Leave of the Pope to Travel to *Jeruſalem*; but finding the peace broken between the *Turk* and *Venetian*, they go to *Venice*, and there did dreſs the Wounds and Sores of poor people in Hoſpitals. Seven of theſe ten companions of *Ignatius* took the Prieſt-hood upon them, and Preached up and down the Territories of *Venice*, having neither Temporal nor Eccleſiaſtical means to ſuſtain them. After this they all go to *Rome*, where they are hated and moleſted by

by the Clergy, yet their Society increased daily, and procured a Confirmation of their Order from Pope *Paul* the third, which since was ratified by *Julius* the third, *Paul* the fourth, *Pius* the fourth; and the Council of *Trent*. At first they were not to have " above sixty of their Society, but afterward the Pope perceiving " how needful this Order was to the decaying *Roman* Religion, " permitted all that were fit to enter into the same. They have their Chief or General, their Coadjutors in Spiritual things, such are their Priests, and Professors of Divinity, Philosophy, and inferiour Arts. Their Coadjutors in Temporals, who look to their cloathing, dyet, and domestick affairs; their Scholars and Novices are maintained, lest this Order or Society might fail, who are bound to obey their Superiours without doubting or inquiring into the nature of the thing enjoyned them. " This Order differs from " others, in that besides the three ordinary Vows of Chastity, Po- " verty, and Obedience, they bind themselves to the Pope, in un- " dertaking chearfully, readily, and without charging them, any " journey he shall command for propagating the *Roman* Faith. The title also of Professor among them is more honourable than of Priests; for one may be a Priest many years, before he be admitted Professor. The *Jesuites*, instead of a Hood, wear a Philosophical Cloak, that is long and black; their Cap resembling a Cross is called *Bareta*; this they do not wear abroad; their Cassocks they call *Solannas*, which they tye with silk girdles, and they spread so fast over the world, that above sixty years ago they had 256. Colleges.

See Christianus Franken in Colloq. Jesuit. Surius, Hospinian, &c.

Q. 3. *What be the general Rules to which the* Jesuites *are tyed?*

Jesuites, their Rules.

A. To examine their Conscience twice daily; to be Diligent in Prayer, Meditation, and Reading; to be daily at Divine Service, at the times appointed to confess their Sins; to renew their Vows every Year twice; to be abstinent on Fridays, not to preach without the Superiors leave; nor to keep Money by them, nor to have any thing in proper; To read no Books without leave, nor to meddle with any thing that is not theirs; To learn the language of the country where they live; not to lock their Chests, or Chamber doors; Not to sleep in the night with window open, or naked, or to go out of their Chamber without their Clothes; Not to teach or learn without the Superiors leave; Not to drink between meals, or to eat abroad without leave, or to take Physick, or to consult with the Physician, till they be permitted by the Superior; to hearken to the Bell when it rings; to keep their Beds neat, and Chambers clean; To acquaint the Superior, when any is grievously tempted; To be obedient, humble, and reverent in uncovering the head to their Superiors, not to complain of one Superior to another; To be silent, or else to speak briefly, with moderation and submission; To avoid contentions, contradictions, or speaking evil of one anothers Native Country; let him only reprove and command who is authorized so to do. Let none enter into another mans place, office, or Chamber, without leave; whilst

two

Sect. 11. *of* EUROPE. 231

two are in one Chamber, let the door stand open: Let no man mock another, Let no Man at Table put off his hat, except to his Superiour; No talk with strangers, or commerce by letters without leave; Let no man report idle rumours, nor divulge abroad what is done at home. None without leave may write any thing of instruction or consolation, nor meddle at all with secular affairs. Every one ought to instruct and exhort his Brother to confess; Let none go abroad without leave, and he must shew the cause of his going abroad, and what effect it took, when he doth return; he must also write down his name, and acquaint the Porter whither he goeth, and must return before night. That when any travelleth he shall lodge no where but in a *Jesuits* College, if there be any in that place; and shall be as obedient to the Superiour there, as to his own. Let every one have these rules by him, that he may read, or hear them read, once every month. But the Coadjutors must read their rules every week. They have also their constitutions, wherein is shewed that the end of their Society is to do good to their own souls and the Souls of their Neighbours, and that therefore they are bound to travel to and fro in the World; to confess their sins to the Priest every sixth Month, and then to receive the body of Christ; to cast off all inordinate affections of Kindred, Friends, and Worldly things, to deny themselves, to take up the Cross of Christ, and to follow him; to study Humility, to aim at Perfection and all other Virtues, chiefly Charity; to have a special care of the inward man; to imbrace Poverty with chearfulness, to give freely of their Spiritual things, as they have received freely; to study purity and chastity; and to be very vigilant over their senses, chiefly over the eyes and tongue. To be temperate, modest, decent, and devout in all things, chiefly at table. To labour diligently for Obedience, and to refuse nothing that the superiour shall command. In confession to conceal nothing from the Ghostly Father. To study unity and conformity in judgments, and affections. To avoid Idleness and secular affairs. To be careful to preserve health, and to avoid all excess that may impair it, as too much watching, fasting, labouring, or any other outward pennance, and in sickness to be humble, patient and devout. To desire the Superiour once every year that he would enjoyn them some Pennance for their failings in the observation of their rules and constitutions, which ought to be heard or read every Month. *Of these passages see the Jesuites Rules printed together in one Book at Lyons, Anno 1607.*

Q. 4. *What other Rules have they besides the common Rules and Constitutions?*

A. They have Rules for every particular Officer amongst them. As the Provincials Rule is to use diligence, fidelity, mildness, bounty tempered with severity in his government, to alter or add nothing in the rules and customs of the Province, without the consent of the General; in his absence or sickness, he may name (if the General do not) a Subprovincial; he must always have with him four Counsellors, with whom he may advise in matters of weight. *Jesuites, their constitutions and rules for Provincials.*

Q 4

weight. He hath power to chuse divers Officers, such as Masters of the Novices, the Governours in spiritual things, Confessors, Preachers, and Readers, &c. He may dispense in divers things, and admit such as he thinks fit for probation; and may dismiss also in some cases, if the General hinder not: None must be admitted, who have forsaken the Society, or dismissed, without a new examination and probation; he is to take care of the Masters and Teachers in Schools and Colleges, what proficiency there is, what Books are Read, who are to study Divinity, and the Learned Tongues; that no Stage-plays be acted, but in Latin, and such as are modest, &c. He must confer no degrees in Divinity or Philosophy without the General's leave. The degree or title of Master and Doctor, must not be used among them. He may chuse Coadjutors in Spiritual and Temporal affairs. He must look to the Edifices, Revenues, and Lands of the society within his Province; to avoid Sutes in Law, yet to maintain their Rights by Law, if need be; to look to all expenses and accounts, to avoid running in Debt, and to have a care of the Wardrobe, and all the Utensils; that if any Lands or goods be given to the society, the General be acquainted therewith, and some share thereof be given to the poor of that place, where the Goods or Lands are. He is to be obedient, faithful, and reverent to his General; to call Provincial Assemblies at fit times, and to help other Provinces when need requires. To see that Masses be had, and Sacraments administred according to the custom of the *Roman* Church; That Preachers and Confessors do their duties; That none be made Confessors, chiefly to Women, but such as are well struck in years; That in time of Infection he appoint such as may look to the sick; That he depart not out of his Province without the General's leave; nor the Provost or rector from his House, or College without leave from the Provincial. That he be careful what Labourers he sends abroad into the Lord's Vineyard; that he give them full instructions; that they travel on foot rather than ride. He must visit every place within his Province once a year, and first the Church, the place where the Eucharist is kept, the holy Oyl, the Relicks, *Altars*, Seats of the Confessors, &c. then the persons, with whom he must deal prudently: and lastly the Superiour of the House or College.

Of these passages see more fully in the forenamed Book.

Q. 5. *What Rules have they for the Provosts of Houses, Rectors of Colleges, Masters of Novices and Counsellours,* &c.

Jesuites, their rules for Provosts.

A. The Provost is bound to observe the common and particular rules; as also, all customs approved by the General or Provincial, to be careful of his Under-Officers, and Confessors; to impose ordinary pennance, such as publick reproof, to eat under the table, to kiss the feet of others, to pray in the refectory, to impose fasting, &c. He must have a Book, in which he must record what concerns the good of his House. He must see rules and constitutions of the House be duly observed. That confessions be

Sect. 11. *of* EUROPE.   233

be made at the appointed times. That Scholars and Coadjutors not formed, renew their Vows twice a year. That every other *Friday* he make an exhortation to obedience, pennance, patience, charity, humility, and other vertues. That he carry himself sweetly and wifely to his inferiours, moderate in reproving and punishing; to send (if occasion be) one whom may beg alms from door to door, for the Hospital, or who may accompany the Caterer, or who may preach in the streets. He must chiefly preserve love and unity in his House, and must read all Letters, that are either sent to, or from any under his charge, and must suffer none to have a Seal, without the Provincial's leave; let there be no arms nor musical instruments, nor wanton of Books, nor idle recreations within his house. The Provost may, if need be, preach and hear confessions, but must not suffer Priests of the Society to preach, and hear the Nuns confessions, except upon extraordinary occasion. He must take care that all spiritual exercises be duly performed, and divine service every day. Let there be seven hours allotted for sleep, and eight hours between dinner and supper. Let the Table be blessed, and thanks given according to the *Roman Breviary.* Let an hour be allowed for recreation after Dinner and Supper, and on *Friday* after evening collation half an hour, Let there be conferences touching cases of Conscience held twice a week, at which all the Priests should be present. Let there be an account taken every Month of what is received and expended in the House. Special care must be had of those that labour in the Lord's Vineyard, that they may not want. If any thing of moment is to be done in the House, let the Provincial be acquainted therewith. Let no Man keep a Horse, except upon urgent Occasion, and with the General's leave. Women must not be permitted to enter into the house. Lands given by Will must be sold for the use of the Society, but not without the General's leave. Let no Man walk abroad without a Companion; let Travellers of the Society be entertained kindly, &c. The Rectors of Colleges also have their Rules, which are in a manner the same with those of the Provosts. Which Rules and Constitutions, must be read twice or thrice a year in the Refectory. The Examiner also of those that desire admission, hath his Rules; he must be a man skilful and discreet, who must signifie to his Superiour how he finds the party affected and qualified. If unfit, he must be chearfully dismissed; if fit, he must ask him if he be resolved to forsake the World? and why? and what induced him to be of this Society; if he be in debt, or subject to any Infirmity; what is his Age, his Country, his Parents, and their condition; if he be born in Marriage, of Christian Parents, or of Hereticks; if he be a Scholar, where? and how long he hath studied? if he will be a Coadjutor, and content with *Martha's* Lot? then he must be well instructed in the constitutions and Rules of the Society. The Master of the Novices by his Rules is tyed to be Courteous and Loving to his Novices, to help, comfort, and instruct them upon all occasions;

The Rules for Rectors of Colleges and the Examiner.

Their Rules for Masters of the Novices.

occasions; he hath power in some cases to enjoyn Pennance on them, and in some cases to absolve them. He must also be well exercised in *Basil's*, Rules, *Gregorie's* Morals, *Austin's* Confessions and Meditations, in *Bernard*, *Bonaventure*, *Cassian*, *Dorotheus* his Homilies, *Cæsarius*, *Ephraim*, *Hugo* and *Richard de S. Victore*, *Umbertus de Eruditione Religiosorum*, *Innocentius* of contempt of the World, *Thomas de Kempis* of the Imitation of Christ, and such like Books; for Histories, he must read *Gregorie's* Dialogues, *Gregory Turonensis* of the Glory of confessors, and Life of St. *Martin*, *Eusebius*, his Ecclesiastick History, *Sulpitius* of Saint *Martin's* life, the select Lives of the Fathers, the Lives of *Lippoman*, and *Surius*, *Pet. Damianus*, *Pet. Cluniacensis* of Miracles, the *Indian* Letters and the Life of *Ignatius*. The Probationer for the first three weeks is to be used as a Guest: in which time he is to be instructed in the rules and constitutions of the house: Then must be examined, and must promise that in a Years space after his Entrance he shall part with all his estate: If he be a Scholar, he must read some lectures; if no Scholar, he shall do some handy-work. A General confession must be also made; what he brings with him into the house must be inventoried in a Book, where the Day and year of his Entrance, with his Country, must be registred, and subscribed with his own hand; he must also perform some spiritual exercises in his second probation, and he must be tried how he can serve for a Month; and then for another Month, he must be imployed in Begging from Door to Door, to shew how willing he is for the love of Christ, to forsake all worldly hopes. And for a fourth experiment, he must be exercised in some base employments, about the house. After this he shall be imployed in teaching the Ignorant and Children the Doctrine of Christianity, and must be tired with mean Cloaths and Diet, and with moderate Pennance also: And must be instructed in the practice of Devotion and Mortification, and Modesty, and must be made a chamber fellow to one by whom he may profit. He must not speak with his kindred without leave and witnesses, and therefore must not be in any such office as hath relation to strangers, as Caterer, Porter, &c. The Novices once a week must have a day of Recreation, The Coadjutors must be taught the Rosary. After all this, the Novices must be asked if they are able to undergo the burthens of that society; if they be, let it be recorded, and then let them confess to the Priest. In the Morning after the ringing of the Bell, they must by their private Devotion, prepare themselves for publick prayer. Half an hour is allowed them for dressing up their Beds and Chambers, then they must hear Mass, and Exhortations, which are made to them twice a week for half an hour, the other half hour they shall repeat and confer. Then the next day their Master shall propose them ways to overcome Tentations and Difficulties, the rest of the time till Examination before dinner, shall be imployed in some Exercise. Having recreated themselves an hour after Dinner, at the ringing of the Bell, they shall repair to their Chambers

Sect. 11. *of* EUROPE. 235

to study; an hour after they shall repeat something to their Master, and twice a week they shall ask one another the grounds of Christianity; they must be silent, except in times of Exercise and Recreation: before Supper they shall pray, and so before they go to bed. After two years of Probation, they are examined again touching their Resolution and Constancy in that Order, and then certain Rules of Modesty and Behaviour are prescribed them. The Rules for Councellors are; That they be sincere, judicious, faithful, intelligent, free from partiality, considerate and not rash in giving Sentence, to use few words, to submit to the judgments of the Superior, to divulge nothing without him, to maintain his Dignity, and with submission to give him their best advise, &c. *Their Councellors Ruels. Of these things see the Jesuites Book afore-named.*

Q. 6. *What Rules have they for Travellers, or Pilgrims, for the Minister, for the Admonitor, and other officers?*

A. Travellers must ease the wearisomness of their journey, with Spiritual Fruits; every day when they begin their journey, they must say all the *Letanies* and other prayers; their talk must be of heavenly things, that Christ may be their fellow-Traveller. They must beg Alms for the love of Christ, who was poor himself. Let them accustom themselves to Patience in bearing all injuries; let the stronger follow the weaker, and not go before; if any fall sick by the way, let one stay with him, to look carefully to him, to edifie in the Lord all such as give them entertainment. Let them in all places shew good Examples of Holiness and Modesty. If they travel near any House or College of the Society, they must not beg of Strangers without Leave from the Superiour of that House or College. Let none Travel without his Superiors Letter Patents. The *Minister* or *Controller* of the House, is bound by his Rules, to be assistant to the *Provost* or *Rector*, to be exact in all their Rules, constitutions, and customs of the House, to visit every other day all the Offices and Chambers in the House or College. In the *Spring* and *Autumn* he must acquaint the Superior that the Diet and Cloaths of the Society must be changed. Let him be present with the Physician when he visits the sick; every day he must know the Superiors Mind touching the Houshold Affairs; and must acquaint him with what is fit to be done, and what is amiss. He must see that all things be in good order, and clean, that the Gates be shut every night, to look to the windows, candles, fire, and linen. Let him see there be no disorders or quarrelling; he may supply the Superiors place in his absence, and may have an under-Minister. The *Admonitor* is tyed by his Rules, to put the Superior in mind wherein he faileth in his Office. But this he must do with Reverence and Submission, and with Advice of the Councellors, and must not acquaint others what is done in this case. If the Superior be Incorrigible after divers warnings, he must acquaint the higher powers, he must have a Seal for those Letters which are sent to the Superiour. The *Jesuites* have also Rules in writing of Letters. The Superior or Rector of House or College, is to write every week to the Provincial, and so *Their Rules for Travellers. Their Minister or Controuller Rules. Admonitor his Rules.*

is

is he that is sent abroad to Preach or Convert, of all matters of moment concerning their Society; the Provincials are to write once a Month to the General; but the Superiors and Rectors of Houses and Colleges once in three Months; The Provincials must write once a Month to Provosts, Rectors, and those that are sent Abroad in Messages; the General shall write to the Provincials once in two Months, but to Rectors once in sixth Months, except there be urgent occasion to write oftner: Lest letters be lost or intercepted, they must be written divers times: and the Copies thereof, if they be to the General, must be recorded in a Book: secrets must be written in characters of mystical Terms. The Letters written at *Rome*, by the General, shall be read in the Houses and Colleges, and there safely laid up: He that hath the charge of Spiritual things, is tyed by his Rules, to be careful over the Souls committed to him, in admonishing, Instructing, Exhorting, and Examining.

Over-seer of the Church his Rules. The Over-seer of the Church, is by his Rules both to acquaint the Provost every Saturday of the next Feasts and Fasts, that warning may be given on Sunday in the *Refectory* at Supper-time: He must every Saturday set down in writing, what Ceremonies are to be used the next week at the high Altar. He must take care of the Masses and Prayers be used for their deceased Founders and Benefactors, as also for the defunct of their Society. He must see that the Priests be shaved, and that they observe their Rules. He must suffer no Alms to be given for hearing of Confessions, or saying Divine service. He must have special care of the Host, of the Holy Oyl, Crosses, Chalices, Reliques, &c. When the Reliques are to be shewed, two Wax-candles must be lighted. He must look to the Fabrick of the Church, and must admonish the Superior to nominate Preachers for the next day. He must take care of all the Church Moveables, and keep an Inventory of them. He must also take care of the linen, Candles, prayers, graves. When the holy linen groweth old and useless, let it be burned, and the Ashes thereof cast into the Holy Pond or Lake. A Catalogue also must be kept of all the Masses that are to be celebrated by the Priests, and the Prayers to be said by those that are not Priests, yearly, monthly, and weekly, besides extraordinary times. The

Priests their Rules. Priests are tied by their rules, to be devout, holy and reverent in the Exercise of their Function; to observe all the *Roman rites*, uniformity, and decency; to be expert in cases of conscience, and diligent in hearing confessions; but the Confessor and Penitent must not see one another in time of confession; and there must be an eye-witness present, though not an ear-witness, if the Penitent be a Woman. Confessions must be heard from the morning until noon. The Priests may exhort the sick to make their wills, but not to

Preachers, their rules. assist them in making thereof. Preachers are tyed by their Rules to teach sound and wholsom Doctrine, tending not to curiosity, but Edification; to be diligent in reading the Scripture, and Fathers, to be exemplary in their Conversation, to abstain from reproving Princes, Bishops, and Magistrates in their Sermons, or any Religious

Orders;

Orders; to forbear any Expressions that may move Laughter, or Contempt. Let them beware of Pride, Arrogance, vain Glory, or affected Eloquence; let their gestures be modest and grave; let them chiefly commend the frequent use of confession, of the Eucharist, of Good Works of Obedience, of the Church Ceremonies, of Pennance, Prayer, &c. and let not their Sermons be Extemporary, or exceed an Hour. They that are sent to preach abroad in remote places, are tied by their Rules to walk on foot, to live upon Alms to lodge in Hospitals, to ask leave of the Ordinary to preach, to take notice of the most devout people in every place where they come. They shall not only preach, but likewise confer, catechize, pray, administer the Sacraments, visit the sick, resolve doubts of conscience, compose differences, &c. They must strive to make all men their friends, and to pray for their persecutors, and bear their burthens patiently. Let them write every week to their superiors, what progress they make in their preaching, and other spiritual Exercises; to preach to themselves as well as to others; and to do nothing but what they are enjoyned by their Superior. The Generals Proctor is tied by his Rules, to entertain no Suits in Law, if he can otherwise avoid them: to give an account of all his Actions to the provost General, to keep in Books all Accounts of Expences and Receivings; to keep a List of all Church Benefices united to their Colleges; to have a great care of all the Writings, Popes Bulls, Records, and other Papers committed to his charge, &c. The Protector of the House is tied by his Rules, chiefly to have care of the Houses, Records, and Money, how it is expended; and to give an account thereof to his Superiors. The Protector of the College and House of probation is tied by the same rules to be careful of the Records and Moneys; to keep a good account of what is laid out and received; and to write down all in his Book. He that hath charge of the Readers at Table is bound by his rules, to take care that they have a loud, clear, and distinct voice; that they be perfect in what they read; that first they read a Chapter in the Bible; except in chief Festivals, for then Homilies must be read concerning the Day. Letters also from the *Indies* are to be read yearly. In the beginning of every Month their Constitutions and Common rules, with *Ignatius* his Epistle of Obedience, must be read. In the evening after the lesson, must be read the *Martyrology* of the next day. *Leviticus* and the *Canticles*, with some obscure Chapters in the Prophets, are not to be read at all *Eusebius* his History, *Nicephorus*, *Gregorie*'s Dialogues, *Ambrose*, *Austin*, *Bernard*, with such like books, (whereof the Catalogue is set down in the rules) are to be read. The Superior is to appoint what is to be read every day. He that hath the overseeing of the sick, is tied by his rules to be careful of them, of their diet, Physitian, and all things else that may concern them; that his substitute called by them *Infirmarius*, have all kind of physical Drugs; that he acquaint the Superior with the sickness and quality of it; that every eighth day the sick receive the Eucharist, that Prayers be made

Generals Proctor, his Rules.

Readers, their Rules.

Infirmarius.

made for him, and all things performed which may tend to his comfort and recovery; if he die, that the Corps (if without offence) be kept above ground four and twenty Hours, and then decently interr'd. The Library Keeper by his rules, must have still by him *Index Expurgatorius*, and that he keep no prohibited Books, to keep the Library locked, except to those who are permitted to be in it, to keep the Books clean, to write down their Titles, to have a Catalogue of them, to lend no Book without their Superiors leave, &c. The under Minister of the House is to look to the Chambers, Refectory, Kitchin, Buttery, and other places, that all things be fit and in order. The *Ædituus*, or Sexton must be subject to the *Præfectus*, or him that hath the charge of the Church, to have a care of the sacred Vestiments, of the Linen, of the Host and Wine; he must in Divine Service, light two Candles, and at the Elevation of the Host a wax Torch, or Taper, and then shall ring the Bell; he must keep clean the Church Plate; before Mass or Sermon, let him ring the Bell, and the Virgins Salutation Bell, in the Morning, at Noon, and in the Evening; and to Ring the passing Bell when any of the Society is departing: He must have a Light continually burning before the Host, and there must never be wanting Holy Water; he shall deliver to the *Præfectus* all Oblations that he shall find; he must be careful of the Church-doors, to shut them at Noon, and at Sun-set: and whil'st they stand open, he, or one for him, must not be wanting; he must suffer none to walk up and down, to make any noise, and let all things be kept clean. The Porter must have a List of all the Domesticks Names, he must suffer none to go out without the Superiors leave: All Letters he shall deliver to the Superior; none that returns from the Country, must be let in till the Superior know it; if Bishops or great Men come in, let a Priest attend them whil'st he acquaints the Superior. Let the Keys of the Gate be delivered every night to the Provost or Rectors: he must acquaint the Superior if any Poor be at the Gate, or if any Alms be given there, &c. The Keeper of the Wardrobe must have an Inventory of the Cloathes in the House, and Linen thereof, of which he must be careful; he must every Saturday Night, furnish each Chamber with clean Linen, and carry away the Foul every Sunday Morning to the Washer. In Summer every fifteenth Day he must give out clean Sheets; and in Winter, every three Weeks, &c. The Servants of the House must be careful of the Wine and Water and Dyet of the Society; and to have the Water casks kept clean. He that hath the charge of the Hall or Refectory, must look there be not wanting Water, Towels, Napkins, Table-cloaths, which must be changed once or twice a week; that the due hours of refection be observed by ringing the Bell; that he have a list of all their names who are in commons; that the remainders of the meat be reserved for the poor; and that he have the names of the Waiters at Table every week, and of the Readers, &c. The Cook hath his rules, to be cleanly, frugal, diligent, to touch no meat in cutting

Librarii.

ting or dividing with his hands, but with a fork; to cut as he is directed by the Superior; to dress nothing for any particular man, except he be sick, not to be Wastful of the Wood; to keep a list of all things belonging to the Kitchin. The *Excitator* who wakeneth the *Jesuites* in the morning, must go to rest half an hour before others, that he may rise so much the sooner, ring the Bell, and carry lights to every chamber: a quarter of an hour after, he must visit each chamber again, and if he find some in bed yet, he must tell the Superior: another quarter of an hour after, he must ring to Prayers; he that visits the chambers at night must ring or knock, that every one may examine his conscience: about a quarter of an hour after, he must ring to bed: and a quarter after that, he must see if every one be in bed and the Candles put out, if not to acquaint the Superior. Each House or College hath one who buyeth all things necessary for the house; his rule is to be diligent and faithful in buying and employing the money delivered to him, that he may give a just account thereof. *These are the principal rules to which every Office and Member of the Society is bound. Some of lesser note I have omitted for brevities sake, which may be seen at large in the* Jesuites *own rules, set out by themselves in one Book at* Lyons, *by their Superiors permission, Anno 1607.*

Q. 4. *What Privileges have been granted to this Society from the Popes?*

A. Pope *Paul* the third, gave them power to make what, and how many rules and constitutions they pleased, towards the advancement of their Society: to admit as many into their Orders, as their General shall please, whereas in the beginning they were stinted to sixty only: he also excommunicates all such as shall either hinder, or not aid this Society. He gave them also power to preach, administer the Sacraments, hear Confession, Absolve, &c. in any place where they please, and to have their Coadjutors, both spiritual, as Priests, and temporal, as Cocks, Bakers, Caterers, Butlers, &c. on whom the *Jesuites* professed can confer sacred Orders. The *Jesuites* have this privilege also to change their General, and he power to send them whither he pleaseth, and call them back again without asking leave of the Pope. They may also absolve all Hereticks confessing, and the General may excommunicate and imprison Delinquents. They are exempted from the secular power, and from all Taxes and Tythes; they may carry with them moveable Altars when they travel, and may disguise themselves into any habit; he that visits a *Jesuites* House or College, shall have a plenary indulgence. They have also power to exercise all Episcopal Functions; namely to ordain, anoint, exercise, confirm, consecrate, dispence, &c. All these privileges were given to them by *Paul* the third, in several Bulls. Pope *Julius,* the third, *Paul*'s successor, gave them a privilege to erect Universities where they pleased, and to confer what degrees they will; to dispense also with fasting, and prohibited meats. Pope *Pius* the fourth,

Privileges granted by divers Popes to the Jesuites.

240   *A View of the Religions*   Sect. 11.

fourth, confirmeth all the former privileges. *Pius* the fifth, grants that such *Jesuites* as forsook their Order by leave from the Pope or General, shall enter into no other order except the *Carthusian*, if they apostatize without leave; they shall be excommunicate; he gives them also power to read publickly in any University they come to, without asking leave, and that none must hinder them, but all are bound to hear them. *Gregory* the thirteenth gave them power to have their *Conservators, Judges,* and *Advocates,* and to recite their Canonical hours without the Quire, and to correct, change, interpret, expunge, and burn such Books as they dislike, and to be the Popes Library keepers, and exempteth them from being necessarily present at Processions or Funerals. By reason of these and other privileges granted to this order, besides their own industry, they grew so numerous in the space of 75 years, that they had *Anno* 1608. as *Ribadeneira* sheweth, 293. Colleges besides 123 Houses, and of their Society were reckoned 10581. Out of their Colleges they raise a revenue of twenty hundred thousand Crowns yearly.

Of all their privileges see the Popes Bull and Apostolical Letters, printed at Rome by their Superiors leave, in the Jesuites College Anno 1568.

Q. 8. *Are there no other orders in the Church of Rome?*

A. There are divers more, but of less note, whose original is uncertain, both in respect of their Author and time, besides there be many subdivisions of one and the same order, as the *Franciscans* are subdivided into *Observantes, Conventuales, Minimi, Capucini, Collectanei,* whose charge was to receive the money that is given them. *Amadeani, Reformati de Evangelio; Chiacini cum barba, de Portiuncula, Paulini, Bosiani, Gaudentes, de Augustinis* with their open shooes, *Servientes*. All these differ little except in some small matters. There be also some Monks called *Ambrosiani*, who wear red cloaks over white coats. Others are called *Capellani*, whose Garments are partly black and partly blew, *Chalomeriani* wear a white Cross upon a white cloak. *Cellarii*, from their cells are so called, and *Brothers of mercy* from visiting the sick, and carrying the dead to the grave; in the inside they wear black linen, on the out side a sooty colour Garment. *Clavigeri* wear upon a black cowl two keys, intimating by this, that they have power to open and shut Heaven. They make Saint *Peter* the Author of their order. *Cruciferi*, these bow their bodies and their heads as they walk, go bare-foot, and wear a white cloak girt with a rope, they carry always in their hands a little wooden Cross. The *Brothers* of the *Cross* wear a black cloak without a hood and bear the Cross before their breast. *Forficiferi*, so called from wearing a pair of sheers on their cloak, by which they shew that they clip off all carnal lusts, as it were with a pair of sheers. They wear a black cloak and hood, these we may call *Sheer-Brothers*. The *Brothers of Helen,* brag that they were instituted by *Helen, Constantine's* Mother, after she had found out the Cross, they wear a white garment, and on it a yellow Cross. *Hospitalarii*, so called from looking to *Hospitals*, they wear black; they differ from the former of this name, and so do the *Cruciferi*. The *Brothers* of Saint *James* wear a sandy

Francis-cans subdi-vided into divers Orders. Observantes. Ambrosiani.

Capellani.

Cellarii.

Clavigeri.

Cruciferi.

Forficiferi.

coloured

coloured garment, and shells hanging at it; they make Saint *James* their Patron. The Order of *Ignorance*: These Monks think it mans chief happiness to know nothing. "*This Order of Ignorance is now* "*the greatest in the world, and is like to swallow up all the Orders and* "*Degrees of Learning, as* Pharaoh's *lean Kine did devour the fat. So much the more happy will this Order be, when it is fed with Tythes and Colleges.* There is an Order of *Johannites* differing from the former; these wear a red garment to represent Christ's blood, and on the breast thereof is woven a Chalice, to shew that in his Blood our sins are washed; they also hold a Book still in their hand. The order of the Valley of *Josaphat* goeth in a Purple Garment; these appoint Judges to decide controversies of marriage. The order of *Joseph* was erected in honour of *Mary's* supposed Husband: These wear ash-coloured cloathes, and a white hood. The order of *Lazarus* or *Magdalen* wear a green Cross upon a black cloak with a hood: there be two sorts of them, some contemplative, who are black within, and white without, using ordinary food, the others wear a brown or tawny colour, and are active, their food is only herbs and roots. The order of *Nuns* of Saint *Mary de decem virtutibus*, that is, *Of the ten virtues*, which consist only in repeating the *Ave Mary* ten times: They wear a black Veil, a white coat, a red Scapular, and an ash-coloured cloak. There be two other orders of Saint *Mary*, the one wears a white coat, and a black cloak like *Carmelites*, the other are all white; there is also the order of *Mary's* Conception. The order called *Reclusi*, shut themselves up between two walls, or in narrow cells, whence they never go out so long as they live. The order of Saint *Ruffus*, instituted by him; these go like the *Canon Regulars*, wearing a Scapular over a linen Surpless, and black a coloured hood. There is an order so free Nuns, who maintain themselves, and may marry when they will. The order of *Specularii* are so called from their looking-glasses which they always carry; their inward garment is black, their outward white; They wear on their breast a black cross. "*Among the* Romans *it was accounted an* "*Effeminate trick for men to carry about a looking-glass, therefore* Otho *is mocked by* Juvenal, *who speaking of the Looking-glass,* "*calls it, Pathici gestamen Othonis.* The order of the *Stellati*, wore Stars on their cloathes, some of them have black gowns and black hoods, some have cloaks without hoods. Some other petty orders there are of small account.

Of which see *Seb. Frank* in *Chron. Franc. Mo- dius, Heu- terus de reb. Bur- gund, Hof- pinian,* &c.

Q. 9. *How are the Abbots consecrated at this time?*

A. If the Abbot be not a Monk, he is thus consecrated: On the consecration day, which is some Festival, or the Lords day, both the Bishop, and the Abbot elect, confess, and fast the day before. In the Church two Chappels are trimmed up, the bigger for the Bishop, the lesser for the Abbot. On the Altar of the greater Chappel, stands a Cross and four Candlesticks. At the foot of the Altar the ground is covered with Turky Carpets, or Tapestry: there is also in the Chappel a Table placed for the Bishop; on which is clean linen, two Candlesticks, Basons with

Abbots, how consecrated.

R   Towels,

Towels, the holy water-pot, with the *Aspersory*, the censer, &c. Likewise the Bishops Mass-Ornaments; there be also three chairs, one for the Elect Abbot, the other two for the two assistant Abbots. The Bishop hath three Chaplains. In the lesser Chappel for the Abbot is an Altar with the Cross and two Candlesticks, with the Pontifical and Missal; There is also a Table covered with clean linen, with Basons, and two Candlesticks, and the Ring which is to be consecrated, &c. The Bishop having prayed at the Altar, ascendeth his Chair of State over against the Altar, with his Mitre on his head; the Elect Abbot sits in his ordinary cloathes, between two Mitred Abbots his assistants; then the Elect boweth himself to the Bishop, who riseth, taketh off his Mytre, and saith some prayers: after this the Bishop without his Mytre blesseth the Elects new cloaths, and besprinkles them with Holy water, then he sits down, puts on his Mytre, and takes off the Elects secular garment; saying, *The Lord take off from thee the old man*, &c. And then cloaths him in a Monastical Habit; saying, *The Lord cloath thee with the new man*, &c. This done, the Bishop laying aside his Mytre, riseth and prayeth, and sits down again. Then the Elect riseth, and beseeching him with bended knees, and his hand on his breast, that he would receive him, the Bishop riseth and prayeth over him; then the Elect being now made a Monk, promiseth Canonical obedience to the Bishop and his Successors, fidelity to the Convent, Continency and Renunciation to his own Estate; with this the Bishop receiveth him into the Society of the Monks, and withal into the kiss of peace. After this the Elect Abbot goeth into his Chappel, where he is habited like a Priest, and thence brought between the two Abbots assistants to the Bishop, who uncovering their heads, bow to him, and the Elder of the two presents him to the Bishop, desiring he would ordain him Abbot of such a Monastery, according to the Apostolical Authority committed to him. Then the Popes Mandate is read; the Elect sweareth upon the Gospel, the Bishop asketh if he will be faithful over the Flock committed to him, if he will reform his life, be sober, humble, chast, and patient; if he will be subject, obedient, and reverent to the Pope and his Successors, if he answereth *I will*, then the Bishop prayeth that God will keep and strengthen him; if the Abbot be not exempted from Episcopal Jurisdiction, he is to promise Obedience to the Diocesan and his Successors. This done, The Elect kisseth the Bishops hand, who standing before the Altar makes confession, kisseth the Gospel and the Altar, which he doth also incense, and sayeth Mass. After this the Elect goeth to his Chappel, where he is trimmed in the Abbots Ornaments; and is brought again before the Bishop, to whom he boweth himself, and then the Musick begins: the Bishop after this takes the Pastoral staff, blesseth it, and prayeth for the Elect Abbot, who all the while is on his knees, then the Bishop layeth both his hands on the Abbots head, prayeth, and giveth to him the Rule of the Order, whereof he is to be head, and with

Sect. 11. *of* EUROPE. 243

an Exhortation to be careful over them. After the Bishop hath blessed the Staff, he besprinkleth the Elect with Holy water, delivereth him the Staff, with an Exhortation to use it with discretion. Then he blesseth the Ring, and casts Holy water on it, and puts it on the Ring finger of his right hand, and prayeth for him; this done, the Abbot receiveth the kiss of peace, then retireth to his Chappel, thence returneth with his two assistants, and presenteth to the Bishop two burning Tapers, two Beads, two vessels of Wine, and kisseth his hand. Then Mass is said, the Sacrament administred, and the Abbot is solemnly blessed, at length the Mytre is blessed, and washed with Holy water, which the Bishop puts on the head of the Abbot; saying, *Lord we put on the head of this thy Servant the Helmet of Salvation, that he having his head armed, may with the horns of both Testaments appear terrible to the Adversaries of the Truth,* &c. At last the Gloves are blessed and washed, and put on the Abbots hand, who with his Mytre on his head, is by the Bishop brought to the Quire and set in his Predecessors chair; whence he riseth, blesseth the people present, and thanks the Bishop. The rest of the day is spent in good cheer. The Consecration of the Abbatess and Nuns is much after this manner.

Steven Albertus Capellanus in Pontificali and Hospinian out of him.

Q. 10. *Wherein do the Christian Orders of Knighthood differ from one another?*

A. In the times, Authors, Occasions, Habits, Ends, Ornaments and Ceremonies of their institution. The first Order of Knight-hood in *France* was that of the *Genet*, instituted by *Charles Martel*, in memory of the great Victory he obtained against *Abdiramo*, in whose Camp were found good store of *Gennets*, which are Beasts like *Spanish* Cats in bigness with long and slender Snowts, their Furies (whereof good store were found in the Enemies Camp, and presented to *Charles Martel*) do smell like those of *Civit* Cats. From this beast the order is so called, consisting of sixteen Knights only, who wore collars of Gold made of three chains, linked with red Roses enamelled; at the end of this collar hung a Golden *Gennet*. The order of the Crown Royal, (instituted by *Charlemaigne*, in favour of the *Frisons*, who had done him good service in his Wars against the *Sesnes* or ancient *Saxons*) wore on their breasts a Crown Royal in embroydery of Gold, wherefore this was called *L' Ordre de la Coronne Royal*. The order of the Star instituted by King *Robert* of *France*; Anno 1022. was composed of thirty Knights, whereof the King was chief. Those wore cloaks of white Damask; on the left side of the breast, was embroydered a Star wrought in Gold, with five pointed beams. Their Oath was to say in honour of the Virgin *Mary*, (whom they called Star of the Sea, and Lady of the Star) a *Corona* or *Chaplet* made up of five tens of *Ave Maries*, and five *Pater Nosters*, with an Anthem. The order of the Broom Flower, instituted by Saint *Lewis* the French King, did wear a collar composed of broom husks, or codds, interlaced

Knights of the Genets.

Of the Crown Royal.

Of the Star.

Of the Broom flower.

R 2

interlaced with flowers *de Lys*. King *Lewis* chose this broom for his emblem, adding these words, *Exaltat humiles*, intimating that God had exalted him for his humility to the Royal Throne of *France*, in stead of his Elder Brother, *Philip* of *France*. The Knights of this order wore caffocks of white Damask. The

Of the Ship. order of the Ship, instituted also by Saint *Lewis*, for incouraging the French Nobility to attempt the Seas with him against the *Saracens*, wore a collar interlaced with double *Scallops* (signifying the sandy shore) and double crescents or half Moons, which with the Ship hanging thereat declared his enterprise was to fight with *Infidels* and *Mahometans*, and to plant the Christian faith; Therefore these Knights were tied by their order to hear daily the office of our Saviours passion, to defend the Catholick Faith, Church and Ministers thereof, and to protect Widows, *Of S. Michael.* Orphans, and other afflicted people. The order of St. *Michael* was instituted by *Lewis* the eleventh, Son to *Charles* the seventh, in honour of Saint *Michael* the French tutelar Angel, who commanded *Aubert* Bishop of *Auranches* to erect a Church to him on that Hill, which ever since hath been called *Mount Saint Michael*, frequented yearly with Pilgrims from all parts of *France*: to whom also is dedicated the nine and twentieth day of September, in memory of this Angel who fought against the English at *Orleans*; here upon *Charles* the seventh took for his *Oriflamb* the Image of Saint *Michael*, which was always carryed before the King when he went to Wars. They wear a collar of Gold made of Scallops fastned on small chains, from which hangeth the Image of *Michael* treading on the Dragon. As often as any Knight misseth the wearing of this collar, he is to cause a Mass to be said, and to pay seven Sols and six *Deniers Tournois*. All the Knights are bound on the Vigil of Saint *Michael* to wait in their habits on the King from his Palace to the Church. On Saint *Michael's* day, they are to wait on the King in the same ornaments to Mass, and to offer each man a piece of Gold; that day the King is to entertain them at his Table; The next day they offer (being cloathed in black) wax candles for the dead, for whom Mass and Prayers are said. Their oath is to maintain the dignity of the French *Of the Holy* Crown, and the Church. The order of the Holy Ghost was *Ghost.* instituted by *Henry* the third of *France Anno* 1579. in memory of his Nativity, election to the Crown of *Poland*, and his coming to the Crown of *France*, all which happened upon Whit-Sunday, when the Holy Ghost descended on the Apostles. The Knights of this order wear a collar made of Flowers *de luce* of Gold, cornered with flames of fire interwoven with some Letters, the first whereof is *H*. the first letter of *Henry's* name. From the collar hangs the Image of a Dove in the mid'st of a Cross like that of *Malta*, all beset with beams and four Flowers *de luce*. The King is chief of the order, whose oath is to maintain the Catholick Religion, and unity amongst his Subjects. The Knights are

all

all bound to community every first day of the year, and on the day of Pentecost, and to swear their zeal to the Catholick Faith, and their fidelity to the King and his Successors. This order consisteth of the King, and one hundred Knights; among which are four Cardinals, five Prelates, the Chancelor, Provost, Master of the Ceremonies, the High Treasurer and Register. All the Knights are bound to wear the Cross on their garment. The feast of this order is kept on the first of *January*, in which the King is accompanied to the Church by the Knights, and they after Mass are feasted by him at the Palace. At Even song; they for the deceased Knights were black, and the next day offer wax candles for their souls, and then dine with the King again. The order of *Christian Charity* was instituted by the same *Henry*, for the benefit of poor Captains and maimed Soldiers, to whom Rents and Hospitals were by him assigned. They wear on their cloaks an anchored Cross embroydered with white Sattin. These Knights of *Lazarus* had their original at *Jerusalem*, but being expelled thence were by Saint *Lewis* brought from thence, and entertained with great revenues, to the end they might look to the cure of leprous and other infected persons; but when these Knights became idle, and married, their Rents were taken from them, and a part thereof given to the **Knights** of Saint *John* of *Jerusalem*. By *Gregory* the thirteenth *Emanuel Philbert* Duke of *Savoy* was chosen great Master of this order of Saint *Lazarus*, to whom he gave the command of all spitles for Lepers. The order of the Virgin *Mary* in mount *Carmel*, consisting of one hundred French Gentlemen, was instituted by King *Henry* the fourth of France, and confirmed by Pope *Paul* the fifth, *Anno* 1607. They are tied to keep a feast every year the sixteenth of *May*, to the Virgin *Mary* of mount *Carmel*, to wear on their cloaks a Cross of tawny velvet, in the mid'st whereof shall be the Image of the Virgin *Mary*, entowered with beams of Gold; about their necks they shall wear an anchored Cross of Gold, in the mid'st whereof shall be the Virgins Image enamelled. They may not marry above twice. They must fight for the Catholick faith. The orders of *Orleans* was instituted by Monsieur *Lewis* of *France* Duke of *Orleans*, An. 1393. it is called also the Order of the *Porcupine*, because there hangs the picture of the beast from three chains of Gold, which Monsieur took for his Device, to let *John* of *Bourgogne* his mortal enemy know, that he wanted not Arms and Courage to be revenged on him, for his wicked and bloody intentions. The Order of the *Golden Shield* was instituted by *Lewis* the second, third Duke of *Burbon*, sirnamed the Good Duke; in the Golden Shield was a bend of Pearls, whereon was written *Allon*, which is as much as *Allons* in French, that is, Let us go all together to the service of God, and defence of our Country. He instituted also the Order of the *Thistle*, called also the order of *Burbon*, in honour of the Virgin *Mary Anno* 1370. consisting of six and twenty Knights,

Of Christian Charity.

Of Saint Lazarus.

Of the Virgin Mary a Mount Carmel.

Of Orleanor Porcupine.

Of the Golden Shield.

Of the Thistle.

who were a Belt, in which was embroydered the word *Esperance* in Capital Letters; it had a Buckle of Gold, at which hung a tuft like a Thistle; on the Collar also was embroydered the same word *Esperance* with Flowers *de Luce* of Gold, from which hung an Oval, wherein was the Image of the Virgin *Mary*, entowered with a Golden Sun, crowned with twelve Stars of Silver, and a Silver Crescent under her Feet; at the end of

Of Anjou. the Oval was the head of a Thistle. The Order of *Anjou*, or of the Crescent or half Moon, was instituted by the good King *Rene*, being Duke of *Anjou*, and King of *Sicily*: The Symbol of the Order was a Crescent of Gold, whereon was engraven this word *Loz*, which signifies Praise; this the Knights wore on their Cloaks or Gowns; there were of this order six and thirty

Of Saint Magdalen. Knights. The Order of St. *Magdalen*, was instituted by *John Chesnel*, a Noble Gentleman of *France*, *An* 1614. out of a Godly Zeal to reclaim the French from their Quarrels, Duels, and other sins; that by remembring the Repentance of *Mary Magdalen* they might with her learn to repent. The Cross which might serve to wear on the cloak, or about the neck, had at three ends three Flower *de Luce*; the foot stood in a Crescent, in the mid'st was the shape of *Magdalen*; the Cross is beset with Palms, to shew this Order was instituted to encourage Voyages to the Holy Land; within the Palms are Sun beams, and four Flowers *de luce*, to shew the glory of the *French* Nation. The Knights are tied by their vow to abandon all hazardous gaming, blasphemy, reading of prohibited and vicious Books, &c. Their habit is of skie colour. Their collar is made up of the letter *M.* doubled with *L.* and *A.* to express *Mary Magdalen*, King *Lewis*, and Queen *Anne*, interlaced with double hearts, wounded with darts of Gold crossed; the Ribband is Crimson, from which hangs an Oval, having *Mary Magdalen* on the one side, and Saint *Lewis* on the other. The device about the Oval on the cloak is, *L' amour de dieu est pacifique.* They had a house allotted them near *Paris*, wherein were ordinarily five hundred Knights, bound to stay there during two years probation; at the end of which, they shall take the oath of the order, of charity, obedience and conjugal chastity; they must also abjure all duels, quarrels and assassinates. The Knights that live abroad shall meet every year at their house called the lodging Royal on *Mary Magdalen*'s Festival day, to communicate and to give an account of their actions to the great Master. The Knights that live in the house, must on all Sundays and Festivals be assistant at Divine Service, the Knights have their Academy for all kind of exercise. But this order as it began, so it ended in the person of *Chesnel*. The order of *Bretaigne*, or of the *Hermine*, and *Ears* of *Corn*, was instituted by *Francis* Duke of *Bretaigne*, *Anno* 1450, it was called of the *Ears* of *Corn*, because the Golden Collar was made in the form of Ears of Corn, at the end of which hung by three small Golden chains a little white

beast,

beast, called an *Hermine*; his word or Motto was, A *Ma Vie*, intimating, that whil'st he lived he would preserve his courage, purity and integrity, resembled by the *Ermine*, which is so loth to defile his white skin by running through dirty and boggy places when he is hunted, that he will rather suffer himself to be caught; whose skin is in great request for Furs. This order consisteth of five and twenty Knights of the *Ears of Corn*, so called, to signifie, that Princes should be careful to preserve Husbandry.

Of Bretaigne or Hermine. They that would see these orders described at large, let them read the History of Andrew Favine, Parisian, and Advocate in the Court of Parliament.

Q. 11. *What other Orders of Knight-hood were there in Christendom, besides those of the French.*

A. In *Flanders*, was instituted the Order of the Golden Fleece, by Duke *Philip*, in the City of *Bruges*, Anno 1429. in memory of the great Revenues which he raised by Traffique of Wools, or else in memory of *Gideon*'s Fleece, or of the Golden Fleece at *Colchos*. The Order consisted of thirty Knights, the Duke being chief. The great Collar was made of double Fusiles enterwoven with Stones and Flints, sparkling flames of fire. The Flints were the Arms of the ancient Kings of *Burgundy*; the Flames did signifie the Swiftness, Fierceness, and Terror these Knights should shew to their Enemies, to this purpose was this Motto, *Ante ferit quam flamma micet*. From the Collar hung a Golden Fleece. The Patron of this Order was Saint *Andrew*: The Knights were to keep three Festivals: on the first day they wore a Scarlet, to shew that Heaven and Glory is god by Martyrdom and Effusion of Blood. On the second day black, to shew their grief for the Dead. The third day white Damask, to shew their purity. The Order of the Garter was instituted in *England*, Anno 1347. by King *Edward* the third, consisting of five and twenty Knights, under the patronage of Saint *George*. The great Collar was of Gold, composed of white and red Crosses, knit in manner of true Love Knots; instead of which Knots, the Thistles of *Scotland*'s Order were combined, by King *James*, who united the two Orders as he did the Kingdoms. From the Collar hangeth St. *George* on horse-back with the Dragon at his feet. In *England* were instituted the Knights of the Bath by King *Henry* the fourth, as some write, who made six and forty Knights, who having their several Chambers in the Tower, watched and bathed themselves on Saturday night, and on Sunday they were made Knights; At high Mass in the Evening before the Ceremony, they were cloathed with Gray cloath like *Eremites*, to shew they were willing to renounce the World for Christ, the next day they swear, *To love God, defend the Church, honour the King, and to protect the oppressed*: and then they lay aside their Monks habit, and are richly cloathed; then they mount on Horse-back, having on the Frontstall the sign of the Cross, and so they ride to the King, who girdeth them with the Girdle and Sword, and commandeth two Ancient Knights to put on their gilded Spurs. At dinner they wait on the King, after which they present their Swords to God on the high Altar and redeem them again with money. These

Of the Golden Fleece.

Of the Garter.

Of the Bath.

and other Ceremonies of the Knights Batchelors, or of the Bath, may be seen at large in our own Histories. The order of the Thistle, or of Saint *Andrew* in *Scotland* was instituted by King *Achaius*, who made a League offensive and defensive with *Charles* the Great, *Anno* 809. The Collar is made up of Thistles and Rue, the one being full of prickles, and not to be touched without hurting the skin, the other is good against Serpents and poyson. The Motto is *Nemo me impune lacessit*, intimating, that he wanted not power to defend himself, and offend his enemies. At the Collar hangeth the picture of Saint *Andrew* with his Cross. The Order of the *Lily*, or of *Navarre*, was instituted by Prince *Garcia* the sixth of that name, in the City of *Nagera Anno* 1048. where the Image of the Virgin *Mary* issuing out of a Lily, was discovered in the time of the Kings sickness, who thereupon suddenly recovered his health; and in token of Gratitude, instituted the Order of Knights of Saint *Mary* of the Lily consisting of eight and thirty Knights; whereof he was chief. They swear to expose Goods and Fortunes to preserve the Kingdom of *Navarre*, and to expell the *Moors*. Each of these weareth a Lily on his breast, made of Silver, and a double chain of Gold, enterlaced with this *Gothish* letter M. which stands for *Mary*. At the end of the chain hangeth a Flower *de luce*, carrying the same Letter crowned. The Knights are tied to divers services and prayers, to confess also and to communicate. The Order of Saint *James* of the Sword was instituted *Anno* 1158. under the reigns of *Alphonso* the ninth King of *Castile*, and of *Ferdinand* King of *Leon*. The Knights wear on their breasts, and on the left side a Scallop-shell. About their neck they wear three chains of Gold, from which hangs the form of a Sword, being of red Sattin embroydered, and a Scallop shell upon the same Sword. The red Sword signified their Victory over the *Arabians*, with whose blood their Swords were died. The Scallop shell was a mark of their Pilgrimage to the holy Sepulchre of Saint *James*; these they gather on the Sea shore, and fasten them to their hats or hoods, who go on Pilgrimage. This order took first beginning in *Galicia* under the homage then of *Leon*; at first these Knights lived in common with the Monks of Saint *Helie*, and shaved their Crowns, vowing chastity, poverty, but afterwards they married; they both were of Saint *Austin's* rule. This order was also established in *Portugal*; above six hundred Knights were of this order. Many Lords of *Spain* hold it an honour to wear the habit of Saint *James*. The great Mastership of this order was incorporated to the Crown of *Castile*, *Anno* 1493. by Pope *Adrian* the sixth. The order of Saint *Julian*, called of the *Pear Tree*, was instituted in the Kingdom of *Leon*, *Anno* 1179. and was approved by Pope *Alexander* the third, *Lucius* the third, and *Innocent* the third; the Knights have the Pear-Tree for their Arms. But after *Alphonso* the ninth King of *Leon*, became Master of the City *Alcantara*, which he

took

took from the *Moors*, and bestowed it on the Great Master of *Calatrava*, and this gave it to the Master of the Pear Tree; These Knights of the Pear Tree stiled themselves Knights of *Alcantara*, and forsaking their former Arms, wore the *Green Cross Flower de Inced* on their breasts; they live under the order of *Benedict*. They first professed Chastity, but Pope *Paul* the fourth permitted them to marry. The Great Mastership of this order was by Pope *Alexander* the sixth a *Spaniard* united to the Crown of *Castile*, in favour of King *Ferdinand* of *Arragon*, and Queen *Isabel* his Wife. The order of *Calatrava* was founded in the Kingdom of *Castile Anno* 1158, under the Reign of *Sancio* the third, and sixth King of *Castile*. They were called *Calatrava* from a Castle of that name taken from the *Moors*, and given to the Knights *Templars*, but they fearing their own weakness, surrendred it to the King *Sancio* of *Castile*, who gave it to certain Monks of the *Cistertian* Order, who offered themselves to keep this Frontiered Castle; *Hence arose the order of* Calatrava. They wear a red cross Flower deluced. Pope *Alexander* the third approved this Order; at first these Knights wore Scapularies and robes of white, but Pope *Benedict* the third dispensed with them for that Monkish habit, and they were permitted by Pope *Paul* the third, to marry once only. At last the Masterships of Saint *James* of *Calatrava*, and of *Alcantara* were annexed to the Crown of *Spain* in favour of *Charles* the fifth, Emperour and King of *Spain*, who enjoy the Revenues of these three great Masters. The Order of the *Band*, or *red Scarf*, was instituted in *Castile* by *Alphonso* the 11th. *Anno* 1330. King of *Leon* and *Castile*. The Knights wore a broad ribband of red Silk, and are bound to accompany the King in his Wars, to be Valiant, Sober, Courteous, Discreet, &c. The Order of the *Dove*, or *Holy Ghost*, was instituted in *Segobia* in *Castile*, *Anno* 1379. by *John* the first of *Castile*. They wore a collar linked with Sun-beams, whereat hung a Dove of Gold, Enamelled with white, as if it were flying down from Heaven. But this Order ended with the institutors life, to wit, the same year of his institution. The Order of Saint *Saviour* of *Montreal* called the Order of *Arragon*, was instituted in *Arragon*, *Anno* 1120. by *Alphonso* the eighteenth King of *Navarre*, and first of *Arragon*. The Knights wore a white Robe, red cross; their Rule was like that of the *Templars*, to whom and on the breast an Anchored they succeeded in *Montreal*, but only that they had power to marry. The Order of our Lady of *Montesia*, or of *Valencia*, was instituted in the Kingdom of *Valencia*, *Anno* 1317. by *James* the second King of *Arragon*, upon the extermination of the *Templars*. The Statutes of this order were answerable to that of *Calatrava*, under the rule of the *Cistertians*, whose cloathing they were dispensed withal to wear. Their Cross was that of St. *George*, a full Red Cross which they wore on their breast. The Order of the *Looking-Glass* of the Virgin *Mary* was instituted by *Ferdinand* the Infant of *Castile*, upon a memorable

Calatrava.

Of the Band or Red Scarf.

Of the Dove.

Knights of S. Saviour of Montreal.

Of Montesia.

Of the Looking Glass.

ble Victory he had over the *Moors*. The Collar of this order was composed of Bough-pots full of Lilies, interlaced with Griffons. The order of *Jesus Christ* was instituted in *Portugal*, Anno 1320. by *Dionysius* the sixth King of *Portugal*: the Knights wear black, and upon their breasts a red cross, and another white over the red. Pope *John* the twenty second confirmed this order, 1320. gave them the rule of St. *Bennet*. Pope *Alexander* the sixth gave them leave to marry. This order as that of *D. Avis* was annexed to the Crown of *Portugal*. This order D. *Avis* was instituted in *Portugal* under the first King *Alphonso Henriquez*, Anno 1147. under the rule of St. *Bennet*. They bear for their Arms the cross like that of *Alcantar* with two black Birds like Ravens.

Of Jesus Christ.

Of D. Avis.

See *Famine*, &c.

Q. 12. *What were the orders of Knight-hood in* Germany, Hungary, Bohemia, Poland, *&c.*

Of the Dragon.

A. The order of the *Dragon* was instituted in *Germany*, by the Emperor *Sigismund*, Anno 1418. upon the condemnation of *Husse*, and *Hierom* of *Prague*. The Knights did wear on High Days a Scarlet cloak, a double Golden Chain, at the end whereof hung a Dragon overthrown, her wings seeming broken; and daily they wear a Cross Flower deluced with Green. This order was famous throughout *Germany* and *Hungary*. The order of *Austria* and *Carinthia*, or of Saint *George*, was instituted by the Emperour *Frederick* the third, first Arch-Duke of *Austria*, Anno 1470. The Knights wear a white Coat, and a red Cross; they were bound to guard the Frontiers of *Germany*, *Hungary*, *Austria*, *Styra*, and *Carinthia*, against the *Turks*. The Order of *Poland*, or of the white Eagle, was instituted by King *Ladislaus* the fifth, Anno 1325. The Kings wear a tripple chain of Gold, whereat hangs an *Eagle* crowned. The Order of *Denmark*, or of the *Elephant*, was instituted by *Christierne* the first, King of *Denmark*, Anno 1478. The Collar which the Knights wear, is composed of Elephants, with silver Castles on their backs, at the end whereof hangeth the picture of the Virgin *Mary*, beset with Sun-beams, and a Crescent under her feet. The order of *Sweeden*, or of *Jesus*, or of the *Seraphims*, was instituted by *Magnus* the fourth King of *Sweeden*, Anno 1334. The Collar of this order is composed of Cherubims, and Patriarchal Crosses, in memory of the siege laid to the chief City of *Upsala*. At the end of the Collar hung an oval, bearing these three letters, I. H. S. that is *Jesus Hominum Salvator*, with four Nails enamelled white and black to shew our Saviours passion. The order of *Cleve*, or of the *Swan*, is at this day held up by the Princes descended of the house of *Cleve*, who do bear the *Swan* for their Order, Crests, and Supporters of their Arms. Of the order of *Prussia*, called the *Marian*, or *Teutonick*, we have spoken already. The order of *Livonia*, or of the Sword bearers, was instituted Anno 1203. by *Albert* a Monk of *Breme*, with some rich Merchants, who out of zeal to fight against the Infidels of *Livonia*, renounced the world, and vowed obedience, and chastity, in the presence of

Of S. George.

Of the white Eagle.

Of the Elephant.

Of the Seraphims.

Of the Swan.

Of the Sword-Bearers.

Bishop

Sect. 11.   *of* E U R O P E.   251

Bishop *Albert*, who prescribed them the rule and habit of the *Cistertians*; a long white Cassock, with a black hood, having on the left side, near to the shoulder, a red sword, and on the breast two swords a cross, with the points downwards. This order was confirmed by Pope *Innocent* the third. The order of S. *Gall* in *Switzerland*, was instituted by *Frederick* the second, Emperour, *Anno* 1213. when he came on Pilgrimage to the Abby of St. *Gall*, and instituted that order which he called the order of the *Bear*, giving to the chief Lords thereof collars, and chains of gold, at the end whereof hung the form of a Bear in gold enamelled with black. The Abbot was to confirm this order every sixteenth day of *October*, being the Feast day of St. *Gall*, the Apostle of the *Germans*. This order was instituted to the memory of St. *Ursus*, Martyred before the Temple of the Sun at *Solleverre:* The Cantons of the *Switzers* honoured this order, till they fell off from the House of *Austria*; now it is quite lost. *Of St. Gall. See the Histories of thefeplaces.*

Q. 13. *What are the orders of Knight-hood in Italy?*

A. The Popes have been Founders of divers Orders. Pope *John* the twenty second at *Avington*, instituted the order of *Jesus Christ*, *Anno* 1320, They did wear a Cross of Gold enamelled with red, and inclosed with another Cross. Pope *Paul* the second instituted at *Rome* the Order of the *Holy Ghost*, *Anno* 1468. The Knights wear a white Cross. Pope *Alexander* the sixth, instituted the Order of Saint *George*, *Anno* 1498. They carried a Cross of Gold, entowered with a wreath made in form of a Crown. *Leo* the tenth instituted the Order of Saint *Peter*, *Anno* 1520. These wore within an Oval of Gold the Effigies of Saint *Peter*, at the end of a Tortis of Chains of Gold. These were to guard the Sea Coasts against the *Turk*. *Paul* the third established the order of, St. *Paul*, *Anno* 1540. Pope *Pius* the fourth, erected the order of the *Pies*, *Anno* 1560. Their charge was to carry the Pope when he went abroad in publick. He would have them to take place of the Knights of *Malta*, and of the Empire. *Sixtus Quintus* ordained the Knight-hood of *Lauretto*, *Anno* 1587. to whom he Erected our Lady Church at *Lauretto*, for a Cathedral. At *Rome* also, there be some Churchmen of the order of Knight-hood, as the Knights *Hospitallers* of Saint *Anthony*. The General of this Order is called Abbot of St. *Anthony* of *Vienna*; the principals of this Order do wear on their black Cassocks, Cloaks, and Gowns, a double Saint *Anthony*'s Cross; that is, two T. T. of blew Sattin; the meaner sort wear but one. The Knights of the Virgin *Mary*, were instituted by Brother *Bartholomew*, Bishop of *Vicenza*, a *Dominican*, *Anno* 1233. and confirmed by Pope *Vrban* the fourth, the Knights follow St. *Dominick*'s Rule, wearing a white Cassock, with a red Cross on the breast, with two Stars: Their cloak is of Gray colour. Their charge is to take care of Widows and Orphans, and to reconcile Differences between Man and Wife.

Divers Orders of Knights at Rome.

They

They lived at Home with their Wives and Families, and not in Convents. Hence they were named *Fratres Gaudentes*. Brethren of joy. The Order of the *Glorious Virgin Mary* was instituted at *Rome*, *Anno* 1618. by three Brothers, *Pedro*, *John Baptista*, and *Bernardo*. They were confirmed by Pope *Paul* the fifth, who with his successors were to be great Masters thereof. Their Convent is in the Palace of *Lateran*. They are bound to defend the Christian Faith, the Catholick Church, to suppress the *Turks*, to be Nobly extracted. The Knights *Layicks* of this order, and *Knights Priests* that are beneficed, are to wear about their necks a Ribband of blew. Silk, and a Golden Cross enamelled with blew, and on the Cloak a Cross of blew Sattin to shew the colour of the Virgins Garment which she wore, to wit, of a blew Skie-colour; but the Knights *Chaplins* are to wear the blew Cross on their Cloaks, but not about their necks. Within the Cross is a round circle, wherein is M.S. standing for *Maria Sancta*, with a Crown. About the circle are twelve Silver-beams, representing the twelve Apostles; each branch of the Cross hath nine Tracts, demonstrating the nine Orders of Angels; the four ends of the Cross are four Lilies, to shew that the Virgin is the Lily of the Valleys; at the ends of the Cross are four Stars, figuring the four Evangelists. At *Venice* there

Knights of Venice. is the order of Saint *Mark*'s Knights, instituted when Saint *Mark*'s Body was brought thither from *Alexandria*. At *Genoa* are the

Of Genoa. Knights of Saint *George*, and so divers Cities of *Italy* have their peculiar orders of Knight-hood: In *Savoy* there is the order of the

O Savoy. *Annunciation*, of which we have already spoken. The Collar of this order is composed of Roses and Love knots, whereunto hangs an Oval, containing the Angel, holding a Scepter, and saluting the Virgin, over whom hovereth a Dove. We have also spoken of the orders of Saint *Maurice*, and Saint *Lazarus*. The former of these two began *Anno* 1440. when *Amadeus* the seventh, first Duke of *Savoy*, retired to the Desart of *Ripaille*, to preserve the memory of that valiant Knight, as of his Lance and Ring. They follow Saint *Austin*'s rule. The order of Saint *Lazarus* was united by *Gregory* the thirteenth, to that of Saint *Maurice*; these are *Cistertians*, and have divers privileges and immunities.

Of Florence. The order of *Florence*, or of Saint *Stephen* Pope, was instituted by *Cosimo de Medici*, first Duke of *Florence*, *Anno* 1561, in honour of Pope *Stephen* the ninth Patron of *Florence*. They follow Saint *Bennet*'s rule, and have the same Priviledges with the Knights of *Malta*. They wear a long Gown of White Chambler, on the breasts, a red Cross like that of *Malta*. The order of the *Precious Blood of Christ*, was instituted by *Vincentio de Gonzago*

Of Mantua. the fourth Duke of *Mantua*, and second of *Monsferrat*, *Anno* 1608 in honour of Christ's Blood, some drops whereof are kept in Saint *Andrew*'s Church at *Mantua*. The Collar is composed of Ovals of Gold, and these two words, *Domine Probasti*; in the Ovals are flames of fire, burning about Gold-Smiths melting

pots

pots full of pieces of Gold. At the end of the Collar within an Oval, are two Angels standing upright, holding a Chalice and Pixe-Crowned, on the Table whereof are three drops of blood, with this Legend about the Oval, *Nihil isto triste recepto*.

See the above named authors.

Qu. 14. *What were the Christian Military orders in the East?*

A. The order of *Cyprus* and of *Luzignan*, or of the *Sword* was instituted by *Guy* of *Luzignan*, King of *Jerusalem* and *Cyprus Anno* 1195. The Collar of his order was composed of Cordans of white Silk twined into love knots, interlaced with the Letters S. and R. at this hung an Oval of Gold with a Sword in it, about the Oval was engraved these words, *Securitas Regni*. Of the other Eastern order we have already spoken; namely, of that of the Holy Sepulchre, instituted by *Baldwin* the first of that name, and second King of *Jerusalem*, Brother to *Godfrey of Bulloigne*, *Anno* 1103. They were at first *Canons Regular* of Saint *Austin*'s order, permitted to live in *Jerusalem*, by the *Saracens*: after they were Knighted, retained their white habit, wherein they carried the Cross of *Jerusalem*, such as the Kings bare in their Arms. Pope *Innocent* the eighth, *Anno* 1484, united these Knights to the *Hospitallers* of Saint *John*; but this Union lasted not long; for the Knights married, whereupon Pope *Alexander* the sixth took the power of conferring this order himself, giving power to the *Guardian* of the holy Sepulchre, who is always a *Franciscan*, who confer this Order on Pilgrims to the Holy Land, provided they take their Oath on the Holy Sepulchre. We have also spoken of the *Hospitallers* of St. *John* Baptist of *Jerusalem*, instituted by *Baldwin*, first King there, *Anno* 1104. Likewise of the Knights *Templars*, instituted under *Baldwin* the second, third King of *Jerusalem*, *Anno* 1119. Of these I will make no further mention. There were other Orders in the Holy-Land, as the Knights of St. *John of Acres*, of St. *Thomas*, of St. *Gerion*, of St. *Blaze*, &c. but these were of small note; and are now lost. See *Favine*'s Theatre of Honour.

Knighthood in the East.

The

The Contents of the twelfth Section.

The Opinions of the Anabaptists, *and wherein they agree with the old Hereticks.* 2. *The Tenets of the* Brownists. 3. *Of the* Familists. 4. *The* Adamites, *and* Antinomians. 5. *The Religion of the* Socinians. 6. *Of the* Arminians *Tenets.* 7. *Of the Church of* Arnhem, *and the* Millennaries *Opinions.* 8. *Of many other Sects at this day amongst us.* 9. *The Opinions of the* Independents. 10. *The Tenets of the* Presbyterians, *whereby way of a Chatechism is delivered their whole Doctrine concerning the Ministery, Episcopacy, Presbytery, Lay-Eldership, Deacons, Civil Magistrates, the Election of Ministers, Ordination, power of the Keys, Excommunication.* 11. *Divers erroneous Opinions which have been lately revived, or hatched since the Fall of our Church Government,* &c.

SECT. XII.

Quest. I. **W**Hat *Opinions in Religion are there held at this day among them that are fallen off from* Rome?

A. We have already spoken of the Opinions of *Luther*, *Calvin*, *Oecolampadius*, *Zuinglius*, and other Protestants; whose Tenets are followed by many thousands at this day: We have also spoken somewhat of the Original and Increase of *Anabaptism*; now we will briefly set down their Opinions, as they are recorded by *Pontanus*, *Bullinger*, *Gastius*, *Sleidan*, *Osiander*, and others, and will shew wherein they agree with the Old condemned Hereticks. They hold that Christ took not his flesh from the Virgin *Mary*; "So held the "Heretick *Valentinus*. 2. That Christ is not true God, " so held *Arrius*. 3. They deny baptism to Infants, " so did the *Pelagians*. 4. They re-baptize, so did the *Novatians*, *Arrians*, *Ætians* and *Donatists*. 5. They believe to enjoy here after the day of judgment, an earthly Monarchy, so did the *Cerinthians*, *Nepotians* Millennaries, and *Mahometans*. 6. They say our righteousness depends upon the works of charity and affliction, not upon faith in Christ; "so did the *Cathari*, *Meletians*, *Donatists*, and *Pelagians*: 7. They maintain free-will in spiritual things; so did the *Pelagians*. 8. They account themselves the only pure Church without sin; so did the *Donatists*. 9. They say Lay-men may administer the Sacraments; so did the *Marcionites*, and *Pepusians*. 10. They reject Magistracy among Christians; "so did the *Manichees*. 11. They say that Christian Magistrates are not to punish Malefactors

Anabaptists their Opinions and Names.

factors with death, "so said the *Tertullianists*. 12. They will have all things in common, "with the old *Nicholaitans*. 13. They teach that a man may put away his wife though not for adultery; "so taught the *Jews*. 14. And that a Christian may have many wives, which is the Doctrine of *Mahomet*. 15. They will not swear at all; *in this they follow the Tenet of the old Pelagians*. Now all these opinions are ancient Heresies as we have shewed, which have been refuted sufficiently by the ancient Doctors of the Church, and condemned by General and Provincial Councils, besides that divers late writers, both of the Roman and Protestant Church, have fully refelled these opinions; whose writings they that are at leisure may peruse. And by the way we must observe, that as the *Anabaptists* have divers opinions, so they have divers names. Some are called *Munzerians*, from *Munzer*, who raised the Boors in *Germany* against their Lords. He taught that all things shall be common. 2. *Separatists*, for separating themselves from the affairs of the World. 3. *Catharists*, for thinking themselves more pure than others; therefore deny original sin, nor will they pray, *Forgive us our sins*. 4. *Apostolicks*, who like the Apostles go without staff or scrip, up and down the World Preaching. 5. *Enthusiasts* pretend revelations, and brag they have the gift of prophecy. 6. *Silentes*, who place all their holiness in silence. 7. *Adamites* who believe that the wearing of Cloaths, is a cursed thing, therefore they affect nakedness. 8. *Georgians*, so called from *David George* the *Familist*, who boasted he was greater than Christ. 9. *Liberi*, who think they are made free by Christ from payments of Taxes or Debts, and free from obedience to humane Laws. 10. *Hutites*, so called from one *Huta* who denied Christ's Divinity, and made himself the only Son of God. 11. *Melchiorists*, so named from one *Melchior* of *Strasburg*, who taught that *Mary* was the Conduit through which Christ did pass, as water through a Pipe. 12. *Menonists* so called of *Menon* a *Frieslander*. 13. *Beucheldians*, so called from their Author, these affirm *Polygamy* to be an holy kind of life. 14. *Augustinians* from *Augustine* a Bohemian who bragged he was the first that opened Paradise for himself and followers. 15. *Servetians*, so called from *Servetus* the *Arrian*, who was burned at *Geneva* for denying Christ's Divinity, 1553. These will not Baptize Children till they be thirty years of age. 16. *Denkians* from one *Denkius* their Authour, who with *Origen*, would have the wicked and Devils to be saved. 17. *Monasteriensies*, so called from *Munster*, where *John* of *Leiden* their King reigned, who taught that he had a commission from Heaven to take many wives. 18. *Libertines*, who make God the Author of sin, and deny the Resurrection. 19. *Deo Relicti*, who rejected all means and relied only upon God. 20. *Semper Orantes*, who with the old *Euchites* are still praying, thinking they are tyed to no other duty.

Of these Altstedius *in his History of Anabaptists, and* Bullinger *in his first Book against them; have made a collection, and* M. Pait *out of them.*

Q. 2. What

A View of the Religions

Q. 2. *What were the Tenets of the* Brownists?

Brownists their Kinds and Tenets. *A.* These being so called from their Author, Master *Robert Brown* of *Northamptonshire*, sometimes a School Master in *Southwark*, hold there is no other pure Church in the World but among them; so did the Donatists *of old*. 2. They reject the Lord's Prayer; in this they are Jews, *and agree with the old Hereticks, called* Prodiciani. 3. They will not serve God in consecrated Churches, nor will communicate with those they called impure *in this they follow the old Cathari.* 4. They reject tythes, and affect parity, *in this they are Anabaptists.* 5. They hold all the Church Ceremonies to be Popish. 6. That the love which is in God is not Essential. 7. That Ordination of Ministers, by Bishops is Antichristian. 8. That the word preached, and Sacraments administred by scandalous Ministers, are altogether ineffectual. 9. That Church Musick is unlawful. 10. That Lay-men and Mechanicks may preach and expound Scripture. 11. That set forms of prayers are abominable in the sight of God, *whereas notwithstanding we have divers set forms, both in the Old and New Testament, at which they quarrel, and chiefly at the Lord's prayer.* 12. There be divers sorts of this profession; some *Brownists*, of which we have spoken; some *Barrowists*, so called from *Barrow* their first Martyr. He called the Church of *England*, *Sodom*, *Babylon*, and *Egypt*. Some are called *Wilkinsonians*, from *Wilkinson* their Master, who taught that he and his Followers were truly Apostles, and therefore denied Communion with such as did not give them that Title. A fourth sort there is of *Anabaptistical Brownists*, who hold themselves the only true Church, and condemn the other *Brownists* for *Pædobaptism*; therefore they re-baptize such as come to them. They that would see more of this Sect, let them read the Book called *The profane Schism of the Brownists*; another called *The foundation of Brownism*, Mr. *White*'s *Discovery of Brownism*; Doct. *Hall*'s *Apology against the* Brownists; *Gifford*'s *Declaration against the* Brownists; *Pagit*'s *Heresiography*, &c.

Q. 3. *What are the Familists?*

Familists, their Heresies. *A.* The *Familists*, or *Family of Love*, are so called from the love they bear to all men, though never so wicked; and their Obedience to all Magistrates, though never so tyrannical, be they *Jews*, *Gentiles* or *Turks*. Their Founder was one *David George*, of *Delph*, who called himself the true *David*, that should restore the Kingdom to *Israel*. He held, 1. That neither *Moses*, nor the *Prophets*, nor *Christ* could by their Doctrine save the People, but his Doctrine was the only means of Salvation. 2. That whosoever spoke against his Doctrine should never be forgiven, neither in this life nor in the life to come. 2. That he would set up the true House of *David*, and raise the Tabernacle of God, not by suffering, but through love and meekness. 4. That he was the right Messiah, the beloved Son of the Father. 5. That he should not die; or if he did, he should rise again. His Successor, *Henry Nicholas* of *Amsterdam*, maintained the same Doctrine, but in his

his own name, calling himself *The Restorer of the World, and the Prophet sent of God.* To the former Tenets he added, 1. That there is no other Christ but Holiness, and no other Antichrist but Sin. 2. That the *Family of Love* hath attained the same perfection that *Adam* had before he fell. 3. That there is no Resurrection of the flesh. 4. That the day of judgment is already come, and that this *Nicholas* is the Judge of the World. 5. That there hath been eight great Lights in the World, whereof Christ was the seventh, but himself the eighth, and greatest of all. 6. That none should be baptized till the thirtieth year of their age. 7. That the joys of Heaven shall be only here on the Earth, and so likewise Hell. 8. That they ought not to bury the dead, nor to give Alms to such as are not of their profession. 9. That Angels are born of Women. 10. That every day of the week should be a Sabbath. 11. That the Law may be fulfilled in this Life. 12. That there was a World before *Adam* was made. 13. That there is no other Deity but what man partakes of in this World. 14. That such Wives as are not of their Belief, may be rejected for Whores. 15. That in *Henry Nicholas* dwelleth all Perfection, Holiness, and Knowledge, and that their illuminated Elders are deified in this life, and cannot sin. There be also divers sorts of *Familists*, as *Castalians, Grindletonians,* of the *Mountains,* of the *Vallies,* of the scattered *Flock,* &c. which hold with these former Opinions, that the Scriptures are but for Novices; that we ought not to pray for Pardon of sin after we are assured of God's Love; that wicked men sin necessarily, and such more stuff.

As may be seen in Dr. Denisons white Wolf. M. Knowstub in the Familists Confession Mr. Jessop, and others.

Adamites.

Q. 4. *What be the* Adamites *and* Antinomians?

A. Of the *Adamites* in St. *Austin's* time, we have already spoken, as also of the *Bohemian Adamites*. Of late years there were some of them in *Amsterdam,* where the men and Women did pray in their meetings, and perform other divine services naked. This posture they call the state of innocency, and their Meetings Paradise. In their opinions they were *Anabaptists*. The *Antinomians* are so called from opposing and rejecting of the Law, which they say is of no use at all under the Gospel, neither in regard to direction, nor correction, and therefore ought not to be read or taught in the Church. 2. They say that good works do neither further, nor evil works hinder salvation. 3. That the child of God can no more sin than Christ could, and therefore it is sin in him to ask pardon for sin. 4. That God never chastiseth his children for sin; nor is it for their sins that any Land is punished. 5. That murther, adultery, drunkenness, are sins in the wicked, but not in the children of grace, nor doth God look upon them as sinners, and consequently that *Abraham's* lying and dissembling was no sin in him. 6. That the child of grace never doubteth, after he is once assured of Salvation. 7. That no man should be troubled in his conscience for any sin. 8. That no Christian should be exhorted to perform the duties of Christianity.

Antinomians.

9. That

A View of the Religions   Sect. 12.

9. That an Hypocrite may have all the graces that were in *Adam* before his fall, and yet be without Christ. 10. That Christ is the only subject of all graces, and that no Christian believeth or worketh any good, but Christ only believeth and worketh. 11. God doth not love any man for his Holiness. *Sanctification is no evidence of a man's justification. " Of this and such like stuff you " may read in *Pontanus* his Catalogue of Heresies, who makes one *John Agricola* the Author of this Sect. *Anno* 1535.

See also Gataker in his preface, Edwards in his Gangrena, P. git and others

Q. 5. *What is the Religion of the* Socinians?

A. *Faustus Socinus*, an *Italian* of *Siena*, placed all Religion in these Old condemned Heresies, so greedily embraced by his Disciples. 1. That man before his fall was naturally mortal. 2. That no man by the light of nature can have any knowledge of God. 3. That man before his fall, had no orginal righteousness. 4. That there is no original sin in us, as it imports concupiscence, or deformity of nature. 5. That there is a free will to goodness in us, and that we may here fulfill the Law. 6. That God hath no fore-knowledge of Contingencies determinately, but alternatively. 7. That the causes of predestination are not in God, but in us, and that he doth not predestinate to salvation any particular or certain person; and that predestination may be frustrated. 8. That God could justly pardon our sins without any satisfaction. 9. That Christ by his death did not satisfie for us, but only obtained power for us, to satisfie for our selves, by our faith and obedience. 10. That Christ died for himself; that is, not for his sins (for he was without sin) but for the Mortality and Infirmities of our nature - which he assumed. 11. That Christ became not our High Priest nor impassible before he ascended into Heaven. 12. That Death eternal, is nothing else but a perpetual continuance in death, or Annihilation. 13. That everlasting fire, is so called from its effect, which is the eternal extinction or annihilation of the wicked which shall be found alive in the last day. 14. That Christs Incarnation is against reason, and cannot be proved out of Scripture. 15. That Christ is not truly God. 16. That the Holy Ghost is not God; that there is not a Trinity of Persons in one God. 17. That the Old Testament is needless for a Christian man. " *These opinions are but Renovations of old Heresies, broached* " *by Ebion, Photinus, Arrius, Samosatenus, Sabellicus, Servetus,* " *Anti-trinitarians,* and others.

Socinians, their Tenets.

He that would see these opinions at large, let him read Socinus himself, Crellius, Lubbertus, the Racovian Catechism, Volkelius, Ostorodius, and others.

Arminians, their Tenets.

Q. *What be the* Arminian *Tenets* ?

A. *James Arminius*, Divinity-reader in *Leyden, Anno* 1605. published and taught five Articles, which have occasioned great Troubles in *Holland*, being eagerly maintained by his Followers called *Remonstrants*. They hold, 1. That Election to Life, is the will of God to save such as will Believe, and persevere in Obedience; that men may be elected to Faith, and yet not elected to Salvation; that election is sometimes absolute, sometimes

times conditional; that the act of Faith is chosen as a condition to salvation, and that in election to Faith, the condition of using the light of reason is required. That Faith and Obedience are fore-seen by God, as already performed by those who are to be chosen peremptorily and compleatly. That election sometimes is changeable, and some elect may finally perish; and consequently no certainty of our elections immutability. That God hath not decreed to leave any man in the state of sin and damnation, meerly out of his will and pleasure; and consequently it is not Gods meer will that one Nation should receive the Gospel, and not another, but a fore-sight of the goodness and worth of one Nation above another. 2. They teach that God so ordained his Son to die, that he did not determine to save any particular man expresly, so that Christs death was powerful and sufficient, in respect of impetration, though there had been no actual application thereof to any particular man: that Christ did not establish a new Covenant of grace by his blood, but only procured a right to his Father, to make with men any Covenant whatsoever: that Christ by his satisfaction did not merit faith and salvation to any man in respect of effectual application, but only obtained power, that the Father might make what conditions he pleased, with man, the performance whereof depends upon his free will: that the Covenant of grace consisteth not in being justified and saved by faith in Christ, but in this, that God esteemeth our imperfect faith and obedience as meritorious of life eternal, as if we had fulfilled the Law: that all men are received into the Covenant of grace, and all freed from original sin: that Christ died not for those whom God elected and highly loved, seeing such stood in no need of Christ's death. 3. They teach that original sin of it self was not sufficient to condemn mankind to temporal or eternal punishment: that an unregenerate man is not totally dead in sin, nor destitute of all strength to spiritual good things, but that he may hunger and thirst after righteousness and life: that a natural man can (by using the gifts of nature rightly) obtain saving-grace, and salvation, and that God affords sufficient means to bring men to the knowledge of Christ. 4. They teach that Holiness and Righteousness could not be seated in man's will when he was created, and therefore in his fall could not be separated from it: that in spiritual death, spiritual gifts were not separated from the will of man; seeing the will of it self was never corrupted, but intangled by the darkness of the intellect, and unruliness of the affection, that in man's conversion no new gifts are infused; and therefore the faith, by which we are converted, is not a quality infused, but only an act of man: that the grace by which we are converted, is only a gentle perswasion, so that Moral grace makes natural men become spiritual: and that God by Moral reason produceth the consent of the will: that God in mans conversion, doth not use his omnipotent power to bend the will infallibly, so that man may and

doth

doth oftentimes refist and hinder our own converfion: that grace and free will are co-operating caufes in our converfation, fo that grace in order of caufality doth not precede the action of the will. 5. They teach that perfeverance is not the effect of Election, but a condition of the new Covenant to be performed on man's part before his peremptory Election, and that by his own free-will, that God furnisheth the faithful man with fufficient means to perfevere; yet it is in the choice of man's will to perfevere, or not to perfevere: that regenerate men may and do fall totally and finally from grace and falvation; and that they may fin againft the Holy Ghoft: that on affurance of perfeverance can be had in this life without fpecial Revelation: that the Doctrine of affurance is hurtful to all holy exercifes, and a means of prefumption and fecurity, whereas doubting is commendable: that temporary, and true juftifying faith, differ only in continuance: that it is no abfurdity, if man be oftentimes regenerated, his former regeneration being extinct: that Chrift never prayed for the faithfuls infallible perfeverance in faith. Thefe are the five Articles of *Arminianifm*, as they are fet down in the Book called, *The Judgment of the Synod of* Dort.

Q. 7. *What are the Opinions of the new Church of* Arnhem?

The Church of Arnhem, and the Millennaries their opinions.

A. They hold that Independency is a beginning of Chrift's temporal Kingdom here on earth: that within five years, (but thefe are already expired) Chrift was to come in the flefh, and with an Iron Sword to kill moft of his enemies, and then that he fhould raign here on earth with his Saints a thoufand years, in all carnal delights. 2. That God is not only the author of fin, but alfo of the finfulnefs or *Ataxie* thereof. 3. That all men are bound to know God *in abftracto* without Chrift, without grace or Scripture. 4. They held extream unction to be a Sacrament and neceffary for the fick, and of divine inftitution, fo they held the holy kifs of peace a religious and needful ceremony. 5. They put down finging Pfalms, and fet up in lieu thereof finging Prophets, who are to chant out alone in the Congregation their own hymns. 6. They teach that the foul is mortal. 7. That juft men's fouls go not into Heaven till the laft day, but remain in the upper element of fire, whither *Enoch* and *Eliah*, with the Soul of Chrift before his refurrection, and the foul of the good thief went, and no higher: they teach alfo that the fouls of the wicked go not before the laft judgment into Hell, but remain in the lower region of the air or in the bottom of the fea. 8. They fay that after the day of judgment, all the World fhall be Hell, except that part of Heaven where God refides with his Angels. 9. In preaching, they will have their Minifters covered, and the people bare, but in adminiftring the Sacraments they will have the people covered, and the Minifter bare.

Of thefe opinions, fee the forenamed Authors.

Q. 8. *Upon what grounds do thefe Millennaries, build Chrift's temporal Kingdom here on earth for a thoufand years?*

Anfw.

Answ. Upon that place of the *Revelation.* 19. 4, 5, 6. *I saw the Souls of them, who were beheaded for the witness of Jesus, and they lived and reigned with Christ a thousand years:* " but this place " proves no such Kingdom, for it is mystical, and symbolical Divi-" nity, not argumentative. Again, in this place there is no menti-" on at all of any earthly presence of Christ, nor of any earthly " reign with him: besides the Kingdom of Christ is everlasting, " *for of his Kingdom, saith the Angel, there shall be no end;* there-" fore here is put a definite number for an indefinite. Christ saith, *his Kingdom is not of this World,* " the Kingdom of Christ " is spiritual and within us, and if we speak of Christ's Kingdom, " as he is Mediatour, and reigning in his Church by his Word, " Sacraments, and Discipline, we must conclude that he hath " reigned already above 1600 years; and how long more he shall reign here on earth we know not. 2. They build their opinion upon *Dan.* 12. 2. *Many of them who sleep in the dust shall arise, &c.* Hence they infer two resurrections, in the first, many shall rise to reign with Christ here on earth, in the second they say, all shall rise to judgment; *but this interpretation is ridiculous; for the first resurrection mentioned in Scripture is spiritual, to wit, a rising from the death of sin, of which the Apostle,* if you be risen with Christ, seek the things that are above; *for as sin is called death, you are dead in sins and trespasses, so the forsaking of sin is called a resurrection; this is the rising of the mind, the other of the body.* A-gain in Scripture, many *and* all *are promiscuously taken for the same, as here, many shall arise, that is all.* So Matth. 4. •Christ healed all Diseases; *that is, many*: Besides the Words of Daniel are di-rectly spoken of the second resurrection to judgment, and not to a tem-porary Kingdom: for he saith, that some of those shall rise to life eternal, not to a temporary of a thousand years, and others to everlast-ing shame, which yet the Millennaries deny, in saying, the wicked shall not rise till the expiration of the thousand years; and where they say, that the Saints shall shine as the Stars, or the firmament in the first resurrection, but as the Sun in the second, it is vain; for in the second resurrection shall be degrees of glory, as the Apostle sheweth, 1 Cor. 15. *For as one Star differeth from another Star in glory, so is the Resurrection of the dead; Some shall shine as the Sun who is the brightest of all the Stars; and some shall be lesser Stars in glory,* they do also vainly call their first Resurrection, a hidden mystery, where-as indeed it is the second Resurrection that is a mystery, and so hid-den, that the wisest Philosophers understood it not; and thought Paul had been mad when he Preached this mystery at Athens, that which cannot be apprehended by reason, but by faith only, may be truly called a hidden Mystery. 3. They misapply divers places of Scripture to prove this imaginary reign of Christ here on earth, as *Psal.* 102. 16. *When the Lord shall build up Sion, he shall appear in his glory.* " This Scripture was fulfilled when *Jerusalem* was rebuilt, after " the captivity. So they alledge, *Acts* 3. 20, 21. *The Heavens* " *shall*

The grounds upon which they build Christs tem-poral King-dom here on earth for a thousand years.

shall receive Christ, till the times of Restitution of all things. "But
" this is spoken of the second Resurrection, for then shall be a
" Restitution of all things, and not before, in their thousand
" years Reign : For they confess that then all the Jews shall not
" rise, nor all Christians, it must then follow, that there shall not
" be a restitution of all things, at that time. That place of *Rom.* 11.
" 12. concerning the calling of the Jews is impertinent ; for we
" deny not but they shall be called to the faith of Christ, but that
" they shall return, to build *Jerusalem*, and be under Christs
" earthlily reign 1000 years, is not at all spoken in that place :
No less impertinent is that place of 2 *Pet.* 3. 13. *We look for new
heavens, and a new earth, wherein dwelleth righteousness;* " For this
" is spoken of the last judgment, wherein all things shall be re-
" newed by fire, and not before ; as the circumstances of the
" Scripture do shew, and all interpreters do agree : So with-
" out any sence or reason, they apply the 65th chapter of *Isaiah* to
" their Millennary reign, which is plainly spoken of the calling of
" the Gentiles, and of Christs first coming to preach the Gospel,
" and to gather a Church, which there, and elsewhere, is called
" *Jerusalem*, and the Prophets usually under the terms of plant-
" ing, building, eating, and drinking, new Heavens, and new
" Earth ; the joy of Hills, Forests, and Trees, *&c.* do express
" the happy estate of the Church of Christ under the Gospel.
· *When the Mountain of the Lord's House shall be exalted on the top of
the Mountains, and all nations shall flock to it, then* Jerusalem *that
is the Church shall be the throne of the Lord.* Then out of *Sion* shall
go forth a Law, and the word of the Lord from Jerusalem; " Then
" shall the God' of Heaven set up a Kingdom, which shall never
" be destroyed ; Christ shall reign over the House of *Jacob* for ever,
" to this City of the Church, shall the Kings of the Earth bring
" their glory and honour : *in that day, he that is feeble shall be like*
David, *and the house of* David *shall be as God.* See *Isa.* chap. 2.
chap. 55. and chap. 5. *Jer.* 16. *Ezech.* 2. *Dan.* 2. *Zach.* 12. *Luke* 1.
Rev. 21. and many more places, which speak of the Churches felicity under the Gospel, but not a word of a Millennary Reign.
Q. 9. *Wherein doth the vanity of the Millennaries opinion consist?*

The vanity of the Mil-lennaries opinions.

An. 1. In giving to Christ a temporal Kingdom of a thousand
years, whereas his kingdom is eternal, it shall stand for ever,
of his Kingdom shall be no end saith the Angel.

2. In giving him an earthly Kingdom, whereas his Kingdom is
heavenly, *My Kingdom (faith he) is not of this World*; It is not
from hence, it is within us.

3. In making his Kingdom to consist in earthly pleasures, in
eating, drinking, fighting, *&c.* all which are directly against the
nature of his Kingdom, which as the Apostle saith *Rom.* 14. 17.
*Is not meat and drink, but righteousness, peace, and joy in the Holy
Ghost,* the end of his coming was to fight with no other weapon,

but

but with the two-edged sword of his Word, proceeding out of his mouth; he was the Prince of Peace, the Dove that brought the Olive branch in her mouth: he brought peace in his birth, he preached peace in his life, and recommended peace to us at his death: and as Saint *Austin* saith *pacem nobis reliquit, iturus ad Patrem, & pacem nobis dabit perducturus ad patrem*, his peace he left with us, and his peace he will bring again to us.

4. In this their imaginary Kingdom, they bring Christ down from heaven before his time; *for the heavens must contain him till the restitution of all things*, which cannot be till the last judgment, it is an Article of our creed, that Christ shall come down from heaven to judge the quick and the dead, which shall not be till the last day.

5. He is to sit at God's right hand, *untill he hath made his enemies his footstool, Psal.* 110. 1. But these men will bring him from thence before he hath obtained this conquest and triumph, which is not to be obtained till the last day, and consummation of all things. 6. They are injuries to Christ, to bring him from his place and condition of glory, to play the part of a Butcher and Executioner in murthering of men with the sword, here on earth, an office ill beseeming him, and no way suitable to his glorious condition, and mercy, who came to save sinners, and not to destroy them. 7. The Scripture mentioneth no other Resurrection of the bodies, but such as shall rise at the last day, *John* 6. 39, 40, 44. in the end of the World, when he shall have delivered up the Kingdom to God, 1 *Cor.* 15. 22. *Where we shall be caught up in the clouds to meet the Lord in the Air, and shall be ever with the Lord,* 1 Thes. 4. 15. But this Millennary Resurrection is long before the last day, and end of the World, neither in it shall we be ever with the Lord, if we are with him but a thousand years. 8. The Scripture doth not speak of three comings of Christ, but of two only; the first when he came in Humility, the second when he shall come in glory: *Unto them that look for him shall he appear the second time without sin unto salvation*, Heb. 9. 28. Let them shew us out of Scripture a third coming, and we will believe them. 9. Christ tells us, *John* 13. 2. *That in his Fathers house*, that is in Heaven, *are many mansions*; thither he is gone to prepare a place for us, and not here upon earth; for so we shall not be where he is, but he shall be where we are; which is repugnant to his own words. 10. They make the time of Christ's second coming to Judgment certain, in affirming it shall be at the end of their thousand years; but this is repugnant to Christ's words, who saith, that his coming shall be sudden, secret, and unexpected, like the coming of a Thief in the night: like the coming of *Noah's* flood, or the fire of *Sodom*: *So that of that day and hour knoweth no man, no not the Angels in Heaven*; nor Christ himself as he is man. 11. Whereas the condition of Christ's Church here on earth in mixed, consisting of Saints and Reprobates,

bates, of sheep and goats, of good and bad fishes, of wheat and chaff, of corn and tares; they give Christ such a Church, as is without sin and sinners, as need no preaching nor Sacrament, no Pastors and Teachers, no Advocate with the Father, no Christ to appear for us in the presence of GOD: and lastly, such a Church as is not subject to persecution, affliction, sufferings and trouble; all which is directly repugnant to Gods word; and condition of the Church militant here, which is subject both to infirmities and afflictions. 12. Antichrist shall not be destroyed, till Christs second coming to judgment, as the Apostle sheweth, 2 Thes. 2. 8. That *Christ shall destroy him with the brightness of his coming*; but the Millennaries will have him to be destroyed before the beginning of their thousand years which is flat against Scripture. 13. They do exceedingly wrong the Martyrs, in bringing their souls down from heaven, where they have the fruition of God and his Angels, to reign here on earth, and to enjoy carnal and sensual pleasures; the meanest of the Saints in heaven must be in a far better condition, than the greatest martyr in this earthly Kingdom. 14. The reward that is promised to the Saints after this life, is not a Kingdom here on earth, but the Kingdom of heaven; *a house made without hands, eternal in the heavens*; a mansion in our Heavenly Fathers house, to sit with Christ in his throne; to be caught up in the clouds; to meet the Lord in the air; and to be ever with the Lord; to be with Christ in paradise, to enjoy life-eternal, *&c.* 15. Whereas they dream that *Jerusalem* shall be rebuilt, and the Jews shall reign in *Juda* a thousand years with Christ, is directly also against Gods word, which *Ezek.* 16. 54, 55. sheweth that the Jews shall be restored to their former state, when *Samaria* and *Sodom* shall be restored, which will never be, and *Gen.* 49. 10. The Scepter shall depart from *Juda* when *Shilo* cometh: *Jerusalem* saith St. *Hierom, est in æternos collapsa cineres*, fallen into everlasting ashes, and never to rise again. 16. Whereas they dream, that in the Millennary Kingdom, sacrifices, circumcision, and all other Jewish ceremonies shall be used, 'tis plainly to deny that Christ ever came in the flesh; or that he offer'd himself a propitiatory sacrifice, to put an end to all Jewish rites, which were but shadows of Christ's sufferings; the substance being come, the shadows were to vanish: therefore the Apostle saith, *Gal.* 9. That *they who turn to these beggarly elements again, desire to be in bondage again*, and in the next chapter, he tells the *Galatians*, that *if they be circumcised, Christ shall profit them nothing*. Lastly, this millennary Kingdom of eating, drinking, and sensual pleasures, was fitly devised by *Cerinthus* the Heretick, as best suiting with his swinish disposition; for he was noted for a person given to Gormandizing, and libidinous sports.

Q. 10. *What other Sects and Opinions are there now stirring amongst us?*

A. We

A. We have *Anti-trinitarians*, or *Polonian Arrians*, which Sects of this
sprung up in *Poland, Ann.* 1593. These deny the Trinity of Per- Age.
sons, the Divinity of Christ, and of the Holy Ghost ; that Christ
was the Son of God essentially, but in respect of his dominion, and say that the eternal generation of the Son, is against
truth and reason. We have also *Millennaries*, the spawn of *Cerinthus* the Heretick ; these dream of a temporary Kingdom here
on Earth, which they shall enjoy with Christ a thousand years.
*But indeed they aim at the enjoyment of the temporal estates of such
as they call wicked, who (as they think) have no property in their
estates.* We have *Traskits*, so called of one *Trask*, who would
have no Christian Sabbath kept, but the Jewish Laws observed,
and the Sabbath or Seventh-day to be perpetually kept holy till
the World's end. Others we have, who will keep no Sabbath
at all: these we call *Anti-Sabbatarians.* We have likewise *Anti-Scripturians*, who reject all Scriptures as man's inventions ; there
are among us *Divorcers*, who hold that Men may put away their
Wives upon small occasions. We have also *Soul-Sleepers*, who
with the *Arabick* Hereticks, hold that the Soul dieth or sleepeth with the Body : *Whose souls I think are asleep before the body* Seekers or
dyeth ; Amongst other professions, we have of late *Seekers* or *Ex-* Expecters.
pecters, who deny there is any true Church or Ministry, and
therefore they are seeking one, *But they know not where to find this
Church, except it be in the Land of* Utopia. There was one *Aetherington* a Box-maker who rejecting all Church-discipline, published that the Sabbath of the *Jews* was abolished by Christ, and
that every day now is a Sabbath ; that the Books of *Esdras* were
Canonical Scripture, and in other Opinions agreed with the
Familists.

Q. 11. *What Opinions in Religion are held by* Theaurau
John.

Ans. He calls himself, *Priest of the Jews, sent as he saith from* Theaurau
GOD, *to convert them* : his wild whimsies are these ; 1. He John his
calls it nonsence and a lye to say that GOD is Father of us all. 2. That opinions.
we Gospellers (as he call us) *worship the Devil, because* (saith he)
the spirit of man is a Devil. 3. *That it is a monster, and absolute
blasphemy to say, the Godhead dwelt in Christ bodily.* 4. *He wonders
how he that created all, could be born of a Woman* : by which we
may plainly see he is a circumcised Jew. 5. He saith, *that the
child which the Virgin brought forth, is love, as if the generation of
Christ were altogether mystical, and not real.* 6. He saith, That
Mary *is Christ, and Christ is* Mary, *and these are but names of one
thing.* 7. He denyeth, *That Christ was properly born, or that he
was born in one, or that he was begotten ; or that he could be flesh
properly ; or that he did descend into our flesh, but into our spirits
only ; or that he could be included in the Virgins womb ;* and withall he belyeth us in saying, *That we have brought the humanity to
be very* GOD: *whereas we say, the same person is God and Man,*

are not by conversion of the God-head into flesh, but by taking of the manhood into God. One altogether, not by confusion of substance, but by unity of person. 8. He calls the English Clergy thieves, robbers, deceivers, founding from Antichrist, and not from the true Christ, in which we see the impudent spirit of an heretick, who can no other ways defend his lyes, and blasphemies, but by railing. 9. He prateth, That the Gospel cannot be preached by another, but by it self; so that man's voice or outward sound, is a lye and Antichrist. 10. That our Ministers, are not Christ's Embassadors, but that their Call is a lye, for 'tis learning, and learning is that Whore which hath deceived the Nations, and compleated the work of Antichrist, "See the "impudence and boldness of this blind ignoramus. 11. He denieth, that the Priest's lips can preserve knowledge, though the Scripture is plain for it; but by the Priest, he understands knowledge it self, and so he will make the Holy Ghost to speak Tautologies, in saying, Knowledge shall preserve knowledge: Here we see the fruits of ignorance. 12. He makes the spirit of Man to be a quintessence abstracted one of the elementary motions, "such is his dull Philosophy. 13. Out of his kind respect to the Devil, by whose instinct he writeth: he affirms, That he with the false prophet shall receive mercy at last; because GOD will not punish a finite thing infinitely. "But here he again bewrays his ignorance; "for the Devil is infinite à posteriore, both in regard of his essence, and of his desire in sinning; besides, that God whom he offendeth, is infinite. 14. He ignorantly saith, That he who confers God's gift, is as great, yea, greater than GOD himself; if so, then it must follow, that the Apostles were greater than God, when they gave the gifts of the Holy Ghost by imposition of hands. 15. He impiously saith, that Saint Paul wrote many things which he understood not. 16. And as impiously doth he say, that in them Books, which we call Scripture, is the lye, as well as in other Books. 17. After his ignorant manner, he confounds the gift of prophecy with the prophet himself, in saying, Man is not the prophet, but the light in Man from God. 18. He will not have us to seek for Antichrist abroad, for Man in darkness is Antichrist, "I deny "not, but every Man in darkness, is in some sort an Antichrist: "yet there is one great Antichrist to be sought for abroad. 19. The Trinity which he acknowledgeth is, God the Son, and man: "this Trinity is hatched in his crasie brain. 20. He is so mad, that he saith, he can make one word bear forty significations: so he can make [ru] thou stand for dark or light, or Hell, or Heaven, or Sea, or Land, or Angel, or Sun, or the Devil. 21. He will not have Christ's body that suffered to be our Saviour, nor Christ's body; for Christ's body, saith he, is obedience: thus he would fain make Christ our Saviour, a meer allegory; and therefore in plain terms affirmeth, that true Christ hath not, nor cannot have any true corporal body; for he is a spirit and a spirit is free from flesh, "as if forsooth a spirit "and flesh could not be united in the same person: then he concludes "that the body or flesh which suffered at Jerusalem was not Christ's
"body,

" body. 22. He makes the soul of Man to be all one with the Gospel: and the body of Christ to be the whole Creation; " by this and
such like stuff with which his books are fraughted, we may see that he
deserveth to have his brains purged with Hellebor, rather than his
crazy opinions refuted by arguments, or Scripture. In the mean while,
we may perceive to our great grief, the lamentable fruits which are
begot of too much liberty in Religion. These impious opinions are in
his printed Pamphlets lately published. One *Richard Coppin* holdeth
some of the before-recited Opinions, and withal, lately before a confused multitude, in an usurped Pulpit, asserted the lawfulness of
Women's preaching, *For such Ranters, a Pillory were more fit than
a Pulpit.*

Q. 12. *What opinions in Religion are lately broached by* John
Reeve, *and* Lodowick Muggleton?

A. These two would perswade us, that they are the two last wit- *John Reeve*
nesses, and Prophets of Christ, sent by his spirit to seal the fore- and *Lodo-*
heads of the Elect and Reprobate: that one *John Robins* is the last *wick Mug-*
great Antichrist, and Son of perdition, spoken of by the Apostle *gleton their*
in the *Thessalonians*, because he sheweth lying signs and wonders, opinions.
and assumes to himself the Titles of the only God, in that he calls
himself *Adam* and *Melchisedech*, and Father of Jesus Christ; in
saying, the three Persons in Trinity are *Adam*; that is, himself,
Abel, that is his Son Jesus; and *Cain*, that is, the holy Ghost:
" Many such blasphemies they ascribe to him. They affirm also
that Christians using the sword of Steel, are ignorant of Jesus, and
enemies to his Gospel, and they teach, that the two uncreated
substances of earth and water, were eternally resident in the
presence of God the Creator: that death was from Eternity:
that the person of the Reprobate Angel or Serpent, entered into
the womb of *Eve*, and there died, but quickned in her all manner of uncleanness: that there is no Devil at all without the body of Man or Woman, but what dwells within them; so that the
Devil spoken of so often in the Scripture is man's spirit of unclean
reason, and cursed imagination: That God the Father, was a
spiritual man from Eternity, and that in time his spiritual body
brought forth a natural body: that if the very God-head had not
died; that is, (say they) the Soul of Christ, which is the Eternal Father had not died, all men had perished eternally: that
Moses and *Eliah* are Angels, and did represent the person of the
Father in heaven, as they did the person of the Son on earth, that
Eliah was made Protector of God: when God became a child;
and that he filled the Lord Jesus with those great revelations of
his former glory which he possessed in heaven, when he was the
immortal Father, and that it was *Eliah* who spake these words
from heaven, saying, *This is my beloved Son in whom I am well-plea-
sed*: They say also, that all the Ministry in this World, whether
Prophetical or Ministerial, with all the worship taught by them,
is all a lye, and abomination to the Lord. Again they declare,

that

that whereas, *there are three witnesses on earth, water, blood, and the spirit*: that by water is meant the Commission given to *Moses* and the prophets under the Law: by blood the Commission given to the Apostles, and ministers of the Gospel: and by the Spirit is meant the Commission of the two witnesses, that were to come in this last age, whose ministry is invisible and spiritual, cutting off all formal worshipping of an invisible, spiritual, personal God: they say there is hardly a minister in the World, that confesseth an invisible God, but they preach a God of three persons, that is a Monster instead of one true personal God: they say, that the true God is a distinct body or person, as a Man is a distinct body or person: again, they say, that there is no Christian Magistrate in the World, that hath any authority from Christ, to set up any visible form of worship; and that the spirits and bodies of men, are both mortal, both begot together, and both of one nature: that the spirit is nothing, without the body, and that it is the spirit alone, that walks and works, eats and drinks, and dies, for the spirit is a natural fire of reason: they say also that the bodies or persons of holy men, wherein they lived and died, shall not appear again any more; but when the Saints are glorified, they are absolutely of the very same glorious nature, both in spirit and body, as God is: and that believing spirits are of the very same divine nature of God. " This is the summ of their divinity, and
" Philosophy, as may be seen in their transcendent spiritual Trea-
" tise, (as they call it) which is full of transcendent nonsence,
" and blasphemies, for here they lay their axe to the very root
" of Christianity; in giving a new Father to our Saviour Jesus
" Christ, in calling the blessed Trinity a monster in denying the
" creation, whilst they make earth and eternal; in making an-
" gels, and men's souls mortal; in making weak man, God's
" Protector, and author of that divine knowledge which was in
" Christ; in denying the Ministry of the Gospel, and the power
" of the Magistrates, and the outward worship of God, and ma-
" king the souls of men corporeal; in denying also the Resur-
" rection of the flesh, and transforming men into the Divine na-
" ture. By this and other wicked tenets, permitted and coun-
" tenanced among us, at this time; we see what Christian Re-
" ligion is come to in this Land; so famous heretofore for piety
" and zeal: we received Christianity as soon as any Nation in
" *Europe*: whether by the preaching of St. *Peter*, or St. *Paul* or *Si-*
" *mon Zelotes* or *Joseph* of *Arimathea*, I know not, but all agree,
" we received it very early, and have continued ever since in the
" profession thereof; neither was there ever any Nation more de-
" vout and zealous in the advancement thereof, as our goodly
" Temples, Monasteries, Hospitals, Colleges and Schools can
" witness, but alas! now *Quantum mutamur ab illis Angligenis?*
" what is there left among us, but the bare skelliton of Religion,
" the vital substance thereof being eat up and consumed by here-
.sies

" fies and blasphemies, worse than any *Sarcophagus*. I may here
" with *Jeremiah* complain that from the daughter of *Sion*, all her
" beauty is departed, her Princes are become like Harts, *&c.*
" How is the gold become so dim and the most fine gold changed,
" and the stones of the sanctuary are scattered in every corner of
" the streets, *&c.*

Q. 13. *What are the Opinions of the Quakers?*

A. These fanatical spirits are called Quakers, because they use to quake and tremble when they prophesie; so did the Heathen soothsayers of old, *Non vultus, non color unus, non comptæ manse're comæ, sed pectus anhelum, & rabie fera corda tument,* &c. but the Spirit of God, is the Spirit of peace, quietness, and tranquility; he is not in Fire, Earthquakes and Whirlwinds, but in the soft and still voice; it's not the quaking of the body, but humility and reverence of mind which he requires; these sectaries *deny all ministerial Ordinances; and knowledge got by study and industry,* pretending an inward light from the spirit, and that all our Learning got by Preaching, Hearing, Reading, or Catechising, is but notional and carnal and hanging upon the tree of knowledge: they blasphemously prate also, that Christ had his failings, and that he distrusted GOD on the Cross, when he cried out *My God, My God, why hast thou forsaken me?* by which they overthrow the work of our Redemption, which none could perform, but he that knew no sin, in whose lips was found no guile, whom his enemies could not accuse of sin. *They will not have Ministers to preach for tithes, which they call wages,* and yet our Saviour saith, *That the labourer is worthy of his wages,* and the Apostle, *That they who serve at the altar, should live by the Altar,* and if they communicate of their spiritual things, why should they not participate of the peoples temporal things. *That will not have particular houses for preaching and prayer;* and yet among the Jews was the Temple, and Synagogues and after Christianity was settled, Churches were erected. *They cannot abide studied or methodical Sermons, nor expounding, nor learning in matters of Divinity,* by which we see how ignorant these people are, who despise such helps as GOD hath given for propagating the Gospel. Is it not better to study and premeditate, than to utter *quicquid in buccam venerit,* undigested, immethodical, ignorant trash. Christ and his Apostles expounded and opened the Scriptures; and yet these men reject expounding; these men are also against singing of Psalms, a duty practised by Christ, and urged by Saint *Paul,* and Saint *James.* They *reject Infant-Baptism,* and yet to infants belong the Kingdom of Heaven. *They will have no set-days for Divine worship,* and consequently the Lord's-day must be of no account with them. *They will have no prayer before and after Sermon;* and yet the Apostles joyn'd prayer with their Doctrine and breaking of bread, *Acts,* 2. 24. neither did they ever undertake any weighty business without prayer. They condemn *set-hours of*

prayers

[marginal note: Quakers, or as some call them Shakers, their opinions.]

prayers, and yet we read in the *Acts* of the Apostles, that the third and ninth hours, were set hours of prayer: but by these wild Fancies we may see, how cross-grained these people are in contradicting every thing, even God's Word it self; if it be not consonant to their shallow reason, which they call the spirit, but it is indeed the spirit of giddiness, with which they are troubled, and trouble others; for the rejecting of all outward forms, and decent ceremonies in Religion is the overthrow of Religion it self; which though it consist not in ceremonies, yet without them it is like a man strip'd naked of his garments, and so for want of them exposed to all injuries of weather, and danger of death. The leaves of a tree are not the fruit thereof, and yet without them the fruit will not prosper.

Q. 14. *What other Opinions do the Quakers hold?*

Other opinions of the Quakers.

Answ. Not to mention their horrid blasphemies, in saying that some of them are Christs, some God himself, and some equal with God, because they have the spirit in them which is in God. They maintain that the Scripture is not the Word of God: that our Preaching is conjuration; that expounding of Scripture is adding to it; that the letter of Scripture is carnal; that the word is not the rule to try the spirits: that the soul is a part of God, and long existent before the body: that there is no Trinity: that Christ hath no other body but his Church: that Christ's coming in the flesh was but a figure: that all men have a light in them sufficient to salvation: that the man Christ is not ascended into Heaven: that there is no imputation of Christ's righteousness: that prayer for remission of sins is needless: that we are justified by our own inherent righteousness: that there is no other life or glory to be looked for, but in this World: that there is no local Heaven nor Hell, nor resurrection of the body: that many of them cannot sin: that the calling of our Ministry is Antichristian: that our preaching is altogether useless: that themselves are immediately called by God: that our worshipping of God in the Church is heathenish: that the sprinkling of children with water in Baptism, is Antichristian: that we have no Sacraments: that *David*'s Psalms are carnal, and not to be sung: that in our Churches, " which they call beast-houses, God is not worshipped: that Christ came to destroy all property; and that therefore all things ought to be common: that no man is to be called Master or Sir, or to be saluted by the way; and that one man ought not to have power over another: *Here we see that these men despise Magistracy, reject the Ministry, slight all decency and ordinances in Christ's Church, and in a word, overthrow, as much as in them lieth, all Religion and Piety, setting up a Babel of their own, full of impiety, ignorance and blasphemy: these are the fruits of the too much liberty, and the effects of reading Scripture, by ignorant and malicious spirits; who like Spiders, suck poyson out of the sweetest and wholsomest flowers, and like mad-men, use that sword of the word to destroy themselves*

See what hath been written against them by Samuel Eaton, Robert Sherlock, and others.

and others, which was ordained to save and defend us from our Enemies.

Q. 15. *Wherein do the Absurdities and Impieties of their Opinions consist?*

A. 1. In rejecting all University-Learning, because Christ and his Apostles were never taught in Schools: But this Opinion is ridiculous; for Christ and his Apostles, taught no other Divinity for the matter, than what is taught in Universities; the difference is only in the manner of attaining this knowledge, for they had it by Inspiration, we by Study, Labour and Instruction; and yet the Prophets had their Schools and Colleges both, on the Hill of God, 1 Sam. 10. 5, 10. and at *Bethel*, 2 *Kings* 2. 3. and at *Jericho*, v. 5. and at *Naioth*, 1 *Sam.* 14. 20. *Elisha* had his College, 2 *Kings* 6. 1, 2. *They will not have us expound Scripture, because the Apostles expounded them*: But this conceit is also frivolous; for to what purpose did Christ appoint Doctors and Pastors to continue still with his Church, if they are not to expound Scripture? where the Apostles expounded briefly, we expound more fully. In their Expositions, there be many intricate, obscure, high, and figurative passages, which require a further exposition. God did never reveal all his truth at one time. Among the Jews we read that *Ezra* the Scribe, and the Levites expounded the Law, *Nehem.* 8. Christ took a Text and expounded it, *Luke* 4. and so did *Philip*, *Acts* 8. 3. *They will not have Ministers to be called Masters*: But I would know of these men, whether they that labour in the Word and Doctrine deserve not honour, even double honour; that is, honourable titles, and honourable maintenance; 'tis true, they should not ambitiously affect honours, nor ought they to reject them. Christ was oftentimes called Master, and yet he never reproved any for calling him so. 4. They quarrel *with the word Sacrament, because not found in Scripture*; but I would know, whether the *thing meant* by this word Sacrament be not found in Scripture? where hath the Scripture forbid us to call sacred things by significant terms? they may as well say, that God is not every-where, or that he knows not all things, because these words *omnipresent* and *omniscient* are not in Scripture. 5. *They will not have Ministers to take Tithes*; then they will not have those who wait at the Altar, to partake with the Altar, which thwarts the Apostles words directly; why should not the Ministers under the Gospel as well receive Tithes, as the Priests under the Law? is our burthen easier, or our calling less deserving? it's too much presumption to discommend what Christ hath commended; but he commended the Scribes and Pharisees for paying their Tithes, *Luke* 11. 42. 6. *They rejected Infant-Baptism, because the Scripture speaks not of it*, but the Scripture speaks of baptizing whole Families, and Nations, *Acts* 16. 33. but Infants are included in these: Infants were circumcised, were admitted to Christ; to them belongs the Kingdom of Heaven. *Jeremiah* an Infant, was sanctified by the holy Spirit, *Jer.* 1. 5, 6. The hand of the Lord was with *John Baptist* an Infant, and he grew strong in the Spirit, *Luke* 1. 66, 80. *Can any man then forbid water, that these should not be baptized, which have received the Holy Ghost?* 7. *They Quarrel with publick prayers in the Church, because Christ bids us pray in private;* this is a childish consequence; for the one should be done, and the other not to be left undone: Our Saviour prayed sometimes privately by himself, and sometimes publickly with his Disciples: he calleth his Temple the House of prayer; but the prayers there used were publick. St. *Paul* both prayed in publick, and taught in publick. *Acts* 20. 36. and 21. 5. Publick prayers were used among the Jews also, *Neh.* 9. 3, 4. Are we not commanded to pray continually, and to lift up pure hands in all places? is it not by prayer that our preaching is sanctified, and made useful? it's true, we ought not to make publick places, (*as the Pharisees did the Temple and Synagogue*) the places for our private prayers; we have Chambers at home to pray in private; but this privacy doth no more exclude publick prayers, than private instructions at home by the Master to his Family, do exclude publick preaching. 8. *They will not have David's Psalms to be sung in meter.* These dull souls do not know, that *David* made his Psalms in meter, and did sing them; and why may not we do the same in our language, which *David* did in his? besides, did not Christ sing a Hymn? did not *Paul* and *Silas* sing Psalms to God at midnight? *Acts* 16. Doth not the Apostle exhort us to Psalms and Hymns? *Ephes.* 5. and doth not Saint *James* will us to sing Psalms, when we would be merry? there are in the Psalms as in a storehouse, all sorts of materials for devotion, and for all occasions. 9. *They make faith and repentance necessary concomitants of Baptism,* this they hold to exclude Infants from Baptism, but they should know, that though Infants have not faith, and repentance actually, yet they have both in possibility; the seed of both are in them, and the actual faith of their parents, supplies the actual defect of the Children: besides *Simon Magus, Alexander,* the Copper-smith, and others, were baptized, who neither had true faith, nor repentance; and repentance is enjoyned to *Simon,* long after his Baptism, *Acts* 8. 13, 22. and Christ was baptized, who needed neither faith nor repentance. 10. They say, *That the Church is in God;* therefore *God is in the Church,* by the same reason they may say, that God is not in Heaven, because Heaven is in God; or that Christ is not in us, because we are in Christ; Christ is in us as the Head, we are in him as the Members. The Church is in God, because in him we live, move, and have both our natural and spiritual being: God is in his Church by his assistance, providence, and spiritual presence, and so he hath promised, that where two or three are gathered together in his Name, there is he in the midst of them. *Mat.* 18. 20. Divers other absurd Opinions they maintain; as namely, against Tithes, against maintenance for preaching, against Clerks saying *Amen* in

the

Church, and such like; of which we have already spoken, and indeed all or most of their opinions are Anabaptistical, and this Sect is the spawn of Anabaptists, who are subdivided into different factions, and such diversity there is amongst them, that the Anbaptists in *Holland* will not admit those of *Moravia* and *Suevia*, without Rebaptization. *Sebastian Francus* in his Chronology, reckons seventy Sects of them.

Q. 16. *Now you have satisfied me as to the Quakers; I pray do me the like favour concerning a sort of people they call Ranters, which I have received divers horrid relations of, and such, as for their strange and impious assertions, I have not yet admitted into my belief?*

A. The Ranters are a sort of beasts, that neither divide the hoof, nor chew the cud; that is to say, very unclean ones, such as hold no small correspondency with the *Quakers*, their lives and demeanors are much alike, only what the ranters act upon the stage, by an open profession of lewdness and irreligion, the other do it within the curtain, by crafty and seemingly innocent insinuations and pretences of sanctity, and the contempt of the things of this World. These are they that make a laughing-stock of Christianity by their bitter invectives, and derision at the ordinances and ceremonies of Christian Religion; These are they that make no distinction between *Forms* and *Order*, for having cried down the former, their dispensations will not bear with the latter; it being their main design to bring the business of Religion to that condition, wherein Man was before he had assum'd thoughts of government; that is to say, into Anarchy and Confusion. As for their blasphemies and horrid expressions of Christian things! *Mahometans, Jews,* and *Pagans,* own more modesty, and less prophaneness. But to retail their opinions; or to anatomize this Monster, we must come to particulars. 1. They hold that God, Devils, Angels, Heaven, Hell, &c. are Fictions and Fables. 2. That *Moses,* the Baptist, and *Christ,* are Impostors! and what Christ and his Apostles acquainted the World with, as to matter of Religion, perished with them, and nothing transmitted to us. 3. That Preaching and Praying is useless; and that it is but publick Lying. 4. That there is an end of all Ministry and Administrations, and people are to be taught immediately from God. 5. They hold Baptism a pure, legal administration, not proceeding from Christ, but from *Joh.* 9. They jest the Scriptures, *That Divine Legacy of our salvation!* out of all life, reverence, and authority, quoting it in driblets and shreds, to make it the more ridiculous. In their Letters, they endeavour to be strangely prophane, and blasphemous, uttering Atheistical curses and imprecations, which is a kind of canting among them, as among Gypsies; as for example, in one you have this style, *My own heart blood, from whom I daily receive life, and being, to whom is ascribed all honour,* &c. *thou art my garment of needle-work, my garment of Salvation. Eternal plagues consume you all, rot, sink and damn your bodies and souls into devouring fire, where none but*

Ranters their Character, and Opinions.

those who walk uprightly can enter. *The Lord grant that we may know the worth of Hell, that we may scorn Heaven.* 7. Sin is only what a man imagines, and conceives to be so within himself. 8. Ordinances they account poor low things, nay, the perfections of the Scriptures is so inconsiderable in their apprehensions, that they pretend to live above them! *Their lives witness they live without them.* 9. If you ask them what Christian liberty is, they will tell you that it consists in a community of all things, and among the rest, of women; which they paint over with an expression call'd *The enjoyment of the fellow-creature.* 10. The enjoyment of the fellow-creature, cannot but be seconded with lascivious songs, drinking of healths, musick, dancing, and bawdry. Lastly, They are (with the *Anabaptists*) those that most of all kick against the pricks of Authority: for Magistracy cannot have in it any thing more sacred than the Ministry, so that they wish as much Policy in the State, as Government in the Church, which is none at all; so to bring an Ægyptian darkness upon both: that the World might be the less scandalized at their madnesses and extravagancies. *But this age, which is much more fruitful of Religions, than of good works, of Scripture-phrases, than of Scripture-practices, of opinions, than of piety, had spawned more Religions, than that Lady of* Holland *did Infants; to mention all which, were to weary both my self and the Reader; therefore I will content my self to mention some few more, as the* Independents, Presbyterians, *&c.*

Q. 17. *What are the Opinions of the* Independents?

Independents their Tenets.

A. 1. These are so called, because they will have every particular Congregation to be ruled by their own laws, without dependance upon any other in Church-matters. 2. They prefer their own gathered Churches (as they call them) in private places, to the publick Congregations in Churches, which they slight, calling them Steeple-houses. 3. They hold there is no use of learning or degrees in Schools, for preaching of the Gospel; and withall, that maintenance of the Ministry by Tithes, is Superstitious and Judaical. 4. They are against set-forms of Prayer, chiefly the Lord's-prayer, accounting such forms, a choaking of the spirit. 5. They give power to private Men, who are neither Magistrates nor Ministers, to erect and gather Churches; and to these also, they gave the power of Election and Ordination, (if we may call this Ordination) of Deposition also, and Excommunication, even of their own Officers, and final determination of all Church-causes. 6. They commit the power of the Keys in some places to Women, and publickly to debate and determine Ecclesiastick Causes. 7. They admit private Men to administer the Sacraments, and Magistrates to perform the Ministers office in Marrying. 8. They permit Divorces in slight cases. 9. They hold Independency to be the beginning of Christ's Kingdom, which is to be here on Earth a thousand years. 10. They place much Religion in names, for they do not like the old names of Churches, of the days of the week,

of the month of the year; of *Christmas, Michaelmas, Candlemas,* &c.
11. In preaching they will not be tied to a Text, nor to prayer, but they make one to preach, another to pray, a third to prophesie, a fourth to direct the Psalm, and another to bless the people.
12. They permit all gifted Men (as they call them) to preach and pray, and then after prophesying is ended, they question the Preacher in the Points of his Doctrine. 13. Some of them allow no Psalms at all to be sung in publick calamities, and will not suffer Women to sing Psalms at all. 14. They will baptize no Children, but those of their own Congregations; whom they esteem not Members of their Church, until they have taken their Covenant.
15. They in divers places communicate every Sunday among themselves, but will not communicate with any of the Reformed Churches. 16. Whilst they are communicating, there is neither reading, exhortation, nor singing; nor have they any preparation, nor catechizing before the communion; and either they sit at Table, or have no Table at all; and because they would not seem to be superstitious, in the time of administration, they are covered.
17. They allow their Ministers to sit in civil Courts, and to voice in the choosing of Magistrates. 18. They are against violent courses in matters of Religion; nor will they have the Conscience to be forced with fear or punishment, but gently to be inclined by perswasion and force of argument; *In which point, I commend their Christian moderation; for in propagating the Gospel, neither Christ nor his Apostles, nor the Church for many hundred years, did use any other sword, but the word, to bring men to Christ.*

Of the Independents Tenets, see the Antidote against Independency, Bayly's dissuasives, Edwards, Paget and others.

Q. 18. *What Tenets are held by the Independents of* New-England?

A. Besides those opinions which they hold with other Independents, they teach that the Spirit of God dwells personally in all the Godly.
2. That their Revelations are equal in Authority with the Scriptures.
3. That no man ought to be troubled in his Conscience for sin, being he is under the Covenant of Grace.
4. That the Law is no rule of our Conversation.
5. That no Christian should be press'd to practice Holy Duties.
6. That the Soul dieth with the Body.
7. That all the Saints upon Earth have two Bodies.
8. That Christ is not united to our fleshly body, but to the new body, after the manner that his Humanity is united to his Divinity.
9. That Christ's Humanity is not in Heaven.
10. That he hath no other body but his Church.
11. They reckon all Reformed Churches, except themselves profane and unclean.

Independents of New-England their Tenets.

All these Opinions savour of nothing but of pride, carnal security, blasphemy, and slighting of God's written Word, which is able to make the man of God perfect, and wise unto salvation.

Of these opinions, see Bayly's dissuasives, Edwards his Gangrena, &c.

Q. 19. *Upon*

Q. 19. *Upon what grounds do the* Independents *forsake our Churches?*

The grounds whereupon the Independents forsake our Churches.

A. Because they do not see the signs of grace in every one of our members; "but this ground is childish, for many are in the state of grace, in whom we see no outward signs; so was *Saul* when he persecuted the Church, he was then a vessel of mercy, and many in whom we see the outward signs of grace, may be in the estate of damnation; such are hypocrites, whose wolfish disposition is covered with sheeps-cloathing: *Moses* did not separate himself from the Jewish Church, because most of them were a stiff-necked people, a rebellious generation of uncircumcised hearts and ears, a people that erred in their hearts, and knew not the ways of God. Neither did Christ separate himself from the Apostles, though there was a *Judas* amongst them. Neither did St. *Paul* abandon the Church of *Corinth*, because of the incestuous person, and other wicked men among them. Will the husbandman forsake his field, because there are tares among the Corn? or will he abandon his Barn, because of some chaff among the wheat? there will come a time of separation, when the sheep and goats, the good and bad fishes, the green and withered trees shall be parted, which shall be in that great day, when all secrets shall be disclosed, and the vizard of hypocrisie, removed: till then, the true *Israelites* must be content to have some *Canaanites* live among them. 2. They say, that many among us profess the faith of Christ outwardly, which have not the Spirit of God within; "but I say, that whosoever among us professeth Christ outwardly, hath the Holy Ghost for ought we know; we are to judge of the Tree by the fruits; it is only God that exactly knoweth who are his: It were uncharitably done, of us to expell or exclude any man from the body of Christ that professeth him outwardly; it's true, there be many hypocrites, such as are among us, but are not of us; these we cannot discern, whilst they continue in their outward profession, but by revelation; the servants that invited and compelled all sorts of guests to the wedding-feast, knew not who wanted the inward wedding-garment of grace; it was only the Master of the feast that could find that out. 3. They say that we receive divers into our Churches, which shall not be saved. *I answer, that no man is certain who shall be saved, or not saved, we are to judge charitably of all men, till we know the contrary; we receive none into our Church, but such as profess Christianity, and the children of believing parents, to whom also the covenant of grace belongeth; and though we did know such, as were not to be saved, yet we are not to debar them from the Church, so long as they joyn in outward profession with God's people. So Christ knew that* Judas *should not be saved, yet he received him into the fellowship of the Apostles; but I would be informed, how these men can so exactly know, who shall be saved or not; seeing in outward profession, the hypocrite can go as far as the best Saint;*

so

Sect. 12. *of* EUROPE. 277

so likewise, the best Saint may for a time seem to be in the state of damnation : besides, John Baptist *admitted Scribes, Pharisees, and all sorts of people to his Baptism, if they confessed their sins and repented ; and so* Philip, Acts 8. *admits to his Baptism all outward professors of faith, which is many times without the inward grace of Sanctification.*

Q. 20. *Upon what grounds do the* Independents *and* Anabaptists *allow Lay-men to preach, without call or ordination ?*

A. Because the Sons of the Prophets did preach ; so did *Jehosaphat* and his Princes ; so did the Disciples before Christ's Resurrection ; so did *Paul* and *Barnabas*; likewise the Scribes and Pharisees, and many in the Church of *Corinth*, who were not Church-men : besides, *Moses* wisheth, that all the Lord's people were Prophets. " But these are all weak and groundless reasons ; For,
" 1. The Sons of the Prophets were destinated for the Ministry,
" and therefore were by probation-sermons to give testimony of
" their gifts ; which they acquired by their pains, and industry in
" the Schools of the Prophets, which were their Colleges. 2. *Je-*
" *hosaphat* and his Princes, in an extraordinary time of Reforma-
" tion, made an exhortation or speech to the people, to stir up
" the Levites and Judges, to discharge their duty : neither do we
" read, 2 *Chron.* 17. that the Princes did preach or expound the
" Law, but only that they accompanied and countenanced the
" Levites whilst they preached. 3. The Disciples were called to
" the Apostleship, and to preach the Gospel before Christ's Resur-
" rection. 4. And so were *Paul* and *Barnabas* called to preach
" the Gospel. 5. Likewise the Scribes and Pharisees sate in *Mo-*
" *ses* chair, in that confused time, and they were Doctors of the
" Law ; therefore Christ wills the people to hearken to them :
" they had their Synagogues, as well as the Levites had the Tem-
" ple. 6. In the Church of *Corinth*, there were some extraordi-
" nary Prophets endowed with infused gifts and revelations, which
" can be no warrant for Lay-men, who want these gifts to under-
" take the ordinary function of preaching. 7. We deny not, but
" *Moses* wished that all God's people were Prophets, and so do we,
" but neither he nor we wish that they should prophesie without a
" calling, either ordinary or extraordinary ; for *how shall they
preach, except they be sent,* saith the Apostle ? *Rom.* 10. 15. *No man
taketh the honour of sacrificing to himself, but he that is called of God,
as was* Aaron, *Heb.* 5. 3. " Much less should any without a call take
" upon him the office of preaching, which is more noble than sa-
" crificing : and therefore the Apostle preferrs preaching to bap-
" tizing, 1 *Cor.* 1. 17. And surely if Lay-men may preach, they
" may also baptize ; for Christ joyneth these two together, in his
" Apostles and their successors, with whom he is by his assistance
" and spiritual presence, to the end of the World : but we see how
" far they are from being sent by God, or from having the gift
" of preaching, by the Errors and Heresies daily hatched among

T 3 " them ;

The grounds whereupon the *Independents* and *Anabaptists*, allow Lay-men to preach without call or ordination.

"them; and how can it be otherways, seeing they are not bred
"in the Schools of learning, whereby they may be fitted and set
"a-part for this great employment, which will require the whole
"man; and *who is sufficient for it*, saith the Apostle? Neither do
"we read in the Scripture, that this ordinary gift of preaching,
"was communicated to any but to Apostles, Evangelists, Prophets,
"Pastors, and Doctors; and to give way that all men may preach
"without Call or Ordination, is to make him who is the God
"of Order, to be the God of Confusion.

Q. 21. *What are the Tenets of the* Presbyterians?

Presbytery the Doctrine and Tenets thereof.

A. The *Presbyterians* are so called, for maintaining that the Church in the beginning was governed by Presbyters or Elders; and that it should be so governed still, because the office of a Bishop came not to be distinct from the Presbyter, till almost three hundred years after Christ; before which time they had the same name, for Presbyters were Bishops, as they shew out of the fifth, sixth, and seventh verses, of the first chapter to *Titus*; likewise out of *Hierom ep. ad Evag. & ad Ocea. Irenæus l. 4. cont. hæret. c.* 43, 44. *Eusebius Hist. l.* 5. *cap.* 23. and others. And as they shew their names to be one, so likewise that their office of preaching and administring the Sacraments was the same out of 1 *Pet.* 5. 2. the power also of Ordination they prove to have been in the Presbytery, 1 *Tim.* 4. 14. which *Hierom* calls the Ecclesiastical *Senate*, *Isa.* 3. and *Ignatius Epist. ad Magnes.* the Apostolical *Senate*. And that in ruling there is no difference, they prove out of *Hebr.* 13. 17. and 1 *Thes.* 5. 12. But because much hath been written in defence of this opinion, by the Presbyterians of *England, France, Scotland, Netherlands,* and divers parts of *Germany*, I have therefore out of their writings reduced the whole summ of their Doctrine and Discipline into 95 Questions, or a short Catechism, by way of Question and Answer.

Quest. *What is the Ministery of the Gospel?*

Answ. It is the dispensation of Divine mysteries, manifested by Christ's coming in the flesh.

Q. *How many parts hath this Ministery?*

A. Three; to wit, the preaching of the Gospel, the administration of the Sacraments, and the exercise of Church-discipline, commonly called the power of the Keys, and of binding and loosing.

Q. *Wherein consisteth Church-discipline?*

A. In two things; to wit, in Imposition of hands, and in correction of manners.

Q. *Are all Church-Ministers properly Ministers of the Gospel?*

A. No; for they are properly Ministers of the Gospel, who preach and give the Sacraments; but Deacons who look to the Poor, and Deaconesses are only Ministers of the Church, not of the Gospel.

Q. *Are Prophets in the New Testament, and Ministers of the Gospel the same?*

A. No; for *Philip*'s four daughters were Prophetesses, yet not Ministers

Ministers of the Gospel. Many of the Laity had the gift of Prophecy, which were not Ministers of the Gospel.

Q. Are Presbyters and Priests all one?

A. No; for he is a Priest that offers sacrifice, but Presbyter is an Elder, which sometimes is called a Bishop, as *Acts* 20. mention is made of many Bishops, that is, many Elders or Presbyters. The Apostles also are called *Elders*, 1 Pet. 3. *Presbyter, Bishop,* and *Pastour* are taken for the same office, *Acts* 20. We read also of many Bishops in *Philippi, Phil.* 1. which is meant of many Elders: the Apostle useth promiscuously the word *Bishop* and *Presbyter*, Tit. 1. For indeed *Bishops* or *Pastors ought to be Elders; that is, excell others both in years and knowledge.*

[margin: Presbyters their Office.]

Q. Were the 70 Disciples subject or subordinate to the 12 Apostles?

A. No; for though they were called later than the Apostles, yet I find not that their power in working Miracles, in preaching, in administring the Sacraments, in Ecclesiastick discipline, was less or subordinate to the Apostles; for both were immediately called by Christ, and equally subject to him without subordination, or subjection to the Apostles, no more than of old the Prophets were subject to the High Priests.

Q. Is the Ordination of the Church of Rome *lawful?*

A. Yes; for neither *Huss, Wickliff, Luther,* and other worthy men, who forsook the Errors of the *Romish* Church, did ever reject her Ordination, no more than they did her Baptism. She retains the faith of the Trinity, the two Testaments, the Sacraments or Seals of the Covenant, the two Tables of the Law; therefore though she be a wife of fornications, as the Church of *Juda* sometime was, yet she may bring forth sons to God.

Q. In what things did the Apostles differ from their successors?

A. 1. The Apostles were immediately called by Christ, but their successors by men. 2. The Apostles were sent abroad into all the World, but their successors were confined to peculiar places. 3. The Apostles Doctrine was the Rule and Canons by which their successors must frame their Sermons. 4. The Apostles were the first that gave the Holy Ghost by imposition of hands; as for preaching, administring the Sacraments, and discipline, in these they agreed with their successors.

[margin: Apostles and their office.]

Q. Who founded the first Christian Churches?

A. The Apostles, either immediately, as *Peter* and *John* founded the Church of *Samaria, Acts* 8. 5, 6. *Peter* the Church of *Cæsarea, Acts* 10. 44, 45. *Paul* the Church of *Corinth,* 1 *Cor.* 3. 6. and 4. 25. and the Church of the *Galatians, Gal.* 4. 19. or else immediately by their Deputies, or Evangelists, as *Barnabas* founded the Church of *Antioch, Acts* 11. 22.

Q. Had any Apostle power or jurisdiction over the rest?

A. No; but they were all of equal power and authority; whence it follows, that neither the Pope should usurp any power over other Patriarchs, nor Bishops lord it over their fellow Bishops or Presbyters, (for these I take here for one) except by consent for a time a super-intendency be given for quieting of troubles in the Church; which perhaps was given to one of the Apostles, it may be to *Peter*, whilst they lived together at *Jerusalem*, before their dispersion; but if so, it was only temporary, and by consent.

Q. *Was it the chief office of the Deacons in the Primitive Church to preach the Word?*

A. No; but to take care of the Poor, of Widows and Orphans, and to attend on the Tables; that is, on their Love-feasts, called *Agapæ*; of which burthen they desired to be eased, who preached the Word, as not being able to do both: yet we read that *Steven*, *Acts* 6. 6, 8, 10. did preach; but indeed in that place it is more likely that he disputed in the *Jewish* Synagogues, than preached in the Temple; and if he had preached, it will not follow, that the Deacons office is to preach; for this act of *Steven*'s was extraordinary, as having an extraordinary measure of the Spirit; and so we read that *Philip*, another Deacon of those seven, preached in *Samaria*, *Acts* 8. 5. but this he did, as being an Evangelist in *Cæsarea*, *Acts* 21. 8. not a Deacon in *Jerusalem*.

Deacons and their Office.

Q. *Doth the care then of the Poor rely only upon the Deacon?*

A. The care of collecting the charitable benevolence for the Poor, and distributing of the same, relies upon the Deacon; but the care of exhorting to benevolence, of recommending the Poor, of inspection into the Deacons fidelity and industry, relies upon the Presbyter; from which the Apostles exempted not themselves.

Q. *Did the Apostles in all the Churches, which they planted, appoint Presbyters and Deacons?*

A. Yes; otherwise they had left these Churches as sheep without Shepherds, or ships without Pilots, to be devoured by Wolves, and to be swallowed by the Waves of confusion, Heresies and Schisms; therefore *Paul* having preached the Gospel in *Crete*, and having settled some Presbyters there, he gives order to *Titus* to set up Presbyters in every Town; and it is unlikely that *Paul*, who had continued at *Corinth* a year and six months, *Acts* 18, 11. would leave that Church destitute of Presbyters and Deacons, seeing the Lord testified to *Paul* in a Vision, *that he had much people in that City*, ver. 10. And writing to the *Philippians*, he salutes the Bishops and Deacons there.

Q. *Why did he not salute the Presbyters there also?*

A. Because in that place a Presbyter is all one in effect with a Bishop; for if Presbyters had been distinct from Bishops, *Paul* would not have left them unsaluted; for why should he salute the Deacons, and not the Presbyters, which are a higher degree?

Q. *Why were the Pastors called Bishops and Presbyters?*

A. To put them in mind of their duty and dignity; for the word *Episcopus* or Bishop, signifieth the care, inspection, and oversight, which they should have of men's souls, in guiding, instructing, and feeding them with the Word and Sacraments. *Presbyter* signifieth

Presbyters their office

nifieth the age, dignity, and experience that ought to be in Ministers, whose grave carriage, wisdom, and knowledge, should procure Reverence of the People to that high calling, and obedience to their Doctrine.

Q. *Are young men then fit to be made Presbyters or Bishops?*

A. No; except there be extraordinary gifts in them, as were in *Timothy*; or in extream necessity, when grave and ancient men cannot be found; *Temeritas florentis ætatis, prudentia senectutis*; Young men are rash, inconstant, head-strong, proud, inconsiderate, and indiscreet in their words and carriage for the most part, which hath brought this high calling into obloquy and contempt. They have not that experience, wisdom, gravity, and knowledge; that are in old men; nor are they Masters of their passions and affections, and how are they fit Over-seers of others, who cannot over-see themselves? A young Presbyter is a contradiction, and a young Bishop is incongruous. Young and green heads have been the cause of so much distemper, so many Heresies and Schisms in the Church of Christ. *Therefore little hope there is, that ever Peace, Religion, and Truth shall flourish in that Church, were giddy young men are Bishops or Presbyters, and hotspurs, or green heads are preferred to gray hairs; ancient Divines are fittest to serve the ancient of days.*

Q. *But if* Paul *constituted Presbyters and Deacons in all the Churches which he planted, why doth he not salute them, as he did these of* Philippi?

A. For brevities sake, he oftentimes omits them, thinking it sufficient to have saluted the Church in general in which they are included; being Members thereof.

Q. *Is not the degree of Bishops higher than that of Presbyters?*

A. Sometimes to avoid heresie, schisms, and troubles in the Church; the Presbyters have chosen one of their own Society, to precede or oversee the rest; but this was only in some places, and at sometimes, and, rather an Ecclesiastick custom, than a Divine tradition, saith *Hierom.*

Bishops.

Q. *But why did* Paul *besides his custom salute the Deacons at* Philippi.

A. Because by *Epaphroditus* they had sent him relief, therefore he would particularly thank them; besides he would shew, that under these two names of Presbyter and Deacon, is contained the whole Ministry of the Church; the Presbyter caring for the things of the Soul, the Deacon for the things of the Body.

Q. *What doth the word Deacon signifie?*

A. A Minister or servant, for so the Magistrate is called, *Rom.* 13. a Deacon or Minister; *Paul* calls himself the Deacon of the Gospel, *Ep.* 5. and he calls Christ the Deacon of Circumcision, *Rom.* 15. but this word is appropriated to him that hath the charge of the poor and strangers, in collecting and laying out the Church money for their relief. Such were those seven mentioned *Acts* 6.

Deacons and their Office.

Acts 6. and as Christ had twelve Apostles, so one of them, to wit, *Judas* was a Deacon, for he kept the bag.

Quest. Were there in the Church preaching Presbyters only?

A. No; there were also ruling Elders, of which *Paul* speaketh, 1 *Tim.* 5. 17. *Let the Elders that rule well, be counted worthy of double honour, especially they who labour in the Word and Doctrine:* for the preaching Presbyters thought it too great a burthen to preach, and to have the inspection of men's manners, therefore they desired some of the Laity to assist them, whom they called ruling Elders.

Q. What difference is there between a Minister and a Deacon?

A. The Greek word signifieth both promiscuously, but we have appropriated the word Minister to a Preacher, and the word Deacon to the Overseer of the Poor.

Q. How doth it appear that Presbyter and Bishop was the same?

A. Because the Apostle, *Phil.* 1. salutes the Bishops of *Philippi*; but in one Town, there is only one Bishop, usually so called. So *Acts* 20. having called together the Presbyters, he bids them take heed to the flock, whereof the Holy Ghost hath made them Bishops: And leaving *Titus* at *Crete* to establish Presbyters, sheweth that a Bishop must be without reproof.

Q. Have there not been sometimes two Bishops in one Town?

A. We read in *Sozomen*, l. 4. c. 14. that the Bishops assembled at *Sirmium*, wrote to *Fælix*, and the Clergy of *Rome*, to admit of *Liberius* as an assistant Bishop to *Fælix*; but the Council of *Nice* forbids two Bishops to be in one City, *Can.* 8.

Q. Why do not the Reformed Churches now call our Ministers by the name of Bishops and Priests?

A. Because these Offices have been abused in Popery, the one to Pride and Tyranny, the other to Superstition and Idolatry.

Q. May a man exercise the office of Presbyter or Bishop without a calling?

A. No; for no man takes upon him this office, but he that is called of God, as *Aaron* was. *Uzza* was struck with sudden death, for his rash touching of the Ark, 2 *Sam.* 6. God complains of those Prophets that run, and yet were not sent, *Jer.* 23. and how can such preach if they be not sent? *Rom.* 10. Leprosie shall seize upon King *Uzziah*, if he stretch out his hand to touch the Ark, 2 *Chron.* 26. Christ himself spoke not of himself, nor was his Doctrine his own, but his that sent him, *John* 5. and 7.

Q. How must a man be called?

Ministerial calling.
A. First, Internally by the Spirit moving his heart, and furnishing him with graces fit for so high a calling. Secondly, Externally, by the Church, to which twofold calling we must yield obedience, and not resist and run from it as *Jonah* did.

Q. How shall we know the inward call of the Spirit, from the flattering conceit of our Fancies?

A. If we are called by the Spirit, we have no other ends but

the falvation of fouls, we feek Chrift for his
loaves; we will not truft to our own ftrength,
ice, but will difclaim our own fufficiency with
ccufe our own uncircumcifed and defiled lips
fay, and will rely only upon the goodnefs and
vho will give us wifdom, and will put in our
hall fpeak.

ts of callings are there in the Church?
, extraordinary, as that of the Apoftles, Evan-
; ; and ordinary as the callings of Prefbyters,
hing Prophets, or Paftors, and of Deacons.

e callings be in one man?
my and *Ezekiel* were ordinary Priefts and Le-
raordinary Prophets. So *Luther* had an ordi-
he Church of *Rome*, yet was called extraordi-
e Gofpel in purity.

e power of Election and Ordination of Prefbyters

inciently in the Laity and Clergy, till the Cler-
ty. And the Pope excluded the Emperor, from
other Bifhops were wont to receive their In-
ng and Crofier-ftaff; not in reference to their
but to their temporal means, which they en-
cence of Princes; but Ordination is only from
fhop was wont to ordain alone, but that was
of Ecclefiaftick cuftom, than out of Divine in-
ntly Ordination did belong to the whole Prefbytery,
y be feen alfo in divers Canons and Counfels.

ch now without Calling or Ordination?
ery one that pretends to have the fpirit fhould
h, preaching would grow contemptible, Here-
ld multiply. Now the Church is eftablifhed,
n, and an ordinary Calling, muft be expected.
y of Chriftianity, before the Church was fet-
times of perfecution difperfed themfelves, and
, *Acts* 8. 4. and fo the men of *Cyprus* and *Cyrene*
at *Antioch*, *Acts* 11. 20. So *Apollos*, a private
w the Baptifm of *John*, and ftood in need of
ctions by *Aquilla* and *Prifcilla*, yet he taught
Acts 11. 25, 26. But fuch Examples were extra-
when no Preachers were found, no ordinary
no Church at all fettled.

of Apoftle, Prefbyter and Bifhop, of equal extent?
Apoftles are called Prefbyters, 1 *Pet.* 5. 1: but
Apoftles, the higher dignity includes the leffer,
rary; fo Apoftles are Bifhops; *Judas* his Apo-
Bifhoprick, *Acts* 1. 10. but all Bifhops are not

Q. Be-

Q. Because an Elder must be apt to teach, will it therefore follow that there ought to be none but preaching Elders?

A. No; for a Ruling Elder should also be apt to teach his Children and Family, and likewise apt to teach, that is, to advise and give counsel in the Consistory, though he preach not in the Pulpit.

Q. Is a Pastor and Doctor all one?

A. No; for all Pastors are Doctors or Teachers; but all Doctors are not Pastors: *Paul* in the Synagogue at *Antioch* did the part of a Doctor or Teacher, when he uttered words of Exhortation, yet he was not the Pastor. The Prophets, Christ, and *John* Baptist were Doctors or Teachers, but not Pastors.

Q. Should there be any superiority of Presbyters over their fellows?

A. Yes, of order, or at sometimes, as when they meet in Synods to determine matters, there ought to be Moderators or Speakers, as we know there were among the Apostles; sometimes *Peter*, sometimes *James*, see *Acts* 15. and perhaps, such was the superiority, that *Samuel* had over the Prophets, in *Naioth* in *Rama*, 1 *Sam*. 19. 20. Such authority had *Eliah* and *Elisha* over the other Prophets in their time. The superiority of the High-Priest over the inferiour Priests was typical, as it had relation to Christ the High-Priest of our profession, the Prince of Pastors, and Bishop of our Souls.

Q. Is it a Novelty to have Lay-Elders in the Church?

Elders.

A. No, for such were in the Church of the *Jews*, *Jer.* 19. 1. Elders of the People, as well as Elders of the Priests; which the Apostle means, 1 *Cor.* 11. 28. For besides Apostles, Prophets, Teachers, *&c.* he speaks of Rulers under the abstract word of Governments: for having mentioned before in the same Chapter, the diversity of gifts. Now in this verse, he speaks of the diversity of Functions in the Church.

Q. Are Lay-men excluded from Church-Government, because they are Lay-men?

A. No; for though they be no part of the Clergy, yet they are a part of the Church, and Members of Christ's mystical body, as well as the Clergy. And it is for the Clergies advantage, that there be Lay-Rulers; for by these means, the Ministers are eased of much trouble, and they are backed with the greater power; besides they are less obnoxious to envy and opposition, which the *Romish* Clergy hath brought upon themselves, by excluding the Laity from Church-Government; proudly monopolizing all to themselves. Lastly, Many Clergy-men, though good Scholars, yet are indiscreet in their carriage, and unskilful in matter of government.

Q. May a Lay-Elder with a safe Conscience, leave his Function at the years end, seeing it is not lawful to put the hand to the plough, and look back, Luk. 9. 62.

A. If there were not choice of such Elders, he could not leave the Church destitute of Government, with a safe conscience. 2. He
may

may not out of diflike to the Function, or of his own head, leave it, but by order and authority he may, where there be others to fupply his place. 3. That Plough in *Luke* is not meant of the Plough of Ruling, but of Preaching; which no man called thereto may leave off, feeing it is of fuch neceffity for the erecting of Chrift's Kingdom.

Q. Is the Function of a Lay-Elder unlawful, becaufe he is not called to preach and baptize?

A. No; for preaching and adminiftring the Sacrament do not belong to the ruling, but to the preaching Presbyter; neither is ruling neceffarily annexed to preaching and baptizing, but that it may be feparated from them; yea it is fit they fhould be feparated, for the reafons above alledged; Minifters fhall have more time to ftudy, and to follow their preaching better, if they be taken off from the trouble of ruling; and God, who giveth to divers men divers gifts, and not the fame to all men, hath made fome fitter for preaching, others fitter for ruling. And it is fit that fome of the Laity fhould have place in the Confiftory, that nothing may be there concluded partially or prejudicially to the Laity; for fo they fhall avoid all fufpicion of tyranny.

Q. Of what Elders doth Ambrofe *fpeak in his Expofition of the fifth Chapter of* 1 Tim.

A. Both of Elders by age, and of Elders by office; for having fhewed that Old age is honourable among all nations; from thence he inferrs, that both the Synagogue and Church of Chrift had Elders, without whofe advice nothing was done in the Church; which office in his time (as he there complains) was grown out of date by reafon of the pride of the Teachers, that they alone might feem to be fomewhat.

Q. Can Ruling-Elders be proved out of the fifth Chapter of 1 Tim. v. 17.

A. Yes, for the Apoftle wills that *the Elders who rule well, be counted worthy of double honour, efpecially they who labour in the Word and Doctrine*: In which words, there is no oppofition made between the teaching Presbyters, as if they who teach and preach, were worthy of double honour, efpecially they who labour in teaching and preaching; for there is no teaching and preaching without labour; and where there is no labour, there can be no double honour merited, but the oppofition is plain between the Ruling-Elders, and the other Elders that labour in the Word. The Ruling-Elder deferves much honour, but much more deferves the Preaching-Elder, that labours in the Word; for Preaching is a toilfome labour, compared to Ruling; and fo this Expofition doth not force the words, as the former doth.

Q. What priority had the High Prieft, or Chief Priefts over the other Priefts?

A. The priority of order, but not of authority and command, all being equal in the Office of Priefthood; fuch a priority was among

mong the Presbyters, but when the Church began to spread, and heresies to increase, there was some power or authority given to the chief Presbyters, whom they called Bishops; but there was no distinction of Parishes till 267 years after Christ, as *Polydor Virgil* witnesseth, so it is thought there could not be in that time any Diocess, or Diocesan Bishops.

Q. *Did all Christian Nations upon their Conversion to Christianity receive Episcopacy?*

Bishops.
A. No, for the *Scots* admitted of no Bishops for 290 years after their conversion, if we may believe *Johannes Major l. 2. Hist. de gest. Scot. c. 2.* And the *Cantabrians* or people of *Biscay* in *Spain*, as yet admit of no Bishops; as it is recorded in the *Spanish* Story.

Q. *Was the power of Jurisdiction in the Bishop or Presbytery?*

A. It was thought to be in both joyntly: for in the time of *Cornelius*, lapsed Christians were not admitted into the Church at *Rome*, untill they confessed their sins before the Presbytery, *Cyprian Epist. 6.* and *Epist. 46.* Yet the peoples consent also was required, as may be seen in the same *Cyprian Epist. 55.* and *Epist. 12. ad plebem.*

Q. *Were* Timothy *and* Titus *Bishops or not?*

A. They were probably Evangelists who were not to reside in one particular place, as Bishops or Presbyters, but to attend on the Apostles, and to perform their messages, by *preaching* the *Gospel* from place to place: for *Paul* left him with *Silas* at *Berœa*, *Act. 17. 14.* then *Paul* sent for him to *Athens*, ver. 15. from thence he sends him to *Thessalonica*, 1 *Thess.* 3. 2. from hence he returned to *Athens*, and is sent by *Paul* into *Macedonia*, and returns from thence to *Corinth*, *Act. 18. 5.* after this he went to *Ephesus*, and from thence was sent by *Paul* to *Macedonia*, *Act. 19. 22.* whom *Timothy* accompanied thence into *Asia*: and then to *Miletum*, where having sent for the Elders of *Ephesus* gives them a charge to feed the flock of Christ; not naming *Timothy* at all, to whom the charge should have been given, had he been a settled Bishop there, which title is not given to him at all in Scripture. So *Titus* travelled with *Paul* through *Antioch* to *Jerusalem*, *Gal. 2. 1.* through *Cilicia* he went to *Crete*, where he was left a while, and sent for by *Paul* to *Nicopolis*, *Tit. 3. 12.* he was expected at *Troas*, 2 *Cor. 2. 13.* he met *Paul* in *Macedonia*, 2 *Cor. 7. 6.* and conveyed that Epistle of *Paul* to the *Corinthians*, 1 *Cor. 13. Postscript.* He was with *Paul* at *Rome*, and went from thence to *Dalmatia*, 2 *Tim. 4. 10.* by which 'tis plain, he was not a settled Bishop in *Crete*.

Q. *Were there any Lay-Elders or Senators in* Austin's *time?*

A. Yes, for *L. 3. Con. Cresconium Grammaticum* he speaks of Bishops, Presbyters, or preaching Elders, Deacons and Seniors, or Lay-Elders, and *c. 56. ibid.* he speaks of *Peregrinus* Presbyter, and Seniours, by the one meaning the preaching, by the others the Ruling-Elders. And in his 137 Epistle he speaks of the Clergy, the Elders and the whole people; and in divers other places of his Works, he speaks of these Elders, as being distinguished from the Clergy, and the rest of the Laity, and having a charge of Church affairs, whence it appears, that to have ruling Elders is no novelty.

Q. *What were those Elders which are mentioned* Tit. 1. 5.

A. They were Bishops or preaching Presbyters; for *Act.* 20. *Elders,* ver. 17. are named *Bishops,* ver. 28. so in *Titus,* chap. 1. *Elder,* ver. 5. is called *Bishop,* ver. 7. every City then and Village had their Elder, that is, their Bishop, and this is witnessed by *Sozomen* L. 7. these were then parochial Bishops, not Diocesan in all likelyhood.

Q. *Whether did the power of Jurisdiction and Ordination belong to the Bishop alone, or to the Church?*

A. To the Church, for Christ saith, Dic Ecclesiæ, go tell the Church, and to all the Apostles together, which were then the Church Representative he gives the Keys or power of binding, &c. and this is Jurisdiction. So likewise Ordination belongs to the Church or Presbytery, as we shewed before out of 1 Tim. 4. 14.

Q. *Is it not lawful for one Clergy-man to exercise Dominion or Lordly authority over another?*

A. No; for Christ will not have any of his Apostles to aim at greatness or superiority, but will have such become Ministers and Servants, Mat. 20. 25. Mar. 10. 42. Luk. 22. 25. for Christ's Kingdom is spiritual and not of this World, as the Kingdoms of earthly Princes are; neither did he mean to set up an earthly dominion for a thousand years, as the *Millennaries* thought: and the Apostles themselves had a conceit of an earthly Kingdom, when they thought that Christ did purpose to restore the Kingdom to *Israel*: neither doth Christ forbid tyranny or the abuse of dominion, but all kind of dominion; for the one Evangelist used the word Κυριεύειν, as the other doth Κατακυριεύειν. Yet some respect is to be given to the Ministers that have the greatest gifts, by those that have lesser. And a priority of order, though not of jurisdiction.

Q. *What part of the Apostolical Function ceased with the Apostles, and what was to continue?*

A. The Universality of their Function, and the infallibility of their authority were to cease with them, for they were temporary gifts: but the preaching of the Word, the administration of the Sacraments and the exercise of Discipline, were to continue in their successors; these gifts were ordinary, but perpetual; the other extraordinary and temporary.

Q. *Is the power of the Keys and Apostolical authority the same thing?*

A. No; for the power of the Keys is the Church-Discipline, which was to continue for ever in the Church. But the Apostolical authority, which consisted in their immediate calling from Christ in the Universality of their Embassage, in the infallibility of their Judgments. In giving of the Holy Ghost by Imposition of their hands, and such like priviledges were not to continue longer than themselves.

Q. Had not Timothy *and* Titus *the same power of the Keys, and Apostolical authority that* Paul *had?*

A. They had the same power of the Keys; that is, of preaching, administring the Sacraments and censuring; but not the same Apostolical authority; that is, an immediate call from Heaven, the same infallibility of Judgment, or power of giving the Holy Ghost, that the Apostles had; nor was their Doctrine otherwise authentical, than as it was conformable to the Doctrine of the Apostles.

Q. But was not the Church after the Apostles decease left an Orphan, being destitute of these extraordinary Apostolical graces?

A. No; for though she was deprived of the personal presence of the Apostles, yet she is not destitute of their infallible judgment left in their writings with her, which supply the Apostles absence till the end of the World.

Q. Could one man at the same time be both an Apostle, and Bishop or Presbyter?

A. Yes, in case of necessity; for *James* was an Apostle and Bishop of *Jerusalem* too; because that was the Mother-Church, to which resorted Jews of all Nations for instruction and knowledge; therefore it was fitting that none less than an Apostle should reside there, for the greater authority and satisfaction.

Episcopacy, what among the Presbyterians.

Q. Can Episcopacy be proved by the Canons of the Apostles, and Council of *Antioch*?

A. Those Canons are much doubted, if they be the Apostles or not; however it is probable to me, that the parochian, not the diocesan Bishop is there meant; for there is no superiority there given, but of order and respect, partly because of the eminency of the place or City where he lived, partly by reason of his own worth and learning, without whose advice matters of moment should not be done by the other Bishops or Presbyters; nor should he do any thing without them; but should together ordain Presbyters and Deacons, for that is a matter of moment, yet he is only named there, because, he being as it were the head; the rest are understood.

Q. Was Aerius *an Heretick for affirming there was no difference between a Bishop and a Presbyter?*

A. No; Though for this opinion *Epiphanius*, and out of him *Austin* place him among the hereticks: for the Scripture puts no difference between these. The Church of *Alexandria* was the first that put difference between them, as *Epiphanius* seems to affirm, when he saith *Haeres.* 68. that the Church of *Alexandria* doth not admit of two Bishops. But though *Aerius* was not in this an *Heretick*, yet he was in an error, if he thought that there was no difference at all among Bishops or Presbyters, for one is above another

another in gifts, in honour, in order; though perhaps not in jurisdiction; authority and pastoral Function.

Q. *Is the Church to be ruled by the Civil Magistrate.*

A. No; for the Church being Christ's spiritual Kingdom, and not of this World, is to be guided by her own spiritual Officers, as the State is ruled by temporal Officers, *Cæsar must have what is Cæsar's, and God that which is God's*; And for this cause the Church and State have their different Laws and Punishments. Neither had the Apostles chosen Elders, and other Officers in the Church; if the Civil Magistrate had been to rule it; and had the Church of *Jerusalem* been all one with the State thereof, or the Church of *Crete*, all one with the Kingdom of *Crete*, the Apostles had incroached upon the temporal Government, had been guilty of Rebellion, and proved enemies to *Cæsar*, when they set up Elders and other Church-Officers, in those and other places: besides Women sometimes, and Children are Magistrates and Princes, but the one must not speak in the Church, 1 Cor. 14. 34. The others are not fit to be made Bishops, 1 Tim. 3.

Church, how to be governed. For this cause the Magistrates Office different from the Church-Governours.

Q. *Are Church-Governours by Divine Institution?*

A. Yes; for Christ appointed Apostles, Prophets, Evangelists, Teachers, and other helps of Government, 1 Cor. 12. 28. Paul left *Titus* in *Crete* to ordain Elders in every City, Tit. 1. 5. The Apostles ordained Elders in every Church, Acts 14. 23. Which Officers were in the Church, before there was any Christian state or Christian Magistrate. And as Christ appointed Rulers for his Church, so he gave them the Keys of Heaven, or power to bind and loose, Mat. 16. 19. and 18. 17, 18. and to remit and retain sins, John 20. 23. these are said to have the rule over us, Heb. 13. 17, 24. this ruling power was exercised by *Paul* against *Hymenæus* and *Alexander*, 1 Tim. 1. 20. and injoyned to the Elders of *Corinth*, 1 Cor. 5. 3, 12, 13. and was practised before them, by the Priests upon *Uzziah*, 2 Chron. 26. 17, 18, 21. by *Phinehas* the Priest, Num. 25. by Christ himself, in whipping the buyers and sellers out of the Temple.

Church-Governours.

Q. *Have we any president for appeals from the classical to the higher assemblies?*

A. Yes; for there was an appeal from the Church of *Antioch* concerning some Jewish ceremonies to the assembly of the Apostles and Elders at *Jerusalem*, Acts 15. 1, 2, 6.

Q. *Who are to judge of scandals?*

A. The Ministers, 1 Cor. 5. 11. for they succeeded the Priests and Levites in the old Law; but these were appointed Judges by God in such cases, Deut. 17, 8. 9.

Q. *Is the Church-Government by Elders or Bishops, Deacons, Doctors and Teachers, alterable?*

A. Not in the substance or essentials thereof, but in the circumstances or adjuncts it is alterable, as in the manner, time, place, and other circumstances of Election. So the Government by El-

Church-Government, alterable.

ders and Deacons is not to be changed, but that they should be elected by all the people, and that there should be the strict number of seven Deacons in each parish is not needful, though at first, as *Acts* 6.5. there were but seven chosen, and that by the multitude.

Q. *Wherein is moderate Episcopacy different from Presbytery?*

Episcopacy, how different from Presbytery.

A. Presbytery, is Episcopacy dilated, and Episcopacy is Presbytery contracted; so the government is in effect the same differing only as fist, or hand contracted, from the same hand expanded, or dilated, only Episcopacy is more subject to error and corruption than Presbytery, and this more Subject to disorder and confusion, by reason of parity, than Episcopacy, the peace of the Church, the suppression of schism and heresie, the dignity of the Clergy are more consistent with Episcopacy than with Presbytery; but this again is less obnoxious to pride and tyranny, than Episcopacy, by which we see that no Government is perfectly exempted from corruption in this life, *nihil est ex omni parte beatum*. But I find that as the *Romans* in their greatest dangers betook themselves to the Dictatorship, so hath the Church in her extremities had recourse to Episcopacy.

Q. *May the Civil Magistrate change the Church-Government?*

Magistrates Office.

A. He may alter the outward form thereof, as it depends upon the circumstances of time, place, and persons; but the substance of it he cannot change; he can also by his Laws force the observation of the Government, and punish the disturbers of the Church's peace.

Q. *May the same man be both a Magistrate and a Minister?*

A. Though among the *Gentiles* it was lawful as we see in *Anius*, that was both King and Priest, *Rex hominum Phœbique sacerdos*; and in the Emperours of *Rome*, that were also chief Pontiffs: and though *Melchisedech* was King and Priest among the *Jews*, *Abraham* was a Prince and a Priest, *Heli* a Judge and a Priest, the *Macchabees* were Princes and Priests; yet this was not ordinary, for *Abraham*, *Melchisedech*, *Heli*, were Types of Christ; the *Macchabees* by usurpation undertook both governments, but ordinarily these offices were distinct among the *Jews*, therefore *Moses* who gave Laws concerning the Priesthood, did not exercise it himself, neither did *Joshua*, *David* nor *Solomon*; but on the contrary, *Saul* and *Uzziah* were severely punished for medling with the Priests Office; *Saul* for offering sacrifice lost his Kingdom, and *Uzziah* was struck with Leprosie; but among Christians these Offices are much more distinct; for Christ's Kingdom is not of this World; and the Ministry is burden enough without other addition: *Who is sufficient for it*, saith the Apostle? besides it is Christ's prerogative, to be alone King and Priest of his Church. Yet so far may the Magistrate meddle with the Ministry, as to reform what is amiss, both in their life and doctrine; examples hereof we have in *Jehosaphat*, *Ezechiah*, and *Josiah*, and in *Solomon* too, who deposed *Abiathar* the Priest.

Q. *Was*

Sect. 12. *of* EUROPE. 291

Q. *Was the Presbytery in use among the Jews?*

A. Yes, for besides the Civil Judicature, which by *Moses* his appointment, consisted of 70 men, and had its seat in the City Gates, there was a Spiritual or Ecclesiastick Judicature kept in the Synogogues, which judged of things holy and clean, and discerned between holy and profane, clean and unclean things, and declared the Statutes of God: and because of the Scribes among them, they decided matters of their Civil Law, *Levit.* 10. 10. This Judicature consisted of Priests and Levites, as also of the chief fathers of *Israel*, which we may call Lay or Ruling-Elders, as we may see 2 *Chro.* 19. 8. *Jehosaphat* did not only restore and reform the Civil Courts called *Sanhedrim*, in each City, the chiefest whereof was at *Jerusalem*, but also he reformed the Presbyteries, or Ecclesiastick Judicatures, as may be seen there, placing *Amariah* the chief Priest over these; but *Zebadiah* Ruler or Prince of the house of *Juda*, over the *Synedria*, or Civil affairs, called there, ver. 11. *the King's matters*, because the King was chief over these Courts; as the High-Priest over the Presbyteries; but afterward through the corruption of time: *These Courts were confounded and the Presbyteries did not only judge de jure*, as anciently they used, but also *de facto*, even of life and death; as in the time of the *Macchabees*, but under the *Romans* this power was taken from them for they could neither put *Christ* nor *Paul* to death; As for *Stephen* he was stoned; not by the sentence of the Court, but in a popular tumult.

Presbyters among the Jews.

Q. *How are these two Courts named in the New Testament?*

A. The Civil Court is called συνέδριον, the Council; the Ecclesiastick Court is named the Synagogue, *Mat.* 10. 17. The chief of the Synagogue was the High-Priest; but of the Council was the Judge, *Deut.* 17. 12. *Jeremiah* was condemned by the Synagogue, *Jer.* 26. 8. but absolved by the Council or secular Judges in the Gate, ver. 16.

Q. *Why are Ministers called Presbyters and Bishops, but not Priests in the New Testament?*

A. Because they were to be put in mind of their Dignity and Function, which consisteth in the care and inspection of their flock, not in *offering of sacrifice*, which was the proper work of the Priest, but ceased when Christ our propitiatory sacrifice was offered; besides Christ would reserve this prerogative to himself, he being the only Priest of the New Testament, not after the order of *Aaron* which ended when he was sacrificed; but after the order of *Melchisedech*, which was in him to continue for ever without successor. Therefore the Ministers of the New Testament are no otherwise Priests, than they are Kings, but these titles are common to all Christians, who by Christ are made Kings, and Priests to God the Father.

Ministers called Presbyters.

Q. *How are Ministers to be elected?*

A. They must be examined, whether they be apt to teach,

V 2 and

How to be elected. and well reported of by them who are without. Therefore Timothy must not lay hands suddenly on any man, 1 Tim. 5. 22. and 3. 7. Secondly, the Bishop or Pastor must be chosen by all the Bishops or Pastors of the province, or by three at least, as was ordained by the Council of *Nice*, *Canon* 4. Thirdly, the election of the Minister must be made known to the people, as we may see in the sixth *Canon* of the Council of *Chalcedon*. Fourthly, the people must give their approbation, *Acts* 6. 5. therefore S. *Austin Epist.* 110. presented his successor *Eradius* to the people for their consent. Fifthly, there must be imposition of hands, a custom used not only in the Christian Church, *Tim.* 4. 14. and 5 verse 18. but also among the *Jews*, *Num.* 27. 18. *Deut.* 34. Sixthly, in the reformed Churches the other Ministers give to him that is elected the hand of fellowship; as *James*, *Peter* and *John* gave to *Paul*, *Gal.* 2. Seventhly, the new elected Minister subscribes the confession of faith, and discipline of the Church; which custom was used in the Churches of *Africa*.

Q. *Are* Romish *Priests (converted to our Church) to be reordained?*

A. There is no necessity of a *new ordination*; *for though their commission in the Church of Rome*, was to offer the body and blood of Christ in the *Eucharist*, yet they were ordained *to preach the word*, and to administer the Sacraments. Which ordination is not nullified, when they shake off the errors of Doctrine, and preach the word in purity, *neither was their ordination* originally from the Pope, or his subordinate Bishop, but from Christ; neither must their Oath be taken in Ordination to maintain the *Romish* Doctrine, hinder them from preaching the Word in purity; for an unlawful Oath must not be kept. Therefore *Luther* and others who forsook the Errors of *Rome*, received no new Ordination.

Q. *Had the Presbytery power to excommunicate?*

Presbytery, their power to excommunicate. A. Yes; and not the Bishop alone, for *Paul* would not by himself excommunicate the incestuous *Corinthian* without the Presbytery, or the Church gathered together, 1 *Cor.* 5. 4. for indeed the whole congregation should have notice given them of the Excommunication, that they may avoid the party excommunicated.

Q. *Upon what is this power grounded?*

A. Upon God's own practice, who excommunicated *Adam* out of Paradise, and *Cain* from his presence. 2. Upon his command who prohibited the unclean from entring the Temple till they were purified; and from eating the passover, or commercing with God's people who commanded every soul not circumcised the eighth day to be cut off from the people. 3. Upon Christ's words, *Whomsoever you bind on earth, shall be bound in heaven.* 4. Upon Christ's counsel, forbidding *to give that which is holy to dogs, or to cast pearl before swine.* Upon the Apostles practice, *Peter* excommunicated *Simon Magus* in keeping him off from imposition of hands. *Paul* excom-

excommunicated the inceſtuous *Corinth*, and delivered over to Satan thoſe two blaſphemers, *Hymenæus* and *Philetus*. 6. *Paul* will have the *Corinthians* purge out the old leaven, and not eat with ſuch as are notoriouſly wicked; and pronounceth *Maranatha* againſt ſuch as love not the Lord Jeſus, and *Anathema* againſt ſuch as preach another Goſpel, than what the *Galatians* received, and wiſhed they may be cut off who trouble them. And wills us to beware of ſuch as cauſe diſſention and ſtrife, and to reject an *Heretick*. *John* will not have us receive ſuch men within our houſes, nor bid them God ſpeed; by all which it is apparent that Excommunication is both ancient and neceſſary in the Church.

Q. *May an excommunicate perſon be debarr'd from publick prayers and preaching?*

A. Yes; for though meat is not to be denied to him that is hungry, yet we may juſtly refuſe to feed him who is glutted, and hath taken a ſurfeit. An Heathen or Infidel may be admitted to hear the word, becauſe he ſins of ignorance, which is cured by preaching; but a wicked or profane brother, who ſins of wilfulneſs and perverſeneſs, is not to be admitted to that which he deſpiſeth; for that pearl is not for Hogs, and ſuch by hearing the Word, do but aggravate their own damnation. Therefore Saint *Paul* permits us to eat with an Infidel without ſcruple, 1 *Cor.* 10. 27. but with a profane brother he will not have us to keep company, 1 *Cor.* 5. 11. So we read in *Tertullian*, that *Cerdon* the Heretick was not ſuffered to enter into the Church: and *Theodoſius* had the Church-doors barred againſt him by *Ambroſe*. Yet in this caſe private Exhortations, Comminations are not to be neglected, *that the prodigal Son may be induced to return again to his Father's houſe.*

Excommunicate perſons, their condition.

Q. *May a man that is excommunicate remain ſtill in the ſtate of election?*

A. Yes; for the ſentence of the Church is declarative only, and not effective: Election, as the other gifts of God, is without repentance. Though *Peter* fell dangerouſly, yet in his fall he was the child of election, for Chriſt pray'd that his faith ſhould not fail: the Tree in Winter may ſeem to be dead when it is ſtript of its leaves, yet in the Spring it revives again, becauſe the vital faculty lurking all that while in the root, breaks out and ſhews its vertue upon the approach of the Sun. So the root of grace remains alive in the Godly, though the leaves be dead, for which they are or may be excommunicate.

Q. *If Excommunication was in uſe among the* Jews, *why did not the Prophets excommunicate notorious ſinners, nor the Phariſees excommunicate the Sadduces, who were dangerous Hereticks, nor the Prieſts and Elders of the people excommunicate Chriſt and his Apoſtles, who they accounted pernicious Seducers?*

A. The Prophets had no Eccleſiaſtick Juriſdiction, they were ſent to preach againſt ſin, but not to excommunicate for ſin. The Phariſees and Sadduces were Sects different in opinions, but had

The Prophets, Phariſets, &c. could not excommunicate.

no Ecclesiastick Jurisdiction one over the other. Though Christ and his Apostles were hated by the Priests, yet the Priests durst not excommunicate them, partly for fear of the People, partly for fear of the *Romans*; neither had *John Baptist* any power to excommunicate the Pharisees and Sadduces, though he knew them to be a Generation of Vipers; nor had he any reason to exclude them from his baptism, seeing they came to confess their sins, *Matt.* 3. 6.

Q. *Why did not Christ excommunicate* Judas, *whom he knew to be unworthy of the Sacrament?*

Why Christ did not excommunicate Judas.

A. Because the sin of *Judas* was not yet known, nor scandalous; for though it was known to some of the Priests, yet it was not known to the Disciples; and though it was known to Christ as he was God, or else by revelation, as he was man, yet it was not publickly known; and though it had been publick, yet without admonition, conviction, and condemnation, he should not have been excommunicate. Therefore Christ bids them all eat and drink, but yet by this he doth not give way, that such as are notoriously and scandalously wicked, should be admitted to the Sacrament without repentance; especially obstinate despisers of admonition, but only that such as are admitted, though Hypocrites, should not refuse to eat and drink.

Q. *May the Presbytery excommunicate any man for his absence?*

Excommunication and excommunicate persons considered.

A. If his absence be prejudicial to Church or State, or joyned with obstinacy, he may be excommunicated for being absent; but if he be absent upon unavoidable occasions, or upon the certain knowledge that he hath of the prejudicate opinion which the Presbytery hath of him, he may absent himself till they be better informed. Thus *Chrysostom* absented himself from the Synod of *Constantinople*, because he knew that *Theophilus* Bishop of *Alexandria*, and *Epiphanius* of *Cyprus*, before whom he was convented, were enemies to his Cause: therefore he was injuriously by them for his absence condemned.

Q. *How many sorts of Excommunication were there?*

A. Three. 1. Of those that were kept off a while from the Sacrament, they were called *Abstenti*. 2. Of them who were excluded from the Sacraments, but not for any certain time; these were named *Excommunicati*. 3. Or them whose condition was desperate, they were named *Anathematisati*, which decree of Excommunication or *Anathema* was denounced rather against the Doctrine, than persons of men; of whom we should not despair while they live; and being dead, are not in our power: yet I find the persons of *Julian* the Apostate, of *Arrius* the Heretick, and some others, were *Anathematized*.

Q. *Was excommunication used only among Christians?*

A. No; for the *Jews* had this punishment among them, as we may see *Joh.* 9. in casting the blind man out of their Synagogue; and threatning to do the like to those that should profess Christ, which

Christ

Chrift alfo foretold to his Difciples. This kind of fpiritual punifhment was moft ftrictly obferved among the *Effens*, *Jofeph de bell. Judaic. l.2. c.7.* for not only did they excommunicate notorious finners, but fuffered them alfo in the time of their Excommunication to ftarve for want of food. This punifhment alfo was in ufe among the *Gentiles*. For the *Druides* among the *Gauls* ufed to debar from their Sacrifices fcandalous Livers, as *Cæfar* witneffeth, *de bell. Gall. l.6.* and *Devoveri Diti*, or *Diris*, was a kind of Excommunication among the *Romans*.

Q. *What benefit hath the Church by Excommunication?*

A. By this the Word, *Sacraments*, and other things, are kept holy, and vindicated from Profanation; Swine are kept off from treading upon Pearls, and Dogs from tearing us; the fheep are kept within their fold, the loft fheep is recovered, the prodigal Son is brought home, the Reputation of the Church's Holinefs is kept up, and all occafion of obloquy cut off; the Body is preferved by cutting off the gangrened Member, and the Tree profpers by lopping off the wither'd Branches; and the contagion is ftayed from creeping further, which without this remedy would infect others: Men by this are deterred from fin; by this alfo God's Anger is appeafed, and his Judgment removed or averted, and our communion with God is renewed and confirmed. Therefore we are commanded, *Deut.* 1.3. *to remove the evil from amongft us, and to depart out of Babylon; and not to communicate with the unfruitful works of darknefs.*

Q. *Are excommunicate perfons members of the Church?*

A. As they are excommunicate, they are not members; for how can they be members of the Church, from whofe Union and Society they are feparated? or how can *Heathens* and *Publicans* be members of the Church, for fuch are excommunicate perfons to be accounted? yet in refpect of their faith, which is not quite extinguifhed; and as they are fubject to the external Government of the Church, they may be called members thereof.

Q. *Are we Proteftants juftly excommunicate by the Pope?*

A. 1. No; for we are not Hereticks, but Orthodox Profeffors. 2. He hath no power to exclude us out of the Church, who himfelf is fcarce a member of the Church. 3. 'Tis no wonder that we are rejected by thofe who feem to be the only builders; whereas *Chrift himfelf, the chief corner-ftone, was rejected by the builders.* 4. By being excommunicate from *Babylon*, we are made members of *Jerufalem*; and indeed we had not been partakers of the true light, fo long as we remained in darknefs; nor had we been the Servants of Chrift, fo long as we ferved Antichrift. 5. *No fooner had the Hirelings caft out Chrift's fheep out of the fold, but Chrift the true fhepherd found them out, and brought them home with joy:* So the blind man, *Joh.* 9. was no fooner caft out of the Synagogue, but he was received and entertained by Chrift. So we have gained Heaven by being excommunicate from *Rome*; and *Balaam's* curfe is turned to a bleffing.

Q. *What*

Q. *What hath* Rome *got by Excommunication?*

A. Though she kept the World a-while in awe, and thereby got wealth, yet by her Excommunications she hath lost more than she hath got; for she lost all the *Eastern* Countries, when Pope *Victor* inconsiderately excommunicated the *Eastern* Churches about the matter of *Easter*. What the Popes got by Excommunicating the *German* Emperors, and *French* Kings, Histories can tell us; they lost *England* by Excommunicating *Henry* the Eighth, and his Protestant Children.

Q. *Who are to be Excommunicate?*

A. 1. Not *Jews* and *Turks*, but *Christians*; for we are not to judge them who are without, but if any be called a Brother, who is a Fornicator, &c. 2. Not every sinful Brother, but he who sins of perverseness, after admonition; for he doth wilfully by his sins separate himself from God, therefore deserves to be separate from the Church by Excommunication; and consequently to be delivered over to Satan, who reigns without the Church, as Christ doth within; and this delivering over is to the Destruction of the flesh, that is, of the Old Man, or body of sin; but that the Spirit may be saved; that is, that Grace or the New Man may be strengthened. 3. A Brother must not be excommunicate for every sin, but for that which is publick and scandalous; private sins are to be punished by him who knows all Secrets. 4. A Brother must be excommunicate for his own sins, but not for the sins of another; every man must bear his own burthen; therefore Bishop *Auxilius* was justly reproved by St. *Austin, Epist.* 75. for Excommunicating the whole Family for the Masters offence alone.

Q. *Can Excommunication consist with Charity?*

A. Yes; for there can be no greater charity than to save the soul; but the end of Excommunication is to save the soul or the spirit; it is charity to keep a man from blaspheming; but *Hymeneus* and *Alexander* were delivered up to Satan, that they might learn not to blaspheme, 1 *Tim.* 1. It is charity to stay an Infection or Plague; but Excommunication is such a means; therefore *Paul* wills the *Corinthians, to take away the Evil from among them; for know you not,* saith he, *that a little Leaven will sowre the whole lump?* 1 *Cor.* 5. It is charity to keep a man from eating and drinking his own Damnation; but unworthy Eaters of the Sacrament, eat their own Damnation, if they be not suspended, or kept off by Excommunication.

Q. *Is the Civil Magistrate prejudiced by the censure of Excommunication?*

A. No; for the weapon of the Magistrate is the Sword, but the Minister useth only the Word. The end of the Ministers censure is to save the sinner. The end of the Magistrates is to kill the sinner; the Minister is content to receive the sinner into the Church again upon his repentance; but the Magistrate regards not the repentance and sorrow of the Malefactor; the Minister takes

Sect. 12. *of* EUROPE 297

takes notice of many sins, which the Magistrate doth not, because they are such as trouble not the State, as private grudges of Neighbours, &c. There be also Magistrates that wink many times at great sins; as for example, Drunkenness, which the Minister should not forbear to censure.

Q. *May the Minister or Presbytery excommunicate any man without the consent of the Church?*

A. No; for excommunication, or separation from the body of Christ, is of that consequence, that it concerns all to take notice of it; but the Minister may suspend from the Sacrament without the Church's consent, such as he knows are scandalous and profane; and this he ought to do, though the Church should refuse to assent; for he is commanded not to give that which is holy to Dogs; nor must he suffer any of his flock to eat his own damnation; this is to put the Sword into his hand that would kill himself; which is to be guilty of his sin. *Qui non vetat peccare, cum possit, jubet.*

Q. *From what things can we not be excommunicate?*

A. 1. From the love of God in Christ Jesus our Lord no man can separate us; for the Foundation of God remaineth sure. 2. Nor from the practice of those Duties which are grounded on the Laws of Nature, can we be hindred by Excommunication; such as are the Duties of Husbands and Wives, Fathers and Children, Masters and Servants, Princes and People; therefore the Pope's Excommunication cannot loose People from their Allegiance to their Prince. 3. Nor can Excommunicate persons be hindred from practising such things as are grounded on the Law of Nations; such as traffick and commerce; for an excommunicate person must be to us as a *Publican* and *Heathen*; but with such the *Jews* might have commerce and traffick. 4. Excommunication doth not debar us from exercising the works of Charity; for we are bound to feed the hungry, and not suffer them to starve, because they are excommunicate. 5. Excommunication doth not debar us from hearing the Word, except we be Scoffers of it.

Q. *Is the Christian Magistrate subject to the censure of Excommunication?*

A. Yes; for though he be a Father as he is a Prince, yet he is a Brother as he is a Christian; and therefore liable to be censured as a Brother. Hence King *Uzziah* was excommunicate by the Priest *Azariah*, and *Theodosius* the Emperour by *Ambrose*.

Q. *Will it follow that there must be no Excommunication, because Christ will not have the Tares pluckt up till Harvest?*

A. No: 1. For Christ speaketh there of Hypocrites, which cannot be pluckt up by the Church, because she knoweth them not; but in the great Harvest, they shall be pluckt up by the Angels, at his command who knows the secrets of the heart. 2. If the place be meant of Hereticks, they are not to be pluckt up at such times, as may endanger the Church's peace; but they
must

must be left to a convenient time, when the Church may excommunicate them without danger; or else be left to the judgment of the great day. 3. All Tares cannot be pluckt up, whilst the Church is here Militant; for there will be found still some Tares amongst the Corn; some Goats among the Sheep; a *Judas* among the Apostles, as there were *Canaanites* and *Jebusites* among the *Israelites*. 4. Christ by this condemns their rashness, who presently go to pluck up and fly to Excommunication, before they use reproof and admonition.

Q. *Can the Minister exclude any man from the Kingdom of God?*

A. 1. He cannot by his own power, but by the power of him whose Minister he is. 2. He cannot exclude any man from Heaven, but he can pronounce and declare that such a man is excluded thence.

Q. *Can the delivering of a man over to Satan, be a means to save his spirit?*

A. Yes, accidentally; for God can draw good out of evil, and light out of darkness: thus the buffetings which *Paul* suffered by the Angel of Satan, caused him to pray heartily: it is the special work of God's mercy, to save our souls by afflictions and misery.

Q. *Can an excommunicate person be accounted as a Brother?*

A. Yes, for Excommunication takes not away true Brotherly love and affection; and excommunicate persons may be shut out of Heaven, but not out of hope; we may exclude him out of our Society, but not out of our Bowels of compassion and mercy: we draw the Sword of Excommunication against him, not to kill, but to cure him. Who would be more fully resolved of these Presbyterian Tenets, let him read their own Writings.

Q. *How many Erroneous Opinions in Religion have been lately revived or hatched since the fall of our Church-Government?*

Divers erroneous opinions which have been lately revived or hatched, since the fall of our Church-Government.

A. It were almost endless to number every particular; it may suffice that I shall name more than one hundred of the most ordinary and latest received of them; which are, 1. That the Scriptures are a Humane invention, insufficient and uncertain, and do not contain half of his revealed Will. 2. That they are all Allegorical, and written according to the private spirit of the Penmen, and not as moved by the Holy Ghost. And that the Old Testament is now of no force. 3. That Reason is the Rule of Faith. 4. That Scripture binds us no further than the Spirit assureth us that such is Scripture. 5. That Scripture should not be read to a mixt Congregation without present Exposition. 6. That God is the Author of the pravity and sinfulness of men's actions. 7. That *Turks, Jews, Pagans*, and others, are not to be forced from their Opinions. 8. That God loves a crawling Worm as well as a Holy Saint. 9. That God's Will, not sin, is the cause of man's Damnation. 10. That Man was a Living Creature before God breathed

breathed into him; and that which God breathed, was a part of his Divine essence. 11. That God is the only Spirit, and that Prince of the Air, who ruleth in the children of disobedience. 12. That the soul dieth with the body. 13. That reprobation cannot be proved out of Scripture. 14. That there is no Trinity of Persons in God. 15. That every creature is God, every drop in the River is water. 16. That Christ is not essentially, but nominally God. 17. That Christ was polluted with Original sin. 18. That Christ was true man when he created the World, yet without flesh. 19. That Christ died only for sinners, and not for unbelievers; for sins past before our conversion, but not for sins done after conversion. 20. That no man is damned but for unbelief, and that man can satisfie for his own belief. 21. That Heathens have the knowledge of Christ by the Sun, Moon, and Stars. 22. That the end of Christ's coming was to Preach God's love to us, and not to procure it for us; therefore did not obtain life for the Elect, but a resurrection only, and deliverance from death temporal. 23. That Christ Preached not the Gospel, but the Law; for the Gospel was taught by his Apostles. 24. That our unction is all one with Christ's Divinity. 25. That Christ with the Church of *Jews* and *Gentiles*, shall reign on Earth a thousand years in carnal pleasures. 26. That the Heathens are saved without Christ. 27. That the Spirit of God neither dwells nor works in any, but it is our own spirit which both works in the children of disobedience, and sanctifies the Elect. 28. That God seeth no sin in his Elect. 29. That a man baptized with the Holy Ghost, knows all things, as God doth. 30. That we may be saved without the Word, Prayer, Sacraments, &c. 31. That there is no inherent sanctification in believers, but all is in Christ. 32. That *Adam* had died, though he had not sinned. 33. That we have no Original sin, nor is any man punished for *Adam*'s sin. 34. That God's Image consisteth only in the face, which Image was never lost. 35. That men who know the Gospel, are of themselves able to believe. 36. That one man is not more spiritual than another. 37. That we have no Free-will, not so much as in our Natural estate. 38. That the Moral Law is of no use among Christians. 39. That we are not justified by Faith: and that neither Faith, nor Holiness, nor Repentance, are required in Christians. 40. That the Child of God can no more sin, than Christ himself can. 41. That there should be no Fasting-days under the Gospel. 42. That God doth not chastise his children for sin. 43. That God loves his Children as well when they sin, as when they do well; and therefore *Abraham*, in denying his Wife, sinned not. 44. That God's Children ought not to ask Pardon for their Sins; for though they have Sin in the Flesh, they have none in the Conscience. 45. That the body of Iniquity is the great Antichrist mentioned in Scripture. 46. That Men shall have other bodies given them in the Resurrection, and not

the

the same they had here on Earth. 47. That Heaven is empty of souls till the Resurrection. 48. That Infants shall not rise at all, yet Beasts and Birds shall rise again. 49. That after this life, there is neither Heaven, nor Hell, nor Devil; but Hell is in this life, in the terrours of Conscience. 50. That there is no true Ministry, nor Church of Christ upon the Earth. 51. That none are damned, but for rejecting the Gospel. 52. That now many Christians have more knowledge than the Apostles had. 53. That Miracles necessarily attend the Ministry. 54. That there ought to be no Churches built, nor should men worship in consecrated places. 55. That the Apostles were ignorant of the Salvation to be revealed in the last days. 56. That all Men ought to have Liberty of Conscience, and of Prophesying, even Women also. 57. That Circumcision and the Old Covenant was only of things Temporal. 58. That Pædo-baptism is unlawful and impious; and that others, besides Ministers, may baptize; and that a man may be baptized often. 59. That the people should receive the Lord's-Supper with their Hats on: but the Ministers in giving it, should be uncovered. 60. That the Church of *England* is Antichristian. 61. That there is no Divine Right to call or make Ministers: that Ministers should work for their living, and that Tithes are Antichristian. 62. That Christians are not bound to observe the Lord's-day; and that we should observe still the Old Sabbath. 63. That humane Learning and Premeditation is useless to Preaching; and that Preaching should only consist in Disputing, Reasoning, and Conferring. 64. That the Saints must not joyn in Prayer with wicked Men, nor receive the Sacrament with them, nor with any Members of the Church of *England*. 65. That publick Prayers are not to be used but by such as have an infallible Spirit, as the Apostles had. 66. That set-hours of Prayer are needless. 67. That Singing of *David*'s Psalms, or other Holy Songs, except they be of their own making, are unlawful. 68. That wicked Men ought not to Pray at all. 69. That all Government; which, in the Church ought to be Civil, not Ecclesiastical. 70. That the Power of the Keys is as well in six or seven gathered together, as in the greatest Congregation. 71. That neither Miracles nor Visions, nor anointing the Sick with Oyl are ceased. 72. That in these days many are with *Paul*, rapt up into the third Heaven. 73. That the Magistrate is not to meddle with Matters of Religion, nor Forms of Church-Government; which if they do, they are not to be obeyed. 74. That there ought to be a Community of Goods, seeing all the Earth is the Saints. 75. That a man upon slight causes may put away his Wife, and that one man may have two Wives. 76. That Children ought not at all to obey their Parents, if wicked. 77. That Parents should not instruct their Children, but leave them to God. 78. That Christians ought not to maintain Religion by the Sword, nor to fight for their Lives and Liberties, nor to fight at all, nor to kill any thing, nay not a Chicken for our use. 79. That it stands not with God's Goodness to damn his own Creatures eternally. 80. That it's unlawful for a Christian to be a Magistrate. 81. That Man lost no more by *Adam*'s fall, than the rest of the whole Creation. 82. That Christ hath not purchased Eternal life for Man, more than for the best of the Creation; and that he offered up himself a full and perfect Sacrifice; not only for Man, but for all that Man kept, even the whole Creation. 83. None are sent to Hell before the last Judgment. 84. It is not the Law, but the Gospel which threatens us with Hell-fire. 85. If God shew not mercy to all, he is not infinite. 86. Christians are not bound to meet one Day in seven for publick Worship. 87. The Saints are justified, not by Christ's Obedience, but by the Essential Righteousness of God. 88. A Woman committeth not Adultery, in lying with another Man, if her Husband be asleep. 89. That the Saints may put away their unbelieving Wives or Husbands. 90. There is no other Seal but the Spirit, the Sacraments are no Seals at all. 91. The Magistrate may not put to Death a Murtherer, being a Member of the Church, till first he be cast out of the Church. 92. The Promises belong to sinners, as sinners, and not as Repenting sinners. 93. Apocrypha-Books are Canonical Scripture. 94. To use Set-forms of Prayer, even the Lord's-Prayer, is Idolatry. 95. Bells, Churches, and Churchyards, Preaching in Pulpits, in Gowns, by an Hour-glass, the names of our Months and Days are all Idolatry. 96. That the Apostles Creed is to be rejected as erroneous. 97. That there ought to be no other Laws among Christians, but the Judicial Law of *Moses*; and that the Magistrate hath no Legislative Power at all. 98. That all Learning, Schools, Universities, Arts, Degrees are to be rejected as pernicious. 99. That Angels and Devils are not Substances, but meer Qualities; and that mens Souls are but terrestrial Vapours, perishing with the Bodies. 100. That some in this life are perfect without all sin, and need not pray for Pardon. 101. That in God there is some composition, and corporeity, and mutability also. 102. That Christ took not his Flesh of the Virgin *Mary*, but that his Body was created without all Consanguinity with the first *Adam*. 103. That God doth personally subsist in every creature. 104. That the World is eternal. 105. That the Lord's-Supper may be celebrated in Inns rather than Churches, and that in the end of a feast. 106. That the Devils have no sin. But I will leave these Devils, though I could mention many more; but that it delights not my self, nor can it the Reader, to be taking in such filthy mire and dirt. These are some of the poysonous Weeds, which have (too much of late) infested our *English* Garden; I mean the Church, once admired (both at home and abroad) for the beauty of her Doctrine and Discipline; and envied of none but Ignorants, or Men of perverse Mind. The Poet bewailing the Ruins of *Troy*, said,

Church England

[*Seges deplored.*

[*Seges ubi Troja fuit.*] Corn grows where *Troy* stood; but I may sadly complain, that instead of Corn, that is, sound and wholsome Doctrine, which should be the Food of our Souls: Now grows Tares and Weeds, that choak the good Word with which we were formerly fed; and might have been, unto a Life of Glory everlasting, if we had therein abode. But lest I should bring thee into danger, by giving thee only a sight of these Rocks and Precepices; to prevent that, I shall commend to thy serious perusal Master *Wollebius* his *Abridgment of Christian Divinity*, which for the good of my Country-men I Englished, Enlarged, and Cleared in obscure places, and have now fitted for a second Impression. A Book worthy to be written in Letters of Gold, and imprinted in the Heart of every good Christian; the Knowledge therein contained (by Prayer, and through the assistance of God's Spirit) will root and establish thee in every good Word and Work, to the Coming of our Lord and Saviour Jesus Christ: Which God of his infinite Mercy grant.

The Contents of the Thirteenth Section.

The Doctrine *of the Church of* Rome *concerning the Scriptures.* 2. *Their Tenets concerning Predestination, the Image of God, Original and Actual Sin, and Free-will.* 3. *Their Opinions concerning the Law of God, concerning Christ, Faith, Justification, and good Works.* 4. *Their Tenets concerning Penance, Fasting, Prayer, and Alms.* 5. *Their Opinions concerning the Sacraments and Ceremonies used in those controverted.* 6. *What they believe concerning the Saints in Heaven.* 7. *Their Doctrine concerning the Church.* 8. *What they hold concerning Monks, Magistrates, and Purgatory.* 9. *Wherein the outward Worship of the Church of* Rome *consisteth, and first part of their Mass.* 10. *Their Dedication of Churches, and what observable thereupon.* 11. *Their Consecration of Altars,* &c. 12. *The Degree of Ecclesiastical Persons in the Church of* Rome: *Their sacred Orders, Office of the Bishop, and what colours held Sacred.* 13. *Wherein the other part of the Mass consisteth.* 14. *In what else their outward Worship doth consist.* 15. *Wherein consisteth the seventh part of their Worship, and of their Holy-days.* 16. *What be their other Holy-days in which they observe Canonical Hours and Processions.* 17. *Wherein the eighth part of their Worship consisteth; their Ornaments and Utensils used in Churches dedicated to Christ and the Saints; their Office performed to the Dead.*

SECT. XIII.

Quest. 1. **W**Hat *is the Doctrine of the Church of* Rome *at this day, and first of the Scriptures?*

A. Though they maintain the same Scriptures with us, the same Commandments, Lord's-prayer, and the three Creeds of the Apostles, of *Nice* and *Athanasius,* yet in many points they differ from other Churches, which briefly are these. 1. They hold that *Apocryphal* Books are for regulating our Faith and Manners, of equal authority with the Canonical Scripture; such are *Judith, Tobias,* third and fourth of *Esdras,* the Book of *Wisdom, Ecclesiasticus, Baruch,* the Epistle of *Jeremy,* the thirteenth and fourteenth chapters of *Daniel,* the book of *Maccabees,* and that part of *Hester,* which is from the tenth verse of the third chapter. 2. They preferr the vulgar Latine Edition to the Hebrew and Greek Texts. 3. They hold that there is no necessity to translate the Scripture into vulgar Languages. 4. That the Scripture is not to be read

Church of Rome *different from other Churches about the Scriptures.*

of Lay-people, except of such as are discreet, judicious and learned, and are authorized by the Ordinary. 5. That the Mass is not to be celebrated in the vulgar Tongue. 6. That the sence and interpretation of the Scripture depends upon the Church's approbation. 7. That the Scriptures by reason of their difficulty and obscurity, are not fit to be read by the Laity, or to be judges of Controversies. 8. That the Scriptures have four different senses; namely, the *Literal, Allegorical, Tropological,* and *Analogical*; *See Bellar-* which are to be expounded according to Traditions written and un-*mine, Ec-* written, according to the practice of the Church, the consent of Fa-*kius, Pig-* thers, and Interpretation of Counsels confirmed by the Pope. 9. That *hius, and* the Scriptures are not of absolute necessity for the being of a *the other* Church, seeing there was a Church from *Adam* to *Moses*, for the *Writers of* space of two thousand years, without any Scripture, being only *Controver-* guided and instructed by Traditions, without which the Scrip-*sies in the* tures are not perfect, as not containing all Doctrines necessary to *Roman* Salvation.
Church.

Q. 2. *What are the Tenets concerning Predestination, the Image of God, Original sin, and Actual, and Free-will?*

Roman A. 1. They hold Election mutable, because the Elect may to-*Church* tally fall from Faith and Righteousness. 2. That sin foreseen, *different* was the cause of Reprobation, in respect of the positive act of *from others* condemnation; and some of them hold, that foreseen works were *about Pre-* the cause of Election. 3. Concerning the Image of God, they *destinati-* hold that it consisteth most in Charity; and that this is, *Gratia on, God's gratum faciens : Grace which makes us acceptable* ; and that it is a *Image and* habit infused ; whereas they say, that *Gratia gratis data*, is the *Sin.* gift of Miracles. 4. That man in the state of Innocency, did not stand in need of any special assistance, by which he might be excited to good works. 5. That original sin is not in the understanding and will, but in the inferiour part of the soul only, which they call the flesh; that concupiscence and ignorance are only infirmities, and remainders of original sin. That the Virgin *Mary* was without original sin. That infants dying in original sin only, are punished with the pain of loss, not with the pain of sense. That original sin is taken away by Baptism, and that in the regenerate it is remitted, and not imputed, or to be called a sin, but only as it is the cause and punishment of sin; that some actual sins are of their own nature venial, and some mortal. That the sin against the Holy Ghost is pardonable. 6. They hold that in free-*See the a-* will is required, not only a liberty from coaction, but also from *bove nam'd* necessity ; that an unregenerate man, can by his own strength, *Authors,* without God's special help, perform some moral good, in which *and the* there may be no sin found : That an unregenerate man hath *Catechism* freedom of will in matters of Salvation, though not without the *of the Coun-* help of grace ; so that he may hinder or further his conversion, *cil of* and may by his natural power co-operate with grace.
Trent.

Q. 3. *What*

Q. 3. *What are their Opinions concerning the Law of God, concerning Christ, Faith, Justification, and good works?*

A. 1. They divide the two Tables so, that they make but three Commandments in the first, and seven in the second; making one Commandment of the first two, and two of the last. They hold that Idols and Images are not the same, and that the Images of Christ, and of the Saints may be worshipped without Idolatry. That Equivocation may be used in some cases, and an officious Lye. **2.** Concerning Christ they hold that he was not ignorant of any thing, and that he did not attain to knowledge by Learning. That he descended truly into Hell, in respect of his soul, and there preached to the Fathers in prison, and delivered them from their *Limbus*; so that they had not as yet entered into Heaven, till Christ by his Death had opened the Gates thereof, which *Adam* shut by his sin: That Christ did merit by his sufferings, not only for us, but also for himself that glory which he enjoys after his Ascension. **3.** Concerning Faith, they say that Historical, Miraculous, and saving Faith are one and the same: that the special Application of the promises of grace belongs not to Faith, but to presumption: that Faith hath its residence only in the Intellect, and not in the Will: that Faith is an Assent, rather than Knowledge: that justifying Faith may be totally lost in the Regenerate: that true Faith may be without Charity: that we are not justified by Faith alone: that Man by the natural strength of Free-will, can prepare himself for future Justification, being assisted by the Holy Spirit. In his preparation are contained these acts, namely, *Fear, Hope, Love, Repentance, a purpose to receive the Sacrament, a resolution to live a new life, and to observe God's Commandments.* **4.** Concerning Justification, they say, that the first is when a sinner of a wicked man is made good, which is by Remission of sins, and infusion of inherent Righteousness. The second Justification is, when a just man becomes more just; and this is in doing of good works; by the Merit of which, he can make himself more just. They say Christ is the meritorious Cause of our Justification; but the formal Cause is either intrinsecal, to wit, the Righteousness of Christ; or actual, which are our good works; so that here is a threefold formal Cause: they teach that Justification consisteth not in the bare Remission of sins, but also in the inward Renovation of the mind. That we are not only justified, but also saved by good works, as efficient Causes. **5.** Concerning good works, they teach that the good works of just men are absolutely just, and in a manner perfect; that a just man may fulfill the Law; that a man is justified by works, not in the first but second justification; yet not without the assistance of grace. That an unregenerate man by the works of Repentance may merit the grace of justification, *ex congruo*, as doing works agreeing to the Law of God: that they who are justified by the first justification, do merit life Eternal by their works *ex condigno*.

Romanists differ about the Law of God, Christ, Faith, Justification, and good works.

See the Catechism of Trent, with Bellarmine and the other Writers of Controversies.

Q. *What are their Tenets concerning Penance, Fasting, Prayer, and Alms?*

Differ about Penance, Fasting, Prayers, and Alms.

A. They teach that Faith is no part of Penance; that Repentance may be totally lost; that the parts thereof are not Mortification, and Vivification, but Confession, Contrition, and Satisfaction. That Penance is a Sacrament; that Contrition is to be ascribed partly to Grace, partly to Free-will. That it is necessary to Justification, and the cause of Remission of sins, and that by it all sins are pardonable. That auricular Confession to the Priest is necessary to reconcile us to God. That a sinner before Baptism, is received into grace without his own satisfaction, only by the satisfaction of Christ, but after Baptism, he must make satisfaction himself. That after the fault is forgiven, there remains oftentimes the Guilt of temporary punishment either here or in Purgatory, which must make satisfaction; that the punishments of Purgatory may be redeemed by Fasting, Prayers, Alms, &c. Concerning Fasting; They hold it a sin, and deserving Death, to eat of Meats prohibited by the Church. That Fasting consisteth only in Abstinence from Meat, not from Drink. That the times of Fasting, chiefly Lent, are of Apostolical institution. That Fasting is satisfactory and meritorious. That the Tradition of the Church in such indifferent things, obligeth the conscience. 3. Concerning prayer. They say that it is meritorious; that the Canonical Hours of prayer should be observed; that they are not to be said or sung in Latine by the Clergy and Monks. That the titles given to the Virgin *Mary* are true and holy. That to prayer in the Quire ought to be joyned Singing, Organs, Trumpets, and other musical Instruments. 4. Concerning Alms; They hold that the giving thereof is Meritorious. That there is not only a corporal, but also spiritual Alms, consisting in comforting, counselling, teaching, &c. That Alms may be raised of ill-gotten goods, and filthy lucre, as of Whore-houses, &c.

See the Author abovenamed.

Q. 5. *What Opinions do they hold concerning the Sacrament?*

Differ from others about the Sacraments.

A. They teach that the efficacy of the Sacraments depends upon the intention of the giver. That the Sacraments are not Seals to confirm the promises of grace. That grace is contained in, and conferred by the Sacraments *ex opere operato*; and that the receivers thereof, by their justifying vertue, are saved. That three Sacraments, namely, *Baptism, Confirmation,* and *Order,* do imprint an indelible character, form, or figure, in every substance of the soul; the character of *Baptism* is *Passive,* making a man capable of all other Sacraments; that of *Order* is *Active*; that of *Confirmation* is partly *Active,* partly *Passive.* That there are seven Sacraments of the New Testament. That all the Ceremonies used by them in the Sacraments are necessary. 2. Concerning Baptism, they say that Lay-men and Women in case of necessity may Baptize. That the Baptism of *John* was not the same with that of Christ, nor had the same efficacy, and that after.

ter *John's* Baptism, is was necessary to receive Christ's Baptism. That to Water in Baptism should be added Oyl, Spittle, Salt, &c. The sign of the Cross, Exorcism, Exsufflation, a white Garment, &c. That Baptized Infants have, if not actual, yet Habitual Faith infused into them. That Infants cannot be saved without Baptism; that Baptism began to be absolutely necessary on the day of Pentecost. That it totally abolisheth Original sin. 3. Concerning the Eucharist. They say, that only unleavened bread is to be used. That Christ by way of *Concomitance* is wholly in the Broad; that is, his Body, Blood, Soul, Divinity, &c. That the whole Essence of the Sacrament is in the Bread alone. That there is no necessity to communicate under both kinds. That the Wine ought necessarily to be mixed with Water. That the Priests may participate alone. That the Eurcharist is profitable for the dead. That the Bread should be dipt in the Wine, that it should be elevated, carried in Procession, adored, &c. That there is no trope in these words, *This is my body*, &c. That Christ's body is not only really, but substantially in the Sacrament. That it may be at one time in many places. That the bread is transubstantiated into Christ's body. That the form of consecration consisteth in these words, *This is my body*. That the Mass is a Propitiatory Sacrifice for the quick and the dead. 4. Concerning *Confirmation, Penance, Extream Unction, Orders* and *Matrimony*. They teach that these are Sacraments properly so called: that there is vertue in *Extream Unction*, either to cure the body, or do away the remainders of sin; for this cause they anoint six parts of the body; to wit, the Eyes, Ears, Mouth, Hands, Reins, and Feet. That Ordination is a Sacrament as well in *Deacons, Sub-Deacons Acolouthi, Exorcists, Readers,* and *Door-Keepers*, as in Priests.

See the former Authors.

Q. *What Ceremonies do they use in the five controverted Sacraments?*

A. In *confirmation*, the Bishop anointeth the child's forehead with Chrism, making the sign of the Cross thereon; and saying; *I sign thee with the sign of the Cross, and confirm thee with the chrism of salvation, in the Name of the Father*, &c. Then he strikes him on the cheek, to shew he must not refuse to suffer for Christ. In *Penance*, the Bishop goeth to the Church-door where the Penitents lie prostrate on the ground, saying; *Children come to me, and I will teach you the fear of the Lord*. Then he kneeleth and prayeth for them; and having used some words of admonition, he brings them into the Church: this is done on the day of the Lord's-Supper, that they might be partakers thereof; all the Church-doors are then opened to shew that all people have access to Christ. The Penitents being received into the Church, cut their Hair and Beards, and lay aside their penitential garments, and put on clean cloathes, after the example of *Joseph* when he was delivered out of Prison. This casting off their old cloathes puts them in mind of putting off the old man. In *Extream Unction* the Priest first besprinkleth the sick person, and the whole room with holy wa-

Ceremonies used in the five controverted Sacraments.

ter, then he anointeth the Organs of the Five Senses, because by them sin infecteth the Soul; the reins also and feet are anointed to expiate the sins that are in the concupiscible and motive faculties. They only must be anointed of whom there is no hope of recovery. Of the Ceremonies used in *Sacred Orders*, we will speak hereafter. In *Matrimony* the Priest blesseth the married couple with Prayers, and oblations; if they were never married before; but they are not to bless the second marriage. The Woman is covered with a Veil, after the example of *Rebecca*; and to shew her subjection to the man, she is united to the man by a Lace or Ribband tied in a knot, by a Ring also put upon the fourth finger of the left hand, because of the Vein that reacheth from thence to the heart; signifying the mutual love that ought to be between them; but marriages are not to be celebrated in Lent, and other times of humiliation.

See besides the above-named Authors Eckius in his Homily upon this subject.

Q. 7. *What are their Tenets concerning the Saints in Heaven?*

A. They register their names in their Calenders after the Pope hath canonized them, or given a testimony of their Sanctity, and decreed honours for them; namely, publick Invocation, dedication of Altars and Temples to them, oblation of Sacrifices, celebration of Festival days, setting up of their Images, and reservation of their Reliques. The honour they give to God is called by them *Latria*, that of the Saints is *Dulia*; but the honour which they give to Christ's humanity and the Virgin *Mary*, is *Hyperdulia*. 2. They say that the Saints make intercession for us, not immediately to God, but through Christ they obtain their requests. 3. That we ought to invocate both Saints and Angels. 4. That their Images are to be worshipped; that the Images of Christ, and of the Saints are not Idols because Idols are representations of that which is not, and in Scripture the word *Idol* is spoken only of Heathen Images; that it is not unlawful to represent God by such Images as he hath described himself, therefore they paint God in the form of an old man, the Holy Ghost in the form of a Dove; that though the Images of Christ and the Apostles, are to be honoured in relation to the persons which they represent, yet we must not think there is any Divinity in them, or that they can help us; or that we ought to ask any thing of them. 5. That the Images of Christ and the Saints shall be placed in Churches, because the Images of the *Cherubims* were placed in *Solomon*'s Temple, and before in the Tabernacle. 6. That the Reliques of Christ and of the Saints are to be honoured, and kissed, as holy pledges of our Patrons, yet not to be adored as God, or invocated as Saints. 7. That the true Cross of Christ, the Nails, the Thorns, &c. By way of analogy and reduction, are to be worshipped with the same kind of Worship or *Latria* that Christ is: that the sign of the Cross in the forehead, or in the air, is a sacred and venerable sign, powerful to drive away evil spirits. 8. That Pilgrimages ought to be undertaken to those holy places, where the Images and

Roman Church differeth from others about the Saints in Heaven.

Of these passages see Thomas in his summes Gregory de Valentia, Bellarmine, and the other above named.

and Reliques of Christ and of the Saints are kept. 9. That days should be kept holy in memory of the Saints; the observation of which is a part of Divine Worship.

Q. *What is their Doctrine concerning the Church?*

A. They teach that the government of the Church is Monarchical, as being the most excellent form of government. That the government of the Church was founded on the person of Saint Peter. That *Peter* was Bishop of *Rome*, and so continued till his death. That the Pope is *Peter's* Successor, and Christ's Vicar, by whom he is made Head of the Church-Militant. That the Pope is not Antichrist, but that the great Antichrist shall be a particular man, of the Tribe of *Dan*, who shall reign in *Jerusalem* three years and a half, and shall be acknowledged by the *Jews* as their Messiah, whom he will make believe that he is of the Tribe of *Juda*, and descended of *David*. 2. They hold that the Pope is the supreme Judge in Controversies of Faith and Manners; that his judgment is certain and infallible; that he can err in particular controversies of fact, depending upon men's testimony, and that he may err as a private Doctor in questions of right, as well of faith as of manners; but that he cannot err, when with a General-Council he makes decrees of faith, or general precepts of manners; and that the Pope is to be obeyed, though either by himself, or by a particular Council, he err in some doubtful matters: But they generally now believe, that though the Pope were an Heretick, yet he cannot prescribe or define any Heretical Doctrine, to be believed by the whole Church. That the Pope hath a spiritual coactive jurisdiction in making Laws to bind the Conscience, by his sole authority, without the consent of Priests or People; and that he can judge and punish the transgressors of his Laws. That as the Apostles had their immediate authority from Christ, so the Bishops have the same immediately from the Pope. That the Pope hath a supreme Power over the temporal estates of Christians to depose Kings, and dispose of their Kingdoms in order to spiritual things, and so far as is necessary to the salvation of souls. That it is not repugnant to God's Word, for the same man to be both a Political and Ecclesiastick Prince, seeing *Melchisedech, Moses, Eli, Samuel* and the *Maccabees* exercised both Powers. 3. They believe that the true Church of Christ is only that Society which acknowledgeth the Pope to be head thereof, and Christ's Vicar upon earth. That they which are not baptized, and the *Catechumeni*, are not properly and actually members of the Church, but only in possibility. That Hereticks, Schismaticks, and excommunicate persons, are not member of the Church. That Reprobates are members of the Militant Church: *Because in Noah's Ark were unclean Beasts; in the same Net are good and bad Fishes; at the same Wedding-feast many were called, but few chosen; in the same Sheep-fold are some Goats; in the same Houses are vessels of dishonour;* Judas *was one of the Apostles,* &c. That the true Catholick

A View of the Religions Sect. 13.

Catholick Church is always visible; for it is compared to a Mountain, to a Candle, to a City on a Hill, &c. That the true visible Church can never fail totally, *Because it is built on a Rock, against which, Hell Gates cannot prevail*, &c. That the true Church cannot fall into errour : *Because it is the Pillar and Ground of Truth*, &c. That the true notes of the Church are Universality, Antiquity, Continuance, Multitude, Succession of Bishops from the Apostles Ordination, Unity in Doctrine, Unity among the members themselves, and with their head, soundness of doctrine, power and efficacy of doctrine, holiness of life, miracles, the light of prophecy, the testimony of her enemies, the unhappy end of those who oppress the Church, and the temporal felicity of such as have defended her.

See the above nam'd Authors.

Q. 9. *What do they hold concerning Councils, Monks, Magistrates, and Purgatory?*

Romanists differ about Councils, Monks, Magistrates and Purgatory.

A. They teach that Diocesan Councils are to be convocated by the Bishops; Provincial by Arch-Bishops, National by Patriarchs or Primates, but General Councils by the Pope alone, and not by the Emperour without the Pope his approbation; except it be when the Pope is either imprisoned, or dead, or mad; in such cases the Cardinals may call a Council. That ordinarily Bishops have the power of decisive suffrages, but by custom and privileges; Cardinals, Abbots, and Generals of Orders, have the same power, though they be not Bishops. That in a General Council should be present all Bishops, at least of the greater Provinces, except any be excommunicate. That the Pope and the four Patriarchs of *Constantinople, Alexandria, Antioch*, and *Jerusalem*, or their Deputies be also present, and at least some of the greater part of Provinces. That the Pope is the supreme President, and Judge of Councils. That Christians are bound to obey the decrees of Councils. That General and Particular Councils, confirmed by the Pope, cannot err. That the Scripture is above Councils, as it is the infallible Word of God; but in respect of interpretation, it is dependent from Councils. That the Pope is above Councils, and not to be judged by any. 2. Concerning Monks, they teach that their original is of divine right; That their institution is grounded upon Evangelical Council, not Precept. That Counsels are not commanded, but commended to us: That commands are of things easie to be performed, and taken out of the principles of nature: Counsels are of things difficult, and above nature, and of things better than those of commands. By Precepts we are tied to Obedience, by Counsels we are left to our Free-will: Precepts have their rewards and punishments; but Counsels have no punishments, but great rewards: *Hence arise the works of Supererogation.* That children, if they be come to years of puberty, may enter into a Monastery without their Parents consent, if so be their Parents need not their help. And so may Wives without their Husbands consent. That Vows, though

though of things not commanded, are a part of God's worſhip. That the promiſe made in Baptiſm, to renounce the Devil, the World and the Fleſh, is not properly a Vow. That the Vows of Poverty, Obedience, and Continency, are lawful. That the Pope may diſpenſe with Vows. That the habits and ſhaving of Monks, are of a great uſe and antiquity. 3. Concerning Magiſtrates, they teach that their Laws do no leſs bind the conſcience, than Divine or Eccleſiaſtick Laws. That Magiſtrates are ſubject and inferior to the Clergy in matters of Religion. That Magiſtrates may inflict death on Hereticks. 4. Concerning Purgatory, they ſay, that it is one of theſe four Contignations or Rooms under-ground; the lowermoſt is Hell, where the pain of loſs and ſenſe is eternal. The next above that is Purgatory, where pain of loſs and ſenſe is temporary. Above that is the Receptacle of Infants, where only is the pain of loſs eternal. The uppermoſt was that of the Fathers, where was only temporary pain of loſs: now it is empty ſince Chriſt's deſcent thither. That in Purgatory are thoſe ſouls which depart hence with venial ſins, or whoſe ſins are pardoned, but not the puniſhment. That the Suffrages of the living are beneficial to the dead; namely, Maſſes, Prayer, and ſatisfactory Works, as Alms, Pilgrimages, Faſts, &c. To which may be added Indulgences.

Who would ſee more at length the Doctrines of the Church of Rome, let him read the above-named Authors; and withal Baronius, Bonaventura, P. Lombard, Canus, Caniſius, Caſſander, Alphonſus de Caſtro, Coccius, Gerebrard, Gerſon, Gretſerus, Suarez, Taurianus, Vaſquez, Hugo de S. Victore, *and others.*

Q. 10. *Wherein doth the outward worſhip of the Church of* Rome *conſiſt, and the firſt part of their Maſs?*

A. In Churches, Church-yards, Bells, Altars, Pictures, Crucifixes, Images, Curtains, and other Church-Ornaments, as Tapeſtry, Candleſticks, &c. In dedication alſo of Churches, conſecration of Altars, Anointings, Sacraments, &c. In Miniſters, Eccleſiaſtical Orders, and their Functions; ſuch are *Singers, Pſalmiſts, Door-keepers, Lectors,* or *Readers, Exorciſts, Acolyths,* who are to light the Tapers, and hold them whilſt the Goſpel is read, and to furniſh Wine for the *Chalice,* &c. *Sub-Deacons, Deacons, Prieſts,* and *Biſhops,* &c. the office alſo of the *Acolyths* is to make *Agnus Dei,* of conſecrated Wax, mixed with Chriſm diſtributed by the Pope in the Church. Theſe *Agni* or Lambs, repreſent *the Lamb of God, who taketh away the ſins of the World;* for as the Wax is begot of the Bee, without libidinous copulation, ſo was Chriſt of the Bleſſed Virgin; and as the Honey is hid within the Wax, ſo was the Divinity hid under the Humanity. Thyme or Chriſm mixed with the Wax, ſignifieth, that mercy and gentleneſs which was in Chriſt. They ſay that theſe Lambs are preſervatives againſt Lightning and Tempeſts, by vertue of their conſecration. O *Catholicks, great is your Faith, be it to you as you believe.* - 3. In the Garments or Ornaments of Biſhops, Prieſts, and other Church-Miniſters; ſuch are the *Amictus,* which, like the *Ephod,* covers the head

The outward worſhip of the Roman Church and firſt part of their Maſs.

Acolyths, their Offices.

head and shoulders of the Prieſt or Biſhop; t
S...... A.ba, or Cemiſia, is the Surpli
Gir le or Belt with which the Prieſts loins are
... in form of a Chain about the Prieſts nec
his fides, and hangs down to the knee: it is o
cau'e it is the habit of Orators, that preach t
people. Manipulus or Sudarium, or Mappula,
theſe names it hath) is a Towel or Handkerc
Miniſter or Prieſt in his left hand, or in his
or C.ppa, Planon, is an upper garment which c
dy, as it were a little Cottage, called in Latin
Ornaments are common to Prieſts and Biſhops
naments peculiar to Biſhops; namely, Calig
hoſe, or ſtockings; Sandalia, a kind of ſlippe
cincterium, a kind of girdle; Orale, a linen
head; Tunica, a long coat down to the heels, t
laris; Dalmatica, ſo called from Dalmatia, th
was firſt woven in a garment with long and l
ſenting the Croſs; Chirothecæ are white glo
Mitra is the Mitre or Ornament of the head; .
which the Biſhop wears, to ſhew he is betrothe
ius Paſtoralis, is the Biſhops Croſier-ſtaff; Pall
the Ornament of Arch-Biſhops and Patriarchs,
to be worn but in the Church, and in time c
Gregory permitted it to be worn in ſolemn L
Church: upon it are four red croſſes, ſignifyi
nal vertues, Juſtice, Prudence, Fortitude, and T
ought to be in Prelates, which Vertues are not
but as they are ſanctified by the Croſs of Ch
they ſhould glory with the Apoſtle, for the Gen
tues, but knew not Chriſt his Croſs. There a
three pins or bodkins, ſignifying the three C
Faith, Hope, and Charity, without which he
or retain his Pall; they may ſignifie alſo a thr
compunction which ought to be in Prelates.
towards thoſe that are in miſery. 2. Of ca
conſcionable execution of their office. 3. Of f
4. Their worſhip conſiſteth in the Maſs, whc
ceremonies; firſt the Biſhop or Prieſt before h
Pſalms: then he combs his head, and waſheth
eth the aſperſion of holy water; then is the .
at the Prieſts approach towards the Altar; wl
ſinging, the Prieſt or Biſhop walketh towards tl
Prieſt and a Deacon, before whom walketh the
rying the Book of the Goſpel ſhut, before who
per-bearers, and before them is carried the Co
When the Prieſt or Biſhop comes to the Altar
Mitre, makes confeſſion, openeth the Book and

the Bishop also, a linen cloth full of pictures is carried by four Ministers in form of a Canopy. In their four solemn processions, to wit, at *Candlemas, Palm-Sunday, Easter,* and *Ascension*-day, they have crosses in Banners, seven Tapers born by seven *Acolyths,* seven *Deacons* following, then the seven *Priors,* three *Acolyths* with Incense, one *Sub-Deacon* carrying the Gospel, then the *Bishop* in great state, whom the people follow with the *Porters, Readers, Exorcists, Singers,* &c. Before the Bishop or Priest ascends the Altar, he boweth himself to the ground, and then confesseth; and during the time of Mass, he boweth his body eight times before the Altar. After confession and absolution, the Priest blesseth the incense, and puts it in the censer; then he kisseth the Altar and the Book, and takes the censer from the Deacon, with which he fumeth the Altar, and then removeth to the right side of the same, and withall *Kyrie Eleeson* is said not less than nine times in the Mass. *Gloria in Excelsis* is also sung, which was the Angelical Hymn at Christ's Nativity; then the Priest turning to the people, salutes them in these words, *The Lord be with you*; to whom the Quire answereth, *And with thy Spirit*. Seven times in the Mass the Priest salutes the people, but turneth to them only five times. Then the collects or prayers are said, and after them the Epistle is read, with the face towards the Altar; it's the Sub-Deacon's office to read the Epistle; which done, he delivers the Book (shut to the Bishop, who layeth his hand on the Sub-Deacon) which he kisseth. After the Epistle, is sung the *Gradual,* so called from the steps of humility, by which we ascend to Heaven; it's called also the *Responsory,* because the matter thereof answers the matter of the Epistle. Next to this, *Hallelujah* is sung, but from *Septuagesima*-Sunday till *Easter*; instead of *Hallelujah,* the *Tractus* is sung, so called a *Trahendo,* because it is sung with a long drawing tone, as containing the mournful condition of man in this life, as *Hallelujah* is the joyful song of Heaven. After *Hallelujah,* is sung the Prose, which by them is called *Sequentia,* it is a song of exultation. This done, the Priest removeth from the right to the left side of the Altar, whence the Deacon takes the Gospel, and ascends into a high place, where he reads it, with his face to the north; the cross, the censer, and two lights, are carried before the Gospel, which is laid upon a cushion, to shew the yoke of Christ is easie; at the reading of it, all stand up, and cross themselves, and give glory to God. After this, the Creed is rehearsed, and the Sermon followeth, which concludeth the first part of the Mass.

Of these particulars, see *Stephanus Durantus de ritibus Ecclesiæ, Gul. Durandus* his *rationale, Alcuinus de divinis officiis, Incocent 3. de myster. missæ. Hugo de sanct. Victor. de offic Eccles. & in specul. Ecclesiæ Bern. de offic. missæ,* and divers others.

Q. 11. *What is their manner of dedicating Churches?*

A. In the Church to be dedicated or consecrated, are painted twelve Crosses on the Walls, before which burn twelve Tapers. The Bishop in his

Romanists, their manner of dedicating of Churches.

Pontificals

Pontificals with his Clergy, and the people come to the Church-door being shut, where he prayeth, and then besprinkleth the Wall with holy Water, whilst the Clergy and People go singing about the Church. The holy Water is sprinkled out of a bundle of Hysop. Then the Bishop with his whole Train returning to the Church-porch, prayeth again, and with his crosier-staff knocketh the door thrice, saying these words: *Lift up your heads, O ye Gates; and be ye lift up, ye everlasting Doors, and the King of Glory shall come in.* Of whom the Deacon within the Church asketh, *Who is the King of Glory?* to whom the Bishop answereth, *The Lord strong and mighty, the Lord mighty in Battel.* Then the door is opened, the Bishop with three of his servants entereth, the rest remain without; after the Bishop hath wished peace three times to that house, the door is shut again, and he on his knees before the Altar prayeth, whilst the Clergy without sings the Letany, and the Priests carry on their shoulders a Chest or Coffin, containing the Relicks of that Saint to whom the Church is dedicated. The Altar, with all belonging to it, are sanctified. The Walls with certain Letters are painted; Salt, Water, Ashes and Wine are exorcised, and mingled together, into which he dips his thumb, and makes the sign of the Cross on the Altar, Walls and Pavement. Then he offers Incense, and blesseth the Church in the Name of the *Father, Son,* and *Holy Ghost:* this being done, the Bishop before the Church-door preaching to the people concerning the Anniversary-dedication of that Church, of honour due to the Clergy, of tenths also and oblations. After Sermon all are admitted into the Church singing. The twelve Lights and twelve Crosses, do signifie the Doctrine of the twelve Apostles which shineth in the Church, by which they preached the Cross of Christ. The Bishop representeth Christ making intercession for his Church, and by the staff of his Word knocking at the doors of our hearts. His compassing the Church three times, and his three times knocking at the door, signifie his three-fold power in Heaven, Earth, and Hell: And his three-fold right or interest he hath in us, to wit, by Creation, by Redemption, and by the gift of life eternal promised to us. The making of Greek and Latine Letters with a Cross on the Pavement with ashes, shew that the Gentiles are made partakers of the Cross of Christ, but not the Jews; besides that, the rudiments and alphabet of Christianity must be taught to the weaker sort; the Oyl, Salt, Water, Ashes, and Wine, which are used in the dedication, have mystical significations. The Water and Wine represent the two Sacraments of Baptism, and the Eucharist; Oyl sheweth our Spiritual unction; Salt, that wisdom which should be in us; our mortification; Hysop, our purity and sanctification; and the Incense, our prayers.

What observable thereupon.

Q. 12. *What else is observable in the dedication of Churches?*

A. 1. They hold that no Church is to be dedicated till it be endowed; for he that buildeth a Church, is, or should be like a Hus-

rrieth a Maid, on whom he ought to bestow a
the Feast of dedication, which from the Greek
ought to be kept every year; for so it was
ews; which if it had been unlawful, Christ
noured it with his presence. 3. They say that
urches is a terror to evil spirits; an incitement
everence; a means to move God to hear our
; a testimony of our zeal, that Christians are
inferiour to the *Jews* and *Gentiles*, who would
ke use of their Temples for prayer and sacri-
eir Priests they had consecrated and dedicated
s. 4. That what is in the dedication of Chur-
ought to be in us invisibly effected; namely,
be holy, we should not be profane; shall they
the service of God, and not we? shall their
with hallowed Images, and our souls defiled
imaginations? shall the Church be called the
d our bodies (which ought to be the Temples
) dens of Thieves? we are lively stones, but
re dead; we are capable of grace and holiness,
s; for it is confessed on all sides, that Temples
not made capable of actual holiness, but only
Divine Service. Is it not a great shame that in
ts continually shine, and in the Temples of
ere is nothing but darkness? That they should
eir Altars; and we be quite destitute of zeal
r hearts: They make use of outward unction,
the outward unction of the Church, nor the
. When we see them make use of Salt, and Holy
be careful to have Salt within us, and that
, without which we cannot be regenerated.
t Churches may be re-dedicated, if they are
llen down, and built again; or if it be doubt-
have been consecrated heretofore; but if they
ltery, or such like uncleanness, they are only
Holy Water. 6. That Churches must not be
t Mass, and the Reliques of some Saints, and
pe or a Bishop, not by a Priest or any inferi-
t gifts or presents which they call *Anathemata*,
w Church; after the example of *Constantine*
ndowed with rich presents and ornaments the
ilt at *Jerusalem* to the honour of our Saviour.
they dedicate or consecrate their Altars?
aving blessed the water, makes with the same
e four Horns of the Altar, to shew that the
preached in all the four corners of the earth.
out the Altar seven times, and besprinkleth it
loly Water, and Hysop; this is to signifie the

But of this subject concerning dedication, read Durandus and Durantus Turrecremata, Hostiensis, Hugo de S. Victore de Sacram. Hospinian, Raibanus Ivo, &c.

Their consecration of Altars, &c.

seven

seven gifts of the Holy Ghost, and the f(
Christ's blood; to wit, 1. When he was cir(
he sweat blood in the Garden. 3. Whe1
4. When he was Crowned with Thorns.
6. When his Feet were nailed to the Cross ; a
was lanced. The Bishop also makes a cross
Altar, to shew that Christ was crucified in th
for so *Jerusalem* is seated. At this consecra
water, but salt also, wine, and ashes, to :
necessary for Christianity; namely, Purit)
joy, and Humility. The Altar must not
other material, but of stone, to represent
which the Church is built, the corner-stone
refused, the stone of offence at which the
the little stone cut out of the mountain with
Altar is anointed with oyl and chrism, so wa
ces of the spirit, and the oyl of gladness abc
anointing also of the stone Altar, is in imita
ting the stone on which he slept. So the r
water is poured out at the foot of the Alta
of old used to pour out the blood of the sacri[
Altar. The holy Reliques are laid up i
grains of incense, as the Manna of old wa
our hearts should be the Coffins in which t[
Saints with faith in the Trinity, or with the t
Faith, Hope, and Charity, should be caref(
liques are laid under the Altar, because, *I*
those who suffered for Christ were seen b)
Altar. It is also to be observed, that as th
with water, so is it anointed in five plac
with chrism, to signifie the five wounds of (
more fragrantly than any Balsam, and by v
the five senses also are hereby signified, wh
fied. After unction, incense is burned, to
supplications follow sanctification ; At las
all that belong to it are hallowed, the Altar
Mass is said, and Tapers lighted ; to shew
devotion must be accompanied with goo

See the for-
mer Au-
thors.

shine before men here if we should shine l
ment hereafter.

Q. 14. *What else do they consecrate besid*
A. Besides these they consecrate all the O1
the *Patine* for making the body of Christ ;
vering thereof; the *Chalice* for the blood ;
the Altar is covered : the *Eucharistial*, or]
dy is kept, representing Christ's Sepulch(
and *Capse,* that is, Chests or Coffins wl
Saints are kept. They consecrate also t]

nd *Easter-Tapers*, their *Fonts, First-fruits, holy Water, Salt, Church-yards, Bells*, &c. Every one of which have their peculiar prayers; besides, Washing, Crossing, Anointing, Incense, &c. They hold that Bells succeeded the Jewish Trumpets; by which we are awaked, and admonished to put on the Armour of God, to fortifie our selves with prayer against our spiritual enemies. Bells are more durable than Trumpets, and their sound louder, by which is signified that the preaching of the Gospel exceedeth that of the Law, both in the continuance and efficacy. *Bells have clappers, and Preachers have tongues? it is a shame that the one shall be vocal, and not the other; how is that congregation served, which hath sounding Bells, and dumb Preachers; or that which hath sounding brass, and tinckling cymbals for their Preachers; such as have clappers, but no hands; good words, but no good works; which Preach to others, and are cast away themselves? like Bells, they call upon others to hear Sermons, but are not thereby bettered or edified themselves.* In the *Roman* Church they baptize their Bells, and give them names; for this, alledging the example of *Jacob*, who gave the name of *Bethel* to *Luz*, the place where he had the Vision of the Ladder. Their Bells seldom are heard in *Lent*, and three days before *Easter* are quite silent, to shew the sadness of that time. Church-yards, in Greek κοιμητήρια, that is, Dormitories (because our bodies sleep there till the resurrection) are consecrated with Crosses, holy Water, Fumigation and Prayers, as the Churches are; they be also as well as Churches, Sanctuaries, and places of refuge; none must be buried here, but Christians who have been baptized? such as die without baptism, or without repentance after Murther, Adultery, Self-Homicide, or any other grievous sin, though baptized, must not be buried there. In the Church-yard are set up five crosses, one whereof stands in the middle; before each of them are placed three burnings Tapers, fifteen in all; the Bishop beginning at the middle cross, maketh a speech, then prayeth, and puts the three Tapers on the top of the cross: the like he doth to all the rest, and in the interim the Letany is sung, and each cross besprinkled with holy Water and fumed with incense.

Q. 15. *What degrees of Ecclesiastical persons are there in the Church of* Rome?

A. They divide their Church-offices into dignities and orders; their dignities are these; the *Pope, Patriarch, Primata, Arch-bishop* or *Metropolitan, Bishop, Arch-Presbyter, Arch-Deacon* and *Provost* or *Præpositus*. For the Quire there are the *Dean, Sub-Dean, Præcentor, Succentor, Treasurer*, &c. The Popes, Senators, or Counsellors, are named *Cardinals* from *Cardo*, the hindge of a door, because on them, as the door on its hinges, all weighty affairs of the Church are turned. Their orders be seven, to wit, *Door-keeper, Readers, Exorcists, Acolyths*, or *Taper-bearers, Sub-Deacons, Deacons*, and *Priests*. These three also are only sacred

The degrees of Ecclesiastical persons in the Church of Rome.

Orders,

Orders, the other four are not. The door-keeper is first instructed in his office by the Arch-Deacon, who presents him to the Bishop, and he ordains him, delivering to him from the Altar the Keys of the Church, and saying, *So do, and so live as thou were to give account to God of the things locked up by these Keys.* The Lecturers or Reader's office is to pronounce and read clearly, and distinctly the Lessons appointed to be read in the Church: none must exercise this function but he who is ordained by the Bishop, who in the presence of the people delivers the book to him, in which he is to read, *Take and read the word of God ; if thou art faithful in thine office, thou shalt have a share with them who dispence the same word.* The Exorcist is he who calling on the name of Jesus, by that name doth adjure the unclean spirit to depart out of the possessed, on whom he layeth his hands. When the Exorcist is ordained, he receiveth the book of Adjurations from the Bishop, saying, *Take and learn this by heart, and receive power to lay thy hands on the possessed, whether he be baptized, or a Catechumenus as yet.* The Acolyths or Taper-bearers are they who carry the lights whilst the Gospel is reading, or the Sacrifice is offered, to represent Christ the true light of the World, and to shew the spiritual light of knowledge, which should be in us. Their office also is to provide vessels for the Eucharist. The Bishop doth instruct them in their function when he ordains them, and then the Arch-Deacon delivereth to them a candlestick with a wax light in it, and an empty Tankard, to shew their office is to provide lights and vessels for Divine Service. These be the Lesser Orders which are not sacred, and which they teach Christ himself did exercise; for he performed the Porter or Door-keepers office, when he whipped the Money-changers out of the Temple. The Reader's office, when he took up the book and read that passage in *Isaiah*, *The Spirit of the Lord is upon me,* &c. The Exorcist's office, when he cast seven Devils out of *Mary Magdalen*. The Acolyth's office, when he said, *I am the light of the world, he that followeth me walketh not in darkness,* &c.

Q. 16. *Which be their Sacred Orders?*

Their sacred Orders.

A. These are three ; the first is the Sub-Deacon whose office is to read the Epistle, to receive the peoples oblations, and to bring them to the Deacon; to carry also the Patin and Chalice to the Altar; to hold the Bason whilst the Bishop, Priest, or Deacon washeth their hands before the Altar, to wash also the Altar-linen. When the Bishop ordains him, he delivers into his hand the empty Patin and Chalice, saying ; *See whose Ministration this is, which is delivered to thee.* From the Arch-Deacon he receiveth then the Tankard with Wine and Water, and the Towel. He wears a Surplice and Belt, as the four former Orders do. His Coat is girt to him, and he holds a Handkerchief, or Towel. They say that Christ performed the Sub-Deacon's office which he turned water into wine in *Cana,* and when after Supper he poured

water

water into a Bason, and washed his Disciples feet. Their second Sacred Order is the Deacon or Minister, whose office is to preach to the people, and to serve or assist the Priest at the Sacraments; to cover the Altar, to lay the Oblations thereon; to read the Gospel, and the Epistle also in the Sub-Deacons absence; in Processions to carry the Cross, to say the Letanies; to rehearse the names of those who are to be ordained and baptized, and to name the holy-days, &c. They must not administer the Sacraments, but in case of necessity, and by permission of the Bishop, or Priest; nor must they without leave sit in the presence of a Priest. When the Deacon is ordained, the Bishop alone layeth his hands on him, and blesseth him, and delivers (using certain words) the Book of the Gospel and the *Stola* to him. When he reads the Gospel, the *Acolyths* hold two Tapers before him; not to illuminate the air, by day, but to shew what joy and spiritual illumination we have by the Gospel. The Censer also with the Incense is carried, not only to represent Christ, in the sweet smell of whose Sacrifice the Father is well pleased; but also to shew Preachers that their prayers must like Incense ascend before God, and that the good fame of their Life and Doctrine, must be like the fume of Incense smelling sweetly among all men, The Deacon also reads the Gospel in a high place, that it may be heard the better; and to shew that it ought not to be preach in corners, but, as Christ saith, on the house-tops: this is also in imitation of Christ, who when he would teach his Disciples, went up into an high mountain. The Gospel is read with the Deacon's face against the North, that the frozen and could hearts of the Northern Nations might be warmed and melted by the comfortable heat of this bright Sun of the Gospel. When the Deacon salutes the people, he signs himself with the Cross on the forehead, to shew, he is not ashamed of the Cross of Christ; and likewise on the breast, to put us in mind that we should be ready to crucifie our affections with Christ. At the reading of the Gospel all stand up bare-headed, to their reverence: Swords and Staves are laid aside, to shew their peaceable minds; and the Book is kissed, to declare by this their love and affection to the Gospel. They say that Christ performed the Deacon's part when he preached and prayed for his Apostles. Their third and highest Sacred Order is Priesthood; when the Priest is ordained, the Bishop with some other Priests lay their hands on his head, and anoints his hand with oyl, to signifie that not only must the Priest have his head stuffed with knowledge, but his hands must be supple and ready to do good works; the Bishop also delivers into his hand the Chalice with the Wine, and the Patin with the hoast; saying, *Receive power to say Mass for the quick and dead, and to offer Sacrifice to God in the name of the Lord.* Then the Bishop kisseth the Priest, to shew he is his equal in respect of order; whereas, the Deacon and Sub-Deacon kiss the Bishop's hand, to shew they are of an inferiour order. The Priest must not say Mass, till he first have washed, and confessed if he be guilty of any deadly sin, and have put on first the *Amictus*, which like a veil covers his head and shoulders, to shew how Christ's Divinity was veiled by his humanity. 2. The *Alba* or *Talaris*, because it reacheth to the heels, in Greek ποδήρης, which by its whiteness signifieth innocency, and by its length perseverance, two vertues fit for Priests. 3. The Girdle or Belt about their loins, to shew the subduing of their concupiscence. 4. The *Stola* or *Orarium* about the neck, and hanging cross-way on the breast, signifieth that the Priest must undergo the yoke of Christ, and still meditate on his Cross. 5. The *Mappula* or *Manipulus*, which is a Towel or Handkerchief, for wiping away the sweat from their faces, and moisture from their eyes, representing also the purity that ought to be in the Priests lives. 6. The *Casula* over all the other garments, signifying Charity, which is above all vertues. Christ exercised the Priests office when he administered the Eucharist, when he offered the propitiatory Sacrifice of his body on the Altar of the cross, and yet whilst he is making intercession for us in heaven.

Of these passages, see Innocent 3. l. 1. Myst. Missae, c. 58. Stephan. Eduensis de sacr. altaris. c. 10. Amalar. Fortunat. l. 6. de Ecclef. offic. c. 19. l. 2. & l. 3. Rab. Maurus l. 1. de instit. cler. c. 18. Alcuin. de divin. offic. Alexand. de Ales part 4. Quaest. 26. Hugo de S Victore l. 2. de sacram. Part 4. Besides the Councils of Rhemes, of Lateran, of Braccara, and divers others.

Q. 17. *Wherein consisteth the office of the Bishop?*

A. Under this name are comprehended Popes, Patriarchs, Primats, Metropolitans, Arch-Bishops, and Bishops. Some will have the Bishop to be a particular order; but indeed the order of the Priest and Bishop is all one, in respect of catechizing, baptizing, preaching, administring the Eucharist, binding and loosing. The Bishop then is an office of dignity, not of order; he hath nine priviledges above the Priest, namely, of Ordination, Benediction of Nuns, consecration of Bishops, and imposing hands on them, Dedication of Churches, Degradation, holding of Synods, making of Chrism, hollowing of Cloathes and Vessels. Because Bishops are superintendents and overseers, therefore they have the highest Seat in the Church; they are consecrated on the Lord's-day only, and at the third hour, because then the Holy Ghost descended on the Apostles, to whom Bishops have succeeded. At the Bishop's Consecration, there must be present at least three; to wit, two Bishops, and the Metropolitan; that the gifts of the Spirit may not seem to be given by stealth and in corners; in this they follow the example of St. *James*, who was made Bishop of *Jerusalem* by *Peter*, *James*, and *John*. In the Bishops consecration two hold the Bible over his head, one pouring the benediction on him, and the rest laying their hands on his head. By this Ceremony is signified not only the conferring of the gifts of the spirit, but also the knowledge which the Bishop must have of the Gospel, and the care he must undergoe to support it. On the Sunday in the evening he is examined concerning

See also Guliel. Durand. l. 2. c. 10. Office of the Bishop.

cerning his former life, and the Trinity is three times called upon for a blessing. The next morning he is examined concerning his future conversation and faith; and then his head and hands are anointed, and the Mitre is set on his head, the Staff also and Ring are given him. The Priest is anointed with Oyl, but the Bishop with Chrism, that is, Oyl and Balsam; to shew that the higher he is in dignity, the more fragrant must his fame and conversation be. He must excell in knowledge and good works, represented by the anointing of his head and hands: *Christ performed the Bishops office, when he lifted up his hands, and blessed his Apostles*; saying, Receive the Holy Ghost; whose sins you forgive, they are forgiven, &c.

Q. 18. *What colours do they hold sacred in the Church of Rome?*

A. Four; namely, White, Red, Black, and Green; White is worn in the Festivities of Saints, Confessors, and Virgins, if they be not Martyrs, to shew their integrity and innocency; In festivities also of Angels, because of their brightness, in the feast of the Virgin *Mary*, of *All-Saints*, (yet some then wear Red) of *John* Baptist's Nativity, of St. *Paul*'s Conversion, of St. *Peter*'s Chair; also of the Vigil from Christ's Nativity, to the eighth day of *Epiphany*, except there be some Martyrs days between. On Christ's Nativity, on the Feast of *John* the Evangelist, on the Epiphany, because of the Star that appeared to the wisemen; on the day of the Lord's-Supper, because then the Chrism is consecrated; on the holy Sabbath till the eighth day of the Ascension; on the Resurrection, because of the Angel that appeared in white; on the Ascension-day, because of the bright cloud that carried Christ up to Heaven, and the two Angels then in white; on the Feast of Dedication, because the Church is Christ's Spouse, which ought to be innocent and immaculate. The Red colour is used in the solemnities of the Apostles, Evangelists, and Martyrs, for they shed their blood for Christ in the festivity of the Cross, also in Pentecost week, because the Holy Ghost appeared in fire: in some places white is worn on the festivities of the Martyrs, because it is said *Cant.* 5. *My beloved is white and red*. White in his Confessors and Virgins, Red in his Martyrs; these are the Roses and Lilies of the Valley. Black is worn upon *Good-Friday*, on all Fasting-days, on the Rogation-days in Masses for the dead, from Advent till the Nativity; and from *Septuagesima* till *Easter-Eve*; on *Innocent*'s day some were Black, because of the Mourning in *Rama*; some Red, because of the blood of those young Martyrs; Green, which is made up of the three former colours, White, Red and Black, is used between the eight of *Epiphany* and *Septuagesima*: likewise between *Pentecost* and *Advent*; but in the City of *Rome* the violet colour is worn sometimes instead of Black and Red.

What colours held sacred.

See Durandus Rationale, L. 3. C. 18.

Q. 19. *Wherein consisteth the other parts of the Mass?*

A. The second part begins with the offertory which is sung, and so called from the Priest offering of the Hoast to God the Father,

The other parts of the Mass.

ther, and the peoples offering of their gifts to the Priest. Then the Priest before he offereth the immaculate Hoast, washeth his hands the second time, in the interim the Deacon casteth over the Altar a fair linen cloth, called *Corporale*, because it covers Christ's body, and represents his Church the mystical body: it's called also *Palla*, from palliating or covering the mystery above named. There is also another *Palla* or *Corporale*, with which the Chalice is covered. Then the Deacon presenteth the *Patina* with the round Hoast on it, to the Priest or Bishop; the Deacon alone can offer the Chalice, but the Priest consecrates it; who also mixeth the Wine and Water in the Chalice, which the Deacon cannot do; the Priest poureth out a little on the ground, to shew that out of Christ's side, water and blood issued out, and fell on the ground. The water is blessed by the Priest when it is mixed, but not the wine, because the wine represents Christ, who needs no blessing; the Hoast is so placed on the Altar, that it stands between the Chalice and the Priest, to shew that Christ is the Mediatour between God (who is represented by the Priest) and the People, which the water in the Chalice resembleth. Then the Priest fumeth the Altar and the Sacrifice three times over, in manner of a Cross, to shew *Mary*'s three-fold devotion in anointing Christ's feet, then his head, and at last her intention to anoint his whole body; then the Priest boweth himself, kisseth the Altar, and prayeth, but softly to himself: this prayer is called *secreta* and *secretella*; but tho' it be said in silence, yet the close of it is uttered with a loud voice, *Per omnia secula seculorum*; then follows the *Præfatio*, which begins with Thanksgiving, and ends with the Confession of God's Majesty: the minds of the people are prepared with these words, *Lift up your hearts*: the answer whereof is, *We lift them up unto the Lord*: Then is sung this Hymn, *Holy, Holy, Holy*, &c. *Heaven and earth is full of thy Glory*, &c. Then follows *Hosanna*, and after this the *Canon*, which containeth the Regular making up of that ineffable mystery of the Eucharist; it is also called *Actio* and *Secreta*, because in it is giving of Thanks, and the Canon is uttered with a loud void. The Canon by some is divided into five parts, by others into more: in it are divers prayers for the Church, for the Pope, for Bishops, Kings, all Orthodox Christians, for Gentiles, also Jews and Hereticks; those in particular are remembred, for whom the sacrifice is to be offered, whose names are rehearsed, for those also that be present at the Mass, and assistant, and for himself likewise: then is mention made of the Virgin *Mary*, of the Apostles, Evangelists and Martyrs; but the Confessors are not named, because they shed not their blood for Christ: then follows the Consecration after many crossings, these words being pronounced, *For this is my body*; the people answer *Amen*: then the Hoast is elevated, that the people may adore it; and that by this might be represented Christ's Resurrection and Ascension: when the Priest mentioneth Christ's passion, he stretcheth out his

arms

Sect. 13. *of* EUROPE.

arms in manner of a cross: the Hoast is crossed by the Priest five times, to shew the five wounds which Christ received; but indeed, in the Canon of the Mass, there are seven several crossings of the Hoast and Chalice; in the first the sign of the Cross is made three times; in the second, five times; in the third, twice; in the fourth, five times; in the fifth, twice; in the sixth, thrice; and in the seventh, five times; so all make up twenty-five crossings: Prayers are also made for the dead. The Deacon washeth his hands, to shew how *Pilate* did wash his hands, when he delivered Christ to be scourged. The third part of the Mass begins with the *Pater-Noster*, and some other prayers; the Sub-Deacon delivereth the *Patina* covered to the Deacon, who uncovereth it, and delivers it to the Priest; kisseth his right hand; and the Priest kisseth the *Patina*, breaks the Hoast over the Chalice, being now uncovered by the Deacon, and puts a piece of it in the wine, to shew that Christ's body is not without blood. The Hoast is broken into three parts, to signifie the Trinity: then the Bishop pronounceth a solemn blessing: then is sung *Agnus Dei*, &c. that is, *O Lamb of God, that takest away the sins of the World*, &c. and then the kiss of peace is given according to the Apostles command, *Salute one another with a holy kiss*. In the fourth part of the Mass, the Priest communicates thus; he takes the one half of the Hoast for himself, the other half he divides into two parts; the one for the Deacon, the other for the Sub-Deacon: after these three, the Clergy and Monks communicate, and after them, the People; the Priest holdeth the Chalice with both hands, and drinks three times to signifie the Trinity: the Hoast must not be chewed with the teeth, but held in the mouth till it dissolve; and after the taking thereof, he must not spit, but must wash his hands *Of these* left any of the Hoast should stick to his fingers. The three washings of the Priests hands in the Mass, do signifie the three-fold *Ceremonies* purity that ought to be in us; to wit, of our Thoughts, Words, *see the a-* and Works: then follows the Post-communion, which consisteth *bove named* in thanksgiving and singing of *Antiphones*: This done, the Priest *Authors*, kisseth the Altar, and removes again to the right side thereof, *and Ga-* where having uttered some prayers for the people, and blessed *briel Biel* them, the Deacon with a loud voice saith, *Ite, missa est*; that is, *de canone* *Go in peace*; *the Hoast is sent to God the Father to pacifie his anger.* *Missæ.*

Q. 20. *In what else doth the outward Worship consist?*

A. The fifth part of their Worship consisteth in their Divine *Other parts* Service or Office, as they call it; whereof be two sorts; one composed by St. *Ambrose* for the Church of *Millan*; the other by *worship.* St. *Gregory*, which the Angel in the night by scattering the leaves up and down the Church did signifie, that it was to be spread abroad through the World. In the sixth part, they place much Religion in the observation of Canonical hours of prayer, whereof at first were eight; four for the night, and four for the day;

the diurnal hours are, the first, third, sixth, and ninth; the night hours, the *Vespers, Completory, Nocturnals*, and *Mattins*, or Morning-prayers: But now these eight are reduced to seven, to signifie the seven gifts of the Holy Ghost, or the seven deadly sins, or the seven-fold passion of Christ; the Nocturnals are said with the Mattins, and not a-part, as heretofore: every one of these Canonical hours begins and ends with a *Pater-Noster:* the *Nocturnal* Office is the first, and is sung at mid-night, in memory that about that time Christ was born and apprehended by *Judas*, and that about mid-night, he shall come to judgment: The *Mattins* or *Praises* are said and sung in memory of Christ's Resurrection, and the Creation of the World about that time; the first hour is kept in memory of Christ's being delivered by *Pilate* to the Jews about that hour, and that then the Women who came to the Sepulchre, were told by the Angels that Christ was risen: the third hour is in memory of Christ's being at that time condemned by the Jews, and scourged; at that time the Holy Ghost was given to the Apostles, who then spoke the great Works of God: the sixth hour is in memory of Christ's Crucifixion at that time, and of the Sun's miraculous defection: the ninth hour Christ gave up the Ghost; his side was then pierced, and then he descended into Hell; the Vail of the Temple was rent, and the Graves opened: At that hour also *Peter* and *Paul* went up into the Temple to pray, and so did *Peter* into an upper Chamber, where he fell into a Trance: the *Vespers* are observed, because in the evening Christ's body was taken down from the Cross; at that time he instituted the Sacrament, and did accompany the two Disciples to *Emaus*; at this time is sung the *Magnificat*, because the Virgin *Mary*, who compiled this Song, is the bright evening Star of the World. Then also the Tapers are lighted, to shew we must have our Lamps ready with the wise Virgins: The *Completory* is so called, because in it are compleatly ended all the diurnal Services; it is observed in memory of Christ's sweating of blood at that time; he was then also put in the Grave. The Song of *Simeon*, *Nunc dimittis*, &c. is sung in the *Completory*; because as he before his death sung it, so should Christians before they sleep, which is a resemblance of death. In each one of these Canonical or Regular hours are sung *Gloria Patri*, with Hymns, Psalms, and spiritual Songs; peculiar Lessons are read, and Prayers said.

See Durandus and Durantus.

Q. 21. *Wherein consisteth the seventh part of their Worship?*

A. In observation of Festival-days; to every one of which are appropriated Divine Services or Offices. They begin their Feasts from the Four Sundays in Advent, kept to put us in mind of Christ's four-fold coming; to wit, in the flesh, in the minds of the faithful, in death, and in judgment at the last day. In the third week of *Advent* begins the first of the four Fasts, called *Jejunia quatuor Temporum:* and this Fast is for the Winter-quarter, the Vernal Fast is in the first week of Lent. The Æstival is the first week

Days Festival in the Church of Rome.

week after *Whitsontide*, and the Autumnal in the third week of *September*. These four Seasons of the year resemble the four Ages of man's life; to wit, his Childhood, Youth, Manhood, and Old age; for the sins of which we ought to fast. They observe also the Fasts of Lent, and of Fridays, and on the Eves of the Apostles. Saint *Laurence* alone of all the Martyrs, and Saint *Martin* of all the Confessors, have their F.sts. On the Eve or Vigil of Christ's Nativity, a Lesson is read out of *Exod.* 16. concerning the *Manna* that fell in the Desart, to prepare the people for the due receiving of the true *Manna*, Christ Jesus the next day, in which are sung three Masses, to shew that Christ was born to save those that lived before, under, and after the Law: The first is sung at midnight with the Angelical Hymn, the second at the breaking of the day, in which mention is made of the Shepherds that came to see Christ; the third Mass is at the third hour, in which are read Prophecies, Gospels, and Epistles, shewing Christ's Nativity. On the Sunday following, are Lessons of the same Nativity: The first of *January* being the eighth day after the Nativity, is observed in memory of Christ's Circumcision, who in this would be subject to the Law, would teach us humility, and mortification, and would shew himself to be true Man, and the Messiah. The *Epiphany* is kept in memory of the Star that appeared, and of the three wise Men that offered him gifts; and because on the same day Christ was baptized, when the whole Trinity appeared, it is called *Theophania*: and because on the same day Christ turned water into wine at the marriage in *Cana*, it is called *Bethphania* from the house where the miracle was done. The eighth day after the *Epiphany*, is kept in memory of Christ's baptism. Every Sunday throughout the year hath its peculiar Service or Office: chiefly *Septuagesima, Sexagesima, Quinquagesima*, and *Quadragesima* Sundays. Their Lent-Fast, which is kept in memory of Christ's forty days Fast, begins on Ash-Wednesday, in which consecrated Ashes are put on their heads in sign of humility, and mortification, and to shew we are but Dust and Ashes. During the Lent every day in the week, as well as the Sundays, have their proper service and devotion: on the fifth Sunday in Lent, they begin the Commemoration of Christ's Passion. *Palm-Sunday* is kept in memory of the branches of trees cut down by the people, and born by them, when Christ was riding in triumph to *Jerusalem*: therefore this day the Priest blesseth and distributeth branches of trees. The three days immediately going before *Easter* are kept with much sadness and devotion: their *Mattins* end in darkness, the Bells are silent, all lights are put out, &c. Three sorts of Oyl are blessed on this day; to wit, that of Baptism, that of the Sick, and that of the *Catechumeni*; the Bishop breatheth on the Oyl three times, to signifie the Trinity; whereof the Holy Ghost, represented by the Oyl, is one of the Persons. After evening Service the Altars are stript naked, to shew Christ's nakedness on the Cross.

In some places also they are washed with Wine and Water, and rubbed with Savin leaves, to represent the blood and tears with which Christ, our true Altar, was washed, and the thorns he was crowned with. In the *Parasceue* is kept a strict fast and silence; no Mass is said this day: Christ's Passion is read in the Pulpit uncovered; the dividing of Christ's garment is represented by the *Sub-Deacons*; much Adoration is given to the Cross. Christ's body is carried by two Priests to the Altar, which body was consecrated the day before; for on this day, and on the holy Sabbath, the Sacrament is not celebrated, because the Apostles those two days were in great fear and sadness: And so there is no divine Office this Sabbath. On this day the *Agnus Dei*, or Lambs of Wax are consecrated, to defend those that carry them from Thunder and Lightning. The *Paschal* Taper is also consecrated, and the fire which was put out, is renewed by new sparks out of a flint, to represent Christ the true Light of the World, and that stone cut out of the Mountain: on the Taper (being lighted) are fastned five pieces of frankincense, to represent the Spices brought by the Women, and Christ's five Wounds. The Taper hath three things in it representing Christ. The Cotton or Wick signifieth his Soul: the Wax, his Body: and the Light, his Divinity. It also putteth the people in mind of the fiery Pillar which went before the *Israelites* to *Canaan*. The Light of the Taper also signifieth both the Light of the Gospel here, and the Light of Glory hereafter. The Lessons are read without title or tone; the Fonts or *Baptisteria* are also blessed this day, to shew that by baptism we are buried with Christ: the Priest in consecrating the water toucheth it with his hand, dips the Taper in it, bloweth on it, and mixeth the chrism with it: baptism is to be administred but twice a year; to wit, at this time, and on the day of Pentecost, except in case of necessity: besides divers ceremonies used in baptism, the Priest bloweth three times on the Infant, gives him chrism, and a white garment. Four sorts are excluded from being witnesses in Baptism; namely religious persons, Infidels, such as are not confirmed, a man and his wife together; for becoming spiritual parents, they are not to know one another carnally any more. They say divers Letanies in baptism; Confirmation is done by the Bishop, who anoints the Child with Chrism on the forehead, as the Priest had done on the crown of his head in baptism. The reason why the Child is twice anointed with Chrism, is, because the Holy Ghost was given twice to the Apostles; once here on earth before Christ Ascension, and once from heaven in a fuller measure after Christ's Ascension. By the first they receive a new birth, or regeneration; by the second growth, strength and perfection. Therefore this Sacrament of confirmation is called by the Greek Fathers πλήωσις, perfection or confirmation. The Chrism wherewith they are anointed, is made and consecrated on the day of the Lord's Supper, because two days afore *Easter*, *Mary Magda-*

len anointed Christ's head and feet. The Priest must not confirm except by deligation from the Pope; this belongs only to the Bishop, because it is an Apostolical Function, and Bishops are the Apostles successors. Confirmation is not to be given to those that are not baptized; because the character of this Sacrament, presupposeth the character of baptism. Neither must Children be confirmed till they be able to give an account of their faith. Then the Bishop strikes the Child on the cheek with his hand, to shew he must be content to suffer for Christ. On the holy Sabbath, the Altars begin to be covered again, *Gloria in Excelsis* is sung; the Bells are rung, as preparatives for the Resurrection; but before the Gospel, Incense is carried instead of Light, to shew that the Light of the World was supposed to be yet in the Grave by the Women that went to embalm him. And the Post-Communion is not sung, to shew how the Apostles were silent, when Christ was apprehended.

Of these and other Ceremonies, see the aforenamed Authors.

Q. 22. *What be their Holy-days which they observe?*

A. The chief is the Feast of *Easter*, in which their Churches, Altars, Crosses, and Priests, are cloathed in their best ornaments; nothing this day must be eat or drunk without the Priest's benediction, and signed with the Cross. In *Easter* week the custom was in Salutations, to say, *The Lord is risen*; and to answer thus: *Thanks be to God*, and then to kiss each other; which custom is yet observed by the Pope to the Cardinals when he sayeth Mass this day. The next Sunday to *Easter* is called *Dominica in albis*, because they that are baptized on the Holy Sabbath, lay aside on this day their white Garments. The second Sunday is called *Expectationis*, the day of expectation or looking for the Coming of the Holy Ghost. On *Easter* day before Mass, there is a solemn procession of the Priest's cloathed in white, singing the Resurrection; before whom are carried Tapers burning, Crosses, and Banners. There are also Processions all the week after to the Fonts singing, in imitation of the *Israelites* rejoycing for the drowning of their enemies in the red Sea: Baptism is the sea, and our sins are our enemies; every day also this week the *Neophytes* are led to the Church by their God-fathers and God-mothers, with wax Tapers before them, which on the next Sunday, called *in albis*, they offer to the Priests. From the Octaves of *Easter* till *Whitsunday*, are sung two *Hallelujahs* every Sunday, and one every working-day, to shew that the joys of Heaven are represented, which the soul only participates till the Resurrection; and after that, soul and body together, which is a double *Hallelujah*. Every day in *Easter* week hath its peculiar Epistle and Gospel, mentioning the Resurrection of Christ, and our happiness in Heaven: to this same purpose hath every Sunday after *Easter* its peculiar Mass and Service. *Rogation*-Sunday, which is the fifth after *Easter* is so called from praying or asking; for being *Ascension*-day is near, and we cannot follow Christ corporally into heaven, therefore we are taught to follow him by our prayers: three days then before Afcenfion-day, are *Rogations*, *Letanies*, or Prayers both for fpiritual and temporal Bleffings; the Letany ufed at this time is called the Leffer, and invented by *Mamertus* Bifhop of *Vienna*, in a time when Wolves and other wild Beafts had broke out of the Woods, and killed divers people; the greater Letany was the invention of *Gregory* the firft, when *Rome* was afflicted with a great Plague, caufed by the poyfonable breath of Serpents; on thefe Rogation-days there ufed to be Proceffions, with Croffes, Reliques, and Banners carried before, finging alfo and praying for divers bleffings; among the reft, for the fruits of the earth: the Vigil or Eve of Afcenfion hath its proper Mafs; on Afcenfion-day is a folemn proceffion; on the Sunday after; Promifes are read concerning the Coming of the Holy Ghoft: on Whitfun-Eve Baptifm is celebrated as it was on Eafter-Eve; for as we are dead with Chrift in Baptifm, fo we are Baptized with the Holy Ghoft, which was accomplifhed when he came down on the Apoftles: The Feaft of Pentecoft is kept feven days; at which time, becaufe of Baptifm, white is worn; this colour fignifieth that all who are Baptized, are made Priefts to God the Father, for the Priefts Garment is white: it fheweth alfo the innocency and purity that ought to be among Chriftians: and it puts them in mind of the refurrection, and glory of the life to come. They pray ftanding, in fign of liberty obtained by the Spirit: *Hallelujah* and *Gloria in excelfis* are fung often this week: from Eafter till this time, no man is bound to faft: this feaft is obferved feven days, to fhew the feven gifts of the Holy Ghoft: and every day three Leffons are read, becaufe all the feven gifts are included in thefe three, Faith, Hope, and Charity. The next Sunday is kept to the honour of the Trinity: for as Chriftmafs was ordained to be kept in honour of God the Father who fent his fon into the World, and Eafter to Chrift the fecond Perfon, and Whitfunday to the third Perfon: fo this Sunday was inftituted to the three Perfons together, and from this day are named the other Sundays till Advent, whereof are twenty fix: to each of which is appropriated a peculiar Mafs, with Leffons and Pfalms fit for each day.

See the Authors above named.

Q. 23. *What be their Canonical hours of prayer?*

Their canonical hours of prayer and obfervation there upon.

A. Their fet-hours of prayers are called canonical, becaufe they are prefcribed by the Canons of the Church, and regularly obferved by devout people. Thefe hours they ground upon the practice of *David* and *Daniel*, who prayed three times a day, Thefe hours are feven, becaufe *David* fpeaketh of calling upon God feven times a day, becaufe the gifts of the Holy Ghoft, are feven; and the foul fpirit bringeth feven fpirits worfe than himfelf; there be feven deadly fins; the Walls of *Jerico* fell down at the blowing of the feven Ram-horn Trumpets; there were feven Afperfions in the Levitical Law, *Levit.* 14. and 16. We read alfo of feven Lamps, and feven golden Candlefticks. Thefe Canonical

cal hours are not only for the day, but also for the night, after the example of *David* and Chrift, who fpent fome part of the night in prayer; and of the Church in the *Canticles*, which fought Chrift in the night. The Prince of darknefs is moft bufie in the night to affault us, therefore we ought to watch and pray, that we be not flain with the Ægyptian firft-born in the night. The *Nocturnals* or Night-praifes, are faid at mid-night, becaufe at that time *Paul* and *Silas* praifed God: and fo did *David*. About that time Chrift rofe from the Grave, as the Greek Church believeth, but the Latine Church holdeth that he arofe in the morning. The firft hour of the day is dedicate to prayer; that whilft the Sun rifeth, we may call upon the Sun of Righteoufnefs, who bringeth health under his wings. About that hour he was mocked, fpit upon, and buffeted: and at that hour after his Refurrection, he was feen by his Difciples ftanding on the Sea-fhore. To whom the firft fruits of the earth were offered in old time; to him alfo fhould the firft-fruits of the day be offered. The third hour is confecrated to Prayer, becaufe then Chrift was crowned with thorns, and condemned by *Pilate*. It was the third hour alfo that the Holy Ghoft defcended on the Apoftles. The fixth hour is Canonical, becaufe then Chrift was crucified; at that hour *Peter* went up to the top of the houfe to pray, *Acts* 10. and then it was that Chrift asked water from the Woman of *Samaria*. The ninth hour is for prayer, becaufe then Chrift gave up the ghoft; fo *Peter* and *John* went up into the Temple at the ninth hour of prayer, *Acts* 3. The evening alfo is a time for prayer; then they have their *Vefpers*, becaufe the *Jews* had their evening Sacrifice: then it was that Chrift inftituted the Sacrament of the Eucharift at his laft Supper. And then was his body taken down from the Crofs. The hour of the *Completory* about the beginning of the night is Canonical alfo; in memory of Chrift's burial. And becaufe *David* would not go up into his bed, nor fuffer his eye-lids to flumber, till he had found out a place for the Temple. Then is fung the Song of Old *Simeon*, *Nunc dimittis*.

Of thefe hours *Caffianus fpeaketh, Rabanus Maurus, Ifidore, Amalarius, Fortunatus, Rupertus Tuitenf.* &c.

Q. 24. *What elfe may we obferve about thefe Canonical hours?*

A. That all Priefts, Deacons and Sub-Deacons, are bound to obferve thefe hours, fo are alfo Monks and Nuns, if they be not Novices. But the inferiour Orders of Clergy that are not beneficed, as they are not debarred from Marriage, fo they are not tied to thefe Canonical hours. They alfo that are excommunicate and degraded, are to obferve thefe hours, for the character is indelible; but fick perfons, and fuch as have any natural impediment, are excufed. Again, thefe Canonical prayers are not to be faid every-where, but in the Church, becaufe the multitude of petitioners makes prayers the more efficacious; otherways, they acknowledge that private prayers may be faid any-where. The times alfo, Order and Reverence muft be obferved in faying of thefe prayers, and diligent attention muft be ufed without wandring

dring thoughts; the attention must be fixed, not only on the words and sense thereof, but chiefly on God the object of our prayers; and devotion must be used both outward in prostrating of the body, and inward in humility and submission of the mind. But on Sundays and all the time between *Easter* and *Pentecost* they pray standing, to shew their readiness (being risen with Christ) in seeking the things that are above. Beneficed men who neglect in six months time to say the Canonical Prayers, are to lose their benefices. In the first Canonical hour the *Kyrie Eleeson* is said; so is the Lord's-Prayer, and the Creed, but with a low voice, to shew that Prayer and Faith consist rather in the heart than in the tongue. In the third hour Prayers are said for the dead, as well as for the living. The sixth hour they say *Adam* fell, and was cast out of Paradise, therefore they hold it then a fit time, by Prayer to enter into God's favour again. The ninth hour Christ's side was pierced, out of which flowed water and blood, the two Sacraments of the Church; then the Vail of the Temple rent asunder, the Graves opened, and Christ descended into Hell; all which do furnish sufficient matter for Prayers and Praises that hour. In the end of the day are said the *Vespers* or Evening-service, to signifie that Christ came in the end of the World. In the evening Christ washed his Disciples feet, and was known to the two Disciples in breaking of bread, as they were going to *Emaus*. Five Psalms are then said, in reference to Christ's five Wounds, and to expiate the sins of our five senses. In the evening is sung the *Magnificat*, to shew that in the evening of the World, the Virgin brought forth Christ, in whom is our chiefest rejoycing. And then are Lamps lighted to put us in mind that with the wise Virgins we should have our Lamps ready to meet the Bridegroom. The *Completory* is a fit time for prayer, because then Christ prayed, and sweat blood in the Garden. The song of *Simeon* is then sung, for as he immediately before his death uttered these words, so should we before our sleep, which is a resemblance of death. Four Psalms are then said, to expiate the sins of our child-hood, youth, man-hood, and old age. The Creed is said the first hour and *Completory*, to shew that all our works must begin and end in faith. About mid-night are said the *Nocturnals*, because about that time the *Egyptian* first-born were slain; then Christ was born; then was he apprehended by the *Jews*; then are we in greatest danger; then is the Prince of Darkness most busie in his works of Darkness.

See Gabriel-Biel in can. missæ. Navar. de orat. & hor. can. Durandus in rationali, Durantus de ritibus Ecclesia, &c.

Q. 25. *What may we observe concerning their Processions?*

Their Processions and Observations therein.
A. They ground their Processions on the practice of *David* and *Solomon*, when the one accompanied the *Ark* in Triumph to the Tabernacle, the other to the Temple: They have four solemn Processions; namely, on the Purification of the Virgin, on Palm-Sunday, on Easter-day, and on Holy-Thursday, being the fortieth day after Easter, and the days of Christ's ascension, kept

in memory of that Procession which Christ made with his Disciples, when they walked to the Mount of *Olives*, from whence he ascended to Heaven; as there is a Procession every Sunday in memory of Christ's Resurrection, so there was wont to be another every Thursday in remembrance of his ascension; but because of the multitude of Festivals, this is kept but once yearly solemnly, yet every Sunday it is remembred in that day's Procession. They hold also that these Processions were typified by the *Israelites* coming out of *Ægypt*: For as *Moses* delivered them from the Tyranny of *Pharaoh*, so hath Christ freed us from the oppression of Satan. The Tables of the Law were received on *Sinai*, and carried before the people, so the Gospel is taken down from the Altar, and carried in their Procession. A fiery Pillar went before the *Israelites*, and burning Tapers are carried before the people, in these solemnities: as every Tribe had their arms and colours carried before them, so here are carried Crosses and Banners. Their *Levites* bore the Tabernacle, and our Deacons carry the Coffer or Pix. Their Priests carried the Ark, and our Priests carry the holy Reliques. In their Procession *Aaron* followed in his Ornaments, and in ours, the Bishop in his Pontificals. There was the sounding of Trumpets, here the noise of Bells; there was sprinkling of Blood, here of holy Water, &c. They carry Banners and Crosses in memory of that Cross seen in the air by *Constantine*, and which after he always wore in his Banners. Besides these triumphant Processions, they have also in times of publick Calamity, mournful Processions, which they call *Rogations*, and the Greeks *Litaniæ*, that is, prayers or supplications, of which there is the greater *Letany* kept on St. *Mark*'s Feast, and invented by *Gregory* the first in a great Plague at *Rome*. The lesser Letany is kept three days before the Ascension, and was invented at *Vienna* by *Mamertus* Bishop there, in a time when there were great Earth-quakes and Irruptions of Wolves, which in *France* did great hurt: this is called the lesser Rogation, because it was found out in a lesser City than *Rome*, and by a lesser Bishop than *Gregory*, yet the lesser is more ancient by eighty years, for it was devised in the time of *Zeno* the Emperour of *Constantinople*; whereas the other was found out in the time of *Mauritius*, who was Contemporary with *Gregory* the Great. Pope *Liberius* appointed there should be Letanies, when Wars, Plague, or Famine do threaten; which commonly fall out about the time of the year, wherein the memory of Christ's Ascension is observed. *Of these things see the foremed writers.*

Q. 26. *Wherein consisteth the Eighth part of their Worship?*

A. In the Worship of the Saints, whom they Honour with Temples, Chappels, Altars, Images, Holy-days, mentioning of their names in the Mass, reserving and worshipping their Reliques, praying to them, &c. They divide them into four ranks; namely, *Apostles*, *Martyrs*, *Confessors*, and *Virgins*. The Festival-day's of the Saints, kept in memory of their Martyrdom, are called *Natales*, that is, Birth-days; For *then they began truly to live, when Saints* *Festival days of the Saints.*

they died for Christ in the Kalender. These following Saints have their Holy-days; *Fabian* and *Sebastian, Agnes*, the Conversion of St. *Paul, Julian, Agatha*, the Purification of *Mary*; this day is a Procession in memory of that procession which *Joseph* and *Mary* made to the Temple: this Feast was instituted in the time of *Justinian*, upon a great Mortality which then hapned, and Candles this day are carried with great solemnity, to shew that our Light should shine before men; that Christ who was this day presented in the Temple, is the true Light of the World; and that like wise Virgins, whereof *Mary* was the chief, we should have our Lamps ready: the Feast of St. *Peter's* Chair is kept in memory of his advancement first to the Bishoprick of *Antioch*, then of *Rome*: the Feast of the Annunciation is kept in memory of the tidings which the Angel brought to *Mary* of her conception: on the first of *May* is the Feast of *Philip* and *James* the Lesser, the Son of *Alpheus*, and Brother of our Lord. Who was the first Bishop of *Jerusalem*, had seen Christ's Transfiguration, and for preaching Christ, was thrown down from the pinacle of the Temple by the Jews the other called the greater, and of *Compostella*, was the Son of *Zebedeus*, and brother to S. *John* the Evangelist: on the third day of *May* is the invention or finding of the Cross by *Helena, Constantine's* Mother: the Feast of S. *John Baptist* is kept the 24. of *June*, in which are fires made, and Torches carried, to shew that he was a shining and a burning Lamp: the Feast of *Peter* and *Paul* is kept the 29 of *June*, in memory that they both suffered in one day under *Nero*: on the 25. of *July* is the Feast of S. *James*, S. *John's* brother who preached the Gospel in *Spain*, and returning to *Jerusalem*, was beheaded by *Herod*: the Feast of the seven *Sleepers* is on the 27 of *July*; these flying from the persecution of *Decius*, hid themselves in a Cave, where they slept about 300 years, and being awaked, thought they had slept but one night, the Feast of Saint *Peter's* Chains is kept *August* the first in memory of *Peter's* miraculous delivery from *Herod's* prison, when the Chains fell from him of their own accord: the Feast of Saint *Laurence* is kept *August* the tenth, in memory of his Martyrdom under *Valerian*; he was Arch-Deacon of *Rome*, after whom, none there have had that title: The Assumption of *Mary* is on the fifteenth of *August*; this is her greatest Feast, for it is ushered in with a Fast, and hath its *Octave*: on this day herbs and flowers are gathered and blessed, because she is compared to the Rose and Lily: S. *Bartholomew's* Feast is on the 24th of *August*; he preached in *India*, and then in *Albania* of *Armenia*, where he was first flea'd, and then beheaded, therefore some keep the Feast of his Excoriation, others of his Decollation: Saint *John Baptist's* Decollation is kept the 29th of *August*; his head hath been removed from divers places: the Nativity of St. *Mary* is celebrated the 8th. of *September*; it was kept in Heaven by the Angels, (so goeth the story) long before it was observed by men here on earth; the

Roman

Roman Church celebrates no Nativities, except that of Chriſt's, of his Mother, and of his Forerunner: The Exaltation of the Croſs is kept the 14th. of *September*, in memory of the Croſs recovered from *Coſroes*, King of *Perſia*, by the Emperour *Heraclius*, and by him carried in Triumph into *Jeruſalem*: the Feaſt of Saint *Matthew* the Apoſtle and Evangeliſt is on the 21ſt. of *September*, in Remembrance of his Sufferings for Chriſt in *Æthiopia*, where having planted the Goſpel, he was beheaded there: S. *Luke*'s day is on the 18*th*. of *October*, he was a Painter, Phyſician, and Evangeliſt, and the Diſciple of Saint *Paul*: the Feaſt of *Simon* and *Jude* is kept on the 28th. of *October*; theſe were brothers, and Sons to *Mary Cleophas*, who married to *Alpheus*; they had two Brothers more, to wit, *James* the Leſſer, and *Joſeph* called *Barſabas*, and ſurnamed *Juſtus*: *Simon* was called, *Zelotes*, and *Cananæus*, from *Cana* of *Galilee*: *Jude* was named *Thadæus* and *Lebeus*; *Simon* preacht in *Ægypt*, afterward he ſucceeded *James* in the See of *Jeruſalem*, where he was crucified; *Jude* preached to the *Medes* and *Perſians*, and ſuffered at *Perſis*: the firſt of *November* is dedicated to all the Saints, becauſe there be more than can have particular day's aſſigned them. The old *Romans* worſhipped all their gods together in one Temple called *Pantheon*; *Chriſtians* held it fitter to worſhip all the Saints and Martyrs in the ſame Temple, under the name of Saint *Mary*; this Feaſt is uſhered in with Faſting the day before, and backed with Prayers for all Souls in Purgatory the day after. Saint *Martin*, Biſhop and Confeſſor, is Honoured the Eleventh of *November*, for his Charity to the Poor, in parting with his own Garments to cloath them; and for his Humility, in that he would Die on no other Bed but on a heap of Aſhes; this Feaſt hath its *Vigil* and *Octave*. They thought that he ſhould be thus Honoured by Men, who had been Honoured by Angels. The thirtieth of *November* is Saint *Andrew*'s day; he preached in *Scythia*, *Achaia*, and other places thereabout, and ſuffered death on a Croſs; his bones, with thoſe of Saint *Luke*, were tranſlated to *Conſtantinople*, in the time of *Conſtantine* the ſecond. The ſixth of *December* is for Saint *Nicholas*, the Biſhop, famous for his Charity, Boldneſs, and Conſtancy in the maintenance of Chriſtianity. They write that being an Infant, he would never ſuck his Mothers breaſts but once on Wedneſdays, and Fridays. The 21*ſt* of *December* is for Saint *Thomas*, who preached to the *Indians*, and by their Idolatrous Prieſts was firſt ſhot with Arrows, and then thruſt through with a Launce, as he was at his prayers. Saint *Stephen* is celebrated the ſix and twentieth of *December*; as he was the firſt Martyr, ſo he deſerved to be the firſt in the Kalendar: the firſt Martyr is placed next to Chriſt's Nativity, to ſhew Chriſt was born, that we might ſuffer; and Chriſt's Nativity here on earth was the cauſe of *Stephen*'s Nativity in Heaven. Saint *John* the beloved Diſciple, is honoured on the ſeven and twentieth of *December*: he eſcaped

miracu-

miraculously, first Poyson, and then burning Oyl. The eight and twentieth of *December*, is for the *Innocents*, who suffered in their Infancy by *Herod*, for the Infant King of the *Jews* Christ Jesus; there are multitudes of Saints more, who are placed in the *Kalendar*, as *Ambrose*, Bishop, on *December* 7. *Anselm*, Bishop, *April* 21. *Augustine*, Bishop, *August* 21. *Babylas*, Bishop, *January* 24. *Barbara* the Virgin, *December* 4. *Barnabas* the Apostle, *June* 11. *Basil*, Bishop, *April* 26. *Basil* the Great *January* 1. *Bernard*, Abbot, *August* 20. *Bonaventure* the Cardinal, *July* 14. Three *Bonifaces*, and three *Katharines* on several days. *Christopher*, Martyr, *July* 25. *Clemens*, Pope and Martyr, *November* 23. Saint *Paul*'s Conversion, *April* 25. Saint *Austin*'s Conversion, *May* 5. *Cyprian*, Martyr, *September* 26. *Dionysius* the *Areopagite*, *October* 9. *Epiphanius*, Bishop, *May* 12. *George*, Martyr, *April* 24. *Gregory* the great Pope, *March* 12. *Gregory Nazianzen*, Bishop, *May* 9. *Gregorius Thaumaturgus*, *November* 17. *William*, Confessor, *February* 10. *Hierom*, *September* 30. *Ignatius*, Bishop and Martyr, *February* 1. *Ignatius Loyola*, *July* 31. *Johannes Chrysostom*, Bishop, *January* 27. *John Damascen*, *May* 6. *Joseph*, *Mary*'s husband, *March* 19. *Irenæus* Martyr, *August* 26. *Julianus*, Martyr, *January* 9. *Justinus*, Martyr, *April* 13. *Lanfrancus*, Bishop, *July* 3. *Laurence* Martyr, *August* 10. *Lewis*, King *August* 25. *Mary Magdalen*, *July* 22. *Matthias* Apostle, *February* 24. *Michael*, Arch-angel, *September* 29. *Narcissus*, Bishop, *October* 29. *Olaus*, King, *July* 29. *Patrick*, Bishop, *March* 17. *Polycarpus*, Bishop, *January* 26. *Severinus Boethius*, *October* 23. *Thomas*, Bishop, *December* 29. *Thomas Aquinas*, *March* 7. *Vigilius*, Bishop, *June* 26. There are multitudes more in the *Roman Kalendar*, but these are the chief which I have culled out: They have also Holy-days for some eminent *Jews*, as *Daniel* the Prophet, &c. For Angels also; and for dedication of Churches, which the *Greeks* call *Encænia*, a custom borrowed from the Jews.

But of these passages see the *Romans Martyrology, Baronius, Surius, Durandus, Fasti Mariæ, Lippelus*, &c.

Q. 27. *What Ornaments and Utensils do they use in their Churches dedicated to Christ and the Saints?*

Their ornaments and utensils, used in Churches dedicate to Christ and the Saints.

A. They have in them their Reliques, Pictures, Images, Crosses also and Crucifixes; the Images also of Angels, which they paint with wings to signifie their swiftness, and sublimity of their nature; with white garments also to shew their purity. The Images of Christ and of the Saints, are painted with the Sun beams about their heads, to represent the glory they are in. God the Father is represented like an old man, because he is described by *Daniel* like the ancient of days. The Holy Ghost is painted like a Dove; because in that form he appeared on Christ. They have Chalices not of Glass, because subject to breaking; not of wood, because that is porous and drinks in the liquor; not of brass nor copper, because of the bad smell thereof, rust, and canker; but of silver or gold. They have also Candlesticks, Tapers and Lamps, which they burn to the Saints by day, to shew they are not in darkness, but in light. Their Censers and Incense represent Christ, and the Prayers of the Saints; which like Incense ascend before God; these Odours are burnt in their Churches, both to expel bad vapors, and to refresh the senses. They have also their flaps or fans to drive away flies from the Chalice, after the example of *Abraham* who drove away the birds from his sacrifice, and to teach us that we should drive away all wandring thoughts when we pray. Their *Patina* and other vessels shining bright, put us in mind how we should shine in our conversation. The Corporal is the linen cloth in which the Eucharist is covered, signifying how Christ's body was wrapped up in fine linen; for as linen is first washed, and then wrung, and lastly dried; so must our souls be first washed in tears, then wrung by repentance; and lastly, dried by the heat of the love of God. Organs are also used in Churches to excite the mind, and to stir up devotion. Yet in the Popes Chappel there are none, perhaps to shew that he needs no such helps. Their Altars are inclosed with Rails, to keep off the people, for the Priests only have access to them; they were anciently places of refuge, and are covered all the year, except in the Passion-week, then they are stript, to represent Christ's nakedness on the Cross. Ordinarily the Altar is placed towards the East, yet in the Church of *Antioch* it was placed towards the West. On the Altar stands the *Pixis*, or *Ciborium*, which keepeth the Hoast for strangers, sick persons and travellers; but it must not be kept above seven days, lest it mould; therefore the Priest must eat it himself, and put in a fresh one. They have Fonts, called *Baptisteria*, of stone, in which the water of Baptism is consecrated by the Priest, who poureth oyl into it; he also by breathing, and by certain words exorciseth the evil Spirit. Salt is consecrated, and put in the child's mouth: to shew that he must have spiritual Salt within him; Then the Priest laieth his hand on the childs head, in sign he is reconciled and made a member of the Church. Then he signeth his fore-head with the sign of the Cross, that hereafter he may not be ashamed of Christ crucified. He puts his finger into his ear and into his nostrils also with spittle; saying to his right ear, *Ephata*; that is, *Be thou opened*, to shew that by nature we are deaf in spiritual things, as was that man whom Christ after this manner cured in the Gospel. The touching of the nostrils sheweth that the child must remember his vow in Baptism, so long as he hath breath in him. Then he anoints the Child two times, that he may renounce the devil and all his works, &c. The breast is first anointed, then the shoulders to shew the strength of our love, and faith in the Trinity, and that withall we must be wrestlers against all spiritual wickedness. The child is three times dipt in the water, and in some places only sprinkled; to shew Christ's three days burial, and our faith in the Trinity. After baptism the child is anointed by the Priest on the fore-head with chrisin, and cloathed in white, to signifie he must cast off the old

man,

man, and be cloathed with innocency: Anciently those that were baptized at Easter, wore white all that week, which they laid aside the Sunday following, called therefore *Dominica in albis*; this also signified the glory of the Resurrection. Then a Wax-candle burning is given to him, to shew the light of faith and knowledge that should be in him, and with which he should be ready to meet the Bridegroom: Then the God-fathers are instructed concerning their duty to the child.

See Innocent.3. L.2. de myst. missæ. Rab. Maurus de instit.cleric Amalar. Fortunat. de ecclesiof- ficiis. Isidor. de ecclef.officiis. Alcuin. de celeb. missa. Durantus, &c.

Q. 28. *What other utensils have they in their Churches?*

A. They have three viols or flaggons for oyl, which the Priest carrieth on the day of the Lord's-Supper; one holds the oyl of the *Catechumeni*, the second is for the Chrism, and the third for the oyl of the sick. With the Chrism, the baptized are anointed on their crown; and they that are confirmed, on the forehead, and so are they who be ordained. The *Catechumeni* and sick are anointed with single oyl. They have also in their Churches holy Water-Pots, which by some are called *Amulæ*, by others *Situlæ* and *Aquiminaria* and χερνιβα and περιρραντερια. This pot must be of Stone or Marble, at which is tied with a chain the holy Water-spunge; with this salt-water they are sprinkled that enter into the Church, because anciently they washed before they entered into the Temple, to shew that with pure and sanctified minds we must come before God. They have also Bells which they sprinkle with water, and consecrate with certain prayers; these have succeeded the Trumpets used by the Jews, to call together the Assembly. They have also Altars which they anoint, and consecrate; and Holy Reliques, *Whereof many doubtless are suppositious and false?* therefore no new Reliques are to be received without the Bishop's appprobation, nor to be honoured without the Pope's authority. And because the Altar represents Christ, therefore the Priest after Mass, in sign of reverence and subjection kisseth the Altar; by which also he sheweth the great desire the Church hath to enjoy Christ when she saith, *Let him kiss me with the kisses of his mouth*. The Vestry is the place where the sacred Vestments (which we have already spoken of) are kept. Here the Priest before Mass puts on his Holy Garments; this place they say Represents the Virgin's Womb, in which our great high Priest put on the Garment of our Humane Nature, that in it he might offer the true propitiatory sacrifice to God his Father; for the sins of the World. They make also every part of their material Temple, to have a mystical signification; the Quire represents the Church Triumphant, the main body the Church Militant; the Porch or great Door is Christ, by whom only we have access to the Father; the Windows are the Scriptures, which give light to the spiritual Church; the Pillars are the Apostles, by their Doctrine supporting the Church; the Pavement is Humility and Faith; the Cover is God's protection; the Tower, with the Bells, are the Prelates, which ought to be eminent in their conversation,

Of these and many more see Durandus in his Rationale & the other writers above named.

conversation, and founding in their preaching; the Cock, on the top thereof, is to put them in mind of their vigilancy; the Lights that shine continually in their Churches, are to signifie our good works which should shine before men.

Q. 29. *What office do they perform to the dead?*

A. They have a peculiar Office or Service for the Dead in Purgatory, which some perform every third day, that they might be partakers of Christ's Resurrection, who over-came death that day; some again every seventh day, that they may attain to the Eternal Sabbath or rest in Heaven, whereof God's resting from the Works of Creation on the seventh day, was a Type. Others perform this Office the thirtieth day, because the *Israelites* mourned for *Moses* and *Aaron* thirty days. Others again the fortieth day, because *Joseph* and his Brethren bewailed *Jacob* forty days. Others the fiftieth day, because the fiftieth year is the Jubilee, or year of liberty, which they wish these imprisoned Souls may partake eternally. Others perform this Office yearly, and make it anniversary; but if this day fall upon a Sunday or any other solemn festivity; then it must not be kept, or put off till the next day, as the Feasts of the Saints are, but must be kept the day before, that the Souls may the sooner partake the Fruits of our Devotion. No Mass must be said on festival-days for the dead, except the body be present. And although in the Mass for the living Incense is burned, to shew that their prayers like Incense ascend before God, yet in the Mass for the dead Incense is not burned, because their prayers are of no Efficacy; for *Do the Dead praise thee?* saith *David.* The Corps may not be brought into the Church, whilst Mass is saying for the living, but must be set in the Porch till Mass be done, and the Mass for the dead begun; in which Mass the kiss of peace must not be given, because there is no communion between us and the dead, neither can they answer us; the dead Corps is washed and anointed; then it is carried to the Church; but by the way the Bearers rest three times, to signifie Christ's three days rest in the Grave. Holy water and Frankincense is put in the Grave with the Corps, to keep off evil spirits thence, and to shew that the deceased party hath offered to God the Incense of his prayers and good life whilst he lived. He is buried with green bays, to shew that his Soul is alive, and that it doth not wither with the body; and with his face upward, and his feet towards the East, to shew his expectation of Heaven, and his readiness to meet Christ in the Resurrection, whose appearance (is believed) shall be in the East. Every Christian that is buried out of the Church, or Church-yard, hath a Cross set at his Head, to shew he was a Christian; Clergy-men that have taken Orders, are buried in the habit of their Orders; all are wrapt in linen, because Christ was so; yet some are buried in Sack-cloth to shew their Repentance. And early the names of Holy men departed were registred in scrolls or folding Tables called Δίπτυχα, *Diptycha,* which word the Latine Church retained;

Their Office performed to the dead.

these words were kept by the Bishops, and the names publickly read, in time of divine Service, to *shew that the just shall be had in everlasting remembrance*. The prayers that are made for the dead are not for the Saints in Heaven, for they need not our prayers, but our praises to God for them; nor for the damned in Hell, seeing our prayers can avail them nothing, but only for those who dying in venial sins unrepented, make satisfaction in Purgatory: Lastly, there is neither *Gloria in excelsis*, nor *Hallelujah* sung in the office for the dead. Of these passages see *Alcuinus de divin. Offic. Amular Fortunat. de Ecclef. officiis, Stephanus, Durantus de ritibus Ecclef. Cathol. Guliel. Durandus in rationali*, &c.

The Contents of the Fourteenth Section.

Of the Eastern Religions, and first of the Greeks. 2. *Of the Church-dignities, and Discipline in the* Greek *Church at this day.* 3. *Of the other Nations, professing the* Greek *Religion, chiefly the* Moscovites *and* Armenians. 4. *Of the Monks, Nuns, and Eremites of* Moscovia. 5. *Of the Form of Service in their Churches.* 6. *How they administer the Sacraments.* 7. *The Doctrine and Ceremonies of the* Russian *Church at this day.* 8. *Of their Marriage and Funeral Ceremonies.* 9. *Of the profession of the* Armenians. 10. *Of the other* Greek *Sects; namely, the* Melchites, Georgians, *and* Mengrelians. 11. *Of the* Nestorians, Indians, *and* Jacobites. 12. *Of the* Maronites *Religions.* 13. *Of the* Cophti. 14. *Of the* Abyssin *Christians.* 15. *Wherein the Protestants agree with, and dissent from other Christian Churches.*

SECT. XIV.

Quest. 1. *Having taken a view of the differences in Religion among the* Romanists *and* Anti-Romanists *in the West, what Religion do the Christians in the East profess?*

Greek Religion at this day.

A. In the East the *Greek* Religion prevaileth in many places, chiefly in these Countries of *Europe*; namely, *Greece, Macedonia, Epirus, Bulgaria, Thrace, Servia, Rascia, Moldavia, Walachia, Bosnia, Podolia,* and *Moscovia*; In the Islands also of the *Ægean* Sea, and in some parts of *Poland, Dalmatia,* and *Croatia*; in some parts also of *Asia,* namely, in *Natolia, Circassia, Mengrelia,* and *Russia*. The *Greeks* place much of their Devotion in the worshipping the Virgin *Mary*, and of painted, but not carved Images; in the intercession, prayers, help, and merits of the Saints, which they invocate in their Temples. They place justification not in faith, but in works: School-divinity, chiefly the works

Sect. 14. of EUROPE.

works of *Thomas Aquinas*; which they have in Greek, are in great request with them. The Sacrifice of the Mass, is used for the quick, and the dead; and they use to buy Masses; they do not hold a Purgatory-fire, yet they believe there is a third place between that of the blessed and the damned, where they remain who have deferred repentance till the end of their life; " *but if this place be not Purgatory, I know not what it is, nor what the souls do there.* " Though they deny the procession of the Holy Ghost from the Son, yet they baptize in the name of the Three Persons. Priests among them may marry once, but not oftner. That marriage is unlawful, which is contracted within the seventh degree of Consanguinity and Affinity. They use leavened bread in the Sacrament, and administer in boths kinds; they have four Lents in the year; they deny the Pope's Supremacy, abstain from blood and things strangled; observe the Jewish Sabbath with the Lord's-day. They use neither confirmation, nor extream unction, and will not have either the blessed souls in Heaven to enjoy God's presence, or the wicked in Hell to be tormented till the day of judgment; preaching is little used among them, but Masses often, therefore one of their Monks, whom they call *Caloieri*, for Preaching, sometimes in Lent, and at Christmass, and Easter, was accused and banished to Mount *Sinai* by the Patriarch of *Constantinople*, as *Chytræus* witnesseth. They esteem equal with the Scriptures, the Acts of the seven Greek Synods, and the Writings of *Basil*, *Chrysostom*, *Damascen*, and their Traditions. They believe that the Souls of the dead are bettered by the Prayers of the living. They are no less for the Churches authority and for Traditions, than the Roman Catholicks be; when the Sacrament is carried through the Temple, the people by bowing themselves adore it, and falling on their knees, kiss the earth.

See the Council of Florence, Boterus, Chytræus, Brerewood, Jeremy, Patriarch of Constantinople, in resp. ad German. Possevin. de reb. Moscov. &c.

Q. 2. *What Ecclesiastical Dignities and Discipline is there in the Greek Church at this day?*

A. They have their Patriarch, who resides at *Constantinople*, who is elected by his Metropolitans and Arch-Bishops, but is confirmed by the great Turks chief Bassa, who upon promise of some thousand Duckets from the Patriarch, doth ratifie his privileges. He hath no more authority with the great Turk, than any Christian Embassadour, who thinks it a great honour to be admitted to fall down at the Seignior's feet, and to kiss his Cloak. Next to the Patriarch are the Metropolitans, who are placed according to their antiquity: Of these Metropolitans are 74; under whom are Arch-Bishops, and Bishops. The Metropolitan of *Thessalonica* hath ten Bishops under him; he of *Athens* hath six; *Corinth* hath four Bishops, and one hundred Churches; *Mytilene* had five Bishopricks, but now none; *Chalcedon* hath a Metropolitan and sixty Churches, but no Bishops. The Metropolis of *Nicæa* hath fifty Churches, but no Bishop at this time: *Ephesus* hath fifty Churches, but no Bishop: *Philippi*, the Metropolis of *Macedonia*, hath one hundred and fifty Churches: *Antiochia* of *Pisidia*, is

Greeks, their Church-dignities and discipline at this day.

Z 2 Metropo-

Metropolis of forty Churches: *Smyrna* is Metropolis of eighty Churches: but forty or fifty persons make a Church in *Greece*. Most of the Metropolites in *Asia* are ruined. The *Greeks* at *Constantinople* are distributed into certain Churches, where they meet on Sundays and Holy-days: their greatest Congregations scarce exceed three hundred persons. Their chief Feast is that of *Mary's* Assumption: every Lord's-day in Lent, the Patriarch sayeth Mass, sometimes in one Church, sometimes in another, where he collects the Alms of well-disposed people. They have no Musick in their Churches: the Women are shut up in their Churches within Latices, that they may not be seen by the Men. In the Patriarch's own Church are to be seen the bodies of *Mary Salome*, of Saint *Euphemia*, and the Marble Pillar, to which Christ was bound, when he was scourged. They have also in the Greek Church *Hieromonachi* and Priests whom they call Popes: these may consecrate, and say Mass. They have their Lay-Monks, Deacons, and Sub-Deacons, and their *Anagnostes*, who read the Dominical Epistle and other things. The Monks, who are all of Saint *Basil's* Order, have their *Archimandrithes* or Abbots: Their Monks are not idle, but work; they are called *Caloieri*: the Patriarch, Metropolites, and Bishops are of this Order, and abstain from flesh; but in Lent, and other Fasting-times they forbear Fish, Milk and Eggs; the Greeks celebrate their Liturgies in the old Greek tongue, which they scarce understand. On Festival-days, they use the Liturgy of *Basil*, on other days that of *Chrysostom*. They have no other Translation of the Bible, but that of the 70.

See the above named Author and the Letters of Stephen Gerlochius to Crusius, An. 1575.

Q. 3. *What other Nations profess the Greek Religion, besides those already named?*

Moscovites, their Religion and discipline.

A. The *Moscovites* and *Armenians*; as for the *Moscovites*, they, with the *Russians*, were converted by the *Greeks*, and are with them of the same Communion and Faith, saving that they differ from the Greeks, in receiving Children of seven year old to the Communion, in mingling the Bread and Wine in the Chalice with warm water, and distributing it together in a spoon: besides, they permit neither Priest nor Deacon to officiate or take Orders, except they be married; and yet when they are actually in Orders, will not allow them to marry: they dissolve Marriage upon every light occasion: the Arch-Bishop of *Mosco*, their chief Metropolitan, was wont to be confirmed by the Patriarch of *Constantinople*, but is now nominated by the Prince or Great Duke, and consecrated by three of his own *Suffragans*, whereof there be but eleven in all that Dominion; but the Bishops of South *Russia*, subject to the King of *Poland*, have submitted themselves to the Pope; and whereas the *Russian* Clergy were wont to send yearly Gifts to the Patriarch of *Constantinople*, residing at *Scio* or *Chios*; now the great Duke himself sends him somewhat yearly towards his maintenance: the Bishops of *Moscovia*, besides their Tithes, have large Rents to maintain them according to their Place and Dignity;

Sect. 14.   *of* EUROPE.   341

nity; and they have as large an Ecclesiastical Jurisdiction, as any Clergy in Christendom: they do so highly esteem the Scriptures and four General Councils, that they touch them not without crossing and bowing: besides their Patriarch and two Metropolitans of *Novograd*, and *Rostove*, they have four Arch-Bishops, and six Bishops; besides Priests, Arch-Priests, Deacons, Monks, Nuns, and Eremites. The Patriarch of *Mosco* was invested in his Jurisdiction by *Hieronymo*, the banished Patriarch of *Constantinople*, or *Scio*; because in the Isle *Chio* or *Scio*, was the Patriarch's Seat, after he was banished by the *Turk* from *Byzantium*. The Bishops in their Solemnities wear rich Mitres on their heads, embroydered Copes with Gold and Pearl on their backs, and a Crosiers staff in their hands; when they ride abroad, they bless the people with two fore-fingers. All Bishops, Arch-Bishops, and Metropolites are chosen by the Great Duke himself, out of their Monasteries; so that first they must be Monks, before they can attain these Dignities; so they must be all unmarried Men. The Ceremonies of the Bishops inauguration are in a manner the same that are used in the Church of *Rome*. Preaching is not used in this Church; only twice a year; to wit, the first of *September*, which is their New-years-day, and on Saint *John Baptist*'s day; in the Cathedral Church a short Speech is made by the Metropolite, Arch-Bishop, or Bishop, tending to Love with their Neighbours, Obedience and Loyalty to their Prince, to the Observation of their Fasts and Vows, and to perform their Duties to the Holy Church, &c. The Clergy there keep out Learning, to keep up Tyranny. The Priests Crowns are not shaved, but shorn, and by the Bishop anointed with oyl; who in the Priests Ordination puts his Surplice on him, and sets a white Cross on his breast, which he is not to wear above eight days; and so he is authorized to say, sing, and administer the Sacraments in the Church. They honour the Images of Saints; their Priests must marry but once; the Lay-people pray not themselves, but cause the Priests to pray for them, when they go about a business or journey. Every year there is great meeting to solemnize the Saints-day that is Patron of their Church; and to have prayers said to that Saint for themselves and friends, and so an offering is made to the Priest for his pains, for he lives on the peoples benevolence, and not on the Tithes; once a quarter the Priest blesseth his Parishioners houses with perfume, and holy water, for which he is paid; but whatsoever benefit the Priest makes of his place, he must pay the tenth thereof to the Bishop. The Priest wears long tufts of hair, hanging down by his ears, a gown with a broad cape, and a walking-staff in his hand. He wears his surplice, and on solemn days his cope, when he reads the Liturgy. They have their regular Priests, who live in Covents. In Cathedral Churches are Arch-Priests, and Arch-Deacons; every Priest hath his Deacon or Sexton.

See the above named Authors, and withall the History of Russia by G. Fletcher, Possevin. de reb.Moscov Sigism. de Mosco-via, Guagin.descrip. Moscov &c.

Q. 4. *Are there any store of Monks, Nuns, and Eremites in Moscovia?*   A. Every

Z 3

Monks and Nuns in Moscovia.

A. Every City abounds with Monks of St. *Basil*'s Order; for many out of displeasure, others out of fear to avoid punishment, and others to avoid taxes and oppression, do embrace this life; besides the opinion of Merit they have thereby. When any is admitted, he by the Abbot stript of his Secular Garments, and next to his skin, is cloathed with a white Flannel shirt; over which is a long Garment, girded with a broad leathern Belt. The upper Garment is of Say, of a sooty colour; then his crown is shorn; to whom the Abbot sheweth, that as his hairs are taken from his head, so must he be taken from the World: this done, he anoints his crown with Oyl, puts on his cowl, and so receives him into the Fraternity, having vowed abstinence from the flesh, and perpetual chastity. The Monks do not only live upon their rents, but they trade also, and are great Merchants; as for Scholarship they have none. *Sergius* is a great Saint amongst them, to whom the Empress goeth sometimes in Pilgrimage. They have divers Nunneries; some whereof are only for Noble Mens Widows and Daughters, whose stock the Emperor means to extinguish. They have Eremites also who go stark naked, except about the middle, they wear long hair, and an Iron collar about their neck or middle. The people esteem them as Saints, and Prophets, and whatsoever they say is received as Oracles, even by the great Duke himself. He thinks himself in great favour with God, who is reproved; or robbed of any part of his goods by them. But of these Eremites there be very few in that cold Country.

See the above named Authors.

Q. 5. *What form of Service have they in their Churches?*

A. They have their Mattins every morning; the Priest attended by his Deacon, in the middle of the Church, calls on Christ for a blessing, in the name of the Trinity; and then repeats three times, *Lord have mercy upon us*: this done, he marcheth into the Chancel, whither no man may enter but the Priest alone; and there at the Altar he saith the Lord's-prayer, and twelve times *Lord have mercy upon us;* Then *Praised be the Trinity*: The Deacon and people answer *Amen.* Then he reads the Psalms for the day, and with the people turns to the Images on the Wall; to which they bow three times knocking their heads to the ground. Then he reads the *Decalogue,* and *Athanasius* his Creed. After this the Deacon standing without the Chancel door, reads a part of their Legend of Saints lives, which is divided into so many parts as there be days in the year; then he addeth some Collects or Prayers. This Service lasteth about two hours, all which time many Wax Candles burn before their Images, some as big as a mans wast; such are vowed and enjoyned by penance. They have about nine of the morning another service, and on Festival days they have solemn devotion. The evening service is begun like the mornings; after the Psalms the Priest singeth the *Magnificat* in their Language, and then all with one voice, *Lord have mercy upon us,* thirty times together; and the Boys answer thirty times; then is read by the Priest, and on holy days sung, the first

Moscovites, their Church-service.

first Pfalm, and *Hallelujah* repeated ten times. Then the Prieſt reads ſome part of the Goſpel, which he ends with three *Hallelujahs*, and withall that evening ſervice with a collect for the day, all this while the Prieſt ſtandeth at the high Altar. The Deacons ſtand without the Chancel, whither they dare not come during ſervice-time. The people ſtand together in the body of the Church, for they have no Pews to ſit in. *See the Hi- ſtories of Ruſſia.*

Q. 6. *How do they adminiſter the Sacraments?*

A. Eight days after the Child is born, he is brought to the Church-porch, where the Prieſt receives him; and tells the witneſſes their duties in the Childs education after baptiſm, namely to teach him how to know God and Chriſt, and withall what Saints are the chief mediatours; then he conjures the Devil out of the water, and ſo after ſome prayers, he plungeth the Child three times over head and ears in a tub of warm water, holding it neceſſary that every part of the Child be dipped. They uſe the ſame words that we do; *In the name of the Father, Son, and Holy Ghoſt*, and not *By the Holy Ghoſt*, as ſome Hereticks have uſed. Then the Prieſt layeth Oyl and Salt mixed together on the Childs fore-head, on both ſides of his face, and on his lips praying that God would make him a good Chriſtian, *&c.* This done, the Child now being made a Chriſtian, is carried from the Porch into the Church: the Prieſt matching before, who layeth him on a cuſhion before the feet of the chief Image in the Church, to which he is recommended as to his Mediatour. After baptiſm the Childs hair is cut off, wrapped up in wax, and reſerved as a relique in the Church. The *Ruſſians* uſe to re-baptize their Proſelyte Chriſtians, and in ſome Monaſtery to inſtruct them in their Religion; firſt they cloath the new convert with a freſh *Ruſſian* Garment, then they crown him with a Garland, anoint his head with oyl, put a wax light into his hand, and for ſeven days together pray over him four times a day, all which time he is to forbear fleſh, and white meats. After the ſeventh day he is waſhed, and on the eighth day is brought into the Church and there inſtructed how to bow, knock his head and croſs himſelf before their images. The *Ruſſians* communicate but once a year, in Lent, after confeſſion to the Prieſt; who calls them up to the Altar, asks them if they be clean from ſin; if they be, they are admitted: but never above three at one time. Whileſt the Prieſt prayeth, the communicants ſtand with their arms one folded within another, then he delivereth, to them a ſpoonful of bread and wine tempered together, ſaying, *Eat this Drink this*, without any pauſe. Then he delivereth bread by it ſelf, and wine mingled with warm water, to repreſent the water and blood that iſſued out of Chriſt's ſide. Then the Communicants follow the Prieſt thrice about the Altar, with their folded arms. At laſt after Prayers the Prieſt chargeth them to make good cheer, and be merry for ſeven days together, and to faſt the next ſeven days after. *Their Sa- craments.*

See the a- bove men- tioned H. ſto- ries.

Q 7. *What is the Doctrine and Ceremonies of the Ruſſian Church at this day?*   *A.* The

Their Doctrine and Ceremonies.

4. They hold that the Books of *Moses* (except *Genesis*) are not to be read in Churches, and are of no use since Christ's coming; nor the Prophets, nor the Revelation. 2. They teach that their Church traditions are of equal authority with the Word of God. 3. That the Greek Church, chiefly the Patriarch and his Synod, have full authority to interpret the Scripture; and that their interpretation is authentick. 4. That the Holy Ghost proceedeth not from the Son. 5. They hold Christ to be the only Mediator of Redemption, but not of Intercession; this honour they give to the Saints, chiefly to the Virgin *Mary*, and St. *Nicholas* who they say is attended upon by three hundred of the chief Angels. 6. Their doctrine and practice is to adore the Images or Pictures of the Saints, whereof their Churches are full, and richly adorned. 7. They teach that in this life there can be no assurance of salvation. 8. And that we are justified not by faith only, but by works also; which consist in prayers by number on their beads, in fasts, vows, alms, crossings, offerings to Saints, and such like. 9. They ascribe great power to auricular confession in doing away sin. 10. They hold all to be damned, that die without baptism. 11. Extream Unction is with them a Sacrament, though not of such necessity as baptism, yet they hold it a cursed thing to die without it. 12. They re-baptize Christians converted to their Church. 13. They esteem some meats more holy than others, and are very strictly superstitious in their fasts. 14. They disallow Marriage in their Clergy; yet they permit their Priests to marry once. 15. They place such virtue in the Cross, that they advance it in all their high-ways, on the tops of their Churches, on the doors of their Houses, and are upon all occasions signing themselves with it on their fore-heads and breasts: They adore it, they use the signs thereof instead of prayers and thanksgiving in the morning and evening, when they sit down to meat and rise from table; when they swear, they swear by the Cross, &c. 16. Such virtue they place in holy Water, that after the Bishops have consecrated the Rivers on the *Epiphany*, as their custom is then every year, people strive who shall first plunge their children, and themselves therein, and think their meat is blessed that is boiled in that water; and that the sick shall either recover, or be made more fit and holy for God, if they drink thereof. 17. They have their solemn Processions on the *Epiphany*, in which go two Deacons bearing Banners in their hands, the one of our Lady, the other of Saint *Michael* fighting with the Dragon; after them follow the other Deacons and Priests, two and two in a rank, with Copes on their backs, and Images hanging on their breasts. After these march the Bishops in their Robes, then the Monks and their Abbots: and after them the Patriarch in rich attire, with a ball on the top of his Mitre, as if his head supported the World; at last comes the great Duke with his Nobility; when they are come to the River, a hole is made in the Ice, then the Patriarch prayeth, and conjureth the Devil out of the water; which done, he

he casteth Salt, and censeth the water with incense, and so it becomes holy. This is the Procession at *Mosco*; where the people are provident, lest the Devil (being conjured out of the water) should enter into their Houses, they make Crosses with Chalk over their doors. In their Processions also they carry the Image of Christ within a Pix upon a high pole, which they adore, and think this Image was made without hands. 18. Such holiness they place in their Priests benediction, that when they brew, they bring a dish of Wort to the Priest within the Church, which he consecrates, and this makes the whole brewing holy. In Harvest they do the like, by bringing the first fruits of their corn to the Priest to be hallowed. 19. On Palm-Sunday, when the Patriarch rideth through the *Mosco*, the Great Duke holds his Horse bridle, and the people cry *Hosanna*, spreading their upper garments under his Horse feet. The Duke hath for his service that day a Pension from the Patriarch of 200 Rubbels. 20. Besides their Wednesdays and Fridays fasts, they have four Lents in the year: The first and great Lent is as ours, before Easter, the second about Midsummer, the third in Harvest-time, the fourth about All-hollow-tide; the first week of their great Lent they feed upon Bread and Salt only, and drink nothing but water; in this Lent they have three *Vigils*; in the last whereof, which is on Good-Friday, the whole Parish watcheth in the Church from nine a clock in the evening, till six in the morning; all which time they stand, except when they fall down and knock their heads against their Images, which must be 170 times in that night. 21. They have a Saint for every day of the year, which is held the Patron of that day. The Image whereof is brought every morning with the Cross into the Great Duke's Chamber, by the Priest his Chaplain: before which Image the Great Duke prayeth, crosseth himself, and knocks his head to the ground: then he is with his Image besprinkled by the Priest with Holy Water. On his Chair where he sitteth, he hath always the picture of Christ, and of his Mother; as often as he, or his Nobles, drink or change their dishes at table, they cross themselves. *See Fletcher, Botero, Les Estats du Monde, and other relations of Moscovia.*

Q. 8. *What Ceremonies use they in their Marriages and Funerals?* *Their Marriages.*
A. Their Marriages are performed with such words of contract as are used among us, with a Ring also, and delivery of the Bride's hand into the Bridegroom's by the Priest, who stand both at the Altar, opposite to each other. The Matrimonial-knot being tied, the Bride comes to the Bride-groom, and falleth down at his feet, knocking her head upon his shooe, in sign of her subjection; and he casteth the lap of his upper garment over her, in token of cherishing and protection: then the Bride's friends bow low to the Bride-groom, and his friends likewise to hers, in sign of affinity and love: and withall, the Bride-groom's Father offers to the Priest a loaf of bread, who delivers it to the Bride's Father, with attestation before God and their pictures, that he delivers the Dowry wholly at the appointed day, and keep love with one another;

another; hereupon they break the loaf and eat it. This done, the married couple walk hand in hand to the Church-Porch, there the Bride-groom drinketh to the Bride, who pledgeth him; then he goeth to his Father's House, and she to hers, where either entertain their friends a-part. In token of plenty and fruitfulness, corn is flung out of the windows upon the Bride and Bride-groom, at their entring into the House. In the evening the Bride is brought to the Bride-groom's Father's House; there she lodgeth that night in silence and obscurity; she must not be seen by the Bride-groom, till the next day; for three days she must say little or nothing; then they depart to their own House, and feast their Friends. Upon any small dislike the man may enter into a Monastery, and so forsake his Wife. At their Funerals they hire Women to mourn, who howl over the Body after a barbarous manner, asking him what he wanted, and why he would die? They use to put in the dead party's hands a Letter to Saint *Nicholas* their chief Mediator, to intercede for him. They use both anniversary and monthly Commemorations of their dead friends, over whose Graves the Priest prayeth, and hath a penny for his pains. They that die in the Winter, because the ground then cannot be digged, have their bodies piled up together in a place which they call *God's house*, till the spring; what time the bodies and the earth being resolved and softened, every one taketh his dead friend and burieth him in the same apparel he used to wear when he lived.

Their Funerals.

See the above named Writers.

Q. 9. *What is the profession of the* Armenians?

A. They were altogether of the *Greek* Religion, and subject to the Patriarch of *Constantinople*, but now are fallen off in most Tenets, and have two Patriarchs of their own; the one resideth in *Armenia* the greater, called *Turcomania*; the other in *Armenia* the lesser; but now the one sits in *Persia*; the other, to wit, the lesser, in *Cilicia*. They are in some sort *Eutychians*, holding a coalition of Christ's two natures, into one compounded nature, but by their late confession, it seems they have renounced their opinion. Their Patriarchs they call Catholicks: they administer the Sacrament with unleavened bread; and will not have Christ's body to be really in the Sacrament under the species of bread and wine; nor do they mingle water with wine. With the *Greeks* they deny the procession of the Holy Ghost from the Son. They give the Eucharist to Infants presently after Baptism; they pray for the Dead, yet deny Purgatory; they re-baptize Converts from the *Latine* Church. They fast the 25th of *December*, and keep Christmas-day on the *Epiphany*, or rather Christ's baptism. They keep the Feast of Annunciation the 6th day of *April*, the Purification the 14th of *February*. They eat Flesh on Fridays, between Easter and Ascension-day. In Lent they feed only on Herbs, Roots, Fruits, and Pulse; they abstain from such beasts they account unclean: they hold that the souls of good men obtain not felicity till the Resurrection: They admit none to be secular Priests till they are

Armenians, their Religion.

See Baronius, Boterus, Chytræus, Boemus, Vitriacus *his Oriental History; the* Armenian Confession, &c.

re married; but must not marry the second time. They will not have the Sacraments to conferr grace. They administer the Cup to all, and celebrate no Mass, without distributing the Sacrament. They invocate Saints, and insert divers words into the Creed which are neither Greek nor Latin.

Q. 10. *What other Sects are there of the Greek Religion?*

A. The *Melchites*, so called from *Melech*, a King, because they have always followed the Faith of the Emperors of *Constantinople* according as it was established by the Council of *Chalcedon*, against *Eutyches* and *Dioscorus*. They are so called *Syrians*, from the Country where they inhabit. These are altogether of the Greek Religion and Communion, but none of the jurisdiction of the Patriarch of *Constantinople*, but of the Arch-Bishop of *Damascus*, under the title of Patriarch of *Antiochia*; for this City, where Christianity had its first residence and name, and where *Peter* sate seven years Bishop, being wasted and forsaken, the Patriarch's Seat was translated to *Damascus*, where it remaineth. 2. The *Georgians* are also of the *Greek* Religion, but are not subject to the Patriarch of *Constantinople*, having a Metropolitan of their own, whose residence is in the Monastery of Saint *Katherine*, in Mount *Sinai*, a great way from *Iberia*, lying between the *Euxin* and *Caspian* Seas, where the *Georgians* inhabit; who are so called from Saint *George*, as some think, who converted them to Christianity, and whose picture they carry in their Banners; but doubtless they were called *Georgians* before Saint *George* was born: For *Mela* speaks of them in the first book of his Geography, who lived in the time of *Claudius* the Emperor; and *Vadianus* on that place, thinks they were called *Georgians* from their Husbandry, to which they were much addicted. 3. The *Georgians* next Neighbours, to wit, the *Mengrelians*, called of old *Colchi*, and the ancient *Zychi*, now called *Circassians*, whence the *Sultan* had his *Mamalukes*, are of the Greek Communion, and subject to the Patriarch of *Constantinople*; but they baptize not their children till they be eight years old: In other points they are of the Greek Religion, being converted to Christianity by *Cyrillus* and *Methodius* the Apostles, or Ministers of the Patriarch of *Constantinople*.

Q. 11. *What is the Religion of the Nestorians, Christians of Saint Thomas and Jacobites?*

A. 1. The *Nestorians*, so called from *Nestorius* the Heretick, whose opinion concerning two persons in Christ they held a long time, and spread themselves through a great part of *Asia*, by reason of *Cosroes* the *Persian* King, who in hatred to *Heraclius* the Emperor, caused all Christians within his Dominions to become *Nestorians*: these were subject to the Patriarch of *Mussal*, which some think to be *Bagded* or *Babylon*, others *Selucia*, and others a part of old *Ninive*; but at this day most of them are subject to the Pope, both in jurisdiction, and partly in religion, and have renounced their old errors concerning the two Persons in Christ, that *Mary* should not be called the Mother of God; that the

Melchites.

Georgians.

Mengrelians.

Circassians. See Belloniu̇s his observations, Boterus, Chytræus de stat. Eccles. Thomas à Jesu Brerewood, Prateolus de Sectis, &c.

Nestorians.

Council

Council of *Ephesus*, and all other Councils after it, are to be rejected: These errors, I say, they have renounced; but they administer the Sacrament with leavened bread, and in both kinds, and permit their Priests to marry the third or fourth time; they have Crosses but not Crucifixes, nor confirmation, nor Auricular confession. 2. The Christians of *India*, or of *St. Thomas*, so called because converted by him. They were heretofore *Nestorians*, and subject to the Patriarch of *Musa*, but now are subordinate to the Pope, both in profession, and jurisdiction. They did use to give the Eucharist in both kinds, to season the bread with Salt, instead of Wine to drink the juice of Raisons, to baptize their Children when forty days old; to reject all Images except the Cross, the Pope's supremacy, extream unction, and second marriages of their Priests, &c. but now they are of the *Roman* Religion. 3. The *Jacobites*, so called from *Jacobus*, the *Syrian*, a great *Eutycnian*, are spread through many Kingdoms in the East. They are named also *Dioscorians*, from *Dioscorus* Patriarch of *Alexandria*, a great Patron of *Eutyches*. They belonged anciently before the Council of *Chalcedon*, to the jurisdiction of *Antiochia*: but since, they yield obedience to a Patriarch of their own, whose residence is in *Caramit* the Old Metropolis of *Mesopotamia*, but yet retains the name of Patriarch of *Antiochia*. They held there was in Christ but one nature, will, and operation, and therefore in signing with the Cross they used but one finger, whereas the other Eastern Christians used two. Before baptism they imprinted on their Children the sign of the Cross with a Hot Iron. They deny Purgatory, and prayers for the dead, and say that the Angels are made of fire and light. They hold that just men's souls remain in the earth till the Resurrection; their Priests are married, they deny auricular confession, give the Eucharist in both kinds, and the bread unleavened. They circumcise both Sexes, they condemn *Eutyches* as an Heretick, and yet honour *Dioscorus*, and *Jacob* the *Syrian* as Saints; but now they have utterly rejected the Heresie of one nature in Christ, and with the Latine Church acknowledge two distinct natures, with their distinct properties, as may be seen by the *Jacobites* confessions.

Q. 12. *What is the Religion of the* Maronites?

A. The *Maronites* are so called from *Maron*, a holy man; their chief residence is in Mount *Libanus*, though some inhabit *Aleppo*, *Damascus*, *Tripoli* of *Syria* and *Cyprus*. Their Patriarch is a Monk of Saint *Anthony*, having nine Bishops under him; he is always called *Peter*, and will be styled Patriarch of *Antiochia*, which title is claimed by the *Jacobite Patriarch*, who is always named *Ignatius*. The *Maronites* were *Monothelites*, and with the Greeks denied the Procession of the Holy Ghost from the Son; abstained from blood and strangled things; observed the Sabbath with the Lords day; condemned the fourth marriage as utterly unlawful; rejected confirmation; administred the Sacrament in leavened bread, and in both kinds, and excluded the blessed souls from Heaven, till the Resurrection; they did besides hold that

all

all mens fouls were created together in the beginning; that Hereticks are to be re-baptized; that the Child is not to be baptized till the Mother be purified, which is forty days after a Male Child, and eighty after a Female; that Children should receive the Eucharist, as soon as baptized; that the Father may dissolve the Matrimony of his Child, if he dislike it; that the Eucharist is not to be reserved, nor to be carried to sick persons, in danger of death; that Priests and Deacons must be married; that Children of five or six years old may be made Sub-deacons; that Women during their monthly purgations are not to be admitted into the Church, nor to the Eucharist. But these Opinions the *Maronites* renounced, when the Christians had the command of *Syria* and *Palestine*; but when *Saladine* recovered those parts, the *Maronites* fell off from the Roman Church, and embraced their former Tenets; but in the time of *Gregory* the thirteenth, and *Clement* the eighth, they reconciled themselves again to the Roman Church.

See the above-named Author, withall Possevin. apparat. sacr. Thomas à Jesu de conver. Gent. Vitriacus, Histor. Orient. Tyrius de bello sacro, &c.

Q. 13. *What are the* Cophti?

A. The *Cophti* are the *Jacobites* of *Egypt*, for the *Egyptians* were anciently named *Ægophti*; we call them *Cophti*, that is, Egyptian Christians, as the *Jacobites* of *Syria* are named *Syrians*, and in no country were these *Eutychians* more patronized than in *Syria* and *Egypt*; yet these *Jacobites* differ from *Eutyches* in this, That He taught the two Natures in Christ to be one by confusion or commixtion; whereas They say, that they are one by co-adunation; but so, that the properties of each nature remain distinct, so that in effect they hold two Natures, but dare not say so, for fear of *Nestorianism* of the two Persons; not being able to discriminate between the Nature and the Person. These *Cophti* are subject to the Patriarch of *Alexandria*, whose residence is now in the City of *Caire*. They used heretofore to be circumcised; but by the Popes perswasion have left it. They baptize not children till the fortieth day: to whom they give the Eucharist immediately after baptism, and then also confer on them all sacred Orders under Priesthood; their Parents promising for them (and performing what they promise) till they be sixteen years old, Chastity, Fasting on Wednesdays, Fridays, and in the four Lents. They administer the Eucharist in leavened bread, and in both kinds. With the *Greeks* they leave out the words of the *Nicene* Creed, *and from the Son*; they deny the Sacrament and Extream Unction to the sick, reject Purgatory, and prayer for the dead, and all General Councils (chiefly *Chalcedon*) after that of *Ephesus*. They keep no Lord's-day, nor feasts except in Cities. They marry within the second degree of consanguinity without dispensation, they account the Roman Church heretical, and in their Liturgies use to read the Gospel of *Nicodemus*.

Cophti of Egypt.

See the above-named Authors, with Baronius and Thevet's Cosmography of the Levant, c. 48.

Q. 14. *What are the* Abyssin *Christians*?

A. These be they which inhabit the Mid-land *Æthiopia*, under *Presbyter* or *Precious John*; they have a Patriarch of their own, whom they call *Abunna*, whose garment is white, his upper Vestment

Abyssine. their Religion.

ment is like a Cardinals Cloak buttoned before. When he rides abroad on his Mule, he is attended on with a great train; three Crosses or Staves are carried about him, and holdeth a Cross in his own hand. They have many Mytred Priests or Bishops, and great store of Monasteries. All their Patriarchs and Bishops are of S. *Anthony's* Order, as are the Patriarchs of *Alexandria*, to whose jurisdiction anciently *Æthiopia* did belong; and yet at this day they are tied to chuse their *Abunna*, (whom they call Catholick) of the jurisdiction of *Alexandria*, by the Patriarch of which place he is confirmed, consecrated and invested in his Ecclesiastical Rights. In their Liturgy also they pray particularly for the Patriarch of *Alexandria*. The *Æthiopian* Religion consisteth in circumcising Male and Female; whether out of Religion, or the ancient custom of their Nation (as being descended from the ancient *Æthiopians* or *Arabians*, *Ismael's* posterity, who used to be circumcised) is uncertain, but most likely they are circumcised in memory and imitation of Christ, who was also circumcised. They use also every year to Baptize themselves in Lakes and Rivers on *Epiphany* day, in remembrance of Christ's baptism, who was baptized on that day in *Jordan*. The other points of their Religion be these: they abstain from such beasts as the old Law accounteth unclean; they keep the Sabbath and Sunday together: The Thursday before Easter they administer the Sacrament in unleavened bread; but ordinarily in leavened bread; all communicate (standing) in both kinds. The Wine they receive from the Deacon in a spoon; and that in the Church only. The day they receive in, they must not spit till Sun-set. After forty days the Males are baptized, the Females after eighty, except in case of necessity; and then also they give them the Eucharist, they think the Children dying without baptism shall be saved by the Faith of their Parents. They confess after every sin committed, and then receive the Eucharist. They are *Jacobites* in acknowledging but one nature and will in Christ: therefore they reject the Council of *Chalcedon*, for condemning *Dioscorus* the Eutychian. So they deny Confirmation and Extream Unction. They hold traduction of souls, admit of painted, not Massie Images; they usually excommunicate none but murtherers, and this only belongs to the Patriarch. Priests and Monks have neither Tithes, nor Alms by begging, but live by their labour. They permit not their Bishops and Priests to marry twice. Flesh is eaten every Friday betwixt Easter and Whitsunday. The King conferreth all Ecclesiastick promotions, except the Patriarchship. Of these passages see the above-named Authors, and withall the *Æthiopian* Liturgy in *Bibliotheca patrum*, tom. 6. *Alvarez* the King of *Portugal's* Chaplain who lived in *Æthiopia* six years, and wrote the *Æthiopian* History. *Zaga Zabo* an *Æthiopian* Bishop sent into *Portugal* by King *David* the *Abyssin*; who set out the Confession of the *Æthiopian* faith, translated by *Damianus à Goes*, &c.

Q. 15. *Wherein doth the Protestant Church agree with, or dissent from other Christian Churches?* A. They

Sect. 14.   *of* EUROPE.   351

A. They agree with the *Greek* Church, in giving the Sacrament in both kinds, in admitting Priests to marry, in rejecting Images, Purgatory, and extream unction, and in denying the Pope's Supremacy; in the same points also they agree, with the *Melchites* or *Syfians*, with the *Georgians*, *Mengrelians* and *Circassians*, and with the *Moscovites* or *Russians*, who are all of the Greek profession, though in some things they differ. The Protestants agree with the *Nestorians* in rejecting auricular confession, in permitting Priests to marry, in communicating in both kinds, and in rejecting Crucifixes. With the Christians of Saint *Thomas*, they agree in administring the Sacrament in both kinds, in rejecting Images and Extream Unction, and permitting Priests to marry, and denying the Pope's supremacy. They agree with the *Jacobites*, in confessing their sins only to God, in rejecting Purgatory, and prayers for the dead, in giving the Sacrament in both kinds, and in unleavened bread, and in tolerating Priests mariages; in the same points also they agree with the *Cophti* or Christians of *Egypt*, with the *Abyssins*, *Armenians* and *Maronites*. But the Protestants differ from the above named Churches in these subsequent points. 1. They believe that the Holy Ghost proceedeth from the Son. 2. They use unleavened bread in the Sacrament. 3. The English Priests allow Confirmation. 4. They hold that the blessed souls enjoy God presence, and that the wicked are tormented in Hell, immediately after their departure hence. 5. They permit Priests after ordination to marry. 6. They reject pictures as well as Massie-Images. 7. They observe not the Saturday or Sabbath, 8. They have but one Lent in the year. 9. They make no scruple in eating of blood; in these points the Protestants dissent both from the *Greeks*, *Melchites*, *Georgians*, *Mengrelians*, *Circassians*, *Moscovites* and other Sects above-named. They deferr not Baptism till the eighth year with the *Circassians*; they pray not for the dead, nor give the Sacrament in a spoon, nor divorce their Wives upon every light occasion, with the *Moscovites*; they affirm not two persons in Christ, nor deny *Mary* to be the Mother of God, nor reject the Council of *Ephesus*, and all other Councils after it, with the *Nestorians*. They deferr not Baptism till the fortieth day, nor exclude Priests from second marriage, with the Christians of Saint *Thomas*. They did not ascribe one nature only, one will, and one operation to Christ; nor do they use circumcision, and a hot Iron in Baptism; nor do they teach that Angels are composed of fire and light, with the *Jacobites*. They give not the Eucharist to Infants; they marry not in the second degree of consanguinity; not do they read the Gospel of *Nicodemus*, with the *Cophti*. They do not hold traduction of souls by seminal propagation, nor baptize themselves every year, nor suffer they their Ministers to live by mechanical labours, with the *Abyssins*. They use not rebaptization, nor fasting on Christmas-day, nor abstain from eating of unclean beasts prohibited

Protestant Church, its agreement with, and dissent from other Christian Churches.

hibited by the old law, with the *Armenians*; they do not hold that all souls were created together, nor that parents ought to dissolve their childrens marriages when they please, nor that children should be made Sub-Deacons, nor that Menstruous Women should be excluded from the Sacrament, with the *Maronites*. The Protestants do not celebrate their Liturgy in an unknown tongue, as the *Maronites, Cophti, Jacobites, Indians* and *Nestorians* do, who make use of the *Chaldee* or *Syriack* language in their Divine Service, which few understand; nor with the *Greeks, Melchites, Georgians, Circassians* and others, do they use the Ancient Greek tongue in their Liturgies, which these above-named know not, and yet make use of it in their Churches; nor with the Roman Catholicks do they read and pray in Latin, but in their own vulgar languages; which are intelligible by all; in which point they agree with the *Abyssins, Armenians, Moscovites, Russians, Sclavonians*, anciently called *Illyrians*. Lastly, Protestants differ from the Roman Catholicks in these points: 1. Of the number of canonical books of Scripture, of their sufficiency, authority and interpreter. 2. Of Christ's descent into Hell. 3. Of the Head of the Church, and of the Pope's Supremacy. 4. Of the true Catholick Church. 5. Of their Clergy, their Orders, Immunities, and Cœlibate. 6. Of the Monastical life, Vows, and Evangelical Councils. 7. Of the power of the Civil Magistrate. 8. Of Purgatory. 9. Of Invocation of Saints. 10. Adoration of Images and Reliques. 11. Sacraments, their number, efficacy, and ceremonies. 12. Baptism, its necessity, effects, and ceremonies. 13. Transubstantiation, and the consequences thereof. 14. Of administring in both kinds. 15. The sacrifice of the Mass. 16. Auricular confession. 17. Satisfaction. 18. Indulgences. 19. Extream Unction. 20. Original sin. 21. Free-will, Predestination, and Grace. 22. Justification, Faith, and Good works. 23. The Latine Service. 24. Traditions. *Some other small differences there are, and fewer there might be, if men would be moderate on either side; but the spirit of contention and contradiction, hath hitherto hindered, and will yet hinder the peace of the Church, till the Prince of Peace, or true* Solomon, *who built this mystical Temple, without noise of Axes or Hammers, put an end to all jarrs and discords, till he whom both the Winds and Seas do obey, awake, who now seems to be asleep? till he, I say, awake and rebuke the stormy winds, and proud billows, on which his Ship is tossed to and fro; that at last she may enjoy a calm time, and some Halcyonian-days, and may cast Anchor in the safe harbor of tranquility, where we may find our Saviour not in the Earth-quakes, Whirlwinds, and fire of contention; but in the still and quiet voice of peace, concord, and unity, which he left to us as a Legacy, but we have lost it by our pride, sacrilege, envy, ambition, covetousness, profaneness, and vain-glory.*

The

The Contents of the Fifteenth Section.

Religion is the ground of all government and greatness. 2. By divers reasons it is proved that Religion of all Common-wealths, and humane societies, is the foundation. 3. That Princes and Magistrates ought to have a special care in settling and preserving of Religion. 4. That one Religion only is to be allowed in a Common-wealth publickly. 5. In what respect different Religions may be tolerated in private. 6. A Christian Prince may not dissemble his Religion. 7. Why GOD blesseth the professors of false Religions and punish the contemners thereof. 8. False Religions are grounded upon policy, and what use there is of Ceremonies in Religion. 9. The mixture and division of Religions, and of Idolatry. 10. How the Gentile Religion in worshipping of the Sun, seems to be most consonant to natural reason; with divers observations concerning Sun-worship, and the knowledge the Gentiles had of a Deity, and the Unity thereof, with some glimmering of the Trinity. 11. That the honour, maintenance, and advancement of a Priesthood, is the main supporter of Religion. 12. That the Christian Religion is of all others the most excellent, and to be preferred for divers reasons, being considered in it self, and compared with others; with an exhortation to the practice of Religious duties, which is true Christianity.

SECT. XV.

Quest. I. Having now past through all Religions known in the World, it remains that we make some use of what we have viewed: let us know then to what end and purpose hath this view been taken?

A. First to let us see, that there is no nation so barbarous, or brutish (except some particular fools, who have said in their heart, *there is no God*) which hath not made profession of some Religion, by which they are taught to acknowledge and worship a Deity: For Religion is the pillar on which every Common-wealth is built; so long as the Pillar is stable and firm, which is the foundation, so long will the house stand immovable; *Though the rain descends, and the winds blow, and the floods come, and beat upon that house, yet it shall not fall because it is founded upon a Rock.* Mat. 7. But if blind *Sampson*, if people void of understanding, trusting to their strength, shake once this pillar of Religion, down falls the whole Fabrick of Government, Law and Discipline. Of this, examples in all ages may be brought, to shew,

Religion the ground of government and greatness.

how States and Religion like *Hippocrates* Twins do live and die together; so long as Religion flourished in *Judea*, so long did that State flourish; but when the one failed the other fell. *Judah* and *Israel* were not carryed away into Captivity, till they had Captivated Religion: As *Sampson*'s strength consisted in his Hair, so doth the strength of a Common-wealth in Religion; if this be cut off, the *Philistines* will insult over the strongest State that ever was; and bring it to destruction: This is the *Palladium*, which if once removed, will expose the strongest City in the World to the enemy. The *Greek* Empire had not fallen from the *Palæologi* to the *Turk*, had the Christian Religion stood firm in *Constantinople*. The Poet could acknowledge that so long as *Rome* stood religious, so long she continued Victorious; *Dis te minorem quod geris, imperas, Horat.* And *Tully* confesseth that the instruments by which the *Romans* subdued the World, were not strength and policy, but Religion and Piety: *Non calliditate & robore, sed pietate ac Religione omnes gentes nationésque superastis. Orat. de Arusp. resp.* For this cause the Senate and people of *Rome* were careful to send their prime youth to *Hetruria*, (the University then of the *Roman* Religion) to be instructed in the ground of all their sacred and mysterious learning. Therefore *Mæcenas* in *Dion. Cassius L.* 3. adviseth *Augustus*, πάντη πάντως, by all means and at all times, to advance the worship of God, and to cause others to do the same, and not to suffer innovations in Religion, whence proceed συνωμοσίαι, συστάσεις κ̓ ἑταιρεῖαι conspiracies, seditions, and conventicles, or combinations. Religion is the Bulwark, as *Plato* saith, of Laws and Authority; it is the band of all humane society; the fountain of justice and fidelity; beat down this Bulwark, break this band, stop this fountain, and bid Adieu to all Laws, Authority, Unity, Justice, and Fidelity.

Qu. 2. *How doth it appear that Religion is the Foundation of Common-wealths, or humane societies?*

The Foundation of all Common-wealths. A 1. Because Religion teacheth the fear of God, without which men should live more securely among Lions and Bears, than among men; therefore *Abraham Genesis*, 20. knew that at Gerar he should both lose his Wife and his life too, because *he thought, surely the fear of God was not in that place*; 'tis not the fear of the temporal punishment, or of corporal death that keeps men in awe, but of eternal torments and spiritual death; therefore when *men will not fear those that can destroy the body, they will stand in awe of him who can cast body and soul into Hell-fire, Mat.* 10. It was this fear that begot Religion in the World, *Primus in orbe Deos fecit timor*, and it is Religion that cherisheth, increaseth and quickneth this fear; the end then of Common-wealths, and of all societies, is, that men may live more comfortably and securely than they can do alone, but without Religion there can be no security nor comfort, no more than there can be for Lambs among Wolves; for *homo homini lupus*. 2. There can be no durable Common-wealth where the people do not obey the Magistrate; but there can be no obedience or submission of Inferiours to their Superiours without Religion, which teacheth that Princes and Magistrates are Gods Vice-Gerents here on Earth; whom if we do not fear and obey, we cannot fear and obey God; who commands *Rom.* 13. *That every soul be subject to the higher Powers, for there is no power but of God.* 3. There is in all men naturally a desire of happiness and immortality; which cannot be attained without the knowledge and worship of God; whom we can neither know nor worship without Religion, which prescribeth the rules and way of worshipping him; and likewise sheweth us that there is a God, That he is one, invisible, eternal, omnipotent, the maker of all things, *&c.* 4. The Essence and Life of a common-wealth consisteth in Love, Unity, and Concord; but it is by religion that these are obtained; for there is no band or tye so strict and durable, as that of Religion, by which all the living stones of the great buildings of Kingdoms and States are cemented, and like the planks of *Noah's* Ark, are pitched and glewed together. 5. As each particular man is subject to death and corruption, so are whole States, Corporations, and Kingdoms; but the means to retard and keep off destruction and ruin from them is, Religion; hence those States continue longest; where Religion is most esteemed and advanced; whereas on the contrary, the contempt of Religion is the fore-runner of destruction, this we see that when the whole World was united into one corporation and society, for slighting Religion, were all overthrown in the General Cataclysm, except eight religious persons, saved in the Ark. The Poet acknowledgeth that all the miseries which befell *Italy,* proceeded from the neglecting of Religion; *Dii multa neglecti dederunt* Hesperiæ *mala luctuosæ,* Horat. 6. As all Common-wealths and States know and are assured that they cannot subsist without the protection of Almighty God, who is the Author of all humane societies; so likewise they know that God will not own and protect them who either cannot or will not serve, worship, and honour him, which without Religion is impossible to be done by men; for as all Nations know, even by the comely order and harmony, the strange operations of Nature, and the beauty of the world, that there is a Divinity, which is also plain by the actions of Providence; so likewise they know that this divine power must be honoured and obeyed, except they will shew ingratitude in the highest degree, to him, whence they have their living, moving, being, and all they enjoy; but without Religion they can neither know how nor where, nor when to worship him. 7. Every man knows he hath a spiritual, reasonable, and heavenly soul, which naturally delights in the knowledge and contemplation of heavenly things; which shew that he cannot reject all Religion; except he will shake off nature and humanity. 8. The veriest *Atheists* in the world, who denied God, (at least in his providence, though they

they could not in his essence) yet affirmed that Religion was necessary in all societies, without which they cannot subsist, as is already said. 9. As subjects will not obey their Princes, but fall into rebellions, so Princes will not protect their Subjects, but become Wolves and Tyrants, if it were not for Religion that keeps them in awe, and assures them that there is over them a King of Kings, and Lord of Lords, to whom they must give an account of their actions. *Regum timendorum in proprios greges. Reges in ipsos imperium est Jovis. Horat.* 10. If it were not for the force of Religion, few Common-wealths could defend themselves; what Soldier could fight with that courage, or expose his life to danger, if he did not expect a greater reward, a more durable Garland hereafter, than any they could expect here? This made the *Jews* so resolute against their neighbour *Gentiles*; this animated the *Romans* against their enemies; they fought *Pro Aris* for their Altars in the first place; this animateth the *Turks* against Christians, and these against the *Turks*.

Q. 2. Ought not then Princes and Magistrates to have a special care in the settling and preservation of Religion?

Religion, most requisite in Princes and Governors, they should be careful of it.

A. Yes: for no means is so powerful to establish and perpetuate their Thrones and authority as Religion; no Guard so strong as this; no Castle so impregnable; no Spur so sharp to stir and extimulate peoples affections towards the defence, obedience, reverence, and maintenance of their Governours, as Religion; therefore the wise *Roman* Emperors took more pride and delight in the titles of *Pius* and *Sanctus*; of *Picus, Holy, Religious*, than to be stiled, Wise, Fortunate, Stout, or Valorous; and to let the people know what care they had of Religion, they alone would be called *Pontifices Maximi*; or chief Bishops. There is no Epithet that the wise Poet gives to *Æneas* so often, as that of *Piety*; *Pius Æneas, pietate insignis & armis, insignem pietate virum*, &c. *Quo justior alter, nec pietate fuit*, &c. *Virgil*. That good Emperor *Antoninus*, who succeeded *Hadrian*, preferred the title of *Pius* to all his other honorable titles; and as wise Princes have been chiefly careful of Religion, to preserve it pure, and uncontaminate, so have they been diligent in suppressing *Atheists* the chief enemies thereof, for they saw that *Atheism* did introduce *Anarchy*; for he who is an enemy to God, cannot be a friend to Gods Vice-gerents; therefore in all well governed States they have been either put to death or banished, as being enemies to government and humane society. Wise Princes find that as Religion uniteth peoples affection to them, so it makes them fortunate and successful in all their actions and undertakings; never was there a more religious Prince than King *David*, and never a King more successful against his enemies; the like we may see in *Constantine, Theodosius, Charles* the great, and many others no less famous for their Religion, than for their Victories; and because wise Law-givers are not ignorant how much Religion is prevalent with the people, therefore they delivered them no Laws, but

what

what either they received, or said they received from some Deity; so *Lycurgus* gave out that his Laws were delivered to him by *Apollo*: *Minos* received his Laws from *Jupiter*, with whom he was familiar nine years together. *Zaleucus* makes *Minerva* the Author of his Laws. *Numa* ascribes his Laws to the Nymph *Ægeria*, with whom he had Familiar conferences in the night. And *Mahomet* will have his Law backed by the Authority of the Angel *Gabriel*; *such is the force of Religion*; that without this, men would neither receive nor obey Laws: for this cause God himself appeared often to the Patriarchs, and came down in lightning and thunder upon Mount *Sinai*, when he gave the Law. Neither hath there been any more forcible way to appease tumults and popular seditions, than the conceit of Religion. When the City of *Florence* in a civil dissention was washed with her own blood, *Francis Sodorinus* the Bishop, in his Pontificals, having the cross carried before him, and accompanied with his Priests, struck such an awe of Religion into the hearts of the Citizens, with his very presence, that they flung down their arms: the like religious Stratagem was used by *Jaddus* the High Priest of the Jews, to obtain the favour of *Alexander*, as he was marching against *Jerusalem* with his Army, who was so struck with the Priests majestical presence and Vestments, that he both adored the Priests, spared the City, and conferred on it divers benefits. The like respect and success had Pope *Urban* from *Attilla* when he besieged *Aquileia*; and many more examples may be alledged.

Q. 4. *Are Pluralites of Religions tolerable in a State?*

A. 1. Publickly One Religion only is to be allowed, because there is but one God, who is the Object of Religion; therefore as his Essence is most simple and indivisible, so should his worship be, because diversities of Religion breed diversities of opinions concerning God. 2. As there is but one truth, so there ought to be but one Religion; for false Religions either teach to worship false Gods, or else in a false manner to worship the true God; therefore God himself prescribed to the Jews the rule and manner of his worship, strictly commanding them not to alter any thing therein; and Saint *Paul* sheweth, *That the Gospel which he taught, was the only true Gospel, so that if an Angel from Heaven should preach any other Gospel, let him be accursed.* Galat. 3. As there is but one Church which is the ground and pillar of truth, and one faith to lay hold on that truth, and one spirit to lead the Church into the way of truth, so there should be but one Religion, which is the Doctrine of that truth. 4. There is but one way to Heaven and life Eternal; but the ways to destruction are many; therefore there ought to be but one Religion to conduct us in that way to eternal happiness. 5. Religion (as is said) is the Foundation of all States and Kingdoms; therefore in one State or Kingdom there ought to be but one Religion, because there can be but one foundation; for one building cannot have many Foundations. 6. Religion is the band and cord

But one Religion to be allowed publickly.

by which the unity of the State is preserved; if this band be broken into many pieces, how can it bind the affections of people, and preserve their unity, either amongst themselves, or with their Princes and Governours: As therefore *a city divided against it self cannot stand*; neither can that State subsist, which is divided into different Religions, which occasioneth diversity of affections, and withal many jars and contentions. 7. As in bodies natural, contrary qualities cause distruction; so in bodies Politick, contrary Religions; for if there be but one true Religion, the rest must needs be false; and what can be more contrary than truth and falshood; so that the belly of *Rebecca* must needs be tormented, where such opposite twins do struggle: Hence proceed heart-burnings, emulations, strifes, proscriptions, excommunications, and such like distempers, by which the seemless coat of Christ is torn in pieces. 8. Diversity of Religions beget envy, malice, seditions, factions, rebellions, contempt of Superiors, treacheries, innovations, disobedience, and many more mischiefs, which pull down the heavy judgments of God upon the State or Kingdom where contrary Religions are allowed, because whilst every one strives to advance his own Religion above the other, all these distempers now mentioned must needs follow. We could instance the condition of the *Jews*, how they flourished whilst they adhered to the Religion prescribed them by God: But when they admitted the *Gentile* Religions also among them, they fell into all the mischiefs mentioned, and God cast them off as a prey to their Enemies. But we have sufficient and experimental proof of this in our neighbouring Countries of *France* and *Germany*; what distempers and civil wars not many years ago have ensued upon the differences of Religion, to the desolation and ruine of many Towns and Cities? *Tantum Religio potuit suadere malorum.*

Q. 5. *May a State tolerate different Religions in private?*

Different Religions how and when to be tolerated.

A. 1. If there be such Religions as do not overthrow the fundamentals of truth. 2. Nor such as impugn or disturb the government established in that State or Kingdom. 3. If the professors thereof be such as are not factious, ambitious, or pertinacious; but honest, simple, tractable, obedient to Superiors, having to other end in holding their opinions of Religion, but God's glory, and satisfaction of their own conscience, so far as they can conceive, and withall are willing to submit to better judgments, and to renounce their opinions when they are convinced to be erroneous; in these regards I say a State may, and wise States do tolerate diversities of opinions in Religion, upon good grounds; because (as *Solomon* saith) *There is a time for all things under the Sun*; There will come a time when *the tares shall be separated from the corn, though the wise Husbandman suffers them to grow together a while.* The wise Physician will not presently fall to purging out the noxious humours of a *Cacochymical* Body; for in some diseases nothing is more dangerous than precipitate and untimely Physick; Chronical diseases are not cured by Physick and motion, but by time and rest. The nature of man is such (saith *Seneca*) that he will be sooner lead than drawn, *facili-*

us ducitur, quàm trahitur. Stubborn and violent courses in reformation, beget stubborn and violent opposition. The warm Sun will prevail more with the traveller, than the cold and boysterous wind; the Goats blood will break the Adamant, which the hardest hammers cannot do. God also hath his times for calling of men to the knowledge of his truth; some he calls at the ninth hour, and some not till the eleventh. Christ sends abroad his Disciples to preach and work miracles among the *Jews*: but into the way of the *Gentiles* they must not yet go till his Ascension. It falls out many times that the remedy is worse than the disease; and while we go about to cure the State, we kill it; and instead of purging out the peccant humours of the body Politick, we cast it into a *Calenture* or a burning Fever. This was not unknown to that wise and good Emperour *Theodosius*, who could not be perswaded by the *Catholicks* to exterpate, or use violent courses against the *Arrians*, but permitted them to enjoy their Churches and opinions, knowing how dangerous it would prove to the State, if the quietness thereof should be disturbed; this had been to kindle the fire which was lately extinguished, and to raise a conflagration in the Empire, which could not be quenched without an inundation of blood, this had been *Camerinam movere*, or to awake a sleeping Dog. For this cause though the *Turk* is zealous in his Religion, yet he permits *Christians, Jews, Persians, Æthiopians*, and others, to enjoy their several Religions. The like liberty is permitted in *Germany, France*, and other places, for avoiding further mischief; For this purpose that their may not be a breach of peace, and disturbance in the government of the State. The *Turks* and *Muscovites* inhibit all disputations in point of Religion on pain of death. The like inhibition was made by the Emperour and Princes of *Germany*, after their Civil Wars, that there should be no dispute or contention between the Catholicks and Protestants; for indeed by such disputes, Religion it self is weakned, and the State endangered; for if it be not tolerable to question Laws once established, how can it be safe either for State or Church to call in question Religion once settled and confirmed by authority? By questions and disputes the Majesty of Religion is slighted; and that made dubious, which ought to be most certain; The objects and high mysteries of our faith, are not to be measured by our shallow reason. The many disputes about Religion, commonly, overthrow the practice of Religion, which consisteth not in talking, but in doing; the one indeed is more easie than the other, as *Seneca* saith, *Omnes disputare malunt quam vivere*; *We had rather dispute of salvation, than work it out with fear and trembling.* If Heaven could be obtained with wrangling and disputing, a profane Sophister should sooner have it than a holy Christian, who knows that life eternal is not obtained by talking *of*, but *by* walking *in* the way of GOD's Commandments. But to return to our former discourse, and to end this question, as we began; diversity of Religions, with the limitations aforesaid, may be connived at; especially when it cannot be avoided without the danger and ruine of the State; and the rather, because the Conscience cannot be compelled, nor faith forced. There never was a wiser State than the *Romans*, and more zealous in the worship of their Gods, κατὰ τὰ πάτρια, according to the custom and Laws of their Nation; yet they admitted the worship of *Isis* and *Æsculapius*, foreign Deities; and a *Pantheon*, or Temple for all Gods. And though they abhorred the *Jews* above all other people, yet *Augustus*, that wise and happy Emperor, permitted them to exercise their own Religion. Princes and Magistrates must, like wise Ship-Masters, rather strike Sail, and cast Anchor, than make Ship-wrack in a Storm, and rather sail back with safety, than venture upon the Rocks in the Harbour with danger: *Præstat recurrere quam male currere*. As *Constans* the Emperor, and *Theodosius* the Great, though Catholick Princes, yet for quietness sake tolerated the *Arrians*. So did *Leo* make the edict of Union, called ἑνωτικὸν, that all the different Religions within his dominions might live peaceably and friendly together. For the same cause *Anastasius* made a law of *Amnesty*, and accounted those the best preachers that were moderate.

Q. 6. *May a Christian Prince dissemble his Religion?*

Princes may not dissemble in Religion.

A. 1. He may not; because God abhorreth Hypocrisy, condemneth a double heart, and rejecteth such as draw near to him with their lips when their hearts are far from him. Christ denounceth more woes against Hypocrisy than any other sin: of those who are Wolves in Sheeps cloathing, he will have us take heed, and threatneth to deny those before his heavenly Father, who deny him before men. Who are commanded to love God *with all our heart, with all our strength*, &c. which we do not, if we dissemble. He requires faithfulness, truth, and sincerity in the inward parts, he abhorreth liars, and deceitful men. Shall we think it lawful to dissemble with God, and are offended if our neighbours dissemble with us? God will not have us wear a Linsy-Woolsy Garment; nor plow with an Ox and an Ass: nor sow different seeds in the same ground. *Simulata sanctitas duplex impietas*; The Devil is never more dangerous, than when he transforms himself into an Angel of light; *Malus, ubi se bonum simulat pessimus est*, saith *Seneca*. 2. God is the chief good, in whom is no impurity nor guile; therefore he requires of us pure and sincere love; he is omniscient, *there is nothing hid from him, he knoweth the hearts, and searcheth the reins, and knoweth our hearts long before: all things are naked and open to his eyes*; Therefore though we can delude men, we cannot deceive God; he knows what is within painted Sepulchres, and in those platters that have washed out-sides. God is truth it self, therefore is an enemy to falshood. He is zealous of his glory; but there is nothing wherein he is more dishonoured, than by dissimulation and Hypocrisy. 3. Never was there any good Prince a dissembler, nor did ever any dissembler prove a good Prince; but cruel, tyranical and impious, as we see by the examples of *Herod, Tiberius, Nero*, and many more, who at first made great shew of Religion and Virtue: but when the Vizard was taken off, they proved monsters and not men, and Woolves in Sheeps cloathing; nay there is more hope of him that in the beginning professeth his own infirmities, than in him that concealeth them; for the one is more corrigible than the other: as *Bodin* instanceth in King *John* of *France*, who could not hide his weakness, yet never committed any wicked act. And indeed dissembling Princes fall into this inconveniency and mischief, that they cannot be long hid under the Vizard of Religion and Vertue, but their nature will break out, and then will become more odious to their people, than if they had at first detected their natures. *Dionysius* the younger, so long as *Plato* was with him, played the counterfeit egregiously, making show of sobriety, temperance, and all other Princely vertues: but as soon as *Plato* was gone, his wicked nature broke out, like a running stream that hath been damned up. And how can a people put confidence in that Prince, who dissembleth with God? he that is not true to his maker, but playeth fast and loose with him, can never be true to his people. And indeed for a Prince or State to dissemble with God; who had raised them out of the dust, to make them rulers over his people, is ingratitude in the highest degree; and much worse than of any private man, by how much the higher he is advanced above others. To be brief, among all the wicked qualities of *Cataline*, there was none that was more exaggerated by the Historian, than his dissimulation and counterfeiting; *Cujuslibet rei simulator ac dissimulator; aliud in lingua promptum, aliud in pectore clausum habebat.*

Q. 7. *Seeing there is but one true Religion, why doth God bless the professors of false Religions, and punisheth the contemners thereof?*

A. 1. Because in false Religions there is the acknowledgment of a Divinity, though the conceptions men have of this Deity be erroneous, and the worship they give be superstitious. 2. Because by false Religions men are kept in awe and obedience to their Superiors, and in love and concord among themselves; therefore God, who is the Author of all goodness, and tender of the welfare of mankind, will rather have a false Religion than none, and Superstition rather than Atheism, for even in false Religions both Prince and People are taught their duties to each other. The *Romans* stood so much in awe of their Heathenish Superstitions, that they would rather loose their lives, than falsify the Oaths they took in the presence of their Gods; and were more moved to the performance of their duties, by the hope of rewards, and fear of punishments hereafter, than of any they could expect or endure here. Humane society, fidelity, justice, temperance, fortitude, and other vertues, are upheld even by false Religions: therefore the defenders of such have been outwardly rewarded by God, and the enemies thereof punished. *Philip* of *Macedon*, for defending *Apollo*'s Temple against the *Phocenses*, who came to rob it, obtained a glorious Victory, and they an ignominious overthrow, to the loss of the whole Army. The Soldiers of *Cambyses*, who went to

Falſe Religions why bleſſed, and the contemners puniſhed.

pillage the Temple of *Jupiter Hammon*, were overthrown by the Sands, and he, for his many Sacrileges committed in *Egypt*, was slain by his own Sword in the midst of his age, glory, and Army: God punished the Sacrilege of *Xerxes* the Son of *Darius*, for robbing the *Delphick* Temple, with the loss of his innumerable Army, by a handful of *Grecians*, and the overthrow of his 4000. sacrilegious Soldiers, with lightning, hail, and storms, so that not one was left to bring rydings of the destruction of those wretches who were sent to rob *Apollo*. *Brennus*, Captain of the *Gauls*, had the like judgment fell upon him, for the like Sacrilege upon the same *Delphick* Temple; his Army was overthrown by storms and an earthquake; *Brennus* himself, out of impatience, was his own executioner. *Sextus Pompeius*, for robbing *Juno's* Temple, was exercised ever after with miseries and calamities, so that never any action he undertook prospered; and at length lost both his Army and himself miserably. I could speak of the wretched end of *Antiochus*, who robbed the Temple of *Jupiter Dodonæus*, and of those who stole the gold of *Tholouse*; but these examples are sufficient to let us see, what severity God hath used against sacrilege, even among the Gentiles. What then shall they expect, that with sacrilegious hands have spoiled the Temples of Christians? If he be such a favourer of Superstition, will he not much more patronize the true Religion, and persecute with his plagues sacrilegious Christians, who hath not spared sacrilegious Gentiles? God prospereth false Religions; when conscientiously practised, and curseth wicked professors of the true Religion; for he prefers practice to knowledge, and honest Gentiles to wicked Israelites.

Q. 8. *What other observations may be made of this View of all Religions?*

A. That all false Religions are grounded upon Policy; for what else were the variety of Oracles, Soothsayers, or Divinations by Stars, by Flying and Chattering of Birds, by feeding of Poultry, by Inspection into the intrails of Beasts, &c. What were their multitudes of Sacrifices, Priests, Deities, Festivals, Ceremonies, Lights, Songs, Altars, Temples, Odors, and such like, used among the Gentiles, but so many devices of humane Policy, to keep people in obedience and awe of their Superiors? whereas the true Christian Religion is, of it self, so powerful to captivate and subdue all humane wisdom, and exorbitant affections, to the obedience of Christ, that it needs not such weak helps of mans wisdom or earthly Policy. Yet I do not condemn such policy as is conducible towards the advancing of knowledge in divine Mysteries, or of Concord, Justice and Obedience; for God himself prescribed mutitudes of Ceremonies to the *Jews*: And since the first establishing of the Christian Church, she hath always made use of some decent Ceremonies; which do not argue any defect or want in Religion, but the weakness only of those that are children in Religion, who must sometimes be fed with such milk. Religious Ceremonies, are like the Priests ornaments, which are not parts of his essence, and yet

Ceremonies in Religion.

pro-

| Sect. 15. | of EUROPE. | 363 |

procure him reverence, which *Jaddus* knew, when in his robes, he presented himself to *Alexander*; who doubtless, had he appeared without them, had gone without either reverence or benevolence; so that *Jerusalem* did own her safety and deliverance to the high Priests vestments. Religion without ceremonies, is like solid meat without sauce. Though in the Church of God some are so strong, that they need no sauce of Ceremonies to the solid meat of Religion, yet most stomachs are so weak, that they cannot digest the one without the other. Christ deals not so niggardly with his Church, as to afford her cloaths only to cover her nakedness, he is content to see her in rings, bracelets, jewels, and other ornaments. Thus he dealt with his first spouse of the Jewish Church; *I cloathed thee* (said he) *with broydered work, and shod thee with badgers skins, &c. I girded thee about with fine linen, and I covered thee with silk: I decked thee also with ornaments, and put bracelets upon thine hands, and a chain on thy neck, and a frontlet upon thy face, and ear-rings in thine ears, and a beautiful crown upon thine head,* Ezek. 16. 10. &c. If God was so bountiful to his first Wife, why should he be so sparing to his second, as to afford her no outward ornaments at all? Is she so rich, that she needeth not any? I wish it were so, but I find it otherwise; for she stands in as much need of some outward decent and significant, ceremonies, to help her knowledge and devotion, as the Jews did, though not of so many, nor of the like nature. I observe, that where are no ceremonies, there is small reverence and devotion, and where some cost is bestowed, even on the outside of Religion, there some love is manifested: as our Saviour proves that *Mary Magdalen* had more love to him than *Peter* had: because she had washed his feet, wiped them with her hairs, kissed them, and anointed his head with precious ointment, which *Peter* had not done: This cost was not pleasing to *Judas*, yet Christ commends her for it: I know the Kings daughter is glorious within, yet her cloathing is of wrought gold, and her raiment is of needle-work. This I write not to commend either superfluous, needless, or too costly and frivolous Rites, but to shew how requisite it is to have some decent, significant, and such as may further knowledge and devotion.

Ceremonies in Religion.

Q. 9. *What else may we observe in the view of all these Religions?*

A. That some of them are meerly *Heathenish*, some *Jewish*, same meerly *Christian*, some mixed, either of all, or some of these; *Mahometanism* is mixed of *Judaism*, *Gentilism*, and *Arrianism*: the *Muscovite* Religion is, partly *Christian*, partly *Heathenish*: In the East are many Sects, partly *Christian*, partly *Jewish*, observing Circumcision with Baptism, and the Sabbath with the Lord's day. Among the *Corinthians* some professed Christianity and yet with the *Gentiles* denied the Resurrection; but God always

Mixed Religions.

ways abhorred such mixed Religions, as joyn with *Micah*, the *Ephod* and *Teraphim*, and halt between *God* and *Baal*; *Who are* Hebrews, *and yet with the* Gentiles *round the corners of their heads, and cut their flesh,* &c. *Levit.* 19. 27. God will not have any mixture in the ointment, flour, myrrh, or incense, that is offered to him, but will have all pure: he would not have the Ox and Ass yoked together: therefore the Apostle reproveth sharply the *Galatians*, for using their *Jewish* Ceremonies with *Christianity*: The *Samaritans* are condemned for worshipping the Lord and *Idols*; Christ hated the works of the *Nicolaitans*, who were partly *Christians*, and partly *Gentiles*, and punished the *Gergasites*, by drowning their Swine in the Sea; *For being Jews, they rejected Circumcision, and eat Swines flesh with the Gentiles.* For this cause, *That the* Jews *might not learn the Religion of the* Gentiles, *God would have them dwell apart by themselves, and not mix with other Nations, nor dwell near the Sea-side; and yet we see how prone they were to Idolatry, by the Golden Calf, the Brazen Serpent, the Ephod, Teraphim, and graven Image, taken out of the house of* Micah, *and set up in* Dan. Judges 18. 20. *The Chariot and horses of the Sun set up in the Temple,* as we may read in *Ezekiel*: *The Golden Calves set up by* Jeroboam: *The Idolatry of* Solomon, Manasseh, *and other Kings, and the falling away of the Ten Tribes from God.* The reason of this proneness in them to Idols, was their education in *Egypt*, the mother of strange Religions, where they had been seasoned with Idolatry; and so pleasing his Idolatry to flesh and blood, that they will spare no cost, nor time, nor pains, nor their own lives and children, to please their Idols: thus the *Hebrews* could rise early in the morning and part with their golden Ear-rings to make a Calf: The *Baalites* could cut their flesh with knives and lancets, till the blood gushed out, and could cry from morning till evening: Yea, many Idolaters did not spare to offer their children to *Moloch*: but there is no sin more hateful to God than Idolatry, which the Scripture calls

Idolatry condemned. abomination; *and Idols lying vanities, and sorrows.* And Idolaters are named *Fornicators, and Adulterers, and God will have the very places of Idolatry to be destroyed, Deut.* 12. 2. 3. The *Jews* must not eat of things offered to Idols, nor marry with the Heathen, who having forsaken the true God, made gods of their Forefathers and Benefactors; by setting up their Images at first in memorial only, and then fell to adoration of them; and because they could not see God, who is invisible, they would have his visible presence in some outward Image or representation, thinking they could not but be in safety, so long as they had his Image with them. This made the *Trojans* so careful of their *Palladium*, the *Tyrians* of their *Apollo*, and other places of their tutelar gods.

Q. 10. *Which of all the Religions we have viewed seems to be most consonant to natural Reason?*

A. The barbarous and butcherly Religions of the *Gentiles*, in
sacrificing

sacrificing men, in worshipping stocks and stones, &c. Divers Tenets also in *Mahometanism*, *Judaism*, and many opinions in heretical sects among Christians are against reason. The doctrine of the true Orthodox Christian is above natural reason: for the natural man saith the Apostle, *understandeth not the things of the Spirit*: But the Religion of those *Gentiles*, who worshipped the Sun, seemed to be most consonant to their natural reason; because they could not conceive what God was, being a Spirit incomprehensible: for all knowledge comes by the senses, and finding that no sensible entity was comparable to the Sun in glory, light, motion, power, beauty, operation, &c. but that all things in a manner had dependance from him, in respect of life, motion, comfort, and being, they concluded that the Sun was the only Deity of the world: and however the *Gentiles* might seem to worship divers chief gods, because they expressed them by divers names, and effects, or Offices; yet indeed the wiser sort understood but one supream Deity, which they worshipped under divers Names, Epithets, and Operations. Now that this Deity was none other but the Sun, whom they called by the name of *Apollo*, *Jupiter*, *Mercury*, *Mars*, *Hercules*, &c. is apparent, by the *Gentiles* own writings; for in *Nonnus*, *lib.* 40. *Diony.* we see with how many names the Sun is called; namely, ἄναξ πυρός, King of the fire, ὄρχαμος κόσμου, guide of the world. *Belus* of *Euphrates*, the *Lybian Ammon*, *Apis* of *Nilus*, the *Arabian Saturn*, the *Assyrian Jupiter*, the *Egyptian Serapis*, *Phaeton*, with many names, *Mithras*, the *Babylonian* Sun, the *Grecian Delphick Apollo*, *Pan*, *Æther*, or the Heaven, &c. So *Orpheus in Hymno* under the name of *Vulcan* understands the Sun, when he calls him ἀκάματον πῦρ, a perpetual fire, λαμπόμενον φλογίαις αὔγαις, shining in the flaming Air or Skie. So by *Mars* they meant the Sun, as appeareth by that Image of *Mars* adorned with the Sun-beams, and worshipped anciently in *Spain*, thus adorned. They made him the god of War, because all strife and contentions arise from the heat of the blood, caused by the Suns influence. They meant also the Sun by *Apollo*, so called from πάλλειν, that is, darting or casting of his beams: or because μόνος ὅτι καὶ ἐ πολλοί, he shines alone, and not others with him; therefore in Latin he is named, *Sol quasi solus*: Other reasons and derivations of this name may be seen in *Macrobius lib.* 1. *Saturn.* Some call him *Apollo*, ὡς ἀπολλύντα, from killing or destroying of the creatures, with his excessive heat; whereas with his temperate warmness he cures and drives away diseases, ὡς ἀπελαύνων: and in this respect he was called *Apollo*, and the God of Physick; and was painted with the Graces in his right hand, and in his left holding his bow and arrows, to shew that he is ready and nimble to help and cure, but, slow to hurt, and kill; he was called also *Phaeton* and *Phœbus*, from his brightness and light; *Delius*, from manifesting or revealing all things, therefore was held the God of divination. He was named *Loxias*, to shew his oblique motion in the *Ecliptick*. He

Gentiles worshipped the Sun under diverse names and shapes. Their Religion most consonant to natural reason. Sun the Gentiles chief and only god. Apollo, the Sun. Mars, the Sun.

is called by *Callimachus* πολύχρυσ☉, abounding in Gold, becauſe Gold is generated by his influence, and his beams repreſent Gold in their colour, for this cauſe his Garments, his Hap, his Quiver, Arrows, and Shooes, are by the Poets ſaid to be all of Gold. The Sun was alſo called *Adonis*, which in the *Phœnician* tongue ſignifieth a Lord, for he is the Lord of this inferiour world, and of the ſtars too, by imparting light to them. This *Adonis* was ſaid to be killed by a Boar, and to converſe ſix months with *Proſerpina*, as being dead under the Earth, for which he was bewailed by the Women: but the other ſix months he revived again, and converſed above with *Venus*; which turned the womens ſorrow into joy. By this was meant, that the Sun in the ſix Southern ſigns ſeemeth to die, and to be killed by the Wild Boar, that is, by the Winter; for that beaſt delights moſt in cold Countries, and proves beſt in the Winter. By *Proſerpina* is meant the inferiour Hemiſphere; and by *Venus* the Superior, with whom *Adonis*, or the Sun converſeth, whil'ſt he is in the ſix Northerly ſigns. This *Adonis*, is that *Thammuz Ezek.* 8. 14. (as S. *Hierom* thinks) for whom the Women did mourn. But at his return the *Alexandrians*, ſent by Sea to the mourning Women at *Byblus*, letters ſhut up within a Veſſel of Bull-ruſhes, to ſignifie that *Adonis*, or *Thammuz* was returned, and that therefore they ſhould rejoyce: of this cuſtom ſpeaketh *Procopius*, *Gazæus*, *Cyril. in Eſaiam*, c. 18. 2. as ſome think, and ſo *Orpheus* in *Hymn* by *Adonis*, underſtands the Sun, as may be ſeen in this Verſe:

ΣϐεννυμΨε λάμπωνlε λαλᾶς ἐν κυκλάσιν ὥραις.

Adonis, the Sun.

Atys, the Sun.

That is, *Thou who art ſometimes extinct, and ſhineſt again in the beautiful circling hours*. The Sun alſo is the ſame with *Atys*, a fair boy beloved of *Cybele*, by which they meant the earth, which is in love with the Sun, with whoſe beautiful beams ſhe is comforted. Him they painted with a Scepter and a Pipe, by that repreſenting his power, by this the harmony of his motion, or elſe the Whiſtling of the Winds raiſed by his heat. His feſtivals alſo they celebrated with joy, therefore called *Hilaria*; about the 22. of *March*; becauſe then they perceive the day to exceed the night in length. By *Oſiris* alſo the Sun was meant, whoſe genitals, being caſt by *Typhon* his brother into the River, were notwithſtanding honoured by *Iſis*, and after by the *Greeks*, under the name of *Phallus*, *Ithiphallus*, and *Priapus*, becauſe all ſeminal vertue proceeds from the Sun. Saint *Hierom*. *Ruffinus*, *Iſidore*, and others think, that this was the ſame Idol, which the *Moabites*, *Edomites*, and other *Gentiles* worſhipped under the name of *Baal-Peor*. The Sun alſo is called *Liber* by *Virgil Geor* 1. Becauſe by his light he freeth men from the fears and dangers of the night; ſo he is called *Dionyſius* by *Orpheus* in *Hymns*, Διονυσ☉ ἠ ἐπεκλήθη ὔτεκα δινεῖται ἀπείρονα μακρὸν Ὄλυμπον; He is called *Dionyſius*, becauſe he is rouled about the immenſe and long Heaven. He was worſhipped by the *Egyptians*, under the name of *Apis*, and *Mnevis*, and ſhape of a Bull or Calf, to ſhew his ſtrength, and benefits we receive

Priapus, the Sun.

Apis, the Sun.

Sect. 15. *of* EUROPE. 367

receive by the Sun, especially in the fruit of our grounds; therefore the Golden Calf, which the *Hebrews* did worship in the Desart, and afterwards *Jeroboam* set up, signified nothing else but the Sun who was also worshipped under the name of *Serapis*, as his Image shews; which was made of Gold and Silver, with beams, and painted over with blew, to shew that the Sun at his rising and falling look like Gold, but in his Meridian blew, and like Silver, and so he is called λαμπρὸν φῶς Ἡελίοιο, the glittering light of the Sun. So in Hebrew he is called *Achad*; that is, One; as being the sole light and beauty of the world. And so may that place of *Isai*. c. 66. 17. be understood; *They purifie and sanctifie themselves in Gardens behind One*; that is behind the Image of the Sun, which there is called *Achad*, One of this opinion is *Joseph Scaliger*, in *l. ad fragment. Grec. Veter. de Diis Germ. c.* 4. and *Elias Schedius*; save only that they speak of the Temple behind which they purified themselves; but I think rather, it was the Image of the Sun, which they had in their Gardens; for it is unlikely that the Temples of the Sun, were built in Gardens. *Moloch* also was the Sun; for he is *Melech*; that is, King of the world, to whose sight and power all things are obvious; therefore the *Egyptians* represented him by a Scepter, with an eye on it: now this *Moloch* had on his forehead a precious stone shining like *Lucifer*, or the Sun, εἰς Ἐωσφόρου τύπον saith *Theophylact*. in *Act*. c. 7. and *Cyril* upon *Amos*. The *Valentinian* Hereticks, by the word *Abraxas*, meant the Sun, as I have shewed; for in this word are contained 365, which is the number of days the Sun makes in the Zodiack: And it is derived from *Abrech*. *Ab* in Hebrew signifieth Father; and *Rech*, *King*, in the *Aramæan* tongue. So they made the Sun, Father, and King of the Universe; he was also called *Mithres*, which signifieth Lord, as *Joseph Scaliger de emend. temp. l.* 6. sheweth, and *Claudian* in that verse *l.* 1. *de Stilic*. *Moloch, the Sun. Abraxas, the Sun.*

Et vaga testatur volventem sidera Mithram.

For they thought that *Mithra*, or the Sun, did regulate, and govern the other stars; and in the world Μίθρης is found the number of 365. days. The Sun also was expressed by the name of *Jupiter*, or *juvans pater*, the Father that helps and supports all things; therefore he was painted with *Jupiter's* Thunder in his hand. I know *Jupiter* is most commonly taken for the Heaven, or Air; but I rather think that by this name was meant the Sun. So when *Virgil*, *Ecl*. 7. speaks thus: *Mithra, the Sun. Jupiter, the Sun.*

Jupiter & largo descendit plurimus imbre.

He means not that the Heaven comes down in rain, but the Sun rather, who by his heat elevated the vapors and by desolving them into rain, may be said to come down in a shower. So in another place, *Fæcundus imbribus æther conjugis in lætæ gremium descendit*, Geo. 2. There is also meant the Sun, who is named *Æther*, from αἴθειν shining, or from ἀεὶ θεῖν his constant race or motion. By *Mercury* also was meant the Sun; for he is *Mercurius, quasi medius currens*, keeping his Court in the midst of the Planets. *Mercury, the Sun.*

And

And *Hermes* from ἑρμηνεύειν interpreting; for by his light he expoundeth all dark places. He was painted with wings, to shew the Suns swift motion. He killed many eyed *Argus*, that is, he puts out the light of the Stars, which are as it were, the eyes of *Heaven*. *Mercury* is still painted young, to shew that the Sun never groweth old or feeble: he was pictured with three heads upon a four corner stone, to shew the Suns three virtues, of heat, light and influence upon the four parts of the world, or four seasons of the year. He was held the god of Merchants, because without light there can be no trading. The Sun also was worshipped by the Eastern Nations, under the name of *Bel*, *Baal*, *Belus*, and *Baal Samen*, or *Baal-Shammajim* that is, Lord of the heavens; and by the old *Celtes* and *Noricks*, under the name of *Belenus*; now *Belus*; as *Macrobius Sat. lib.* 1. *v.* 19. sheweth us is the same that *Jupiter*, and *Jupiter* is the same that *Sol*, as I have said, and which *Orpheus in Hym. ad Jovem*, confirmeth Ἀγλαὲ, Ζεῦ, Ἥλιε παμφαέτος, &c. that is, beautiful *Jupiter* the Sun, generator of all things; therefore the Sun is called by *Pluto* in *Phædro*, μέγας ἡγεμὼν ζεὺς ἐν οὐρανῷ, &c. *Jupiter the great commander in heaven, driving his swift Chariot, whom the Army of gods follow divided into twelve parts*, and *Vesta alone stands immoveable in the Court of the gods*, he means the motion of the Sun and Stars, through the twelve signs of the Zodiack, and the Earth standing in the middle. That under the name of *Belenus* was meant the Sun, is apparent by the number of 365. which is found in the letters thereof, answering the 365. days, which the Sun finisheth in his annual motion. By *Hercules* also was meant the Sun, as his name sheweth, being ἥρας κλέος, the glory of the air, his twelve labours are the twelve signs of the Zodiack, through which he laboureth every year; he is called *Alcides*, from ἀλκὴ, strength; for like a strong Giant, he rejoiceth to run his course: *Juno* endeavoured to obscure the glory of *Hercules*; so doth the Air, which the Poets called *Juno*, oftentimes obscure by clouds, mists, and vapors, the glory of the Sun. *Hebe*, the Goddess of Youth was *Hercules* his best beloved; so is the spring-time, wherein the youth of the earth is renewed, the Suns lovely wife. *Hercules* overthrew *Geryon*, and rescued his Cattle; so doth the Sun by destroying Winter, preserve the beasts. The Tenths of the Earths increase were offered to *Hercules*, to shew their gratitude to the Sun for his heat and influence, by which the earth fructifieth. *Hercules* is noted for his fecundity; for in one night he begot eighty Sons, this was to shew that generation and fruitfulness is from the Sun: he was called, ἀλεξίκακος, the driver away of all evils and diseases, by which was meant, that grief of mind is driven away by the Suns light, and infirmities of the body by the Suns heat: he is also much noted for his voracity in eating and drinking; by which was signified the rapid heat of the Sun, consuming the moisture of the earth, and exhaling the Lakes, and Brooks. In the name also ἡρακλῆς is contained the number of 365. He was expressed

sed also by *Antæus* the Giant, whose strength increased as he touched the ground, but being lifted up from thence, he grew weak; so doth the Sun begin to gather force when he is in his lowest declination, and near the earth; but when he is in his *Apogæum* or highest elevation, his strength begins to decay. *Pan* also signified the Sun, whom they painted with a red face, horns, and a long beard, to shew the colour and beams of the Sun. *Pan* was covered with a spotted skin, so is the Sun covered in the dark, with the spotted or starry mantle of the night; his wings and crooked staff was to signify the Suns swiftness, and oblique motion in the Zodiack; he was the God of shepherds, and driver away of Wolves; therefore called *Lycæus*, and so was *Jupiter*; the Sun by his heat and light is a friend to shepherds and their flocks, who by his presence drives Wolves, and other wild Beasts into their dens: the perpetual fire kept by the *Arcadians* in the Temple of *Pan*, was to shew that the Sun was the fountain of heat, which stirs up Venery; therefore *Pan* is described by his fallacious nature: the Suns monthly conjunction with the Moon was expressed by *Pan*, being in love with the Moon. They meant also the Sun by *Bellerophon*; who by the help of winged *Pegasus* overcame *Chimæra*; for the Sun by the help of the winds overcometh the pestilential and infectious vapors of the air. By *Polyphemus* also, they meant the Sun; which is that great Giant with one eye, put out sometimes by mists and vapors arising out of the earth. *Endymion* was the Sun, with whom the Moon is in love, visiting him once every month. *Janus* also was the Sun, who is keeper of the four doors of heaven (to wit East, West, North, and South;) he hath two faces, seeing, as well backward, as forward; in one hand he hath a Scepter, in the other a Key; to shew that he rules the day, and that he openeth it to us in the morning, and shuts it in the evening. *Janus* was the first that taught men Religion, and doubtless, men became Religious, and did acknowledge a Deity, by beholding the Beauty, Motion, Power, and Influence of the Sun. By *Janus* was placed a Serpent, biting his tail, intimating, that the Suns annual motion is circular, beginning where it ends, *atque in se sua per vestigia labitur annus*. By *Minerva* also was meant the Sun, as appears by the golden Lamp dedicated to her at *Athens*, in which burned a perpetual light maintained with oyl; which not only shews the Suns golden beams; and inextinguished light, but also that oyl, as all other fruits, are begot by his heat; for the same cause she was the inventer of Arts and Sciences, and held the Goddess of Wisdom and Learning; for by the moderate heat of the Sun, the Organs of the brain are so tempered, and the spirits refined, that all Arts by men of such temper have been found, and wise actions performed: she had a golden Helmet, and a round Target, the one signifying the colour, the other the Orb of the Sun. The Dragon dedicated to her, signified the Suns piercing eye, as the Cock was dedicated to *Minerva*, so he was to the Sun, to shew,

Pan, the Sun.

Polyphemus, the Sun. Endymion, the Sun. Janus, the Sun.

Minerva, the Sun.

that by these two names, one Deity was meant: no man could look upon her Target, having *Gorgons* head in it, without danger; nor may any without danger of his eyes, look upon the Sun. The *Athenians* preferred *Minerva* to *Neptune*, because the benefits men have by the Sun, are greater than those they have by the Sea, and that hot and dry Constitutions are fitter to make Scholars, than cold and moist: for the fire, which *Prometheus* stole from the Sun, brought Arts to perfection. The Image of *Pallas* was kept in *Vesta*'s Temple, where the sacred fire burned perpetually, to shew, the Sun, the fountain of heat and light, is the same that *Minerva*, **Pallas, the** who was called *Pallas*, from πάλλειν to signifie the shaking and **Sun.** brandishing of the Sun beams, expressed also by the brandishing of the Spear. She had power to use *Jupiter*'s thunder, and to raise storms, to shew that thunder and storms are caused by the Suns heat: she, and *Vulcan* the God of fire, were worshipped on **Vulcan,** the same Altar, to shew, these two were but one Deity, to wit, **the Sun.** the *Sun*, who is the God of Fire, which *Homer* also expressed, by giving her a fiery Chariot, and a Golden Lamp, holding out a bautiful light, she made her self invisible, by putting on the dark Helmet of *Orcus*; so is the Sun to us, when he is covered with mists, clouds, and vapors, which arise from *Orcus*, or the lower parts of the earth; and so he is invisible to us, when he goeth un-**Nemesis** der *Orcus*, of our Hemisphere. By *Nemesis*, the Goddess of Re-**the Sun.** venge, was also meant the Sun; for he punisheth the sins of men, by pestilence, famine, and the sword; for he, by his heat either raiseth infectious vapors, or inflameth the blood, burns up the fruits of the earth, and stirreth up the spirits of men to strife and Wars: as *Nemesis*, raised the humble, and humbled the proud, so doth the *Sun* obscure lucid bodies, and illustrate obscure things. The *Egyptians* to shew, that the Sun, and *Nemesis* were the same, they placed her above the Moon. By beautiful *Tythonus* also they meant the Sun who is the beauty of the world; *Aurora* was in love with him, and rejoyced at his presence; it is the approach of the Sun, that gives beauty, loveliness, and chearfulness to the morning. *Tithonus* in *Aurora*'s Chariot, was carried to *Æthiopia*, **Tithonus,** where he begets black *Memnon* of her; to shew that the Sun in **the Sun.** the morning, having mounted above our Hemisphere, moves towards the South parts of the world, where by his excessive heat in the Meridian, he tawns or blacks the *Æthiopians*. *Tithonus*, in his old age became a weak grashopper, so, in the Evening, the light and heat of the Sun weakneth and decayeth to us. By *Castor* and *Pollux*, they signified the Sun and Moon; the one, that is the Sun, being a Champion, subdueth all things with his heat; the other, to wit the Moon, is a rider, if we consider the swiftness of its motion: they may be said to divide immortality between them; because when the one liveth, that is, shineth, the other is obscured, and, in a manner dead to us: they ride on white Horses, to shew their light and motion. They that will see more of the Sun, let them read what we have written elsewhere

where *in Myftag. Poetico.* But befides what we have written there, we now make it appear, that the Sun was in a manner the only Deity they worfhipped: for the honour they gave the Moon, Fire, Stars, Air, Earth, and Sea, was all in relation to the Sun, as they are fubfervient to him; and the many names they gave to the Moon; as *Minerva, Vefta, Urania, Luna, Juno, Diana, Ifis, Lucina, Hecate, Cybele, Aftarte, Erthus,* were only to fignifie the different operations of the Sun by the Moon; fo that as *Ariftotle de mundo* faith, Εἶς ἢ ὢν, πολυώνυμός ἐςι, God being One, hath many names, from his many effects, which he produceth in the world.

The Sun then in regard of the feminal Vertue, generative faculty, and defire of procreation, which he gives to fublunary creatures, for eternizing of their feveral *fpecies*, is called *Venus à venis*, from the veins and arteries (for thefe alfo were anciently called veins) in which are the blood and vital fpirits, the proper vehicles of *Venus*, or the feminal virtue, and of which the feed of generation is begot; which the Prince of poets knew, when he faid of *Dido's* Venereal love: *Vulnus alit venis.* Every Spring when the Sun returneth to us, he brings this venereal faculty with him; therefore he may be called *Venus à veniendo*, from coming; for he cometh accompanied every year in the Spring with this generative defire which he infufeth in the creatures, which the fame learned Poet; *Geor. l.* 2. acknowledgeth in thefe divine Verfes.

Ver adeo frondi nemorum, ver utile fylvis.
Vere tument terræ, & genitalia femina pafcunt,
Tum pater omnipotens fœcundis imbribus æther
Conjugis in gremium lætæ defcendit, & omnes
Magnus alit magno commiftus corpore fœtus.
Avia tum refonant avibus virgulta canoris,
Et venerem certis repetunt armenta diebus.
Parturit omnis ager, &c.

And in another place *Geor.* 3. he fheweth the reafon why in the fpring, living creatures are more prone to venery, becaufe the Sun infufeth then a moderate heat into the body. *Vere magis, quia vere calor redit offibus,* &c. This venereal defire, is by the Poets called *Urania*, and *Olympia*, becaufe it proceeds from heaven, namely from the Sun, the chief ruler in heaven. And to fhew that by *Venus*, they meant the Sun, as he is the God of love, they fpeak of her in the Mafculine Gender, fo doth *Virgil Æn.* 2. *defcendo ac ducente Deo flammam inter & hoftes.* They paint her with a beard, hence *Venus barbata*, to fhew the Sun-beams. They gave her the Epithets of the Sun, in calling her golden *Venus*, fo doth *Virgil. Æn.* 10. *Venus aurea*, and by the Greek Poets χρυσῆ Ἀφροδίτη, and by the Eaftern people fhe was called *Baaleth Shammajim*, the ruler of Heaven, and Ἐωσφόρος *Phofphorus* or *Lucifer* from the light of the Sun; which *Venus* or the Moon borroweth. So what *Orpheus* in *Hymnis* fpeaks of *Venus* is to be underftood of the Sun: γυιᾶς ἢ τὰ πάντα ὅσα τ᾽ ἐν ἐρανῷ ἐςὶ ᾗ ἐν γαίῃ πολυκάρπῳ ἐν πόντῳ τε βυθῷ τε, that is, thou procreateft all things in Hea-

[marginal note: Venus, the Sun.]

ven, in the fruitful earth, and in the sea or depth. She is called καλλίκομος, fair haired, to shew the beauty of the Sun-beams; And *Euripides* in *Phæniss.* gives her ἐύγω χρυσόκυκλον, a golden circled light. By *Cupid* also was meant the Sun, who was painted young, with wings, crowned with Roses, and naked; to shew the eternity, swiftness, colour, and native beauty of that great Luminary; who may be called the God of love, in that by his heat he excites love in all living creatures, as is already said.

Moon the same Luminary with the Sun. By *Luna* or the Moon, they understood the Sun; for though these be two different Planets, yet in effect they are but one Luminary; for the Moon hath her light from the Sun; therefore she is called sometimes the sister, sometimes the daughter of *Phœbus*; she is painted with a Torch, and Arrows, and with Wings, to signifie her motion, and that her light and operations are originally from the Sun. As the Hawk was dedicated to the Sun, because of her high flying and quick sight, so the Moon was represented by a white skinned man with an Hawks head; for her whiteness is

Moon her properties. not from her self, but from the Hawks head, that is the Sun. They held her to be both male and female; to shew, that she is the Sun in acting, the Moon in suffering; she receiveth her light and power from the Sun, in this she is passive: she imparts this light and power to the inferior world, in this she is active: she is called *Lucina* also from this borowed light, and *Diana* from the divine qualities thereof; for which cause *Diana* was held to be the sister of *Phœbus*: and *Juno* from helping; she was painted with beams about her face, sitting upon Lions with a Scepter in her hand, by which was meant the Dominion she hath received from the Sun; and whereas they made a rain-bow to attend upon *Juno*, they meant hereby that the Sun makes the rain-bow; therefore by *Juno* they meant the Sun. So when they make *Vulcan* the son of *Juno*, they understand the Sun, for he by his heat causeth fire, and not the Moon. And so *Mars* the God of fire, is said to be *Juno*'s son, that is, the Sun, for it is he that inflameth mens bloods, and not the Moon. They expressed the power of the Sun over the Sea and other waters by the names of *Neptune, Nereus, Glaucus, Triton*, and other

Pluto the Sun. Sea Deities. When they would express his operations on the earth, they give him the names of *Vesta, Cibele, bona dea*, &c. when they would shew his power under the Earth, then they used the names of *Orcus, Pluto, Proserpina, Charon, Cerberus*, &c. *Orcus* is from ὅρκος an oath, because they used to swear by the Sun: *Esto mi sol testis ad hæc, & conscia Juno, Æn.* 12. and in another place, *Æn.* 4. *Sol qui terrarum flammis opera omnia lustras: Pluto* is from πλοῦτος wealth, for all wealth, both upon and within the earth, is begot of the Suns heat and influence. When he is under our Hemisphere, he is called the God of Hell, he is said to ravish *Proserpina*, that is,

Proserpina the Sun. the seminal vertue of vegetables, which in the Winter and the Suns absence, lyeth hid in the bowels of the Earth, his influence upon the corn, and other seeds cast into the Earth, and causing them to creep out, thence is called *Proserpina*. *Charon* is from

Charon the Sun. χάρων

χάρα Joy; the Sun is joyful to us by his presence, and as he is *Phœbus* or light of the World; he is also joyful to us by his absence, and as he is *Charon* under the earth, for then he permits the air to receive refrigeration, by which all things are refreshed, *Cerberus* is as much as κρεοβόρος a flesh eater, for as all flesh is generated by the Sun, so is all flesh consumed by the same. *Cerberus* had three heads, to shew that time which devoureth all things had three heads, one present, the other past, and the third to come, now the Sun by his motion is the measurer of time, in which respect he is called *Cerberus*: and so he was represented by *Saturn*, cutting down all things with his Sickle; for all things are consumed by time. *Tempus edax rerum, tuque invidiosa vetustas omnia destruitis.*

Cerberus the Sun.

By what we have said, appears that the wise *Gentiles* did acknowledge but one Deity, giving him divers names, from his divers effects and operations. This Deity was nothing else but the Sun, as we have shewed; whose power is diffused every where, and nothing, as *David* saith, is hid from the heat thereof: *Jovis omnia plena* saith *Virgil*, *Ecl.* 3. all things are filled with *Jupiter*: and elsewhere he sings *Geor.* 4. that God runs through all parts of the earth, of the sea; and of the heaven, *Deum namque ire per omnes, terrasque tractusq; maris, cœlumq; profundum, Æn.* 6. And in his divine Poem he sings that this spirit (for so he calls the Sun, and so did *Solomon* before him in the first of *Ecclesiastes*) cherisheth Heaven, Earth, Sea, Moon, and Stars, and that he diffuseth himself through all parts of the world, and produceth Men, Beasts, Birds, Fishes, which he animates and foments.

Gentiles acknowledge but one Deity.

> *Principio Cœlum, ac terram camposque liquentes*
> *Lucentémque globum Lunæ, Titaniáque astra*
> *Spiritus intus alit, totamque infusa per artus*
> *Mens agitat molem, & magno se corpore miscet;*
> *Inde hominum, pecudúmque genus vitæque volentum;*
> *Et quæ marmoreo fert monstra sub æquore Pontus*
> *Igneus est illis vigor & cœlestis origo,* &c.

But here it may be objected, that seeing the *Gentiles* acknowledged the power and vertue of the Sun to be every where, why did they devise so many petty Deities? I answer, this multiplication of Deities was for the satisfaction and content of the rude people, which could not comprehend, how one and the same Deity could be diffused through all parts of the Universe; therefore the wiser sort were forced to devise as many Gods, as there were *species* of things in this world: And because the ignorant people would worship no Deity, but what they saw, therefore their Priests were fain to represent those invisible powers by Pictures and Images, without which the people thought they could not be safe or secure, if these Gods were not still present with them. They wear affected with fear and joy, according to the absence or presence of their Gods: this *Virgil, Ecl.* 1, imitates when he saith,

Gentiles, their superstitious fear

Nec tam præsentes alibi cognoscere divos.

and elsewhere, *Geor.* 1. *& vos præsentia numina Fauni*; so they held nothing propitious if their Gods had not been present; this made *Æneas Æn.* 3. so careful to carry his Gods about with him, wheresoever he went; *Feror exul in altum, cum sociis, natoque, Penatibus, & magnis diis.* Therefore he foretells the ruin of *Troy*, by the departure of her tutelar Gods, *Excessere omnes adytis, arisq; relictis Dii, quibus imperium hoc steterat, Æn.* 2. Hence such care was taken by the *Grecians* to steal away the *Palladium*; the presence of which made *Troy* impregnable, as they thought: And the *Romans* had a custom, that before they besieged any City, they would first by conjuration or exorcism, call our their tutelar Gods, Therefore when *Carthage* was in any danger of the Enemy, the Priests used to bind *Apollo* their tutelar God to a Pillar, lest he should be gone from them. Hence it appears that they were forced to have Deities in every place: at home they had their *Lares* and *Penates*, in the fields they had their *Ceres, Pales, Bacchus, Pan, Sylvanus, Fauni*, &c: At Sea they had their *Neptune, Triton, Glaucus*; in the Harbour they had their *Portunus*, besides that every ship had its tutelar God set in the stern thereof: *Aurato præfulget Apolline puppis, Æn.* 10. The woods have their *Dryades*: the Trees *Hamadriades*: the Flowers *Napææ*: the Hills *Oreades*: the Rivers *Naiades*: the Lakes *Limneades*: the Fountains *Ephydriades*: and the Sea *Nereides*: But notwithstanding this multiplicity, the wiser sort acknowledged but one Deity, as may be seen in *Orpheus*, who thus singeth.

Gentiles, their Deities under diverse names.

Εἷς δ' ἔς' αὐτοφυὴς ἑδὸς ἔκγονα πάντα τέτυκ]αι.

That is, *He is only one, begot of himself, and of him alone are all things begot.* So elsewhere:

Ζεὺς πρῶτ⊙ γένετο. Ζεὺς ὕςατ⊙ ἀρχικέραυν⊙.
Ζεὺς κεφαλή, Ζεὺς μέσα, Διὸς δ' ἐκ πάντα τέτυκ]αι,
Ἐν κρατ⊙. Εἷς Δαίμων γένετο μέγας ἄρχος ἁπάντων.

Gentiles acknowledged one God.

That is, *Jupiter was the first, and Jupiter is the last thunderer, Jupiter is the head, Jupiter is the middle, from Jupiter alone are all things.* There is but one power, one God the great Lord of all things, *Trismegistus*, confesseth there is but one divine nature, μία φύσις τῇ Θεῦ. In defence of this truth, *Socrates* died, when he was forced to drink poyson for affirming there was but one God. And *Diagoras* laughed at the multiplicity of Gods, and at the simplicity of those who held the wooden Image of *Hercules* a God; therefore in derision he flung it in the fire, saying, Thou hast served *Euristheus* in twelve labours, thou must serve me in this thirteenth. The *Sybils* in their verses prove the same, that there is but one God, Εἷς θεὸς ὃς μόν⊙ ἐςιν ἀπέμεγέθης ἀγένητ⊙. that is, *There is one God, who alone is immense, and ingenerable.* And again; Εἷς μόν⊙ εἰμι θεὸς, κ̀ οὐκ ἔςιν θεὸς ἄλλ⊙. *I alone am God, and besides me there is no other God.* So *Horace, Divosque mortalesque turmas imperio regit unus æquo: He alone ruleth in justice all things.* I could alledge many testimonies out of the Greek and Latin Poets: out of the Philosophers also, to prove that the *Gentiles* did acknowledge but one Deity, howsoever they gave him many

ny names, besides their practise in uniting all the Gods in one, by dedicating the *Pantheon* to them, intimating; That as all the Gods were united in one Temple; so they were indeed but one in essence: the Altar also at *Athens*, erected to the *Unknown God*, doth confirm the same. But this task hath been already performed by S. *Austin*, *Lactantius*, *Eusebius*; and other ancient Doctors of the Church, besides what hath been written of latter years, by *Philip Morney*, *Elias Schedius*, and others, who also alledge many testimonies, that the *Gentiles* were not ignorant of the Trinity of Persons, as well as of the Unity of Essence, which was the *Pythagorean Quaternity*, wherein they held all perfection consisted. Hence they used to swear by Τετρακτὺν, that is, *Quaternity*, which they called παγὰν ἀενάε φύσεως, *The fountain of perpetual nature*; and this doubtless was the same with Τετραγράμματον, the Hebrew name of God יהוה which consisteth of 4. letters; and so doth the Greek Θεὸς, the Latin *Deus*: the *Italians*, *French*, and *Spaniards* express the same name in four letters, so did the ancient *Germans* in their word *Diet*, the *Sclavonian Buch*, the *Panonian Istu*, the *Polonian Buog*, and the *Arabian Alla*, are all of four letters; and so is the name *Jesu*, which was given to Christ by the Angel. The *Egyptians* expressed God by the word *Teut*. The *Persians* by *Sire*, and the *Magi* by *Orsi*: all intimating this *Quaternity*, or Trinity in Unity. So the Greeks expressed their chief God Ζεὺς and the *Egyptians* their *Isis*, and the *Romans* their *Mars*, and the ancient *Celtes* their *Thau*, and the *Egyptian* their *Orus*, by which they meant the Sun, in four letters: and perhaps they meant this *Quaternity*, when they gave the Sun four horses, and four ears, and placed four pitchers at his feet. And it may be that the Queen of Cities and Lady of the World, understanding the Mystery of this *Quaternity*, would not have her own name *Roma*, to exceed or come short of four letters. So *Adon* and *Baal* signified the Sun.

Gentiles acknowledge a Trinity.

Now having shewed that the Sun was the only Deity the *Gentiles*, worshipped under divers names; in whom likewise they acknowledged a Trinity, though not of persons, yet of powers, or vertues; to wit, of light, heat, and influence; so the orb, beams, and light, are the same Sun in substance. I should now shew how superstitious they were in their Sun-worship; some offering horses, and chariots to him, which the *Jews* also sometimes did; others used to kneel to him at his rising; the *Messagets* were wont to sacrifice Horses to him; the *Chinois* and other *Indians* honour him with singing of Verses, calling him the Father of the Stars, and the Moon their Mother; the *Americans* of *Peru* and *Mexico* adored the Sun by holding up their hand, and making a sound with their mouth, as if they had kissed: of this custom we read in Job. 31. 26. *If I have kissed my hand beholding the Sun*, &c. the *Rhodians* honoured them with their great *Colossus*; and many Barbarous Nations did sacrifice men and children to him; such were the sacrifices offered to *Moloch*, by whom they meant the Sun; the

Superstitious Sun-worship.

Gentiles also to shew their devotion to the Son, used to wear his colours, and to prefer the red or purple, the golden or deep yellow, to all other colours, hence the *Germans*, as *Diodor. Sic.* lib. 5. *Biblio* sheweth; *Cæsariem non modo gestant rufam, sed arte quoque nativam coloris proprietatem augere student*; they used to make their hairs red by art, if they were not red enough by nature: of this custom of painting or dying the hairs red, *Martial* speaks, shewing that they used some hot medicaments;

Caustica Teutonicos accendit spuma capillos.

This red colour saith *Clemens Alexandrinus* l. 3. *Pædag.* c. 3. was used to make them more terrible to their enemy, for it resemb'eth blood συγχρὲς τι χρῶμα τῷ αἵματι. I deny not this reason but I believe they had a further aim; for they thought themselves safe, and under the Suns protection, if they wore his colours; and because the Sun-beams look sometimes yellow and like Gold, therefore hair of this colour was of greatest account; hence *Virgil. Æn.*4. gives yellow hair to Queen *Dido*, as *Flaventesque Abscissa comis*; and again,

Nec dum illi flavum Proserpina vertice crimen.

Abstulerat: Ibid. So likewise he gives yellow hairs to *Mercury*, by whom as we have said, was meant the Sun;

Omnia Mercurio similis, vocemque, coloremque,
Et crines flavos, & membra decora juventæ.

Ibid. *Tertullian* sheweth, that women of his time use to die their hairs with saffron, *Capillos croco vertunt*, to make them look like the flame, or Sunny-beams; and so the Bride always wore a vail called *Flammeum*, of a red or fire-colour; and so *Flamminica* the wife of the Priest called *Flamen*, wore always such a veil, as resembling the colour of the Sun, whereof her husband was Priest, but Saint *Hierom* forbids Christian women to dye their hair of its colour, as resembling the fire of hell, *Ne capillos inrufes, & cia liquid de gehennæ ignibus aspergas*: the *Athenians*, to shew how much they honored *Apollo*, by whom they meant the Sun, used to wear in their hairs golden pictures of grashoppers: for these creatures were dedicated to the Sun: τέττιγας χρυσοῦς ἐν τοῖς θριξὶν πλέγμασιν εἶχον, as the Scholiast of *Aristophanes* witnesseth, and so doth *Thucydides*. *Julius Capitolinus in Vero*, affirms of *Verus* that to make his hairs look the yellower, and to glitter like the Sun, he used to besprinkle them with Gold dust; *Tantum habuit curam capillorum flavorum, ut & capiti auri ramenta inspergeret quo magis coma illuminata flavesceret*: and because these two colours of yellow and red were sacred to the Sun; hence Kings and Priests were wont to be adorned with these two colours; for Kings and Priests have been held the great Luminaries within their Dominions; therefore they shined with artificial ornaments, as the Sun doth with his native: hence Q. *Dido* by the Poet, *Æn.*4. is painted with Gold and Scarlet;

Cui pharetra ex auro, crines nodantur in urum;
Aurea purpuream subnectit fibula vestem:

So elsewhere, *Æn.* 11. he describes the ornaments of *Chlorus* the Priest, of Gold and Scarlet also;

Ipse peregrina ferrugine clarus & ostro
Spicula torquebat Tyrio Cortynia cornu!
Aureus ex humeris sonat arcus & aurea vati
Cassida: tum croceam chlamidemque sinusque crepantes
Carbaseos fulvo in nodum collegerat auro.

The Priest is commanded to cover himself with Scarlet whilst he is sacrificing;

Purpurea velare comas adopertus amictu, Æn. 3. It was also a part of Sun-worship to erect high Altars, and to sacrifice to him under the name of *Jupiter* upon the highest hills, because they thought it fit, that he, who was the chief God, should be worshipped on the chief places, and the highest in dignity, should be honoured on he highest places of situation, hence he was named, ἐπάκριῷ Ζᾴς. *Jupiter* on the mountain; of these high places we read in Scripture; they used also to the honour of the Sun, to build their Temples, and erect their Altars towards the East.

Illi ad surgentem conversi lumina solem.

and elsewhere, *Æn.* 12.

——— *ætherei spectans orientia solis*
Lumina, rite cavis undam de flumine palmis
Sustulit———

and to shew the Suns inextinguishable light and heat, they used to maintain a perpetual fire upon their Altars; whence they were called *aræ, ab ardendo*: for the same cause both the *Persian* Kings and *Roman* Emperors used to have the sacred fire carried in great solemnity before them, by this, intimating how careful they were to maintain the worship of the Sun: and so superstitious were the Gentiles in advancing of this Sun-worship, that they spared not to sacrifice their children to *Moloch*, which was nothing else but the Sun: " This was a preposterous "zeal; for that glorious Lamp required no such sacrifice at their "hands, though he be the cause of generation; he gave life to "their children by his influence, but they had no warrant from "him to use violence, or to destroy that nature by Elementary fire, "which he by cœlestial fire did animate. The milder sort of them were content to let their sons and daughters pass through the fire, or between two fires as some will have it, which was their Purgatory, though some were so bold as to run through the fire, and tread with their naked feet upon the burning coals without hurt, which might be done without miracle, as we have shewed elsewhere, *Arcan. Microcos.* of this custom the Poet *Æneid.* 11. speaketh;

Summe Deum, sancti custos Soractis Apollo,
Quem primi colimus, cui pineus ardor acervo
Nascitur, & medium freti pietate per ignem
Cultores multa premimus vestigia pruna.

Lastly, as the Sun by the *Asians*, and *Africans* was described under divers shapes, according to his diverse effects and operations,

Sun, how painted and worshipped by the Northern Nations.

ons, so was he also expressed in the Nothern part of the European world, as he is the measurer of time, and cause of different seasons; namely of Summer and Winter, of Seed-time and Harvest: they described him like an old man standing on a fish, wearing a coat girt to his body with a linen girdle, but bareheaded and bare-footed, holding a wheel, and a basket full of corn, fruit, and roses; by this old age and coat girt to him, was signified Winter, by his naked head and feet, Summer; by the corn and fruits, Harvest; and by the roses, the Spring; his standing on a Fish, which is slippery and swift in its motion, and silent withal, shewed the slipperiness and swiftness of time, which passeth away without noise, ———— *nulloque sono convertitur annus,* and old age comes *tacito pede.* with a silent foot: the wheel signified the roundness of the Sun, and the running about of the year's and the linen girdle might signifie the *Zodiack* or *Ecliptick* line, within which the Sun containeth himself. I think this may be the genuine meaning of the *Saxon* Idol, which by them was called *Crodo,* which *Shedius de Diis Germanis,* thinks to be *Saturn,* and do otherwise interpret it: when they did express the Sun as King of the Planets, and chief ruler of the world, they painted him sitting upon a throne, holding a Scepter in his left hand, and a Sword in his right; out of the right side of his mouth came out thunder; out of the left lightning: on his head sat an Eagle; under his feet was a Dragon; and round about him sate 12. gods; the Throne, Scepter and Sword may signify the Majesty and power of the Sun, who by his heat causeth thunder and lightning; the Eagle sheweth the swiftness of his motion, and his piercing eye, as discovering all things by his light, his treading on the Dragon may shew, that he by his heat, subdueth the fiercest creatures, and most pestiferous vapors; the 12. gods may signify the 12. signs in the Zodiack, or 12. months of the year: when they did express the heat, light and motion of the Sun, they painted him like a man, holding with both his hands a flaming wheel: when they did present the martial courage, and military heat of soldiers, excited in their hearts, by the heat of the Sun, they set him out like an armed man, holding a banner in one hand with a rose in it, in the other a pair of scales; on his breast was the picture of a bear, on his target a lion; the field about him full of flowers by which they signified valour and eloquence, both requisite in a Commander; the arms, bear and lion were to shew the fierceness, courage and defence, that is, or ought to be in military men; the rose and flowery field, did represent the sweetness and delight of eloquence; the scales were to shew, how words should be weighed in the balance of discretion, before they be uttered: when they expressed how the Sun by his heat and influence, stirreth up *Venereal* love in living creatures, they painted him like a woman, for that passion is most impotent in that sex; on her head she wore a myrtle-garland, to shew she is a Queen, and that love should be always green, sweet and pleasant as the

Myrtle;

Myrtle in one hand she holds the world, in the other three golden Apples, to shew that the world is upheld by love, and so is the riches thereof; the three golden Apples also signified the threefold beauty of the Sun, to wit, the Morning, Meridian and Evening; in her breast she hath a burning Torch, to shew both the heat and light of the Sun, and the fire of love which burneth in the breast;

Ardet in ossibus ignis; cæco carpitur igne.
Vulnus alit venis, est mollis flamma medulas.
Ardet amans Dido, traxitque per ossa furorem, Virg. when they did express the Suns operation upon the Moon, they painted him like a man with long ears, holding the Moon in his hands, to shew that she receives her light and power from him; his long ears I think did signifie his readiness to hear the supplications of all men, though never so far distant. These interpretations I suppose are most likely to be consonant to the meaning of those, who first devised those Images or Idols, though the *Saxon* Chroniclers, *Albertus, Crantzius, Saxo Grammaticus, Munster, Schedius,* and others do think these Images were erected to the memory of some *German* Princes or Commanders: but it is unlikely, that the *Germans*, who were as *Tacitus* saith, such great adorers of the Sun and Stars, would give that worship to dead mens statues. *Cæsar lib.* 6. *de bel. Gall.* tells us, that the *Germans* only worshipped for gods those which they saw, and received help from, as the Sun, Moon, and fire, other gods they never heard of. but of the *European* Idolatries, we have spoken more fully before.

Q. 11. *What hath been the chief supporter of all Religions at all times?*

A. The honour, maintenance, and advancement of the Priesthood; for so long as this is in esteem, so long is religion in request; if they be slighted, Religion also becometh contemptible. Whereupon followeth *Atheism*, and *Anarchy*, which wise States considering, have been careful in all ages to maintain, reverence, and advance the Ministers of Religion; for if there be not power, maintenance, and respect given to the publick Ministers of States, all Government and Obedience must needs fail; the like will fall out in the Church, if the Priest-hood be neglected. Therefore among the *Jews*, we read what large maintenance was allowed to the Priests and Levites; how they were honored and reverenced by the people, and how the high Priest had no less, or rather more honor than the Prince, the one being honored with a Mitre, as the other with a Crown, and both anointed with precious oyl. Among the *Gentiles*, we find that the Priesthood was in such esteem, that the Prince would be honoured both by the Priests office and name; as we read of *Melchisedech* King of *Salem*, and Priest of the most High God: *Numa* was both King and Priest: so was *Anius* in the Poet; *Rex* Anius, *Rex idem hominum Phæbique sacerdos*. *Augustus* and the other *Roman* Emperors held it no less honour to be stiled *Pontifices Maximi*, High Priests, than to be called Emperors:

Religion, how supported. Priests their dignity and necessity.

Dignity of Priests among the Greeks.

Emperors: For this cause Priests wore Crowns or Garlands, as well as the Emperors. Some were Crowned with Bays, as the Priests of *Apollo*; some with popular leaves, as the Priests of *Hercules*; some with Myrtle; some with Ivy; some with Oaken leaves, &c. All Priests among the *Romans*, were exempted from Taxes, Wars, and secular imployments. The High Priest at *Rome*, as *Dionysius* witnesseth, L. 2. had in some respect more privilege than the Emperor, and was not to give any account of his actions to people and senate. And *Cicero in orat. pro domo ad Pontif.* doth acknowledge that the whole dignity of the State, the safety, life and liberty of all men: and the Religion of the gods depended from the High Priests. The great King of the *Abyssins*, at this day will be called Prester, or Priest *John*; though I know some deny this. Among the *Mahometans* none of the *Musulmans*, or true Believers, as they call themselves, must take upon him the Title of *Lord*, but the *Calipha*, or High Priest only: and to offer the least wrong to the meanest Priest, is there a hainous and punishable crime. The Priest of *Mars*, called *Salii*, among the *Romans*, were in such honour, that none was admitted to this dignity, but he that was *Patricius*, or Nobly born. In *Tyrus* the Priests of *Hercules* were attired in Purple; and had the next place to the King. In old time among the *Germans*, none had power to punish offenders, but the Priests. The *Trallii* honoured none with the privilege of a Palace, but the King and Chief Priest. Among the *Egyptians* none were Priests but Philosophers; and none chosen Kings, but out of the Priest-hood. *Mercury* was called *Trismegistus*, because he bore three great Offices, to wit, of a Philosopher, of a Priest, and of a King. Among the *Phœnicians* the Priests of the Sun had the honour to wear a long Robe of Gold and Purple; and on his head a Crown of Gold beset with Jewels. The ancient *Greeks* also privileged their Priests to wear Crowns, whence they were called ςεφανοϕοϱοι; in *Rome* the *Flamen Dialis* or *Jupiter's* Priest, had this honour, that his bare word had the force of an Oath; and his presence was instead of a Sanctuary, if any guilty person had fled to him, he was free that day from any punishment. He had power to exercise consular authority and to wear Consular garments; and whereas none had the Honour to ascend the Capital in a Sedan or Litter, save only the *Pontifex* and Priests, we see in what reverend esteem they were in old *Rome*; and no less honour, but rather more, the Priests and Bishops of modern *Rome* have received from Christian Princes. Among the *Jews* we find that *Eli* and *Samuel* were both Priests and Judges: the Levites were as Justices, and by their word used to end all strife, *Deut.* 21. in *David's* time 6000 of the Levites were Judges: and after the captivity some of the Priests were Kings of *Juda*, 1 *Chron.* 23. in the Christian Church, we see how at all times the Clergy hath been honoured; in Scripture they are called *Fathers, Embassadors, Friends of God, Men of God, Prophets, Angels*, &c. *Tertullian* L. *de pœniten.* shews that in the Primitive Church,

Penitents ufed to fall down at the feet of their Priefts; and fome write, that they ufed to kifs their feet. In what efteem the Bifhops of *Italy, France, Germany,* and *Spain* are now in, and in *England* have been in, is known to all that read the Hiftories of thefe places; in *Mufcovia,* the Bifhops not only are endowed with rich Revenues, but alfo with great honours and privileges, and ufe to ride in rich apparel, and in great ftate and magnificence. What refpect the great *Turk* giveth to his *Mufti,* or High Prieft, and in what efteem he hath the Chriftian Patriarch of *Conftantinople,* is not unknown to thofe that have lived there, or read of Hiftory. In a word, Religion flourifheth and fadeth with the Priefts and Minifters thereof; it rifeth and falleth, floweth and ebbeth as they do; and with *Hippocrates* Twins, they live and die together; fo long as the *Gentile* Priefts had any maintenance and refpect left them, fo long their fuperftition continued in the Empire, even under Chriftian Emperors; but as foon as *Theodofius* took away their maintenance, *Gentilifm* prefently vanifhed, and went out like the fnuff of a Candle, the tallow or oyl being fpent.

Religion which is beft

Q. 12. *What Religion is moft excellent, and to be preferred above all others?*

Chriftianity

A. The Chriftian Religion which may be proved: firft from the excellent Doctrines it teacheth, as that there is a God, that he is but one, moft perfect, infinite, eternal, omnifcient, omnipotent, abfolutely good, the author of all things, except fin, which in a manner is nothing; the governour of the world, and of every particular thing in it; that Jefus Chrift the fon of God died for our fins, and rofe again for our juftification, &c. 2. From the reward it promifeth, which is not temporal happinefs promifed by *Mofes* to the *Jews* in this life; not fenfual and beaftly pleafures, promifed by the *Gentile*-Priefts to their people, in their *Elyfium*; and by *Mahomet* to his followers in his fools Paradife; but eternal, fpiritual, immaculate, and Heavenly felicity, in the full and perpetual fruition of God, *In whofe prefence is fulnefs of joy, and at his right hand are pleafures for evermore: fuch as the eye hath not feen, nor the ear heard, and cannot enter into the mind of man.* 3. From teaching the faith of the Refurrection, which none of the *Gentiles* did believe, and not many among the *Jews,* for the *Sadducees* denied it; only Chriftianity believeth it, being affured, that he, who by his power made the great world of nothing, is able to re-make the little world of fomething; neither can that which is poffible to nature, prove impoffible to the author of nature: for if the one can produce out of a fmall feed a great tree, with leaves, bark, and boughs: or a butter-fly out of a worm, or the beautiful feathered Peacock out of a mif-fhapen Egg: cannot the Almighty out of Duft raife our bodies, who firft out of duft made them? 4. No Religion doth teach how God fhould be worfhipped fincerely and purely, but Chriftianity; for other Religions confift moft in facrifices, not of beafts and birds only, but of men alfo; likewife in multitude of unneceffary ceremonies whereas

it's excellency

as the Christian Religion sheweth, that God is a spirit, and will be worshipped in spirit and truth: That outward Ceremonies are but beggarly rudiments: That he *will have mercy and not sacrifice: That the sacrifice of God is a broken and contrite heart*: That he is better pleased with the circumcision of our fleshly lusts, than of our flesh, with the mortification of the body of sin, than of the body of nature. *He eateth not the flesh of Bulls, nor drinks the blood of Goats, but we must offer to him thanksgiving, and must pay our vows.* The best keeping of his Sabbath, is rather to forbear the works of sin, than the works of our hands: and to wash our hearts in innocency, rather than our hands in water. The service he expects from us, is the presenting of our bodies a living sacrifice and holy, which is our reasonable service. No Religion like this doth teach us the true object of our faith and hope, which is God; of our charity which is our neighbour: of temperance, which is our selves: of obedience, which is the Law: of prayer, which is the Kingdom of Heaven, and the righteousness thereof in the first place, and then things concerning our worldly affairs in the second place: no Religion but this, teacheth us to deny our selves, to forgive our enemies, to pray for our persecutors, to do good to those who hurts us, to forget and forgive all injuries, and to leave vengeance to God, who will repay: no Religion like this, teacheth the conjugal chastity that ought to be between one man and one wife; for other religions permit either plurality of wives, or divorcers upon light occasions, or fornication amongst young people unmarried, *Crede mihi, non est flagitium adolescentem scortari*, Teren. or that which is worse and not to be named; but Christianity forbids unchast talk, immodest looks, and even unclean thoughts. Other Religions forbid perjury, this swearing at all, except before a Judge to vindicate the truth. No Religion doth so much urge the mutual justice or duties, that ought to be between masters and servants, parents and children, Princes and people, and between man and man; all theft, oppression, extortion, usury, bribes, sacrilege, &c. are forbid even all kind of covetousness, and immoderate care, but to *cast our care upon God, to depend on his providence, to use this world, as if we used it not, to cast our bread upon the waters, to make us friends of our unrighteous* Mammon, *to be content with food and raiment, to have our conversation in heaven, and to seek the things that are above, to lay up our treasures in heaven; where neither moth can spoil, nor thieves break through and steal.* 5. The excellency of Christianity may be proved from the multitude of witnesses, or Martyrs, and Confessors, who have not only forsaken father and mother, lands and possessions, and whatsoever else was dear to them, but likewise their lives, (and that with all chearfulness,) for the name of Christ: and which is most strange, in the mid'st of flames and other torments, they did sing and rejoice, and *account it no small honour and happiness, to suffer for Christ, being fully perswaded that the afflictions of this life were not worthy of the glory that should be revealed*; and that *after they had fought the good fight and finished their course; a Crown of righteousness was laid up for them.* 6. The excellency of the author commends Christianity above all other religions, which have been delivered by men only, and those sinful men too; as, *Moses, Lycurgus, Minos, Solon, Numa,* and *Mahomet, &c.* But the author of Christianity was both God and man, whose humane nature was without spot or sin original, and actual; for though he became sin for us, yet he knew no sin, *there was no guile found in his mouth; he had done no violence, he was oppressed and afflicted yet opened he not his mouth, but was brought as a Lamb to the slaughter, and as a Sheep before his shearers was dumb, &c.* Isa. 53. his very enemies could not accuse him of sin, he prayed for those that crucified him, and died for his enemies, he was obedient to his Father, even to the death of the Cross; *he did not lay heavy burthens upon other mens shoulders, which he did not touch himself;* but as well by practise, as by precept, he hath gone before us in all holy duties; and as he died for sinners, so he rose again for them the third day, ascended into Heaven, where he now sits at the right hand of his Father, and will come again to judge the quick and the dead. He is the true Messias, who in the fulness of time came, upon the accomplishing of *Daniel's* seventy weeks, not long before the destruction of *Jerusalem,* as was foretold by the Prophets, by whose presence the glory of the second Temple far exceeded the glory of the first, though in all things else inferiour to it. He is the true *Shilo,* at whose coming the Scepter departed from *Juda*; and as it was foretold, that he should come of *David,* be born in *Bethlem*? have a Virgin for his Mother, preach in *Galilee,* and heal all manner of infirmities, and shall reign over the *Gentiles,* so these things came to pass. 7. Never was there any Religion propagated through the world, in that wonderful manner, as this was, if we consider either the Authors that spread it, who were illiterated fisher-men, and yet could on a sudden speak all Languages, or the manner how it was spread, without either, violence or eloquence; whereas *Mahometanism,* and other Religions have been forced upon men by the Sword, Christianity was propagated by weakness, suffering, humility, patience, plainness, and working of miracles, the suddenness also of its propagation, the great opposition it had by the Potentates of the world; whom notwithstanding these fishermen conquered: the largeness of this religious extent, as being spread over the four parts of the habitable earth: I say, all these being considered, must needs shew us what preheminence this Religion hath above all others, the course whereof could not be retarded either by the force, policy, or cruelty of Tyrants, who exposed Christians to a thousand sorts of Torments, yet in spite of all opposition, it went like a mighty Torrent through the world, and like the Palm, the more it was suppressed, the more it flourished: *Per tela, per ignes, ab ipso ducit opes, animumque ferro:* What Religion could ever name such Martyrs, either for number or constancy, as the Christian can?

To be brief, how far Truth exceedeth Error, one God, multiplicity of gods; his sincere and pure worship, the Idolatry of worshipping evil Spirits, Stars, dead Men, brute Beasts, yea, meer accidents and phansies; and how far Divine power exceedeth all Humane power, so far doth Christianity exceed Gentilism. Again, how much Christ exceedeth *Moses*; and the Gospel the Law; and how far the precept of patience and meekness taught by Christ, exceedeth the precept of revenge delivered by *Moses*; how far Baptism excelleth Circumcision, and the Lord's Supper, the *Jewish* Passover, the true propitiatory sacrifice of Christ's body, all the sacrifices of beasts and birds, how far the easy yoke of Christ is lighter than the heavy burthens of *Moses*: and the true Messiah already come, exceeds the *Jews* supposed Messiah yet expected: so far doth the Christian Religion excel the *Jewish* superstition. Lastly, how far *Jesus* in respect of his humane nature exceedeth *Mahomet*; the one being conceived of the holy Ghost, and born of a Virgin; the other being conceived and born after the manner of other men; the one being without sin, the other a thief and robber: the one teaching love, peace and patience; the other hatred, war and revenge: the one curbing mens lust, by *Monogamy*; the other letting loose the reins to uncleanness by *Polygamy*; The one planting Religion in the soul, the other in outward Ceremonies of the body: The one permitting the moderate use of all Gods creatures, the other prohibiting Wine, and Swines flesh: The one commanding all men to search the Scriptures. The other prohibiting the vulgar to read the *Alcoran*, or to translate it into other tongues out of the *Arabick*; the one working by miracles, the other only by cheating tricks: The one propagating Religion by suffering, patience, and humility, the other by cruelty, oppression, and tyranny: The one chusing for his followers, innocent and holy men, such as followed their trade of fishing; the other wicked and prophane persons, whose trade consisted in thieving, robbing, and murthering: The one teaching sound and wholesom Doctrine; the other ridiculous and savourless fables in his *Alcoran*: I say, how far in all these things the man Christ Jesus (not speak of his Divinity) did exceed *Mahomet*: so far doth Christianity excel Mahometanism. And thus have I with as much brevity as I could, taken and given a view of all known Religions, and have set down what use is to be made thereof; and withal have shewed the excellency of Christianity above all other professions in the world: God grant that as it is the best of all Religions, so we of this Land may prove the best of all the professors thereof, learning *to deny our selves, to take up the Cross of Christ, and follow him in meekness, patience, humility, justice, sobriety, holiness, love,* and all other virtues, wherein the life of religion consisteth; laying aside self-interest, idle quarrels, needless debates, unprofitable questions in points of religion, but let us maintain the Unity of the Spirit in the bond of love, and know that Religion is not in words, but in works; not in opinions, but in assurance: not

Christian duties urged.

in speculation, but in practice. *Pure Religion and undefiled before God is, to visit the Fatherless and Widows, &c. to do good and to communicate; for with such Sacrifice God is well pleased,* that not the hearers of the Law, but the doers shall be justified, that not they that cry *Lord, Lord,* shall enter into heaven, but they who do the will of our Father; that without peace and holiness no man shall see the Lord, that they who feed the hungry, and cloath the naked, &c. shall inherit the Kingdom prepared for them from the beginning of the World: And God grant that we may run the ways of Gods Commandments, *walk in love,* tread in the paths of righteousness, fight the good fight, run the race set before us, *with patience,* looking unto *Jesus the Author and Finisher of our Faith;* that having finished our course, and wrought out our *salvation with fear and trembling,* may at last receive the Crown of righteousness. In the mean while let us not forget our Saviour's Legacy; which is, *Love one another, and my peace I leave with you;* Are we not all the members of one body, the sheep of one fold, the children of one Father? Do we not all eat of the same bread, drink of the same cup, live by the same spirit, hope for the same inheritance? are we not all washed with the same Baptism, and redeemed by the same Saviour? why then should we not be of the same heart, and mind with the Apostles? why is there such struggling in the womb of *Rebeccah,* such a noise of hammers in building Christ's Mystical temple; such clashing of arms under the Prince of peace; is this Christianity? Alas we are *Mahometans* or *Gentiles* in practice, and Christians in name. *Now the God of peace that brought again our Lord Jesus from the dead, give us the peace of God that passeth all understanding;* that we may think and do the same thing. That as there is but one shepherd, so there may be but one sheepfold: The Church of God is a little flock beset with many Wolves, of *Jews, Turks, Pagans, Atheists,* why then should we not be careful to preserve peace, love, unity among our selves, the only thing to make us formidable to our enemies; *Concordia res parvæ crescunt.* A bundle of Arrows cannot be broken, except they be separated and disjoyned; nor could the horse tail be plucked off (as *Sertorius* shewed his *Romans*) so long as the hairs were twisted together; as hard a matter it will be to overcome us, so long as we are united in love; but let this band be broken, and we are a prey to every enemy: *imbelles damæ quid nisi prædæ sumus.* If we will needs fight; let us buckle with our professt and common enemies, with the Devil, the World and the Flesh, with Principalities, and powers, with spiritual darkness, and chiefly with our selves: *Nec longè scilicet hostes quærendi nobis, circumstant undique muros.* We have a *Trojan* horse, full of armed enemies in the Citadel of our hearts; we have *Jebusites* within us, which we may subjugate, but can never exterminate; and such is our condition, that we are pestered with enemies, whom we can neither fly from, nor put to flight; *Nec fugere possumus nec fugare.* If we did exercise our selves oftner in this spiritual *Militia,* we should not quarrel so much as we do, not raise such tragedies every where in the Church of Chrift, about controverfies and opinions, quarrelling about the fhell of Religion, being carelefs what become of the kernel. With *Martha* we bufie our felves about many things but negleƈt that *Unum neceſſarium*: playing Philofophers in our difputes, but *Epicures* in our lives. I will end in the words of *Laƈtantius*, *Inſtit* 6. c. 1 & 2. *Innocentiam folam ſi quis obtulerit Deo, ſatis pie, religioſeque litavit* ; *He is the moſt religious man, who offers to God the beſt gift, which is innocency*. *For Chriſtian Religion conſiſteth not in words, but in gifts and ſacrifices; our gifts are perpetual; our ſacrifices but temporary; our gifts are ſincere hearts, our ſacrifices are praiſes and thankſgivings. No Religion can be true, but what is grounded on Goodneſs and Juſtice.*

The Alphabetical TABLE of the chief things contained in the feveral Seƈtions of *The View of all Religions*, &c.

A.

Abbots, how eleƈted,	194
how confecrated,	241
Abraxas, the Sun,	367
Abyſſins, their Religion,	349,&c.
Adamites,	257
Adonis, the Sun,	366
Africa, the Religions thereof,	68
African Iflands their Religions,	73
Albati,	225
Albigenſes, and their opinions,	158
America, the Religion thereof,	74
Southern *America*, the Religion thereof,	81
Americans, their fuperftitious fear and tyranny thereof,	84
Anabaptiſts, of *Moravia*	163
their opinions and names,	254
Angola, its Religion,	72
Antinomians,	257
Apis, the Sun,	366
Apollo, the Sun,	365
Apoſtles, and their office,	279
Arabians, their Religion and difcipline	49,
Armenians, their Religion,	346
Arminians, their tenets,	258
Aſia, the Religions thereof,	1
Aty, the Sun,	366
S. *Auſtin*'s girdle,	183

B.

Babylonians, their ancient Religion,	42
Bel and *Belenus*, the Sun,	368
Bengala, its Religion,	60
Biſhops,	181. & 286
Biſnagar, its Religion,	63
Braſil, its Religion,	82
S. *Bridget*'s Order,	221
Browniſts, their kinds and Tenets,	256
Buildings firft ereƈted for divine fervice.	3
Burial of the dead, an aƈt of juftice and mercy,	94

C.

Calvin's doƈtrine,	168
Camaldulenſes,	200
Cambaia, its Religion,	60
Canons of S. *Saviour*,	225
Of S. *George*,	ibid.
Of *Lateran*,	226
Carmelites,	212
Carthuſians,	201
Cerberus, the Sun,	373
Ceremonies in Religion,	362
Charon, the Sun,	372
Chinois, their Religion,	57
Chriſtianity, its beginning.	128
It yields to *Mahometaniſm*,	129
Its excellency,	381
Chriſtian duties urged,	384

Churches

Churches from the beginning, 1, 2. set Day, Sacrifices, and Church Government from the beginning, 4. and Under *Moses*, 4. After *Moses*, 5. Under *David* and *Solomon*, 6. and After *Solomon*, 7. Among the ten Tribes, 8. In, and after the Captivity of *Babylon*, 20. Among the *Jews* at this day, 21. *Church* Offices sold among the *Jews*, 35. *Church* how to be governed, 289. *Church* Governors, *ibid*. Alterable, *ibid*.
Church of *Arnhem*. Vide, Millennaries.
Church of *England*, deplored, and Remedy against her growing errours 301. &c. Of Protestant *Churches*.
Churches of *Rome*, wherein different from other *Churches*, 303
Cluniacenses, 199
Colours of the Sun worn, 376
Congo, its religion, 73: the Religion of its Northern neighbours, *ibid*.
Cophti of *Egypt*, 349
Creation, the knowledge the *Pagans* had thereof, 50. of it and *Noah*'s flood, what knowledge the *Americans* had, 79

D.

Dayes festival in the Church of *Rome*,
Deacons, and their office, 280
Dead. *Vide* Burial.
Death, how worshipped, 103
Dominicans

E.

Earth, how worshipped, 101
Egyptians, their ancient Religion, 65
Their idolatrous worship, 66. and continuance thereof, *ibid*. Their modern Religion, 67
Elders, 284
Endymion, the Sun, 369
Episcopacy, what among the Presbyterians, 288. How different from Presbytery, 290
Eremites, or Anchorites, 172
Their first manner of living 173
Their too great rigour, 174
Of S. *Austin*, 211. Of S. *Paul* in *Hungary*, 220. Of S. *Hierom*. 224.

Ethiopians of *Africa*, their ancient Religion, 71. Their Religion at this day. *ibid*. The Religion of the lower *Ethiopians*, 72
Europe the Religions thereof, 87
Excommunicate persons their condition, 293. Prophets, Pharisees, &c. could not excommunicate, *ibid*. Why Christ did not excommunicate *Judas*, 294
Excommunication and excommunicate persons considered, *ibid*.

F.

Familists, their Heresies, 256
Superstitious *Fear*, its cruelty, 84
Festival days of Christ,
Of the Saints.
Fez the Religion and Church discipline thereof, 68, &c.
Their times of prayer, 70
Fire, how worshipped, 101. &c.
Florida, its Religion, 75
Franciscans, 215. &c. subdivided into divers orders. 240
Fraternities, 198
Fratricelli, 225
Friars Mendicants, 211. Predicants, 213. Minorites, 216

G.

Gentiles, their gods, *vide* Gods, worshipped the Sun under divers names and shapes, 365. &c. acknowledged but one deity, 373. under divers ra nes, 374. Their superstitious fear *ibid*. acknowledge a Trinity, 375
Georgians, 347
Goa, the Religion thereof, 61
God, acknowledged by the *Americans*, 79. but one *God* acknowledged by the wiser sort of *Gentiles*, 91
Gods of the *Gentiles*, 111. How ranked and armed, *ibid*. Their Chariots how drawn, 112. In what peculiar place worshipped, *ibid*. One God acknowledged by them, 91
Greeks, their Religion and gods, 96, &c. their worship, and how painted, 98. The *Greeks* sacrifices, 103. Their Priests and Temples, 104. their chief festivals,

festivals, 113, &c. Greeks Religion at this day, 338. &c. their Church dignities and discipline. 339
Groves and high-places condemned in Scripture, 3.
Guinea, its Religion, 70,&c.

H.

Hercules, the same with the Sun, 368
Heresie, an Enemy to Christianity, 130
Hereticks and heresies, namely Simon Magus, 130. Menander, 133. Saturnius, ibid. Basilides, ibid. Nicolaitans, Gnosticks, ibid, &c. Carpocrates, Cerinthus, 134, &c. Ebion, Nazarites, 135. Valentinians, ibid. Secundians, Ptolomeans, 136, &c. Marcites, ibid. Colarbasii, ibid. Heracleonites, ibid. Ophites, 137. Cainites, and Cerbites, ibid. Archonticks, and Ascothyptæ, 138. Cerdon, 138. Marcion, ibid. Appelles, 139. Severus, ibid. Tatianus, ibid. Cataphrygians, 140. Pepuzians, Quintilians, ibid. Artotyrites, ibid. Quartodecimani, 141. Alogiani, ibid. Adamians, ibid. Melchisedecians, 142. Bardesanists, Noetians, Valetians, ibid. Cathari, ibid. Angelici, Apostolici, 143. Sabellians, Origenians, Origenists, ibid. Samosatenians, 144. Photinians, Manichees, ibid. Hierachites, Meletians, 145. Arrians, Audians, Semi-Arrians, Macedonians, 146. Aerians, ibid. Aetians, 147. Eunomians, ibid. Apollinarists, Antidicomarianites, Messalians, ibid. Metangismonites, Hermians, Proclianites, Patricians, Ascitæ, 148. Patalorinchitæ, Aquarii, Coluthiani, Floriani, Æternales, Nudipedales, 149. Donatists, ibid. Priscillianists, 150. Rhetorians, Feri, Theopaschitæ, Tritocitæ, Aquei, Melitonii, Ophei, Tertullii, Liberatores, ibid. Nativitarii, Luciferians, Jovinianists, and Arabicks, Collyridians, Paterniani, Tertullianists, 151. Abellonitæ, Pelagians, Prædestinati, Timotheans, 152. Nestorians, Eutychians, and their spawn, 153. Hereticks of the seventh Century, 155, &c. of the eighth Century, 156. of the ninth and tenth Centuries, ibid. of the eleventh and twelfth Centuries, 157. of the thirteenth Century, 159. of the fourteenth Century, 160. of the fifteenth Century, 162, &c. of the sixteenth Century, ibid.
Hierapolis, the Religion thereof, 45.
High places, vide Groves, &c.
Hispaniola, its Religion, 85
Hussites, their tenets, 162, &c.

I.

Jacobites, 348
Janus, the Sun, 369
Japan, its Religion, 63, &c.
Idolaters, their cruelty and cost in their barbarous sacrifices, 77. The making, worshipping of Images, and bringing in Idolatry, 43
Idolatry of the Gentiles, and of all kinds condemned, 45, and 364
Idolatry, further condemned, 85
The Gentile Idols were dead Men, 43
Jesuits, 229, &c. their rules 230, &c. their constitutions and rules for Provincials, 231. Provosts, 232, &c. Rectors, and Masters, 233. Counsellors, 235. Travellers, ibid. Rule for the Admonitor, ibid. &c. Overseer of the Church, 236. for the Priests, ibid. &c. Preachers, ibid. for the General Proctor, 237. for the Readers, Infirmarii, ibid. Librarii, and under Officers, 238. their privileges granted by divers Popes, 239, &c.
Jews, their Church discipline from the beginning, till their last destruction, 4, &c. The difference of the High Priest, from other High Priests, 5. Solomon's Temple and the outward splendor of the Jews Religion, 8, &c. what represented by Solomon's Temple, and the utensils thereof, 11. office of the Levites, 12. Prophets, Scribes, ibid. Pharisees, ibid. Nazarites, 13. Rechabites, ibid. Essenes, Sadduces, Samaritans, ibid.
Jews, their ancient Observation on the Sabbath, 14. how they observed their passover, ibid. &c. their Feast of Pentecost, 15. their Feast of Tabernacles, ibid, their new Moons, 16. their

their Feasts of Trumpets, *ibid*, their Feasts of Expiation, 17. their Sabbatical year, *ibid*. their Jubilee, *ibid*. their Excommunications of Old, 18. how instructed by God of Old, 19. their maintenance or allowance to their Priests and Levites, *ibid*. &c. their Church Government at this day, 21. their manner and time of Prayer. 22. they hear the Law three times a week, 23. their Ceremonies about the Book of the Law, *ibid*. their manner of observing the Sabbath, *ibid*. &c. how they keep their Passeover, 25. their manner of eating the Paschal Lamb, 26. their modern Ceremonies are Rabbinical, *ibid*. observations concerning the Jews at this day, 27. whether to be permitted (amongst Christians) to live and exercise their own Religion, 29. whether Christians are not to communicate with Jews, 30. they spend eight days in their *Easter* Solemnities, *ibid*. their Pentecost, 31. their feast of Tabernacles, *ibid*. they fast in *August*, 32. their solemnities in beginning the New year, 33. their preparation for Morning Prayer, *ibid*. their feast of reconciliation and Ceremonies therein, 34. their rites after the Law is read over. 35. their Church Offices sold, *ibid*. their feast of Dedication, 36. of *Purim*, *ibid*. their Fasts, 37. their Marriages, *ibid*. their Bills of Divorce, 38. the separating of the Wife from the deceased Husband's Brother, 39. their Circumcision and rites thereof, *ibid*. how they redeem their first-born, 40. their duty to the sick, *ibid*. their Ceremonies about the Dead, *ibid*.

Ignatius Loyola, 229
Independents, and their tenets, 274
Independents of *New England*, their tenets, 275
The grounds whereupon they and the Anabaptists allow Lay-men to preach, without call or Ordination, 277

Indians, their ancient Religion, 58. and at this day, 348
John Tany, vide, *Theaurau John*.
Jucatan, its Religion, 80
Jupiter, the Sun, 367

K.

Katherine of *Sena*, 224. *Knights* hospitallers of St. *John*, 205, &c. of *Rhodes*, 206, &c. of *Malta*, 207. Templars, *ibid*. &c. the *Teutonicks* or *Marians*, and their installment, 208, &c. of St. *Lazarus*, of *Calatrava*, and St. *James*, 210. Divers other Orders of Knighthood, *ibid*.&c.
Knights of the holy Sepulchre, 218, &c. Gladiators, 219.
Knights of St. *Mary*, of redemption, *ibid*. of *Montesia*, 220. of the Annunciation, of St. *Maurice*, of the golden Fleece, 226. of the Moon, of St. *Michael*, of St. *Stephen*, and of the holy Spirit, 227, 244.
Knights of the Gennet, 243. of the Crown Royal, of the Star, and of the Broom flower, *ibid*. of the Ship, and of St. *Michael*, 244. of Christian charity, and of St. *Lazarus*, 245. of the Virgin *Mary* in mount *Carmel*, of *Orleans*, or *Porcupine*, of the golden shield, and of the Thistle, 245. of *Anjou*, and of St. *Magdalen*, 246. of *Britain* in *Ermin*, of the golden fleece, of the garter, and of the Bath, 247. of St. *Andrew*, or the Thistle of *Navarre*, of the Lily, of St. *James*, of the Sword, and of St. *Julian*, or the Pear-Tree, of *Alcantara*, 248. of *Calatrava*, of the band or red scarf, of the Dove, of St. *Saviour*, of *Montreal*, of our Lady in *Montesia*, and of the Looking-glass, 249. &c. of *Jesus Christ*, of D. *Avis*, in *Germany*; of the Dragon in *Austria*, of St. *George*, in *Poland*; of the white Eagle, in *Denmark*, of the Elephant, Sweden, of the Seraphims, in *Ceos*, of the Swan, and in *Livonia*, of the Sword-bearers, 250. in *Switzerland*,

of *St. Gall*, and divers orders of Knights at *Rome*, 251
Knights of *Venice*, *Genoa*, *Savoy*, *Florence*, and of *Mantua*, 252. of Knighthood in the East, 253

L.

Liber, the Sun,
Life. Vide *Sociable*.
Luther, his Opinions, 162. and sects sprung out of *Lutheranism*. 164

M.

Magistrates Office, 290
Magor, its Religion, 60
Mahomet, not that great Antichrist spoken of by St. *Paul*, and St. *John*, 118
Mahometans, their Law, 116, &c. their opinions, 117, &c. their sects, 119, &c. their religious orders, 120, &c. secular Priests, 121. their devotion, 122, &c. their pilgrimage to *Mecca*, 123, &c. their Circumcision, 124. their rites about the sick and dead, ibid. &c.
Mahometanism, its extent, 125, and of what continuance, 126
Malabar, its religion, 61
Maronites, 348
Mars, the Sun, 365
Melancholy, its danger, 57
Melchites, 347
Mendicants of St. *Hierom*, 226
Mengrelians, 347
Mercury, the Sun, 367
Mexico, its Priests, and sacrifices, 78
Millennaries, their opinions, 260. the grounds upon which they build Christ's temporal Kingdom here on Earth for a thousand years, 261. the vanity of their opinions, 262
Minerva, the same that the sun, 369, &c.
Ministerial calling, 282
Ministers, called Presbyters, 291, &c. how to be elected, 292. three ways whereby Satan deludes Men ● false Miracles, 53, &c. the fear of Satans stratagems (though illusions) whence it proceeds, 55, &c. our duty respecting the many stratagems and illusions of Satan, 56, &c.
Mithra, the Sun, 367
Moloch, the Sun, ● ibid.
Monasteries and their Laws, 196, &c.
Monks, who were the first, 176
Monks of St. *Basil*, and their rules, 177, &c. of St. *Hierom*, 180. of St. *Austin*, ibid. &c. they are not to beg, 181, &c. the Monks first institutions and exercises, 183. why they cut their hair and beard, 184, &c. whence came this custom, 185, &c. in what account Monks are in *Rome*, 188, &c. how consecrated anciently, 189. Benedictine Monks, ibid. &c. Authors of other Orders, 190. their rules, 191. their habit and diet, 192. Rules prescribed to the Monks by the Council of *Aix*, 193
Monks of *Cassinum*, 194. *Cluniacenses*, 199, &c. *Camaldulenses*, 200. of the shadowy Valley, ibid. *Silvestrini*, and *Grandimontenses*, 201. of St. *Anthony* of *Vienna*, 202, *Cistertiani*, ibid. *Bernardines*, *Humiliati*, and *Præmonstratenses*, 203. *Gilbertins*, *Cruciferi*, and *Hospitalarii*. 204. *Trinitarians*, and *Bethlemites*, 205. *Augustinians*. 212. *Carmelites*, ibid. *Dominicans*, 213. *Franciscans*, 215. &c. their Habits, Schisms, Families, Rules and Privileges, 216, &c. *Vallis Scholarium*. St. *Marks* Canons regular, 220. *Boni homines*, 220. of St. *Maries* servants, 221 *Cælestini*, *Jesuiti*, ibid. of St. *Bridget*, ibid. of St. *Justina*, 224. of mount *Olivet*, 225. of the holy Ghost, of St. *Ambrose ad Nemus*, *Minimi*, of *Jesu Maria*, 226.
Monks in *Moscovie*, 342
Moon, how worshipped, 101. the same luminary with the Sun, 372. her properties, ibid.
Morocco, its Religion, 70
Muscovites religion and discipline, 340, &c. their Monks and Nuns, 342 their Church service, ibid. their Sacraments, 343. their doctrine and ceremonies, &c. 344. their Marriages, 345, &c. their

THE TABLE.

&c. their Funerals, 346
Muggleton. Vide *Reeve*,

N.

Narsinga, its religion, 63
Nemesis, the Sun, 370
Nestorians, 347,&c.
New Spain, its Religion, 76
Festival days there, 80
Nuns in the Primitive times, 187, &c.
How consecrated, 189,&c.
Nuns of St. *Bennet's* Order, 195,
&c. of St. *Clara,* 220. of St. *Bridget,*
221,&c. of St. *Catherine,* 224, &c.

O.

Divers Erroneous *Opinions* which have been lately revived or hatched since the fall of our Church Government, 298,&c.
Orders of Pilgrims, 228, &c. of *Indians,* 228. of divine love or *Theatini,* of *Paulini,* and of *Jesuits,* 229,&c. *Observantes, Cellarii, Ambrosiani, Capellani, Clavigeri, Cruciferi,* and *Hospitalarii,* 240,&c.
See Monks,
Ordination in the beginning of the World, 2

P.

Pallas, the Sun, 370
Pegu, its Religion, 59
Persecution an Enemy to Christianity, 130
Persians, their ancient Religion, 49
Persius, his notable saying, 77
Peru, its Religion, 82. festival days, 83. the *Peruvian's* belief of the departed souls, ibid.
Philippinæ, their Religion, 64
Phœnicians, their Religion and discipline, 48
Poor Pilgrims, 228,&c.
Pilgrims, *vide,* Orders,
Pluto, the Sun, 372
Polyphemus, the Sun, 369
Poverty, threefold, 218
Presbytery, the doctrine and tenets thereof, 278. the office of *Presbyters,* 279. among the Jews, 291. their power to Excommunicate, 292

Priapus, the Sun, 366
Priests and *Levites* among the *Jews,* 4, &c. among the *Mexicans,* 78, &c. the dignity of *Priests,* and their necessity among the *Greeks,* 379. *Romans,* or elsewhere, 380
Princes should be careful of Religion, 356, they must not dissemble in Religion, 360
Proserpina, the Sun, 372
Protestants, 167. wherein they agree with, and dissent from other Christian Churches, 351

Q.

Quakers, their opinions, 269: other opinions of theirs, 270. wherein the absurdities, and Impieties of their opinions consist, 271

R.

Ranters characterized, and their opinions, 273, &c. *John Reeve,* and *Lodowick Muggleton,* their opinions, 267
Religion of the Northern Countries near the pole, 53, &c. of the Nations by West *Virginia* and *Florida,* 75, &c. of the Northern Neighbours of *Congo,* 73: of the *African* Islands, of new Spain, ibid. &c. of the parts adjoyning to *Jucatan,* 80, &c. of the Southern *Americans,* 81, &c. of *Paria Guiana,* and *Debeiba,* 82. of *Asia,* 1, &c. of *Africa,* 68, &c. of *America,* 74, &c. of *Europe,* 87. of *Greeks,* and *Romans,* 96. of *Germans, Gauls,* and *Britains,* 106, &c. of *Danes, Swedes, Moscovites,* and their Neighbours, 108. of the *Scythians, Getes, Thracians, Cymbrians, Goths,* 109, &c. of the *Lithuanians, Polonians, Hungarians,* 110, &c. of the *Mahometans,* 117, &c. of *Christians,* 128, &c. by what engines battered, 130. pestered with divers opinions, 170, &c. of the *Greek's* Religion at this day, 338. of *Moscovia,* 340, &c. of *Armenia,* 346. of the *Melchites,* 347. of the *Georgians,* ibid. of the *Circassians,* of the *Nestorians,* 347. of the *Indians,*

ans, and *Jacobites*, 348. of the *Maronites*, ibid. of the *Cophti*, 349. *Abyssins*, ibid.
Religion the ground of government and greatness, 353. the foundation of all Common-wealths, 354, &c. most requisite in Princes and Governours, 356. one Religion to be taught publickly, 357, &c. different Religions how and when to be tolerated, 358. dissimulation in Religion rejected, 360, &c. false Religions, why blessed, and the contemners punished, 361,&c. religious policy and ceremonies, 362, &c. mixed Religions, 363. what Religion most consonant to natural reason, 364
   Religion, how supported, 379
   Religion, what is best, 381
Romans, their old Religion, 87. their chief Festivals, 88. their chief Gods, 90. their Priests, 92. Sacrifices, 93. their Marriage rites, *ibid.* their Funeral rites, 94
Roman Church different from others about the Scriptures, 303. about Predestination, God's Image, and sin, 304. about the Law of God, Christ, Faith, Justification, and good works, 305. about Penance, Fasting, Prayer, and Alms, 306. about the Sacraments, and their ceremonies in those controverted, *ibid.* &c. about the Saints in Heaven, 308. about the Church, 309. about Councils, Monks, Magistrates, and Purgatory, 310. the outward worship of the *Roman* Church, and first part of their Mass, 311
Roman Acolyths, their offices, ibid.
Romanists their manner of dedicating Churches, 313. and what observable thereupon, 314. their consecrating of Altars, &c. 315, the degrees of Ecclesiastical persons in the Church of *Rome*, 317. their sacred Orders, 318. office of the Bishop, 320. and what colours held sacred, 321. the other parts of the Mass, *ibid.* other parts of their Worship, 323. their Festival days, 324. their Canonical hours of prayer and observations thereon, 328. their processions and observations thereon, 330. their ornaments and utensils used in the Churches, dedicated to Christ and the Saints, 334. their office performed to the dead,
Russians, see *Moscovites*.

S.

Satans stratagems, *vide* miracles.
Old *Saxons* worshipped their Gods under divers shapes and forms, 107
Scythians their old religion, 50
Sea, how worshipped, 102
Sects sprung out of *Lutheranism*, 164
Sects of this age, 265
Shakers, vide *Quakers*.
Siam, its Religion, 59
Simon Magus and his Scholars, vide, Hereticks.
Sociable life preferred to the solitary 175
Socinians, their tenets, 258
Solomon's Temple, vide *Jews*,
Soul, its immortality believed by the idolatrous Pagans, 62. its immortality and life after this believed by the *Americans*, 79. by the *Brasilians* also, 82
Spain, vide *New Spain*,
Sumatra, its Religion, 64,&c.
Sun, how worshipped, 365. the Gentiles chief and only God, *ibid.* his divers names and worship, *ibid.* superstitious *Sun*-worship, 375. how painted and worshipped by the Northern Nations, 378
Syrians, their gods, 47

T.

John Tany, vide, *Theaurau John.*
Tartars, their old Religion, 50. their diversities of Religions, 52. *Theaurau John*, his Opinions, 265
Tithonus, the Sun, 370
Trinity, acknowledged by the *Americans*, 79. denied by *Simon Magus*, and his Scholars, with others, besides *Jews* and *Mahometans*, and why, 131.
Turlupinũ,

Turlupini,	225	**W.**	
V.		*Wickliffe's* Opinions,	161
Venus, all one with the Sun,	371	**Z.**	
Virginia, its Religion,	74	*Zeilan*, its Religion,	64
Vulcan, the Sun,	370		

FINIS.

---

1 THOMAS MUNTZER.

His Opinions, Actions, and End.

The Contents.

MUntzer's *Doctrine spreads, his aims high, his affirmations destructive; He asserts* Anabaptism, *rests not there, but grows worse and worse in his opinions and practices; his large promises to his party and the common people; he endeavours to set up himself, pretending to restore the Kingdom of Christ; being opposed by the* Landgrave, *his delusive animation of his followers; their overthrow; his escape; he is found, but dissembles himself; is taken, but yet obstinate; the* Landgrave *convinceth him by Scripture, when being racked, he laugheth, afterwards relenteth; his last words; is deservedly beheaded, and made an example.*

2 JOHN MATHIAS.

JOHN MATHIAS *repairs to* Munster, *his severe edicts, he becomes a malicious executioner of* Hubert Trutiling, *for contumelious expressions touching him; his own desperate end.*

3 JOHN BUCKHOLD or JOHN of LEYDEN.

JOHN BUCKHOLD *his character, his disputing and contention with the Ecclesiasticks concerning Pædobaptism; he succeeds* John Mathias, *he comforts the people with a pretended revelation; he makes* Bernard Knipperdoling *of a Consul, to become common executioner.* Buckhold *feigneth himself dumb, he assumes the Magistracy, he allows Polygamy, he takes to himself three wives, he is made King, and appoints Officers under him, his sumptuous apparel, his Titles were, King of Justice, King of the new* Jerusalem; *his throne, his Coin and Motto thereon; the King, Queen and Courtiers wait on the*

people

people at a Feast, with other digressions. The King endeavours to raise commotions abroad, is happily prevented. He suspects his own safety, his large promises to his Captains, himself executes one of his wives, he feigns himself sick, and deludes the people with an expectation of deliverance, in the time of famine forgets community; he is betrayed by his confident, is brought prisoner before the Bishop, who checks him; his jesting answer and proposal; he is put to a non-plus, is convinced of his offence; his deserved and severe execution.

4 HERMANNUS SUTOR.

HERMAN the Cobler professeth himself a Prophet, &c. He is noted for drunkenness; The ceremonies he used in Anabaptism. Eppo his Host discovers him and his followers to be cheats. Herman's wicked blasphemies, and his inconstancy in his opinions; his mothers temerity; his Sect convinced, and fall off from him; by one Drewjis of his Sect he is handled roughly; Herman is taken by Charles Lord of Guelderland, &c. and is brought prisoner to Groeninghen; when questioned in his torments, he hardened himself and died miserably.

5 THEODORUS SARTOR.

THEODOR the Botcher turns Adamite, he affirms strange things, his blasphemy in forgiving of sins, he burns his cloaths, &c. and causeth his companions to do the like. He and his rabble go naked through Amsterdam in the dead of night, denouncing their woes, &c. and terrifie the people. They are taken and imprisoned by the Burghers, but continue shameless. May 5. 1535. they are put to death; some of their last words.

6 DAVID GEORGE.

DAVID GEORGE, the miracle of the Anabaptists. At Basil he pretends to have been banished his Country for the Gospels sake; with his specious pretences he gains the freedom of the City for him and his. His Character. His Riches. He with his Sect enact three things. His Son in Law, doubting his new Religion, is by him questioned; and upon his answer excommunicated. His wife's death. He had formerly voted himself immortal, yet Aug. 2. 1556. he died, &c. His death troubled his disciples. His doctrine questioned by the Magistrates, eleven of the Sectaries secured. XL. Articles extracted out of the writings of David George. Some of the imprisoned Sectaries acknowledged David George to have been the cause of the tumults in the lower parts of Germany, but disowned his doctrine.
Conditions whereupon the imprisoned are set at liberty.
The Senate vote the Doctrine of D. G. impious, and declare him unworthy of Christian burial, and that his body and books should be burned, which was accordingly effected.

7 MICHAEL

The Contents.

7 MICHAEL SERVETUS.

SERVETUS *his converse with Mahometans and* Jews. *He disguiseth his monstrous opinions with the Name of Christian Reformation. The place of his birth. At the* 24 *year of his age, he boasted himself the only* Teacher *and* Seer *of the world. He inveighed against the deity of Christ.* Oecolampadius *confutes his blasphemies, and causeth him to be thrust out of the Church of* Basil. Servetus *held but one person in the God-head to be worshipped, &c. He held the Holy Ghost to be* Nature. *His horrid blasphemy. He would reconcile the* Turkish Alcoran *to the Christian Religion. He declares himself Prince of the Anabaptists. At* Geneva, Calvin *faithfully reproves* Servetus, *but he continues obstinate. Anno* 1553, *by the decrees of several Senates, he was burned.*

8 ARRIUS.

Arrianism *its increase, Anno* 323.

THe General Council at Nice, Anno 325 *called as a remedy against it, but without success. The* Arrians *mis-interpret that place,* John 10. 30. *concerning the Father and the Son. They acknowledged one only God in a Judaical sense. They deny the Trinity.* Arrius *his wretched death, Anno* 336.

9 MAHOMET.

MAHOMET *characterized. He made a laughing stock of the* Trinity. *He agreed with* Carpocrates, *and other Hereticks. He renewed Circumcision, and to indulge his disciples, he allowed them* Polygamy, &c. *His Iron Tomb at* Mecca.

10 BALTHAZAR HUBMOR.

HUBMOR *a Patron of Anabaptism. He damned usury. He brought in a worship to the virgin* MARY, &c. *The Senate of* Suring *by a Council reduced him. He renounced the heads of his former doctrine. Himself or Sect still active. He is taken and imprisoned at* Vienna *in* Austria. *He and his wife both burned.*

11 JOHN HUT.

JOHN HUT *the prop and pillar of Anabaptism. His credulity in dreams and visions. He is accounted a true Prophet by his proselites. At* Methern, *his Fraternity became as it were a Monastery.*

12 LODO-

12 LODOWICK HETZER.

LOdowick Hetzer *a famous Heretick.* He gains *Proselytes in* Auſtria *and* Switzerland, Anno 1527. *At a publick diſputation* Oecolampadius *puts* Hetzer's *Emiſſaries to their ſhifts.* Hetzer *denied Chriſt to be co-eſſential with the Father. His farewell to his Diſciples. He is put to death for Adultery.*

13 MELCHIOR HOFMAN.

HOFMAN *a* Skinner, *and Anabaptiſt,* Anno 1528. *ſeduced* 300 *men and women at* Embda *in* Weſt-Friezland. *His followers accounted him a Prophet. At* Strasburgh, *he challenged the Miniſters to diſpute, which was agreed upon,* Jan. 11. 1532. *where being mildly dealt with, he is nevertheleſs obſtinate. Other Prophets and Propheteſſes delude him. He deluded himſelf, and voluntarily pined himſelf to death.*

14 MELCHIOR RINCK.

MElchior Rinck, *an Anabaptiſt. He is accounted a notable interpreter of dreams and viſions. His diſciple* Thomas Scucker, *in a waking dream cut off his brother* Leonard's *head, pretending for his murther obedience to the decree of God.*

15 ADAM PASTOR.

ADam Paſtor *a derider of Pædobaptiſm. He revived the* Arrian *hereſie. His fooliſh interpretation of that place,* Gen. 2. 17. *ſo often confuted.*

16 HENRY NICHOLAS.

HENRY NICHOLAS, *Father of the Family of Love. He is againſt Infant Baptiſm. His deviliſh Logick.*

THOMAS MUNTZER.

*Hei mihi quot sacras iterans: Baptismatis undas
Muntzerus Stigys Millia tinxit aquis.*

His OPINIONS, ACTIONS, and END.

THE CONTENTS.

MUntzer's *Doctrine spreads, his aims high, his affirmations destructive*; He *asserts* Anabaptism, *rests not there, but grows worse and worse in his Opinions and practices; his large promises to his party, and the common people: he endeavours to set up himself, pretending to restore the Kingdom of Christ; being opposed by the* Landgrave, *his delusive animation of his followers, their overthrow; his escape; he is found, but dissembles himself; is taken, but yet obstinate; the* Landgrave *convinceth him by Scripture; when being racked, he laugheth, afterward relenteth; his last words; is deservedly beheaded, and made an Example.*

About

THOMAS MUNTZER.

Anno 1521, 1522.

About the year of our Redemption, M.D.XXI. and M.D.XXII. there rose up in *Saxony* near the River *Sales* a most insolent Sect of certain *Enthusiasts*, among whom *Nicholas Storkius* was no ordinary person.

Hereticks, their usual pretence.

These presumptuously boasting that their *Dreams, Visions* and *Revelations*, were inspired into them from heaven, had slily scattered it among other seditious persons of the same kidney; *That the world was to be reformed by their means*, which done, and the wicked utterly cut off from the face of the earth, it should be governed by Justice *it self*. All that gave not up their names, and embraced their Sect, they branded with the name of *ungodly*.

Muntzer a quick Scholar in a bad school. His Doctrine spreads. His aims high. The end that Hereticks propound to themselves, in opposing the Ministry and Magistracy. His affirmations destructive.

Out of this Sodomitical lake sprung *THOMAS MUNTZER*, one that boasted that he had had communication with God. This man's Doctrine incredibly spred, as being in the first place levell'd at the holy Doctors of the *Reformed Religion*; and from thence discharged at the *Magistrates* themselves; for the Christian flock being once deprived of these two constitutions of men, there were nothing to hinder the greedy Wolves to break out into all rapine, and oppression. And this is the reason why the *Wolves*, that is to say the *false Teachers*, have ever most violently opposed the *Ministry* and the *Magistracy*, in hopes, if possible, to draw these from the care and charge of their flocks, or at least to bring them into contempt with their sheep which by that means should stray into their parties. This *Muntzer* did both by his teaching and writings publickly affirm, that the *Preachers of that time that contributed their endeavours to the advancement of the Gospel, were not sent by God; but were meer Scribes, and impertinent interpreters of the Scriptures; that the Scriptures and the written Word, were not the pure word of God, but only a bare Testimony of the true word; that the true real word was something that was intrinsecal and heavenly, and immediately proceeding out of the mouth of God, and consequently to be learned intrinsecally, and not out of scriptures, or by any humane suggestion.* With the same breath he brought *Baptism* into contempt, most inconvincibly affirming that there was no warrant from God for *Pædobaptism*, or baptism of children, and that they ought to be *baptized after a spiritual and more excellent dispensation*. He further endeavoured to teach that *Christ's satisfaction for us was necessary, whatever honest and weak understanding men could urge to the contrary; That matrimony in the unfaithful and incontinent was a pollution, meretricious and diabolical; That God discovered his will by dreams (whence it was that he was mightily infatuated with them) holding that those were (as it were) communicated by the Holy Ghost.*

Anabaptists their leading principles. Seldom rest there, but grow worse and worse.

Sectaries like tinder, are soon on fire.

Hereupon was he acknowledged by his followers for some heavenly and spiritual Prophet, and it was believed that he was thus taught by the spirit of God, without any humane assistance. This doctrine did he disperse throughout all *Germany* by printed Books and Epistles, which the tinder brain'd disciples of his seditious sect were soon fir'd with, read, approved, and propagated.

THOMAS MUNTZER.

propagated. The same man in the years M.D.XXIII. and M.D. An. 1523, XXIV. taught at *Alsted*, which is a City in *Saxony*, near *Thuringia*; and when not only the *Ministers*, but also the *Magistrate* lay under the lash of his calumny, insomuch that his, Sermons were stuff'd with most seditious and bitter invectives against them, and pretending to groan for the return of lost liberty, and for the insufferable pressures of the people under Tyranny, he complained of it as a great grievance, that their wealth and estates were the prey of the magistrate, and therefore would perswade them that a remedy was timely to be applied to these things. Being for this doctrine dispatched out of *Alsted*, he comes to *Norimbergh*, and thence without discontinuing his journey into *Basil*, and thence into *Switzerland*, from whence at length he came to *Cracovia*, where at a certain town called *Griessen*, he continued some weeks. In the mean time he was no less idle than ever, and that especially in the County of *Stuling*, where he sowed so much of his contagious seed among his factious disciples, as afterwards thrived into an extraordinary harvest. At the same time he publickly scattered abroad his doctrine of *Baptism*, and the *word of God*, in such sort as we have touched before. Departing out of this Countrey, and wandering up and down to *Mulhusium* in the Countrey of *During*, he writ letters to some of the most confident to his Religion; by whose countenance and assistance factious spirits were sometimes more and more exasperated against the Magistrate. Some small time before the Countrey people took up arms, he sent up and down certain Briefs by Messengers, wherein were divers things, and among the rest was represented the greatness of those warlike instruments which were cast at *Mulhusium* upon occasion of this sedition, so to encourage and enflame the fiery followers of his faction. For having stayed two months at *Griessen*, and that he thought he could not so much advance his designs if he returned into *Saxony*, because his affairs prospered not according to his desires in those places, he returns back to the people of *During* and *Mulhusium*. But before he was arrived thither, *LUTHER* had by letters forewarned the reverend Senate of *Mulhusium* concerning him, that they should beware of him as of a destroying wolf, and fitter to be shunned than Serpents, or whatever Mankind bears any antipathy to, for that both at *Swickaw*, and not long before at *Alsted*, he was accounted a tree sufficiently evil and corrupt, which bore no other fruit but Tumult and inevitable destruction; and one, who, no more than his Comerades, could ever be brought to make any defence of their opinions, among which was, *That they all were God's elect, and that all the children of their Religion were to be called the children of God; and that all others were ungodly, and designed to damnation.* And divers other things to the same purpose were contained in the foresaid letter, which was dated from *Weimaria*, on Sunday, being the day of the Assumption of *Mary*, in the year M.D.XXIV. *Muntzer* in the mean time with

An usual pretence to raise sedition.

Hereticks restless.

Luther adviseth the Senate to beware of Muntzer, and his opinions.

words

THOMAS MUNTZER.

Muntzer's large promises to his party, and the common people.

Words plaufibly fweetned, drew away the minds of all he could to favour his party, and by promifing mountains of gold to the common people, to the end they fhould cry him up with the general acclamations of being a true Prophet, it came to pafs that a very great concourfe of the dregs of the people repaired to him from Mulhufium and other places; nay, by his fubtilty and the authority he had gotten, he perverted the very Magiftrate of Mulhufium, and made him a new abettor of his opinion. And this was the firft original of the mifchief; and thence divers other *Hydra's* of feditions like fo many excrefcencies took a fudden growth from this. For all mens goods became common, and he taught that no man had any propriety in what he enjoyed. To which he added, that it was revealed to him from God, that *the Empire and Principalities of this world were to be extirpated, and that the fword of Gideon was put into his hands to be employed againft all Tyrants, for the affertion of true liberty, and the reftauration of the Kingdom of Chrift*: and at this time he gave orders for the repairing of certain warlike engines. While he was wholly taken up about thefe things, that is, in the following year MDXXV. the Countrey people throughout *Sweedland* and *Franconia*, and diverfe other places, rife up againft their *Magiftrates*, forced away a great part of the Nobility, plundered Towns and Caftles, to be fhort, made an abfolute devaftation by fire and fword. The *Landgrave Henry* being moved at thefe things raifes a war, and fought the country people, the firft time near *Frankenhufium*, the fourteenth day of *May*, which done, he prepared himfelf for a fecond fight to be fought the next day, which *Muntzer* having intelligence of, faid by way of animation to his followers, What are thofe Canon bullets? I will receive them in my gloves, and they fhall not hurt me: whereby the country people being encouraged, were the next day beaten by the *Landgrave*, five thoufand flain, and three hundred taken, who had all their heads cut off; fo that, while they were ambitious of *Liberty*, they loft even the liberty of *life* it felf. And herein was the ancient Proverb verified, War is moft delightful to thofe that had never experienced it. The difcreeter part of the country people having laid down their arms, put their hands to the golden plough, to hold which they had been defigned, rather than to manage Lances and Pole-axe. *Muntzer* efcapes to *Frankenhufium*, and hid himfelf in a houfe near the Gate, where a certain Noble man had taken up his quarters. This mans fervant going up into the upper rooms of the houfe to fee how they were accommodated, finds one lying upon a bed, of whom he enquired, whether he were of thofe who had efcaped the fight, which he denied, averring that he had lain fome time fick of a fever: whereupon looking about, he perceives a little bag lying carelefly near the bed fide; he opens it and finds letters from *Albert* Count of *Mansfield* wherein he dehorted *Muntzer* from his wicked purpofe, and from promoting the tumult already raifed. Having read them, he asked him whether they were directed to him, who denying he threatens to
kill

kill him; whereupon he cried quarter, and confessed himself to be *Muntzer*. He is taken, and brought before *George Duke* of *Saxony* and the *Landgrave*, whereupon they having made him confess that he was the cause of the popular insurrection, and sedition, he answered that he had done but his duty, *and that the Magistrates who were opposers of his Evangelical doctrine, were by such means to be chastised*. To which the *Landgrave* made answer, and proved it by several testimonies of Scripture, that all honour is to be given to the *Magistrate*; and that all tumult raised in order to a mans particular revenge, was by God forbidden *Christians*. Here *Muntzer* being convinced, held his peace. Being laid upon the rack, while he cried out a loud and wept, the Duke of *Saxony* spoke to him to this purpose; Now thou art punished, *Muntzer*, consider with thy self by what unspeakable ways thou hast seduced and brought so many to destruction! whereat *Muntzer* broke out into a great laughter, saying, This is the judgment of the Country people. But when being brought to his death, he was thrust into close prison, 'tis wonderful how faint-hearted he was, and stood extreamly troubled in mind, not being able to give any account of his Faith, but as the Duke of *Saxony* pronounced before him, and which he told him he was to make a confession of before God. Being surrounded with souldiers, he openly acknowledged his wickedness, and withall addressed these words to the Princes that were present; shew mercy and compassion, ye Princes, left hereafter you incur by my example the punishment I now suffer; Read and attentively consider the holy Books of the *Kings*. Having said this, his head was struck off, and fastened to a stake, for a monument and example to others.

Muntzer taken, yet obstinate.

The Landgrave convinceth him by Scripture.

Münster when racked, laugheth, but afterward relenteth.

His last words.

Is deservedly beheaded.

Dd JOHN

JOHN MATHIAS.

Primus hic è Batavis Trutzeri dogma sequutus
Turbavit muris Westphala regna modis.

THE CONTENTS.

JOHN MATHIAS *repairs to* Munster, *his severe edicts, he becomes a malicious executioner of* Hubert Trutiling, *for contumelious expressions touching him; his own desperate end.*

Anno 1532.

IN the year of our Lord God, MDXXXII. at *Munster* (which is the Metropolis of *Westphalia*) a certain Priest called *Bernardus Rotmannus* undertook to preach the Gospel of *Christ*; which being done with great success, certain Messengers were sent to *Marpyrgum*, a place in *Hassia*, whose business was to bring along with them some men of learning and good conversation, who should be helpfull in the propagation of the Gospel. From *Marpyrgum* were there some dispatched, who arriving at *Munster*, reduced the principal heads of Christian Religion into *thirty nine Articles*, which they proposed to the Magistrate, being ready, (as they

they pretended) to make good and prove the said heads, by pla- *Pretenders*
ces of the holy Scriptures; which was effected. The *Religious*, *to Religion,*
and (as they are called) the *spiritual* who were possessed of the *proveusual-*
chiefest Church, could by no means digest this, so that departing *ly the di-*
the City, they caused much trouble to the Citizens. Upon this *sturbers*
weighty business, the Magistrates and Citizens sate in long and *thereof.*
prudent Consultations. At length there was a certain agreement,
upon these terms, *viz.* That all injuries committed in those Tumults should be pardoned, and that the Gospel should be freely
preached in six Parish Churches, and that the Church *of our Lord*
only should be absolutely reserved to them. These conditions
were readily subscribed to by both sides, and thereupon all things
laid asleep in peace. But this peace was not long undisturbed by
the *Devil*, (that irreconcilable enemy of peace and virtue) and *The devil*
therefore by doing at *Munster* what he had done at other places, *an enemy of*
that is, by raising up out of the jaws of Hell the seditious and pe- *peace.*
stiferous *Anabaptists*, those importunate disturbers and *turn-pikes*
of the *Gospel*, his design was not onely to discourage the good and
godly, but withall, shamefully to destroy the Gospel it self. For
in the same year there rose up at *Harlem* a *Baker* called *John Mathi-* *John Ma-*
as, a man utterly unlearned, yet crafty and boldly eloquent. *thias a Ba-*
This man being excessively lecherous neglected and slighted his *ker at*
own wife, who being somewhat well stricken in years was so much *Harlem.*
the less fit for the exercises of *Venery*. Being therefore over head *His lechery*
and ears in love with a certain *Virago* who was an Alehouse- *notorious.*
keepers daughter, he could not resolve of any way more advanta-
geous to seduce, than by an *Angelical carriage,* and a counterfeit
sanctity. He made frequent visits to her, and entertaining her with
his visions and revelations, he thereby drew her to his opinion,
and conveighed her into a secret place in *Amsterdam*, where he *At Am-*
professed himself a Doctor and a Preacher, affirming that God had *sterdam he*
revealed certain secrets unto him, not yet revealed to others, and *professeth*
that he was *Enoch* the second high Priest of God. Upon some he *himself a*
laid hands and sent them two by two as *Apostles* and messengers of *Doctor, and*
Christ, dispatching to *Munster* one *Gerard* a Bookseller, and *John* *a Prea-*
Buckhold the Botcher of *Leyden*, and others into other places. These *cher.*
emissary messengers of Christ, or rather of Satan, boyled over
with their various opinions, held marriages of no account, and
dreamed divers other things. Some taught by parables, and
their own illusive dreams; others acknowleged not him a *Brother*
who defiled his Baptism with sins; others preferred the *Baptism*
of *John* before that of *Christ* ; others taught that all Magistrates, *A murthe-*
and whoever were unsatisfied with their Religion, ought to be *rous opini-*
destroyed root and branch; some would acknowledge nothing but *on.*
their own visions and prophecies; others that all the Prophets and
Teachers that were departed this life, should shortly arise again,
and should reign with Christ upon earth a thousand years, and
should receive a hundred fold for what ever they had left behind
them. Some of these men affirmed that they had communication
with

with God, some with Angels; but the more discreet and wiser sort of men conceived that their conferences had been with the Devil. Hereupon the great Prophet *John Mathias* (upon whose account his most vain Apostles already proclaimed a Peace) perceiving an occasion by this means of domineering in this world, consecrated in his stead his disciple *James Campensis*, a Sawyer, Bishop at *Amsterdam*, committing unto his charge the people, to be seduced with the same zeal, as he had begun. These things being thus fairly carried, he repaired to *Munster* to his Apostle and Ambassador *John Buckhold*, whom he made Governour of the City, who presently published these severe edicts, *That every man should bring his gold and silver, and whatever were of greater importance, into the common heap, and that no man should detain any thing at his house for the receiving of which things so collected a place was appointed.* Though the people were not a little astonished at the rigour and severity of the edict, yet did they submit thereto. Moreover he forbad the reading of all books but the *Bible*, all which that they ought to be burnt, the divine authority had by him it's witness commanded.

John Mathias repairs to Munster. His severe edicts.

At this very time a certain Tradesman, whose name was *Hubert Trutiling*, had scattered some contumelious expressions concerning this great Prophet; whereat he being immeasurably incensed, even to the loss of all compassion, caused the foresaid *Trutiling* to be brought into the Market place, where he is accused and sentenced. Whereupon he himself laying his violent hands upon this innocent man, lays him along upon the ground; in that posture he runs him through with a spear; but finding by the palpitation, that there was some remainder of life, he made him to be conveighed thence, and taking a musket from one that stood by, which was charged, killed him, intimating that he was commanded by God, that is to say, his own, (who was a murtherer from the beginning) to do what he had done. This noble exploit performed, he took a long lance in his hand, and hastily ran about the City, crying out that he was commanded by God the Father to put to flight the enemy, which at that time had closely besieged *Munster*. Having taken the said weapon, and running like a mad man upon the enemy, he himself was run through by a souldier of *Misna*.

He becomes a malicious executioner of Hubert Trutiling, for not siding with him.

His desperate end.

JOHN

JOHN BUCKHOLD,

*Agressusque nefas magnum et memorabile Regnum.
Somniat abjecta forfice sceptra gerens.*

THE CONTENTS.

JOHN BUCKHOLD *his character, his disputing and contention with the Ecclesiasticks concerning Pædobaptism; he succeeds* John Mathias, *he comforts the people with a pretended revelation; he makes* Bernard Knipperdoling *of a Consul, to become common executioner.* Buckhold *feigneth himself dumb, he assumes the Magistracy, he allows* Polygamy, *he takes to himself three wives, he is made King, and appoints Officers under him, his sumptuous apparel, his Titles were, King of Justice, King of the new* Jerusalem; *his throne, his Coin and Motto thereon; the King, Queen and Courtiers wait on the people at a Feast, with other digressions. The King endeavours to raise commotions abroad, is happily prevented. He suspects his own safety, his large promises to his Captains, himself executes one of his wives, he feigns himself sick, and deludes the people with an expectation of deliverance, in the time of famine forgets community; he is betrayed by by his confident, is brought prisoner before the Bishop, who checks him; his jesting answer and proposal; he is put to a non-plus, is convinced of his offences; his deserved and severe excution.*

<small>John Buckhold his Character. His disputing and contention with the Ecclesiasticks concerning Pædobaptism.</small>

JOHN BUCKHOLD was a Botcher of *Leyden*, a crafty fellow, eloquent, very perfect in the Scriptures, subtle, confident, more changeable than *Proteus*, a serious student of sedition, briefly, a most fervent *Anabaptist*. This man being sent by *John Mathias* to *Munster* was a perpetual thorn in the sides of the Ecclesiasticks, craftily sifting them about the business of *Pædobaptism*, in which employment he spent nine whole months, and most commonly making his party good with them, both as to disputation and litigious contention, while in the mean time he secretly spawn'd and scatter'd the doctrine of Anabaptism, as much as lay in his power. About that time a certain unknown Preacher of the word of God, one *Hermannus Stapreda* of *Meurs* came to *Munster*, who supplying the place of *Rotmannus* in preaching, seduced him, and leavened him with *Anabaptism*, and he also publickly anathematized *Pædobaptism*. This gave occasion of raising of tumults among them people; they who before were only secretly instructed by *John Buckhold*, discover themselves openly to the world, and lay aside all disguises of their intentions; in most parts of the City, they have their frequent meetings in divers houses, but all in the night time, whereat the Magistrates being incensed, and offended, prohibited their Conventicles, and some they banished; but they weigh not this any thing, and being sent out at one gate, they came in at another, and lay concealed among those that were the favourers of their Sect. Hereupon the Senate caused all the *Ecclesiasticks* to assemble at the Palace, to dispute the business of *Pædobaptism*. In this assembly, *Rotmannus* stood tooth and nail for the *Anabaptists*; but those of the Reformation fully refuted their errors, as the publick acts concerning that business do abundantly testifie. At this very time the ministers of the Church of *Argentoratum* signed and set out an account of their Faith in a printed Book. Hereupon the Senate of *Munster* by a publick edict banished the *Anabaptists* out of the City; which edict, they, persisting in contention, opposed, being now arrived to that rashness and impudence, that they thrust a reformed Preacher, one *Peter Werthemius* out of the Church. Yea, some of them rioting about the City, (whereof the ringleader was *Henry Rollius*) cryed out as they went, *Repent and be rebaptized, otherwise will the heavy wrath of God fall upon you!* These things happened about the end of the year M. D. XXXIII. and the beginning of M. D. XXXIV. Some honest-hearted and harmless men, partly out of an apprehension of divine wrath (as they made them believe) partly for fear of men, suffered themselves to be washed with the laver of *Anabaptism*. For, the *Anabaptists* leaving their dens, broke into the City without any controul, and with an unanimous violence assaulting the Market place, they soon possessed themselves of the Palace and the

<small>Conventicles usually the nurseries of Tumults.</small>

<small>Anno 1533. &c.</small>

<small>Anabaptists their bold attempts.</small>

the Magazine, sentencing with loud conclamations, such as required a greater voice than that of *Stentor*, that all were to be destroyed as so many Heathens and Reprobates, that did not embrace Anabaptism. In this tumult, a certain young man of *Burchstenford* was killed. This gave occasion both to the *Papists*, and to those of the *Reformation* to provide for their safety. These chiefest Patrons of the Anabaptistical Heresy were, *Bernard Rotman, John Buckhold, Bernard Knipperdoling, Gerard Knippenburgh, Bernard Kratching*, &c. These two parties having skirmished with as great eagerness and animosity as greater armies exasperated one against another, for some days, there followed a Truce, whereby it was agreed that every one should quickly enjoy and persevere in his own Religion. However the surges of Anabaptism were not yet laid, till they had entered into a conspiracy to drive those of the Reformation out of the City. The most eminent of the Conclave writ to the Anabaptists of the Cities adjoyning, *viz.* to those of *Dulmen, Coesvelt, Soyst, Warendorp*, and *Osenburgh*, that leaving all things behind them, they should repair with all speed to *Munster*, promising they should have ten fold what ever they left. Being enticed by these propositions, husbands and wives leaving all behind them, came in swarms to *Munster*. A great number of the more religious Inhabitants looking on that strange rabble as an insufferable grievance to their City, left it to the disposal of the Anabaptists, who being by this means increased in number, became also more extravagant, degraded the Senate, and chose another out of themselves, wherein were Consuls, *Gerard Knippenburgh*, and *Bernard Knipperdoling*, whose Effigies is the Ensuing.

Quo non fastus abit quid non Rex impius audet
Carnificem serit qui modo Consul erat

Anabaptists were Masters, most insolent.

BEing now become Lords and Masters, they in the first place seized on *Maurice* Church, and burnt it, and the houses all about it, thence falling forcibly upon other holy places and Monasteries, they carried away Gold and Silver Ornaments and Utensils, and whatsoever else was of any consequence. Upon the fourth day after those rapines, trudging up and down the streets and high-ways, they with a horrible howling, uttered, *Repent, Repent!* to which is added, *Depart, depart, be gone ye wicked, otherwise woe be to you!* This done, they immediately went armed in multitudes, and with unspeakable barbarism and cruelty, turned out their miserable fellow-citizens, as enemies to their Religion, out of their houses and possessions, and thrust them out of the City without any consideration of age or sex, so that many women with child had this misfortune seconded with that of dangerous abortions. The *Anabaptists* presently by what right they please, seize to themselves

selves the possessions of the banished, so that the honest and godly party being cast out of the City, fell into the hands of the Soldiers, who had block'd up the City and all the *avenues*, as among enemies, by whom some were taken, others unadvisedly killed; at which entreaty the other honester part of citizens being discouraged, and seeing that guilty and not guilty faired alike, would not stir a foot out of the City; which being closely besieged by the Bishops Army, all places were filled with blood, sighs, tears. Now do the mad men of *Munster*, and such as no Hellebore can have any effect upon, grow insufferably insolent, and above all, that great Prophet *John Mathias*, of whom we have spoken before: But that sally of his out of the City, those of *Munster* looked on as a great *Omen* of their destruction, and thought that the unexpected death of that most holy man did signify that some great calamity did hang over their heads. But *John Buckhold* must be his successor, a lid fit for the other pot; who addressing himself to the people, comforted them, perswading them that they ought not to mourn for that unlooked for miscarriage of the Prophet, for that it had long before been revealed to him, and withal, that he should marry his widow. Upon *Easter* Eve they fell upon all the Churches and places of devotion about the City, and pulled down all the Brass works. Some few days after, *Bernard Knipperdoling* prophesied that all the chiefest men ought to be disqualified and degraded, and that the poor and the humble were to be exalted. He also declared, that it was the command of the divine Oracle, that all Churches should be demolished, which indeed was sufficiently performed. The very same day *John Buckhold* putting into the hands of *Bernard Knipperdoling*, the Executioners Sword, conferred on him withal his employment, and that according to Gods Command; so that he who had discharged the office of a Consul, was now to execute that most dishonorable employment of a common executioner. This most excellent condition he chearfully accepted. By this time had the City been besieged some months by the Bishops forces when resolving to storm it, they lost both Gentlemen, Commission Officers and others, to the number of about four thousand, upon which they quitted all hope of taking it by force. Some few days after *Whitsuntide*, the City being notwithstanding the dis-execution of that assault still besieged, was wholly taken up to rest and imaginary dreams, wherein there were spent three whole days; which done, *The Anabaptist* being awake, acted the part of *Zacharias*, *John Baptist*'s father; for pretending to be dumb, he desired to have a Table-Book; wherein he wrote down the names of twelve men, who should be as it were the twelve Elders of *Israel*, and should administer all things at *Munster* as if it were the New *Jerusalem*, and this he affirmed that he was commanded to do from Heaven. By this brokery did this crafty knave chalk out his way to that soveraign dignity whereof he was so ambitious. But in the mean time, consider by what a strange *Stitch* this excellently wicked *Botcher* did utterly

John Buckhold succes-sor of John Mathias.

He comforts the people with a pretended revelation.

He makes Knipperdoling common executioner.

About four-thousand men lost at the siege of Munster.

Buckhold feigneth himself dumb.

dif-

JOHN BUCKHOLD,

He assumes the Magistracy. dis-repute that Magistrate whom God had ordained, and by the assistance of most illusive dreams and his own excellency of playing the impostor, he possessed himself of that dignity. A while after our *Prophet* advanced certain conclusions tending to the allowance *He allows Polygamy.* of *Polygamy*, whereat the Ecclesiasticks made some opposition, but afterwards were content to sit still. So that, not long after the Pro- *He takes to himself three wives.* phet at one bout took to him three wives, whereof the most eminent was the widow of the deceased Prophet *Jo. Mathias*, and whom *A bad example soon followed.* he afterwards dignified with the title of *Queen*. This example of Kingship, some other knaves like himself did without any difficul- *Godly and loyal citizens hate usurpation.* ty admit; but divers of the more godly citizens, looking on this thing with the greatest indignation that might be, repairing to the Market-place laid hands on the prophet *Knipperdoling*, which occa- sioning the people to take up arms, they set upon those Citizens in *Loyalty not always successful.* the palace, and having taken them, they delivered the Prophet, and the Ecclesiasticks out of their hands. Nine and forty of the said Citizens were after a most barbarous manner put to death. Here- *Hereticks, their cruelty.* upon the Prophet cried out, that all those who should do any vi- olence to those enemies of God, should do God a very high piece of service, whence it came to pass, that some were torn in pieces with Hooks, and not a few killed by *Knipperdoling* himself. Up-

ANNO 1534.

on the four and twentieth of *June*, which is the day of the nativi- ty of *John Baptist*, in the year one thousand five hundred thirty four at *Munster* or rather *Monster*, (for so may that place be called from the *monstrous* and portentous pullulation of *Anabaptists*) there *John Tuysen schreever an upstart, and abetter of John Buckhold.* sprung from Hell another new Prophet, one *John Tuysentschrever*, a Goldsmith of *Warendorp*. The people being generally summon- ed to the Market place, this man acquainted them, that the most ho- ly prophet *John Buckhold* of *Leyden* was to be exalted to Kingly Dignity, and that he should inherit the eternal seat of his Father *J. Buckhold confirms his delusive prophecies.* David, and should possess it with far greater Majesty. Having prophesied these things, *Buckhold* kneeling down confirmed all, saying, that so much had been revealed to him from God the Father ten days before; though it was against his inclination to undertake the difficulties of Government. The common people being asto- nished at this extravagant piece of villany, tore their hair as they went; yet however some might smell out the cheat, fear was able to sti- fle all muttering. For, this Beast fatten'd for destruction, having been very successful in some encounter, had now assumed what *He is made King.* Authority he pleased. Behold he that at *Leyden* was but a *Botcher*, is made *King* at *Munster*; *John Buckhold* is invested with all the *Regalia* of supream Authority. Having hereupon immediately de- *He appoints Officers under him.* graded the twelve Councellors of State, according to the wonted manner, he constitutes a Vice-roy, a Comptroller of his houshold, four *Huissers* or common Cryers, a Noble-man, a Chancellour, Cup- bearers, Carvers, and Tasters, and Master-builders, and disposed of all other Offices as Princes use to do. The Kingly Robes were *His sump- tuous appa- rel.* some made of water'd stuffs, some made of silk, some of pure silk, some scarlet, some made more sumptuous with the Gold of the

Or-

Ornaments which the sacrilege had furnished him with, so that it can hardly be expressed how artificially, how gallantly, how indeed Emperour-like they were interwoven, being embroyder'd with Gold, edg'd, scollop'd, and disposed into divers colours. His spurs were gilt with Gold, and he had two Crowns of solid Gold, and a golden scabbard. The King walking in these ornaments, two young men in a Courtly and magnificent habit, one of each side of him accompanied him, whereof one carried a naked Sword, the handle whereof glitter'd with gold and precious stones; the other held up the *Holy Bible*, together with a golden Crown shining with most excellent Pearls. A certain Jewel dazling the beholders with the bright sparkling of a Diamond, and whereat was hanged a golden apple (to represent as it were the World) wounded through with two swords a cross, hang'd at his neck. His Scepter was set forth with three golden incirculations. His Nobles, who were eight and twenty in number, clad in green and ashie coloured garments, and having on white Turbants, accompanied him. The Kings Title was, *The King of Justice, The King of Justice, of the New Jerusalem.* In the Market-place there was erected a Throne for him of three steps high, which, when the King sate in it, was adorned with ornaments of more than *Attalick* sumptuousness. Some Money he caused to be coin'd, whereon was this Latin Inscription, VERBUM CARO FACTUM QUOD HABITAT IN NOBIS, that is, *the word made flesh, which dwelleth in us.* The City being all this while besieg'd, the Prophets and the Doctors published the Book called THE RESTITUTIONS, wherein they endeavoured to defend that *Monstrous* (I would say *Munstrous*) and seditious tumult, and all those almost infinite inconveniences that were consequent to it: but to prevent that poisonous Hydra, a Gospel antidote was prescrib'd in the month of *August*, about St. *Bartholomews* day, *John Tuysentschrever* went sounding a Trumpet through all the streets, thereby inviting all to the Lords Palace, where there being a sumptuous feast prepared, he magnificently entertained all that came. The King himself, the Queen, and all the Courtiers waited on them. At the last course he gave to every one a loaf of unleavened bread, saying, *Take eat, and celebrate the Lords death*; which done the Queen in like manner carried about the *Cup*, by which ceremony, the Supper of the Lord, or rather that Scene of pleasure, wantonness and temerity, was certainly very frolickly celebrated. Hunger being banished far enough by this feast, the Prophet *Tuysentschrever*, goes up to preach, requiring of them obedience and complyance with the word of God, whereunto (with one head and as with one eye) they unanimously consented. This obtained; he acquaints them, that it was revealed from the heaven, Father, that eight and twenty Ecclesiasticks should depart out of this City, that should preach our doctrine throughout the World, whose names he recommended, and designed the way they were to take their journey, that is to say, six for *Osenburg*, as many for

His Titles were King of Justice, King of the new Jerusalem. His Throne. His Coin and Motto thereon.

The King, Queen, and Courtiers wait on the people at a Feast. A mock Sacrament.

A Seditious Sermon.

their Rendezvous at the house of *Peter Gael*, broke out in the night time to the Market place, wherein being more and more seconded by some of their own, they killed some of the watch and some they kept prisoners. But the Burghers making head, discharged some Musquets at the Anabaptists, who most unworthily, when their Consuls were cruelly killed, entrusted their safety to their heels; so that the others courages being heightned by this, they violently ran upon the *Deuterobaptists*, and after a most bloody engagement put them to the worst, wherein *John Geel* and *Gotbeit* were slain, *James Campensis* was taken and put to death. Now other Tumults had already forced others from those places, the prevention whereof could not be possibly without the infinite inconveniences which fell upon the honester sort. There wanted not also some clandestine vipers, who disguisedly waited for the restauration of the kingdom of *Israel* (as they called it) whereof one being apprehended at *Leyden*, and upon examination put to the question, confessed, That the King of the Anabaptists, who was a *Hollander* sojourned then at *Utrecht*; and had not yet began his reign, but that according to the good hope they had conceived of him, and the confidence placed in him, they doubted not but he would undertake it. Having with what's above, gotten out of this fellow, that some gold and silver vessels and other ornaments had by a most wicked surprise, been take out of their Churches by the means of their King, and who with his followers had attempted some most detestable villanies, it was discover'd that there could no other be meant than *David George*. I crave thy pardon, courteous Reader, if I acquaint thee, that it is not any thing the less for thy advantage, if, in the description of these rotten and contemptible rags and menstruous clouts of humanity, I have woven a longer web of discourse than thou did'st expect. Although *John Buckhold*, and the other Prophets had entertained the ignorant greedy vulgar with hopes of more than *Arabian* wealth, yet the citizens being daily more and more streightned by the siege, were accordingly brought into greater perplexities, and being brought low by the famine, which is the consummation of all misery, began, as it for the most part happens, upon the barking of the stomach, to snarle at one another, to grumble and complain, and to hold private consultations about the taking of their King, and by delivering him to the enemies, to better the terms of their composition. But the King, the stitcher, and botcher of all deceit, being afraid of himself, chose out of all the people twelve men in whom he could place most confidence, and these he called his *Captains*, assigning to them their several guards and posts in the City, which they were to make good. This done, he promised the Citizens that the close siege should be raised before *Easter*; for he was confident that a certain emissary, whom he had sent into *Zealand*, *Holland*, and *Friezland* should return with such supplies, as by a furious and desperate assault made upon the besiegers should deliver the City;

They break out in the night time.

They are worsted.

Famine the consummation of all misery.

The King suspects his own safety.

City: But hope it self was to him become hopeless, nor could safety it self save him. To his Captains as he called them, 'tis incredible what wealth he promised, such as the fabulous riches of *Pactolus* and the treasures of *Midas* should not make good, with oceans of goods (which haply must be paid them out of his dreams) and that after the City were relieved, they should be *Dukes* and Governours of *Provinces*, and particularly that *John Denker* should be Elector of *Saxony*? But behold, in the month of *February*, a sad face of things appeared, many being meerly starved to death, which occasioned, that one of his *Queens* (for he had gotten a many) *Elza* or *Elizabeth*, who was distinguished by the name of the *Glove-maker*, had been often heard to say, that the most cruel sword of *Famine* came not from God, which though he had not heard himself, having caused her to be brought with his other wives into the market place, he struck off her head, kneeling in the mid'st of them, which done, insulting over her, he affirmed that she had carried her self as a common prostituted whore, and had been disobedient to him, while in the mean time her fellow Queens sung this hymn, *Glory be to God on high* &c. *Easter* day being now dawning: and no hope of deliverance shining on them, the common people with just reason were extreamly astonished; nor, considering how things were carried, could they have any longer patience. In this conjuncture of affairs, to elude the people, according to his wonted insinuations, he feigns himself to be sick, and that after six days, he would appear publickly in the Market-place, but that as to the *deliverance* which they were to expect according to his intimation, it was to be understood after a *spiritual manner*, and so it should certainly come to pass. For he affirmed for a most certain truth, that in a divine dream he saw himself riding on an Ass, and bearing the unspeakable weight of sin, and that all that had followed him were freed from their sins. But indeed they may be fitly said to be like Asses that rub one another; or to the blind leading about the blind. It is a great affliction, it is a penance to repeat the miseries and the woful consequences of Famine and want. There were a many who being impatient of so long hunger, revolted to the enemy, not so much out of hope of compassion, as to accelerate their own deaths; not a few creeping upon all four, endeavoured to get away; for being weak and strengthless, they could hardly fasten their feet on the ground; some falling down were content to give up the ghost in the place were they lay. There you might see a sad spectacle of foreheads and cheeks pale as ashes, temples fallen, eyes sunk into hollowness, sharp noses, ears shrivel'd, lips black and blue, throats slender as those of spiders; to be short, *Hypocritical* faces, living carcases, and excellent shadows of men. They had sown certain kinds of seeds and pulses in the City, which for a time served for high delicacies to the grumbling stomach; but these being soon devoured by the hungry belly; *Cats*, *Dormice*, and *Rats*, which themselves were almost starv'd to anatomy, became (doubtful) entertainments,

His large promises to his Captains, both of moneys and preferments, the usual baits of sedition.

He becomes executioner to one of his wives.

He feigns himself sick, and deludes the people with an expectation of deliverance.

Famine it's character, and miseries.

ments. Some were reduced to that inhumane necessity, that they fed on the flesh of the buried carcasses; some drest the feet of sweaty woollen socks, some cut to pieces the parings of tanned leather, and mincing them with some other things, bak'd them and made them serve for bread. To this we may add, that the most wickedly obstinate citizens were not yet convinced, that by crafty insinuations and specious suggestions they were brought into the noose, whom therefore he still entertained with considerations of Magnanimity and the deliverance they were yet constantly to expect from God, but as for those who admitted any thoughts of running away, and endeavoured to avoid their miseries, he peremptorily sends for, and like a publick Robber taking away all that their industry had furnished them with, *depart*, says he, *and be gone* to *Hereticks, and bid farewel to this place*. The King, though he had gotten at his house sufficient provision for two months, yet was he willing to imbrace all occasions whereby he might keep up the heart of the City which now continually barked for sustenance. To which end, behold a certain man named *John Longstrat*, being a Nobleman and privy Councellour to the King, and one of whom he was very confident, boasted that he would within fourteen days relieve this hunger starv'd City, both with provisions and supplies of men, to the number of three hundred. By this pretence he flies to the enemy, and betrays the City to the Bishop, for a certain sum of money with his life included. The Eve of *Saint John* was appointed for the execution of this design, about ten of the clock, at which time he had obliged himself by oath to cause the gate called the Crosse-gate to be opened. This Commissary for provisions returning at length to the City, assured the King upon his faith and reputation, that the said recruits of provision and forces should be ready within the time appointed. The day assigned being come, he acquaints the Guards that the promised forces, were to come in in the night (which would be star-light enough) that so they might receive them as friends. The gates are hereupon set open, and the enemies being admitted into the City as into another *Troy*, upon the Watch word given, soon dispatch'd the Guards and others that were near. Now could be nothing heard for the cry of Arms, Arms. The King and his Courtiers being gotten into a body, drove back the enemies to the Gates, which the citizens had by that time shut again: whereupon the rest of them that were without, were forced to set Engines to force open the Gates, which being once broken open, they flourished and set up their Colours. The Citizens stiffly resisted the first assault, and made a strong body in the Market place, where the fight became very hot and bloody. The *King* himself, *Knipperdoling* and *Kratching* fell into the enemies hands; but *Rotman* seeing there was no possibility of safety, rushing where the enemy was thickest, was trod to pieces; he it seems placing all hopes of life in death. The Anabaptists upon the taking of their King being quite cast down and discouraged, went and hid themselves in

He forgets community.

J. Longstrat his confident betrays him by stratagem.

Larders,

Larders, Kitchins, and other lurking holes. The City was most *The City of* unmercifully plundered; and to make a full search of it, there *Munster* were ten days allotted. There was found by those of the Kings *unmerciful-* Guard at the Royal Palace as much provision as would maintain *ly plunder-* two hundred for two months. O *Goodman King*, where is now *ed.* the *Community* of goods and provisions which your Religion holds forth? This sad fate did that City suffer in the year one thousand five hundred thirty and five. The third day after the sacking of *The King* the City, the King was carried to the Castle of *Dulmen*, three *is brought* miles off. The Bishop having caused the King to be brought with *prisoner be-* all speed before him, said to him, O thou cast away of Mankind, by *fore the* what deplorable means hast thou corrupted and destroyed my peo- *Bishop.* ple! To which the King, with an undisturbed and proud deport- *Who (de-* ment made answer thus; O thou *Pope* have we done thee any in- *servedly)* jury, by delivering into thy hands a most well-fortified and invin- *checks him.* cible City? But if thou thinkest thy self any way injur'd or en- *His jesting* damag'd by us, if thou wilt but hearken to our advice, thou *answer and* shalt be easily enriched. The Bishop hardly abstaining from laugh- *proposal,* ing, desired him to discover that secret, to which he replyed, Cause an Iron Cage or Basket to be made, and cover it with lea- ther, and carry me into all the parts of thy Country to be seen for a shew, and if thou take but a penny of every one for the sight, assure thy self it will amount to more then all the charges of the war. The more eminent Anabaptists wore about their necks a cer- tain medal wherein was the effigies of their King, to which were added these letters, D. W. F. whereby was signified, that *the word was made flesh*. But the King being carried up and down as a cap- tive with his two associates, was shewn to divers Captains and Ec- clesiasticks of the *Landgrave*, which gave occasion of disputation between them about some things, as of the *Kingdom of Christ*, and of *Magistracy*, of *Justification*, and of *Baptism*, of the *Lord's Sup- per*, and of the *Incarnation* of *Christ*, as also of *Matrimony*: in which disputation, they prevailed so far by the divine testimonies of holy writ, that they brought the King of the Anabaptists, *King of the* (though not acknowledging the least satisfaction) to a Non-plus, *Anabap-* who to obtain another disputation out of hopes of life (as was said) *tists put to* promised that he would reduce the Anabaptists, which swarmed in *a Non-plus.* *Holland, Brabant, England*, and *Friezland*; and that he would do all honour to the Magistrate. Upon the twentieth of *January* Ann.1536, one thousand five hundred thirty and six, he is brought with his companions to *Munster*, where they were secured in several pri- sons; two days were spent in weeding and rooting up their errors. The King indeed confessed his offences, and cast himself wholly *He is con-* upon *Christ*, but his companions discover'd a vain obstinacy in the *vinced of* defence of their cause. The next day the King is brought to the *his offen-* place of execution, fasten'd to a stake and is pulled piece-meal by *ces.* two executioners, with pincers red hot out of the fire. The first *His deser-* pains he felt, he suppressed, at the second he implor'd God's mercy. *ved, and* For a whole hour was he pull'd and delacerated with those instru- *severe exe-* ments, *cution.*

ments, and at length, to haften fomewhat his death, run through with a fword. His companions were dipped with the baptifm of the fame punifhment, which they fuffered courageoufly; all whofe carcaffes put into Iron baskets; as anathema's of eternal example hang out of the tower of *S. Lambert*. And this was the retiring room of the Tragedy of *Munfter*.

HERMANUS SUTOR, &c.

Hic, qui se Chriſtum et qui ſe Jactarat IESUM,
Servaſſe haud potuit ſeq; ſuiſq; fidem.

THE CONTENTS.

HERMAN *the* Cobler *profeſſeth himſelf a Prophet, &c. He is noted for drunkenneſs; The ceremonies he uſed in* Anabaptiſm. Eppo *his Hoſt diſcovers him and his followers to be cheats.* Herman's *wicked blaſphemies, and his inconſtancy in his opinions; his mothers temerity; his Sect convinced, and fall off from him; by one* Drewjis *of his Sect he is handled roughly;* Herman *is taken by* Charles *Lord of* Guelderland, *&c. and is brought priſoner to* Groeninghen; *when queſtioned in his torments, he hardened himſelf and died miſerably.*

THat there were divers emiſſaries and Ambaſſadours ſent by the King of the Anabaptiſts into *Holland, Frieſland*, and other places to raiſe ſouldiers, you have underſtood out of the Hiſtory of *Munſter*; which ſouldiers, having raiſed a Tumult, cauſed the Biſhop to diſcamp from before *Munſter*; and of this Herd was
there

there one *Nicholas Alcmariensis* a worthy disciple of *John Mathias*, who being dispatched into *Friezland* for the foresaid negotiation, got together a promiscuous crue of Anabaptists for the relief of *Munster*: but that it might appear how real and effectual he was in the businefs, they sent two of their fellow souldiers, *Anthony Ciftarius*, and a Tradesman whose name was *James*, to *Munster*. These two with some others, having compassed their desires at a Town called *Opt'zant*, having shuffled together from all parts into a kind of a Troop, made their rendezvous at the house of one *Eppo*, about the twilight out of a pretence that they there should meet with some later intelligence, which they receiving from their Ambassadors, out of very joy for those good tidings, absolutely broke forth into Tumults. The Bell weather of these, was one *Herman* [an excellent vamper of all abomination] a *Cobler* of *Opt'zant*, who professed himself *a true Prophet, and that he was the true Messias, the* Redeemer *and* Saviour *of the world*, nay, (which causes horror to me in the relation) that he was *God the Father*. This fellow lay naked in his bed from the privy parts downward, and caused to be laid near him a hogs-head of strong beer, which he desir'd to drink in Healths, which required no small draughts; for he had gotten an excessive thirst, greater than that of any dog; or that which the Serpent *Dipsas* causeth in those that are stung by it; and all through his extraordinary bellowing and bawling. For, having for some days led a life like one of *Epicurus*'s herd; that is to say being drunk even to extravagance, he with a *Stentor*'s voice, and a horrid howling, among other things often repeated this; *Kill, cut the throats without any quarter, of all these Monks, all these Popes, and all, efpecially our own Magiftrate, Repent, Repent, for your deliverance is at hand,* &c. In the mean time, he, with the affiftance of his fellow souldiers, denounced to certain Presbyters of another Religion, that Peace was not to be rejected without incurring the dreadfull effects of the laft judgment, which was now at hand, and thefe were such as both by follicitations and promifes, his main defign was to inveigle into his deceit. Moreover he fent to redeem some of his followers out of a prifon belonging to a certain Nobleman called *John of Holten*, with this charge, that they fhould kill with swords and piftols, whosoever should either by words or blows any way oppose them. When they returned with their delivered captives, they had difpatched a man (it is thought he was a Prieft) looking out at his door, with a Musket, had he not turned his back and fhut the door againft them. The very fame night, which was to be the laft, or wherein the world being to be turned to deceitful afhes, they expected it fhould by the means of this Mediator and Interceffor (as was thought) prefently be reftored to liberty, there were a great many that embraced him where ever they could with those complements which they fhould ufe to one, as without the earneft of whofe baptifm, they were to expect the reward of difobedience, and eternal deftruction to be treafured up for them. The Sacrament of Anabaptifm being according

ding to these ceremonies celebrated, the fore-commended Parent *The Cere-*
exhorted his children to prayer in these words, *Pray, pray, pray,* *monies be*
pray, mouthing it out with an agitation of his lips, like that of our *used in A-*
Storks; which done, falling on their knees, they disgorged, a *nabaptism.*
strange vicissitude of prayers and songs. The owner of that house,
who was an Inn-keeper, and withal lame, sat near this great Fa- *Eppo his*
ther, towards whom the Father turning, said unto him, *Arise and Host, disco-*
walk. But *Eppo* being still lame, and seeing that they were all *vered him*
deceived, and that by a sort of cheats wickedly stitch'd together, *and his fol-*
withdrew from them, and hid himself for fear in another man's *lowers to be*
house far from thence. These things being thus past, there arises *cheats.*
up another, one *Cornelius* *Cæmiteriensis,* who ran about after a ** Supposed*
most strange manner, and when the *Father* (of all execrable teme- *to be a*
rity) lay sick in his bed, tormented with an imaginary, or at least *digger of*
such a disease as puzzled the Physicians to find any name for; this *graves.*
man for an hour together uttered these and such expressions: O
FATHER, *look upon thy people, have mercy upon thy people:* O *let*
thy bowels, O *Father, be moved to compassion!* &c. At which addresses the Father being moved, he commanded a tankard of beer to
be drawn out of the hogshead, which was now almost at the bottom, which he drinking to his son, drank till it came to the Lees,
which presenting to his son, he said to him, *Drink up the holy Ghost.* *Herman's*
The son like his Father, and following his example, having taken *wicked*
it off, he flings out of bed, and falls upon those that stood by; *blasphemy.*
and tossing the tankard from one hand to the other, ran up and
down like a drunken man, and at length joyned with the father
(who was sick of an imaginary extravagance, wherein he was
much given to laugh) in roaring out in these words; *Mortifie the*
flesh, mortifie the flesh; the flesh is a Devil, the flesh is a Devil,
mortifie the flesh; &c. Upon this there immediately starts up a- *Heresie. A*
ther pursued (as he thought) by an extraordinary vision, and *thing, or*
ter their example, roared it out most furiously, which fellow *is mad di-*
was reported) was really advanced to some degrees (if not the *sease.*
supreme) of madness. A certain woman better than middle-aged,
being frighted almost out of her wits, by the bawling and howling of this son, intreated that they would keep in the lunatick
and possessed person, and that he might be carried to *Bedlam.* The
common people being astonished at this impious hellish crue,
were forced to pin their faith upon their sleeves, as a truth confirmed
by the lying of those prophetical mouths. These relapses of fury
and madness, having their intervalls of calmness and serenity, he
admonished them, that all arms and weapons were to be laid aside,
and that they should put off their guarded, edged and scolloped
garments, and their wrought smocks and peticoats, nay that women ought to abstain wearing their necklaces, and all things that
were burdensom, intimating the manner wherein God that needs no
arms, would fight their battels for them, and should discomfit all
their enemies. The cowardly and inconstant vulgar being moved
at the madness of this Doctrine, disburthened their bodies of all

manner

manner of cloathing. A certain harmless man having cast away his knife, takes it up again, which his daughter looking asquint upon rebuked her father; to which he answered, be patient, be patient, daughter, we shall have employment hereafter for this to cut bread withall. O how was this girl once a child, but how was this old man twice! when the Student of *Bedlam*, the *Son*, with his yelling, was exhorting the bewitched people to singing and prayer,

Hereticks in onstant in their opinions.

and to resist the Devil, the *Father* presently with his own son in whom he was well pleased, taught them, that the time of prayer being done, and the time of war coming on, they must take up the instruments of war; whereupon he gets up into a Pulpit, and declared himself to the people who stood all about him with a loud voice, that he was the *Son of God*, and cryed out that he was born a true *Mediator unto them*, &c. His mother being there present, they asked her whether she was the mother of the Son of God? To which between force and fear, she at length answered, though innocently, that she was. This gave occasion to many to be diffident, and to waver in the faith received; insomuch that a certain man discovering his dissatisfaction, and speaking ill of the son, the said Son taking hold of him, flings him into a common shore, saying unto him now art thou deservedly cast into Hell: from whence the said man coming out all dirt, divers others unanimously acknowledged that they were defiled and bespattered with the same filthiness and Abomination. And hence rise up that impious report of the Son of God, that he was thrust out of doors, which that Ambassadour *Antony*, being returned from *Munster*, having heard took it in mighty indignation, and by force breaking into the house, would have vindicated those holy expressions. The Father and Son, were much against it that any should come in; yet he, though the people flocking about him made some opposition, bitterly rebuking that blasphemous wretch broke forth into

Herman blasphemes again. His Mothers temerity.

The Proverb verified vice corrects sin.

these words, *Thou villanous and contagious burthen of the earth; what madness, what extravagance hath besotted thee without fear of divine judgment, to assume to thy self the title of the Son of God?* which spoken, swelling up with the leaven of wrath, he casts himself upon the ground, whereupon the people ran violently upon him, knocking, beating, and kicking him like a foot ball; at last being well loaden with blows he rises, and breaking through the press of the people, he got away and escaped. In his way he comes to a hole in the ice broken for the cattel to drink, twenty foot over, which he made a shift to get over, as it is said, with the help of the Devil; for many that would have found him out, lost their labour: All being now convinced that they were abused, for fear of the most noble *Charles* Lord of *Guelderland*, the viceroy of *Groningen* (called also King of *Guelderland*) who was sent to appease that tumult, got secretly away. But before they were all departed, one of them called *Drewjis* (whom they called Doctor *Nucius*) out of pure spight laying hold of the Father, being sick in his bed, thundred to him in these words; Thou villain, thou fruit

Herman's party are convinced and fall off from him. One Drewjis of his party handles him roughly.

and

or *Herman* the *Cobler*.

and groanings of the Gallows, where, where, is now your governing, and authority? now the time of prayers is past, &c. Having dragg'd him out of bed by head and shoulders, they with some assistance bound him with cords, and delivered him to the custody of the mistress of the house to be safely kept till night. In the mean time the valiant *Charles* surrounds the house with his men, and besieged it, which the woman seeing, cut the cords. Being loose, he takes a trident fork wherewith assaulting them as with a sword, he put to flight forty men through other houses, whom he hastily pursuing, was unawares surprised by others, and brought to *Groningen*. But behold the miracle! to that very place, where this naked [of all truth] *Messias* with his forky Scepter, and this Shoomaker or Cobler beyond his last, had with his Trident put so many to flight, did the water dreading Anabaptists resort, and render unto God, infinite thanks for the religious privileges thereof. Of this lewd *Messias*, who was now well acquainted with the fetters of *Groningen*, it was asked in his torments, whether these routs (of whom he was ring-leader) were out of pretence of sanctity raised to rob the publick treasuries, (as many thought) which yet (as some say) was denied. For, he hardning himself against even the most cruel torments could be inflicted on him, still cryed out; *Destroy, destroy, destroy Monks, Popes, kill all the Magistrates and particularly our own.* In the mid'st of these bawlings being miserably worried out, he gave up the Ghost.

Charles Lord of Guelderland, &c. with his men surrounds the house where Herman is taken and brought prisoner to gen. He is questioned in his torments. He is hardned. He dieth miserably.

THEODORUS SARTOR,

Quis quæso hic Sartor nudus qui deperit ? ille
Qui rogo Cernentis nomine dignus erat ?

THE CONTENTS.

THEODOR *the Botcher turns Adamite, he affirms strange things, his blasphemy in forgiving of sins, he burns his cloaths, &c. and causeth his companions to do the like. He and his rabble go naked through* Amsterdam *in the dead of night, denouncing their woes, &c. and terrifie the people. They are taken and imprisoned by the Burghers, but continue shameless.* May 5. 1535. *they are put to death; some of their last words.*

Anno 1535.

IN the year of our Lord one thousand five hundred thirty and five, upon the third of *February* at *Amsterdam*, in a street called *Salar*-street, at the house of *John Sifrid* a cloath-worker, who at that time was gone into *Austria* about some business, there met seven men, Anabaptists, and five women of the same perswasion, of

which

which flock, the Bell-weather was *Theodorus Sartor*, who rapt into a strange enthusiasm and extasie, stretching himself upon the ground stark naked upon his back before his brethren and sisters, seemed to pray unto God with a certain religious dread and horrour. Having ended his prayers, he affirmed that he had beheld God with his eyes in the excessive and ineffable riches of his glory, and that he had had communication with him, both in heaven and in hell, and that the day of his judgment was at hand. After which he said to one of his companions; Thou art decreed to eternal damnation, and shall be cast into the bottomless pit; at which the other crying out; The Lord God of Mercy have compassion on me; the prophet said to him be of good chear, now art thou the son of God, thy sins are forgiven thee. Upon the eleventh day of *February*, the foresaid year, the persons afore mentioned, unknown to their husbands, repaired to the same *Augeas*'s stable. This Prophet, or Seer, having entertained them with a Sermon of three or four hours long, casts a helmet, a breast plate, a sword, and other arms, together with all his clothes in the fire. Being thus stark-naked, and his companions who yet had their cloaths, being uncovered, he peremptorily commanded them to do the like, as being such as must be as safe as himself. He further affirmed, that the children of God ought to look upon all things of this world with contempt and indignation. And since Truth, which is most glorious in her nakedness, will not admit the deformity of any earthly disguise whatsoever, he affirmed that they ought in all things to conform themselves to that example of Truth and Justice. A great many hearing these things having quite cashier'd all shame, offered up their shirts, smocks, and petticoats, and whatsoever savoured of earth, as a burnt offering unto God. The mistress of the house being awakened by the stinck which these cloaths made in burning, and going up into the upper chambers, she finds this deplorable representation of immodesty and impudence; but the power and influence of prophetical integrity brought the woman to that pass, that she was drawn in to wallow in the same-mire of unshamefac'dness, whom therefore he advised to continue always a constant adherer to the unblameable truth. Going out of the house in this posture, about three of the clock, the other men and women marching barefoot after him, cryed out with a horrid voice *woe, woe, wee, the heavy wrath of God, the heavy wrath of God*, &c. in this fanatick errour did this hypochondriack rabble run about the streets, making such horrid noise, that all *Amsterdam* seemed to shake and tremble at it, as if it had been assaulted by a publick enemy. The Burghers not having the least hint of such a strange and unlook'd for Accident, (for this furious action happen'd in the dead night) took up arms, and getting these people (lost to all shame and modesty) up to the Palace, clapt them into prison. Being so disposed of, they would own no thoughts of shame or chastity, but would justifie their most white and naked Truth. In the mean time the fire being smelt, they into the house where it was, and wondring at their casting

Theodorus Sartor an Adamite.

He affirms strange things.

His blasphemy in forgiving of sins.

He burns his cloathes, &c. and causeth his companions to do the like.

He and his rabble go naked through Amsterdam in the dead of night, denouncing their woes, &c. and terrifie the people. They are taken and imprisoned by the Burghers, but continue shameless.

May the fifth 1535. they are put to death. Some of their last words.

of their cloaths into the fire, which had since reached the bed, they made a shift to quench it. But the other distracted and mad people, such as deserved to be sent to their kindred, the Savages and Heathens, inconvincibly persisted in their pestiferous opinion, and so upon the fifth of *May* the same year, they expiated their wicked impieties, by their death. Ones farewell saying, was, *Praise the Lord incessantly?* Anothers was, *O God revenge thou our sufferings!* Others cryed out, *woe, woe, shut thine eyes.*

THE

DAVID GEORGE.

Heretici plures visi hic cui visus ego illis
Pluribus invisusque. Hæresiarcha fui.

THE CONTENTS.

DAVID GEORGE, *the miracle of the Anabaptists. At Basil he pretends to have been banished his Country for the Gospels sake; with his specious pretences he gains the freedom of the City for him and his. His Character. His Riches. He with his Sect enact three things. His Son in Law, doubting his new Religion, is by him questioned; and upon his answer excommunicated. His wife's death. He had formerly voted himself immortal, yet Aug. 2. 1556. he died, &c. His death troubled his disciples. His doctrine questioned by the Magistrates, eleven of the Sectaries secured. XI. Articles extracted out of the writings of* David George. *Some of the imprisoned Sectaries acknowledged* David George *to have been the cause of the tumults in the lower parts of* Germany, *but disowned his doctrine.*
Conditions whereupon the imprisoned are set at liberty.

DAVID GEORGE.

The Senate vote the Doctrine of D. G. impious, and declare him unworthy of Christian burial, and that his body and books should be burned, which was accordingly effected.

D. George the miracle of the Anabaptists Anno 1544.

DAVID GEORGE, a man born at *Delph* in *Holland*, the miracle of the Anabaptistical Religion, having lived in the lower Provinces forty years, did in the year one thousand five hundred forty and four, with some of his kindred and companions, in the beginning of *April*, began his journey for *Basil*, in the state and condition of which place, he had before very diligently enquired. Whereof having sufficiently informed himself, he pretended that he had been driven out of his Country for the Gospels sake, and that he had been hitherto tost both on the Land and Sea of the miseries of this World; and therefore he humbly

At Basil he pretends to have been banished his Country for the Gospels sake.

intreated, that now at length he might be received into some place of rest. Some being by their representation of his misfortunes and his tears, melted into compassion towards him, he presum'd to entreat the Magistrate, that in tenderness to Christ and his holy Gospel, he might be made capable of the privileges of the City, which if it were granted, he bid them be confident of Gods most particular protection towards their City, and that for the preservation of it he engaged for him and his, that they should be ready to lay down their lives. The Magistrates being moved with these just remonstrances and desires received the viper

With his specious pretences he gains the freedom of the City for him and his.

as a Citizen, gave him the right hand of welcom and fellowship, and made him and his free of the City. What should the Magistrate do? Behold, he hath to do with a man of a grave countenance, free in his behaviour, having a very long beard and that yellowish, sky-coloured and sparkling eyes, mild and affable in the midst of his gravity, neat in his apparel; Finally one that seem-

His Character.

ed to have in him all the ingredients of honesty, modesty and truth; to be short, one, if you examine his countenance, carriage, discourse, and the cause he is embarked in, all things without him are within the limits of mediocrity and modesty; if you look within him, he is nothing but deceit, fraud, and dissimulation; in a word, an ingenious Anabaptist. Having already felt the pulses of the Senate and divers of the Citizens, coming with his whole family to *Basil*, he and his are entertained by a certain Citizen. Having nested a while in *Basil*, he purchased certain houses in the City, as also a Farm in the Country and some other things thereto appurtenant, married his children, and by his good offices procured to himself many friends. For, as long as he remained at *Basil*, he so much studied Religion, was so great an alms-giver, and gave himself so much to other exercises of devotion, that suspition it self had not what to say against him. By these cunning insinuations, (this is beyond a young fox, and smells more of the *Libyan* wild beast) many being surprized, came easily over to his party, so that he arrived to that esteem and reputation in matters of Religion, he pleased himself. This perswasion thus craftily gotten,

was

was heightened by his great wealth (and his riches in jewels, *His riches.* whereof he brought some with him, some were daily brought from other places in the Low countries) and was yet further encreased by his sumptuous and rich plate and housholdstuff, which though they were gorgeous and majestical, yet were they not made to look beyond sobriety, cleanliness, and mediocrity. These people sojourning thus in common houses, desiring as yet to suppress the pernici- *He, with* ous infection of their Sect, very religiously enacted three things: *his Sect en-* First, that no man should prophane or speak idlely of the name of *all three* David George. Secondly, that no man should rashly or unadvi- *things.* sedly divulge any thing concerning his Country, or manner of Life; whence it was that some thought him to be a person of some quality; some, that he was some very rich Factor or Merchant, whence it came that he was so excessively Rich; others had other imaginary opinions and conceits of him, for as much as they themselves being strangers, lived in a Country where they could not be ascertained of any thing: Thirdly, he was very cautious that none of the *Basilians* should be carelesly admitted into his acquaintance, society or correspondence, imitating therein the policy of the *Ferrets* and *Weesels*, which (as is reported) never assault any bird of supremacy in the places where they frequent. And thus did he by letters, writings and emissaries, plant and water the venomous seed of his sect through the lower Provinces, yet kept the ways by which he wrought unsuspected and undiscovered. For, although he had lived two years among them, there was not so much as one man infected; or had privately caught the itch of his Religion. What transcendent Mysteries are these! This man, though he feared not their deceit nor treachery from strangers, yet the fire kindled out of the deceitful *His son in* embers of his own houshold. For, behold; one of his own Re- *Law doubt-* tinue doubting of the certainty of the new Religion, he caused *ing his new* him to be brought before him, and asked him, whether he did *Religion, is* not acknowledge him to be the true *David* sent from Heaven upon *by him que-* Earth, and to be the Horn, Redeemer, and Builder of the Ta- *stioned, and* bernacle of *Israel*? To which the other answered roundly and *upon his an-* peremptorily, that the restauration of the Kingdom of *Israel* and o- *swer excom-* ther things foretold by the Prophets were fulfilled in Christ, the *municated.* true *Messias*, and that consequently there was no other to be expected. Which he hearing, not without great astonishment, did with much commotion of mind and bitter menaces thrust him, though his son in Law, out of doors, and [which is heavy to think on] excommunicated him. These things being thus managed, *His Wifes* David's Wife fell sick of a disease (which afterwards visited him *death.* and many more) that dispatch'd her into the other World. What *He had for-* a miracle is this! He that declared himself to be greater than *merly voted* Christ, and voted himself immortal (upon the second of *August*, *himself im-* one thousand five hundred fifty and six) did die the death, and *mortal, yet* was honourably buried according to the ceremonies of the Parish *Aug. 2.* Church, and his funerals were celebrated in the sight of his Sons *1556. he* and *died, &c.*

DAVID GEORGE.

His death troubled his disciples. and Daughters, Sons in Law and Daughters in Law, servant Men and Maids, and a great conflux of Citizens. This sad calamity of his death extreamly troubled and tormented the minds of his disciples, as a thing that very much thwarted their hopes of his promised immortality, although he had foretold that he would rise again in three years, and would bring all those things to pass which he had promised while he was alive. Upon the death of this man, a great many with resolute minds made it their business not only to *A good resolution.* bring his doctrine into suspicion, but into utter disesteem, unanimously resolving to embrace what ever was good, sound, and consonant to Christian doctrine, and reject the rest as heretical. In the mean time, the report beat up and down, both among the people, and the more learned, that this man of ingenuity, and author of private doctrines, this very *David George*, was a contagion and a distructive pestilence, a devoted incendiary of a most dangerous *A pattern for good Magistrates* Sect, that (though most falsly) he was born a King, and that he accounted himself the true *Messias*. The Magistrate being extreamly moved at these things not deferring his zeal any longer when the glory of God and his Son *Jesus Christ* was so much concerned, caused all those who were conceived to be infected with the pestilence of that Religion to be brought to the Palace, to whom he rubbed over what things had been transacted some years before; that is to say, acquainted them, how that they had been banished their country upon the account of the Gospel, and upon their humble addresses received into the protection, and made capable of the privileges of the City, &c. But that it had appeared since, that they had fled for refuge to *Basil*, not for the propagation of the Gospel, but for that of the leaven of the sacrilegious *David*, though by all outward appearance, they had hitherto been accounted favourers and professors of the true Religion *The Senates enquiry.* In the first place therefore the Senate being desirous to know the truth, required to have his true proper name; for, some have thought (as some authors deliver,) that his name was *John Bruges*. Secondly, whether he had privately or publickly dispersed his Religion and what Tenets he held. To which some made answer unanimously, that they had left the Country for the true Religion sake, nor did they acknowledge themselves any other than the professors and practisers of the lawful Religion. That for his name, he had not called himself by any other than his own proper name; and for his doctrine, they had acknowledged none either privately or publickly, save what he had privately sometimes suggested, which was not disconsonant to the publick. The Magi-*Eleven of the Sectaries secured* strate perceiving this obstinacy of mind caused eleven of them, the better to discover the real truth, to be secured, and more narrowly looked to. In the mean time, the Senate leaving no *In such cases the learned to be consulted with.* stone unmoved in this business, appointed some to bring forth into publick view some books and writings of *David*, which should give no small light in the business, and these the Magistrate recommended to men of the greatest learning to be read over and examine at with the greatest care possible, that so whatsoever they should meet with repugnant to the Truth, they should extract, and give him an account thereof. Those who had this charge put upon them, presented the Senate with this extract of Articles out of his Writings.

1. "That all the Doctrine delivered by *Moses*, the *Prophets*, or by *Articles extracted out* "*Jesus Christ* himself and his *Apostles*, was not sufficient *of the wri-* "to salvation, but dress'd up and set forth for young men, and chil- *tings of D.* "dren, to keep them within decency and duty; but that the do- *George.* "ctrine of *David George* was perfect, entire, and most sufficient "for the obtaining of Salvation.

2. "He affirmed that he was *Christ* and the *Messias*, that well-"beloved Son of the Father in whom he was well pleased, not "born of blood, nor of the flesh, nor of the lust of man, but "of the holy Ghost and the Spirit of Christ; who vanishing hence "long since according to the flesh, and deposited hitherto in some "place unknown to the Saints, was now at length reinfused from "Heaven into *David George*.

3. "He held that he only was to be worshipped, as who should "bring out the house of *Israel* and the true (that is the profes-"sors of his doctrine) tribe of *Levi*, and the Tabernacle of the "Lord, not through miseries, sufferings, crosses, as the *Messias* of "the *Jews* did, but with all meekness, love, and mercy in the Spi-"rit of Christ granted unto him from the Father which is in "Heaven.

4. "He approved himself to be invested with the Authority of "*Saving* or *Condemning, Binding*, and *Loosing*, and that at the "last day he should judge the twelve Tribes of *Israel*.

5. "He further maintained, that *Jesus Christ* was sent from "the Father to take flesh upon him; for this reason at least, that "by his Doctrine, and the use of his Sacraments, men, being as it "were no better than children, and uncapable of receiving the "true doctrine, might be kept within duty till the coming of "*David George*, who should advance a Doctrine that should be "most perfect and most effectual, should smooth out mankind, "and should consummate the knowledge of God and of his Son, "and what ever hath been said of him.

6. "But he further affirmed, That these things should not come "to pass according to *humane* ceremonies, but after a *Spiritual* "dispensation, and after such a manner as had not been heard of, "which yet none should be able to discern or comprehend but such "as were worthy disciples of *David George*.

7. "To make good and prove all these things, he wrested and "misinterpreted many places of the Holy Scripture, as if Christ "and the Apostles whom he commends, had intimated not them-"selves, nor any other Ecclesiastical times, save only the com-"ing of *David George*.

8. "And

DAVID GEORGE.

8. "And thence it was that he argued thus: If the doctrine of *Christ* and his *Apostles* be most true and most effectual for the obtaining of Salvation; the *Church* which they had by their doctrine built up and confirmed, could not possibly have been broken to pieces for (as *Christ* himself testifieth) against the *true* Church the Gates of Hell shall not be able to prevail: But that building of Christ and his Apostles is overturned and pulled down to the very foundation by Antichrist, as may be evidently seen in the Papacy, according to the Testimony of the same Christ. It therefore necessarily follows, that the Doctrine of the Apostles is imperfect and interrupted whence he concluded his own Doctrine and faith to be the only solid and sufficient Doctrine.

9. "Moreover he maintained himself to be greater than *John Baptist*, yea than all the *Saints* that had gone before him, for that the least in the Kingdom of God (according to the suffrage of Truth it self) is greater than *John*. But he said *David George* was one whose Kingdom was Heavenly and most perfect; whence he makes himself not only greater than *John*, but also sets himself above *Christ*, since that he was born of flesh and that himself was born of the Spirit according to a heavenly manner.

10. "He further allowed with *Christ*, that all sins committed against God the *Father*, and against the *Son* may be forgiven, but those that are committed against the *Holy Ghost*, that is to say against *David George*, shall not be forgiven, neither in this world, nor in the world to come; by which means it is apparent that he conceived himself greater and higher than Christ, adulting Christs own Testimony.

11. "He declared Polygamy to be free and lawful for all, even for those that are regenerated by the spirit of *David George*.

Some of the imprisoned Sectaries acknowledged David George to have been the cause of the tumults in the lower part of Germany, but disowned his doctrine.

These heads [without any brains] did the Magistrate deliver to be carried to some that were in the prison, to fish out what confession they would make, who besides these, being provoked and challenged by a number of Questions, answered at last, that this (*Davus*) I would say *David George*, was the same who had embroyled the lower parts of *Germany* with so many tumults and sedition, but that as to that doctrine and the fore-recited Articles, they unanimously affirmed that they had ———— no——ead of any such thing. Nevertheless they were ——————— the Doctrine expressed in those Articles, to be ———————, execrable, and derived not from Heaven, but from Hell, and that it was heretical, and to be banished with an eternal Anathema; and withal, as men miserably seduced, yet desiring for the time to come, to be reduced into the right way, they were, with good reason, to implore forgiveness. Among those that were in close prison, there

An ingenious confession and refutation.

was one formerly of *David's* greatest confidents, who confessed, that indeed he had been infected with that Religion, but that since by the illumination of the grace of God, he discovered and detested the errors springing from it and avoided them as he would

do

do a cockatrice. But there were others who were civilly acquainted with this man, who denyed that they had known any such thing by him, and cried out against the fore-mentioned Articles as impious and blasphemous. These passages, the Judges appointed by the Magistrate, gave him an account of, who perceiving that some that were in custody were not so extravagant, but that they had some remainder of discretion left, he sent to them some learned and able Preachers of the Word, who having diligently weeded out the tares of their errors, should sow into their hearts the saving seed of true faith. Those who were sent, sifting them with all the humanity, mildness, meekness and charity possible, could scrue nothing out of them, more than what the Judges who had been employed before, had done. In the mean time a report was spread about the City, that it was not *David George*, nor any eminent person of any other name that had been buried, but that a meer swine calf, he-goat (haply an Ass) had been carried out and buried, and that the dead carcass embalmed with the strongest spices, was worshipped and adored with great devotion and religion. But this was but a report, and was not true. Those that were in custody abhorring that doctrine, as unheard of, and such as deserved to be anathematized, and desiring to renew their acquaintance with discretion and their senses, are delivered out of those habitations of Iron which they had kept possession of for two months, upon these conditions; That none should make any purchases either within or near the city, without the knowledge and consent of the Magistrate; That they shall not entertain any coming out of the lower Provinces, though of their kindred, but at publick houses or Inns; That the printed books and writings that were translated into the *Dutch* language shall be brought into the Palace. That there should be nothing published that were disconsonant to *Christian* Doctrine; That children should be educated according to incorrupt manners; That they should not make such promiscuous marriages among themselves as they did; That they should take no *Dutch* into their Famalies; That they should submit to amercements and pecuniary mulcts (if any were inflicted on them) as Citizens ought to do; That upon a day assigned, they should in the Parish-Church, in the presence of the whole congregation, make a publick abjuration of the said Religion, and condemn and anathematize the whole Sect of it; That they should hold no friendship or correspondence with any that shall persist in that Religion. To these conditions did they promise to subscribe, with all the reverence and gratitude they could possibly express. These things being thus managed, the most renowned Senate, returning afresh to the business of the Arch-Heretick, passed these votes, viz. That the Doctrine of *David George* upon mature examination thereof, was found impious and derogatory to the divine Majesty. That the printed books, and whatsoever may have seen the light, should have the second light of the fire. That he as the most infamous promoter of that execrable Sect, and a most horrid blasphemer against *God* and *Christ*, should not be

The votes of the reverend Senate. The doctrine of D.G. declared impious.

DAVID GEORGE.

He is declared unworthy of Christian Burial.

And that his body and books should be burned.

A fit punishment for perverse Hereticks.

accounted worthy christian burial. That he should be taken up out of his Grave by the common Hangman, and together with his books and all his writings, and his manuscripts should, according to the Ecclesiastical canons, be burnt in a solemn place. According to the said judgment, the carkass being digged up, was with all his writings, whereof the greatest part was that (truly) *miraculous book* together with his effigies brought by the Hangman to the place of execution, where having opened the direful Coffin, he being found not much disfigured, nay so little, that he was known by diverse (he being covered with a watered garment, having about him a most white sheet, a very clean pillow under his head, his yellowish Beard rendring him yet graceful; to be short, having a silk Cap on, under which was a piece of red cloath, and adorned with a garland of Rosemary) was set up publickly to be seen, and in the third year after his death, was with his writings consecrated to *Vulcan*, that is to say, burned.

MICHAEL SERVETUS.

*Omnia qum potenta voces hominemque Deumque
Infandi Serves nominis opprobrium!*

THE CONTENTS.

SERVETUS *his converse with* Mahometans *and* Jews. *He disguiseth his monstrous opinions with the Name of Christian Reformation. The place of his birth. At the 24 year of his age, he boasted himself the only* Teacher *and* Seer *of the world. He inveighed against the deity of* Christ. Oecolampadius *confutes his blasphemies, and causeth him to be thrust out of the Church of* Basil. Servetus *held but one person in the God-head to be worshipped, &c. He held the Holy Ghost to be* Nature. *His horrid blasphemy. He would reconcile the* Turkish Alcoran *to Christian Religion. He declares himself Prince of the Anabaptists. At* Geneva, Calvin *faithfully reproves* Servetus, *but he continues obstinate. Anno* 1553, *by the decrees of several Senates, he was burned.*

MICHAEL SERVETUS.

Servetus his converse with Mahometans and Jews. He disguiseth his monstrous opinions, with the name of Christian Reformation. The place of his birth. His arrogant Boast. He inveighs against the Deity of Christ. Oecolampadius confutes his blasphemies, and causeth him to be thrust out of the Church of Basil.

MICHAEL SERVETUS, like another *Simon Magus* having conversed long among the *Mahometans* and the *Jews*, and being excellently well furnished with their imaginous opinions, begat both out of Divinity, and the general treasury of Christian Religion, a monstrous issue of opinions, with the coition of what he had received from the extravagant *Mahometans*, and *Thalmudists*, upon which brat this instrument of *Satan*, must needs bestow the disguised name of *Christian Reformation*. From this Cocks egg were bred these Cockatrices, *Gonesus*, *Gribaldus*, *Blandrata*, *Gentilis*, *Alciatus*, *Simanus*, *Casanovius*, *Menno*, and diverse other *Anabaptistical* Vipers, who extreamly increased the restless waves of Sects and opinions. We, recommending the rest to their proper place, Hell, will take a more particular survey of one Religion, and by the horridness of that guess at the others. This *Servetus* was a *Spaniard*, born in the Kingdom of *Arragon*, most unworthy both of his name and Nation. Being wrapt into a most credible Enthusiasm, he boldly lays his unwashed hands upon holy Divinity; and at the four and twentieth year of his age, boasted himself to be the only *Teacher* and *Seer* of the World, making it his main design, and by his impious and worthless writings, to inveigh against the Deity of the Son of God; with which writings being sufficiently furnished, and withall enflamed with hopes of raising no ordinary tumults, he bestirs himself wind and tide for *Basil*; but *Oecolampadius*, an Ecclesiastical Doctor, learnedly before a full Senate confuted the blasphemies of this man, and by the publick authority he had, caused him as a poisonous blasphemer to be thrust out of the Church of *Basil*. From thence he went to *Venice*, where, in regard the *Venetians* had been timely forewarned of him by the wise and learned *Melancthon*, he made no harvest of his incredible blasphemies, nor indeed was he permitted seed-time for them. Religion is no where safe! But having

Servetus held but one person in the God-head to be worshipped, &c.

consulted with the Arch-hereticks his Predecessors, and being bird-lim'd, he held that there was but one person in the God-head to be worshipped and acknowledged, which was revealed to man-kind sometimes under one notion, sometimes under another, and that it was thus that those notions of *Father*, *Son*, and *Holy Ghost*, were to be understood in the Scriptures. Nay, with the same line of his blasphemous mouth, he ~~affirmed~~ that our Saviour *Jesus Christ* according to his humane nature, was not the Son of God; nor coeternal with the Father. The *Holy Ghost* he granted to be nothing but that influence by which all things are moved, which is called *nature*. He most impiously, Ironical, affirmed that to understand the word *Person*, we must refer our selves to *Comedies*. But the most horrid blasphemy of all, was, when by the suggestion of Satan, he imagined, that the most glorious and ever to be worshipped and adored Trinity (who doth not tremble at it?) was most fitly compared to *Cerberus* the Porter of Hell-gate. But he stayed not here; no, he thought it should be accounted nothing but a diabolical phantasm, the laughing-stock

He held the holy Ghost to be Nature. His horrid blasphemy.

MICHAEL SERVETUS.

of Satan, and the monstrous *Gerion*, whom the Poets by some strange mystery of Philosophy feigned to have three bodies. O incredible, and unheard of subtilty of blasphemy! The most glorious name of the most blessed Trinity is grown so odious to this man, that he would personate (being the greatest that ever was) all the Atheists that have quarrelled with that name. Moreover he maintained, that taking but away the only Article of the *Trinity*, the *Turkish Alcoran* might be easily reconciled to the *Christian* Religion; and that by the joyning together of these two, a great impediment would be removed, yea, that the pertinacious asserting of that Article had enraged to madness whole Countries and Provinces. This abomination of God and men held that the Prophet *Moses*, that great servant of God, and faithful steward of the Lord's house, that *Prince* and *Captain General* of the people of *Israel*, one so much in favour with God, that he was admitted to speak to him face to face, was to be accounted no other than an *Impostor*. He accounted the Patriarch *Abraham* and his seed too much given to Revenge, and that he was most unjust and most malicious to his enemy. The most glorious Church of *Israel*, ('tis the swine that loves the mire) he esteemed no better than a Hog-Sty, and declared himself a sworn prince of the Anabaptistical generation. But, keep off, and approach not, O all ye other Heresies, and Hydra's of opinions of this one man, furies not capable of expiation! Being arrived at *Geneva* and being forbidden to spue out and spatter his pestiferous blasphemies, he continued in hostility against all sharp, but wholesome admonitions: which *Calvin*, that famous Minister of the Church perceiving, being desirous to discharge the duty of a soul-saving Pastor, went friendly to *Servetus*, in hopes to deliver him out of his most impious errors and horrible Heresie, and so to redeem him out of the jaws of Hell, and faithfully reproved him. But he being dazled with the brightness of *Truth*, and overcome, returned nothing to *Calvin* (so well deserving of him) but an intolerable obstinacy, and inconvincible recapitulation of his blasphemies, whence it came to pass, that by the just and prudent Decree of the Senates of *Bernen*, *Zuring*, *Basil*, and *Scaffuse*, and by the righteous condemnation of the eternal God, in the month of *December* in the year one thousand five hundred fifty and three, (or as *Sleidan* hath it, in *October*) he was (how great is the obstinacy of blasphemy) being at that time ecstatically hardned and intoxicated, consecrated to the avenging flames.

He would reconcile the Alcoran to Christian Religion.

He declares himself Prince of the Anabaptists.

At Geneva, Calvin reproves Servetus.

Servetus his obstinacy.

Ann. 1553. By the decree of several Senates he was burned.

ARRIUS.

Dividit Trini qui formam Numeris ecce!
Dividitur membris, Visceribusq́; suis.

THE CONTENTS.
Arrianism its increase, *Anno* 323.

THe General Council at Nice, Anno 325 *called as a remedy against it, but without success. The Arians mis-interpret that place,* John 10. 30. *concerning the Father and the Son. They acknowledged one only God in a Judaical sense. They deny the Trinity.* Arrius *his wretched death,* Anno 336.

Arria-
nism, *its*
increase,
Anno 323.

ABout the year of the Incarnation of the Son of God, three hundred twenty and three, Hell was deliver'd of a certain Priest at *Alexandria* named *Arrius*, a man subtle beyond expression, the trumpet of eloquence, one that seemed to have been cut for out all honesty, and elegance, who yet, with the poison of his Heresie, and the *Circæan* cups of his destructive doctrine, did in the time of *Sylvester* Bishop of *Rome* and the Emperour *Constantine*, draw in a
manner

ARRIUS.

manner all Christendom to his opinion, and so corrupted some, even great nations in the East, that except a few Bishops who stood to the true doctrine, none appeared against him. To remedy this disease, at *Nice* in *Bithynia*, in the year three hundred twenty and five, a general Council was called; but to no purpose; for the contagious stocks of *Arrianism* were deeply rooted, so that they were become such ravening Wolves among the flock of Christ, that all that would not embrace their belief, were to expect banishment or death. These imagined that the *Son* was not of an equal nature and *coeternal* with the Father; to confirm which they alledged that place of *John* 10. 30. which says, *I and the Father are one*; and though they called the Son a great God, yet they denied that he was a living and true God, and co-essential with the father: They boasted that they were ready to answer all objections, and acknowledged one only God, in a *Judaical* sense. To that, *I and the Father are one*, they were used to retort thus, Doth the unity in this place denote co-essence? It must therefore follow, that it is as much, where the Apostle says, 1 Cor. 3. 8. *He that planteth and he that watereth, are one*. They accounted the word Trinity a laughing stock and Fiction, that the Son of God was a *Creature*, and that the *Holy Ghost*, was both born of *Christ*, and conceived and begotten of the *Virgin Mary*. All that were baptized in the name of the blessed Trinity, they baptized again. They denied that Christ was the Son of God according to the Spirit and the God-head; they denied God his own Son.

While *Arrius* was disburthening himself of the necessities of nature, his bowels came forth, and with them his life. And so he who was the successor of those Arch-Hereticks, *Artemon* (who lived about the year of our Lord two hundred) and *Paulus Samosatenus* (who lived about two hundred and forty one) came to a miserable death, in the year three hundred thirty six. See *Athanasius*, *Epiphanius*, *Hilarius*, *Hierom*, *Augustine*, *Ambrose*, *Basil*, *Theodoret*, *Eusebius*, *Socrates*, *Nicephorus*, *Sozomen*, and other Ecclesiastical writers, who have treated of these things more at large.

The General Council at Nice, called as a remedy against Arrianism, but without success. The Arrians misinterpret that place, Joh. 10. 30. concerning the Father and the Son. They acknowledged one only God in a Judaical sense. They deny the Trinity. Arrius his wretched death, An. 336.

MAHOMET.

*Adsum Ingens Mahometes ego lachrimabile mundi
Prodigum omnigeni dux et origo Mali.*

THE CONTENTS.

MAHOMET *characterized. He made a laughing stock of the* Trinity. *He agreed with* Carpocrates, *and other Hereticks. He renewed Circumcision, and to indulge his disciples, he allowed them Polygamy,* &c. *His Iron Tomb at* Mecca.

Anno 622.

Mahomet characterized.

IN the year six hundred twenty two, *Honorius* the fifth being Bishop of *Rome*, and *Heraclius Cæsar* Emperour of the *East*, a transcendent Arch-heretick called *Mahomet*, exchanged Hell for Earth; a *Prophet*, by Nation an *Arabian*, but most deprav'd and corrupt. He had sometimes been a Merchant extreamly rich, and withal very subtle; to be short, he was a serious professor of diabolical Arts, a most ungodly instrument of Satan, the Viceroy of Antichrist, or his sworn forerunner. This man endeavoured to extol his brother *Arrius*, with such praises as are correspondent to his

MAHOMET.

his Heaven. He also with *Sabellio* renewed the laughing stock of the *Trinity*. He with *Arrius* and *Eunomius*, most fervently and contumeliously held that Christ was only a Man, and that he was only called God, *secundum dici*, that is to say, according to a certain manner of speaking. He agrees with *Carpocrates* who denied that Christ was a God and a Prophet. This is also he that shakes hands with *Cerdonus* who utterly abjur'd the Godhead of the Son, or that he was co-substantial with the Father. He imagined with the *Manichees*, that it was not Christ but some other that was fastned to the Cross. With the *Donatists* he contemned the purest Sacraments of the Church. With the most impure *Origen* he affirms that the Devils shall be eternally saved according to a humane, yet an invisible manner. He with *Cerinthus* placed eternal Felicity in the lust of the flesh. Circumcision, that was long since abolished and antiquated, he renewed. Upon his disciples he bestowed the privileges of *Polygamy*, *Concubines* and *Divorce*, as *Moses* had done; and with dreams and an imaginary Phrensy was the miserable wretch ever troubled. This man when he dyed was put into an Iron Tomb at *Mecca*, which by the strength of Loadstones, being as it were in the middle and centre of an arched edifice, hangs up to the astonishment of the beholders, by which means the miraculous sanctity of this Prophet is greatly celebrated. All the dominions of the Great *Turk*, profess this mans faith, whom they acquiesce in as a miracle.

He made a laughing stock of the Trinity.

He agreed with Carpocrates, and other hereticks.

He renewed circumcision, and his disciples, he allowed them Polygamy, &c.

His Iron Tomb at Mecca.

+ this acc.t of mahomets Tomb *[illegible handwritten note]* 15=48

THE

*Ille ego cui Undarum misteria sacra negaui
Igne crenor sato disce caueri meo.*

THE CONTENTS.

HUBMOR *a Patron of Anabaptism. He damned usury. He brought in a worship to the virgin* MARY, &c. *The Senate of Suring by a Council reduced him. He renounced the heads of his former doctrine. Himself or Sect still active. He is taken and imprisoned at Vienna in Austria. He and his wife both burned.*

<small>Hubmor Patron of Anabaptism.
He damned usury.</small>

Doctor *Balthazar Hubmor* of *Friburg*, a man excellently well learned, another *Roscius* in his affairs, a Clergy man at *Ingolstade*, was the third eminent Patron of *Anabaptism*, and a sworn promoter of that worthy Sect. This man in his Sermons at *Regenburgh*, inveighed so bitterly and so implacably against the usury of the Jews, that he banished it even to eternal damnation; he brought in a certain Religious worship to be done to the Virgin *Mary*, and some superstitious vows, and was the cause of great tumult tumults and insurrections, and had built up his doctrine upon very firm and solid foundations, until the most wise Senate of *Suring* applied the universal medicine of a Council to these things, and assigned a day to reduce and root out that Sect, which was the seventeenth of *January*, in the year one thousand five hundred twenty five, wherein the Senate being present and a great presence of people, the most learned *Zwinglius*, and other Sons of learning, opposed this our Doctor, by whom, and the strength of truth, after most hot and serious debating on both sides, he ingeniously confessed himself to be overcome. The heads of the doctrine which he before defended, and whereof he afterwards made his abrenunciation, were these: That he detested the cheat, and humane invention of *Anabaptism*; he affirmed that the spirit both before the fall and after was uncorrupt and unblameable, and that it never dies in sin, whence it should follow, that not it, but the flesh, is deprived of liberty; he also acknowledged that the spirit overcomes and triumphs over the flesh. Though his Recantation was made, and divers rebaptized into their better senses, yet the Torrents of this sect neither stood still, nor were dried up, but increased in *Switzerland* into a deluge, which overturned almost all. This man escaping the endeavours of spies, and shunning the Halter, was at length taken with the fig-tree leaf of divine vengeance, and cast into prison at *Vienna* in *Austria*. Being afterwards put much to the question, it being the design of vengeance, the revenging fire turned him to ashes. His wife being also baptized in the same whirl-pool of Baptism; they both, with minds hardned to their own perswasions, were not disengaged of their faith, but with the departure of their lives.

He brough[t] in a worship to the Virgin Mary &c.

The Senate of Suring by a Council reduced him.

He renounced the heads of his former doctrine.

Himself, or Sect, still active.

He is taken and imprisoned at Vienna in Austria. He and his wife both burned.

THE

JOHN HUT.

Huttus ab Hubmero excrescit, cervice resecta
Sic una in geminum pullula Hydra caput.

THE CONTENTS.

JOHN HUT *the prop and pillar of Anabaptism. His credulity in dreams and visions. He is accounted a true Prophet by his proselytes. At* Merhern, *his Fraternity became as it were a Monastery.*

John Hut the prop and pillar of Anabaptism. Anabaptists aim at the advancement of themselves, but destruction of others.

IN the times of the fore-mentioned *Balthazar* rose up *John Hut*, a learned man, the prop and Pillar of Anabaptism, an eminent despiser of Pædobaptism, which kind of baptism he accounted the execrable fiction of the Schoolmen; whence it came, that he perswaded men, that if they were not baptized by him and his they must necessarily incurr great danger to their souls. To which he added, that those who were honoured with the prerogative of his baptism, should be the restored people of *Israel*, and that the wicked *Canaanites* should be destroyed by their swords, and that God himself should reveal from heaven the time wherein these
things

JOHN HUT.

things should be fulfilled. To visions and horrible dreams, (which he thought proceeded to him from God) he gave great credit, and he affirmed that he saw the preparations of the last day, and the Angel going to blow the last Trumpet, by an indisputable revelation from God. *Hut his credulity in dreams, and visions.*

Upon the account of which dreams, his Disciples, as credulous as their Master, spent and destroyed all they had, fearing the difficulties of the times, wherein they should spend them; all which being scatter'd and consum'd before the day came, they suffer'd a punishment, and inconveniencies befitting their folly, having the lash of poverty perpetually at their backs. However they, a generation on whom the greatest quantity of black *Hellebore* would not be much effectual, did still adore this miraculous piece of madness as a true prophet, even to admiration, of which men, some not worthy the face or name of mankind, do at this day in great numbers live at *Merhern* in Palaces and Convents *Hut accounted a true Prophet by his proselytes.*

upon their accidental contributions, and where they get their lively-hood with their hands, and apply themselves to any handycraft, whereof they are the Masters and Governours, who by the commodities gained by them increase the common stock: They have at home with them their Cooks, their Scullions, their Errand-Boys, and their Butlers, who have a care and dispose all things as they do in monasteries and hospitals. They study to maintain mutual peace and concord, being all equal. These even to this day are commonly known by the name of the *Hutsian Fraternity*. *At Merhern the Hutsian Fraternity became as it were a Monastery.*

*Polluit ut metem sectis deformibus error,
Corpore sic Hetzer sodus adulter erat.*

THE CONTENTS.

Lodowick Hetzer *a famous Heretick. He gains Proselytes in Austria and* Switzerland, *Anno* 1527. *At a publick disputation* Oecolampadius *puts Hetzer's Emissaries to their shifts. Hetzer denied Christ to be co-essential with the Father. His farewell to his Disciples. He is put to death for Adultery.*

<small>Lodowick Hetzer a famous heretick.</small> Lodowick Hetzer, famous for his *Heresie* and *Learning*, was first very intimately acquainted with *Nicholas Stork*, and then with *Thomas Muntzer*, yet he agreed not with these in some things, as in that opinion of theirs of the overturning and destroying of all the powers of this world, which opinion he looking on as * malicious and barbarous forsook them, and joyning with *John Denk*, they by their mutual endeavours, sent some Prophets into *Germany*. But dissenting also from *him* in some things, he propagated his own

<small>* An item to the Hotspurs of our times.</small>

LODOWICK HETZER.

Sect in *Austria*, and made many *Proselytes* at *Bern* in *Switzerland*. Which gave occasion that the Reverend Senate appointed a publick disputation at *Soning*, and caused letters of safe conduct to be sent to *Hetzer* and his followers, for which bickering was set apart the first day of *February*, in the year one thousand five hundred twenty seven, where he appeared not himself, but his Emissaries came, who were by the most learned (but withal stinging,) *Oecolampadius* driven unto their shifts and enforced to acknowledge conviction. *Hetzer* was a considerable part, and the firebrand of the Anabaptistical sect, but he stifly denied *Christ* to be co-essential with the Father, which the verses made by him upon the carrying of the Cross, do more than hint.

Hetzer gains Proselytes in Austria, and Switzerland, Ann. 1527. At a publick disputation, Oecolampadius puts Hetzer's Emissaries to their shifts. Hetzer denied Christ to be co-essential with the Father.

Ipse ego qui propriâ cuncta hæc virtute creabam
  Quæris quot simus? Frustra, ego solus eram.
Hic non tres numero, verum sum solus, at isti
  Haud numero tres sunt, nam qui ego solus eram.
Nescio Personam, solus sum rivus ego, & fons.
  Qui me nescit, eum nescio, solus ero.

I who at first did make all things alone,
Am vainly ask'd my number, as being *one*.
These *three* did not the work, but only I
That in these three made this great *Syzygie*.
I know no *Person*, I'm the only Main,
And though they know me not, will one remain.

He was excellent at three tongues, he undertook to translate the book of *Ecclesiasticus* out of the *Hebrew* into *High Dutch*. *Plauterus* hath testified for him in writing, that he very honestly and unblameably bid farewell to his disciples, and with most devout prayers commended himself to God, even to the astonishment of the beholders. He having been long kept in close prison, was on the fourth day of *February*, in the year one thousand five hundred twenty nine, sentenced to die: and thinking himself unworthy of the city, was led without the walls, where he was put to death, not for *sedition* or *baptism* (as *Plauterus* says) but for *Adultery*, which act he endeavoured to defend by some arguments fetcht from the holy Scriptures.

His farewel to his disciples. He is put to death for Adultery.

MELCHIOR RINCK

Discipulos suc Rincke doces Baptisma negare
Sanguine carnifices et scelerata manus

THE CONTENTS.

MElchior Rinck, *an Anabaptist. He is accounted a notable interpreter of dreams and visions. His disciple* Thomas Scucker, *in a waking dream cut off his brother* Leonard's *head, pretending for his murther obedience to the decree of God.*

Melchior Rinck, an Anabaptist.

MELCHIOR RINCK, a most wonderful Enthusiast, was also a most extraordinary promoter of Anabaptism, and among his followers celebrated the festivals of it. He made it his business to extoll Anabaptism above all others, with those commendations (which certainly it wanted not.) Besides he was accounted no ordinary promoter and interpreter of dreams and visions, which it was thought he could not perform without the special indulgence of God the Father; nay, he arrived to that esteem among the chiefest of his opinion, and became so absolutely possessed

He is accounted a notable Interpreter of dreams and visions.

...sed of their minds, that his followers interpreted whatever was scattered abroad concerning dreams and visions, to have proceeded from heavenly inspirations from God the Father. Accordingly in *Switzerland* (to omit other particulars) at *Sangall*, even at a full Council, his disciple *Thomas Scucker*, being rapt into an Enthusiasm, (his Father and mother then present, and his Brother *Leonard*, having by his command, cast himself at his knees before him) calls for a sword, whereupon the parents and divers others running to know what was the cause and meaning of such an extravagant action, he bid them not be troubled at all, for there should happen nothing but what should be according to the will of God; Of this waking dream did they all unanimously expect the interpretation. The aforesaid *Thomas* [guilty alas of too much credulity] did, in the presence of all those sleeping-waking spectators cut off his own brothers head, and having forgotten the use of water, baptized him with his own blood, but what followed? The Magistrate having sudden notice of it, and the offence being fresh and horrid, the Malefactor is dragg'd to prison by head and shoulders, where he, having long considered his action with himself, professed he had therein obeyed the decrees of the Divine power. These things, did the unfortunate year one thousand five hundred twenty and seven see. Here men may perceive, in a most wicked and unjustifiable action, the eminent tracts of an implacable fury and madness; which God of his infinite goodness and mercy avert from these times.

His disciple Thomas Scucker, in a waking dream cut off his Brother Leonard's head.

He pretends (for his murther) obedience to the decree of God, Anno 1527.

HENRY NICHOLAS.

*Vestra Domus Nicholae cadat, quæ exrudere versa
Futile fundamen Religionis habet.*

THE CONTENTS.

HENRY NICHOLAS, *Father of the Family of Love,
is against Infant Baptism. His devilish Logick.*

Henry Nicholas Father of the Family of Love.
He is against Infant Baptism.

There was also one *Henry Nicholas* the Father of the Family Love, (as he called himself) and not the meanest man of his Gang, one who by many means endeavoured to cripple Baptism of Children, as is too known and apparent out of writings, which at a third hand he with all freedom, earnestn and kindness, endeavoured to communicate to *David George* the other of his Fellow-labourers, and his new *Jerusalem* frier This man in a Pamphlet of his, wherein he notably described h self, and which he dedicated to an intimate friend of his under

HENRY NICHOLAS.

...ne of *L.W.* maintaining that the *minute of the last Trumpet ... coming, that should unfold all the Books of unquiet conscien... hell, and eternal Judgment; which should be found to have ...n only things grounded upon meer lyes, and as all wicked and ...h misdeeds were hateful and detestable to God, so also were ...rious and plausible lyes no less odious to him. The same man ...eavoured to perswade people, that he was a partaker of God, ...d the humanity of his Son. He further affirmed, that at the last ...y God should bring all men, nay, the *Devils* themselves into per... ...t happiness. All the things that were said of *Devils*, of *Hell* or ...gels, and eternal *Judgment*, and the pains of *Damnation*, he said ...re only told by the *Scripture* to cause fear of civil punishments, ...d to establish right *Policy*.

As to minute; if be confine not God, we may believe him.

His blasphemy.

Doubtless he hugg'd himself in this opinion.

His divellish Logick.

The Conclusion.

These few things we have brought to light, were not invented ... us, but were extorted out of their own Disciples, with abun...nce of discourse, not without the presence of many men of God...ess and excellent understanding, *they admitting not the uni...rsal rule of the *Scriptures*. But alas! take these away, where is ...ith? fear of God? eternal happiness? But let us believe them, ...t us believe them, and we shall be saved.
Oh! that to Heresies I could say

Hereticks allow not of the Scriptures.

FINIS.

An Alphabetical Table to the Revelation of *Hereticks*

A

A Pious Act.   417
Adam Pastor, a derider of Pædobaptism,   452
...nabaptists their leading principle, 398. usually they grow worse and worse, *ibid.* their bold attempt, 406 were Masters ... insolent, 408. of a Le...lling principle, 412. they, a... the Devil pretend Scripture for their ... actions, *ibid.* they aim at universal Monarchy, *ibid.* the design upon Amsterdam, 413. they aim ... the advancement ... themselves, but destruction of others, ...ey would enforce ...ers to their opinion; yet pretend liberty of conscience as to themselves,   449
Arrius, his character, and wretched death,   438
Arrianism, its increase, *ibid.*

B

John Buckhold, or John of Leyden, His actions and end.   405. &c.

C

Calvin's reproof of *Servetus*,   435.
Godly and loyal *Citizens* hate usurpation.   410
Conventicles usually the nurseries of Tumults.   406

D

The *Devil* an enemy of peace!   403.

E

A Bad *Example* soon followed: 410

Famil...

THE TABLE.

F
FAmine the confummation of all mifery, 414. its character, &c. 415.

G
DAvid George an Anabaptift, his character, doctrine, actions, and death. 427

H
HErefie, a catching, or mad difeafe. 421
Hereticks their ufual pretence, 398. the end that they propofe to themfelves in oppofing the Miniftry and Magiftracy, ibid. they are reftlefs, ibid. their cruelty, 410. they are inconftant in their opinions, 422. they allow not of the Scriptures. 455
Hermannus Sutor; or Herman the Cobler, his blafphemies, opinions, and end. 419
Lodowick Hetzer, a famous Heretick, 444 &c. his end. 445
Melchior Hofman an Anabaptift, 446. pined himfelf to death. ibid.
Balthazar Hubmor an Anabaptift, 440, he and his wife burned. 441
John Hut an Anabaptift, 442

I
JOhn of Leyden, vide Buckhold.
An Item to the Hot-fpurs of our times, 444

K
BErnard Knipperdoling, 408

L
THe Learned to be confulted with, in detection of Sectaries and Hereticks. 430
Loyaltie not always fuccefsful. 410
Luther's advice to the Senate concerning Muntzer. 399

M
MAgiftrates feduced, moft ominous. 400
A pattern for good Magiftrates, Mahomet characterized, 438. his iron tomb, 439
John Mathias a Baker at Harlem, his actions and end. 402
Money and preferments, the ufual baits of fedition, 415
Thomas Muntzer, His opinions, actions, and end. 393

N
HEnry Nicholas Father of the Family of Love, he is againft Infant Baptifm; his blafphemy, and devilifh Logick, 452 &c.

O
OEcolampadius puts Hetzer's Emiffaries to their fhifts. 445

P
AN ill Prefident foon followed, 400
Pretenders to Religion, prove ufually the difturbers thereof. 403

R
A Good Refolution, 430
Melchior Rinck an Anabaptift, 448. his difciple Thomas Scucker cut off his brothers head. 449.

S
SEctaries like tinder, are foon on fire, 398. their ufual pretence to raife fedition, 39
Sedition goes not always unpunifhed, 412
Michael Servetus an Anabaptift, his blafphemous opinions and end, 435
Succefs in bad enterprizes caufes evil men to rejoice. 420

T
THeodorus Sartor, or Theodor the Botcher, an Adamite, his blafphemy, actions and end. 424
John Tuyfentfchrew, an abettor of John Buckhold, 410. his feditious Sermon, 411.

V
VIce corrects fin. 412

FINIS.

www.ingramcontent.com/pod-product-compliance
Lightning Source LLC
Chambersburg PA
CBHW022111300426
44117CB00007B/675